Text, Artifact, and Image

Program in Judaic Studies
Brown University
Box 1826
Providence, RI 02912

Number 346

TEXT, ARTIFACT, AND IMAGE
Revealing Ancient Israelite Religion

Edited by
Gary Beckman and Theodore J. Lewis

Text, Artifact, and Image

Revealing Ancient Israelite Religion

Edited by
Gary Beckman and Theodore J. Lewis

Brown Judaic Studies
Providence, Rhode Island

Library of Congress Cataloging-in-Publication Data

Text, artifact, and image : revealing ancient Israelite religion / edited by
Gary M. Beckman and Theodore J. Lewis.
p. cm. — (Brown Judaic studies ; no. 346)
Includes bibliographical references and index.
ISBN-13: 978-1-930675-28-5 (cloth binding : alk. paper)
ISBN-10: 1-930675-28-3 (cloth binding : alk. paper)
ISBN-13: 978-1-930675-78-0 (paper binding : alk. paper)
1. Judaism—History—To 70 A.D. 2. Middle East—Religion—History —To 1500. 3. Middle East—Religion—Comparative studies. 4. Judaism —Comparative studies. 5. Kings and rulers—Religious aspects—History —To 1500. 6. Idols and images—Middle East. 7. Temples—Middle East. 8. Monotheism—Middle East. I. Beckman, Gary M. II. Lewis, Theodore J.

BM155.3.T49 2006
296.09'01—dc22

2006029504

Printed on acid-free paper conforming to
ANSI/NISO Z39.48-1992 (R1997) and ISO 9706:1994

Contents

Abbreviations vii

Introduction
Gary Beckman and Theodore J. Lewis xi

I. REPRESENTATIONS OF DEITY IN ISRAEL
AND THE ANCIENT NEAR EAST

1 • What Goes In Is What Comes Out—
Materials for Creating Cult Statues
Victor Avigdor Hurowitz 3

2 • The Representation of the Divine in Ancient Egypt
Ann Macy Roth 24

3 • The Structure of Divinity at Ugarit and Israel:
The Case of Anthropomorphic Deities versus
Monstrous Divinities
Mark S. Smith 38

4 • Will the Real *Massebot* Please Stand Up:
Cases of Real and Mistakenly Identified
Standing Stones in Ancient Israel
Elizabeth Bloch-Smith 64

5 • Arad, Qiṭmīt—Judahite Aniconism vs. Edomite Iconic Cult?
Questioning the Evidence
Christoph Uehlinger 80

II. ROYAL CULT

6 • Sumerian Kingship and the Gods
Jacob Klein 115

7 • The Royal Cult in Ḫatti
Harry A. Hoffner 132

8 • Kingship and Divinity in Imperial Assyria
Peter Machinist 152

9 • Israel's Royal Cult in the Ancient Near Eastern *Kulturkreis*
Ziony Zevit 189

10 • Moses as Equal to Pharaoh
Gary A. Rendsburg 201

III. TEMPLES

11 • Parallelism in Popular and Official Religion in Ancient Egypt
Carolyn Routledge 223

12 • Reflections of Ptah and Memphite Theology from the Soil of Palestine: Iconographic and Epigraphic Evidence
Othmar Keel 239

13 • The ʿAin Dara Temple and the Jerusalem Temple
John Monson 273

14 • Were There Temples in Ancient Israel? The Archaeological Evidence
William G. Dever 300

IV. MONOTHEISM, MONOLATRY, AND POLYTHEISM

15 • Monotheism in Ancient Egypt
James P. Allen 319

16 • Concepts of God in Israel and the Question of Monotheism
Nili Fox 326

Abbreviations

AA	Archäologischer Anzeiger
AASOR	Annual of the American Schools of Oriental Research
AASORDS	Annual of the American Schools of Oriental Research: Research Dissertation Series
ABD	Anchor Bible Dictionary. Edited by D. N. Freedman. 6 vols. New York, 1992
ABL	Assyrian and Babylonian Letters Belonging to the Kouyunjik Collections of the British Museum
ADAJ	Annual of the Department of Antiquities of Jordan
AfO	Archiv für Orientforschung
AHw	Akkadisches Handwörterbuch. W. von Soden. 3 vols. Wiesbaden, 1965–1981
ANEP	The Ancient Near East in Pictures Relating to the Old Testament. Edited by J. B. Pritchard. Princeton, 1954
ANET	Ancient Near Eastern Texts Relating to the Old Testament. Edited by J. B. Pritchard. 3d ed. Princeton, 1969
AnOr	Analecta orientalia
AnSt	Anatolian Studies
AOAT	Alter Orient und Altes Testament
AoF	Altorientalische Forschungen
APAW	Abhandlungen der (Königl.) Preussischen Akademie der Wissenschaften
ARM	Archives royales de Mari
AS	Assyriological Studies
BA	Biblical Archaeologist
BAR	Biblical Archaeology Review
BASOR	Bulletin of the American Schools of Oriental Research
BBB	Bonner biblische Beiträge
BDB	Brown, F., S. R. Driver, and C. A. Briggs. A Hebrew and English Lexicon of the Old Testament. Oxford, 1907
BiOr	Bibliotheca Orientalis
BR	Bible Review
BWANT	Beiträge zur Wissenschaft vom Alten (und Neuen) Testament

CAD	The Assyrian Dictionary of the University of Chicago
CAH	Cambridge Ancient History
CANE	Civilizations of the Ancient Near East. Edited by J. Sasson. 4 vols. New York, 1995
CAT	Commentaire de l'Ancien Testament
CBET	Contributions to Biblical Exegesis and Theology
CBQ	Catholic Biblical Quarterly
CHD	The Hittite Dictionary of the Oriental Institute of the University of Chicago
ConBOT	Coniectanea biblica: Old Testament Series
CT	Cuneiform Texts from Babylonian Tablets in the British Museum
CTH	Catalogue des textes hittites (L. LaRoche)
DAB	A Dictionary of Assyrian Botany (R.C. Thompson)
EA	Die El-Amarna-Tafeln (=VAB II)
EEF	Egypt Exploration Fund
EI	Eretz Israel
EJ	Encyclopaedia Judaica. 16 vols. Jerusalem, 1972
EncRel	The Encyclopedia of Religion. Edited by M. Eliade. 16 vols. New York, 1987
ETL	Ephemerides theologicae lovanienses
FAOS	Freiburger Altorientalische Studien
HKL	Handbuch der Keilschriftliteratur
HR	History of Religions
HSM	Harvard Semitic Monographs
HTR	Harvard Theological Review
HUCA	Hebrew Union College Annual
IAA	Israel Antiquities Authority
IEJ	Israel Exploration Journal
IOS	Israel Oriental Society
JANES	Journal of the Ancient Near Eastern Society of Columbia University
JAOS	Journal of the American Oriental Society
JBL	Journal of Biblical Literature
JCS	Journal of Cuneiform Studies
JEA	Journal of Egyptian Archaeology
JIES	Journal of Indo-European Studies
JJS	Journal of Jewish Studies
JMA	Journal of Mediterranean Archaeology
JNES	Journal of Near Eastern Studies
JNWSL	Journal of Northwest Semitic Languages
JPF	Judean Pillar Figurines
JPSV	Jewish Publication Society Version
JSOT	Journal for the Study of the Old Testament

JSOTSup	Journal for the Study of the Old Testament: Supplement Series
KBo	Keilschrifttexte aus Boghazköi
KlF	Kleinasiatische Forschungen
KUB	Keilschrifturkunden aus Boghazköi
LÄ	Lexikon der Ägyptologie. Edited by W. Helck, E. Otto, and W. Westendorf. Wiesbaden, 1972
LAS	Letters from Assyrian Scholars to the Kings Esarhaddon and Assurbanipal (S. Parpola)
LXX	Septuagint
MARI	Mari: Annales de recherches interdisciplinaires
MDAIK	Mitteilungen des Deutschen Archäologischen Instituts, Abt. Kairo
MSL	Materialen zum sumerischen Lexikon
MT	Masoretic Text (of the OT) Hebrew Bible
NEAEHL	The New Encyclopedia of Archaeological Excavations in the Holy Land. Edited by E. Stern. 4 vols. Jerusalem, 1993
NJPS	The Jewish Publication Society's New Translation of the Holy Scriptures
OA	Oriens antiquus
OBO	Orbis biblicus et orientalis
OBO.SA	Orbis biblicus et orientalis, Series Archaeologica
OIP	Oriental Institute Publications
Or.	Orientalia (Nova Series)
OSP	Old Sumerian and Old Akkadian Texts in Philadelphia Chiefly from Nippur (A. Westenholz)
OTL	Old Testament Library
PEF	Palestine Exploration Fund
PEFQS	Palestine Exploration Fund Quarterly Statement
PEQ	Palestine Exploration Quarterly
PJ	Palästina-Jahrbuch
Qad.	Qadmoniot
RA	Revue d'assyriologie et d'archéologie orientale
RB	Revue biblique
RIME	The Royal Inscriptions of Mesopotamia, Early Periods
RlA	Reallexikon der Assyriologie
RS	Ras Shamra (excavation/tablet number)
SAA	State Archives of Assyria
SBLDS	Society of Biblical Literature Dissertation Series
SCO	Studi classici e orientali
SEL	Studi epigrafici e linguistici
SPAW	Sitzungsberichte der preussischen Akademie der Wissenschaften
STT	The Sultantepe Tablets (O. Gurney, J. Finkelstein)

STVC	Sumerian Texts of Varied Contents (E. Chiera)
TA	Tel Aviv
TAMS	Tel Aviv Monograph Series
TCL	Textes cunéiformes. Musée du Louvre
TDOT	Theological Dictionary of the Old Testament. Edited by G. J. Botterweck and H. Ringgren. Translated by J. T. Willis, G. W. Bromiley, and D. E. Green. 8 vols. Grand Rapids, 1974–
TLZ	Theologische Literaturzeitung
TO	Textes ougaritiques by A. Caquot et al. Les Éditions du Cerf: Paris, 1974
UBC	The Ugaritic Baal Cycle by Mark S. Smith. Leiden: Brill, 1994
UBL	Ugaritisch-biblische Literatur
UET	*Ur Excavations, Texts*
UF	*Ugarit-Forschungen*
UNP	*Ugaritic Narrative Poetry.* Edited by Simon B. Parker. SBLWAW 9. Atlanta, 1997
VAB	Vorderasiatische Bibliothek
VAT	Vorderasiatische Abteilung Tontafel. Vorderasiatisches Museum, Berlin
VO	Vicino Oriente
VT	Vetus Testamentum
VTSup	Supplements to Vetus Testamentum
WMANT	Wissenschaftliche Monographien zum Alten und Neuen Testament
WO	Die Welt des Orients
ZA	Zeitschrift für Assyriologie
ZAH	Zeitschrift für Althebräistik
ZÄS	Zeitschrift für ägyptische Sprache und Altertumskunde
ZAW	Zeitschrift für die alttestamentliche Wissenschaft
ZDMG	Zeitschrift der deutschen morgenländischen Gesellschaft
ZDPV	Zeitschrift des deutschen Palästina-Vereins

Introduction

GARY BECKMAN AND THEODORE J. LEWIS

The writings collected in the Hebrew Bible constitute one of the bases of Western Civilization, having contributed many of our religious and moral concepts as well as a large portion of the common repertoire of exemplary narratives and paradigmatic personalities employed in artistic creation and literary allusion. Furthermore, in Europe for well over a thousand years most knowledge of ancient history was drawn directly from the books of the Hebrew Bible/Old Testament.

But in the closing years of the eighteenth century the campaign of Napoleon in Egypt provided a strong impetus to the recovery of the monuments and archives of the civilizations of the Nile valley and of Mesopotamia.[1] It soon became clear that, far from being unique phenomena of pristine origin, the culture and religion of Israel and Judah had significant forerunners. The ancient Israelites were in fact latecomers to the region. High cultures had flourished in northeastern Africa and in the flood plain of the Tigris and Euphrates rivers for more than two millennia by the time of the founding of the Davidic kingdom.

Debate has long raged over the relationship of ancient Israel to its cultural environment. Some writers have claimed that the culture of the Israelites had been almost entirely borrowed from Egypt or Babylonia.[2] Others have maintained that—whatever their degree of dependence on their highly civilized neighbors—the priests, prophets, and writers of

---

1. See John A. Wilson, *Signs & Wonders upon Pharaoh. A History of American Egyptology* (Chicago: University of Chicago Press, 1964); and Mogens Trolle Larsen, *The Conquest of Assyria: Excavations in an Antique Land* (London: Routledge, 1996). Early scientific investigation of Israel/Palestine is summarized in P. R. S. Moorey, *A Century of Biblical Archaeology* (Louisville, KY: Westminster/John Knox Press, 1991).

2. On the latter viewpoint, known as "panbabylonianism," see Reinhard G. Lehmann, *Friedrich Delitzsch und der Babel-Bibel Streit* (Freiburg, Switzerland: Universitätsverlag, 1994).

Israel and Judah radically adapted any borrowed concepts, producing a religious and philosophical achievement *sui generis*.[3]

The purpose of this collection of essays, which grew out of the work of the Center for Advanced Judaic Studies at the University of Pennsylvania (CAJS) during the academic year 1997-1998, is to examine the religion of ancient Israel within the cultural world of the contemporary and earlier Near East. Elements of Israelite religion are here compared with the practices and beliefs of neighboring populations. Although many of the contributors range widely within this field, each primarily considers one of four questions: (1) How are deities represented in physical form? (2) What is the relationship of the monarch to the nation's tutelary god or gods? (3) Where does divinity make its home within the human settlement, and how is access to this numinous place regulated? (4) Is the divine singular or multiple? These four questions, while not exhaustive, reflect the multi-faceted nature of religious faith and practice in the ancient Near Eastern world. The breadth of material that they explore provides varied avenues whereby ancient Israel's orthodoxy and orthopraxy can be compared and contrasted with those of her neighbors.

What is unique in the present volume is the interaction of archaeologists, textual scholars (Hebraists, Semitists, epigraphists, linguists), historians, historians of religion, art historians, and specialists in the various cultures of the ancient Near East (Egypt, Mesopotamia, Ugarit, and that of the Hittites).

The biblical archaeology movement that flourished from the 1930s through the 1960s, synonymous with the names William F. Albright and G. Ernest Wright, used archaeology to demonstrate the uniqueness of ancient Israelite religion. In the time since Albright, Syro-Palestinian archaeology has reasserted its character as an independent discipline capable of unearthing the *practice* of Israelite religion without being subservient to biblical studies. Some archaeologists such as John S. Holladay part ways with the biblical text entirely, reconstructing Israelite religion from an explicitly archaeological approach.[4] In contrast, William G. Dever, in a series of methodological essays dating back to 1983, has called for a true dialogue between archaeology and text (which he calls a "curated artifact"). Only by combining the *realia* of religious practice (both sanctioned and without sanction, public and private) as seen from

---

3. A good example is provided by the works of Alexander Heidel: *The Gilgamesh Epic and Old Testament Parallels* (2nd ed.; Chicago: University of Chicago Press, 1949), and *The Babylonian Genesis* (2nd ed.; Chicago: University of Chicago Press, 1951).

4. See J. S. Holladay, "Religion in Israel and Judah Under the Monarchy: An Explicitly Archaeological Approach," in *Ancient Israelite Religion: Essays in Honor of Frank Moore Cross*, ed. P. D. Miller, P. D. Hanson, and S. D. McBride (Philadelphia: Fortress, 1987), 249-99.

the archaeological record with a sophisticated reading of the biblical text, can historians of Israelite religion achieve their goals.

Ancient Near Eastern archaeology and textual studies have developed in a manner similar to that charted above for Syro-Palestinian archaeology. The fields of Assyriology, Egyptology, and Northwest Semitics (e.g., Ugaritic studies) can no longer be treated as handmaidens of biblical scholarship. Each field has been on a steady march toward the status of a discipline in its own right. The vast number of journals and books devoted to these fields demonstrate this independence.[5] Like archaeological purists, specialists in these fields often disdain making any connection to biblical studies due to past abuses of a comparative method out of control. Yet, just as historians of Israelite religion must embrace the archaeological record, so too must they describe ancient Israel in its ancient Near Eastern cultural setting.

The 1970s saw a new emphasis on the use of iconography as a tool for the study of Israelite religion. Othmar Keel led the way with his *The Symbolism of the Biblical World: Ancient Near Eastern Iconography and the Book of Psalms* published in 1972. In subsequent years, Keel and his "Fribourg School" have continued to produce some of the liveliest areas of biblical research.[6] Several of our authors here reconsider some of the most pressing issues raised by the numerous works of Keel and his collaborators. First, how can transcendent and para-human beings be contained—or even represented—in an object fashioned by human hands?

VICTOR AVIGDOR HUROWITZ ("What Goes In Is What Comes Out—Materials for Creating Cult Statues") addresses the subject of the creation of idols, an activity for which Mesopotamian craftsmen and priests were mocked by the prophets of ancient Israel. He shows that in the eyes of the Sumerians and Babylonians, the materials employed in the construction of these images were inherently of divine nature, and that the artisan was therefore not fashioning something beyond his own powers. This situation was not paradoxical in the context of a polytheism in which most things can be related to as if they were of divine nature.

ANN MACY ROTH ("The Representation of the Divine in Ancient Egypt") explores the nature of visual and onomastic representations of deity in pharaonic Egypt, showing that both were intended to preserve a

---

5. See *The Study of the Ancient Near East in the Twenty-First Century*, ed. J. S. Cooper and G. M. Schwartz (Winona Lake, IN: Eisenbrauns, 1996).

6. See Christoph Uehlinger's overview of these efforts, "Das Buch und die Bilder: 25 Jahre ikonographischer Forschung am Biblischen Institut der Universität Freiburg Schweiz—Dank an Othman Keel," in *Images as Media: Sources for the Cultural History of the Near East and the Eastern Mediterranean (1st Millennium BCE)*, ed. Christoph Uehlinger (Fribourg, Switzerland: University Press, 2000), 399-408.

certain mysterious distance between god or goddess and worshipper. Conventional depictions of particular divinities are often characterized by the phenomenon of "nesting," whereby remnants of each successive manifestation of divine authority—normally inanimate object, animal, and human form—are present within the next realization.

MARK S. SMITH ("The Structure of Divinity at Ugarit and Israel") uses the conceptual categories of "center" and "periphery" to articulate the distinction between anthropomorphic deities and monstrous divine creatures. Within the "center," Smith distinguishes between "home" and "foreign" to map divine space. Deities are accorded sacred sites (e.g., holy mountains) within the "center" or area of human civilization, while cosmic enemies are not. Within the periphery, he differentiates between that which is experienced by men and that which is beyond human experience.

Smith concludes by paying particular attention to Ugaritic and Israelite cosmic enemies. The relationship between the "beloved" monsters and Ugaritic El is expressed through various "terms of endearment." Yet, whereas Yamm is the premier focus of El's favor in the Baal Cycle, the biblical tradition assigns him little mythology. While the texts of Ugarit present cosmic enemies as divine in rank and power, biblical passages do not accord them any status or strength comparable to that of Yahweh. Particularly relevant to this discussion is Genesis 1 and its "monotheistic poetics." Here the cosmic forces of old are muted, downplayed, and even depersonalized to the point that they are no longer divinities.

ELIZABETH BLOCH-SMITH ("Will the Real *Massebot* Please Stand Up: Cases of Real and Mistakenly Identified Standing Stones in Ancient Israel") takes a closer look at the ancient Israelite phenomenon known as "standing stones" (*massebot*). In recent years these stones have been the object of intense scrutiny by biblicists and archaeologists alike attempting to show how they represent a "material aniconism" of divine presence. At the same time, recent archaeological excavations (e.g., at Tel Dan) have produced more examples of standing stones. Bloch-Smith's aim is to develop criteria for identifying *massebot*. This involves rethinking what constitutes a cultic assemblage.

She demonstrates how scholars have mistakenly identified stones originally used as structural supports, construction stones, and even grinding stones as *massebot*. She then turns her attention to the best candidates for *massebot* in the archaeological record. In public space these include stones from Tell el Farah (N), Lachish, and Tel Dan. Examples of *massebot* in sacred space can be found at Shechem, the "Bull Site," Hazor, and Arad. Bloch-Smith concludes that there is no standardized shape or size for *massebot*. It remains to be ascertained to what degree even the best examples of *massebot* served cultic functions.

And what does archaeology tell us about the avoidance of iconic representation in the religious practice of the Levant? CHRISTOPH UEHLINGER ("Arad, Qiṭmīt—Judahite Aniconism vs. Edomite Iconic Cult?") questions how scholars have treated two of the most important late Iron Age sites, Tel Arad and Ḥorvat Qiṭmīt. Scholars regularly contrast the former as a prime exemplar of Judahite aniconism with the latter, an illustration of Edomite iconic cult. But Uehlinger argues that a reexamination of the archaeological record does not support a Judahite-Edomite rivalry. The traditional "ethnic" and "national" labels "Judahite" and "Edomite" assigned to these two sites are ill founded, resting primarily on biblical premises. According to Uehlinger, once one jettisons the idea of the "non-Judahite" character of Qiṭmīt, a body of evidence emerges for the potential reconstruction of the history of Judahite religions.

The role of the king was central in all religions of the ancient Near East. JACOB KLEIN ("Sumerian Kingship and the Gods") reviews the problem of the deification of the monarchs of the Ur III and Isin dynasties of Mesopotamia, suggesting that this measure was political in origin, taken to allow the head of the centralized state to appoint governors over traditionally independent city-states. The inferiority of this newly minted divinity to the major gods and goddesses of the pantheon is demonstrated by his claim to be the son of a pair of deities, but never an equal. Similarly, his role as representative of the secondary god Dumuzi in the sacred marriage rite makes clear his subordination to the more prominent figure of the great goddess Ishtar.

HARRY A. HOFFNER ("The Royal Cult in Ḫatti") considers the role of the monarch in Hittite cult, a topic that has two aspects. The king was the most important officiant in the state worship of the pantheon, as reflected in his numerous religious duties and required presence at certain important rites. But Hittite rulers themselves were also the objects of worship, at least after death. These two sides of the king's religious position can be harmonized by the recognition that he was the indispensable link between the Hittite people and their deities. Partly through the enforcement of rigorous purity regulations, the monarch became so closely associated with the gods that he himself attained semi-divine status. This point is underlined by recently discovered images of later kings that seem to have served as the focus of worship.

In treating Assyrian royal ideology, PETER MACHINIST ("Kingship and Divinity in Imperial Assyria") explores the relationship of the Assyrian king to the divine. After a thorough analysis of the nuances of the titles *iššakku*, *šaknu*, and *šangû*, Machinist concludes that the king is the "representative or administrator" of the gods. During the reign of Tukulti-Ninurta I in the Middle Assyrian period, the royal ideology was elevated to new heights. The king could now be described as of divine birth and/or nurture, and adorned with divine "radiance" or "effulgence." In addition, the king might be portrayed as the "image" (*ṣalmu*) of a particular god. Indeed, his body is on occasion characterized as "the flesh of the gods," a link to the divine statue made from the prized and exotic *mēsu*-wood. Yet, as elaborate as the language of divine status may be, there were limitations to the royal-divine relationship. Though some texts imply that the Assyrian king enjoyed entry into the divine sphere, others make it clear that he did not stand on par with members of the pantheon. Machinist concludes by proposing a more flexible interpretative framework that does not force us to conceive narrowly of the king as either divine or human. The nature of the ruler is rather dual, rooted in his role as the primary nexus between heaven and earth. When viewed from heaven, he is a divine emissary communicating with his earthly realm. When viewed from earth, he is the representative of his community before the gods.

ZIONY ZEVIT ("Israel's Royal Cult in the Ancient Near Eastern *Kulturkreis*") defines the royal cult in ancient Israel vis-à-vis the "cultural zone" of the ancient Near East by posing three questions: (1) Was the king involved in cultic matters? (2) Did the king act as a cultic functionary? (3) Was the king the focus of cultic activity? Zevit argues that Israelite and Judean kings, like their counterparts in the ancient Near East, were very much involved in a wide variety of cultic affairs, politics, and construction. In contrast, the biblical texts present a mixed picture of the role of the king as a cultic functionary. Judean kings did not function as priests (e.g., engage in blood manipulation), yet monarchs of the northern kingdom did officiate on a regular basis (note especially Jeroboam I's "ascending the altar"). Lastly, while Judahite kings did not receive veneration (either in life or in death), they were the objects of cultic concern, receiving, for example, impressive funeral rites.

Egyptian conceptions of royalty form the backdrop to GARY A. RENDSBURG's analysis of the portrayal of Moses in biblical narrative ("Moses as Equal to Pharaoh"). He argues that the author of Exodus was acquainted with Egyptian artistic and textual motifs. The ancient writer exploited these conventions even to the point of letting "literary flavor override biblical theology." In two passages that have up until now defied explanation, Moses is called "god." He is elevated to divine status, argues Rendsburg, so that he might function as an equal to pharaoh, who was considered divine. Rendsburg also points out how other Egyptian texts (e.g., those narrating the birth of Horus) and iconography (e.g., snake-staffs) present the best parallels for the biblical tales about Moses. The Moses story displays the basic elements of the *Königsnovelle*, a well-known genre in Egyptian literature.

Every temple in the ancient Near East was primarily the residence of a divinity or divinities. Access to the innermost precincts was always restricted to the elite, but the temple nonetheless served as a focus of community life. CAROLYN ROUTLEDGE ("Parallelism in Popular and Official Religion in Ancient Egypt") argues against the widely held view that popular religion in ancient Egypt differed in character from the official cult practiced in the great temples. Instead, she interprets the two realms of worship as parallel, with significant points of contact. This viewpoint makes it possible for us to see the temples as instruments for the construction of hegemony within Egyptian society.

OTHMAR KEEL ("Reflections of Ptah and Memphite Theology from the Soil of Palestine: Iconographic and Epigraphic Evidence") demonstrates how far the influence of a particular temple might reach. He collects the amulets created in the orbit of the temple of Ptah in Memphis and brought to Palestine by travelers. Locally produced imitations of these objects attest to the interest of the Canaanites in the deity depicted in this glyptic material. Keel discusses the relevant iconographic and inscriptional evidence from the Middle Kingdom through the Twenty-sixth dynasty, considering the development in the relationship between god and king manifested therein. Since some of the qualities attributed to Ptah in the "Memphite Theology" are similar to those of YHWH in the Hebrew Bible, it does not seem to be excluded that Egyptian conceptions concerning this deity exercised some influence upon the developing understanding of the God of Israel.

Due to its very absence, Jerusalem's First Temple has been the subject of extensive discussion. JOHN MONSON ("The ʿAin Dara Temple and the Jerusalem Temple") offers a detailed analysis of the Iron Age ʿAin Dara temple in northern Syria and its similarities to the description of the Solomonic temple. Previously, scholars have looked to the temple at Tell Tayinat, also in northern Syria, as the best analogue to the Jerusalem shrine. Monson shows, however, that the Neo-Hittite ʿAin Dara temple excavated between 1980 and 1985 is the closest parallel in date, size, and architectural elements. Moreover, it provides new evidence that anchors Solomon's temple in the cultural traditions of the tenth century B.C.E., an important point for the current debate surrounding Judean royal historiography.

WILLIAM G. DEVER ("Were There Temples in Ancient Israel? The Archaeological Evidence") addresses a topic intimately tied up with this same controversy. Taking a phenomenological approach, he defines a "temple" according to its function. By further explicitly defining a "temple" as the house of the deity, Dever is able to exclude cult-corners, outdoor shrines, open-air sanctuaries, and even "high-places" (*bāmôt*). According to this definition, there are only two known candidates for temples in ancient Israel, the Jerusalem temple and the structure at Tel Arad. While the former must necessarily be considered primarily from texts, archaeological parallels from the Middle Bronze, Late Bronze, and Iron Ages serve to ground the descriptive details drawn therefrom in a "*real*-life context." In contrast, the Arad temple is "our only surviving archaeologically-attested ancient Israelite temple." While its stratigraphy and historical correlations will continue to be refined and debated—a discussion that must await the full publication of the excavated pottery—Arad gives us the only extant example of a structure that fits Dever's functional definition of a temple.

Was ancient Israel's insistence on the uniqueness of its God an unprecedented intellectual development?[7] JAMES ALLEN ("Monotheism in Ancient Egypt") ponders the degree to which the pharaoh Akhenaten should be considered a radical religious reformer. He demonstrates that the king's religious views had their origin in henotheism, the focusing of the worshipper's attention on one deity to the neglect or subordination of others. Earlier Egyptian henotheism had usually involved the syncretistic identification of numerous gods and goddesses with the preeminent deity, or with one of his aspects. But Akhenaten's system of belief eventually developed into intolerance for the worship of other gods, becoming in effect true monotheism. In contrast to the God of Israel, however, the pharaoh's chosen deity was not transcendent but immanent in nature, particularly in sunlight. Allen suggests that the true originality of Akhenaten was in his use of "univalent logic," his insistence that only one explanation of reality—in this case the primacy of the sun disk—can be true.

NILI FOX ("Concepts of God in Israel and the Question of Monotheism") approaches the question of Israelite monotheism from an anthropological perspective. She emphasizes that monotheistic and polytheistic notions can co-exist in the same society. Adapting work on African religions, Fox explores the concept of "diffused monotheism," whereby a supreme deity delegates authority to subordinate functionaries, and concludes that ancient Israel had diverse religious expressions. These included a radical monolatry as well as a diffused monotheism co-existing with the worship of אשרות, אשרים, בעלים, and עשתרות.

7. On this question, see the essays collected in *One God or Many? Concepts of Divinity in the Ancient World*, ed. Barbara Nevling Porter (Chebeague Island, ME: Casco Bay Assyriological Institute, 2000).

In an age of specialization, the need for dialogue and cooperation between philologists, archaeologists, and art historians is paramount. Gone are any hopes of "Renaissance" individuals mastering the ancient Near East in its entirety. And yet ancient Israel's religious expression can only be understood in this setting and with the multiple tools these three disciplines offer.[8]

Gary Beckman
Theodore J. Lewis

8. While the present volume is independent of the Center for Advanced Judaic Studies, it grew out of a conference held at the CAJS in 1998. It is our pleasant duty to extend warmest thanks to the staff at CAJS, who cheerfully facilitated our work in the most efficient manner. These remarkable individuals include Sheila Allen, Aviva Astrinsky, Sam Cardillo, Saul Cohen, David Goldenberg, Etty Lassman, and Judith Leifer. Finally, we cannot fail to acknowledge the strong and effective leadership of David Ruderman, director of the Center, whose unceasing efforts have preserved this marvelous institution for scholarship.

We are very appreciative of the time and effort devoted to bring this book to publication by Andrew R. Davis of the Johns Hopkins University, Saul Olyan, the editor of Brown Judaic Studies series, and Paul J. Kobelski of The HK Scriptorium.

I

Representations of Deity in Israel and the Ancient Near East

1

What Goes In Is What Comes Out

Materials for Creating Cult Statues

VICTOR AVIGDOR HUROWITZ

Manufacturing cult statues and ritual figurines was a complex endeavor involving such activities as deciding to make a statue, determining its form, selecting artisans, acquiring materials, forging the statue, ritually purifying and enlivening it, installing it as an object of worship in the temple or elsewhere, or using it in a ritual. This paper will discuss only one aspect of this complex undertaking. It will focus on the materials from which divine statues and figurines were made and in particular the ways in which the materials were procured or prepared and properties attached to them. It will relate to Mesopotamian sources, reflecting beliefs and practices of scribes who revered cult statues, and to biblical accounts of idol making airing views of scribes who abhorred or ridiculed idolatry. I hope to show how the nature of the materials from which idols were made and the ways in which they were acquired were thought to affect the character of the objects into which they were incorporated.

Materials

What were idols made of? The almost total absence of cult statues in archaeological remains from Mesopotamia can hardly be a coincidence. It indicates, rather, that cult statues were not preserved.[1] This can be attrib-

1. Statues used as objects of worship in temples have not been preserved, but this is not the case for figurines used in apotropaic rituals. Several such objects are inscribed, enabling us to identify them, and associate them with figurines prescribed by rituals. Borger, *HKL* III, 85, lists inscribed apotropaic figures of the Pazuzu and Ninšubur types

uted to their being made of costly materials taken as booty, or of perishable ingredients vulnerable to ravages of time and climate. Cult images would have been made, therefore, of precious metals and stones or of wood. Numerous texts indicate that this was in fact the case.

Many biblical passages mention silver and gold idols in both Israelite and non-Israelite worship.[2] More detailed passages mentioning wood probably refer to wooden cores or bodies overlain and decorated with precious metals and clothed with fine fabrics.[3] There are also references to stone idols.[4]

---

along with humans, dogs, lions, snakes, birds, and fish. Preservation of the figurines may be attributed to, among other factors, the cheap materials of which they were made (clay) and their ritual burial.

2. For foreign idols of silver and gold, see Pss. 115:4; 135:15. For Israelite idols of these precious materials, see Exod. 20:19; Isa. 2:20 and cf. Isa. 31:7; Hos. 8:4; 13:2. Micah 1:7 וכל פסיליה יכתו may refer to breaking up metal idols, for which מסכה is suitable. מסכה, derived from נסך, "pour out," and locutions such as פכל ומסכה (Deut. 27:15; Judg. 17:3-4; 18:14; Nah. 1:14; 2 Chron. 34:3, 4), פסל // מסכה (Isa. 42:17) or צלם מסכה (Num. 33:52) may designate fully metallic images but refer in most cases to wood or stone images covered with metal. This is the case of עגל מסכה which designated the Golden Calf made by Aaron (Exod. 32:4, 8; Deut. 9:12, 16; Ps.106:19 עגל // מסכה; Neh. 9:18) or the two calves made by Jeroboam (2 Kgs. 17:16). The only case in the Bible of a copper image is the serpent made by Moses (Num. 21:4-9) and cut down by Hezekiah (2 Kgs. 18:4). Kings reports that this artifact became an object of worship, but its original function was apotropaic. It would seem, therefore, that the Bible knows only of silver and gold being used in idols meant to be worshipped. This material dichotomy between idols for worship and images for other purposes may be paralleled by the archaeological record. O. Negbi (*Canaanite Gods in Metal*, Publications of the Institute of Archaelogy 5 [Tel Aviv: Tel Aviv University, Institute of Archaeology, 1976]) collects and describes numerous images made of various metals including gold, silver, bronze, and lead but points out that most of these objects were not "cult idols" but, rather, votive idols or idols used as amulets or for magical purposes. We may assume that idols used for worship per se have been lost precisely because they were made of wood and covered with precious metals, while the statues that served nonworship purposes have survived because most of them were made of baser materials.

Pseudo-Philo associates the beginning of idolatry with the invention of metallurgy by Tubal-Qain. *Biblical Antiquities* 2:9, elaborating upon Gen. 4:22, says "Sella bore Tobel and Miza and Theffa. This is Tobel who showed men arts in lead and tin and iron and copper and silver and gold. Then the inhabitants of the earth began to make sculpted objects and to worship them." H. Jacobsen (*A Commentary on Pseudo-Philo's Liber Antiquitatum Biblicarum With Latin Text and English Translation*, Arbeiten zur Geschichte des Antiken Judentums und des Urchristentums 31 [Leiden: E. J. Brill, 1996], 304-5) points out that the majority Rabbinic opinion (based on their interpretation of Gen. 4:26b) holds that idolatry started somewhat later, at the time of Enosh. If so, Pseudo-Philo may be of the opinion that idols must be made of metal and that their manufacture started as soon as the necessary technology became available.

3. See in particular Hab. 2:19 "Woe, you who say, 'Wake up' to wood, 'Awaken' to inert stone! Can it give an oracle? Why, it is encased in gold and silver (תפוש זהב וכסף) but there is no breath inside it." תפוש here, rendered "encased" (NJPS, NEB) or "overlaid" (KJV, REV), is equivalent to Akkadian *uḫḫuzu* (cf. CAD A/I, 179-80 s. v. *aḫāzu* 8a), "to mount an object in precious materials." This term applies frequently to overlaying metal on wooden objects and inlaying stones in wooden or stone objects. See "twenty minas of silver" *<ana>*

An episode in the Erra myth (see below), indicates that the preferred material in Mesopotamia for cult statues was wood of the *mēsu*-tree.[5]

ṣalmīka uḫḫuzim, "<to> mount your statues" (*ARM* 1, 74:4); *u inanna aḫuja ṣalmānu uppuqūtu . . . la tušēbila u ša iṣi uḫḫuzūtu tultēbila*, "and now, my brother, you have not sent me the solid (gold) statues, but (only) wooden ones, that are overlaid" (*EA* 27:33—letter of Tušratta); *u inanna Napḫurrija mārka ṣalmāni ša iṣi ūteḫḫizma*, "now Naphurrija, your son, has (only) overlaid (with gold) the statues of wood (yet in the land of your son gold is as common as dust)" (*EA* 26:41—letter of Tušratta); *inanna* RN [*ṣalmāni*] *ša iṣi ūteḫḫizma*, "now RN has covered wooden [images] (with gold)" (*EA* 26:41); URUDU*ṣalam en Nanna ḫurāṣamušaḫḫaz*, "I would like to have the copper statue of the en-priestess of Nanna mounted in gold" (*UET* 5, 75:5—OB letter of Kudur-Mabuk); [. . .] *lu uḫḫizma*, "[. . .] I overlaid" (5R 33 iv 1—Agum-kakrime referring to restoration of statues of Marduk and Ṣarpanitu). I. Ephal ("Isa. 40:19-20: On the Linguistic and Cultural Background of Deutero-Isaiah," *Shnaton* 10 [1986-89]: 31-35, esp. 33 [Hebrew]), points out that the Targum to Isa. 40:19-20 restores the Aramaic equivalent of *uḫḫuzu*, מאחיד, in the context of the description of an idol.

The polemics of Deutero-Isaiah and Jer. 10:1-16 refer to composite idols. *Epistle of Jeremiah*, an apocryphal work purporting to describe Mesopotamian idolatry, mentions gold, silver, and wood images (vss. 4, 11, 30, 57, 70) made by carpenters and goldsmiths. References to burning idols indicate most likely burning the wooden cores. This is most obvious in the case of the Golden Calf, but see also Deut. 7:5, 25; 2 Kgs. 19:18. Cutting down idols in Deut. 12:3 with the verb גדע suits objects of wood. For wooden idols, see Deut. 4:28 ועבדתם שם אלהים מעשה ידי אדם עץ ואבן; and cf. Deut. 28:36, 64; 2 Kgs. 19:18 = Isa. 37:19; Jer: 3:9(?); Isa. 45:20. For the composition of the Golden Calf, see S. E. Loewenstamm, "The Making and Destruction of the Golden Calf," *Biblica* 48 (1967): 481-90; F. C. Fensham, "The Burning of the Golden Calf at Ugarit," *IEJ* 16 (1966): 191-93; L. G. Perdue, "The Making and Destruction of the Golden Calf—A Reply," *Biblica* 54 (1973): 237-46; S. E. Loewenstamm, "The Making and Destruction of the Golden Calf—a Rejoinder," *Biblica* 56 (1975): 330-43; D. Frankel, "The Destruction of the Golden Calf: A New Solution," *VT* 44 (1994): 330-39; C. T. Begg, "The Destruction of the Golden Calf Revisited (Exod 32,20/Deut 9,21)," in *Deuteronomy and Deuteronomic Literature: Festschrift C. H. W. Brekelmans*, ed. M. Vervenne and J. Lust, Bibliotheca Ephemeridum Theologicarum Lovaniensium 133 (Leuven: Leuven University Press and Uitgeverij Peeters, 1997), 469-79. For detailed descriptions from Emar of cult statues overlain with precious metals see J. Goodnick-Westenholz, *Cuneiform Inscriptions in the Collection of the Bible Lands Museum Jerusalem: The Emar Tablets*, Cuneiform Monographs 13, (Gronningen: Styx, 2000), 63-67. Similar practices are recorded at Ebla for which see A. Archi, "Données épigraphique éblaites et production artistique," *RA* 84 (1990), 101-5.

4. See Deut. 4:26; 28:36, 64; 29:16; 2 Kgs. 19:18; Isa. 37:19; Jer. 2:27; 3:9; Ezek. 20:32; Hab. 2:19. אבן always appears together with עץ. This combination makes it unlikely that these passages refer to מצבות, "stone pillars." פסל, derived from the verb פסל, may originally have indicated a stone statue, but biblical Hebrew uses it for statues of any material.

5. The botanical identity of the *mēsu*-tree remains in dispute, and the word is often left untranslated, even in some recent works. No one has discussed why it is preferred as a tree for divine statues, if indeed there was such a preference. H. Zimmern (*Akkadische Fremdwörter als Beweis für babylonischen Kultureinfluss* [Leipzig: Hinrich'sche Buchhandlung, 1917] 53) identified the *mēsu* with Aramaic *maiša*, the Zürgelbaum or Celtis. Thompson (*DAB*, 248) provides no information about this tree or its wood. *AHw* 647 follows Zimmern and translates "Zürgelbaum," which is a sugar-berry or nettle-tree, *Celtis occidentalis*. This meaning is referred to by *CAD* Ṣ, 241b s.v. *ṣulmu*, discussion section. S. Cohen, "Enmerkar and the Lord of Aratta" (Ph.D. diss., University of Pennsylvania, 1973), 159 on l. 27, points out that *Celtia Australis* is white when young but as it grows old becomes black like ebony, therefore accounting for references to both black and white *mēsu*-trees. Professor Cohen has kindly

Marduk implies that without this particular wood his image cannot be refurbished.

This preference notwithstanding, a wider choice was in fact available. The *mēsu*-tree is called on one occasion *šīr ilī*, "the flesh of the gods," but the *bīnu*-tree is designated *eṣemti ilī*, "bone of divinity,"[6] or *eṣemti Igigi*, "bone of the Igigi" (*Maqlu* VI 5), and is used for divine figurines in various rituals.[7] The *bīnu* is also designated as "pure" (*ellu*) or "holy" (*quddušu*) and frequently serves as a purifying agent. A passage from "Inanna's Descent to the Netherworld" indicates the statue's composite nature, but does not mention the *mēsu* at all. In this text the goddess's body is made of boxwood, *taskarin* (ll. 43-46[8]):

---

brought to my attention S. Krauss, "Service Tree in the Bible and Talmud and in Modern Palestine," *HUCA* 1 (1924): 179-217. Krauss discusses the מיש, which is cognate to *mēsu*, and concurs with its identification with the Celtis, or Service Tree. He points out that Rabbinic Halakha prohibits burning מיש wood on the temple altar because it is very hard and tough and could not burn with a blazing flame (p. 199). I. Löw (*Flora* I, 627 and III, 416-17) mentions the appearance of the Zürgelbaum in various places in the Land of Israel and Lebanon and references to it in Rabbinic literature. These discussions notwithstanding, *CAD* M/II, 34 still maintains that the *mēsu* is "an unidentified large tree that is never imported, whose wood is used frequently for furniture; it has no fruit or medically used product." S. Dalley (*Myths from Mesopotamia* [Oxford/New York: Oxford University Press, 1989], 177) describes it as "a dark wood used in making divine statues, probably a form of rosewood (Dalbergia)." However, she seems to be confusing the *mēsu* with the *musukkannu*. Interestingly, an inscription of Simbar-šipak describing the refurbishing of a throne for Ellil gives the *mēsu*-wood the appelative *iṣu darû*, "enduring wood," otherwise reserved for the *musukkannu*. Is it possible that the ancient scribes too confused or deliberately switched the two terms or occasionally used them synonymously? This would be easily understandable given the fact that the *musukkannu* is called in Sumerian giš.mes.má.gan.na, "the mes of Magan," as if mes were a generic term designating several species while mes.magan were specific. For properties of the *Celtis australis L.*, see C. C. Townsend and E. Guest, *Flora of Iraq* (Baghdad: Ministry of Agriculture and Agrarian Reform, Republic of Iraq, 1980), 4:71-73. This species is quite common in the forest zone of Iraq at an altitude of 550-1300 m. It is a "small tree, 7-9 m., with smooth, grey bark." For a discussion of the מיש and a picture of a 110-year-old מיש tree from Jerusalem's Valley of the Cross, see Y. Feliks, *Fruit Trees in the Bible and Talmudic Literature* (Jerusalem: Rubin Mass, 1994), 257-59 (Hebrew).

6. F. A. M. Wiggermann, *Mesopotamian Protective Spirits: The Ritual Texts*, Cuneiform Monographs 1 (Groningen: Styx, 1992), 81. Note the *mīs pî* ritual incantation to the *bīnu* (giš.šinig), tamarisk, stating "from its trunk gods are made." See C. B. F. Walker, M. Dick, *The Induction of the Cult Image in Ancient Mesopotamia, The Mesopotamian Mīs Pî Ritual*, State Archives of Assyria Literary Texts, 1 (Helsinki: The Neo-Assyrian Text Corpus Project, Institute for Asian and African Studies, University of Helsinki, 2001) 97, 100 l. 4. Another incantation mentions eight different types of forests from which the new statue comes out. See, Walker, Dick, *Mīs Pî*, 115, 120 ll. 22-29 and below, n. 25.

7. Cf. *CAD* B, 242.

8. See W. R. Sladek, "Inanna's Descent to the Netherworld" (Ph.D. diss., Johns Hopkins University, 1974), 108-9, 156. Translation here follows G. Buccellati, "The Descent of Inanna as a Ritual Journey to Kutha?" *Syro-Mesopotamian Studies* 4/3 (1982): 3-7, esp. 5. Buccellati cites Paul Gaebelein's suggestion that certain portions of this myth refer to a statue of the goddess.

Father Enlil, let not your daughter be put to death in the Netherworld,
Let not your good metal be covered with the dust of the Netherworld,
Let not your good lapis lazuli be broken up into the stone of the stoneworker,
Let not your *boxwood* (*taskarin*) be cut up into the wood of the woodworker.

A cultic compendium concerning Marduk lists seven statues of Marduk, each of a different substance.[9] A. R. George contends that Marduk's major statue found in the [*bīt papaḫ*]*u* and named Asalluḫi was of *mēsu*. But other statues of the same god listed in the same text were of boxwood (*taskarinu*), *marḫuššu*-stone, alabaster, and haemetite.

Figurines for ritual use (not necessarily objects of worship) were made of numerous types of wood. Two figurines of uncertain character used in the Akitu festival consist of cedar and tamarisk, decorated with gold inlay and *dušû*-stone.[10] An apotropaic ritual prescribes figurines of cornel and tamarisk,[11] while another requires *ḫaluppu*, cedar, *ašūḫu*, juniper, and *ḫutpalu*.

Despite an apparent preference for wood, other materials were also used. The Old Babylonian forerunner of the lexical series Ur_5-ra = *ḫubullu* mentions *lamas* and *alans* of copper, silver, and gold.[12] Some economic documents from Ibbi-Sin's eleventh year refer to manufacturing a statue of the goddess Nanaya of copper, plated with silver, and overlaid with gold for the eyes, mouth, and arms.[13] Some ceremonies require figurines of clay or wax.[14] A Neo-Assyrian letter from Nabû-bān-aḫḫe to Esarhaddon (*ABL* 531:7) mentions an image of silver and another of bronze overlain with gold. Another letter speaks of a golden image (*ABL* 1219: r. 1). There is no indication of the nature of these images, but the costly material may indicate they are divine statues.[15]

---

9. For BM 119282, see A. R. George, "Marduk and the Cult of the Gods of Nippur at Babylon," *Orientalia* 66 (1997): 65-70.

10. *Racc* 133, ll. 201-16. See M. Cohen, *The Cultic Calendars of the Ancient Near East* (Bethesda, MD: CDL Press, 1993), 442. The figurines are not said to represent specific deities. Their divine nature is indicated by the fact that they carry in their hands a scorpion and a snake respectively and are housed in the temple of the god Madānu and given bran from his offering table. Even so, they are subsequently beheaded and thrown into the ashes of a fire burning before Nabû.

11. F. A. M. Wiggermann, *Mesopotamian Protective Spirits*.

12. *MSL* 7 235: 47-48; 237: 71-72; 240: 111-12.

13. *UET* 3, 509, 525, 538, 740. J. Goodnick-Westenholz ("Nanaya: Lady of Mystery," in *Sumerian Gods and Their Representations*, ed. I. J. Finkel and M. J. Geller, Cuneiform Monographs 7 [Groningen: Styx 1997], 57-84, esp. 61) calls these objects cult statues, but their exact nature is unclear. Why were five made? Were they all used in the same place or in the same manner?

14. R. Borger, "Tonmännchen und Puppen," *BiOr* 30 (1973): 176-83.

15. But note *ABL* 114 r. 3-4, which mentions gold images of the king and his mother, showing that not every statue of precious metal need be a divine image.

Great efforts were expended in order to procure superior materials for use in cult images, be it wood, metals, precious stones, or even clay. Various documents reveal details of how such materials were acquired.

In a letter to Esarhaddon the scribes Nabû-aḫḫe-erība and Balasi tell the king that they were shown "eye-stones" for the crown of Nabû and that they were very good.[16] The writers add words of prayer that Nabû bless the king and his progeny. Similarly, a letter from Mār-Ishtar to Esarhaddon reports delivery of twenty-six eye-stones of serpentine and one mina of gold to be used for Nabû's tiara. The eye-stones from the king and the gold from the queen mother arrived guarded by a trusted official and under seal, indicating that they had not been tampered with on the way. Here too, the report of the shipment is followed by a prayer that Bēl and Nabû bless the king and the royal family.[17]

The pseudo-autobiography of Agum-kakrime lists ten types of semi-precious gems lavished upon Marduk and Ṣarpanitum as decorations for their clothing on the occasion of their refurbishing (col. 2, ll. 36-49).[18] After enumerating them they are typified as *ša ina šadîšu nasqū*, "which were *selected* from the mountain." (col. 2, l. 42.) This expression may be compared with Marduk's rhetorical question in Erra I 161 *ali abnū nasqūti*

16. *ABL* 404 = Parpola, *LAS* 58 = *SAA* X 41. For discussion see Parpola, *LAS* 2, 62-63, no. 58. The verb used for showing is *ukallimūnašini*, derived from *kullumu*. In the Sun-disk inscription and the Nabonidus inscription discussed above, this word has the connotation of "divine revelation." It is possible that in this letter too there is some added connotation to the use of this particular verb. The blessing, which occupies half of the letter, ends: *nēmelu ša mār šarri ša aḫḫēšu Nabû ana šarri bēlīni lukallim*, "may Nabu reveal to the king our lord the profit (prosperity) of the son of the king and his brothers." There may be an intended connection between the *kullumu* of the report and the same word in the blessing. Perhaps the revelation of the stones for the crown is a propitious event, announcing prosperity for the royal family. *ABL* 689 = *SAA* X, no. 40, involving the same two people, is also a report about some precious stones (*šanduppu* and *ašgikû*), and they may be related to the same project involving the divine crown.

17. *ABL* 340:13-22 = Parpola, *LAS* 276 = *SAA* X 348: 13-22. For discussion see Parpola, *LAS* 2, 264, no. 276. Parpola notes that the eye-stones were mounted on divine tiaras, perhaps to symbolize the all-pervasive vision of the gods. W. G. Lambert ("An Eye-stone of Esarhaddon's Queen and Other Similar Gems," *RA* 63 [1969]: 65-71) gathers several examples of inscribed eye-stone votives. He also notes an enigmatic line at the end of "Ishtar's Descent to the Netherworld": *īnāte malâ birk[āša]*, "[her] lap was full of eye-stones," and *īnātēša undallâ* GARZA [x(x)], "she filled [. . .] with her eye-stones." These passages indicate that eye-stones were not used specifically for statue eyes but could be placed all over the divine image. Compare Ezek. 1:18 וגבתם מלאת עינים סביב, "their rims were full of eyes." Rashi comments, "to see in every direction, for they did not turn when walking," reminding us of Parpola's explanation for the eye-stones.

18. For the Akkadian text, see T. Longman III, "Fictional Akkadian Royal Autobiography: A Generic and Comparative Study" (Ph.D. diss., Yale University, 1983), 146-212; for translation and discussion, cf. idem, *Fictional Akkadian Autobiography: A Generic and Comparative Study* (Winona Lake, IN: Eisenbrauns, 1991), 85-88, 221-24. Col. ii ll. 36-45 record the assignment of the materials (*lu addinuma*) while lines 46-49 record how they were used (*lu uzaʾʾinuma*). The same structure was found in lines 26-35. First the gold is assigned (*addinuma*, ll. 28-31) and afterwards the gods are clothed with it (*lu ulabbišūšunutima*, ll. 32-35).

binūt tâmtim rapaštim simat agê, "where are the *select stones*, creation of the broad sea, suited for a crown?"[19]

The letters and literary texts alike indicate a selection process to assure using only the finest stones. Moreover, the two literary texts imply that the stones were brought from far away and are not homegrown. They originate and were actually selected outside the realm of human settlement.

Jeremiah 10:9 tells of beaten silver brought from Tarshish and gold from Uphaz(?), indicating the great effort and expense invested in acquiring the best metals for use in idols. If Tarshish is indeed in Spain and Uphaz is a corruption of Ophir, as many scholars suggest, then we must interpret the prophet's words as if to say "idol makers bring silver and gold from the very ends of the earth."[20]

Native Mesopotamian inscriptions too emphasize the exotic origin of gold (and precious stones) used in cult statues. Esarhaddon boasts (Borger, *Esarh.* 83, §53, AsBbA rev. 30-32):

> *[ḫu]rāṣu atru eper šaddîšu ša mamman la iptiqūšu ana šipir nikilti*
> *abnē nasqūti la ki-*ŠID*-ti šamme ša nība la īšû*
> *nabnīt ḫuršāni ša Ea ana šipir bēlūti šīmat melammī rabîš išīmšunūti . . .*
> *qātēšunu ellēti ušamli*
>
> Quality gold, dust of the mountains, which no one had worked for any artistic task, select stones not overgrown(?) by vegetation, which had no number, creation of the mountain region, which Ea, for work of lordship, had greatly determined a destiny of radiance, . . . I placed in their (the craftsmen's) hands.

This passage emphasizes not only the mountain origin of the precious metal and the selection of the stones, but indicates that only virgin materials, which even in their natural state had served no function and are not suspected of having been touched by human hands, were desirable for use in cult statues. Moreover, Ea himself had designated the stones for their exalted use. The *melammū* (radiance) of the gold and stones is the divine characteristic *par excellence*, and this very quality Ea has instilled in the stone. In other words, the property making the stones divine does not occur naturally, inherent in the stones, but itself is of divine origin.

Elsewhere Esarhaddon describes the fashioning of Bēl, Bēltija, Bēlet-Bābil, Ea, and Madānu (Borger, *Esarh.*, §88 para. 57, AsBbE 14-15):

---

19. See also Riekele Borger, *Die Inschriften Asarhaddons Königs von Assyrien*, Beiheft 9 (Osnabrück: Biblio-Verlag, 1967 [1956]) 83, §53, AsBbA rev. 30-32 to be discussed below. One of the *Mīs Pî* ritual incantations mentions at least ten different types of stones, one of which is an *aban nisiqti* (= na_4 suḫ [MÚŠ]). See Walker, Dick, *Mīs Pî*, 140, 150, l. 65-67.

20. On the location of Tarshish in the Iberian Peninsula, see M. Elat, "Tarshish in Isaiah 23 and History," *Shnaton* 10 (1986-89): 17-30.

ina 50 bilti ṣariru ruššê nabnīt šad Arallî
epir šaddîšu ša ana šipri la patqu
ušarriḫ gattašun

With fifty talents of red shining gold, product of the Aralli mountains,
dust of the mountain, which for (skilled) work had not been formed
I made their limbs luxurious.

This passage emphasizes not only the unworked nature of the gold but claims that it originates from *Arallû*-mountain. This is a real place, but its name invokes the Mountain of the Underworld, *šad Arallî*, considered the birth place of demons and gods, so it is quite appropriate that gold used in making divine statues originate in this region[21]

These inscriptions present ideal circumstances, but reality may have been different. Quite another situation is implied in a "day-to-day" document of no ideological or tendentious nature. A letter from Mār-Issar(?) deals with gold needed to plate images of Nanaya, Arkayitu, Anunitu, Palil of the temple of Mummu, and Uṣur-amassa.[22] The letter mentions a reminder to the king that gold has accumulated in the temples of Uruk and there is repair work to be done on the statues. The text does not specify the source or quality of the gold, but there is no reason to think that it was virgin metal, fresh from the mines. It may have originated from private contributions, tribute or taxes.[23]

---

21. Andreas Fuchs, *Die Inschriften Sargons II. aus Khorsabad* (Göttingen: Cuvillier Verlag, 1993) 182, Ann. 426-27: *Ea Sīn Šamaš Nabû Adad Ninurta u ḫīrātīšun rabâti ša ina qereb Eḫursaggalkurkurra šad Arallî kīniš iʾʾaldū. . . .* For *Šadi Arallî* as a toponym, see E. Reiner, "Lipšur Litanies," *JNES* 15 (1956): 132, l. 21, where KUR *A-ra-lu* MIN KUR KÙ.GI appears in a list along with thirty other mountains (and cf. ibid. 147 for geographical list ḪAR.RA = *ḫubullu* XXII 19′ [*MSL* XI, 23 XXII 22]: KUR *A-ra-li* = MIN *ḫu-ra-ṣi*). This is how the term is understood by *AHw*, 64 ("als Berg"), *CAD* A/II, 227 (red gold, the product of the *A*-mountain) and Borger ("des Arallu-Berges"). See also M. Stol, *Old Babylonian History*, 41-42; Sjöberg, "A Hymn to Inanna and Her Self-Praise," *JCS* 40 (1988): 174; W. Horowitz, *Mesopotamian Cosmic Geography* (Winona Lake, IN: Eisenbrauns, 1998), 282, n. 19.

22. *SAA* X 349 = Parpola *LAS* 277 = *ABL* 476; cf. Parpola *LAS* 2, 265, and V. Hurowitz, "Another Fiscal Practice in the Ancient Near East (LAS 277)," *JNES* 45 (1986): 289-94. Joint royal and clerical supervision of temple income and assets is indicated also in *ABL* 498, a letter from Ibašši-ilu to Esarhaddon. The scribe reports that jewels to be used for the crown of Anu are being stored in the treasure house of the Assur Temple (*bīt nakkandi ša bīt Aššur*), which will not be opened without the *šangu* and Nabû-ēṭir-napšati. For joint supervision of temple finances and expenditures on cult in the Neo-Babylonian period, see G. Frame, "Nabonidus, Nabû-šarra-uṣur, and the Eanna Temple," *ZA* 81 (1991): 37-86, esp. 66-80.

23. Likewise, in *ABL* 340 = *SAA* X, 348: 11-17 discussed above, eye-stones and gold for Nabû's tiara are said to have belonged, respectively, to the king and his mother. *ABL* 498, a letter from Irašši-ilu to Esarhaddon, also indicates a mixed origin of materials for divine regalia. We read: "The twelve mina of gold which came to me from the gifts (*šulmānātu*) of Bel I will make into the rosettes and *tenšû*-ornaments of Ṣarpanitum. The seals which the

Scholars have determined that Esarhaddon's work on Babylon, restoring temples and repairing cult statues, took place after his Egyptian campaigns. Since the cost of work in Babylonia must have been enormous, it may have been financed in part from booty taken in conquering Egypt, so some of the precious materials for repairing the divine statues may have been plundered.[24]

The seeming contradiction between the practices assumed by the letter and the evidence of the royal inscriptions shows a gap between the ideal and the real. In practice, gold was acquired from any available source, but for the sake of the gods and posterity the kings announced that the gold was pristine, touched only by the gods.

Deutero-Isaiah twice lists types of wood used in idols, even mentioning that an idol-maker plants a cedar in the forest and rainwater makes it grow (Isa. 40:20; 48:14). Similarly, an incantation in the Mesopotamian *Mīs pî* ("mouth-washing") ritual lists at least eight types of trees populating the forest where the tree for the idol grew,[25] and adds that Ea has irrigated the roots with subterranean water. If so, the raw material itself is already a divinely nurtured product, untouched by human hands. It is even possible that the prophet, by mentioning rainwater, may be polemicizing with the Mesopotamian notion that trees for statues are watered by a god.

As mentioned above, the wood favored for cultic statues was from the *mēsu* tree. The Erra epic describes this tree as a special species. Marduk, in his refusal to undergo renovations and repairs, asks rhetorically:

ali mēsu šīr ilī simat šar gimri
iṣṣu ellu eṭlu ṣīru ša šūluku ana bēlūti[26]
ša ina tâmtim rapaštim mê 1 ME bēru išissu ikšudu šupul arallî
qimmassu ina elâti emdetu šamê ša [*Anim*]

---

king my lord gave me I am now making. The jewels (on hand at this time) will be used for the crown of Anu, but your (the king's) jewels will be used for the sun-disks. They are laid up in the treasure-house of the Assur temple."

24. G. Frame, *Babylonia 689-627 B. C.: A Political History* (Istanbul: Nederlands Historisch-Archaeologish Instituut te Istanbul, 1992), 76; and cf. J. Brinkman, *Prelude to Empire*, Occasional Publications of the Babylonian Fund 7 (Philadelphia: University Museum, 1992), 76-77, n. 368.

25. *STT* 199 (see below). These include *ḫašḫurru*, cedar, cypress, fig, *taskarinnu*, mulberry, *ušû*, and nettle. Interestingly, *mēsu* is missing from this list. We may think at first that the incantation refers to the possible woods that could be used for the image. However, given the known preference for the *mēsu*, we might see this as a list of the woods that were *not* used, and assume that the text describes the neighborhood in which the *mēsu* sprouted and not that tree itself. See Walker, Dick, *Mīs Pî*, 115, 120 ll. 22-31.

26. Cf. Borger, *Esarh.*, 88 r. 16 cited above, which describes the gold *ša ana bēlūtišun maʾdiš šūlukat*.

Where is the *mēsu*-tree, flesh of the gods, suited to the king of the Universe,
The holy/pure, tree, the princely young man, suitable for lordship,
Which in the broad sea its roots extend in the water to below the Netherworld to a distance of an hundred double-hours' walk,
and whose branches above touch the heaven of [Anu] (the highest heaven)?

These lines describe no ordinary tree. The tree depicted is a cosmic tree, filling the universe. It is broad as the sea, tall as the highest heavens, and rooted in the earth deeper than even the Netherworld. Similar descriptions apply in Mesopotamian literature to temples, divine paraphernalia, and gods. For example, a bilingual hymn describes Ellil:

kur.gal den.líl.lá im.ḫur.sag gú.bi an.da ab.di.a zu.ab.kù.ga.bi
suḫ.bi: uš.uš.e: úru.úru.e

šadû rabû Ellil imḫursag ša rēšāšu šamāmi šannā
apsî ellim šuršudū uššūšu

The great mountain Ellil-Great-Mountain, whose head is like the heavens
and whose foundations are established in the pure Deep

According to W. Lambert, such passages ". . . show that the idea of greatness, whether applied to gods, temples, a god's net, or a mythical tree, is expressed in terms of filling the whole universe: based on the underworld and reaching to heaven."[27] F. Greenspahn suggests that encompassing the universe, from the heavens above to the waters below, is a divine trait. R. C. Van Leeuwen notes that the specific divine prerogatives entailed in encompassing the universe would be immortality, super-

27. W. G. Lambert, *Babylonian Wisdom Literature* (Oxford: Clarendon Press, 1960) 327. See also F. E. Greenspahn, "A Mesopotamian Proverb and its Biblical Reverberations," *JAOS* 114 (1994): 33-38; R. C. Van Leeuwen, "The Background to Proverbs 30:4aα," in *Wisdom, You Are My Sister: Studies in Honor of Roland E. Murphy, O. Carm., on the Occasion of His Eightieth Birthday*, ed. Michael L. Barré, S. S., CBQ Monograph Series 29 (Washington, DC: Catholic Biblical Association of America, 1997), 102-21. Cf. Ezek. 31:3-4 הנה אשור ארז בלבנון יפה ענף וחרש מצל וגבה קומה ובין עבתים היתה צמרתו מים גדלוהו תהום רממתהו את נהרתיה הלך סביבות מטעה ואת תעלתיה שלחה אל כל עצי השדה "Assyria was a cedar in Lebanon with beautiful branches and shady thickets, of lofty stature, with its top among leafy trees. Waters nourished it, the deep made it grow tall, washing with its streams the place where it was planted, making its channels well up to all the trees of the field" (NJPS). Thrice more in the same prophecy we find that the roots of the tree were in the מים רבים (vss. 5, 7, 15). The prophet compares pharaoh with the king of Assyria, who is likened in turn to a cosmic tree. Given the association Assyrians made between the king and the sacred tree, Ezekiel may be alluding here to Mesopotamian beliefs.

human knowledge, wisdom and power. I propose that this trait includes what we today call omnipresence, and it is expressed as a merismus by ancient authors.

But the tree is more than divinely omnipresent. It is also personified. It is not only pure or holy, but a bilingual word play, taking *mēsu* as equivalent to Sumerian MES, which means *eṭlu ṣīru*, lets the tree itself be understood as "an exalted/ princely young man, suited for lordship." These titles suit a human or a divine king but hardly a plank of lumber.[28] Interestingly, both *eṭlu* and *ṣīru* are common epithets of gods and kings, but the combination into a single title is very rare. *CAD* E, 410a, s.v. *eṭlu* 2b2′ lists but a single occurrence of GURUŠ *ṣīru*, in an inscription of Nebuchadrezzar II (*VAB* 4, 144, i 32), where it is an epithet of Marduk! It seems that the *mēsu* is no simple tree but is already a god. In fact, the tree already is Marduk![29] When made into a statue it does not change its essence in the least. The new statue is not a new entity but a transformation or metamorphosis of a previously existing divinity. The statue, which we might consider a new god, was in fact always a god and it remains one. At most, the statue is a concentrate of the god which fills the universe, packaged in a form which can be conveniently introduced and worshipped in a temple.

The attitude to the tree reflected in this mythic passage may have been the target of a very late Jewish anti-idolatry polemic. A discussion of the merits of various materials used in idols appears in the Apocalypse of Abraham. This work survives in Slavonic manuscripts from the fourteenth and fifteenth centuries C.E., but may go back to an ancient Hebrew or Aramaic original.[30] The composition begins with an autobiographical account of Abraham, apprenticed as a carpenter in his father's idol shop, and his growing doubts about idolatry. Once upon a time, while ques-

---

28. King Šulgi of Ur is compared to a *mes*-tree. In Šulgi F we read: "On the day of his elevation to kingship, / He radiated like a fertile *mes*-tree, watered by fresh water, / Extending (his) blossoming branches towards the pure water course; Upon his blossoming branches Utu conferred the (following) blessing: / Being a fertile *mes*-tree, he has borne fruit, / Šulgi, the righteous shepherd of Sumer, will truly spread abundance!" Šulgi P a15 describes the king: "He is my *mes*-tree, with 'shining' branches, he *sprang up* from the soil for me." For texts and translation, see J. Klein, *The Royal Hymns of Shulgi King of Ur: Man's Quest for Immortal Fame*, Transactions of the American Philosophical Society 71/7 (Philadelphia: American Philosophical Society, 1981), 11, 24, n. 122.

29. Note also that another writing for Marduk is ^{d}MES.

30. See A. Pennington, "The Apocalypse of Abraham," in *The Apocryphal Old Testament*, ed. H. F. D. Sparks (Oxford: Clarendon Press, 1984), 363-91. For possible Hebraisms, see A. Rubinstein, "Hebraisms in the Slavonic Apocalypse of Abraham," *JJS* 4 (1953): 108-15 and 5 (1954): 132-35. To the suggestions there we may add "with branches and blossoms and praises" in manuscripts R, J, and K. It seems that "praises" may go back to a Hebrew פארי, a term for the upper branches of a tree.

tioning his father Terah why he worships Barisat, who seems to be the weakest of his idols, he compares the materials out of which the idols were made. Zuch, god of Terah's brother Aron (Haran), is made of gold, so he is more honorable than Terah's own god Marumath, who is of stone. This is because gold is highly prized by men and may be repaired while stone cannot be destroyed. Even Joauv, who is made of silver, is more to be worshipped than the wooden Barisat. This is because silver is prized by men for its brilliance and the idol is also reparable. But Barisat, made of wood, has just burnt up in a fire for cooking Terah's food.[31] This passage is followed in three manuscripts by a discourse on the tree from which Barisat had been fashioned:

> But Barisat, your god, when he was still not made, was rooted in the earth, great and wonderful, with branches and blossoms and praises; and then you cut him with an axe, and he was made into a god by your skill. And behold, now he is withered, and his richness has perished, and from the height he is fallen to the ground, and from greatness has he come to littleness, and his outward form has disappeared, and he is burnt up in the fire.

This passage describes the tree from which Barisat was hewn. He was a glorious tree, deeply rooted, tall, and very great. This description has some of the flavor of the portrait of the *mēsu*-tree in the Erra myth. The *mēsu* too was rooted in the subterranean sea and its branches touched the heavens. It would be dangerous to suggest that the two passages are genetically related,[32] but the similarity invites comparison and contrast. Both texts describe an ideal tree from which an idol is made. But, whereas the Mesopotamian passage regards the glorious qualities of the tree to be transplanted and incorporated into the god fashioned from it, the apocryphal polemic takes quite the opposite view. The act of fashioning the tree into an idol obliterates the very qualities which the Mesopotamian author thought qualified the tree to be a god.

Even the basest of materials are rendered sacred for use in divine figurines. A ritual for founding a new temple called for figurines of the god Ninšubur.[33] These figurines were to be of clay prepared in a brief ritual

---

31. See Isa. 47:14: הנה היו כקש אש שרפתם לא יצילו את נפשם מיד להבה אין גחלת לחמם אור לשבת נגדו, which is combined with Isa. 44:19: ולא ישיב אל לבו ולא דעת ולא תבונה לאמר חציו שרפתי במו אש ואף אפיתי על גחליו לחם אצלה בשר ואכל ויתרו לתועבה אעשה לבול עץ אסגור.

32. The ultimate inspiration for the apocalyptic passage may be Ezekiel 31, which describes Pharaoh as the king of Assyria, or Daniel 4, which describes the king of Babylon. They all describe in similar terms cosmic trees which suffer similar fates. However, the association of the tree with the idol found in Erra and the Apocalypse of Abraham has no parallel in these biblical passages and may have come from outside.

33. R. Borger, "Tonmännchen und Puppen," *BiOr* 30 (1973): 176-83. The name given

consisting of sacrifice, prayer, and gesture. Three days before founding the temple, the ritualist was to go to the clay pit. He was to take lapis lazuli, mix together roasted flour and emmer beer, throw them into the clay pit and say: "Clay Pit! Take your purchase price (ŠÁM-ZU). Three days from now I will make a Ninšubur-figure out of your clay." Afterwards he was to bow down and leave. The clay pit and clay are referred to subsequently in the ritual as having been dedicated/ sanctified[34] (*quddušu;* ll. 13, 33). If so, the ritual is an act of dedicating/ sanctifying the clay for the figurine. Dedicating the clay is accomplished by purchasing the clay from the pit and announcing that it will be used for making a god. The figurine is thus not of ordinary, profane clay, but of ritually dedicated/ sacred clay. Dedicating the clay before its use may be compared to "waving" (תנופה) the contributions of precious metals used in making the Tabernacle. In both cases, profane materials are not incorporated directly into the sacred object but must first be turned into holy material.

A similar but longer and more explicit ritual involving clay for figurines designated as "creatures of the Abzu" (*binūt Apsî*) is found in the apotropaic ritual *Šēp lemutti ina bīt amēli parāsu,* "To block the entry of the enemy into someone's house."[35] The clay is consecrated (*kullata tuqaddaš*) and the clay pit is purified (*kullata tuḫâb*). Purification is done by censer, torch, and holy water, while purchasing the clay is accomplished by throwing into the pit seven grains of silver, seven grains of gold, carnelian, and *ḫulalu* stone. A lengthy incantation explains the ritual (ll. 152-57):

> Clay pit, clay pit, clay pit of Anu and Enlil!
> Clay pit of Ea, lord of the deep, clay pit of the great gods are you!
> You have made the lord for lordship, you have made the king for kingship, you have made the prince for future, distant days;
> Your pieces of silver are given to you, you have received them;
> your gift you have received;
> and so, in the morning before Šamaš, I pinch off the clay of NN son of NN;
> May it be profitable, may what I do prosper.

---

to this ritual by Borger is somewhat misleading. The text itself prescribes a ritual for founding a temple and the next tablet in the series is for establishing the threshold. Preparing the Ninšubur figurine is only part of the larger foundation rite.

34. Borger ("Tonmännchen und Puppen," 176-83) translates "geweihen," whereas *CAD* K, 46 s.v. *kullatu* B translates "made ritually clean," and *CAD* Q, 46 s.v. *qadāšu* places the passages under "to make ritually clean, to purify." There is no reason, however, not to translate "to consecrate, dedicate" here (cf. *CAD* Q, 46 s.v. *qadāšu* 4). Such a rendition is justified not only by the etymology of the word but by the fact that the ritual prescribes no acts of purification such as immersion in water or fumigation, and that the ritualist's pronouncement promises to use the clay to make a divine figurine.

35. F. A. M. Wiggermann, *Mesopotamian Protective Spirits,* 12-13, ll. 144-61.

This incantation first proclaims the divine ownership of the clay pit. It belongs to Anu and Enlil, who are chief gods in the pantheon and gods of the heavens and the atmosphere. But it belongs especially to Ea, god of crafts and craftsmen and denizen of the subterranean waters which keep the clay moist and malleable. Associating the clay with these three gods links it to the three cosmic regions, thus achieving omnipresence. The incantation then invokes the clay pit's primordial role as the place of origin of the material from which the highest ranks of human beings were produced. This part of the incantation may be evoking as well associations with the creation myth Atrahasis and the related piece VAT 17019.[36] By evoking Creation and noting that the prince was made for distant days *rubâ tabni ana lubar ūmē rūqūtu* (l. 154), the ritual spans time from beginning to end, giving an eternal temporal dimension to its work.

It is apparent, therefore, that even the basest material is integrated into the divine realm and given divine qualities before it is formed into the body of a divine figurine.

The Bible does not mention idols of clay. Such objects do occur, however, in the Apocrypha. Bel and the Dragon (Daniel and the Priests of Bel) vs. 7 mentions an idol of Bel made of clay within and bronze without. Wisdom of Solomon 15:7-13 in a lengthy, biting diatribe against clay idols refers to idol makers as potters.

An interesting aspect of this diatribe is some allusions to the creation of man in Genesis 2-3. In Wisdom of Solomon 15:8 we read:[37]

> With misspent toil he (the potter/idol-maker) molds a nothing-god out of the same clay, he who but shortly before came into being out of the earth and shortly after returns whence he was taken, when the life that was lent him is demanded back.

This passage echoes Genesis 3:19:

> By the sweat of your nostrils you will eat bread until you return to the earth, for you were taken from the earth, for dust you are, and to dust you shall return.

In Wisdom of Solomon 15:11 we find:

> . . . he knew not the one who fashioned him and infused him with an active soul and breathed into him a vital spirit.

---

36. Cf. W. R. Mayer, "Ein Mythos von der Erschaffung des Menschen und des Königs," *Orientalia* 56 (1987): 55-68.

37. Translation according to D. Winston, *The Wisdom of Solomon*, Anchor Bible 43 (Garden City, NY: Doubleday, 1979), 285.

This reflects Genesis 2:7:

> And YHWH God formed the man of dust from the earth and blew into his nostrils a breath of life, and the man became a living creature.

It is quite remarkable that the Akkadian incantation and the apocryphal passage both draw connections between molding clay idols and the creation of mankind. I suggest that this may be no mere coincidence. Although writing in biblical language, the apocryphal author may have known that makers of idols in clay indeed regarded themselves as rehearsers of the primordial creation of human beings. However, the polemicist rejects the notion that lends efficacy to production of the idol, viewing it, rather, as a supreme act of hubris, stupidity, and fraud. Moreover, the incantation's claim that clay for the idol served also for such noble creations as kings may underlie the apocryphal caricature telling how the clay made into the idol could otherwise go into clean or unclean vessels of all sorts.

Materials Used in Biblical Idols

The Mesopotamian texts praise the high quality and divine origin, ownership, and nature of the materials used in cult statues. This is to be expected. It comes as no surprise that biblical authors too report the idol makers' positive attitudes towards the ingredients used. Isaiah 40:20 tells of selecting wood for the statue המסכן תרומה עץ לא ירקב יבחר. However we understand the particular types of lumber,[38] it is clear that the prophet

38. See in particular H. G. M. Williamson, "Isaiah 40:20—A Case of Not Seeing the Wood for the Trees," *Biblica* 67 (1986): 1-20. Strangely, J. D. W. Watts (*Isaiah 34-66*, Word Biblical Commentary 25 [Waco, TX: Word Books, 1987], 87) rejects Williamson's suggestion. He prefers to translate "The expert in such offerings," following P. Trudinger, "'To Whom then will you liken God?' (A Note on the Interpretation of Isaiah XL 18-20)," *VT* 17 (1967): 220-25. M. C. A. Korpel ("Soldering in Isaiah 40:19-20 and I Kings 6:21," *UF* 23 [1991]: 219-22) also rejects interpreting המסכן as a tree and prefers to re-vocalize it as a D participle *hammesakkēn*. K. Holter (*Second Isaiah's Idol-Fabrication Passages*, Beiträge zur biblischen Exegese und Theologie 28 [Frankfurt am Main: Peter Lang, 1995], 41-59) sees מסכה as a word for "image," parallel to פסל. In my opinion, we should follow Williamson and others with the "tree-rendering," especially in light of I. Ephal's and Ch. Cohen's conclusive suggestion (see below) that עץ לא ירקב is a traditional apellative of מסכן = *musukkannu* equivalent to Akkadian *iṣu dāru*. תרומה too awaits satisfactory explanation. A. Fitzgerald ("The Technology of Isaiah 40:19-20 + 41:6-7," *CBQ* 51 [1989]: 426-46, esp. 442) suggests that the idol the prophet portrays is entirely of metal and that only the base is of wood. Accordingly he explains תרומה as "platform." K. Holter (*Second Isaiah's Idol-Fabrication Passages*, 48) understands it as "offering," as in most other places in the Bible. We prefer to follow Rashi, who doesn't regard it as a tree but as meaning "separate" or "select." There is parallelism between יבחר

emphasizes the care in selection and may even reflect Mesopotamian terminology since the term עץ לא ירקב, "wood which does not rot," is equivalent to Akkadian *iṣ(ṣ)u dāru*.[39] Ezekiel 7:20 relates that Israelite idols too were made from the finest jewelry: "for out of their beautiful adornments, in which they took pride, they made their images and their detestable abominations—therefore I will make them an unclean thing to them." It is most interesting, in light of the Mesopotamian texts, that the material for some idols is said to have come from God (Ezek. 16:17): "You took your beautiful things (i.e. jewelry) made of silver and gold that I had given you, and you made phallic images and fornicated with them."

Despite the similarities, the attitude towards using materials of divine origin for a cult-statue is conditioned directly by the context. What the idol maker regards as a mark of honor and greatness for the idol is portrayed by the prophets with derision, as a sign of stupidity on the one hand and disgrace or ingratitude on the other. The biblical depictions, even when reflecting reality, are in fact caricatures.

Some biblical authors admit that idol-makers carefully chose their ingredients, but others highlight the profane nature or dubious origin of the materials. As a case in point, the silver that Michayehu's mother uses for the statue in her son's temple is tainted (Judg. 17:1-13).[40] The farcical story starts abruptly, telling how the mother has lost eleven hundred shekels of silver which she tries to retrieve by using an אָלָה-imprecation. Unknown to her, it was her son who had "taken" (i.e. stolen)[41] the silver. When, upon hearing his mother's curse, Michayehu returns the loot, she repeals her malediction by blessing her son, and dedicates the returned silver for use in making an idol. Nonetheless, she cuts costs, investing only two hundred shekels in the actual work. We may assume that she

---

and תרומה. Combining these suggestions permits understanding תרומה // עץ לא ירקב יבחר מסכן as "the *musukkannu* tree is (his) selection, a tree which will not rot he chooses." For הרים with בחר see Ps. 89:20: אז דברת בחזון לחסידיך ותאמר שויתי עזר על גבור הרמותי בחור מעם, "Then You spoke to Your faithful ones in a vision and said, 'I have conferred power upon a warrior; I have exalted (תרמותי) one chosen (בחור) out of the people.'"

39. I. Ephal, "Isa. 40:19-20. On the Linguistic and Cultural Background of Deutero-Isaiah," *Shnaton* 10 (1986-89): 31-35 (Hebrew); Ch. Cohen, "Fixed Terms for Trees in Akkadian and Isaiah 40:20" (unpublished lecture, Tenth World Congress of Jewish Studies, Jerusalem, 1993). I thank Professor Cohen for providing me with a manuscript of his paper.

40. See Y. Amit, *The Book of Judges: The Art of Editing*, The Biblical Encyclopaedia Library 6 (Jerusalem: Mossad Bialik, 1992), 300-301 (Hebrew).

41. Y. Kaufman (*Sefer Shofetim* [Jerusalem: Kiryat Sepher, 1962]) idiosyncratically explains: "Micah does not speak about stealing but about taking, apparently to hint that he took the silver for needs of the household and with the intention of returning it. Micah is a well to do, respected person and scripture does not portray him as a crook." For a comparison of Michayehu's actions with theft in a family in the ancient Near East, see M. Heltzer, "Dishonest Behavior of Sons towards Parents in Ancient West Asia," *Altorientalische Forschungen* 25 (1998), 285-88.

has "kept the change." Also, she transfers the silver to a smith.[42] This might be compared to Isa. 46:5-7: "Those who squander gold from the purse and weigh out silver on a balance, they hire a metal worker to make it into a god, to which they bow down and prostrate themselves" (NJPS). Here the precious metals go toward both the smith's wages and the materials for making the idol. The prophet may be referring to a practice by which the idolsmith deducted his own wages from the very materials to be made into a god. If this practice was known to the author of the Michayehu pericope, then the idol would not even contain the two hundred shekels, thus devaluing and debasing the idol even more before it was produced. All told, the silver is twice stolen, of diminished worth, and has been affected by a lightly conceived and easily abrogated imprecation, and that of a woman to boot.[43] This object of veneration, embodying a deity, has certainly not been concocted from the noblest of ingredients.

The Golden Calf story notes that gold for the calf was collected from earrings of the idolators' wives, sons, and daughters. Curiously, the idolators themselves seem not to contribute. The precious metal is simply "broken off" (התפרק) and gathered up (see below). The twice-used verb התפרק may bear negative connotations. In Psalm 7:3 the petitioner asks God to save him from a pursuer "lest he tear up my throat like a lion, breaking up (פרק) with no one to save (me)." Zechariah 11:16 recalls a malicious shepherd who will eat up the fatlings and "break off their hooves" (ופרסיה יפרק). The verb's connotations of violently or suddenly breaking something off, apparent in these passages (see also Ezek. 19:12) are also inherent in positive contexts such as breaking off a yoke to free a slave or captive (Gen. 27:40; Lam. 5:8; Ps. 136:24) or crumbling a mountain (1 Kings 19:11).

Unlike true idolatrous practice the gold is not refined, prepared, or turned over to the god to render it suitable for sacred use. The base nature of the gold for the calf is highlighted clearly when contrasted with the gold used for the Tabernacle.[44] The gold for the Tabernacle is presented as

---

42. Radaq (Judg. 17:3) suggests that the mother gave two hundred shekels to the smith, used nine hundred for the idol, and kept none for herself.

43. Eleven hundred shekels is the sum Delilah takes from each Philistine ruler (Judg. 16:5) as a bribe to betray Samson. Rashi, on Judg. 17:3, rejects a suggestion that the woman was actually Delilah. He remarks nonetheless: "the incidents were juxtaposed because of the wicked silver which was of an equal amount in both instances and both were silver of disaster." See L. R. Klein, *The Triumph of Irony in the Book of Judges*, JSOTSup 68, Bible and Literature Series 14 (Sheffield: Almond Press, 1988), 143, for additional moral and religious flaws inherent in the silver.

44. For parallels between the calf fund and the Tabernacle fund, see R. W. L. Moberly, *At the Mountain of God. Story and Theology in Exodus 32-34*, JSOTSup 22 (Sheffield: University

a free-will offering by everyone (Exod. 35:22), and refined, as indicated by the expression כל הזהב העשוי למלאכה (cf. Exod. 38:24). It was then ritually presented as a תנופה offering (Exod. 35:22). The silver used for the Tabernacle, having derived from the half-sheqel weight silver poll tax, must have been of specified weight and quality, indicating that it too was refined.

Certain similarities between making the Golden Calf and Gideon making an Ephod in Ophrah (Judg. 8:22-28) permit the two stories to be mutually illuminating.[45] The gold used by Gideon originates in booty from the Midianites, having undergone no process of purification or sanctification.[46] In both cases the material used for the illegitimate object is gold earrings (נזמים). Aaron and Gideon acquire the earrings from the males of the community, even though they are not the original possessors of the objects. Most important, according to Judges 8:25 "they (the Israelites) spread out a garment and each person cast into it an earring from his booty." This passage elucidates a somewhat enigmatic statement in Exodus 32:4 ויצר בחרט. This statement is often taken to refer to the way in which Aaron formed the image. Thus it is translated: "He fashioned it with a graving tool," taking חרט as a sharp instrument as it is assumed to be in Isaiah 8:1 where it is used for writing, or "he cast it into a mold" (NJPS, with reference to Zech. 11:13). It is more likely, however that חרט designates some sort of garment and is identical with the woman's garment חריט mentioned in Isaiah 3:22-23, which lists המחלצות והמעטפות והמטפחות והחריטים והגלינים והסדינים והצניפות והרדידים.[47] Accordingly ויצר is not derived from יצר, "to fashion," but from צרר, "to wrap up." It is significant that in 2 Kings 5:23 Naaman the Aramaean, when giving Gehazi his reward, ויצר ככרים כסף בשני חרטים, "bound up two talents of silver in two חרטים," using an identical expression. Although binding up objects of var-

---

of Sheffield Press, 1983), 47, and in greater detail A. (V.) Hurowitz, "The Calf and the Tabernacle," *Shnaton* 7-8 (1984): 51-60, ix-x, esp. 53-55 (Hebrew).

45. See S. E. Loewenstamm, "The Making and Destruction of the Golden Calf—A Rejoinder," *Biblica* 56 (1975): 330-43, esp. 336-37, and W. Zimmerli, "Die Spendung von Schmuck für ein Kultobjekt," in *Mélanges bibliques et orientaux en l'honneur de M. Henri Cazelles*, ed. A. Caquot and M. Delver (AOAT 212; Neukirchen-Vluyn: Neukirchener Verlag, 1983), 513-28.

46. I favor interpreting Gideon's Ephod as a divine garment that clothed a divine statue or indicated the presence of an invisible deity. Even if we follow the majority and view this Ephod as a priestly garment used for divination, our interpretation of the handling of the materials for its fabrication remains unaffected and instructive for the case of the Golden Calf. On Gideon's Ephod and the various opinions concerning its nature, see recently C. van Dam, *The Urim and Thummim: A Means of Revelation in Ancient Israel* (Winona Lake, IN: Eisenbrauns, 1997), 146-49.

47. See Rashi, Rashbam, and most recently S. Gevirtz, "חֶרֶט in the Manufacture of the Golden Calf," *Biblica* 65 (1984): 377-81.

ious types in assorted garments is mentioned elsewhere in the Bible,[48] this particular expression is used only in these two accounts.[49] If so, not only Gideon but Aaron as well collect the gold for their illegitimate objects in a garment.

These descriptions of Gideon's and Aaron's fundraising may be more than innocent statements about how the "hat was passed around." In fact, the deed seems to be portrayed pejoratively. Collecting valuables in a garment is what a thief does.[50] A person's garment is a ready container in which stolen goods can be concealed, as thieves do until this very day.[51] We should note that Gehazi's acceptance of silver from Naaman is clearly an illicit act. His criminal behavior continues as he stashes the ill-earned gifts in his house prior to appearing before Elisha (2 Kings 5:24-25). This criminal behavior begins when he wraps up the silver in the garment—an act described exactly like the collection of gold for the calf. This element of thievery in the manufacture of cult images corresponds with the same motive in the story of Michayehu's idol. In all these instances, the narrators indicate that illegitimate cult images are made of tainted materials.[52]

---

48. Cf. Exod. 12:34: מאשרתם צררת בשמלתם; Hos. 4:19: צרר רוח אותה בכנפיה; Pr. 30:4: מי צרר מים בשמלה.

49. It is most surprising therefore that modern scholars of a literary bent have not commented on this relationship and attempted to exploit it for exegetical purposes.

50. M. Noth ("Zur Anfertigung des 'Goldenen Kalbes,'" *VT* 9 [1959]: 419-22), who mistakenly took חרט to mean "bag" rather than a type of garment, tried to draw implications from Gehazi's actions about Aaron's and suggested that Aaron tried to remove the gold to a secret place where he could manufacture the calf secretly and protect the valuable metal from robbers. Gevirtz correctly observes that this explanation is fantastic, but he too fails to see the criminal overtones of the actions of both Gehazi and Aaron.

51. Note, e.g., *MSheqalim* 3:2: "The one appointed to empty the chamber does not enter it wearing a sleeved garment, etc."

52. The earrings and their ultimate source may come into play in one more place in the Golden Calf pericope. According to Exod. 33:4-6 the Israelites were punished for the debacle by being prohibited from wearing jewelry from the time they were at Mt. Horeb. As U. Cassuto (*A Commentary on the Book of Exodus* [Jerusalem: Magnes Press, 1967] *ad loc.*) points out, they are punished measure for measure, being deprived of jewelry because they sinned with their earrings, which they contributed to the calf construction fund. It is noteworthy that although the divine pronouncement of punishment says ועתה הורד עדיך מעליך, "and now, remove your jewelry from upon you" (Exod. 33:5), the execution of the punishment is described as ויתנצלו בני ישראל את עדים מהר חורב, "and the Israelites divested themselves of their jewelry from Mount Horeb" (33:6). Moberly (*At the Mountain of God*, 61) and others have already suggested that the peculiar word ויתנצלו echoes God's promise in Exod. 3:22: ושאלה אשה משכנתה ומגרת ביתה כלי כסף וכלי זהב ושמלת ושמתם על בניכם ועל בנתיכם ונצלתם את מצרים and its fulfillment in Exod. 12:35-36: וישאלו ממצרים כלי כסף וכלי זהב ושמלת. ויהוה נתן את חן העם בעיני מצרים וישאלום וינצלו את מצרים, indicating that the jewelry which the Israelites possessed and from which they made the Calf was the very jewelry plundered from the Egyptians with divine license and assistance. This coincidence can best be explained in light of

Conclusion

We have seen that both Mesopotamian idol-makers and biblical anti-idol polemicists pay serious attention to the materials from which cult statues were made.

For Mesopotamian iconoplasts, the materials which go into the idols are already of divine nature. They belong to the gods or embody a god, so that when the idol is produced it does not become a god *ex nihilo*. To paraphrase a current TV commercial, "the divinity goes in before the name goes on." Since no new divinity is brought into existence, the craftsman does not face the problem of creating something beyond his power. This is a natural result of a pantheistic religion in which nearly everything can be related to personally as if it were a god.

It is illuminating to compare a description of the fabrication of idols in India[53]:

> . . . the rites of establishment commence with the initial selection of materials. When making a wooden image, for example, priest and artisan undertake a field trip to the forest, and take care to choose only specimens that bear an innate resemblance to the intended deity. "Male" trees are destined to serve male divinities, "female" to serve goddesses. The eastern side of the tree is marked as its "face," since the completed image will also face east. At the same time, it is necessary to persuade any other spirits that may reside in the tree to vacate it. "The officiating priest should offer worship at night to any gods, ancestor spirits, ghosts, demons, snakes, antigods, henchmen, obstacles, and the like [in the tree]," recommends the Brhatsamhita, " and then he should touch the tree and say: `You have been designated to serve as an icon for such-and-such a deity. We bow to you, tree. Please accept these offerings of worship, in proper manner. May those beings who dwell here receive our tribute, which is given properly, and choose another dwelling. May they forgive us. We bow to them'" (BS 59.9-11). After the tree has been properly honored and purified, it is cut and cleansed, transported back to the construction site, and then once again worshiped with mantras and auspicious substances. Even before the first cut of the chisel, the material is treated as a deity in the making.

Ezek. 16:17, where the prophet accuses the people: ותקחי כלי תפארתך מזהבי ומכספי אשר נתתי לך ותעשי לך צלמי זכר ותזני בם "You took your beautiful things (i.e., jewelry) made of silver and gold that I had given you, and you made phallic images and fornicated with them" (cf. as well Hos. 2:10-15). In all these cases the people of Israel have taken God-given gifts and used them for idolatry, indicating their brazenness, ingratitude, and infidelity.

53. R. H. Davis, *Lives of Indian Images* (Princeton, NJ: Princeton University Press, 1997), 34-35.

For the biblical authors too, the idol is nothing new. A tainted idol derives from raw materials already tainted.[54] In the cases of Michayehu's idol and the Golden Calf the material is hot stuff, stolen goods, and deceptively acquired. This quality is by implication transferred to the idol, which remains a dishonest act of deception.[55]

In both cases, what comes out of the idol shop is exactly what went in.

---

54. Apocryphal literature points to another type of blemish. *Wisdom of Solomon* 13:10-11 emphasizes the inherent worthlessness of the idols' ingredients rather than the deceit with which they were acquired. The stone is said to be "useless" (*lithon axreston*). J. Reider (*The Book of Wisdom*, Dropsie College Edition [New York: Harper and Brothers, 1957], 163) suggests that this is a meteorite devoid of shape. See also D. Winston, *The Wisdom of Solomon*, Anchor Bible 43 (Garden City, NY: Doubleday 1979), 259-60. The wood used in idols is from a *tekton eukineton*, which Reider translates "a handy tree" and explains as being "easily manageable," and is meant to contrast with "useless" in reference to the stone. However, verse 13 claims that the idol maker uses "a crooked piece of wood and full of knots." Reider expresses surprise here, remarking, "No possible reason can be assigned why the artisan should purposely choose the most refuse and amorphous fragments to make into idols." This comment surprisingly ignores the perspective of the description. In fact, it is only to be expected that an anti-idolatry polemicist would mock the miserable materials used in the idols, for he believes that the idols are worth no more than the materials from which they were made. D. Winston captures the gist of the polemic by citing a passage from Horace, *Satirae* 1.8.1: "Once I was a fig-wood stem, a worthless log, when the carpenter, doubtful whether to make a stool or a Priapus, chose that I be a god."

55. *Wisdom of Solomon* 15:7-13 depicts the wretched character of the maker of clay idols: ". . . For, says he, one must get wealth whencesoever it be, even out of evil. For this man above all others knows that he sins, fabricating out of earthy matter brittle vessels and graven images" (trans. Reider). The dishonesty inherent in making idols gave rise to or was related in some way to statements in Daniel and the priests of Bel or the *Epistle of Jeremiah*, which tell that idols were robbed by their adherents. The former work mocks the priests of Bel, who would cover up their god's inability to eat by stealing his food and sharing it with their own families. The later reports that the priests sell the sacrifices offered to the idols and pocket the proceeds (vs. 28); and "Sometimes, even the priests filch gold and silver from their gods and lavish it upon themselves . . ." (vs. 10); or "Gods of wood, silvered or gilded, cannot save themselves from thieves and robbers. Men who can will strip them and make off with the gold and silver and the clothing they had on . . . " (vss. 57-58). These ideas may derive from the historical reality that ancient Near Eastern temples were, in fact, robbed and divine regalia pilfered. The danger of robbing the gods was lessened by restricting access to the rooms in the temple where the precious divine garments would be stored—see L. T. Doty, "Akkadian *bīt pirišti*," in *The Tablet and The Scroll: Near Eastern Studies in Honor of William W. Hallo*, ed. M. E. Cohen, D. C. Snell, and D. B. Weisberg (Bethesda, MD: CDL Press, 1993), 87-89. For references in classical literature to robbing divine statues, see D. Winston, *Wisdom of Solomon*, 261.

2

The Representation of the Divine in Ancient Egypt[1]

ANN MACY ROTH

The current scholarly understanding of the representation of Egyptian gods derives largely from Eric Hornung's book, *Der Eine und die Vielen*,[2] which focuses on problems of multiplicity and henotheism, but also covers most other areas of the Egyptian conceptions of divinity. Rather than repeat the findings of this excellent study, the present paper presents investigations into two particular areas of this question that diverge from the views generally held in ways that may be of interest to scholars of other ancient and Near Eastern religions. The first of these areas is the evolution of the representations of the divine, and the second, which will be more briefly treated, is the representation of individual divinities by their names.

The Evolution of Depictions of the Divine

Two-dimensional representations of gods in Egyptian art of all periods are invariably clearly and cleanly drawn, without any blurred edges, shading, or mystery. Like all elements of Egyptian art, both their figures and the details within their figures are normally outlined in a darker color, to separate them from the blank background. The areas inside these outlines are then filled with solid planes of unblended color, as in a child's coloring book. Details are then added, again in outline.

1. This paper was written and presented in 1998, and does not take account of literature published since that date. I am indebted to Kevin Reinhart for guidance in dealing with the literature of Religious Studies.

2. 1971, translated by J. Baines as *Conceptions of God in Ancient Egypt: The One and the Many* (Ithaca, NY: Cornell University Press, 1981).

This clarity and lack of blending and shading is grounded in Egyptian conceptions of cosmology and cosmogony. Non-existence, according to the Egyptian view, was not a lack of physical presence, but a lack of differentiation and individuality. The universe before its creation was not an empty void, but an undifferentiated purée, from which everything that existed later was created by a process of separation. Existence was thus characterized primarily by multiplicity, differentiation, boundaries, and hierarchical order. The blurring of boundaries could lead to the destruction of individual identity and a collapse back into the undifferentiated primeval waters of non-existence. Therefore, our portraits of Egyptian gods, like everything else depicted in Egyptian art, are sharp and clear, underlining their individuality and supporting their existence as separate entities. This emphasis on the demarcation of the boundaries of beings and objects, which is generally viewed simply as a characteristic of Egyptian artistic style, stresses one of the essential characteristics of existence, and hence is a particularly important characteristic of the divine. Throughout the Egyptian evidence there is a tension between the clarity required for the maintenance of the gods' existence and a certain mystery implied by their divinity.

In scenes where they are shown with people, the forms of the gods often closely resemble the king or even the ordinary people who are worshipping them. Many divinities might easily be mistaken for humans, were it not for their position, the captions above them, iconographic elements identifying them as gods, or their divine role in the scene. Even their dress is merely human dress, albeit sometimes in an archaic style.

Despite their clarity and simplicity, Egyptian depictions of gods and goddesses strike most Western observers as mysterious because the deities are so often represented as animals, or, even more bizarrely, in mixed animal and human form. Egyptologists usually explain the animal parts of these forms as simple visual cues that helped to identify the gods,[3] comparable to the animals that the Hittite and Semitic gods stand on, or even to the characteristic implements of torture that identify martyred saints in Christian art.

But although these animal parts may have functioned in practice as markers to help viewers identify the divinity depicted, they had a much more significant role. Their composite forms embody the history of the divinity, and bring to his present manifestation the powerful aura of antiquity conveyed by a sequence of earlier manifestations. The animal characteristics of certain gods are instances of the ancient Egyptians' conservatism. They preserve an artistic tradition from an earlier phase of

3. See, e.g., L. Lesko in *Religion in Ancient Egypt,* ed. B. Shafer (Ithaca, NY: Cornell University Press, 1991), 112-13.

their religion, even though the gods may have been thought of as fully anthropomorphic at the time these older forms were reproduced.

This view is best supported by the myths that mention the gods. In myths, the gods are almost aggressively human in their behavior and, to the small extent that their appearance is described, they are said to have human features (hands, hair, fingers, etc.). The one exception is in the only complete surviving story about a god before the New Kingdom, where the god is explicitly described as an animal. In the story of the Shipwrecked Sailor,[4] dating to the Middle Kingdom, a sailor is marooned on an island. There he meets a 45-foot-long, gold-plated snake-god, with a three-foot beard, and eyebrows inlaid with lapis lazuli. The snake is clearly a snake in some of its actions as well as its appearance: it carries off the sailor in its mouth, which presumably emphasizes its snake-like lack of hands.

Interestingly, however, neither the gold snake statue from the tomb of Tutankhamun[5] nor any other depictions of divine snakes have anything resembling eyebrows or beards. This was clearly not a standard way of representing a divine snake. The story also depicts the snake as entirely human in feelings and in speech (unless a rather cartoonish tendency to repeat himself was thought to be characteristic of animal speech). This snake-god thus seems to have been viewed as simultaneously a snake and a human being rather than as a mixture of the two.

It is also clear from this story and later stories as well that divinities were viewed as composed of rare and valuable minerals,[6] and presumably were thought to resemble their cult images made of these materials. Since cult statues tend to preserve older forms, this circumstance may help explain why older, animal-based forms are conserved long after gods began to be seen as anthropomorphic in their character and actions.

It has been shown that the animal forms are an earlier development than anthropomorphic divinities. Gustav Jéquier described the Egyptian conception of divinity as having begun with the worship of inanimate objects and evolved through a stage of animal divinities to the anthropomorphic gods of the later myths.[7] His suggestion derived from a belief

---

4. Papyrus Leningrad 1115. For a convenient English translation, see *The Literature of Ancient Egypt*, ed. W. K. Simpson (New Haven, CT: Yale University Press, 1972), 50-56.

5. See, e.g., object number 283a, a photo of which is published in N. Reeves, *The Complete Tutankhamun* (London: Thames & Hudson 1990), 131 (lower right corner).

6. For example, the three divine kings, children of the sun god, described in papyrus Westcar 10,10-27 and the sun god described at the beginning of the Book of the Divine Cow—see A. Piankoff, *The Shrines of Tut-Ankh-Amon* (Princeton: Princeton University Press, 1955).

7. G. Jéquier, *Considérations sur les religions égyptiennes* (Neuchâtel: La Baconnière, 1946), as cited in Hornung, *Conceptions of God*, 39.

common among early anthropologists that all religions pass through such phases before arriving at the "higher" concept of anthropomorphic divinities.[8] This evolutionary view of religious development has long been discredited,[9] in particular the assumption of entire complexes of beliefs that can be called "fetishism" or "totemism" or "animism" and that are shared by all cultures at different times in their evolution.[10]

In fact, however, at least for the Egyptian case, an evolution from the depiction of gods as objects, then as animals, and finally as humans, can be demonstrated. Hornung has argued[11] for the validity of the latter part of this hypothesis; that is, that anthropomorphic divinities appear later than divinities in the form of animals and inanimate objects. To do this, he has analyzed the three hieroglyphic signs that could be used to write the word "god" or as determinative signs to mark as divine the names of specific gods. Conveniently, the chief signs used in this way are an object (a cloth-wrapped staff with the ends of the cloth waving like a flag), an animal (a falcon on a standard), and a human (a seated anthropomorphic god).

These hieroglyphic signs are shown in Figure 1.[12] The two signs on the left (1A and 1B) appear simultaneously in some of the earliest hieroglyphic inscriptions. Although anthropomorphic gods occur already in the prehistoric period and are well established by the early Old Kingdom (around 2700 B.C.E.), the third sign did not become a generic determinative for god until the later part of the Old Kingdom (around 2400 B.C.E.).[13] In making this argument, Hornung points out that while the human form is clearly later, it cannot be proved that the worship of objects preceded animal divinities; and, in fact, he doubts that it did.[14]

---

8. Interestingly, this view goes back to a comparison of ancient Egyptian religion with West African religion of the eighteenth century by Charles. R. de Brosses, *Du Culte des dieux fétiches ou parallèle de l'ancienne religion de l'Égypte avec la religion actuelle de la Nigritie* (1760). De Brosses coined the term "fetishism" for the worship of plants and animals.

9. See, e.g., E. E. Evans-Pritchard, *Theories of Primitive Religion* (Oxford: Oxford University Press 1965), 103-5.

10. C. Lévi-Strauss, *Totemism*, trans. R. Needham (Boston: Beacon Press, 1963), has been a particularly influential critic of these assumptions.

11. *Conceptions of God*, 39-40.

12. Hornung also used these signs to illustrate his discussion. His examples were taken from the Old Kingdom tomb of Akhethetep and Ptahhotep. See N. de G. Davies, *The Mastaba of Ptahhetep and Akhethetep* I (London: Egypt Exploration Fund, 1900), pls. 14 (no. 24), 7 (no. 87), and 6 (no. 11). The two signs on the right have been reversed in this figure.

13. Interestingly, this last step took place soon after the anthropomorphic god Osiris appeared and began his reign as the overwhelmingly popular mortuary god, so his importance may have influenced this development.

14. Hornung, *Conceptions of God*, 40: ". . . other Egyptian material does not suggest that this idea is likely to be right, although it is not possible to disprove it."

FIGURE 1: Three hieroglyphs used to write the word *nṯr*, "god," or to indicate the divine nature of other words and names. A and B occur in the earliest texts, C only in the later Old Kingdom. (Drawing by the author, after E. Hornung, *Conceptions of God in Ancient Egypt* [Ithaca, NY: Cornell University Press, 1981], figs. 1 and 2.)

Despite Hornung's doubts, however, a good case can be made for the priority of the flag, based on a general principle within Egyptian religion, that of "nesting."[15] Some fifty years ago, in his valuable essay in *The Intellectual Adventure of Ancient Man*, John A. Wilson suggested the concept of "multiplicity of approaches,"[16] by which the Egyptians gave multiple explanations for the same phenomenon, some of which seem mutually contradictory to modern Western scholars. He saw these multiple explanations as a kind of "pre-logical" thought that characterized and—obviously, in his view, limited—the ancient Egyptians' view of the world. The concept of nesting is a refinement of this idea, but it assumes that these multiple explanations were not viewed as equal in truth value, but instead represent a layered hierarchy, in which the oldest explanation or manifestation is retained, embedded in a sequence of later interpretations. Older explanations were valued for the authority conveyed by their antiquity, while newer explanations were valued for their up-to-the-minute theology. The entire amalgam thus combined the power and advantages of these and all the intervening nested stages. We can see this nesting in many aspects of Egyptian culture, particularly in those connected with religion and magic.

An excellent example of this concept[17] is the burial of King Tutankhamun in three nested coffins, each of increasing antiquity of style as they approach the actual body. The sarcophagus in which these coffins rested was also surrounded by a nested series of three shrines and a canopy. Later, a fourth shrine seems to have been added: The papyrus plan for the tomb of Ramesses IV shows four shrines only two dynasties later. The magical effectiveness of the coffin was enhanced by the inclusion of nested antique and up-to-the-minute forms.

---

15. A. M. Roth, "Buried Pyramids and Layered Thoughts: The Organisation of Multiple Approaches in Egyptian Religion," in *Proceedings of the Seventh International Congress of Egyptologists*, ed. C. J. Eyre, Orientalia Louvaniensia Analecta 82 (Leuven: Peeters, 1998), 991-1003.

16. J. A. Wilson, "The Nature of the Universe," in H. Frankfort et al., *The Intellectual Adventure of Ancient Man* (Chicago: University of Chicago Press, 1946), 32-33.

17. All of the following examples are taken from the fuller argument for this concept proposed in Roth, "Buried Pyramids and Layered Thoughts."

Similar nested forms are frequently found in mortuary architecture, where sequences of older forms were often buried in the masonry of later forms. For example, two early mastaba tombs show a nested mound and a nested stepped platform; and the true pyramids of the Fourth Dynasty often seem to have had Step Pyramids of Third-Dynasty type buried within them. These buried reminders of earlier architectural forms—which represent earlier views of the afterlife—are usually interpreted as earlier phases of construction, often wrongly. The same nesting can be found in myths and rituals, where later redactions do not replace earlier ones, but are simply grafted on to their beginnings.[18]

This nesting phenomenon can also be seen in the evolution of the forms of the divine, and it supports Jéquier's hypothesis that the flag is older than the animal divinities. The flag used to write the word "god" (Fig. 1A) is essentially a staff wrapped with cloth, with the ends of the cloth strips streaming out loose at the top. The central element here seems to be neither the flag-like strips of cloth themselves nor the staff, but the fact of the wrapping, which obscures and makes mysterious the underlying form. Such wrapping, of course, explains the tradition of wrapping the mummified dead in bandages, and it also probably relates to the entire phenomenon of nested layers that I have described.

When examined closely, it is apparent that the falcon hieroglyph (Fig. 1B) incorporates this flag, and hence is a later development. The horizontal bar on which the falcon is perched has some cloth ends hanging off the front. So the bar on which the falcon stood was basically a horizontal flag sign, nested in the later form.[19] From this we may deduce that the flag sign is, *pace* Hornung, earlier than the falcon.

The continuation of the evolution can be seen in the anthropomorphic hieroglyph denoting divinity. Although his body is human, his arms and legs are not distinguished, and he is, in effect, mummiform, entirely shrouded in cloth wrappings with the exception of his head. And, although his head is human in the generic example shown in Figure 1C, when this sign is used in connection with more specific divinities, the head is often that of an animal. Thus the animal form can also be nested in this third version, just as the wrapping associated with the flag occurs in both of the later signs.

The projection of divine authority first upon inanimate objects, then upon animals, and finally upon human forms, can be seen in several

18. These "nested myths" are strikingly similar to the first two chapters of Genesis, where two separate creation accounts are given, probably in reverse historical order of their composition.

19. Other versions of the sign show streamers hanging down from the angle of the standard.

other aspects of Egyptian religious and cultural iconography. Interestingly, these evolutionary changes seem to have taken place at different times in different aspects of the culture. As was already noted above, anthropomorphic divinities occur in iconography long before the appearance of the generic anthropomorphic god as a determinative in writing, and the change from animal divinities to gods of human form in mythological narratives may date as late as the New Kingdom (although there are so few myths from the earlier periods that it is dangerous to generalize). This does not mean, of course, that those who composed myths conceived of divinity differently than those who wrote hieroglyphs or those who decorated temples; instead, it suggests that in different kinds of representations of the gods these changes were adopted at very different rates. In other words, mythological expression was perhaps more conservative than the writing system, which was in turn more conservative than the theologians who dictated the appearance of the individual gods in temple reliefs.

Another apparently conservative aspect of expression of the divine can be seen in the divine emblems that represent different geographic areas of Egypt. Here, too, an evolution from the inanimate object to the animal to the human form can be seen, paralleling the spatial expansion of Egyptian culture. These emblems apparently derive from—and are in some cases identical to—emblems shown on Upper Egyptian pottery from the prehistoric (Nagada II) period, usually in connection with ceremonial boats. Such emblems seem to have represented divinities, as they often rest on standards and are frequently marked as divine by strips of cloth hanging from them. Later, some of these emblems represent the "nomes" or administrative districts of the Egyptian state, and several can be connected with the local gods of the nome in question. Eventually there were forty-two nomes, twenty-two in the Upper Egypt (the south) and twenty in Lower Egypt (the Nile Delta). These emblems (shown in Fig. 2)[20] seem to reflect an evolution of divine forms over the period during which these districts were incorporated into the Egyptian state.

The Egyptian state originated in the south, in the same area where the painted pots with the standards were fashioned in the predynastic period. This area later comprised the first nine nomes of Upper Egypt.[21] By the time that the standards associated with these nomes had been canonized, early in the Old Kingdom,[22] seven of the emblems associated

20. After W. Helck, "Gauzeichen," *Lexikon der Ägyptologie II*, ed. W. Helck and E. Otto (Wiesbaden: Otto Harrassowitz, 1977), 423-24.

21. The nomes were numbered beginning from the south.

22. Helck, "Gauzeichen," 422. Helck argues here that the earliest nomes are those shown on standards, and that they represent distinguishing marks of royal domains founded during the Third Dynasty. However, the consistency of the pattern suggested below would tend to support the idea of an earlier genesis.

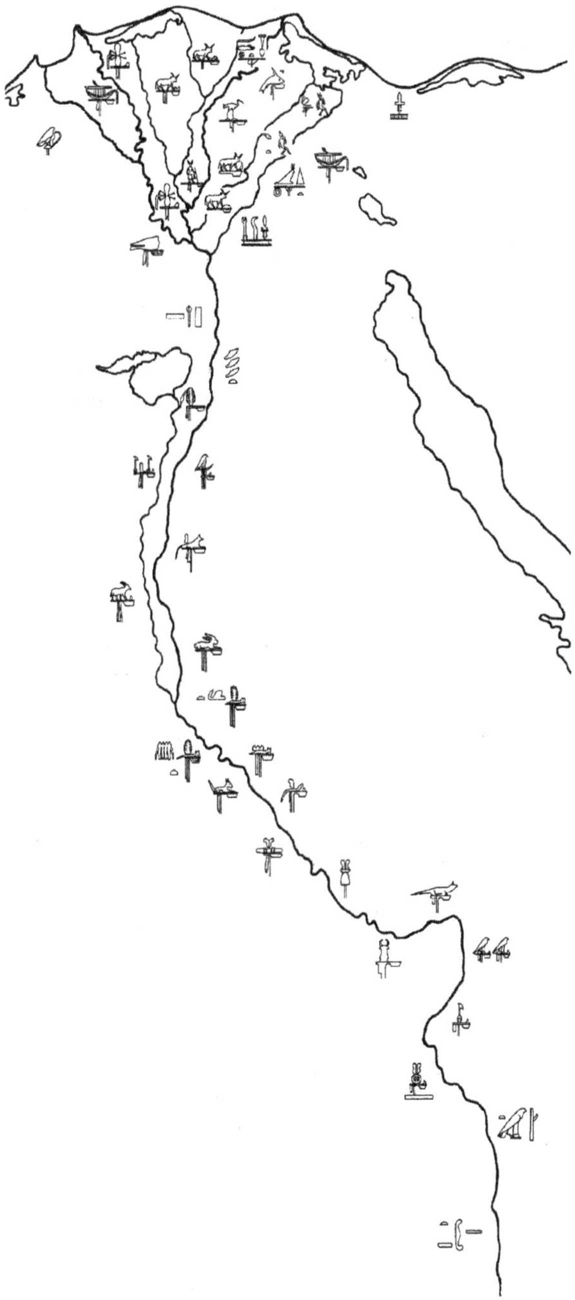

FIGURE 2: The emblems identifying the nomes (administrative districts) of Upper Egypt (the Nile Valley south of the Delta) and Lower Egypt (the Nile Delta). (Figure prepared by the author using nome emblems from W. Helck, "Gauzeichen," *Lexikon der Ägyptologie II*, ed. W. Helck and E. Otto [Wiesbaden: Otto Harrassowitz, 1977], 423-24.)

with these nomes are inanimate objects: a bow (First), the support of Horus (Second), a feathered round emblem (Third), the *w3s*-scepter (Fourth), a cow-headed musical instrument (Seventh), and a fossil (Ninth), as well as a mound-shaped object we cannot identify (Eighth). The two exceptions—the two falcons (Fifth) and the crocodile (Sixth)—may represent additions or subdivisions of larger nomes, reflecting changes which took place before the earliest attestations, since only these two nomes show the later theriomorphic form of emblem. Animal forms are also encountered more frequently as one moves north along the Nile Valley, just as the founders of the Egyptian state did. Most of the northern Upper Egyptian nome emblems take animal form (cobra, Seth-animal, viper, hare, oryx, dog, falcon), with a few inanimate or combined animal and inanimate forms, particularly in the area of the Fayum.

Animal emblems also prevail in the Delta, the last part of Egypt to be divided into nomes. An exception is a group of nomes in the western Delta which are marked by the crossed arrows of the goddess Neith (Fourth and Fifth nomes). Interestingly, this goddess is particularly prevalent in the names of queens from the period of the early First Dynasty, which may point to an alliance with the elite of this area during that period, and the adoption of the earlier inanimate form of standard there.

The Ninth, Eighteenth, and Nineteenth Lower Egyptian nomes have anthropomorphic emblems. The final two of these nomes were among the last to be added to the group in the New Kingdom and later;[23] the anthropomorphic emblem of the Ninth nome, however, dates back to the Fourth Dynasty.[24] Despite the exception of the Ninth nome, however, the general pattern is clear. Again we can see the inanimate forms change to animal forms and ultimately to human forms as the administrative system of the southern rulers extended northward.

Of particular interest is the emblem of the Fourth Upper Egyptian nome, the *w3s*-scepter, the hieroglyph for "power," which is often held by gods. The *w3s*-scepter is a staff with a curving stick attached to its upper end and a divided, usually forked, base. An early example, on a Fourth-Dynasty nome standard, is shown in Figure 3. Cloth strips are also attached to both the scepter and the standard, marking their divine nature, and the scepter is further decorated with an ostrich feather, as are many Upper Egyptian nome standards. In the prehistoric period, from about 5000-3000 B.C.E., the chief town in this area was at the site now

23. W. Helck, "Gaue," in *Lexikon der Ägyptologie II*, 401, notes that the Eighteenth Lower Egyptian nome split off from the Thirteenth at the time of Ramesses II (Nineteenth Dynasty), and that the Nineteenth Lower Egyptian nome did not come into existence until the Third Intermediate Period.

24. Ibid., 397.

FIGURE 3: The standard of the Theban nome (the Fourth nome of Upper Egypt) from a statue of Fourth-Dynasty date. (Drawing by the author.)

known as Nagada. In historical times, Nagada was in the Fifth nome, just to the north of the Fourth, but this was probably a later development, not only because that nome has an animal standard, but because there are clear connections between Nagada and the w^3s-scepter. In hieroglyphic writing, for example, the same scepter with a wavy or spiral shaft is used to write the word "fine gold" or "electrum," tying it to the ancient name of Nagada (Greek "Ombos"), which in Egyptian was called Nubt or "Gold Town." Moreover, a huge example of the w^3s-scepter was actually excavated at Nagada,[25] one of the many large ceremonial objects and representations of divinities found at temples and dating to the early First Dynasty. I would argue that this scepter was in fact the emblem of Nagada, and in the earliest periods probably represented the chief divinity of the city in an inanimate form. (The capital of the Fourth Nome, Thebes, is written with a w^3s-scepter, taking the name of the nome of which it became the capital, which suggests it may have been an artificial formation.)

In later periods, the chief divinity of Nagada was Seth, god of confusion and violence, whose strength and warlike tendencies were often disruptive but could also be exercised in the service of order. His peculiar form (Fig. 4) has long been controversial: It has been called a wholly imaginary animal, a confused mixture of several animals, and identified with the anteater, the tapir, and an assortment of other animals.[26] In fact, the nature of this animal is probably none of these.

He is, in fact, the w^3s-scepter converted into an animal by giving him the body of a greyhound. His head is the head of the scepter, and his unnaturally erect tail ends in the split found at the scepter's base. This would mean that Seth was the chief god of Nagada all along, merely changing his form from a scepter to an animal as animals began to be seen the chief repository of divine power. Then, when gods of human form

---

25. H. te Velde, *Seth, God of Confusion* (Leiden: Brill, 1977), 90.
26. te Velde, *Seth, God of Confusion*, 13.

FIGURE 4: Depictions of the "Seth animal" from the Scorpion Macehead of the late Predynastic period (top), the Old Kingdom (lower left), and the Middle Kingdom (lower right). (Drawing by the author after H. te Velde, *Seth, God of Confusion* [Leiden, 1977], figs. 4 and 6, with some modification to the tail of the uppermost depiction based on photographs and other published drawings of the macehead.)

became more popular, he was represented as a human being, still with his scepter-like head. He is in himself an example of the nesting of earlier forms within later ones. We even have a *w³s*-scepter with a face, from the Eighteenth-Dynasty temple of Deir el-Bahari (Fig. 5), where much of the decor seems to be modelled on much older prototypes;[27] an earlier example dated to Mentuhotep IV of the Eleventh Dynasty, in the very early Middle Kingdom, has recently been excavated at Elephantine.[28]

This argument suggests that the forms a god takes offer clues to the date of his or her origin. For example, the important divinities Osiris and Isis appear quite suddenly in our sources, towards the end of the Fifth Dynasty (about 2425 B.C.E.), and immediately become extremely popular. It is unclear whether they were older divinities that just happened to become popular at this period, or whether they were simply new gods, coming into existence at the time they first appear. Both of these gods are almost invariably depicted in anthropomorphic form, taking animal form only in much later periods, through association with other divinities. But Isis may actually have begun as an object, a divine personification of the royal throne. Her name actually means "throne," and she is generally shown with a throne upon her head. The pattern proposed here suggests that her history may extend back into prehistory, whereas Osiris probably appeared only in the Old Kingdom.

27. The *w³s* scepter and Seth have previously been connected. A. Wainwright, "Some Aspects of Amun," *JEA* 20 (1934): 148, listed many connections; and A. H. Gardiner, *Egyptian Grammar* (3d ed.; Oxford: Oxford University Press, 1957), 509 (sign list S 40), cites Jéquier in identifying the head of the scepter as the head of the Seth-animal. I am simply suggesting that the development was from the scepter to the animal rather than in the other direction, as earlier scholars seem to have assumed.

28. W. Kaiser et al., "Stadt und Tempel von Elephantine, 23./24. Grabungsbericht," *MDAIK* 53 (1997): pl. 20, fragment d. Only the eye is preserved; the bottom part of the scepter is broken.

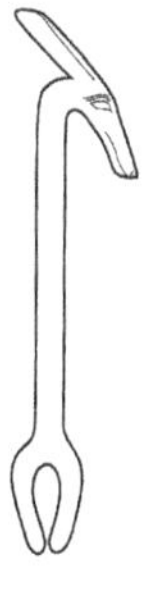

FIGURE 5: A w^3s-scepter from the temple of Deir el-Bahari, with an eye that shows its connection with the Seth animal. (Drawing by the author.)

Names of Divinities

Naming beings and objects was another way that the ancient Egyptians distinguished them from the purée of non-existence. Perhaps because of this function of a name, they believed that knowledge of the name gave one control over whatever the name labeled. One can therefore expect that the names assigned to divinities would be significant and revealing. Divinities are often said to have many names, and this multiplicity again distinguishes them from their human worshippers.

As the example of Isis illustrates, the names of the gods sometimes throw light on their natures as well. The gods connected with creation, for example, tend to have negative names, reflecting the undifferentiated pre-creation primeval waters of non-existence. The name of one of the most important creator gods, Atum, is a form of the negative verb *tm*, "to not do." The name of Shu, another creator god, means "empty," and the name Nefertem is actually a double negative: *nfr*, "to finish or stop something," and *tm*, "to not do," as in Atum. The eight divinities of the Ogdoad, in another creation myth, are named for the negative characteristics of the pre-creation purée. The four gods' names denote the lack of motion, light, limits, and form, while the four goddesses have feminine forms of the same names, implying a lack of gender distinctions.

Goddesses, in contrast, tend to be named for places or things. The name of the goddess Hathor means "the temple of the god Horus"; Horus is her consort, so she is in a sense derived from him, a personification of his temple, although she is clearly also an independent and distinctive deity from a very early period. The name Isis, as mentioned above, means "throne," and interestingly, the name of her consort Osiris is at first written as an eye (possibly the verb "to act") resting on a throne. This suggests that Osiris was derived from Isis in the same way that Hathor was derived from Horus. This supports the suggestion made above that Isis was the older divinity.

But a large number of the most important gods have names to which we cannot assign any specific meaning. This is particularly true of gods popular during the Old Kingdom, such as Ptah, Sokar, Thoth, Anubis, and Seth, as well as the goddess Neith. Some scholars have bemoaned the fact that the meaning of these names has been lost, assuming that if we knew what they meant, we would know more about the nature of these major divinities. But it is more likely that these names are meant to be mysterious: Not only do they not have any obvious meaning, but when they are written phonetically—rather than simply with an emblem or animal, the meaningless names tend to be written exclusively with alphabetic consonantal signs (Fig. 6). The alphabetic spellings completely obscure the pronunciation of these names: Most biliteral and triliteral signs are also words on their own account, and even if the vowels are not noted, the underlying words imply vowels. By writing the words exclusively with single alphabetic signs, scribes avoided implying any vowels, and the true pronunciations of the names remain mysterious, even though an approximation of some sort must have been adopted for purposes of ritual and prayer. These writings constitute an interesting early parallel to the tetragrammaton.

On the other hand, the names of two most important gods of the Old Kingdom, Horus and Reʿ, do have meaning. Horus (Egyptian *Ḥr*) seems to be the preposition *ḥr*, "on, above," obviously descriptive of a falcon deity. And the sun god is called *Rʿ*, which means "sun," or in later periods, *pꜣ Rʿ*, "the sun." This is unusual; all the other cosmological divinities, representing earth, sky, and so forth, have names that differ from the words for those parts of the universe, and their names are rarely preceded by the definite article.

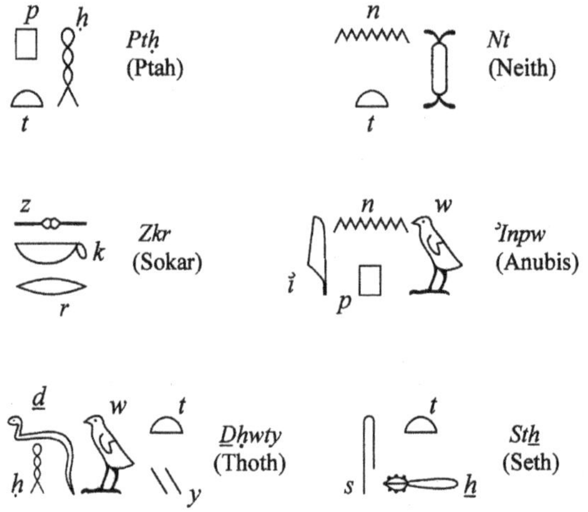

FIGURE 6: The names of six important gods of the Old Kingdom period written almost exclusively with alphabetic signs. (Figure prepared by the author using the Winglyph program.)

The explanation seems to be that both Horus and Reʿ are paraphrastic names that allow the worshipper to avoid naming the divinity altogether. We even have a myth recounting how Isis learned Reʿ's secret, true, name.[29] The myth does not tell us what that name was, but in one manuscript the scribe seems to have tried out several sequences of random alphabetic letters, hoping, we assume, to hit upon the true name by serendipity.[30]

A confirmation of the paraphrastic nature of the names of Horus and Reʿ is the special way they are treated in personal names of the Old Kingdom period. In royal names, Horus is represented by a falcon and Reʿ by a sun disk, in other words, by an image of the divinity's manifestation in nature. But non-royal names spell the name Reʿ alphabetically, as if it were one of those meaningless names, while Horus is written with the face used to write the preposition "upon," flanked by the two alphabetic signs, *ḥ* and *r*. This distinction in the writings again points up the special nature of these two gods, and suggests that while kings' names could represent the actual manifestation of the god, ordinary people treated even the paraphrastic as a name of unknown meaning and pronunciation. This distinction disappeared in later periods, and was not adopted for the "great gods" of later times, so it seems to have been an early phenomenon.

In conclusion, then, it can be said that although the depictions we see of Egyptian gods seem clear and straightforward, both their names and their figures are in fact to some extent shrouded in mystery. There were restrictions about implying pronunciations for the names of the more powerful gods, and the true names of the two most powerful gods of the early period were unknown, save perhaps to their highest priestly attendants. Similarly, the physical forms taken by the gods in art are sometimes literally shrouded by mummy wrappings, despite the clarity of their depictions. In other cases they contain buried layers of references to earlier stages of their own evolution, which obscure whatever their true nature was believed to be. The Egyptians represented their divinities as both well-defined and mysterious beings: The definition and clarity of their names and depictions were necessary to protect their existence and prevent them from reverting to pre-creation chaos. Nonetheless, both names and depictions contained within them obscurities that hid the divinities' true nature and made them almost as mysterious to the people who worshipped them as they are to us today.

---

29. J. A. Wilson's translation of this text is published in J. B. Pritchard, *ANET*, 12-14.

30. The fact that the scribe assumed that the "true name" would be a meaningless combination of alphabetic signs also corroborates the interpretation of the alphabetic names offered here.

3

The Structure of Divinity at Ugarit and Israel

The Case of Anthropomorphic Deities versus Monstrous Divinities

MARK S. SMITH

"There's no place like home."
—*The Wizard of Oz*

Introduction

The customary approach to West Semitic divinity is to list and study individual deities from Ugarit and perhaps further to coordinate this information with data derived from the Bible, West Semitic inscriptions, and other corpora from various sites in Syro-Mesopotamia.[1] The covert or not so covert purpose of these operations is to recover information which advances the understanding of Israel's chief deity. This is the overall thrust, for example, in my book, *The Early History of God*.[2] This atomistic approach may be contrasted with a large-scale comparative approach which ventures a typology of divinity. In his contribution to *The Encyclopedia of Religion*, the historian of religion T. M. Ludwig discusses two

1. I wish to thank the Center for Advanced Judaic Studies of the University of Pennsylvania and all of my co-fellows at the center for the 1997-1998 year. I am especially grateful for the extensive comments provided by T. J. Lewis.

I beg the readers' indulgence for the number of citations, but H. L. Ginsberg's view expressed almost fifty years ago still applies today: "The specialist can not yet dispense with conscientious sifting of all the better writers on Ugaritica since the birth of this discipline" ("Interpreting Ugaritic Texts," *JAOS* 70 [1950]: 160).

2. M. S. Smith, *The Early History of God: Yahweh and the Other Deities of Ancient Israel* (San Francisco, CA: Harper & Row, 1990).

types of typologies, the first a cosmic typology based on geography or realms (deities of sky, meteorology, earth and underworld), and the second a social typology based on functions of vital interest to humanity (creation and guarding society and order; protection and war; fertility and prosperity; home and community; healing, sickness and death; and esoteric knowledge and magic).[3]

This inquiry begins a middle approach, using information about individual deities at Ugarit to tell us about divinity in general. We might approach the issue of divinity by inquiring first into groupings presented by the Ugaritic texts and second into the characteristics of divinity presented in texts and iconography.[4] We might break down the first task by addressing different groupings in the Ugaritic texts from the largest collectivities down to the smallest ones: (1) anthropomorphic deities versus monstrous divine creatures; the main set of deities identified as either (2) the divine council or (3) the divine family; (4) pluralities; and (5) pairings and parallelisms involving two deities. This particular study focuses on the first and most basic division in divinity in the Ugaritic texts, namely the main distinction drawn between anthropomorphic deities and monstrous divine creatures. Following a long line of discussion in anthropology and ancient Middle Eastern studies especially in the 1970s and 1980s,[5] the Assyriologist F. A. M. Wiggermann has adapted to the Mesopotamian organization of the cosmos an important set of distinctions, namely the "periphery" as opposed to the "center" (or "home").[6]

---

3. Ludwig, "Gods and Goddesses," in *The Encyclopedia of Religion*, vol. 6, ed. M. Eliade (New York: Macmillan, 1987), 59-66, esp. 61. See also the thoughtful reflections by R. Panikkar in his contribution "Deity," in *The Encyclopedia of Religion*, vol. 4 , ed. M. Eliade (New York: Macmillan, 1987), 264-76. For further comparative discussions, see J. B. Carmen, *Majesty and Meekness: A Comparative Study of Contrast and Harmony in the Concept of God* (Grand Rapids, MI: Eerdmans, 1994); and the essays in *God: The Contemporary Discussion*, ed. F. Sontag and M. D. Bryant (New York: Rose of Sharon Press, 1982).

4. See A. Caquot and M. Sznycer, *Ugaritic Religion* (Leiden: Brill, 1980); P. Amiet, *Corpus des cylindres de Ras Shamra–Ougarit II: Sceaux-cylindres en hématite et pierres diverses*, Ras Shamra–Ougarit IX (Paris: Éditions Recherche sur les Civilisations, 1992).

5. For example, see E. Shils, *Center and Periphery: Essays in Macrosociology* (Chicago: Universty of Chicago Press, 1975); and the essays in *Centre and Periphery in the Ancient World*, ed. M. Rowlands, M. Larsen, and K. Kristiansen (Cambridge: Cambridge University Press, 1987). For similar reflections on center and periphery for Mesopotamia, see M. Liverani, "The Ideology of the Assyrian Empire," in *Power and Propaganda: A Symposium on Ancient Empires*, ed. M. Trolle Larsen, Mesopotamia. Copenhagen Studies in Assyriology 7 (Copenhagen: Akademisk Forlag, 1979), 306-7; and P. Machinist, "On Self-Consciousness in Mesopotamia," in *The Origins and Diversity of Axial Age Civilizations*, ed. S. N. Eisenstadt (Albany: State University of New York, 1986), 184-91. For the dialectic between center and periphery in historical writing, see P. Burke, *History and Social Change* (Cambridge: Cambridge University Press, 1992), 79-84.

6. F. A. M. Wiggermann, "Scenes from the Shadow Side," in *Mesopotamian Poetic Language: Sumerian and Akkadian*, ed. M. E. Vogelzang and H. L. J. Vanstiphout, Cuneiform

This general set of divisions informs a series of correlations in the conceptual organization of time and space from the perspective of urban elites, between what is perceived by them as culture and cultivated on the one hand, and uncultured and uncultivated on the other. J. D. Schloen, following the work of E. A. Shils, describes the relationship between center and periphery in Ugaritic literature in the following terms:

> the social "center" is "the center of the order of symbols, of values and beliefs, which govern the society;" thus the terms "center" and "periphery" do not necessarily imply spatial separation. For Ugarit, however, it can be argued that the social center was focused in the physical center of the kingdom at Ras Shamra, which appears to have been the main locus of administration, of ritual, and of literary activity. In this case, then, "urban-rural" is more-or-less synonymous with "center-periphery."[7]

Periphery also stands as a transitional zone between the center and the very distant realms of cosmos lying beyond human experience and control. Accordingly, one might prefer to propose three zones, namely "center," "periphery," and "beyond the periphery" (beyond the organized cosmos). A final nuance: at the heart of the "center" lies the household, which connotes safety and protection as well as familial patrimony and land. However, it is not clear that the ancient household conjures up the sensibility of the American English usage of "home," which is imbued further with warmth, hearth, and perhaps nostalgia. Indeed, the ancient narratives often record considerable conflict in the home.

While these general categories have been well delineated for ancient societies, scholars, with the exception of Wiggermann (and to a considerably lesser extent, Schloen), have not extended these categories to the presentation of the cosmos (or universe) in ancient mythological material. Allowing for some flexibility, the following represents an attempt to apply these categories to divinity and the cosmos in the Ugaritic texts. More specifically, these categories may be applied to deities as well as divine geography and topography based on indigenous terminology and distinctions. Within the "center" we may note a further distinction between home and foreign. And within the periphery, there is a differ-

---

Monographs 6 (Groningen: Styx Publications,1996), 207-20. See also Wiggermann, "Transtigridian Snake Gods," in *Sumerian Gods and Their Representations*, ed. I. L. Finkel and M. J. Geller (Groningen: Styx, 1996), 47-48, and *Mesopotamian Protective Spirits: The Ritual Texts*, Cuneiform Monographs 1 (Groningen: Styx & PP, 1992), 151-52. For the function of this dichotomy to support the ruling ideology, see W. van Binsbergen and F. Wiggermann, "Magic in History. A Theoretical Perspective, and its application to Ancient Mesopotamia," in *Mesopotamian Magic: Textual, Historical and Interpretative Perspectives*, ed. T. Abusch and K. van der Toorn, Ancient Magic and Divination I (Groningen: Styx, 1999), 1-34.

7. J. D. Schloen, *The House of the Father as Fact and Symbol: Patrimonialism in Ugarit and the Ancient Near East* (Winona Lake, IN: Eisenbrauns, 2001) 317 n. 1.

ence between what is in the periphery and experienced by humans and what is beyond the periphery and beyond human experience. These subdivisions are primarily expressed in terms of space and place.

Place: Near, Foreign, and Far

In accordance with the scheme above, deities inhabit places that are "near" while "monsters" or "demonic forces" do not. The division of divinity between deities and demons, so to speak, corresponds to the mapping of divine space. CAT 1.23.65-69 casts the contrast marking center versus periphery in agrarian terms, "sown" (*mdrᶜ*) versus "outback, steppe" (*mdbr*).[8] According to this text, the sown contains plenty of food and wine (1.23.70-76). This use of "sown" appears also in administrative lists, twice for royal workers (4.141 III 16 and 4.618.6), and once for a record of wine (4.149.16). This last reference (4.149.14-16) is of further interest, as it shows cultic devotion in the "sown": "five (jars of) wine for the sacrifice of the queen in the sown" (*ḫmš yn bdbḥ mlkt bmdrᶜ*).[9] Failing vegetation is the object of Danil's verbal expression (ritual "prayer"?) in 1.18 II 12-25. Fields (*šd*) are subject to both human cultivation (e. g., CAT 4.39.1-7, 4.72.2-20) and divine ownership (1.23.28).[10]

Within the "center" or area of human cultivation and civilization, deities are accorded sacred mountains or cult sites,[11] while cosmic enemies are not. One of the Ugaritic snake-bite incantations lists the following divinities with their mountains or cult-sites: El at "the meeting-place of the Double-Deeps" (*bᶜdt thmtm*, 1.100.3) known to be at mount *ks* (1.1 III 12);

8. See A. Haldar, *The Notion of the Desert in Sumero-Akkadian and West Semitic Religions* (Uppsala: Lundequistska bokhandeln, 1950); S. Talmon, "The 'Desert Motif' in the Bible and in Qumran Literature," in *Biblical Motifs: Origins and Transformations*, ed. A. Altmann (Cambridge, MA: Harvard University Press, 1966), 31-63; idem, "*midbār*," *TDOT* 8:87-118; N. Wyatt, "Sea and Desert: Symbolic Geography in West Semitic Religious Thought," *UF* 19 (1987): 375-89, esp. 380-85; and idem, *Myths of Power: A Study of Royal Power and Ideology in Ugaritic and Biblical Tradition*, UBL 13 (Münster: Ugarit-Verlag, 1996), 19-115, esp. 26-30, 75-81. For the root **dbr*, see most recently E. Lipiński, "'Leadership': The Roots *DBR* and *NGD* in Aramaic," in *"Und Mose schrieb dieses Lied auf": Studien zum Alten Testament und zum alten Orient. Festschrift für Oswald Loretz zur Vollendung seines 70. Lebensjahres mit Beiträgen von Freunden, Schülern und Kollegen*, ed. M. Dietrich and I. Kottsieper, AOAT 250 (Münster: Ugarit-Verlag, 1998), 501-8.

9. See A. Rainey, "The Kingdom of Ugarit," in *The Biblical Archaeologist Reader 3*, ed. E. F. Campbell, Jr. and D. N. Freedman (Garden City, NY: Doubleday, 1970), 93-94. Should we see here the religious practice of royal women? Cf. "the religion of the palace women" at Mari, discussed in W. G. Lambert, "The Pantheon of Mari," *MARI* 4 (1985): 527.

10. The word *šd* may apply not only to the center but in its meaning "open country," it applies also to periphery (CAT 1.6 II 20; cf. 1.5 VI 6, 29).

11. See R. J. Clifford, *Cosmic Mountain in Canaan and the Old Testament*, HSM 4 (Cambridge, MA: Harvard University Press, 1972), 34-97.

Baal on *ṣpn* (1.100.9); Anat and Athtart on *ʾinbb* (1.100.20); Dagan at *ttl* (Tuttul, 1.100.15); Resheph at *bbt* (1.100.31); Athtart at *mr* (Mari, 1.100.78);[12] Mlk at *ʿṯtrt* (Ashtarot, 1.100.41); Yarih at *lrgt* (1.100.26); and ẒẒ and KMṮ at *hryt* (1.100.36).[13] The Ugaritic texts recognize a distinction between home and foreign divinities and home and foreign cult-sites. Although Kothar wa-Hasis' activity of weapon-making (1.2 IV) and palace-building (1.4 V-VII) clearly take place in the "center," he has no mountain as his abode, but he is said to dwell in Memphis and Caphtor (1.100.46), perhaps a reflection of the center of foreign culture and system of trade which brought artisans at Ugarit the materials necessary for their craft. Indeed, given Ugarit's location as a crossroad for land and sea trade across the eastern Mediterranean, the Levant, and Syro-Mesopotamia, it is hardly surprising to see such locales reflected in the mythological presentation of the outer reaches of the zone of civilization tied to the home. Ugaritic's trade may constitute the basis for the mythological rendering of the connections between home and foreign within the center and to see its agricultural life, its "sown," at the heart of its basic sense of home. In short, the mythological "center" manifests a sub-division between home and foreign.

Within this general home of human and divine order is a center point, Baal's mountain, Mount Sapan.[14] This conceptualization is evident from the description of Baal's palace on the mountain in the Baal Cycle and the heading of one list of deities as "the gods of Sapan" (*ʾil ṣpn* in 1.47.1). It is also reflected in the superscription of one ritual, "the feast of Sapan" (*dbḥ ṣpn* in 1.148.1; 1.91.3).[15] Baal's mountain is also called "pleasant place" (*nʿm*), perhaps garden language which in biblical texts is a recurring motif for the center point of the cosmos.[16] Later West Semitic

---

12. The listing of Anat and Athtart together suggests a different figure here, as surmised by P. Bordreuil, "Ashtart de Mari et les dieux d'Ougarit," *MARI* 4 (1985): 545-47.

13. For the deities and these cult-sites, see D. Pardee, *Les textes para-mythologiques de la 24e Campagne (1961)*, Ras Shamra–Ougarit IV; Mémoire no 77 (Paris: Éditions Recherche sur les Civilisations, 1988), 210-12.

14. Very nicely observed by Wyatt, *Myths of Power*, 27-28.

15. Wyatt, *Myths of Power*, 27-28.

16. As seen by Wyatt, *Myths of Power*, 40 n. 38. See also T. Stordalen, *Echoes of Eden: Genesis 2-3 and Symbolism of the Eden Garden in Biblical Hebrew Literature* (Contributions to Biblical Exegesis and Theology 25; Leuven: Peeters, 2000), 155, 161, where he notes the same word used for the land at the edge of the underworld, perhaps as a reflection of royal garden-graves at Ugarit. If so, this usage might reflect the cosmic connecting point between the royal center of the palace of the living dynasty and the royal periphery of the deceased royal ancestors in the underworld. The deceased ancestors are tied to the living even as they have passed into the realm of the underworld in the periphery. Rituals designed to communicate with the dead (such as CAT 1.161) and myths that reflects aspects of the cultic devotion to the dead (such as CAT 1.5-1.6) express contact of members of the living and deceased royal line between the center and the periphery. For a discussion of these texts, with bibliography, see M. S. Smith, "The Death of 'Dying and Rising Gods' in the Biblical World: An Update, with Special Reference to Baal in the Baal Cycle," *Scandinavian Journal of the Old Testament* 12/2 (1998): 257-313.

cosmology, for example in the Bible (Genesis 2-3 and Ezekiel 28), shows the further development of regarding this sown in particular as a garden,[17] a reflection of the divine fructification of the center. It is for this reason that the mountain of the gods is also regarded as a garden. However, this notion is scarcely developed in the Ugaritic texts.[18] In sum, the sown is the region of human habitation and cultivation, and accordingly within it lies the realm of cultic activity devoted to beneficial deities. To sum up, these distinctions for "center" may be schematized in the following manner:

PLACE: HORIZONTAL SPACE	
HOME	FOREIGN
ʾugrtym (2.81.27, 28)	Egypt/Crete
local cultivation (e. g., Baal)	foreign culture and trade (e.g., Kothar)
SUPERNATURAL	
Home Deities	Foreign deities
Cult/blessing	No cult/with blessing

Just as the center bears a subdivision, the periphery likewise shows a distinction between what humans experience in the periphery and what lies beyond this periphery. This distinction is also expressed spatially:

PLACE: HORIZONTAL SPACE	
Periphery	Beyond the Periphery
Unpopulated zones (outback)	Underworld (*ʾarṣ*)
mdbr, "outback"	Netherworld (e.g., Mot[19]),
Near surface waters	Waters beyond (*thmtm*; e.g., Yamm)

---

17. Wyatt, *Myths of Power*, 27-115. Wyatt also identifies the temple and city as cosmic centers identified in various ways with the divine mountain and the garden.

18. The question is nicely raised by Stordalen, *Echoes of Eden*, 144-61, esp. 156-57. Stordalen explores the question of whether 1.23.66-68a assumes a garden. It would seem, based on the typology discussed above, that lines 68b-76 assume the notion of the sown as an enclosed garden complete with a "watchman of the sown." One problematic aspect of the text involves the command for an offering in the outback (line 65-66). This command would fly in the face of the notion that generally monstrous forces do not receive cultic offerings, possibly even in a sanctuary site in the outback (*mdbr qdš*). However, it is unclear from the context whether such a command can be carried out, since no such offering is described in the narrative, and in fact such a proposed offering may be intended to forestall the monstrous gods' entry into the sown, which takes place in the following lines (lines 68-76). For further discussion of this text, see the recent work by Mark S. Smith, *The Rituals and Myths of the Feast of the Goodly Gods of KTU/CAT 1.23: Royal Constructions of Opposition, Intersection, Integration, and Domination* (SBLRBS 51; Atlanta: Society of Biblical Literature, 2006).

19. Resheph's appearance with other deities, such as Baal, Yarih, Kothar, and perhaps Anat (under the title Rahmay) in 1.15 II 3-6 militates against classifying him easily on this side. So, too, his name in lists of deities (1.47.27 = 1.118.26) and evidently his temple (4.219.3).

In contrast to "home," the periphery or "outback" is characterized as a terrain of "rocks and brush" (*lʾabnm wlʿṣm*,1.23.66).[20] The outback marks a marginal or transitional zone and the site of human activities such as grazing and hunting (for the latter, see 1.12.34-35, 1.92.3) and here begins the area of dangerous forces. Accordingly, in the cosmic geography of the Baal Cycle, *dbr*, "outback," is part of the designation for the locale where Baal meets Mot, the god of "Death" (CAT 1.6 II 20; cf. 1.5 VI 6, 29); this place would appear to be the edge of the underworld (CAT 1.6 I 8-14). The *mdbr* is also the site where Baal's foes are to be given birth and to confront him in 1.12 I 19-22.[21]

Unlike the beneficent gods, Yamm, Mot, *tnn*, and the other cosmic enemies do not have holy mountains. Furthermore, the departures from this divine topography are perhaps as interesting as the general pattern itself. On the one hand, one divine enemy, Mot, is associated with a mountain called *knkny* (1.5 V 13). Yet even this apparent exception is rendered in a manner distinctive from the mountainous homes of the deities, for Mot does not live on top of his mountain. Instead, the mountain is the entrance to the underworld. The home of the astral deities, Shahar and Shalim, understandably is placed in the heavens (*šmmh*, 1.100.52). Athirat is not said to have a divine mountain although it might be argued that she shares her divine husband's home (at least on a part-time basis[22]). El is also of further interest as his home (given in terrestrial terms as a mountain in the mythological texts) is provided with a cosmic location at "the meeting-place of the Double-Deeps" (*bʿdt thmtm*) in one of the snake-bite incantations (1.100.3). The mythological texts refer to the same waters as "the channels of the Double-Deeps" (*ʾapq thmtm*, 1.4 IV 21-22; cf. 1.3 V 6-7; 1.17 VI 47-48). As the expression in the snake-bite text indicates, El's home apparently lies at the edge between what would be considered "near" and "far." Therefore, none of the locations listed in 1.100 lies beyond the orbit of what would have been considered culturally "far." Yet even with the exceptions, the pantheon as a whole is marked by the topography of the sacred mountain, for it meets on Mount Ll, a peak

20. On this expression, see M. H. Pope, "Mid Rock and Scrub, a Ugaritic Parallel to Exodus 7:19," in *Biblical and Near Eastern Studies: Essays in Honor of William Sanford LaSor*, ed. G. Tuttle (Grand Rapids, MI: Eerdmans, 1978), 146-50 = Pope, *Probative Pontificating in Ugaritic and Biblical Studies: Collected Essays*, ed. M. S. Smith, UBL 10 (Münster: Ugarit-Verlag, 1994), 41-46 with "An afterthought (22/12/92) on 'Mid Rock and Scrub.'"

21. S. B. Parker's translation of these pertinent lines renders *mdbr ʾil šʾiy* as "the god-awful wilderness." See *UNP*, 189.

22. See A. van Selms, *Marriage and Family Life in Ugaritic Literature*, Pretoria Oriental Studies 1 (London: Luzac, 1954), 63-64; and Pope, review of van Selms, *Marriage and Family Life in Ugaritic Literature*, *JBL* 74 (1955): 293-94, and *El in the Ugaritic Texts*, VTSup 2 (Leiden: Brill, 1955), 37.

known only in one passage of the Baal Cycle (1.2 I 20).[23] Hence the entire family of the gods is located within the "near" space of a holy mountain.

A further divine mapping involves realms, a feature confined to the second tier of competing males and their enemies. The Baal Cycle includes and builds on this divine topography of mountains and cult sites by organizing divine space additionally according to realms ruled by the second tier of the pantheon held by the males, Baal, Yamm, and Mot. In other words, realms are attributed only to Baal (sky), Yamm (sea), and Mot (underworld), and possibly Athtar (earth?).[24] Space therefore is used in two different ways, mountains to mark proximity of deities enjoying cult and bestowing blessing of various sorts, realms to mark cosmic competition.

Blessing at Home and Abroad versus Destruction

A tripartite division applies not only to space, but also to the supernatural. The first and fundamental division involves human need and functions on the one hand, and human threat or destruction on the other hand. This point can be seen across a number of genres. We see this commonly in the myths where deities largely aid humans or the natural world on which they depend. Many letters include opening greetings that invoke the gods (*ʾilm*) to provide well-being (**šlm*) and to protect (**nǵr*) the addressee.[25] One letter also asks the gods to strengthen the addressee (**ʿzz*, CAT 2.4.4-6; see also the blessing in 1.108.19-27). Another letter specifically asks for "the gods of Ugarit" (*ʾily ʾugrt*, 2.176.4-6) to bestow blessing. While the language in these letters is stereotypical, 1.15 II provides a glimpse into one way that the divinities' blessing was thought to transpire. In this scene, Baal asks El to confer his blessing upon Kirta,[26] with the other deities in attendance. The category of divine blessing apparently includes the deceased royal ancestors. CAT 1.161 invokes

23. The word *ll* appears in Ugaritic otherwise as a time-referent in ritual texts using the expression *lll*, "at night" (1.39.12; 1.49.9; 1.50.7; 1.106.27; cf. *ll* in the partly non-Ugaritic texts, 1.69.3 and 1.132.17, 25, as the apparent recipient of cultic devotion).

24. See T. H. Gaster, "The Religion of the Canaanites," in *Forgotten Religions*, ed. V. T. A. Ferm (New York: Philosophical Library, 1950), 121-30. Contrast the relationship between deities and realms in Mesopotamian myth; for discussion, see A. Livingstone, *Mystical and Mythological Explanatory Works of Assyrian and Babylonian Scholars* (Oxford: Clarendon, 1986), 71-91. Of course, Baal's house (1.4 VII) is located in the sky at a point perceptible to humans.

25. See A. Rainey, *The Scribe at Ugarit: His Position and Influence*, The Israel Academy of Sciences and Humanities Proceedings III/4 (Jerusalem: The Israel Academy of Sciences and Humanities, 1968), 136, esp. n. 58.

26. On this name, see W. G. E. Watson, "The Ugaritic PN *krt*," *UF* 26 (1994): 497-500.

blessing in the context of a ritual involving the deceased heroes and kings, called "god" (*ʾil*) in 1.113.14-26.[27] Finally, personal names show the benevolence of deities, according to A. Caquot: "L'onomastique . . . montrerait sans aucun doute que les noms de personne théophores cristallisent une attitude religieuse semblable: ils demandent à la divinité, quelque soit son nom, salut et bénédiction, protection et faveur."[28] It is to be observed that some deities, especially in their capacity as patrons of one group, may undertake the destruction of others. So for example, Anat defeats human enemies in 1.3 II, El supports Kirta's campaign against king Pabil in 1.14-1.15, and Horon is invoked by Kirta to smash his rebellious son's head in 1.16 VI. These cases, too, may be understood as expressions of blessing for humans. Other cases, such as the mythic rendering of Anat's murder of Aqhat in 1.18, might seem to vitiate the notion of the deities as generally benevolent, yet this case only represents an issue of human disobedience and divine punishment. It is also one of the relatively rare exceptions to the rule. In sum, well-being, including fertility at various levels,[29] was to derive from a number of deities.

In contrast, monstrous powers constitute no benefit, but only a threat to human well-being from the periphery. Yamm, for example, is connected with the demise of Kirta's household (CAT 1.14 I 19-20). Mot is known for his destruction as well (1.127.30-32[30]):

If the city is (has been) taken,	*hm qrt tʾuḫd*
(or) if Mot should attack man,	*hm mt yʿl bnš*
the house of the son(s) of mankind	*bt bn bnš*
will (should) take a goat	*yqḥ ʿz*
and will (should) look to the future (lit. afar).	*wyḥdy mrḥqm*

Here monstrous forces can enter the sown from beyond the periphery to threaten human life, a view expressed in equal conviction in Israelite

27. Regarding the deceased kings in CAT 1.161, see note 16 above.

28. Caquot, "Problèmes d'histoire religieuse," in *La Siria del Tardo Bronzo*, Orientis Antiqui Collectio 9 (Rome: Centro per l'Antichità e la Storia dell'Arte del Vicino Oriente, 1969), 70.

29. For a caution in identifying "fertility" primarily with goddesses or a particular goddess (as opposed to gods), see J. A. Hackett, "Can A Sexist Model Liberate Us? Ancient Near Eastern 'Fertility' Goddesses," *Journal of Feminist Studies in Religion* 5 (1989): 65-76. See the well-placed caution of P. D. Miller against reducing Ugaritic religion to simply a "fertility religion" (Miller, "Aspects of the Religion of Israel," in *Ancient Israelite Religion: Essays in Honor of Frank Moore Cross*, ed. P. D. Miller, Jr., P. D. Hanson, and S. D. McBride [Philadelphia: Fortress, 1987], 59).

30. For this rendering, see A. Rainey, "Gleanings from Ugarit," *IOS* 3 (1973): 51; see also *TO* 2.215; *UBC*, 76. For a more generic translation, "death," see D. Pardee, "Ugarit. Texts and Literature," *ABD* 6:710.

sources (Jer 9:20). One myth, CAT 1.23, narrates how so-called beautiful (but actually monstrous) divinities (*ʾilm nʿmm*) roam the steppe until they come upon the sown realm which provides them with plenty. Unfortunately, the precise import of this text has not yet been determined: does it reflect a similar pattern of threatening divinities reflecting a situation such as drought or famine? In any case, threatening demonic forces may impinge upon the center from the periphery. By the same token, it is to be noted that they are not "at home" in the center. As a general indicator of this distinction, monstrous divine forces generally do not receive cult in contrast to benevolent deities.[31]

The Ugaritic texts witness to a further division between the home deities who provide blessing and foreign deities who also bless. Ugaritic letters distinguish between home gods and foreign gods: *ʾily ʾugrt* in 2.16.4-6 versus *ʾil mṣrm* in 2.23.22 and *ʾil alṯy* in 2.42.8. In 2.42, the gods of Alashiya follow a list of Ugaritic deities invoked in lines 6-8. These letters' opening greeting formulas invoke both home gods and foreign gods to bestow blessing on the addressee. The home deities may be reflected in the heading given to the list of deities in 1.47.1 (absent from 1.118), namely *ʾil ṣpn* (cf. the heading *dbḥ ʾil bldn* in 1.162.1). This expression apparently refers to the "gods of Sapanu,"[32] evidently the home deities of the kingdom of Ugarit, perhaps identified by the mountain of Baal, the divine patron of the Ugaritic dynasty. Foreign deities could stand parallel to home deities through scribal texts listing them in parallel columns, as in 1.47 (and its ritual counterpart, 1.118) on the one hand and on the other hand, RS 20.24.[33] Or, a home god and a foreign deity

31. According to some scholars, *ym* in the ritual texts, e.g., 1.102.3, 1.118.29, 1.162.11, might not be the god Yamm, but a cultic basin; so J. F. Healey, "The Akkadian 'Pantheon' List from Ugarit," *SEL* 2 (1985): 120. Or, it is a deity called "Day"; so E. T. Mullen, *The Divine Council in Canaanite and Early Hebrew Literature*, HSM 24 (Chico, CA: Scholars, 1980), 89. However, de Moor defends the identification ("The Semitic Pantheon of Ugarit," *UF* 2 [1970]: 201). Given the parallel listing of deities in 1.47, 1.118, and 1.148, it is difficult to avoid seeing the god in the list of ritual offerings made in 1.148.9: *ym* in CAT 1.47.30 = 1.118.29 corresponds to ^{d}*tâmtum* in RS 20.24.29 and apparently with *ym* in 1.148.9. Accordingly, the god Yamm and probably not a cultic basin seems to receive an offering in 1.148.9 although it is to be noted that the next entry in 1.47 and 1.118 (but not in 1.148) is a divinized incense burner (*ʾuṯḫt*). On 1.148, see D. Pardee, "RS 24.643: Texte et Structure," *Syria* 69 (1992): 153-70, esp. 158, 160.

32. Certainly not "divine Sapan," as the mountain is mentioned in line 6 of the same text. See J. F. Healey, "The Akkadian 'Pantheon' List from Ugarit," 117. Note that the offering list in 1.148 begins *dbḥ ṣpn*, apparently the sacrificial heading corresponding to the *ʾil ṣpn* in 1.147.1 (see the preceding note).

33. Pardee, "Ugarit: Texts and Literature," 709. For the lists, see J. F. Healey, "The Akkadian 'Pantheon' List from Ugarit," 115-25, and "The 'Pantheon' of Ugarit: Further Notes," *SEL* 5 (1988 = Fs. O. Loretz): 103-12.

may be given a relationship mythologically. The concept of the divine family could be used to represent the relationship of foreign deities. CAT 1.24 not only attests to deities with foreign names, but the relationship of a foreign deity to an indigenous one expressed through the family metaphor of marriage. The Mesopotamian moon-goddess Nikkal (Sumerian nin.gal, "great lady") is to be wed to her West Semitic male counterpart, Yarih. Implicit to this marriage is an identification of the two deities as moon-deities. The text makes a point of mentioning Nikkal's family, indicated by the reference to her father, mothers, brothers and sisters (1.24.33-37). In this case, the divine family retains conceptual coherence in the face of a foreign deity, through marriage, the one ritual that extends family relations.

Animals: Domesticated versus Monsters

Benevolent deities are often rendered anthropomorphically while destructive divinities appear as monstrous in character. Moreover, theriomorphic representations reflect the dichotomy between deities and cosmic enemies. Cosmic enemies are monstrous or undomesticated in character, while the animals associated with benevolent deities ("attribute animals"[34]) lie within the orbit of cultural domestication.[35] This fundamental set of distinctions may be schematized in the following manner:

Benevolent Deities	*Destructive Divinities*
Anthropomorphism	Animal gods, monsters
Domesticated species emblematic of deities: bull, calf, bird, cow	Undomesticated species emblematic of monsters: snake, serpent

34. P. Amiet, *Corpus des cylindres de Ras Shamra–Ougarit II: Sceaux-cylindres en hématite et pierres diverses*, Ras Shamra–Ougarit 9 (Paris: Éditions Recherche sur les Civilisations, 1992), 68: "animaux attributs." Cf. "Animal attribute," in P. Amiet, *Art of the Ancient Near East*, trans. J. Shepley and C. Choquet (New York: Abrams, 1980), 440 no. 787. Amiet also uses "attendant animal," in "Part Five: A Lexicon" of the same work.

35. I prescind from the issue over whether any goddess is to be considered the "mistress of animals." For discussion and references, see I. Cornelius, "Anat and Qudshu as the «Mistress of Animals». Aspects of the Iconography of the Cananite Goddesses," *SEL* 10 (1993): 21-45. For a general treatment of evidence of the goddesses involved, see W. G. E. Watson, "The Goddesses of Ugarit: A Survey," *SEL* 10 (1993): 47-59. For the issue of the goddess' representation as a cow, see M. Dijkstra, "Semitic Worship at Serabit el-Khadim (Sinai)," *ZAH* 10 (1997): 89-97. Since the evidence at Ugarit is unclear, I prescind from this question as well. I would only point out that whatever goddess is involved, it illustrates the association of a domesticated species with a deity.

El often bears the title "Bull" (CAT 1.1 III 26, IV 12, V 22; 1.2 I 16, 33, 36, III 16, 17, 19, 21; 1.3 IV 54, V 10, 35; 1.4 I 4, II 10, III 31, IV 39, 47; 1.6 IV 10, VI 26; cf. 1.128.7). In this connection, the personal name *ʾilṯr*, "El is Bull," may be noted (4.607.32). I am not aware of any other deity coupled with this predicate in a personal name.[36] Baal is presented as a bull-calf (1.5 V 17-21; 1.10 II-III, esp. III 33-37; cf. 1.11; see further below), and here we may note P. Amiet's characterization of the bull as the storm-god's "attribute animal" in Syrian glyptic.[37] In this connection the bull or bull-calf mentioned in the Bible may reflect the iconography associated with El and Baal. El's iconographic representation may underlie the image of the divine as having horns "like the horns of the wild ox" in Numbers 24:8 since this passage shows other marks of El language. Many scholars are inclined to see El's iconography rather than Baal's iconography behind the famous "golden calf" of Exodus 32 and to the bull images erected by Jeroboam I at Bethel and Dan (1 Kings 12),[38] but this iconography has been traced back to Baal as well.[39] Here we might compare not only the depiction of Baal in the Ugaritic texts, but also the "fierce young bull" (symbol) of the storm-god, Adad.[40] Still the tradition in ancient Israel militates in favor of Bethel originally as an old cult-site of the god El (secondarily overlaid — if not identified — with the cult of Yahweh), perhaps as the place-name Bethel (literally, "house of El") would suggest (Genesis 28:10-22).[41]

The case of Anat as a bird is particularly interesting as the evidence is both textual and iconographic.[42] In 1.108.8, the goddess bears the title of

36. The element *ṯr* is not listed in F. Gröndahl, *Die Personennamen der Texte aus Ugarit*, Studia Pohl 1 (Rome: Päpstliches Bibelinstitut, 1967).

37. So Amiet, *Sceaux-cylindres*, 69. For examples from Ugarit, see Amiet, *Sceaux-cylindres*, 68, 71, and 79, no. 146, and 73 and 81, no. 160. For the temporal extent of Levantine bull iconography, see O. Keel and C. Uehlinger, *Gods, Goddesses, and Images of God in Ancient Israel*, trans. T. Trapp (Minneapolis: Fortress, 1996), 37, 50-51, 56, 78, 82, 118-20, 130, 144-45, 158, 169, 172, 191-95, 278.

38. For the bull iconography at Bethel and the close relation of 1 Kings 12 and Exodus 32, see Cross, *Canaanite Myth and Hebrew Epic*, 198-99; Keel and Uehlinger, *Gods, Goddesses, and Images of God*, 191-92. On p. 194 n. 12 the authors suggest that *ʿglyw* in the Samaria Ostracon no. 41 should be rendered not "YW is a bull calf," but "Bull calf of YW" a view that gains in plausibility and sense from the discussion below.

39. See Smith, *The Early History of God*, 51.

40. See *CAD E*: 63a: *būru ek-du ša Adad* in a Middle Babylonian kudurru and ^{d}*AMAR ek-du* in a list of divine symbols.

41. See K. van der Toorn, *Family Religion in Babylonia, Syria and Israel: Continuity and Change in the Forms of Religious Life*, Studies in the History and Culture of the Ancient Near East 7 (Leiden/New York/Cologne, 1996), 321.

42. F. C. Fensham, "Winged Gods and Goddesses in the Ugaritic Tablets," *OA* 5 (1966): 157-64. For iconography of Anat as a bird, see M. H. Pope, "The Scene on the Drinking Mug from Ugarit," in *Near Eastern Studies in Honor of William Foxwell Albright*, ed. H. Goedicke (Baltimore/London: Johns Hopkins, 1971), 393-405 = Pope, *Probative Pontificat-*

"flyer of flyers, she who soars" (*dʾi dʾit rḫpt*).[43] 1.18 IV presents Anat hovering (**rḫp*) among a flock of birds over her prey, the hero Aqhat. As he sits down to eat, she releases her air-to-ground missile in the form of her hired warrior, YTPN. In these two instances the textual evidence is explicit. Thanks to iconographic evidence, Anat's form as a bird is known to underlie also the description of her travel to El's watery home in 1.4 III-IV. The textual evidence does not mention her theriomorphic form, but a drinking mug excavated from Ugarit depicts this scene at El's abode: Athirat stands before the seated El; behind his throne is a fish, signaling the water, and behind Athirat is a bird, namely Anat.[44] The reason for Anat's realization as a bird may not be obvious, but may be related to her depiction as a winged warrior goddess. B. Tessier remarks on the iconography of Baal and Anat depicting them together on seals:

> On Syrian seals the weather god is very often associated with a winged and armed goddess, and a similar association of the weather god and a warlike goddess, Anat, is found in the mythological literature from Ugarit.[45]

These scenes sometimes contain either a bull, Baal's attribute animal,[46] or Anat's, a bird.[47]

In contrast to these deities' animal forms, a number of the cosmic enemies are snake-dragons.[48] The language of dragons, known from Ugaritic

---

ing in Ugaritic and Biblical Studies, 17-27. On Anat's form as a bird, see further F. Gangloff and J. C. Haelewyck, "Osée 4, 17-19: Un marzeah en l'honneur de la déesse ʿAnat?," *ETL* 71 (1995): 370-82. For the lion possibly as her animal (representing her warrior prowess), see Amiet, *Sceaux-cylindres*, 34, 35 no. 46.

43. For the parsing of the expression, see G. A. Tuttle, "*di dit* in UG 5.2.1.8," *UF* 8 (1976): 465-66; *TO* 2:116 n. 356.

44. Insightfully noted by Pope, "The Scene on the Drinking Mug from Ugarit," 393-405. For a different view, see Theodore J. Lewis, "Syro-Palestinian Iconography and Divine Images," in *Cult Image and Divine Representation in the Ancient Near East* (ed. Neal H. Walls; American Schools of Oriental Research Book Series 10; Boston: American Schools of Oriental Research, 2005), 78-79.

45. Tessier, *Ancient Near Eastern Cylinder Seals from the Marcopoli Collection* (Berkeley/Los Angeles: University of California, 1984), 79.

46. Tessier, *Ancient Near Eastern Cylinder Seals*, 243 nos. 476, 477.

47. Tessier, *Ancient Near Eastern Cylinder Seals*, 245 nos. 480(?), 481(?). For the possibility also of the cow as Anat's iconographic representation, see Keel and Uehlinger, *Gods, Goddesses, and Images of God*, 126, 195.

48. For Ugaritic glyptic, see Amiet, *Sceaux-cylindres*, 167-76. For the wider Levantine context, see also Keel and Uehlinger, *Gods, Goddesses, and Images of God*, 76-78, 155. Mesopotamia attests a variety of monstrous forms. See W. G. Lambert, "Ninurta Mythology in the Babylonian Epic of Creation," *Keilschriftliche Literaturen*, XXXIII Rencontre Assyriologique Internationale, ed. K. Hecker and W. Sommerfeld, Berliner Beiträge zum Vorderen Orient 6 (Berlin: Dietrich Reimer, 1986), 55-60; E. Reiner, "Magic Figurines, Amulets, and Talismans," in *Monsters and Demons in the Ancient and Medieval Worlds: Papers Presented in*

and biblical texts, denotes their monstrous form. Here we meet early literary references to the multi-headed dragon of ancient Israel (Psalm 74:13, 14; cf. Job 26:13) and later apocalyptic (Revelation 12:3, 13:1). CAT 1.3 III 40-42 describes Tunnanu (or less likely an unnamed cosmic enemy):

> "Surely I bound Tunnanu and destroyed(?) him.
> I fought the Twisty Serpent,
> The Potentate with Seven Heads."

The god Mot reminds Baal of his defeat of Leviathan in similar terms (CAT 1.5 I 1-3):

> " . . . you killed Litan, the Fleeing Serpent,
> Annihilated the Twisting Serpent,
> The Potentate with seven heads . . . "

Glyptic from Ugarit attests to the anthropomorphic warrior-god with a snake in either hand.[49] Such divine opponents are manifest in incantations as enemies of humans (as in CAT 1.82.1),[50] while mythological contexts describe divine opponents in the same forms yet on a cosmic scale.

Time: Present versus Past

There is one contrast that works poorly for the Ugaritic texts compared to Mesopotamia, and that is the contrast between time present and time past. According to Wiggermann, time present for Mesopotamia marks the epoch of deities and time past signals the ancient era of monstrous enemies. Hence Enuma Elish recounts the ancient past which precedes Tiamat's defeat at the hands of Marduk. The narrative is set in hoary antiquity. In marked contrast, Ugaritic myth has only one case of a text that might involve a "theogony" (1.23).[51] The Ugaritic texts also lack a

Honor of Edith Porada, ed. A. E. Farkas, P. O. Harper, and E. B. Harrison (Mainz: Philipp von Zabern, 1987), 27-36; Wiggermann, *Mesopotamian Protective Spirits*, 143-87. Snakes of the more terrestrial variety may denote other values such as regeneration and they are depicted occasionally with the goddess. See Keel and Uehlinger, *Gods, Goddesses, and Images of God*, 53, 86, 274.

49. Amiet, *Sceaux-cylindres*, 71 and 78, no. 144. See also Amiet, *Sceaux-cylindres*, 74 and 82, no. 166; See E. Williams-Forte, "The Snake and the Tree in the Iconography and Texts during the Bronze Age," in *Ancient Seals and the Bible*, ed. L. Gorelick and E. Williams-Forte (Malibu, CA: Undena, 1983), 18-43. On this type in Mesopotamia, see Wiggermann, "Transtigridian Snake Gods," 210-11.

50. See A. Caquot, "Un recueil ougaritique de formules magiques: KTU 1.82," *SEL* 5 (1988 = Fs. O. Loretz): 31-43; J. C. de Moor, *An Anthology of the Religious Texts from Ugarit*, Nisaba 16 (Leiden: Brill, 1987), 175-81.

51. See F. M. Cross, "The 'Olden Gods' in Ancient Near Eastern Creation Myths," in *Magnalia Dei: The Mighty Acts of God: Essays on the Bible and Archaeology in Memory of*

narrative rendering an ancient conflict between divine warriors and their cosmic enemies issuing in creation (or what F. M. Cross, his students, E. T. Mullen and R. J. Clifford, and a variety of other scholars, call "cosmogony"[52]). To be sure, such old conflicts are topics of conversation. So Anat and Mot both refer to ancient enemies (1.3 III 38-46; 1.5 I 1-3, 28-30; cf. 1.82.1). An ancient cosmogony featuring El as the warrior-creator has often been claimed for the Ugaritic texts, and the idea may be supported by reference to El's weaponry in 1.65.12-14,[53] but even this text which is so focussed on El and his household does no more than allude to this possibility. There is no myth devoted to this topic, in stark contrast with Mesopotamian literary tradition. (A comparable contrast might be made with Israelite tradition as well.) Of course, it might be argued that the Ugaritic literary corpus once included such texts, but that they are no longer extant. This is hardly the end of the matter, since the Ugaritic text usually compared with Enuma Elish is the Baal Cycle, and on the language of time-frame they apparently differ. Enuma Elish explicitly situates its narrative in the distant past. In contrast, the Baal Cycle does not present Yamm and Mot as subjugated foes of the past, but enemies whose struggles with Baal never seem to quite quit. This is clear for Mot who returns after seven years to renew his conflict with the storm-god (1.6 V 8-10); Yamm may also appear after his defeat at Baal's hands (1.4 VII 14). The warrior's battles over Yamm and Mot are not the stuff of high antiquity, but matters of a sort of present; whether timeless or repetitive I doubt anyone can really say (although many scholars do). I would prefer to say that such conflict is represented as part of the present scheme of reality, not simply of the distant past. This presentation reflects the precarious character of the cosmic order represented by Baal's kingship.

G. Ernest Wright, ed. F. M. Cross, W. E. Lemke, and P. D. Miller, Jr. (Garden City, NY: Doubleday, 1976), 328-38; Mullen, *The Divine Council*, 34, 45, 76, 88. Cf. the far-ranging study of N. Wyatt, "The Theogony Motif in Ugarit and the Bible," in *Ugarit and the Bible*, 395-419. For later West Semitic theogony, see further K. Koch, "Wind und Zeit als Konstituenten des Kosmos in phönikischer Mythologie und spätalttestamentlichen Texte," in *Mesopotamia—Ugaritica—Biblica: Festschrift für Kurt Bergerhof zur Vollendung seines 70. Lebensjahres am 7. Mai 1992*, ed. M. Dietrich and O. Loretz, AOAT 232 (Kevelaer: Butzon & Bercker; Neukirchen-Vluyn: Neukirchener Verlag, 1993), 59-91.

52. See Cross, "The 'Olden Gods' in Ancient Near Eastern Creation Myths," 328-38; Mullen, *The Divine Council*, 34, 45, 76, 88; R. J. Clifford, "Cosmogonies in the Ugaritic Texts and in the Bible," *Or* 53 (1984 = Mitchell J. Dahood Memorial Volume): 183-201; P. D. Miller, "Aspects of the Religion of Israel," 59. See also L. Fisher, "Creation at Ugarit and in the Old Testament," *VT* 15 (1965): 313-25; N. Wyatt, "Killing and Cosmogony in Canaanite and Biblical Thought," *UF* 17 (1985): 375-81; T. Fenton, "Nexus and Significance: Is Greater Precision Possible?" in *Ugarit and the Bible: Proceedings of the International Symposium on Ugarit and the Bible. Manchester, September 1992*, ed. G. J. Brooke, A. H. W. Curtis, and J. F. Healey, UBL 11 (Münster: Ugarit-Verlag, 1994), 76-81.

53. On CAT 1.65, see Pardee, "Ugarit. Texts and Literature," 709.

The one myth considered a theogony is often called "the Birth of the Beautiful Gods" (CAT 1.23). Given the birth of two gods sired by El, this text has been regarded as the single instance of a theogony in the Ugaritic corpus. Like the Baal Cycle, this text is not explicitly set in the ancient past (although it could have been thought as having been so, given the text's description of the births of gods long known, namely Shahar and Shalim, that is, Dawn and Dusk). Yet the time of this text is the ritually present, as the many ritual comments of the text would suggest. Whether or not such a "ritual present" likewise informs the narrative presentation of the Baal Cycle I cannot say, even though this would fit very nicely with ritual theories of the text.[54] Yet even here it may be said that ritual perspective and information may be incorporated into a literary text without making it into a text for ritual performance.[55] Accordingly, it may be preferable to investigate the matter of the Baal Cycle's temporal perspective as a literary question. If so, then the cosmic enemies may be divided according to time-frame in the Baal Cycle: most seem to belong to the ancient past which is only a matter of passing reference, but Yamm and Mot belong to the present. Their power is manifest as much in the present cosmos as the kingship of Baal, their warrior-enemy. Cosmic enemies in the present of this sort may be an issue specific to the Baal Cycle, insofar as the text seems to offer a statement about the view of the cosmos in the present. Yet I am not aware of a classic Mesopotamian or Israelite text that so represents the present threat of cosmic enemies in these terms and the help accorded the divine hero by other deities. In sum, whatever more is to be made of the apparent present setting in the Baal Cycle, this feature seems to demarcate it from the very Mesopotamian and Israelite texts commonly compared with it.

The Head God and His Beloved Monsters

The biblical hymn of Psalm 148:7 calls on the cosmic sea creature Tannin to join in praising Yahweh. Mesopotamian culture, too, regarded monstrous creatures as subservient to deities,[56] and so we should be careful not to attribute the kindly attitude toward cosmic monsters as an Israelite innovation. Indeed, this view of the monstrous enemies recalls El's special relationship with these foes, expressed through various "terms of endearment" and other nomenclature. The Ugaritic material is especially rich in terms of endearment between El and the cosmic enemies. The *locus*

54. See *UBC*, 60-61.
55. See *UBC*, 96-100.
56. See E. D. van Buren, "The Dragon in Ancient Mesopotamia," *Or* 15 (1946): 24-25.

classicus for this phenomenon is Anat's speech to Gpn w-Ugr in CAT 1.3 III 36-1.3 IV 1:

> "Why have Gapn and Ugar come?
> What enemy rises against Baal,
> What foe against the Cloud-Rider?
> Surely I fought Yamm, the Beloved of El (*mdd ʾil*),
> Surely I finished off River, the Great God (*ʾil rbm*),
> Surely I bound Tunnanu and destroyed(?) him,
> I fought the Twisty Serpent, the Seven-headed Potentate.
> I fought Desi[re] (*ʾarš*), the Beloved of El (*mdd ʾilm*),
> I destroyed Rebel (*ʿtk*), the Calf of El (*ʿgl ʾil*).
> I finished off Fire (*ʾišt*), the Dog of El (*klbt ʾilm*),
> I annihilated Flame (*ḏbb*), the Daughter of El (*bt ʾil*)
> That I might fight for silver and inherit gold.

Different sorts of images are used for the monstrous cosmic forces' relationship to El. Here Yamm and Arsh are called his "beloved" (*ydd ʾil / mdd ʾil*). Like these cosmic monsters, Mot is cast precisely with the same title elsewhere.[57] This title bears a particular cultural freight and association. Commonly taken as an expression of El's preferred feeling for Yamm, the word may more precisely denote El's legal selection of Yamm over the other gods in his family. H. Z. Szubin has insightfully commented on the legal force of the term in biblical literature:[58]

> This status invested the chosen "beloved" designee with power, authority and title and bestowed upon him special rights and privileges. In the areas of adoption, matrimony, inheritance and succession, such designations were of paramount importance for they not only determined the validity of tranfer of valuable property such as ancestral estates, but also the legitimacy of transmission of office, rank and title.
>
> In controversial and disputable cases the designation of a "beloved" functioned to silence also claims and potential jactations which challenged the legitimacy of the lawfully chosen "righteous" son, king, disciple or teacher in a manner similar to the intended purpose in Solomon's appellation Jedidiah—"beloved of the Lord."

The name of this royal heir signifies David's publicly actualized action which legally defines this particular son as his heir. The titles of

57. Yamm in 1.3 III 38-39, etc.; 'Arsh in 1.3 III 43, and Mot in 1.4 VII 48-49, VIII 23-24, 30-32, etc.

58. Szubin, "The 'Beloved Son' in the Hebrew Bible and the 'Beloved Disciple' in the New Testament in Light of Ancient Near Eastern Legal Texts," Abstract, Society of Biblical Literature International Conference, 1995; used with permission.

Yamm and Mot, namely *ydd ʾil* and *mdd ʾil*, have been compared to the name of Jedidiah,[59] but their possible legal force has gone unnoticed. These epithets mark not only El's preference for them over the other gods, but also their status as his publicly designated successors. They hold a claim to divine kingship from the perspective of divine patrimony. In the context of the narrative, this preference comes at the expense of Baal whose paternity marks him as an outsider to the divine family.

Finally, Fire and Rebel are called El's "pets," specifically "calf" and "dog," while Flame is called his "daughter." The two phrases, *ʿgl ʾil* and *klbt ʾilm*, are terms of endearment, like the expression "beloved of El" and the family term "daughter." (Although many different renderings are philologically possible, the parallel context of the expressions may be seen as militating in favor of understanding the second noun in all of the four expressions, *mdd ʾil*, *mdd ʾilm*, *ʿgl ʾil*, and *klbt ʾilm* as a reference to the god El.[60]) The animal nouns in two of the construct phrases are very clear; they are almost uniformly understood as *ʿgl* as "calf"[61] and *klbt* as a female dog ("bitch").[62] In contrast, the significance of these two terms has received very little attention.[63] Texts proximate in time and space to CAT 1.3 III 44-45 use "dog" and "calf" to denote subservient status. The El Amarna correspondence regularly uses *kalbu*, "dog," to express vassalage to Pharaoh.[64] The juxtaposition of this title with "servant" (*ardu*) is especially indicative of this understanding of "dog": "What is Abdi-Ashirta, servant and dog, that he takes the land of the king for himself?" (EA 71:16-19; cf. 60:1-9; 88:9-11). The question explicitly compares Abdi-Ashirta to a dog that is supposed to be obedient to its owner. The same usage is attested in the Lachish letters (KAI 192:3-4; cf. 195:3-4, 196:3) and

59. *UBC*, 59-60, 150-51.

60. Alternatively, the first and third expressions could allude to El, while the second and fourth phrases may refer generically to the "gods," though perhaps under the assumption that such an expression would still place these "animals" under El's authority. Cf. proper name *mddbʿl* (Gröndahl, *Die Personennamen*, 143).

61. See the discussion of the identification of Akkadian *agālu* in *CAD A/1*, 141b.

62. The gender of this dog presumably derives from the feminine gender of *ʾišt* (so suggested by T. J. Lewis, personal communication).

63. D. R. West has proposed that the title *klbt ʾilm* indicates that *ʾišt* (usually translated as "Fire") was conceived as a cosmic dog, "a native form of Mesopotamian Lamashtu." West, "Hekate, Lamashtu and *klbt ʾilm*," *UF* 24 (1992): 384. The basis for West's comparison is quite general: both Lamashtu and *ʾišt* have fiery and canine associations. Since so little is known of *ʾišt*, it is quite possible that *klbt* has some mythological association along the lines proposed by West. Other parallels, such as Cerberus, might leap to mind as well. For possible Akkadian parallels, see *CAD K*, 71a, 2'f.

64. EA 67:16-18; 76:12-16; 84:6-10, 16-18; 90:19-26; 91:3-5; 108:25-28; 134:11-13; 201:9-16; 320:16-25; cf. 109:44-49; 130:31-38; 138:95-97. These texts are conveniently collected and discussed by J. M. Galán, "What Is He, the Dog?" *UF* 25 (1993): 174.

2 Kings 8:13. To be sure, "dog" was used as a term of derision for a disobedient servant as well. The point of both usages is servitude.[65]

Proper names help to demonstrate this usage for both dog and calf. Ugaritic proper names containing the element **klb*, "dog," are understood in the similar sense of "servant, slave," according to F. Gröndahl.[66] Biblical Hebrew likewise attests to the name *kālēb*,[67] and the same has been suggested for some Phoenician and Punic personal names with the element **klb*.[68] If the metaphorical usage for **klb* (attested in the Amarna and Lachish letters, 2 Kings 8:13, and the West Semitic proper names) lies behind the sense of *klbt* in CAT 1.3 III 44, then the master is El, and *ʾišt* is his servant. An analogous usage may underlie Ugaritic *ʿgl ʾil* in the same context. Akkadian proper names include *A-ga-al-*[d]*Marduk*, "calf of Marduk."[69] As further evidence for this notion of "calf" as a term of subservience, it is possible to point also to personal names which use Akkadian *būru*, "calf," plus divine name.[70]

If this approach to *ʿgl* and *klbt* is correct, Anat's foes, *ʿtk* and *ʾišt*, are said to stand in a subservient relationship to El. Apart from support for this interpretation of *ʿgl* and *klbt* discussed above, this view would also lend coherence to the list of enemies in 1.3 III 38-46, who would seem generally to have a relationship to El. For example, lines 38-39 apply to

---

65. It is possible that such a metaphorical usage lies also behind *keleb*, a category of cultic personnel proscribed in Deuteronomy 23:19, and Phoenician *klbm* in the Kition plaque (CIS 86b = KAI 37, line 10; see also 86a, line 16). See F. L. Benz, *Personal Names in Phoenician and Punic Inscriptions: A Catalog, Grammatical Study and Glossary of Elements*, Studia Pohl 8 (Rome: Biblical Institute Press, 1972), 331; J. C. L. Gibson, *Textbook of Syrian Semitic Inscriptions. Volume III: Phoenician Inscriptions including Inscriptions in the Mixed Dialect of Arslan Tash* (Oxford: Clarendon, 1982), 124-25, 126-27, 130. Some scholars, however, prefer a more literal understanding of **klb* for these cultic personnel. See L. E. Stager, *Ashqelon Discovered: From Canaanites and Philistines to Romans and Moslems* (Washington, DC: Biblical Archaeologist Society, 1991), 35, 36. For further opinions on the two sides of this discussion, see further J. Hoftijzer and K. Jongeling, *Dictionary of the North-West Semitic Inscriptions. Part One: ʾ-L* (Leiden: Brill, 1995), 509. The issues attendant on the Kition plaque are beyond the scope of this investigation.

66. Gröndahl, *Die Personennamen*, 150. For more Akkadian names with the element **kalbu*, see *CAD K*, 696.

67. See *BDB*, 477.

68. See Benz, *Personal Names in Phoenician and Punic Inscriptions*, 131-32, 331.

69. See K. Koenen, "Der Name *ʿGLYW* auf Samaria-Ostrakon Nr. 41," *VT* 44 (1994): 399 n. 5. For further examples, see *CAD A/1*, 141b. The personal name *ʿglyw* in Samaria Ostracon 41 was also interpreted in this manner by Martin Noth, but this view is controverted. See the discussion in Koenen. A verbal form of **ʿgl* could be involved (J. Tigay, personal communication). See also the Palmyrene name *ʿglbwl* discussed in Koenen, 399 n. 2, 400 n. 15.

70. So *AHw*, 141b. For other instances, see *CAD B*, 342a. Note also the comment there: "OB personal names of the type *Būrija*, *Būratum* are probably hypocoristics of WSem. names."

Yamm the epithet, *mdd ʾil*, "darling of El." This relationship is given some context in CAT 1.1 IV where El seems to select Yamm as the champion of the gods; this deputation takes place clearly at Baal's expense. While no such context is provided for *ʿtk* and *ʾišt*, a comparable understanding may be involved: these cosmic enemies opposing the generation of Anat and Baal are likewise the beloved servants of El. The words *ʿgl* and *klbt* then may connote not only animal form, but also subservience, service, perhaps even endearment. While dogs could be a potential problem (Exodus 11:7; Psalms 22:17, 59:6, 14), the use of dog as well as calf and not other animals derived from their domestication; under normal conditions, they are safe and pliable servants. Dogs helped humans care for their flocks (Job 30:1) and accompanied them on journeys (see Tobit 6:1).[71] Humans were also served by calves as beasts of burden (1 Samuel 28:24).[72]

Finally, it may be noted that some of the Ugaritic cosmic enemies are associated with Yamm, others with El. Within the narrative of the Baal Cycle, Yamm and El share a common trait: both are opponents of Baal up through CAT 1.2 I. Perhaps this division of cosmic characters highlights El's relationship with Yamm. Yamm, at least in the Baal Cycle, is the premier figure of El's favor. The situation is quite different in the Bible. Yamm has little mythology left in the extant biblical corpus. The other monstrous enemies will survive as symbols of worldly powers throughout Jewish apocalyptic (presented as a sort of religious science fiction).

Israelite Cosmic Enemies Tamed and Denied

At this juncture, we may take general stock of the Mesopotamian and Ugaritic traditions and the comparable material in the Bible pertaining to the cosmic enemies. First of all, ancient Israel inherited the names of some of the cosmic enemies from West Semitic culture (which it shares with Ugarit). In the Bible and Mesopotamian literature, the warrior-god dominates his cosmic enemies. There are four foes confronted by both Baal in the Ugaritic material and Yahweh in the Bible: Sea (Hebrew *yam*, Ugaritic *ym*); biblical Leviathan (*liwyātān*) and Ugaritic *ltn*[73]; biblical *tannīm*,

71. For domesticated dogs, see CAT 1.16 I 2, 15. For examples of domesticated dogs in shepherding and hunting, see *CAD K*, 71a.

72. For animals in the Bible, see the essays in *Gefährten und Feinde des Menschen: Das Tier in der Lebenswelt des alten Israel*, ed. B. Janowski, U. Neumann-Gorsolke, and U. Glessmer (Neukirchen-Vluyn: Neukirchener Verlag, 1993). See also the surveys of Firmage, "Zoology (Animal Profiles)," *ABD* 6: 1109-67; and P. Riede, "'Denn wie der Mensch jedes Tier nennen würde, so sollte es heissen': Hebräische Tiernamen und was sie uns verraten," *UF* 25 (1993): 331-78.

73. A convenient summary on this figure can be found in J. Day, "Leviathan," *ABD* 4: 295-96.

Ugaritic *tnn* (*tunnanu* in the Ugaritic polyglot[74], spelled Tunnanu in the English translation below); and biblical Mawet and Ugaritic Mot, both literally meaning "Death." For Baal, most are enemies of old, but Sea (Yamm) and Death (Mot) are ongoing threats, a notion entirely missing from biblical or Mesopotamian conflict stories, though not from biblical apocalyptic and other genres.

Second, just as these cosmic enemies are mentioned as Baal's or Anat's old enemies, they are known in Israelite tradition as enemies of Yahweh, the warrior god. Three of these enemies appear in Psalm 74:12-17:

> Yet, O God, my king from of old,
> Maker of deliverance throughout the world,
> You are the one who smashed Sea with your Might,
> Cracked the heads of the Tannin in the waters;
> You are the one who crushed the heads of Leviathan,
> Left him as food . . . [75]
> You are the one who broke open springs and streams,
> You are the one who dried up the Mighty Rivers.
> To You belongs the day, Yours too the night,
> You are the one who established the Light of the Sun.
> You are the one who fixed all the boundaries of the world,
> Summer and winter — it was You who fashioned them.

Here the cosmic enemies' defeat was a prelude to the ancient event of creation. In contrast, Isaiah 27:1 presents Leviathan's defeat as a sign of the end-times. Isaiah 25:8 likewise proclaims a reversal of the power of another cosmic enemy of Death. The image of God there swallowing up Death reverses the comparable image of Death's demanding to swallow Baal (1.5 I 6-8, II 2-6).

Third, biblical texts attest to the cosmic forces as the chief-god's domesticated beasts. The book of Job knows these cosmic enemies both as human enemy and divine playthings. So Job himself expresses the first understanding, when he complains against God: "Am I Sea or Tannin that You set a watch over me?" (Job 7:12; see the reference to Leviathan in Job 3:8, and the mention of the Sea and the serpent in 26:13). Yet Job also declaws these enemies by rendering them not as Yahweh's enemies, but as objects of divine domestication. So God responds to Job that he treated Sea at creation not as an enemy but as a new-born babe (Job 38:8-11), and Leviathan is the sea creature caught by God's "fishhook" (40:25, NJPS),

---

74. See J. Huehnergard, *Ugaritic Vocabulary in Syllabic Transcription*, HSS 32 (Atlanta, GA: Scholars Press, 1987), 72, 185-86.

75. The text-critical difficulties with the end of this line make any translation little more than a hazardous guess.

drawn by a rope and nose-ring. God asks Job: "will you play with him like a bird . . . ?" (40:29). (So Psalm 104:26 identifies this figure as a creature and one for made for play: "Leviathan whom you formed to sport with.") This view of Leviathan as a tamed pet may go against one expectation of an Israelite audience, which knows Leviathan primarily as a monstrous enemy,[76] as in the Ugaritic texts that pit Baal or Anat against such figures. However, the biblical texts treating the monstrous figures instead as pets may echo their "beloved" relationship with El. Just as the biblical material will coalesce the differing imagery involving El and Baal with the national god of Yahweh, so too the differing roles of the cosmic forces as foes and beloved of the divine coalesce.

The Ugaritic material, however, differs from some biblical passages on a number of aspects involving the cosmic enemies and the gods connected with them. First, there is the matter of whether these forces are considered divine or not. On the Ugaritic side, these figures are at a minimum treated as equal in power to the deities who fight them. Note the stalemate between Baal and Mot in 1.6 VI 16-22 or Baal apparently slumped beneath Yamm's throne in 1.2 IV 6-7. Moreover, some of the texts mentioned above treat the cosmic enemies explicitly as divinities. For example, Yamm is clearly treated as divine, as he is included in two god-lists (1.47.30 = 1.118. 29) and equated with "Divine Sea" (ᵈ*tâmtum*) in RS 20.24.29, marked with the divine determinative. River (a title of Yamm) apparently bears the further epithet, "Great God" (*ʾil rbm*) in 1.3 III 39. Included in the same list (1.3 III 38-47) as Yamm are El's beloved or pets, the other cosmic enemies. From this context it would appear that they are comparable in rank or status to Yamm. In 1.14 I 18-20 Yamm's destruction is paralleled with the havoc caused by another god, Resheph. In 1.4 VIII 45-46, Mot receives the title *bn ʾilm* (either "son of El" or "son of the gods"), the same title used elsewhere for members of the pantheon (for example, in 1.4 III 14). Finally, we may mention again the destructive "goodly gods" (*ʾilm nʿmm*) of 1.23.[77] In sum, the Ugaritic texts present these figures at least as divine in rank and power, if not outright as divinities.

In contrast, biblical passages do not accord them a status comparable to the chief god. When they fight against Yahweh as in Psalm 74, such enemies never compare in power to Yahweh. Furthermore, Genesis 1:2 mentions the cosmic waters, but it is an object or abstraction, set in contrast to other raw material of creation. The audience of the creation story of Genesis 1 is set up for a cosmic conflict by the opening references to

76. Among more recent treatments, see T. N. D. Mettinger, "The Enigma of Job: The Deconstruction of God in Intertextual Perspective," *JNWSL* 23/2 (1997): 1-19, esp. 14-15. My thanks go to Professor Mettinger for bringing this article to my attention.

77. For discussion of *nʿm* as "goodly" rather than "beautiful," see Smith, *The Rituals and Myths*, 33-34.

such enemies. In this passage the lack of any conflict, or even any personification of the cosmic oceans or waters, is designed to heighten the picture of a powerful God who but speaks and the divine will is accomplished. So too the passing generic reference to the *tannînīm* in Genesis 1:21 conveys the notion that this God is so powerful that this God is a God beyond any other power, beyond opposition. Such a presentation carries an especially powerful conviction for an audience that knows and presumes the traditional stories of its warrior-God's victories over the ancient cosmic enemies.[78] Indeed, such a presentation assumes that the audience knows how such stories convey its deity's mastery over the universe.[79] Genesis 1 plays on this knowledge and thereby extends the theme of divine mastery.

Yet there is more to this passage. Not only is the conflict role eliminated in Genesis 1; even the old role of cosmic forces as domesticated has been muted by downplaying them, even depersonalizing them. These cosmic monsters are no longer primordial forces opposed to the Israelite God at the beginning of creation. Instead, they are creatures like other creatures rendered in this story. The narrative encloses the order of the divine creation around these monstrous enemies and by omission transforms them into another part of creation. Order then recasts these figures. We may attribute this transformation not only to an alteration of theme, but also literary order. In short, the change of these divine enemies into creatures involves a lexicon of creation. Yet, it is also the text's literary order detailing this creation. Accordingly, the literary order itself contributes to the monotheistic vision of Genesis 1. In this regard the text manifests a "monotheistic poetics,"[80] which alters the perception of real-

78. This point has been made repeatedly by biblical scholars. See the fine presentation of J. D. Levenson, *Creation and the Persistance of Evil: The Jewish Drama of Divine Omnipotence* (San Francisco: Harper & Row, 1988), 53-99. See more recently E. T. Mullen Jr., *Ethnic Myths and Pentateuchal Foundations: A New Approach to the Formation of the Pentateuch*, SBL Semeia Series (Atlanta, GA: Scholars, 1997), 94-98.

79. Levenson, *Creation and the Persistance of Evil*, 3.

80. For the relationship between "a form of discourse and a certain modality of the confession of faith," see P. Ricoeur, *Figuring the Sacred: Religion, Narrative and Imagination*, trans. D. Pellauer, ed. M. I. Wallace (Minneapolis: Fortress, 1995), 39. In this book Ricoeur's own examples suffer from outdated information concerning biblical scholarship since von Rad and about religion since Eliade. Making broader generalizations about the relationship between monotheism and biblical genre is a problematic undertaking. For example, R. Alter associates biblical narrative with biblical monotheism (as opposed to polytheistic myths), but S. B. Parker has provided a devastating critique of Alter's interpretation of biblical genres. See Alter, *The Art of Biblical Narrative* (New York: Basic Books, 1981), 29; Parker, *Stories in Scripture and Inscriptions: Comparative Studies on Narratives in Northwest Semitic Inscriptions and the Hebrew Bible* (New York/Oxford: Oxford University, 1997), esp. 137-42.

ity with its created order. This reading applies not only to these sea creatures; it also works for the sun and the moon, called only "the greater light" and "the lesser light" (Genesis 1:16), titles which were not necessarily polemical as such but quite traditional (cf. "great light," *nyr rbt*, for the Ugaritic sun-goddess in CAT 1.161.19,[81] and "light of the heavens," *nrt šmm*, for the Ugaritic moon-god in 1.24.16, 31). In Genesis 1 these figures are no longer presented as divinities. Instead, like the sea creatures, they are located within the created order. Here ambiguity between Creator and creatures is resolved; there is no middle ground left in Genesis 1's "monotheistic poetics."

As this discussion indicates, Genesis 1 shows some displacement from the traditional picture of both the chief god and the monstrous forces. The book of Job too shows some important differences. The book does not simply echo the earlier roles attested in the Ugaritic texts, at least when it comes to the chief god. For Job modifies the portrait of God compared to either El or Baal. This god appears not in a westerly storm-cloud, a traditional locus of Baal's theophany (or in human dreams, El's usual medium of communication with humans). Instead, God appears in the dust-cloud, the "whirlwind" (*hassĕʿārâ*, Job 38:1), the desiccating wind of the eastern desert, a natural force (that would be associated with Mot, the god of death).[82] This motif signals that God is the God not only of the domesticated human sphere, but also of realms undomesticated, even unknown by humans; therefore, the divine cannot be controlled or tamed by human assumptions. For humans the divine is accessible and therefore to that extent domesticated, yet this is also the God who moves about in the unknown reaches of the universe. This God knows the known and unknown; this God belongs not only to the center, but also to the periphery and well beyond. And so God is the God Job not only knew from of old, but also met for the first time (Job 42:5). "Home is where one starts from," we are told by T. S. Eliott (Four Quartets), and the point applies to human perception of the divine. Yet to know the God of Job only starts at home and requires visiting realms beyond the home, as Job shows in his discovery of the divine in the whirlwind.

---

81. Cf. also the sun-goddess' titles "Great Sun" (*rbt špš*) in 1.16 I 37 and "Light of the Gods, Shapshu" (*nrt ʾilm špš*) in 1.3 V 17, 1.4 VIII 21, 1.6 I 8, 11, 13, II 24, III 24, IV 17, 1.19 IV 47, 49 .

82. See T. McCreesh, "A Carnival of Animals in Job," presented at a meeting of the Old Testament Colloquium held at Conception Abbey in Conception, Missouri, on February 6, 1993. For the east wind as a possible terrestrial manifestation of the god of Death, see Smith, *The Early History of God*, 53; I base this observation on the work of Aloysius Fitzgerald who has noted the role that the east desert wind plays in many biblical passages. See Fitzgerald, *The Lord of the East Wind* (CBQMS 34; Washington, DC: The Catholic Biblical Association of America, 2002), esp. 26.

I would like to end this study with reference to a comment made by G. E. Mendenhall: "Dualistic mythology is always essentially political."[83] Mendenhall intended this statement to apply to polytheistic mythologies of power, but of course if such a comment applies to a polytheistic mythology such as the Baal Cycle or Enuma Elish, it may apply as well to biblical presentations of such conflict. To be more precise, such mythological conflicts may involve either divine strength or power, or its lack. For example, in Enuma Elish, Marduk's mastery is complete, overwhelming against Tiamat, a foe at the outset presented in majestic terms. As noted above, Yahweh's dominion in Genesis 1 is so great that conflict is assumed and transcended. Yet, a passage such as Psalm 74:12-17 appeals to divine strength at a moment of perceived divine weakness or indifference. In this case, Yahweh's mastery is not fully realized; for ancient Israelites this divine dominion is in fact a debatable matter. So, too, in cases where the prospect of divine victory is held out for a future time (Isaiah 27:1). Yahweh here has not yet exercised complete mastery over the cosmos. Such a lack of divine mastery is also apparent in Baal's need for help from other deities and his lack of definitive victory over Sea and Death.[84] Most of these texts are political expressions about deities rendered on the level of the mythological narrative and paralleled by the level of the human experience that inspires such narrative.

We might be content to say that deities' mastery over their enemies expresses the well-being of those who compose such a plot. However, the label of dualistic mythology is not only expressive of political power, it clearly has the flexibility to express political or communal weakness, even desperation. The text of Psalm 74 presents the opposite situation, a recollection of divine victory of the past at a time of human powerlessness. So too Isaiah 51:9-11 can assert and proclaim the power of Yahweh over the cosmic enemy as an expression of hope and herald to human weakness at the time of exile. If Genesis 1 is to be situated against the backdrop of foreign empires' imposing their power upon Judah,[85] then again divine mastery stands in inverse relation to the political status of the text's author. In this case, we might reverse Mendenhall's comment. Here dualistic mythology stands in a mode contrary to political condition of the author's community. Divine power can encode not only human power, but also human powerlessness. This, too, is a political statement that a community has control over its identity despite its political power-

---

83. Mendenhall, *The Tenth Generation: The Origins of the Biblical Tradition* (Baltimore/London: Johns Hopkins, 1973), 211 n. 35.

84. *UBC*, 109-10.

85. The exilic period has been a long-championed backdrop for this chapter. See most recently Mullen, *Ethnic Myths and Pentateuchal Foundations*, 94.

lessness. Whichever is strong or weak, the divine hero and the divine enemy express the identity of community against a threat that may be overwhelming or not. Finally then these mythologies, monotheistic and polytheistic, are ultimately not dualistic. Instead, various lines subtly connect the deities and their blessing on the one hand and the divine monsters on the other. No hero is great without the great enemy to defeat, and no cosmic enemy exists without the hero to vanquish it. Accordingly, pure political power is not the essence of dualistic mythology. Instead, narratives of divine conflict composed at moments of political power or powerlessness are both expressions of vision or hope. Some conflict narratives may be used to present either an existing political order (hence Mendenhall's sentiment), or an emerging order or even a non-existent order that is hoped for. This order, real or unrealized, is seen as a source of blessing or at least it expresses hope for blessing as of yet unknown, of things unseen. Hope then seems to be the key trope to these texts.[86]

86. Cf. Ricoeur, *Figuring the Sacred*, 47: faith "could be called 'unconditional trust' to say that it is inseparable from a movement of hope that makes its way in spite of the contradictions of experience and that turns reasons for despair into reasons for hope according to the paradoxical laws of a logic of superabundance."

4

Will the Real *Massebot* Please Stand Up

Cases of Real and Mistakenly Identified Standing Stones in Ancient Israel

ELIZABETH BLOCH-SMITH

Introduction

In the past decade biblicists and archaeologists have intensified the debate over Israelite aniconism.[1] Recent discussion has included *massebot* (standing stones).[2] Leviticus 26 begins with an admonishment not to fashion objects, including *massebot,* which functioned as images.

> You shall not make idols for yourselves, or set up for yourselves carved images or *massebot,* or place figured stones in your land to worship upon, for I the Lord am your God (NJPS).

Based on the biblical text, C. Graesser distinguished four functions for *massebot* and stones: (a) commemorative stones "commemorate an event for the purpose of honoring the divine and/or human participants in that event," (b) memorial stones "memorialize the dead," (c) legal

---

1. This includes lively and helpful debates with my husband Mark S. Smith of New York University.

2. In 1995 Tryggve N. D. Mettinger published *No Graven Image?: Israelite Aniconism in Its Ancient Near Eastern Context* (Stockholm: Almqvist & Wiksell International, 1995). Christoph Uehlinger countered in 1997 with "Anthropomorphic Cult Statuary in Iron Age Palestine and the Search for Yahweh's Cult Images" in *The Image and the Book: Iconic Cults, Aniconism, and the Rise of Book Religion in Israel and the Ancient Near East,* ed. K. van der Toorn; CBET 21 (Leuven: Uitgeverij Peeters, 1997), 97-155. See too T. J. Lewis, "Divine Images and Aniconism in Ancient Israel," *JAOS* 118, no. 1 (1998): 36-53; and Tallay Ornan, *The Triumph of the Symbol: Pictorial Representation of Deities in Mesopotamia and the Biblical*

stones "witness to a legal relationship between two or more individuals, such as a boundary or a contract," and (d) cultic stones "indicate the place at which the deity is immanent in the cult so that cultic intercourse with the deity can occur."[3] In all four cases, the stone signaled divine presence as witness or participant (for Graesser, only cultic stones marked divine immanence as such). In the case of the dead, erecting a memorial stone associated with divinity was an appropriate marker for the deceased called *elohim* and thus attributed divine status.

Graesser offered three explanations for the biblical prohibition of cultic *massebot*. First, they were associated with indigenous peoples and their cultic practices. Second, *massebot* were connected with local sanctuaries which were closed down with the centralization of worship in the Jerusalem Temple. Third, and most significantly, *massebot* were included among objects banned by the second commandment; "functions proper to images had been transferred to the *massebot* so that they were essentially no better than idols," as attested in Leviticus 26.1 and Micah 5.12, both southern sources.[4]

Archaeological evidence has been selectively cited both to bolster and to debunk the biblical tenet prohibiting the fashioning of divine images including *massebot*. In support of conflicting historical reconstructions, archaeological finds have been cited out of context and without critical re-examination. Excluding structural and functional stones commonly identified as *massebot* and concentrating on the most probable examples, the archaeological evidence supports Graesser's proposed functions of standing stones.

The definition and description of Israelite *massebot* remain vague, as the physical properties such as size, shape, or type of stone are not specified in the Bible. A single reference provides circumstantial evidence of their appearance. Jacob's erecting a stone which he had used as a pillow indicates the relative size, shape, and weight of one particular *massebah* (Gen. 28:18). Based on both biblical and archaeological evidence, Graesser defined a *massebah* as "a plain stone set up by human activity so that it stands higher than it is wide."[5] Even this vague definition fails to include the "Bull Site" stone (see below). A *massebah* is neither structural nor functional; it is prominent or conspicuous, focusing the viewer's attention on a particular spot; its shape is recognizably a standing stone rather than a random rock; and the context and accompanying assemblage support the identification.

Image Ban, OBO 213 (Fribourg: Academic Press; Göttingen: Vandenhoeck & Ruprecht, 2005), 168-82.

3. Carl Graesser, "Studies in Massebot," Ph. D. diss., Harvard University, 1969, 32.
4. Graesser, "Studies in Massebot," 295.
5. Graesser, "Studies in Massebot," 296.

A re-examination of published standing stones in Iron Age Israel and Judah yields prominent examples with clearly functional or structural purposes which should be excluded from the discussion. The remaining examples provide a physical description, the contexts, and accompanying assemblages. Function in each individual case remains a surmise based on patterned behavior and biblical testimony.

Archaeological examples of standing stones in Iron Age Israel are generally assumed to have served a cultic function. Interpretive assumptions bearing on the identification of cultic space in general and *massebot* in particular need to be examined. It is generally presumed that cultic objects render the accompanying assemblage cultic. The assemblage, in turn, leads to the presumption of designated cultic space in the vicinity, either a temple, a public or home shrine, or a storage room for a nearby shrine or temple. Rectangular stones in the vicinity are accordingly identified as *massebot*. The Megiddo shrines, the Taanach "Cultic Structure," and the Jerusalem Ophel "Cultic Structure" are examples of standing stones considered *massebot* on the strength of nearby "cultic" assemblages.

This criterion is problematic on several levels. Criteria defining an object as cultic are vague. Cultic objects need not render the associated assemblage cultic, as they may have been used or stored with profane objects. Prominent or extensive space need not have been dedicated to the display or storage of cultic objects. A designated corner may have served as a public or family shrine.[6] Further issues raised by proposed archaeological standing stones include erecting *massebot* in private as well as public space and using miniature *massebot* at home comparable to larger public examples.

Questionable or Mistakenly Identified "Massebot"

Stones found in neither a temple nor a high place, locations frequently designated "cult shrines," have been identified as *massebot* on the basis of nearby cultic objects such as incense burners or horned altars. In most of these cases, the stones are now agreed to serve a structural or functional purpose, and therefore the sole criterion of proximate "cultic assemblage" is insufficient for the determination of a *massebah*.

Further examples of misattributed *massebot* include miniature "stelae." The Taanach "Cultic Structure" small "stelae," the Lachish Cult Room 49 threshold example, and the Lahav stones with beveled edges and smooth faces are all fragments of grinding stones or stands.[7]

6. Elizabeth Bloch-Smith, "Maṣṣēbôt in the Israelite Cult: An Argument for Rendering Implicit Cultic Criteria Explicit," in *Temple and Worship in Biblical Israel* (ed. J. Day; London: T & T Clark International, 2005), 28-39. All dates in this article, either century or year, are B.C.E.

7. Graesser, "Studies in Massebot," 158-61, identified structural posts falsely identi-

Megiddo

Neither the pair of pillars from Shrine 2081 (early tenth century B.C.E., Stratum VA) nor the stelae from Building 338 (tenth century B.C.E., Stratum VA-IVB) should be considered *massebot*.

The excavator G. Loud reconstructed Locus 2081 in Area AA as the courtyard of an extensive building.[8] The "courtyard" designation is tentative as most of the southern wall and the southeastern corner of the room are missing, a small partitioned room is built into the northwestern corner, and no comparable courtyards were identified in the vicinity.

Two square stone pillars, each 1.5m high, stood side-by-side in the entrance into the interior rooms. Loud identified the building as a shrine and the pillars as *massebot* on the basis of horn-shaped stones in the adjacent open area combined with cultic and domestic objects scattered throughout and concentrated in a corner of the reconstructed courtyard. Two limestone horned altars (one large and one small, comparable to Arad), two offering stands (one large of limestone and one small of limestone and clay), a fenestrated stand, and a "steleform" stone constituted the cultic assemblage. In a "courtyard" corner, both altars and one incense stand lay jumbled among common domestic items including several jars, limestone objects, a jug, and a chalice.

Overlooked is the fact that the vast majority of courtyard objects were common domestic items: 36 jugs, 16 bowls, seven jars, two chalices, one cooking bowl, one lamp, four steatite scarabs or scaraboids, three stamp seals, bone objects (whorl, handle, awl, spindles, miniature mallet), bronze items (toggle pin, fibula, bracelets, finger ring), iron pieces (five arrowheads, an axe), two faience Eyes of Horus, beads, a basalt mortar and pestle, basalt vessels, grain, clay stoppers, two basalt stone rubbers, and sheep/goat or pig astragali in a bowl from an undefined location in the courtyard.[9] The assemblage contains a large number of objects used in domestic activities including hunting, processing grain, cooking, and spinning. This range of items does not typify cultic assemblages. The collection is more likely household goods scattered in the courtyard and stored or dumped in the corner. Household possessions may well include cultic objects, but the presence of such objects does not demonstrate either that the assemblage is cultic or that the associated structure is a designated cult space.

---

fied as *massebot* which have since been dropped from the discussion, including examples from Tell es-Safi, Tell Ta'anach (Sellin), and Tel el-Mutesellim/Megiddo (Schumacher, Lapp, and May).

8. For those who regard the stones as *massebot*, disagreement as to whether the building was private (Yigal Shiloh, Ora Negbi) or public (Uzi Avner, Beth Alpert-Nakhai) is relevant for classifying standing stones as public or private religious expressions.

9. Gordon Loud, *Megiddo II: Seasons of 1935-39*, OIP 62 (Chicago: University of Chicago, 1948), 161-62.

Neither the associated assemblage nor the architectural position of the pillars supports their identification as *massebot*. The two entryway pillars are similar in shape and size to structural pillars in nearby rooms, the pair in locus 2112 and the single pillar in the locus 2162 doorway.[10] At the time of excavation Loud wrote, "The presence of cult objects in locus 2081 arouses the suspicion that two upright stones at the entrance to the central room north of it may, despite their perfect structural positions, bear some cult significance."[11] A later generation more inclined to identify archaeological examples of *massebot* countered Loud and argued that the position of the pillars demonstrated their cultic rather than structural function.[12]

Building 338 was situated in Area BB, the highest point of the mound with a long cultic tradition. The ashlar construction and exceptional quality goods suggest the structure functioned as a public building or palace. Loci 338 and 339 were reconstructed as the shrine forecourt, with a stone laver and a number of stone altars. From the forecourt one entered into the center of the broadroom shrine Room 340, measuring 9.15 x 4.0m. A large and small stele in a line with smaller pillars partitioned the room longitudinally. Also along the line, an "offering table" stood opposite the entrance. Further evidence of cultic function was inferred from nearby and more distant "cultic" assemblages. The jugs, juglets, a cooking pot and a flask, a basalt mortar and pestle, and an "idol" (a hollow, cylindrical torso fragment) retrieved from Room 340 and the adjacent Room 332 were deemed cultic. More convincing was the assemblage uncovered in an open area south of Building 10, about 30m from the "shrine" Room 340. To explain their distant find-spot, the three limestone horned altars, round altars, offering stands, and fragments of five model shrines were assumed to have been removed from the shrine at the time it was reverentially buried.[13]

The Room 340 "stelae" functioned in a partition wall composed of standing monoliths and composite columns now collapsed. A room similarly partitioned with monolithic columns was constructed in a building south of Room 340. The most compelling evidence for the identification of this room as a shrine is provided by the cultic assemblage found 30m away. The lack of direct association between the distant assemblage and Room 340 undermines the cultic identification.

---

10. Loud, *Megiddo II*, fig. 388.

11. Loud, *Megiddo II*, 45.

12. Yohanan Aharoni et al., *Investigations at Lachish: The Sanctuary and the Residency (Lachish V)* (Tel Aviv: Gateway Publications, 1975), 31; Yohanan Aharoni, "Arad: Its Inscriptions and Temple, " *TA* 11 (1968):19.

13. G. Schumacher, *Tell el-Mutesellim I* (Leipzig: Haupt, 1908), pl. XXXV-XXXVIII; David Ussishkin, "Schumacher's Shrine in Building 338 at Megiddo," *IEJ* 39.3-4 (1989):154-67.

The Megiddo examples illustrate two problematic assumptions. First, a biblically inspired assumption of Israelite control and cultural homogeneity permeates the interpretation of archaeological remains. From the tenth century on, the territory from Hazor to Beer Sheba and from the eastern Shephelah to the Jordan Valley is considered under Israelite and Judahite control, and the population is presumed to be Israelite and Yahwistic. Second, given the limitations of our knowledge of Iron I and II peoples and their material culture, each site is treated as culturally and functionally homogeneous. For example, all Megiddo, Ta'anach, and Arad buildings and their contents are regarded as royally sanctioned.[14] On the household level, even though the population may not have been ethnically and religiously homogeneous, all material culture is assumed to be Israelite and Yahwistic. Efforts are needed to distinguish intra- and intersite variation indicative of cultural or religious heterogeneity.

Tell Ta'anach

The "Cultic Structure" consisted of the preserved northwest corner of a building likely destroyed by Pharaoh Sheshonq late in the tenth century. Two partial corner rooms were confirmed as cultic when elaborate cult stands were found discarded in a nearby cistern and in an unspecified location eight meters away, perhaps in a silo. The remaining portion of the smaller of the two rooms, the corner Room 2, yielded two iron knives and sherds of predominantly large jars and jugs. Most of the objects came from Room 1: 80 restorable ceramic vessels (jars—some still with grain, jugs, juglets, pyxides, bowls, cooking pots, lamps, a strainer, and one stand), three lots totaling 140 pig/sheep astragali, more than 58 loom weights, nine iron knife blades and an iron javelin head, a sickle blade, two rubbing stones, multiple querns, eight stone pestles, spindle whorls, weights, beads, an arrowhead, a macehead, a toggle pin, a figurine mold, and three small stelae described as tapering arched slabs measuring .18 x .26m.[15]

From the description and the photo, it is apparent that the three "stelae" identified by P. Lapp were typical grinding stones. Both the Megiddo and Taanach collections appear to be domestic assemblages with tools and vessels for food preparation, storing, and serving; blades, metal points, and a macehead for defense, hunting, and household chores; tools for weaving and perhaps butchering; clothing accessories; and cult objects. Ta'anach "Cultic Structure" Room 2 likely served as a storeroom

---

14. Mettinger, *No Graven Image?*, 158-63, 164-66.
15. Paul Lapp, "The 1963 Excavations at Ta'annek," *BASOR* 173 (1964): 26-28.

for household possessions. Based on the cultic stands and chalices in nearby Cistern 69, W. Rast identified the "Cultic Structure" assemblage as the holdings of a specific priestly family, with no mention of *massebot*.[16]

Lapp also identified an arched slab, 1.5 x .7m wide, found in a nearby stone-built courtyard basin as a *massebah*. Lacking a stratigraphic relationship to Rooms 1 and 2, the basin was considered contemporary on the basis of comparable elevations.[17] Lapp proposed a cultic function for the basin and stone comparable to the nearby Tell el-Farʿah gateway basin with an associated stelae. He concluded that the Ta'anach basin underwent three phases of use. "Only in the third phase does it seem fairly clear that the basin (now nonfunctional) involved cult—perhaps as a repository for cultic stones desecrated by Shishak's destruction."[18]

E. Sellin (and later L. Stager and S. Wolff)[19] considered the basin near Rooms 1 and 2 part of an olive press. Similar basins discovered elsewhere on the site, some filled with charred olive pits, were identified as olive presses by both Sellin and Lapp.[20] The basin near the "Cultic Structure" was most likely part of an olive press, and the alleged *massebah* a crushing stone or a constructional stone from the basin wall or floor.

Lahav

A late eighth century "shrine" was situated in the rear broadroom of a four-room house incorporated into the city's casemate wall (Stratum VIB, Field IV). Cultic artifacts included a Judean pillar figurine head, a fenestrated incense stand, and two rectangular carved limestone blocks with beveled edges and smooth faces—either *massebot* or stands (roughly .15m wide x .25m high). According to the excavators, the shrine continued in use until the destruction of the city in 701 B.C.E., through the period of Hezekiah's religious reforms.[21]

---

16. Walter Rast, "Priestly Families and the Cultic Structure at Taanach," in *Scripture and Other Artifacts: Essays on the Bible and Archaeology in Honor of Philip J. King* (ed. M. Coogan, J. C. Exum, and L. Stager; Louisville: Westminster John Knox, 1994), 355-65.

17. Lapp, "The 1963 Excavations at Ta'annek, 29-32.

18. Paul Lapp, "The 1966 Excavations at Ta'annek," *BASOR* 185 (1967): 30.

19. Lawrence Stager and Sam Wolff, "Production and Commerce in Temple Courtyards: An Olive Press in the Sacred Precinct at Tel Dan," *BASOR* 243 (1981): 99.

20. Garth Gilmour, "Early Israelite Religion During the Period of the Judges: New Evidence from Archaeology," *Kaplan Centre for Jewish Studies and Research Occasional Paper Series* 1 (Cape Town: University of Cape Town: 1997), 10.

21. Oded Borowski, "Hezekiah's Reform and the Revolt Against Assyria," *BA* 58.3 (1995): 151-52.

These stones are dubious examples of *massebot*. All other *massebot* were simple fieldstones or minimally shaped slabs. These highly worked blocks more likely functioned as stands.

Jerusalem

At the base of the eastern slope of the Ophel, K. Kenyon excavated Cave 2 and a "Ceremonial Structure" dated to the end of the ninth century B.C.E. (Phase 2C). A pair of square pillars, each 1.7m high, stood in the center of the "Ceremonial Structure" Room N. Kenyon's identification of the pillars as *massebot* was likely influenced by the nearby eighth century Cave 1 which housed a cultic inventory of more than 1300 objects.[22]

H. Franken and M. Steiner reinterpreted the preserved structural remains as a "guesthouse," with cooking and serving vessels stored in the former tomb partially quarried away to create Cave 2.[23] The pillars were deemed structural supports for a precarious slope, though they more likely functioned in a partition wall similar to other examples in the area.

Lachish

Cult Room 49 (Stratum V, 1000-925 B.C.E.) was a small room, 2.3 x 3m, built against a terrace wall. A plastered stone bench ran around the perimeter of the room, with a raised section in the western corner forming a platform. Scattered vessels cited, "only the more or less complete vessels," included seven chalices and bowls, five jugs, three lamps, two juglets, and one small cooking pot. Four incense burners (two with fenestrated stands), a limestone horned altar, and a small, well-dressed basalt slab broken at its lower part (preserved portion approximately .28 x .12m) lying on the doorsill comprised the cultic assemblage.[24]

J. Holladay recognized the threshold stone, considered by Y. Aharoni to be a *massebah* by virtue of proximity to the cultic assemblage in the room, as a fragment of a basalt saddle quern.[25]

---

22. Kathleen Kenyon, "Excavations in Jerusalem, 1963," *PEQ* 96 (1964): 9.

23. H. J. Franken and M. L. Steiner, *Excavations in Jerusalem 1961-67, Volume II: The Iron Age Extramural Quarter in the South-East Hill* (Oxford: Oxford University, 1990), 19-27.

24. Aharoni et al., *Investigations at Lachish*, 26, fig. 6, pls. 41-43.

25. John Holladay, "Religion in Israel and Judah under the Monarchy: An Explicitly Archaeological Approach," in *Ancient Israelite Religion: Essays in Honor of Frank Moore Cross*, ed. P. Miller, Jr., P. Hanson and S. McBride (Philadelphia: Fortress, 1987), 254.

Beth Shemesh

In 1912 D. Mackenzie excavated a group of five recumbent "betyls" (seventh century B.C.E.) in an open area 30m north of the southern city gate, proximate to a well and above the entrance to an earlier burial cave.[26] Among the five stones, three had rounded tops and two were slabs with square tops.[27] Mettinger cited the Levitical attribution of the city (Joshua 21:16) and the public location of the *massebot* to demonstrate their official sanction.[28] With the benefit of renewed excavation, S. Bunimovitz and Z. Lederman identified the slabs as house pillars.[29]

In sum, large stones identified as *massebot* by virtue of proximity to cultic assemblages are argued to be structural supports (Megiddo, Jerusalem, Beth Shemesh), and construction stones (Ta'anach). The smaller examples were grinding stones (Ta'anach, Lachish) and a stand (Lahav). Stones would not serve both a practical and a cultic function; ambiguity in divine signifiers was unlikely.

The Best Candidates for *Massebot* in the Archaeological Record

1. Examples of Massebot *in Public Space*

Tell el-Far^cah (N)

A basin (.48 x .6 x .3m) and a nearby pillar base, presumed to have supported the square section stone (1.8m x .40 x .40) found in Niveau 1, stood just inside the Niveau 3 western city gate (Period VIIb-VIIe, eleventh/tenth-seventh century B.C.E.). R. de Vaux interpreted the pillar and basin as a libation site for individuals leaving or entering the city.[30]

While the stone stood prominently, its cultic function remains speculative. Stager and Wolff reinterpret the basin and column as a vat and crusher for producing olive oil. Rather than situating the vat just inside the gate, obstructing traffic, they reassign the installation to a Level I courtyard.[31]

---

26. Duncan Mackenzie, "The Excavations at 'Ain Shems, June-July 1912," *PEFQS* (1912): 174; *Excavations at 'Ain Shems (Beth Shemesh) PEF* (1912-13), 16, pls. 1, 2.

27. Graesser, "Studies in Massebot," Appendix.

28. Mettinger, *No Graven Image?*, 153.

29. Shlomo Bunimovitz and Zvi Lederman, "Beth Shemesh, The New Excavations" *NEAEHL* I: 250.

30. Roland de Vaux, "La Troisième Campagne de Fouiles à Tell el-Far'aj, près Naplouse," *RB* 58 (1951): 428.

31. Stager and Wolff, "Production and Commerce," 100.

Lachish

The tenth to eighth century B.C.E. cultic constellation at Lachish consisted of the small Cult Room 49 (Str. V) and, according to the excavators, a *massebah* erected 12m away in the street (Strata V-III) with a possible Asherah in front of it (V only), and 3.5m further down the street, a small pit with broken *massebot* (Stratum IV). A second pit, without *massebot*, was dated to about 100 years later. Due to erosion in the area, the plan and function of adjoining structures are unclear.

A large limestone *massebah* stood in Loc. 81b, approximately 12 meters southeast of Cult Room 49 and lacking any stratigraphic connection to it. The large plano-convex (shaped like a "D") stone, 1.20 x .95 wide x .60m thick, stood on an artifically raised platform or terrace wall. The possible Asherah consisted of a rounded heap of olive tree(?) ash (.5m in diameter) in front of the stone. The tree burned in Stratum V but the *massebah* stood through Strata IV and III (from the second half of the tenth through the end of the eighth century B.C.E.).

Two pits not far from the *massebah* were considered favissae. Pit 136 (Stratum IV, locus 94a), three to four meters west of the *massebah*, in the same street, contained at least four broken stones identified as *massebot*. Each of the stones was .60-.70m high, and roughly dressed in square shape. A stone with seven shallow indentations called "cupmarks" had been discarded along with the "*massebot*." According to Aharoni, the stones were deliberately defaced and broken, and then carefully buried. This pit dates to after the cult room but during the time the *massebah* stood in the street.[32]

Tel Dan

At least four *massebot* shrines were identified in the Tel Dan Area A gate. According to the excavators, they were built by Ahab and destroyed by Tiglath-Pileser III (first half ninth—second half eighth century B.C.E.). All the shrines were positioned on the right-hand side as one enters the city gates. (1) A well-dressed monolith standing .60m high in front of the outer gate and (2) a large basalt monolith near the canopied dias were possible *massebot*. (3) A. Biran uncovered five undressed stones of heights and widths varying from .30-.50m set upright at the foot of the outer wall beside the outer gate. A low platform (.9 x 2.2m x .30m high) with protruding stones at each end extended in front of the five stones. Unspecified numbers of incense burners, plain bowls, plates, seven-wick oil lamps, a lamp on a stand, and animal bones predominantly of sheep and goat lay on the ground to the west.[33] (4) One hundred and twenty five

32. Aharoni et al., *Investigations at Lachish*, 28-32, plan of Str. V.

33. Avraham Biran, *Biblical Dan* (Jerusalem: Israel Exploration Society and Hebrew

feet further to the east at the foot of the city wall was a second, similar shrine with five basalt stones, rising .3-.5m above the street, set against the city wall. No accompanying material culture was cited.[34] A third shrine with five stones set on a stone construction was erected along the facing on the eastern side of the upper gate. All these shrines predate the destruction of the city by Tiglath-Pileser III in 733/32 B.C.E.

Also in Area A, following the destruction of the city, Biran identified an open-ended rectangular compartment (2.5 x 3.0m) with a paved surface as the partial remains of a seventh century B.C.E. "sacred enclosure." At the enclosed end of the compartment stood two side-by-side *massebot*, one large and one small (1. and .73m high). A third, smaller, thinner stone (.54m high) standing beside the other two was tentatively identified as a third *massebah*. The fourth stone in the line had a rectangular top with two hollows. A cultic function for the four stones was confirmed by a basalt bowl containing ashes resting on a carved limestone block in front of the *massebot*, and two small juglets and three broken oil lamps behind the *massebot*.[35]

The Dan *massebot* are exceptional in plan, location, and number. From the limited published information it is not certain that all these stones served cultic functions. A detailed publication of the material culture accompanying each *massebah* or installation, including forms, numbers and find spots, in conjunction with the comparative assemblage from the rest of the gate area would strengthen the cultic attribution. The Beth Saidah gateway shrine, with its carved *massebah*, supports the interpretation of the Dan stones, but the Beth Saidah shrine is considered Geshurite while the Dan shrines are presumed Israelite.[36]

2. *Examples of* Massebot *in Sacred Space*

Shechem

A single, large limestone *massebah* (1.65 x 1.45 x .42m)[37] stood before the entrance to Temple I. In later phases of the temple, two smaller *massebot*

Union College-Jewish Institute of Religion, 1994), 243-45; "Tell Dan—1952," *Excavations and Surveys in Israel* 14 (1995): 5.

34. Avraham Biran, "Tell Dan—1994," *Excavations and Surveys in Israel* 16 (1997): 14; "Sacred Spaces: Of Standing Stones, High Places and Cult Objects at Tel Dan," *BAR* 24.5 (1998): 42-45.

35. Biran, "Tell Dan—1994," 15; "Sacred Spaces," 42-43, 45.

36. Rami Arav, 1998 ASOR Annual Meeting Abstracts, A-24. M. Bernett and O. Keel, *Mond, Stier und Kult am Stadttor: Die Stele von Betsaida (et-Tell)*, Orbis Biblicus et Orientalis 161 (Göttingen: Vandenhoeck & Ruprecht, 1998).

37. Graesser provided these measurements that were not included in the excavation report. See Graesser, "Studies in Massebot," Appendix, 339.

flanked the entrance.[38] L. Stager restores the walls of Temple 2 to the ninth-eighth century "Granary" (Building 5900) and extends the duration of Temple I to ca. 1100 B.C.E., thereby attributing the *massebot* to the Iron I period.[39]

Bull Site

The Iron I "Bull Site" sits atop a ridge seven kilometers east of Dothan. A wall surrounded an elliptical area, 21 x 23m, in the southeast corner of which a rectangular, minimally dressed slab (1.3 x .97 x .55m) had been positioned on its long narrow side. The stone rested on a small pavement of rough, flat stones upon which were recovered "offerings" consisting of the lower parts of two bowls and a fragment of bronze sheet folded over a handle, perhaps part of an Egyptian-type mirror. Nearby lay a ceramic squared corner of an object identified as a cult vessel. A bronze bull found in the enclosure identified the site as cultic and the horizontal slab as a *massebah*.[40]

This example deviates from the conventional shape in that it is wider than it is high. The massive, rough, conspicuous stone is reminiscent of the Lachish Locus 81b stone.

Hazor

The mid-eleventh century *bamah* that was uncovered in Area B Stratum XI in the 1950s has been recently restored.[41] Excavations revealed internal rooms of a building: the southern end of a paved room (Locus 3283) and contiguous paved surfaces of adjoining rooms (Loci 3275, 3279, 3307). At the southern end of the preserved section of the room, a low, narrow (.2-.3m) ledge ran around a low platform or "*bamah*." A large, banana-shaped stone found recumbent would have been propped up on the *bamah*. Too little of the building and its contents were preserved to suggest an overall function.

Objects found in the vicinity were adduced in support of cultic activity. A one-handled, plain grey jug filled with bronzes including a Late Bronze Age seated male figurine was buried beneath the floor near the

38. G. E. Wright, *Shechem: The Biography of a Biblical City* (New York: McGraw Hill,1965), fig. 28.

39. Lawrence Stager, "The Fortress-Temple at Shechem and the House of El, Lord of the Covenant" in *Realia Dei: Essays in Archaeology and Biblical Interpretation in Honor of Edward F. Campbell, Jr. at His Retirement*, ed. P. Williams, Jr., and T. Hiebert (Atlanta: Scholars Press, 1999), 228-49.

40. Amihai Mazar, "'The Bull Site'—An Iron Age I Open Cult Place," *BASOR* 247 (1982): 33-36. See too M. D. Coogan, "Of Cults and Cultures: Reflections on the Interpretation of Archaeological Evidence," *PEQ* 119 (1987): 1-8.

41. Amnon Ben-Tor, "Tel Hazor, 1996," *IEJ* 46 (1996): 266-68.

platform. While the figurine supports cultic continuity, the aggregate bronzes require explanation. In addition to the figurine, the jug contained an axe, two swords, two javelin butts, a needle, a wire, two javelin heads, two possible fibula, a bracelet, a bent rod, and a lump.[42] The bronzes are arguably scrap metal to be smelted and cast anew. Within the room, basalt vessels, a chalice, various types of mortars and pestles, a bronze toggle-pin(?), one bronze arrowhead, and a bone handle lay on the floor. On the pavement outside the cult room to the south (Loc. 3275) were found a complete "incense burner" on a fenestrated stand and fragments of an additional stand, together with a faience bead and a bronze arrowhead. Two more stands lay on the pavement outside the cultroom to the northeast (Loc. 3307).[43]

The concentration of stands, the buried bronze hoard, the perimeter ledge and platform, and the peculiarly-shaped stone all deviate from the expected public, private, or governmental assemblage. This aggregate assemblage likely served a cultic function.

Arad

Arad was the site of a Judahite administrative fortress, with a temple in Strata XI-VII. The excavators date these strata from the late tenth through the seventh centuries B.C.E.,[44] rendering the altar obsolete due to Hezekiah's reforms (Str. VIII) and the temple destroyed during Josiah's reforms (Str. VII). Following Y. Yadin, A. Mazar and E. Netzer, D. Ussishkin challenged the excavators' stratigraphy and dating and Z. Herzog, of the original excavation team, responded.[45]

The sanctuary, constructed in the northwest corner of the fortress, consisted of a 10m square courtyard fronting a narrow broad room (9 x

---

42. Yigal Yadin et al., *Hazor III-IV* (Jerusalem: Magness,1961), pl. CCV.

43. Yadin, *Hazor III-IV*, pls. XXXVII-XXXVIII, CCIII-CCVI; Amnon Ben-Tor, ed., *Hazor III-IV: An Account of the Third and Fourth Seasons of Excavations, 1957-1958* (Jerusalem: Israel Exploration Society and Hebrew University of Jerusalem, 1989), 80-81, plan XVIII; Ben-Tor, personal communication, 1998.

44. Yohanan Aharoni, "Excavations at Tel Arad: Preliminary Report on the Second Season, 1963," *IEJ* 17 (1967): 233-49; Zeev Herzog et al., "The Israelite Fortress at Arad," *BASOR* 254 (1984).

45. D. Ussishkin dates the temple construction in the seventh century and its destruction in the early sixth century (Str VI). See "The Date of the Judean Shrine at Arad," *IEJ* 38 (1988): 151, 155. Z. Herzog, "The Stratigraphy of Israelite Arad: A Rejoinder," *BASOR* 267 (1987): 77-79. Based on published pottery and stratigraphy, all that can be argued with conviction is that the temple existed for an indeterminate period between the tenth or ninth century and the early sixth century, most likely through the second half of the eighth century. In all proposed reconstructions, a *massebah* stood in an official shrine niche down at least through the very end of the eighth century or as late as the early sixth century.

2.7m) with benches along the western and probably southern walls. An elevated niche (1.2m square) approached by three stairs was situated in the rear wall of the broadroom along the central axis. Lying in the northwest corner of this niche was a stone slab (.70m sq.) identified as a "*bamah*."[46]

Also in the niche lay a toppled .9m high limestone arched slab with a rounded back and side and a flat face with red pigment. Two other more roughly formed flint slabs, smaller than the limestone slab, were partially plastered over, perhaps into the walls of the niche. The sequence and possible combinations of stones are impossible to ascertain from the published reports, except that in the final phase the limestone *massebah* stood alone in the niche.

Two hornless incense altars with burnt organic remains on top, .50m and .30m high, were among the accompanying cultic paraphernalia. Though found in Stratum X (late eighth century B.C.E.) laid on their sides and plastered onto the second step, they presumably functioned in the Strata XI and X temples. This pair of altars, one large and the second one smaller, perhaps mirrored a large and small pair of *massebot* standing in the niche.

Conclusions

Standing stones were erected in the region from as early as the Neolithic period. Iron Age examples span the entire period, from the twelfth century B.C.E. (Bull Site, Hazor) through the late seventh/early sixth century B.C.E. (Arad).

Surveying the widely accepted examples of *massebot* demonstrates a lack of standardized shape or size. While the smallest examples were likely all grinding stones, large slabs stood as tall as 1.9m. Standing stones were taller than they were wide (with the exception of the Bull Site), and usually roundish to squarish in section, with a tapered, rounded or flat top. While some stones were chosen or shaped to have a flat face (Dan, Arad), others were left rough and globular (Bull Site, Lachish), and one example was irregularly shaped (Hazor). Limestone was most commonly employed, though flint and basalt were used at Arad and Tel Dan respectively. Most standing stones were isolated, though a pair or trio perhaps stood at Arad, and Dan preserved two examples of installations with five stones each.

46. Y. Aharoni, "Excavations at Tel Arad: Preliminary Report on the Second Season, 1963," 247-48.

Currently the best examples of standing stones are those situated in city gateways or in an architecturally defined shrine or temple. However, it remains to be ascertained whether these *massebot* served cultic functions. Stones erected in public spaces include the gateway stones at Tell el-Fa'rah (N) (following deVaux) and Dan. The tenth to seventh century B.C.E. Tell el-Fa'rah (N) pillar and basin just inside the city gate presented no explicit evidence of a cultic context. While some of the ninth-eighth century B.C.E. Dan gateway *massebot* are likely cultic, comparable to the explicitly cultic iconic example in the Beth Saidah gateway, additional information is necessary to determine each installation's function.

Massebot were associated with architecturally defined temples and high places including the thirteenth to twelfth century B.C.E. Shechem Migdal Temple, the tenth to eighth century B.C.E. Lachish shrine and street cult, the tenth to seventh century B.C.E. Arad shrine, and perhaps the second half of the eleventh century B.C.E. Hazor shrine room.[47]

Within the cultic realm, Graesser distinguished between a *massebah* (to jog one's memory), a sacred stone (or fetish, infused with power), and an image (which bears a resemblance to the deity, to actualize the presence of the deity in that place). He noted these three objects had distinctive but overlapping functions. For instance, a transfer of function would occur when a *massebah* was the focus of worship, a position often occupied by an image.[48] The Arad *massebah/ massebot* exemplify such a transfer of function. The architectural niche served to focus the worshippers' attention at the spot of the theophany, past and/or present. Erected in the niche, the stone functioned like an image, to house or embody the divine manifestation or actualize the presence of the deity. The Arad *massebah/ massebot* support Graesser's third explanation for the biblical prohibition of cultic *massebot*. Functions proper to images had been transferred to stones. In a review of Mettinger's work, V. Hurowitz[49] concurred that standing stones were declared an abomination precisely because the divine may dwell or "inhere" in a physical object such as a stone.

Based on correspondence found in the Arad fort which mentions Yahweh and an Israelite temple, the limestone *massebah/ massebot* in the Arad temple niche arguably represented Yahweh perhaps with one or two accompanying lesser deities. The aniconic principle was perhaps observed in representing Yahweh not with a personified image but by a

---

47. Uzi Avner was unable to date any of the Negev or Sinai *massebot* to the Iron Age. See U. Avner, "Ancient Cult Sites in the Negev and Sinai Deserts," *TA* 11 (1984): 115-31.

48. Graesser, "Studies in Massebot," 113.

49. Victor Hurowitz, "Picturing Imageless Deities: Iconography in the Ancient Near East" *BAR* 23.3 (1997): 46-51, 68-69.

standing stone, an emblem of divine permanence. Alternatively, the stone may have symbolized Yahweh's mountain residence, Mt. Zion. Even more speculative, if the red pigment adhering to the stone was a vestige of writing, Yahweh's presence could have been actualized through his words rather than his image.[50]

---

50. Karel van der Toorn suggests that the Deuteronomists promoted the "book" (better the "word") rather than the image as a symbol for Yahweh. See "The Iconic Book: Analogies between the Babylonian Cult of Images and the Veneration of the Torah," in *The Image and the Book: Iconic Cults, Aniconism, and the Rise of Book Religion in Israel and the Ancient Near East*, ed. K. van der Toorn (Leuven: Peeters, 1997), 229-48. If the Arad stone was inscribed, it would support van der Toorn's thesis.

5

Arad, Qiṭmīt—Judahite Aniconism vs. Edomite Iconic Cult?

Questioning the Evidence

CHRISTOPH UEHLINGER

Introduction

The absence of a cultic image has long been recognized as one of the most distinctive features of Jewish worship since antiquity. Writing *c.* 300 B.C.E., Hecataeus of Abdera provides the earliest extra-biblical comment on this conspicuous custom. According to his *Aigyptiaka*, Moses had led a colony of aliens from Egypt to Judaea, where he founded Jerusalem, established the temple, and instituted the forms of worship and ritual for the new colony:

> But he had no images whatsoever of gods (*agalma theōn*) made for them, being of the opinion that (the) God is not in human form; rather the Heaven that surrounds the earth is alone divine, and rules the universe. The sacrifices that he established differ from those of other nations, as does their way of living, for as a result of their own expulsion from Egypt he introduced an unsocial and intolerant mode of life.[1]

I am grateful to a number of colleagues for helping me to refine an argument that met with considerable skepticism at the Philadelphia colloquium. In spite of the qualified criticism expressed, e.g., by A. Ben-Tor and W. G. Dever, I thought it would be useful to publish a revised version of my paper mainly to stress how necessary it is for our disciplines to reflect on the often unidentified, bibliocentric assumptions that determine the interpretation of much archaeological material from Iron Age Palestine/Israel. I am grateful to Z. Zevit for sending me a then unpublished draft of his discussion of the Qiṭmīt sanctuary, to B. Sass for the suggestion that I should start my case by laying bare some of my own presuppositions, to J. Eggler for help with figs. 1 and 3, and to G. Beckman and T. Lewis for their editorial patience.

1. *Apud* Diodorus Siculus, *Bibliotheca Historica*, 40.3,4; M. Stern, *Greek and Latin Authors on Jews and Judaism. Vol. 1: From Herodotus to Plutarch* (Jerusalem: Israel Academy of Sciences

That influential priestly and scribal circles in Jerusalem considered cultic images as unfit for the proper worship of Yahweh at least since the Persian period and appealed to the Mosaic tradition to legitimate aniconism is confirmed by numerous biblical texts. In modern scholarship, however, the *origins* and *reasons* of this programmatic aniconism are disputed.[2]

While much scholarly progress has been achieved in the twentieth century to contextualize Israelite and Judahite culture and religion within its West Semitic environment,[3] the question of Israel's and/or Judah's distinctive aniconism seems to have escaped a thoroughly critical re-evaluation until recently,[4] to the effect that many scholars still take it for granted—*nota bene* against explicit biblical, inscriptional, and growing archaeological evidence—that Israelite and Judahite worship, and particularly the worship of Yahweh, always refrained from the use of cultic images.[5] Other scholars more cautiously limit themselves to acknowledging our present inability to identify positively and with reasonable certitude a pictorial representation of Yahweh.

---

and Humanities, 1976), 26, 28. See P. Schäfer, *Judeophobia: Attitudes toward the Jews in the Ancient World* (Cambridge, MA: Harvard University Press, 1997), 17, 35.

2. See C. Uehlinger, "Bilderkult," "Bilderverbot," in *Religion in Geschichte und Gegenwart: Handwörterbuch für Theologie und Religionswissenschaft*, 4th ed., vol. 1 (Tübingen: Mohr Siebeck, 1998), 1565-70, 1574-77. Tryggve N. D. Mettinger has suggested that the roots of "Israelite aniconism" should be sought in the common West Semitic custom of worshiping standing stones, which is known since Neolithic times. See his *No Graven Image? Israelite Aniconism in Its Ancient Near Eastern Context*, ConBOT 42 (Stockholm: Almqvist & Wiksell International, 1995). While his study has considerably advanced our understanding of massebot worship, it failed to explain the essential motives of a process that would have led from this time-honored *de facto* practice (not unrelated to iconic cults) to programmatic aniconism and even iconoclasm prohibiting idols and standing stones alike. See my review article "Israelite Aniconism in Context," *Biblica* 77 (1996): 540-49; and T. J. Lewis, "Divine Images and Aniconism in Ancient Israel," *JAOS* 118 (1998): 36-53. In response, Mettinger has considerably refined his original position. See now his "Israelite Aniconism: Developments and Origins," in *The Image and the Book: Iconic Cults, Aniconism, and the Rise of Book Religion in Israel and the Ancient Near East*, ed. K. van der Toorn, CBET 21 (Leuven: Peeters 1997), 173-204 where he considers the rise of programmatic aniconism to be a rather late development related to the destruction of the Jerusalem temple, the experience of exile, and the deuteronomistic so-called name theology. If he is right, then we should be cautious about reading too much programmatic aniconism into the cults of Iron Age Judah.

3. See the survey by W. G. Dever, "'Will the Real Israel Please Stand Up?' Part II: Archaeology and the Religions of Ancient Israel," *BASOR* 298 (1995): 37-58; and now Z. Zevit, *The Religions of Ancient Israel* (London and New York: Continuum, 2001).

4. But see now Lewis's article and the collection of studies edited by van der Toorn in *The Image and the Book* (n. 2 above).

5. Mettinger (*No Graven Image?*) distinguishes between the situation in northern Israel, where a Yahwistic cult focussing on bull iconography seems to be attested both by archaeological evidence and biblical texts, and Judahite Yahwism, for which he claims two forms of aniconic cult, namely, one centering on the empty cherubim throne (in Solomon's temple) and another focusing on standing stones (as in the Arad shrine).

I have presented elsewhere a preliminary inventory of material evidence, inscriptional sources, and historical arguments that undermine the somewhat uncritical assumption that Israelite and Judahite religion always adhered to an aniconic cult which would have distinguished Yahwistic worship from the religious practices of neighboring people.[6] In this paper, I shall provide a related case study on the scholarly interpretation of two late Iron age sanctuaries from two neighboring and roughly contemporary sites, namely the fortress shrine from Tel ʿArad and the sanctuary situated *c.* 10 km south/south-west on the hilltop of Ḥorvat Qiṭmīt (see map on fig. 1). The former shrine is generally used as a primary witness to Judahite aniconism, while the latter (a one-period site where hundreds of fragments of cultic statuary, figurines, and stands dated to the late seventh or early sixth century B.C.E. have been recovered since 1984) is understood by most commentators as a typical example of Edomite iconic cult. The two sites are situated in the north-eastern Negev; they lie within only two hours walking distance and can quite easily be seen from each other. Being so close in space and time, but apparently so different in character, they present a real challenge for religio-historical research.

In a number of recent studies, the two sets of evidence have been treated in a thoroughly contrastive way, to the extent that what objects are found at one site are explicitly claimed to be absent at the other, and vice versa. As a consequence, Judahite and Edomite religion are increasingly construed as two mutually exclusive symbol systems. The evidence of purportedly Edomite Qiṭmīt is considered largely irrelevant for the history of Judahite religion, unless taken as a *via negationis* illustration of what late monarchic Judahite cult and religion were *not*. In this paper, I shall question this dichotomic way of handling the evidence. I shall try to find a way out of a framework that operates with a narrow concept of 'nationally' defined religious symbol systems towards a *regional* and *social* approach that could account for the simultaneous presence and functioning of both sets of evidence within a cultural continuum and precise socio-political contexts.

Premises

Before entering the debate, I should clarify some of my theoretical premises that stand at the background of the following discussion. They concern germane issues which cannot be elaborated within the limits of this paper, although each would need thorough reflection.

6. C. Uehlinger, "Anthropomorphic Cult Statuary in Iron Age Palestine and the Search for Yahweh's Cult Images," in *The Image and the Book*, 97-156.

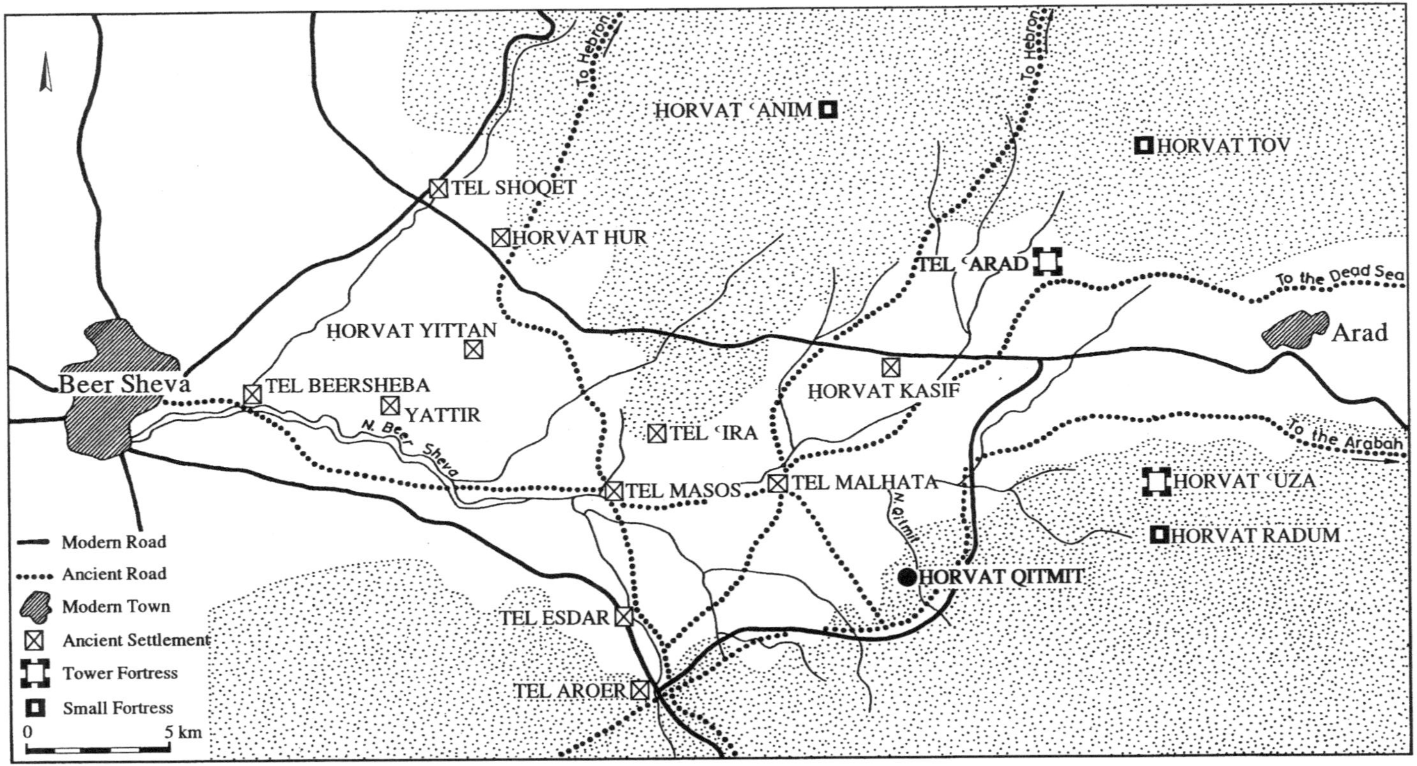

FIGURE 1: Map of the Beersheba valley showing excavated Iron age II sites (adapted from Beit-Arieh, *Ḥorvat Qitmit* [n. 11], 5 fig. 1.5 and *id.*, *Tel ʿIra* [n. 36], 4 fig. 1.2). Courtesy Institute of Archaeology, Tel Aviv University.

The Biblical 'Image Ban'

The so-called 'image ban' texts[7] are often taken to reflect a *general* and *factual* aniconism of Judahite religion. In my opinion, these texts should not be read as mirrors of factual reality. Mettinger has stressed the helpful distinction between *de facto* aniconism, which is characterized by the mere absence of figurative images and may tolerate iconolatrous cults and even co-exist with them within one and the same sacred area; and *programmatic* aniconism, which repudiates and excludes the use of iconic objects in worship and may develop into outright iconoclasm. The biblical 'image ban' texts belong to the second category. They clearly represent programmatic summons excluding iconolatrous worship, whether it be addressed to YHWH or to other gods. According to C. Houtman, followed by Mettinger,[8] the prohibition of cultic images in the decalogue (Exod. 20:4, Deut. 5:8) presupposes the aniconic nature of the cult of YHWH since the prohibition is primarily directed against other deities. However, it seems even more obvious that the prohibition presupposes the knowledge and practice of iconolatry in at least some circles of Judahite society. Why should iconolatrous practices be so emphatically rejected if they were not considered a real danger (or a viable alternative depending on one's viewpoint) to aniconism by at least some members of Judahite society? Moreover, the terminological variations in the 'image ban' texts would appear to be unnecessarily sophisticated did they not reflect real knowledge about real statuary, be it the focus of cult or votive in nature.

The 'image ban' is expressed by a whole set of distinct texts spread over all the major law codes of the Torah, almost each having its own particular wording. I agree with Mettinger and many others that none of these texts in its present form goes back to pre-exilic or even exilic times. Consequently, although the roots of the biblical 'image ban' may be earlier, *biblical* aniconism should be addressed primarily as a phenomenon of the cultic history of 'post-exilic' Yehud. The sheer number of texts and different wordings leads one to assume that the legitimacy of cultic images must have remained a subject of intense debate and reflection in Jerusalem throughout the Persian period. Of course, the possibility remains, and this is Mettinger's thesis, that Judahite Yahwism during the monarchic period was an example of *de facto* aniconism. It is possible that cults focusing on *massebot* were a prominent feature of Judahite religion during the Iron age, although the material evidence for such a statement

---

7. Esp. Exod. 20:3-4; 20:22-23 (. . . 23:13); 23:23-24; 34:17; Lev. 19:4; 26:1; Num. 33:52-53; Deut. 4:15-31; 5:8; 27:15.

8. C. Houtman, *Exodus vertaald en verklaard*, vol. 3 (Kampen: Kok 1996), 30-34; Mettinger, *The Image and the Book*, 176-77.

remains relatively thin.[9] I am also ready to acknowledge the present lack of indisputable, positive evidence for a Judahite cult image of Yahweh.[10] However, this lack of evidence should be put into perspective: after all, it might be due to our general ignorance of Iron age cult sites from Judah (as a matter of fact, Judahite cult sites of the Iron age can still be counted on one hand).

The 'National Religions' Framework

As mentioned above, recent religio-historical research has stressed basic analogies between South-Levantine religions to the effect that Israelite and Judahite religion and its Transjordanian counterparts, i.e. Ammonite, Moabite, and Edomite religion, have been considered as parallel sub-sets within a fundamentally homogeneous West Semitic religious environment. In such an approach, Israelite Yahweh will appear as basically another 'national deity' of the 'Hadad type,' occupying the same position and fulfilling more or less the same roles as Milkom in Ammon, Kemosh in Moab or Qaus in Edom. The model operates with two basic assumptions: on the one hand, it defines the individual profile of 'national' deities by calling him or her by different names (as if a name defined by itself individual personality); on the other, it postulates essential analogy between the religious needs and beliefs of Israelite, Ammonite, Judahite, Moabite, and Edomite worshippers. While such analogies are basically correct and may be helpful for the purpose of fundamental classification, one should not be misled by the model's inherent aesthetics. What holds the model together and at the same time provides the basic divide are the putative borderlines of 'national' states. This, however, is only one possible criterion among many others to define the sub-sets of West Semitic religions: the real picture was undoubtedly much more complex, as Dever's and Zevit's term "religions of Israel" (n. 3) aptly imply. The analysis of the archaeological, iconographic, and textual sources must be refined to include various ecological, geographical, social, and cultural parameters. To many people living in Iron age Palestine the 'national' appurtenance of the deity or deities they worshipped may have had little or no meaning at all.

The 'national religions' model considers the major gods as tutelary patrons of king and state. It is largely based on texts which belong to the

9. See E. Bloch-Smith's contribution to the present volume.

10. The terracotta group, which I discussed in relation to the syntagm "Yahweh and His Asherah" in the afore-mentioned article ("Anthropomorphic Cult Statuary in Iron Age Palestine" [n. 6], 149-52), will remain something of an enigma as long as no parallels are known. Still, it provides important evidence against the assumption that Judahite religion of the Iron Age was generally aniconic.

sphere of the state, the army, and public administration. While it works well for such texts as the Mesha or the Tel Dan inscriptions (although we should still distinguish between territorial, 'national' and dynastic links of specific deities), it suffices to consider the texts from Deir ʿAllā to grasp at once the model's major shortcoming. The controversy whether these represent Aramaean, Israelite or Ammonite religion will probably never come to an end since the source material does not square with the grid of 'national' classification. Similarly, the appearance of two regional forms of Yahweh and his Asherah in closely related inscriptions from Kuntillet ʿAjrud points to the limits of the 'national religions' model. While "Yahweh of Samaria" should probably be identified with the tutelary god of the Israelite state, "Yahweh of Teman" almost certainly was not a state-related god. I would thus suggest that before drawing borderlines and attributing a given set of evidence to, e.g., Judahite or Edomite religion, we should ask ourselves whether the 'national religion' framework really fits the sources under scrutiny. Moreover, we should ask for the social and institutional level on which a set of evidence operated before drawing conclusions with regard to the worshippers' ethnic affiliation. In sum, when comparing Judahite and Edomite religion on the basis of the two cultic structures of Arad and Qiṭmīt, we should take care not to mix up figs with fir-cones.

My working hypothesis follows a 'center and periphery' model and runs as follows: 'National' religion probably had a relatively strong impact in the capitals of the Iron age so-called territorial states, and in the centers of national administration as well. The more one left the center, other factors would become important in the constitution of the religious symbol-system—unless one would get to an outpost of the Judahite state administration such as the fortress of Arad, where the geographically conditioned national fade-out would be counter-balanced by the strong institutional link to the center of the state. Where such a link did not exist, as in Qiṭmīt, one should not expect to find nationally defined 'Edomite religion' but rather ask how this particular set of evidence operated in its primary *regional* context.

Does Arad prove the essentially aniconic character of Judahite Yahwism, and is Qiṭmīt indeed an 'Edomite shrine' which testifies to a distinctively Edomite iconolatry? The present paper aims at a critical re-evaluation of the evidence from both sites. We shall outline the archaeological findings and their interpretation by the excavators and other scholars, discuss the pitfalls of excessive dichotomies based on 'national' or 'ethnic' attributions, and end with some positive suggestions how to integrate both sets of evidence, however contrasting they might appear, within a functional, socio-historical, and regional approach to the religious history of Iron age Palestine.

Two Sets of Evidence in Recent Scholarly Interpretation

The limits of space and time do not allow us to dwell at length on details of the archaeological record. One important difference must however be briefly mentioned before we proceed with our discussion. Only Qiṭmīt is documented in a reasonably detailed excavation report by Y. Beit-Arieh,[11] which contains a meticulous study of the statuary by the late P. Beck.[12] Both authors deserve our greatest appreciation for having produced such a fine volume within ten years. That their presentation of the evidence allows a critical revision of their conclusions is in itself a mark of scholarly quality. In contrast, the late Y. Aharoni, director of the Arad fortress excavations, could not complete a final report. It is thus much more difficult to review the Arad material for which we must still heavily rely on insufficiently documented summary statements. Fortunately, Z. Herzog has recently published a new synthesis[13] which opens some new perspectives, but which still cannot compensate for a fully documented final report.

As different as the two sites might be, they have at least one thing in common: their discovery created a sensation and stirred up public awareness far beyond the usual level of interest. Right since its discovery, the Arad sanctuary was hailed as the first Israelite temple known through archaeological excavations, and it has remained the primary reference for dozens of textbooks and studies concerned with Israelite (and Judahite) religion. Similarly, the Qiṭmīt sanctuary has been praised as "the first Edomite shrine discovered so far, both in Eretz-Israel and in Edom"[14] and

---

11. *Ḥorvat Qitmit: An Edomite Shrine in the Biblical Negev*, ed. Y. Beit-Arieh, TAMS 11 (Tel Aviv: Institute of Archaeology, 1995).

12. "Catalogue of cult objects and study of the iconography," ibid., 27-208; see further eadem, "Ḥorvat Qitmit revisited via ʿEn Ḥazeva," *TA* 23 (1996): 102-14. An abbreviated version of this masterful study has been published posthumously; see P. Beck, "The Cult Objects from Horvat Qitmit," in *Imagery and Representation. Studies in the Art and Iconography of Ancient Palestine: Collected Articles* (Tel Aviv, Journal of the Institute of Archaeology of Tel Aviv University, Occasional Publications 3; Tel Aviv: Institute of Archaeology, 2002, 171-202).

13. "The Arad Fortresses," in *Arad*, ed. R. Amiran et al. (Tel Aviv: Hakkibbutz Hameuchad Publishing House; Israel Exploration Society; Israel Antiquities Authority, 1997), 117-289 (Hebrew), 294-96 (English summary). See also idem, "Arad: Iron Age Period," in *The Oxford Encyclopedia of Archaeology in the Near East*, vol. 1, ed. E. M. Meyers (New York: Oxford University Press, 1997), 174-76, and now idem, "The Date of the Temple at Arad: Reassessment of the Stratigraphy and the Implications for the History of Religion in Judah," in A. Mazar, ed., *Studies in the Archaeology of the Iron Age in Israel and Jordan* (JSOTSup 331; Sheffield: Sheffield Academic Press, 2001, 156-78); idem, "The Fortress Mound at Tel Arad: An Interim Report," *TA* 29 (2002): 3-109.

14. M. Dayagi-Mendels, in I. Beit-Arieh and P. Beck, *Edomite Shrine: Discoveries from Qitmit in the Negev*, Catalogue no. 277 (Jerusalem: Israel Museum, 1987), 8; cf. ibid., 20; I. Beit-Arieh, "New Light on the Edomites," *BAR* 14, no. 2 (1988): 28-41, esp. 32.

for some has quickly become the standard reference for visualizing the nature of Edomite cult. For both sites, scholarly rhetoric has generally stressed *uniqueness* as much as *typicality* for their respective 'national' or 'ethnical' religious symbol system, two notions which to a more distant onlooker would clearly appear to be contradictory.

Arad: Problems of Stratigraphy and Chronology

The excavations of the Iron Age fortress of Tel ʿArad were directed by Y. Aharoni from 1962-1965 and again in 1967. The sanctuary situated in the northwestern corner of the fortress (fig. 2) was discovered during the second season in 1963. The main features of this structure are so well-known that they may be recalled here in a cursory manner (although the details change with almost every published plan of any stratum; fig. 3): an east-west orientation, an entrance from the east into a large courtyard flanked by annex rooms, a large sacrificial altar, a broadroom main hall with benches probably used for votive deposits, and three steps leading

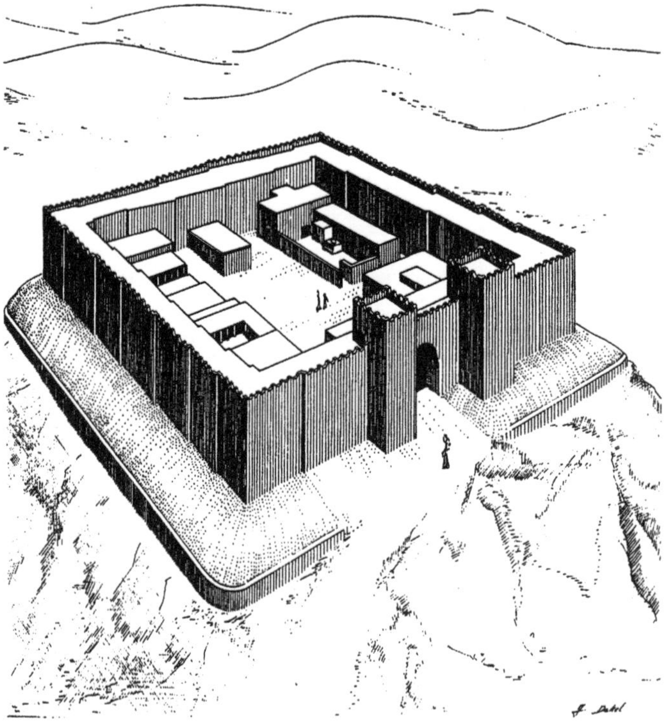

FIGURE 2: Isometric reconstruction of Arad "Str. X" fortress and shrine (Herzog, "The Arad Fortresses" [n. 13], 167 fig. 29). Courtesy Ze'ev Herzog, Institute of Archaeology, Tel Aviv University.

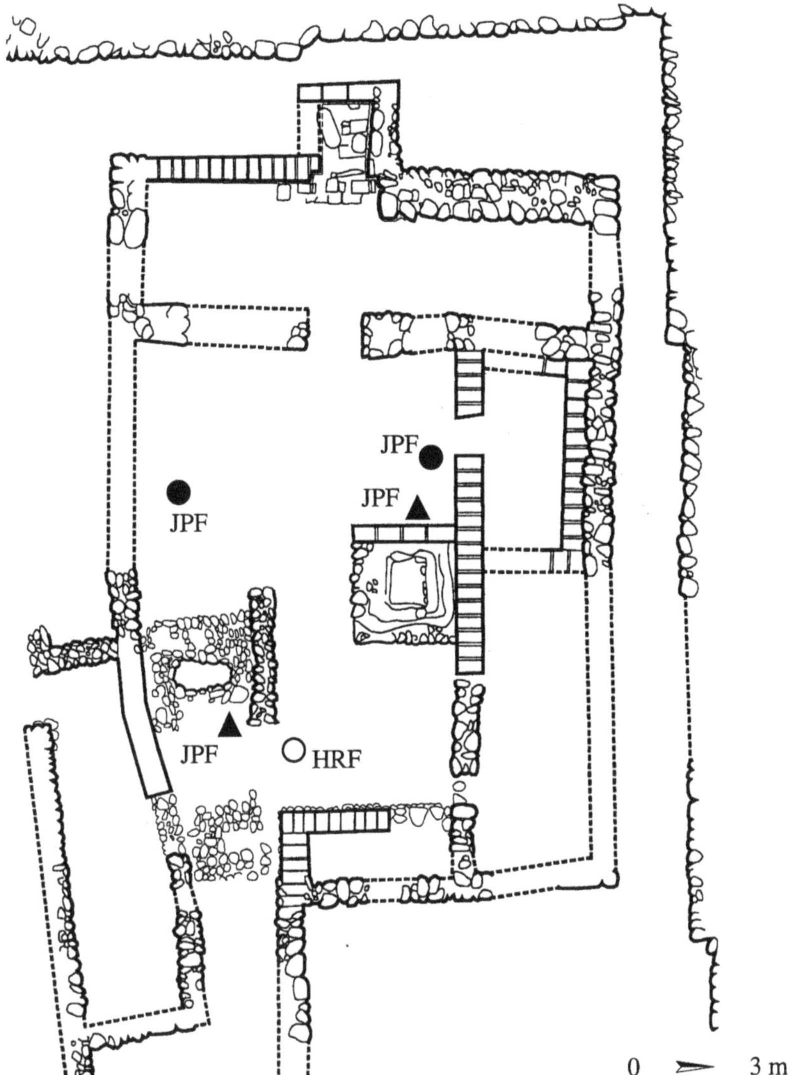

FIGURE 3: The Arad shrine ("Str. IX" plan according to Herzog, "The Arad Fortresses" [n. 13], 201 fig. 56; approximate findspots of Judean pillar figure and horse-and-rider figurine fragments supplemented from Kletter, *The Judean Pillar-Figurines* [n. 53], 108 fig. 35). Courtesy Ze'ev Herzog, Institute of Archaeology, Tel Aviv University.

up to a recessed cella. Two incense altars were found lying on their sides and covered by a thick layer of soil, an arrangement which apparently reflects intentional dismantling. A tall limestone *massebah* painted red represented the divine during the sanctuary's latest use. One or two flint slabs mentioned in passing in preliminary reports were found concealed behind a plaster coating; they may also have stood in the cella in an earlier phase.

According to Aharoni, the sanctuary was in use from the tenth down to the seventh century B.C.E., i.e. from the establishment of the kingdom of Judah until the reign of king Josiah. For the purpose of this discussion, it must be stressed how much Aharoni's interpretation of the archaeological evidence and the site's history and chronology relied on biblical data. From a distance of more than 30 years, Aharoni's attempt to reconcile the sanctuary's plan and metrical standard with the biblical data concerning the Jerusalem temple and the tabernacle despite manifest differences looks astonishing. As its putative biblical prototype in Jerusalem, the Arad sanctuary was thought to have existed for centuries. Aharoni's Qenite cult place of the eleventh century ("Str. XII") owed as much to the Bible and biblical scholarship as the sanctuary's foundation by Solomon in the tenth century ("Str. XI"). All major alterations were related to prominent phases of Judahite cult history according to the biblical text: the first rearrangement of the main hall and adjacent rooms to the period following the division of the Israelite and Judahite monarchies, the abandonment of the sacrificial altar of "Str. X-VIII" to the so-called cultic reform of King Hezekiah, and the dismantling of the "Str. VII" temple, then overbuilt by the "Str. VI" casemate wall, to the cultic reform of Josiah. Not surprisingly, the latter two correlations have had a long career among biblical scholars and archaeologists alike.[15]

True, Aharoni's stratigraphical scheme and general outline of the site's history have been repeatedly challenged since the mid-1960s, with one series of scholars concentrating on issues of architecture and another on pottery typology and palaeography, but biblical scholars have not been very eager to receive these criticisms. Already in 1965, Y. Yadin questioned the dating of the "Str. VI" casemate wall to the late Iron age[16] and soon got support from C. Nylander who suggested a Hellenistic dating because of the manifest use of a 14-15-teeth claw chisel.[17] I. Dunayevsky had early observed the stratigraphical difficulties and considered the

15. See again A. F. Rainey, "Hezekiah's Reform and the Altars at Beersheba and Arad," in *Scripture and Other Artifacts: Essays on the Bible and Archaeology in Honor of Philip J. King*, ed. M. Coogan et al. (Louisville, KY: Westminster John Knox, 1994), 333-54. But note N. Na'aman, "The Debated Historicity of Hezekiah's Reform in the Light of Historical and Archaeological Research," *ZAW* 107 (1995): 179-95; idem, "The Abandonment of Cult Places in the Kingdoms of Israel and Judah as Acts of Cult Reform," *UF* 34 (2002): 585-602; C. Uehlinger, "Was There a Cult Reform under King Josiah? The Case for a Well-Grounded Minimum," in L. L. Grabbe, ed., *Good Kings and Bad Kings* (ESHM 5; Library of Hebrew Bible/Old Testament Studies, 393; London/New York: T&T Clark, 2005, 279-316).

16. "A Note on the Stratigraphy of Arad," *IEJ* 15 (1965): 180.

17. "A Note on the Stonecutting and Masonry of Tel Arad," *IEJ* 17 (1967): 56-59. See further E.-M. Laperrousaz, "Nouvelles remarques sur les pierres à bossages pré-hérodiennes de Palestine," *Syria* 56 (1979): 99-144.

"Str. VI casemate wall" a deep foundation for the Hellenistic casemate fortress of Str. IV, but his insights long remained unpublished before being related by Yadin.[18] A. Mazar and E. Netzer showed the casemate foundations to be a secondary development of the Hellenistic tower and pointed to similar masonry from a Hellenistic tower from Aroer.[19] Moreover, Mazar[20] and O. Zimhoni[21] independently demonstrated that the so-called "Str. X-VIII" represent a single ceramic horizon and concluded that the putative strata represented a series of floor raisings and interior alterations within one single eighth-century stratum. Similarly, the finds of "Str. VII-VI" belong to a single late-seventh to early-sixth-century horizon. This in turn put into perspective the suggestion of F. M. Cross[22] that two "Str. X" offering dishes with inscriptions (the letters *QŠ* scratched on the dishes before firing), which had been found near the altar, should on palaeographical grounds be dated to the later seventh rather than to the tenth or ninth century. Finally, D. Ussishkin[23] argued that the sanctuary could not have been built before but probably post-dates the water system running under the "Str. X" solid wall. In his opinion, the sanctuary was erected at a time when the water system had fallen into disuse, i.e. some time after the destruction of the eighth-century fortress of "Str. X-VIII."

Over the years and after a few attempts to save the heritage of Aharoni's basic intuitions, the members of the Arad excavation team in charge of the final publication have progressively integrated the main criticisms raised by the aforementioned scholars, without however accepting all their suggestions. The Josianic agenda for the sanctuary's final dismantling was abandoned already in 1984, but the foundation in "Str. XI" in continuity with an early Iron Age cult place (now termed "Amalekite") and the early dating of the casemate wall to "Str. VI" were then still maintained.[24] A series of rejoinders demonstrated internal disagreement[25] as much as resistance to criticism.[26] The situation has now changed consider-

---

18. Y. Yadin, "The Archaeological Sources for the Period of the Monarchy," in *The World History of the Jewish People. Vol. 5: The Age of the Monarchies—Culture and Society*, ed. A. Malamat (Jerusalem: Massada, 1979), 187-235, esp. 219-22 (Hebrew).

19. "On The Israelite Fortress at Arad," *BASOR* 263 (1986): 87-91.

20. Ibid., 89.

21. "The Iron Age Pottery of Tel ʿEton and Its Relation to the Lachish, Tell Beit Mirsim and Arad Assemblages," *TA* 12 (1985): 63-90; reprinted in eadem, *Studies in the Iron Age Pottery of Israel: Typological, Archaeological and Chronological Aspects*, Tel Aviv. Occasional Publications 2 (Tel Aviv: Institute of Archaeology, 1997), esp. 203-7.

22. "Two Offering Dishes with Phoenician Inscriptions from the Sanctuary of ʿARAD," *BASOR* 235 (1979): 75-78.

23. "The Date of the Israelite Shrine at Arad," *IEJ* 38 (1988): 142-57.

24. Z. Herzog et al., "The Israelite Fortress at Arad," *BASOR* 254 (1984): 1-34.

25. M. Aharoni and A. F. Rainey, "On 'The Israelite Fortress at Arad,'" *BASOR* 258 (1985): 73-74.

26. E.g., Z. Herzog, "The Stratigraphy of Israelite Arad: A Rejoinder," *BASOR* 267 (1987): 77-79, and now idem, "The Date" (n. 13), 156-78.

ably with the publication of Herzog's reinterpretation.[27] Herzog now relates the sanctuary exclusively to "Str. X," which he dates to the ninth century, and to "Str. IX" of the eighth century (it would thus have overlapped at least in part with the water system), attributing the predestruction dismantling of the entire shrine (not just the sacrificial altar) to the reform of Hezekiah.[28]

To sum up, the scholarly discussion of the Arad sanctuary has followed two different tracks: one, outlined essentially by Aharoni's intuitions, seduced his pupils and numerous biblical scholars fascinated by the apparently unique opportunity to glance into the history of pre-exilic Judahite worship; the other, more restricted to archaeologists, concentrated on issues of chronology. Both groups of scholars, it seems, never really questioned the idea that the Arad sanctuary provides typical and distinctive evidence for the 'aniconic' nature of the cult of Yahweh in pre-exilic Judah.

Ḥorvat Qiṭmīt: The Ethnicity Issue

Identified in 1979 during a survey operation, the hilltop sanctuary of Qiṭmīt was excavated in 1984-1986 under the direction of I. Beit-Arieh. Two main building complexes approximately 15-20 m apart could be distinguished (fig. 4): Building B is an almost square structure. A large standing stone identified as a *massebah* by the excavators stands prominently in the courtyard. Four inscribed vessels with theophoric names(?) including the divine name *QWS* were found in this building. Complex A consisted of a tripartite building (I) and two related stone enclosures (II and III). Hundreds of fragments of cultic statuary were recovered mainly from the two enclosures and their surroundings to the south of building A-I. Further to the north-west and south-west of building A-I, two oval enclosures contained far less finds, possibly some small *massebot* among them, and apparently served a different function, perhaps as animal pens. A shallow pit (loc. 80) located some 70-80 m south-east of complex A was tentatively identified as a potential *favissa*.

Again, many of these finds are well-known and need not be commented upon here in detail. Within the limits of this paper, I would like to concentrate on the *ethnic* labeling of Qiṭmīt as an "Edomite" shrine and its connection with particular notions of Edomite invasion and expansion into the Negev during the late Iron Age II C. The label "Edomite shrine" has been used by Beit-Arieh with continuous emphasis from an early stage of investigation through preliminary articles until

27. See above, n. 13.
28. On which see above, n. 15.

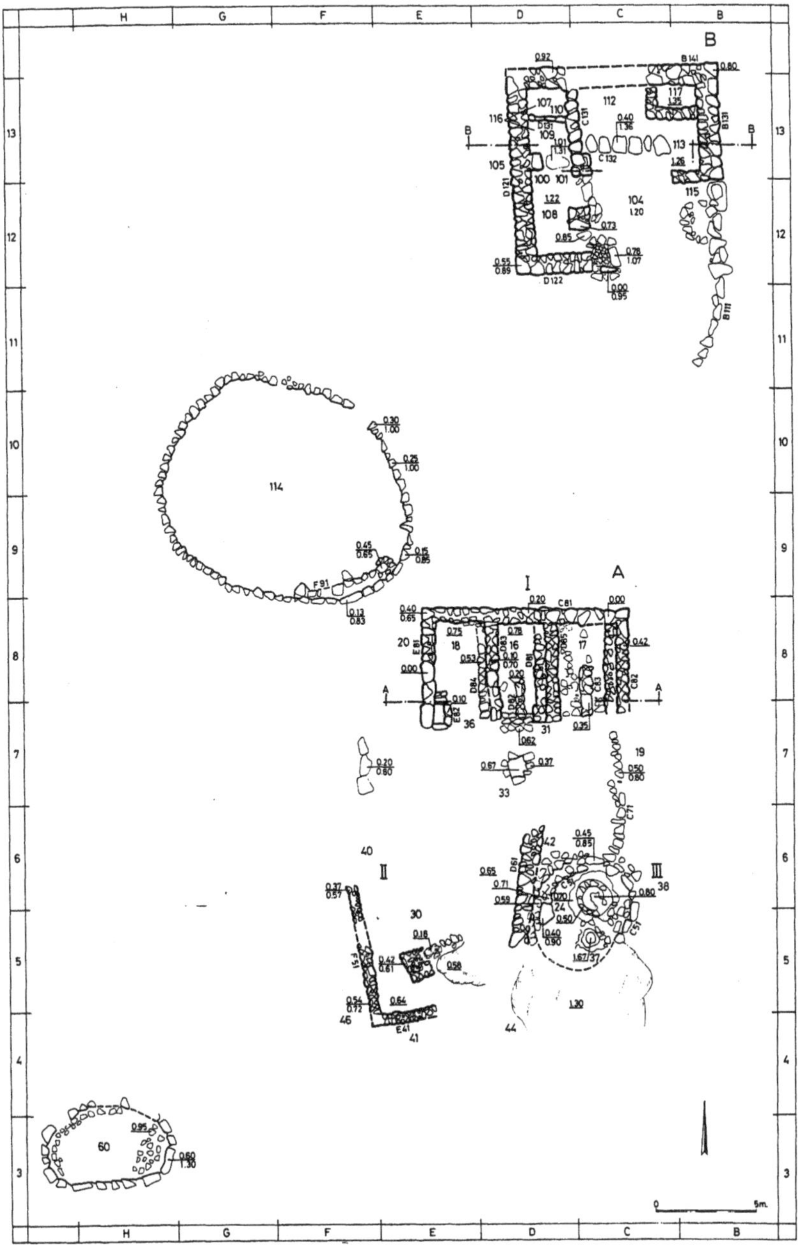

FIGURE 4: The hilltop sanctuary of Ḥorvat Qiṭmīt: general plan (Beit-Arieh, *Ḥorvat Qitmit* [n. 11], 6 fig. 1.6).

the final report published in 1995. Beit-Arieh based himself upon five arguments: a considerable proportion of so-called 'Edomite pottery'; the similarity of some small figurines to comparable objects from Edom; a general resemblance of the three-room building A-I to a building of the Hellenistic period at (then Idumean) Maresha; the orientation of worship (actually the openings of the tripartite building A-I) facing south, i.e. towards the land of Edom (which actually lies in south-eastern direction); the epigraphical finds displaying Edomite script and mentioning the Edomite god Qaus.[29]

The pertinence and validity of these criteria, any of which would deserve detailed discussion, was first questioned by I. Finkelstein.[30] He did not doubt the presence of Edomite features in the material remains of Qiṭmīt but vigorously denied the site's attribution to an Edomite polity. In his opinion, the Negev was firmly under Judahite control during the later seventh century. Qiṭmīt served extra-mural groups, such as pastoral nomads living in the area (which Finkelstein identifies as Arabs), caravaneers and other wayfarers travelling along the southern trade route between Philistia, Transjordan, and Arabia. According to Finkelstein, "the special cultural *mélange* of Ḥorvat Qiṭmīt represents the culture of the different people who were active on the southern routes" and "indicates that it was visited by caravaneers of various origins—Arabs, Phoenicians, Judahites, Edomites and others; at the same time it reflects the special cultural *koine* of the period."[31]

In a recently published overview on Edomite religion, J. A. Dearman raised a number of interesting theoretical questions on how to identify a religious term or practice as "Edomite," distinguishing between a national, cultural or territorial use of the term. In his opinion, "if the patrons of Qitmit were Edomite, the gentilic label should be understood primarily as a cultural designation. . . . Perhaps the materials represent forms of religious expression associated with several clans or population groups who traversed the area, a mixture of Edomite, Amalekite, Arab, Qedarite, and Kenite religious traditions. . . . Like Kuntillet ʿAjrud in the northern Sinai and its eclectic cult, Qitmit may have been a stopping-point that also served as a cultic way-station for several groups."[32]

---

29. See the publications mentioned in nn. 11 and 14 above, and I. Beit-Arieh, "The Edomite Shrine at Ḥorvat Qitmit in the Judean Negev. Preliminary Excavation Report," *TA* 18 (1991): 93-116.

30. "*Ḥorvat Qiṭmīt* and the Southern Trade in the Late Iron Age II," *ZDPV* 108 (1992): 156-70.

31. Ibidem, 162, 166.

32. "Edomite Religion. A Survey and an Examination of Some Recent Contributions," in *You Shall Not Abhor an Edomite for He Is Your Brother: Edom and Seir in History and Tradition*, ed. D. V. Edelman, Archaeology and Biblical Studies 3 (Atlanta, GA: Scholars Press, 1995), 119-36, citation on 122-23.

Although Finkelstein republished his opinions a few years later in a monograph specifically devoted to the archaeology and history of the Negev,[33] his interpretation could not undermine the *communis opinio*. Dearman, who came to rather similar conclusions, shows no awareness of Finkelstein's article. Both authors stressed the eclectic nature of the Qiṭmīt cult, related it to the site's location on a major southern trade route, and gave much weight to nomadic patrons and caravaneers due to the site's apparent isolation. In my opinion, one main difficulty with their alternative approach lies in their supplementing one problematic ethnical, political or cultural label ("Edomite") with others, some of whose identification in the archaeological record is for the time being even more elusive. As far as I know, no one has as yet succeeded in demonstrating an Arab or Qedarite affiliation of specific items of the Qiṭmīt repertoire, and while this does not exclude the possibility that Arab, Qedarite, and other Amalekite tribesmen participated in the Qiṭmīt cult, it seems methodologically unwise to exchange the little known for the as yet almost unknown. Furthermore, both Finkelstein and Dearman seem to have overdrawn the parallel with Kuntillet ʿAjrud, which is an isolated caravanserai in the middle of nowhere, while Qiṭmīt is not a way-station but a regional hilltop sanctuary situated within one or two hour's walking distance from several contemporary settlements and which can easily be seen from Arad, Tel ʿIra or Tel Malḥata.

Instrumental Neutron Activation Analysis undertaken on a representative sample of purportedly 'Edomite' vessels has shown that these were made of local clay.[34] During the 1992 excavations at Tel Malḥata, two figurines were found which originate from the very same potter's workshop as the triple-horned goddess, one of the best-known finds from Qiṭmīt. Beit-Arieh has convincingly argued that most of the pottery and statuary recovered at Qiṭmīt was produced in this nearby settlement.[35] We may conclude that the sanctuary was intimately related to the contemporary settlement of Malḥata, and probably also to other sites in the region such as Tel ʿIra, Tel Masos, Tel ʿAroer and Ḥorvat ʿUza (not to speak about pastoral nomads living in the area).[36] That all these sites are said to have yielded a considerable percentage of so-called 'Edomite' pottery (e.g.,

---

33. I. Finkelstein, *Living on the Fringe: The Archaeology and History of the Negev, Sinai and Neighbouring Regions in the Bronze and Iron Ages*, Monographs on Mediterranean Archaeology 6 (Sheffield: Sheffield Academic Press, 1995), esp. 139-53.

34. J. Gunneweg and H. Mommsen, "Instrumental Neutron Activation Analysis of Vessels and Cult Objects," in Beit-Arieh (n. 11), 280-86 with earlier references.

35. *Ḥorvat Qitmit* (n. 11), 315. See further idem, "Excavations at Tel Malḥata—Preliminary Report," *Qadmoniot* 31, no. 1 (no. 115, 1998): 30-39.

36. For a convenient list of roughly contemporary sites in the area, see now I. Beit-Arieh, *Tel ʿIra: A Stronghold in the Biblical Negev*, TAMS 15 (Tel Aviv: Institute of Archaeology, 1999), 5.

25% of the pottery retrieved during earlier excavations at Tel Malḥata[37]) brings us back to the question of ethnicity: Was Qiṭmīt an Edomite shrine, and Malḥata an Edomite settlement? Did the shrine and the settlements, with the other places mentioned around, belong in any way to an Edomite polity?

Before proceeding, and to complicate the matter, we should mention in passing the recent finds from ʿEn Ḥaṣeva, a site located in the Arava some 45 km south-east of Qiṭmīt and at equal distance west of the Edomite capital Buṣeira. Excavations carried out in 1988-1994 under the direction of R. Cohen have produced remains of a small shrine situated outside at some distance of the small fortress of Str. 4, which is dated by the excavators to the late seventh or early sixth century. A slightly sculpted stela, three anthropomorphic pottery stands, one stand with applied birds, a human couple(?) and quadrupeds, numerous non-figurative stands, and a seal bearing an Arabic(!) name inscribed in 'Edomite' script[38] were among the most conspicuous finds. Mainly on the basis of comparison with Qiṭmīt (and only on second thoughts with pottery from Tell el-Ḫuleifi and sites in southern Transjordan), the structure was soon qualified as representing another "Edomite shrine" while the fortress is considered to be Judahite.[39] Although this process of ethnic labeling tangibly proceeds along circular arguments (Edomites have become fashionable, as long as they stay out of the fortresses[40]) , the finds from ʿEn Ḥaṣeva have strengthened the general perception of Qiṭmīt as a definitely "Edomite" shrine. In response to Finkelstein (and others?), this qualification has been supplemented by repeated comments by both Beit-Arieh and Beck on the definitely "non-Judahite" character of the site, argued specifically by comparison with Arad. This brings us to the question how we should understand the *relationship* between Arad and Qiṭmīt.

So Close, So Different: A Dichotomic Relationship?

A careful reading of early reports shows that Beit-Arieh's emphasis on the distinctly Edomite character of Qiṭmīt ("an Edomite place of worship

37. According to M. Kochavi, "Malḥata, Tel," *NEAEHL* vol. 3 (Jerusalem: Israel Exploration Society, Carta Press, 1993), 934-36, citation on 936.

38. I have my doubts concerning the 'national' labeling of seal scripts; see C. Uehlinger, "Westsemitisch beschriftete Stempelsiegel: ein Corpus und neue Fragen," *Biblica* 79 (1998): 103-19.

39. See R. Cohen and Y. Yisrael, *On the Road to Edom: Discoveries from ʿEn Ḥaẓeva*, Catalogue no. 370 (Jerusalem: Israel Museum, 1995); eidem, "ʿEn Ḥaṣeva—1990-1994," *ESI* 15 (1996): 110-16; eidem, "Smashing the Idols—Piecing together an Edomite Shrine in Judah," *BAR* 22, no. 4 (1996): 40-51, 65 (note that this typical *BAR* title alone contains three questionable assumptions); and see Beck's article mentioned above, n. 12.

40. Note I. Beit-Arieh, "Edomites Advance into Judah—Israelite Defensive Fortresses Inadequate," *BAR* 22, no. 6 (1996): 28-36.

serving an Edomite population located in Judean territory"[41]) presupposes considerable informal discussion and debate at the time on the relationship of Judah and Edom in the Negev during the late Iron Age. As far as I know, however, Finkelstein was first to publish an explicit statement on the relationship of the Arad and Qiṭmīt cult sites in his 1992 article, where he favored a socio-historical instead of an ethnic or political explanation for the "sharp contrast between the finds in (*sic*) the two contemporary cult sites of the region":

> Arad was an "authorized" sanctuary of the Judahite administration in the south, whereas *Qiṭmīt* was a popular, isolated cult place, visited by local Arabs and by caravaneers of varied origins.[42]

Finkelstein acknowledged discussions with P. Beck and referred to her catalogue of cult objects which was at the time largely completed but still unpublished. The subsequent statements on the relationship of Arad and Qiṭmīt made by Beit-Arieh and Beck in the final report clearly reflect internal debate at Tel Aviv and respond essentially to Finkelstein's challenge. While Beit-Arieh stressed the different architectural layout of the two shrines, Beck noted the absence of figurines from the Arad sanctuary. Her meticulous commentary on the Qiṭmīt statuary acknowledged the somewhat 'multi-cultural' references of the Qiṭmīt cult objects and their iconography and emphasized connections with Phoenicia, Philistia, and Transjordan. Yet it also stressed the non-Judahite character of these finds. In Beck's opinion,

> The striking differences between the shrine at nearby Arad and that of Ḥorvat Qitmit undoubtedly testify to independent cult practices at each site: a Judahite shrine at Arad and an 'Edomite' at Ḥorvat Qitmit. It is very difficult to explain historically the co-existence in such proximity of these different cult centres unless they served *two different peoples*.[43]

Beck did not want to commit herself too much with regard to the chronological issue, although it seemed possible to her that the two sites were contemporary. While she insisted on an 'ethnic' explanation for the difference between Arad and Qiṭmīt, the inverted commas she used for the term "Edomite" betrays her own doubts on the precise identification of the Qiṭmīt people. Still, she stressed more than any previous author that

---

41. "New Data on the Relationship between Judah and Edom toward the End of the Iron Age," in *Recent Excavations in Israel: Studies in Iron Age Archaeology*, ed. S. Gitin and W. G. Dever, AASOR 49 (Winona Lake, IN: Eisenbrauns, 1989), 125-31, citation on 129.

42. *Ḥorvat Qitmit* (n. 30), 161 (emphasis added).

43. "Catalogue" (n. 12), 185.

Qiṭmīt was a non-Judahite site, which also implied that Judahites did not worship in this sanctuary. To her, Judahite worship was essentially aniconic, as demonstrated by the Arad evidence. Following an argument made fifteen years earlier by R. Dornemann (who had then commented on the apparent absence of Ammonite-type stone statuary from Judah), she was inclined to explain the Judahite peculiarity by the biblical image ban:

> The striking variance [of the Qiṭmīt statues] from the finds in the Judaean shrines of the period, e.g. Arad, where no statues have been found, perhaps reflects the prohibition of imagery (*sic*) in temples (*sic*) throughout the First Temple period. It appears that despite the claim of some scholars that the absence of Iron Age statuary should be attributed to archaeological chance, the cumulative evidence of a century of archaeological excavations bears eloquent testimony to an intentional abstention from making statues.[44]

One of the latest statements on the relationship of Arad and Qiṭmīt comes from A. Lemaire who published an informative article on Edomite history in 1997. Basing himself largely on the opinions of Beit-Arieh and Beck, this expert historian apparently has no doubts about the ethnic background of the Qiṭmīt worshippers, who were exclusively Edomites. Thinking along the lines of Beit-Arieh's historical reconstruction (increasing Edomite pressure on the Negev and southern Judah towards the end of the seventh century), he pushed the antagonism of Arad and Qiṭmīt even further by explicitly disconnecting the two sites chronologically. According to Lemaire, the Judahite fortress of Arad was destroyed in 597 B.C.E. probably by Edomite raiders, whereas the Qiṭmīt sanctuary functioned between 597 and 587 B.C.E., i.e. in the aftermath of the Edomite conquest:

> En effet, 1. archéologiquement, ce site n'a été occupé que durant une période assez brève, étant érigé vers la fin de l'époque royale judéenne, ou même quelques années après; 2. aussi bien les inscriptions incisées qu'un sceau et la poterie du site montrent qu'il s'agit d'un sanctuaire *typiquement édomite et non judéen*. S'il avait fonctionné en 597, il serait difficile de comprendre qu'on n'y trouve aucune influence matérielle judéenne; 3. le fait que les Édomites aient pu ériger un sanctuaire *à leur unique usage*, au centre du Négev judéen (entre Arad, Horvat ʿOuza, Tel Malhata, Tel ʿIra, Tel Masos et ʿAroër) avant 597 paraît peu vraisemblable.[45]

---

44. Ibid., 182. Against this statement which contains several overgeneralizations, see my call for caution in "Anthropomorphic Cult Statuary" (n. 6), 137-39.

45. "D'Édom à l'Idumée et à Rome," in *Des Sumériens aux Romains d'Orient: La perception géographique du monde*, ed. A. Serandour, Antiquités Sémitiques 2 (Paris: J. Maisonneuve, 1997), 81-103, citation on 91 (emphasis added).

While Qiṭmīt is indeed a one-period site, Lemaire does not take into account that it may have functioned for quite some time. The excavators distinguished two building phases with minor alterations in both complexes. The abundance of finds also seems to testify to a use of the shrine during at least one generation. Furthermore, to squarely state that no Judahite influence is detectable in the material culture is wrong once we consider the utilitarian pottery alongside the cultic vessels, as we shall see below. Finally, that the Qiṭmīt sanctuary should have been reserved by the Edomites for their exclusive use is not borne out by the archaeological evidence, which rather points to a certain 'multi-culturalism.'

According to an early-published statement of Beit-Arieh, "the existence of an Edomite shrine in the midst of an area of Judean settlements in the eastern Negev is best understood against the background of the *continuous conflict* between Judah and Edom, from the very first days of these neighboring kingdoms. This conflict is attested by the biblical account as well as by the archaeological evidence of *Edomite penetration of Judean territory*."[46] As a matter of fact, Beit-Arieh's reconstruction of the Judah–Edom antagonism is not borne out by archaeological evidence but entirely dependent upon biblical texts and related stereotypes perpetuated by later Jewish tradition.

To sum up, a number of recent authoritative statements by experts in the field of archaeology, iconography, and history converge in their putting Arad and Qiṭmīt on a stage where they have essentially antagonistic roles to play, being called to stand for two rival polities, two different societies, two different peoples with radically different cultural background and religious outlook. The distinction of iconic vs. aniconic cult has been recognized as an emblematic feature of this essential difference. The antagonism of Judahite vs. Edomite religion is drawn out so sharply that the two sets of evidence are considered to be mutually exclusive, to such an extent as to even exclude their contemporary co-existence in the same area. It is my contention that this scenario does not adequately reflect the archaeological evidence but is largely determined by biblical premises. Ironically, the scholars responsible for this scenario go even further than the biblical texts, since they project into the realm of religion and worship what the Bible describes as a political and legal conflict. Is it not puzzling that while the Bible contains plenty of polemical texts against Philistine and Phoenician, Ammonite and Moabite gods, goddesses and cults, it apparently does not consider Edomite religion as a particular target for polemics, and certainly not as a characteristic example of paganism and/or iconolatry?

---

46. Beit-Arieh and Beck, *Edomite Shrine* (n. 14), 21 (emphasis added).

Questioning the Evidence

It is time now to proceed towards an alternative interpretation or at least a critical re-examination of the archaeological evidence. I should point out that my alternative approach will only occasionally refer to source material that was recovered very recently and thus would have been unknown to Beit-Arieh, Beck, or Lemaire. Most of the material evidence to which I shall refer is actually Beit-Arieh's and Beck's; my interpretation is thus largely dependent upon their presentation of the finds, although it comes to different conclusions by re-arranging the material to some extent, by putting it into a broader regional and socio-cultural context, and not least by operating with a different conceptual framework. While 'national' or 'ethnic' categories will get their due, I shall rather stress aspects of craft tradition and diffusion, the multiplicity and variety of ancient approaches to worship and ritual, and the importance of social location and function for interpreting cult-related archaeological remains. Readers will have to make up their own mind whether the alternative I shall suggest sounds acceptable to them or not, but it should at least become plain that the objects do not speak for themselves: it is the way we look at them which shapes the basic outlines of the history we tell.

Arad

On the basis of presently available evidence, it is difficult to give preference to one of the two most recent suggestions concerning the dating of the Arad shrine. From the point of view of the material basis, Herzog's latest thesis has to be taken very seriously since he is best placed to control all of the evidence. Unfortunately, however, he fails to refute effectively the two major challenges concerning the typological homogenity of "Str. X-VIII" pottery and the palaeography of the two "Str. X" *QŠ* dishes (*QŠ* for *qodeš*? or *QK* for *qodeš kohanîm*?[47]). From the point of view of methodology, Ussishkin's suggestions present the advantage of an exclusively archaeological discussion which clearly identifies the boundary between arguments based on evidence and hypotheses based on plausibility. I am in full agreement with his urge to provisionally disconnect the discussion of Arad from biblical premises, whether they concern the Jerusalem temple or the tabernacle, the biblical cubit or the religious reforms of Hezekiah and Josiah. I find it more difficult (however tempting) to plainly accept his very late dating of the shrine. While a "post-X" date of the shrine seems more than probable (i.e. late eighth century as

---

47. On these, see most recently J. Renz and W. Röllig, *Handbuch der althebräischen Epigraphik*, vol. 1 (Darmstadt: Wissenschaftliche Buchgesellschaft, 1995), 72-74.

terminus ante quem non), the definite link of the shrine to the "Str. VII-VI" compound (and consequently, to the later seventh and early sixth century) alone cannot (in the absence of any useable section) be firmly demonstrated, although the offering dishes and an Assyrian-type lion-weight[48] seem to favor a seventh-century date (Manasseh or Josiah?).

Whether we follow Ussishkin's or Herzog's scheme,[49] the sanctuary's history has to be drastically reduced from several centuries (Aharoni) to little more than a century (Herzog) if not to one or two lifetimes only (Ussishkin). This chronological shrinkage should make us cautious when addressing the issue of typicality. Thirty-five years after its discovery, the Arad sanctuary still presents something of a unique situation. Although a considerable number of other Judahite fortresses have been uncovered since in different areas once controlled by the Judahite state, not least in the Negev area, none has produced a similar shrine. Conversely, although cultic places from Judah may still be counted on one hand after a century of excavations, not one of them readily compares to the Arad shrine. This situation should be borne in mind and make us hesitate before we give too much weight to Arad as a typical representative of Judahite Yahwism and its cultic traditions.

That the Arad shrine is *genuinely* Judahite is not in doubt, but it is so different from other cult places found in Judah that any statement about its typicality should take into account the particular architectural, and by implication socio-political context of the building. This was first of all a shrine that functioned within a state-run garrison fortress. It was thus almost certainly concerned with tax collection, both for the state and for the state cult. Inscriptions reveal that the fortress shrine must have been closely connected to the central administration in Jerusalem. The Arad evidence may thus inform us on cultic practices on the level of 'official,' state-run religion, but it has little or virtually nothing to say about Judahite popular beliefs and practices. It is only logical to assume that within a state-run fortress shrine prime importance would be given to the head of the dynastic or state cult, i.e. Yahweh, and possibly the latter's paredros (his Asherah). I confess much sympathy for the suggestion by U. Avner, A. Mazar, and others that the replacement of originally two *massebot* by a single one could reflect a cultic realignment from "Yahweh

48. On this, see Herzog et al., "Israelite Fortress" (n. 24), 16, 18 fig. 20 ("Str. IX"); idem, "The Arad Fortresses" (n. 13), 224 fig. 71:3. For interpretation, see most recently C. Zaccagnini, "The Assyrian Lion Weights from Nimrud and the 'mina of the land,'" in *Michael: Historical, Epigraphical and Biblical Studies* (FS M. Heltzer), ed. Y. Avishur and R. Deutsch (Tel Aviv–Jaffa: Archaeological Center, 1999), 259-65.

49. It is interesting to note that Beck seems to have adhered to Ussishkin's late dating since she apparently linked the sanctuary to Str. VI; see her "Catalogue" (n. 12), 185. On the other hand, Herzog's new phasing and dating is supported by L. Singer-Avitz, "Arad: The Iron Age Pottery Assemblages," *TA* 29 (2002): 110-214.

and his Asherah" to "Yahweh alone." Such a move seems to find an echo in the transition of earlier blessing formulae "by Yahweh and his Asherah" (Kuntillet ʿAjrud, Khirbet el-Kom) to "by Yahweh" alone (Lachish, Arad).[50]

Caution is in order with regard to the lack of cultic statuary in the Arad fortress shrine. All the preserved evidence points to the probable conclusion, reiterated by Herzog in his latest study, that the shrine was carefully dismantled some time before the destruction of the fortress. The last *massebah* and the two incense altars were carefully laid on their sides, while the whole sanctuary seems to have been levelled out and filled with earth. When compared, e.g., to Lachish cult place 49 which contained numerous cult-stands, Arad has produced very little finds of the kind. We may perhaps assume that the shrine was intentionally emptied and cleared before the final dismantling and concealing. If this impression is basically correct, the absence of cultic statuary, stands or figurines from the main hall and the cella would come as no surprise but produce a kind of optical illusion. Of course, there might be other reasons for the absence of Qiṭmīt type statuary or figurines from the shrine, e.g. the latter's particular character as a fortress shrine located on Judah's southern periphery. This functional characteristic would (a) not necessarily invite locals to join in the cultic arrangements and could (b) explain why *massebot* rather than cultic images stood in the Arad cella, namely as unsophisticated representatives of the official and ultimately sole authentic cult statue of Yahweh (and his Asherah) in Jerusalem.[51]

Beck mentioned in passing that figurines had been found within the Arad fortress.[52] Rarely if ever mentioned by the excavator and his followers, they have been brought to light again by R. Kletter in his study on Judean pillar figurines.[53] Four or five out of two dozens of figurines or fragments (one of a horse-and-rider, the others of pillar figurines) come from the area of the shrine (two were found together with a zoomorphic figurine in loc. 350, close to the sacrificial altar) and are mostly attributed to "Str. IX."[54] Although their precise stratigraphic position is difficult to

---

50. Cf. O. Keel, C. Uehlinger, *Gods, Goddesses and the Image of God* (Minneapolis: Fortress; Edinburgh: T&T Clark, 1998), § 209; Uehlinger, "Was There" (n. 15), 295-97.

51. On this, see Uehlinger, "Anthropomorphic Cult Statuary" (n. 6), 139-52. In functional terms, a stela or massebah is not very different from a statue as a marker of divine presence; whether a deity is present in the form of his or her cultic image or not says more about a shrine's relative status and administrative setting.

52. "Catalogue" (n. 12), 182, n. 50.

53. *The Judean Pillar-Figurines and the Archaeology of Asherah*, BAR International Series 636 (Oxford: Tempus Reparatum, 1996), 65, 96 fig. 16, 108 fig. 35, 147-48, 210-12. The presence of figurines at Arad was pointed out to me at the colloquium by E. Bloch-Smith.

54. The one exception is Kletter's no. 456, which was found out of context in a Hellenistic pit.

FIGURE 5: Limestone cylinder seal from Arad "Str. IX" (Aharoni, "An Iron Age Cylinder Seal" [n. 55], 53 fig. 1). Courtesy Institute of Archaeology, Tel Aviv University.

ascertain, they would seem to belong to Herzog's "Str. IX" shrine. While the meaning and function of pillar figurines is debated, their presence at sensible places at Arad indicates that not even the Judahites of Arad were strictly aniconic in practice. Consequently, the biblical image ban is a misleading tool for interpreting the Arad shrine. Incidentally, a locally made(?) limestone cylinder seal showing a bird (apparently an ostrich) facing a seated person and three astral symbols (crescent, lozenge and *sebetti*),[55] again a "Str. IX" find, may relate rather nicely—if only in very general terms—to the Qiṭmīt cult (fig. 5).

Ḥorvat Qiṭmīt

If we turn again to Qiṭmīt, better documentation allows for a much more refined discussion. For the sake of brevity, the following remarks will concentrate on the two main structures on the site (A and B), neglecting the hypothetical *favissa* (loc. 80) and the two oval enclosures (loc. 114 and 60) for which the available evidence cannot ascertain an independent cultic setting.

The two building complexes do not appear to be mutually dependent: building B opens towards A, but A shows no functional relationship to B. The very different architectural layout and the distribution of pottery, small finds, and faunal remains confirm the impression of functional dissimilarity.[56] Complex B produced a greater percentage of the so-called

55. M. Aharoni, "An Iron Age Cylinder Seal," *IEJ* 46 (1996): 52-54; see Herzog, "The Arad Fortresses" (n. 13), 223-24 with fig. 71:1-2.

56. B could actually have been built later than A, which is clearly the main focus of the

"Edomite" pottery, especially cooking-pots, one limestone incense burner and four sherds with inscriptions incised (three before, one after firing), containing the divine name *QWS*, but very few if any fragments of stands or figurines.[57] The inscriptions are said to be written in Edomite script (which I would prefer to label a "script of the extreme south of Palestine"[58]). There was evidence for cooking small cattle in room 116 (107 + 109). B may have been the living area of some cultic personnel in charge of the shrine's maintenance. Whether the large stone looking south, in front of which the excavators identified a small "offering surface," should be understood as a *massebah* is unclear. If it was a *massebah*, this would then be the only focus of cult in complex B, implying the worship of a single deity.[59] The latter would most probably have to be identified with Qaus, since the latter's name figures on the fragmentary inscriptions on pottery, which probably refered to the owner(s) of the vessels (one or several resident priests?), and on the bronze seal of one *ŠWBNQWS* from complex A. Qaus is of course mentioned in the blessing formula of the well-known ostracon from Ḥorvat ᶜUza.[60] He may have been the owner of an estate at (or the recipient of revenues from) Aroer.[61] We may consider him to be a very close 'relative' (to say the least) of "Yahweh of the South" (*YHWH TMN*). The close kinship of the two gods is supported by biblical evidence,[62] although it still seems "impossible to untangle the lines that intersect their identities."[63]

Complex A is a much more differentiated ritual compound including

---

sanctuary. However, since the two complexes are not architecturally related, this hypothesis could only be substantiated by pottery analysis. The latter does not seem to allow for a diachronically fine dating.

57. Figurine fragments are mentioned in passing by Beit-Arieh, *Ḥorvat Qitmit* (n. 11), 24, but I could not identify a single fragment in Beck's catalogue (n. 12) nor in the appendix compiled by L. Freud (ibid., 198-208).

58. See above, n. 38, and D. S. Vanderhooft, "The Edomite Dialect and Script: A Review of the Evidence," in *You Shall Not Abhor an Edomite* (n. 32), 137-57, esp. 138 ("extreme south cursive script"). But note that another vessel fragment inscribed before firing which was found in complex A shows a "Phoenician" or rather "Philistine"-type *'alef*: Beit-Arieh, *Ḥorvat Qitmit* (n. 12), 259.

59. Had we only complex B, we would conclude to some 'aniconic' cult, but this optical illusion is of course due only to a heuristic operation.

60. I. Beit-Arieh and B. Cresson, "An Edomite Ostracon from Ḥorvat ᶜUza," *TA* 12 (1985): 96-101; Vanderhooft, "The Edomite Dialect and Script" (n. 58), 142-43.

61. E. A. Knauf, "Qôs," in *Dictionary of Deities and Demons in the Bible*, ed. B. Becking, P. W. van der Horst, K. van der Toorn (Leiden: Brill, 1995), 674-77, esp. 675, following J. R. Bartlett, *Edom and the Edomites*, JSOTSup 77 (Sheffield: Sheffield Academic Press, 1989), 213 n. 4.

62. Note (a) the references to Yahweh's "coming out from Teman/Se'ir/Edom" (Hab. 3:3.7; Deut. 33:2-3; Judg. 5:4-5), i.e., Qaus's homeland; (b) the absence of religious polemic against Qaus; and (c) the strong notion of "brothership" with Edom.

63. See Dearman, "Edomite Religion" (n. 32), 123-27, citation on 127.

a tripartite main building, a large plastered courtyard delimited by a kind of temenos wall, a basin-like installation, and a large horizontally placed stone which the excavators interpreted as an altar. It is in Complex A exclusively that the stands and statuary were found, mainly in the enclosure area. In contrast to the apparently 'monolatric' setting of complex B, the evidence of complex A points to a 'polytheistic' and polymorphous cult. It is tempting to assume that the three parallel oblong rooms of building I had votives and offerings for three different deities, but the evidence is inconclusive. The three rooms may as well have belonged to three different groups of worshippers. That more than one deity was venerated besides the as yet anonymous three-horned goddess can be clearly demonstrated: The fragment of a statue which held the hilt of a sword (fig. 6)[64] is unlikely to have belonged to a worshipper according to a basic principle of ancient Near Eastern religious iconography and ritual etiquette.[65] Other figures representing deities—such as a deity standing on a lion[66]—were applied to stands. Shrine models, some of them displaying moulded plaque figurines of the 'nude pregnant woman' type, may have contained further cult images.[67] These would have been taken from the site when it was abandoned, unless they were made of wood and have thus disintegrated. Various animals depicted on cult stands (e.g., lions, bulls, ibexes, ostriches) may point to different deities. Beck has interpreted the apparent differences in status among these various deities by referring to the concept of resident and 'visiting gods.'[68] One could as well consider

---

64. Beck, "Catalogue" (n. 12), 62-63 no. 46 (and possibly ibid., nos. 45 and 47).

65. This statement requires some further comment since the issue has been raised that on imperial Hittite representations a king with a dagger or sword at his belt could appear in worship in front of a deity.

First, the Hittite examples are quite far removed in time and place from the statuary under consideration, and it would be difficult to demonstrate a connection between the two sets of evidence. On the contrary, scenes of worship on images from Palestine and from first millennium repertoires that had a demonstrable impact on Palestine (e.g., Egyptian, Phoenician, Aramaean, and Assyro-Babylonian iconography) never show, to the best of my knowledge, a worshipper holding a dagger or a sword. Second, there is of course a difference between a weapon carried at the waist and the actual gesture of holding a dagger or sword with one hand in an attitude which denotes potential readiness to use it. Still, one must admit that our knowledge of Arab (and Edomite) iconography of the late Iron Age is sparse. We cannot exclude the possibility that it followed a different iconographic convention (possibly reflecting a different custom in actual cultic behavior) with regard to the representation of worshippers in arms. The three statues from ʿEn Ḥaṣeva and those from Wadi ath-Thamad (see below) were apparently unarmed. As it stands, the available evidence favors the assumption that the fragment once belonged to the statue of a deity.

66. Beck, "Catalogue" (n. 12), no. 110.

67. Ibid., nos. 107-8, 163, 203-10, 763, 765-67, 771, 773.

68. Ibid., 187-88.

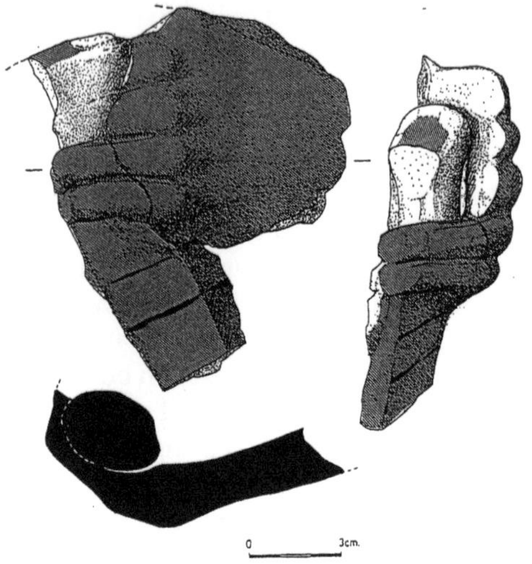

FIGURE 6: Fragment of a anthropomorphic statue grasping the hilt of a sword (Beck, "Catalogue" [n. 12], 63 fig. 3.35). Courtesy Institute of Archaeology, Tel Aviv University.

relating the differences in status and function to the notion of various tiers within the divine world.[69]

Most importantly, although the bulk of cultic objects was produced locally, the Qiṭmīt sanctuary seems to have hosted a rather inclusive community of gods and worshippers which was open for occasional travelling visitors who could deposit objects brought from some distance (the Southern coastal plain, Transjordan, or Edom proper). Beck has conclusively demonstrated that the Qiṭmīt iconography is related to a far greater variety of models than just to Edomite ones. These include implied references to Phoenicia (Sarepta), Philistia (Ashdod), Transjordan as far as Ammon, and Tell es-Saᶜidiyeh. Clearly the Edomite connection is not the only one we should account for at Qiṭmīt. Given the wider exchange patterns that became usual in the Levant with the advent of the so-called *pax Assyriaca*, this broad pattern of 'influences' (or, as I would prefer to say, references) in the Qiṭmīt repertory is not too difficult to understand, but it significantly weakens the site's exclusively "Edomite" ascription.

In fact, what has come to be considered as particularly "Edomite" in recent years may once more be part of an optical illusion. To take but one example, the "Edomite" ascription of the characteristic Qiṭmīt-type vessel statuary has been stressed and even more so since the publication of three more examples from ᶜEn Ḥaṣeva. But this type of vessel statuary has Late Bronze Age forerunners from central Palestine, and isolated contemporary parallels are known from Judahite Tel ᶜErani and Jerusalem.[70] Beck of course knew and acknowledged the latter, but she apparently

69. Cf. Mark Smith's contribution in the present volume.

70. Sh. Yeivin, *First Preliminary Report on the Excavations at Tel Gat (Tell Sheykh 'Ahmed*

considered them as insignificant stray finds. Recently, more such statuary has come to light at Tell Abu al-Ḫaraz in the northern Jordan valley[71] and at site #13 in the vicinity of Ḫirbet al-Mudaynah in Wadi ath-Thamad, northern Moab (seven or eight items apparently belonging to a cult site).[72] We may conclude with reasonable certitude that this type of statuary does not reflect an exclusively Edomite but a more widespread South Levantine tradition.

One of the most basic and intriguing methodological problems of the site's interpretation lies in the relative weight given to so-called "utilitarian vessels" vs. so-called "cultic objects." The excavation report dissociates the former, which are discussed by Beit-Arieh, from the latter which are analyzed by Beck. To some extent, the distinction is artificial. The cultic objects obviously had a utilitarian meaning, too, within the ritual, be it as votives or the focus of worship, offering, and prayer. Conversely, bowls, cups, kraters, and other utilitarian vessels obtain a cultic significance the very moment that they are used within a ritual. The dissociation of the two categories obliterates the fact that they were actually found *together* in a definitely cultic context (note particularly loc. 30). They should thus be interpreted together as one single set of evidence—not only when we study the ritual practices and their symbolism, but also when we address the cultural or 'ethnic' background of the worshippers.

According to Beit-Arieh's discussion of the "utilitarian pottery," the latter includes a very large percentage of vessels in shapes that are generally considered typically Judahite, notably more numerous than vessels which are held to be of a distinctly "Edomite" type. To illustrate this point only with the bowls (i.e. the class of vessels which is attested in greatest quantity): Bowls at Qiṭmīt include shapes with turned-over rim (a type considered characteristically "Judahite," found at all Judean sites dating from the eighth-sixth centuries); they constitute *c.* 50% of all the bowls found at Qiṭmīt.[73] Shapes with flaring walls or so-called shallow bowls

---

el-ʿAreyny), Seasons 1956-1958 (Jerusalem: Department of Antiquities, 1961), pl. III:3; A. D. Tushingham, *Excavations in Jerusalem 1961-1967*, vol. 1 (London—Toronto: Royal Ontario Museum, 1985), 18, 292, 356 fig. 4:10.

71. See P. M. Fischer, "Tall Abū al-Kharaz: The Swedish Jordan Expedition 1992. Third Season Preliminary Excavation Report," *ADAJ* 38 (1994): 127-45, esp. 130-33, 137 fig. 6:1.

72. I thank P. M. Michèle Daviau (Wilfred Laurier University) for sharing then unpublished information with me. See eadem, "Moab's Northern Border. Khirbat al-Mudayna on the Wadi ath-Thamad," *BA* 60 (1997): 222-28, esp. 225-26, and now eadem, "New Light on Iron Age Religious Iconography: The Evidence from Moab," in *SHAJ* VII (Amman 1999): 317-26; eadem, "Family Religion: Evidence for the Paraphernalia of the Domestic Cult," in *The World of the Aramaeans* (FS P.-E. Dion; JSOTSup 325), ed. P. M. Michèle Daviau, J. W. Wevers, M. Weigl, vol. II, Sheffield: Sheffield Academic Press, 2001, 199-229; eadem, M. Steiner, "A Moabite Sanctuary at Khirbat al-Mudayna," *BASOR* 320 (2000): 1-21.

73. Beit-Arieh, *Ḥorvat Qitmit* (n. 11), 210.

are also designated as "Judahite" types. Other types such as bowls with flat rim or carinated bowls are more rarely attested in central Judea but quite common both in southern Judea, the Negev and southern Transjordan.[74] They underline the essentially regional character of much of the Qiṭmīt assemblage, but represent a smaller percentage than the shapes considered definitely "Judahite." The painted and denticulated items usually considered as the hallmark of "Edomite" pottery represent only 2% of the bowls.[75]

The 'ethnic' (let alone 'national') labeling of so-called "Edomite" pottery has been questioned by P. Bienkowski, a leading expert in this field, and other scholars. It ultimately goes back to N. Glueck who had first found this pottery at Buṣeirah and other sites in southern Transjordan. It was only considerably later that it turned up in the Negev too. In Bienkowski's opinion, "Edomite pottery"

> is an unfortunate term that has caused confusion . . . Just because this pottery is called "Edomite" does not mean that wherever it is found it must be Edomite. There is insufficient evidence to indicate that this pottery was confined to a specific ethnic group, rather than being the standard Iron II . . . painted pottery of an area extending beyond Edom proper. The new term that has been proposed is "Buseirah painted ware," which has no ethnic presuppositions, just as elsewhere in the Near East reference is made to "Jemdet Nasr pottery."[76]

Bienkowski's vigorous rejection of the labeling of Qiṭmīt as an "Edomite shrine" comes as no surprise.[77]

The cultural affiliation of the "utilitarian vessels" has to be taken into account when we consider the pottery which is more specifically or even exclusively related to cult and ritual. According to Beck's analysis of both manufacturing techniques and iconography, the cultic objects from Qiṭmīt are of a distinctly "non-Judahite" character. I submit that this judgment results once more from an optical illusion created by the artificial splitting of the evidence into "utilitarian" and "cultic" objects, a distinction which makes little sense at a site like Qiṭmīt where almost every bit of evidence had in some way a cult-related function. Did the worshippers of Qiṭmīt acquire their "utilitarian" bowls, kraters, and cups in Judah, look for cooking-pots and cult inventory in Edom and supplement their repertory by a few acquisitions of Philistine provenance? I can

74. Ibid. 211-12.

75. Ibid. 213.

76. "The Edomites: The Archaeological Evidence from Transjordan," in *You Shall Not Abhor* (n. 32), 41-92, citation on 51.

77. Idem, review of Beit-Arieh, *Ḥorvat Qitmit* (n. 11), *PEQ* 130 (1998): 69-70, and see now P. Bienkowski, E. van der Steen, "Tribes, Trade, and Towns: A New Framework for the Late Iron Age in Southern Jordan and the Negev," *BASOR* 323 (2001): 21-47.

hardly imagine that such were the shopping habits of late Iron Age Negebites. As mentioned earlier, INAA analysis has shown that most of the vessels found at Qiṭmīt were produced from local clay, i.e. by implication, by craftsmen employed in one or several local workshops. This fact forces us to re-define the issue of cultural 'influence': we rather deal with craft traditions which could spread from various centers and be adopted at an intermediary meeting-place by local workshops. One possibility to account for such spreading of techniques, styles and motives from various areas is to assume the existence of itinerant craftsmen moving along major trade routes in an attempt to open new markets for their products. Such itinerant specialists have repeatedly been hypothesized for more sophisticated crafts such as metalwork or glyptics, but there is no reason for categorically excluding potters from such a model. More important, yet, is the recognition that the Qiṭmīt sanctuary's "Edomite" ascription rests on insufficient evidence and unproven assumptions.

What about its "non-Judahite" character? Beck's opinion on this was based on a twin argument: (a) the complete absence at Qiṭmīt, according to her study, of Judahite figurines; (b) "the complete absence of human figures from Judaean and Israelite sites during the Iron age."[78] Besides the fact that both are arguments *e silentio*, and thus not very weighty, there is an obvious contradiction here: The first statement implies the existence of distinctly "Judahite" figurines elsewhere, of which Beck was well aware. Consequently, we must rephrase the second statement to "the complete absence of *anthropomorphic cultic statuary* from Judaean and Israelite sites during the Iron age." This statement, however, is problematic as I have argued elsewhere.[79] At the end of the day, only the first argument can be received.

Beck was undoubtedly right in pointing out the differences between the Qiṭmīt repertory and the figurines commonly related to Judah. As a matter of fact, Qiṭmīt has not produced any distinctly 'Judahite' figurine, be it a Judean pillar or a horse-and-rider figurine. However, what does this mean? The 'national' classification of Judahite figurines largely rests upon late eighth and earlier seventh century material. We should also not forget that what we generally label Judahite figurines first of all represents the Jerusalem and the Shephelah markets. These have seldom been the first providers of goods (and thus, influences in technology or iconography) to the inhabitants of the northern Negev. That Judahite figurines were found at Arad demonstrates that people living in this peripheral fortress were connected to genuinely Judahite production centers (Jerusalem, Lachish, and possibly Tell Beit Mirsim). In contrast, this does

78. "Catalogue" (n. 12), 182.

79. Uehlinger, "Anthropomorphic Cult Statuary" (n. 6); although much of the evidence collected there is admittedly circumstantial, it cannot be ignored.

not seem to have been the case for the Qiṭmīt worshippers. Still, one should note that plaque or pillar-base figurines as well as horse-and-rider figurines of *any* regional or 'national' appurtenance are conspicuously lacking at Qiṭmīt. There may be reasons other than 'ethnicity' to account for the absence of certain types of figurines from the site.

I would concede that Beck was partly right insofar as most inhabitants of the Malḥata and Qiṭmīt area during the late Iron Age would probably not have considered themselves 'Judahites'—but neither, for that matter, 'Edomites.'

Conclusions

Unlike Arad, Qiṭmīt is a one-period site that seems to have functioned during a limited time-span of one or two generations. Whether the site was contemporary with the Arad fortress shrine cannot be firmly determined today mainly because of the uncertainties over the latter's chronology. However, if we can narrow down the dating of Qiṭmīt to the later seventh century, we should probably not go far beyond 600 B.C.E. Beit-Arieh's Edomite invasion model and Lemaire's chronological scheme are entirely dependent on their concept of Judahite–Edomite rivalry and on the ill-founded ethnic labeling of the archaeological finds. Once we abandon the premises of such an essentially antagonistic model, there is no difficulty whatsoever to accept a contemporaneous existence of the two sites and cults. Finkelstein has plausibly argued that the flourishing of late Iron Age Negev settlements was related to the commercial activities linking the southern Levant to the Red Sea and Arabia. This trade came to a rather brutal end with the massive destruction of the cities in the Philistine coastal plain by Nebuchadrezzar II in the years 604/603 B.C.E. If J. Cahill is right in ascribing the rosette stamp impressions to the time of Yehoyaqim,[80] the collapse of the Philistine network and Nebuchadrezzar's 601 Sinai fiasco were exploited by Judah during a very short time in a revolt that did not last. After 598 and until the progressive re-opening of the frankincense road towards the middle of the century under the reign of Nabonidus, there was insufficient material basis for permanent settlement in the Negev. This is the main reason why both the settlement of Tel Malḥata and the regional sanctuary of Qiṭmīt were abandoned.

I have tried to demonstrate that the dichotomic contrasting of Arad

80. "Rosette Stamp Seal Impressions from Ancient Judah," *IEJ* 45 (1995): 230-52.

and Qiṭmīt in recent discussions has led to relatively unproductive and misleading results. The Arad evidence is incomplete, partly unpublished, and it cannot be taken as a representative, even less as a typical sample of Judahite cult. Qiṭmīt, on the other hand, should not be used in a dichotomic way to support the claim of Judahite aniconism, but rather understood as *complementary* evidence which discloses another, equally important segment of the religious history of southern Palestine. Though the martial symbolism of some major statues from Qiṭmīt cannot be overlooked, the site generally hints at ritual practices of farmers and herdsmen. These people, neither genuine Judahites nor Edomites, probably cared more about their living *in between* Judahite garrisons and Edomite raiders and caravaneers than about their own particular 'nationality' or 'ethnicity.'

Let us finally come back to the problem of Judahite (or Israelite) iconolatry. The growth of the biblical tradition prohibiting the production and use of cultic images—first idols, then votive statuary, later even sculpted stones and *massebot*—evidences a debate on the use of different kinds of 'images' in worship over several generations within the religious history of Judah and Judahite Yahwism. Such debate is unthinkable without respective knowledge and practice (see introduction, premise 2). It is unfortunate that after more than a century of archaeological excavations we still have only very limited archaeological evidence for iconic cults from Judah proper. We should not forget, however, that negative evidence is provisional by definition and experience: recall how drastically the finds from Qiṭmīt and ʿEn Ḥaṣeva have re-shaped the mainstream perception of "Edomite religion" within only a decade. Now Qiṭmīt is certainly *not* a Judahite (nor, I argue, an Edomite) site, but a fascinating regional sanctuary in the northern Negev. While geographically it would have been well within the reach of the Judahite administration, it did not belong to Judah proper. Still, for the time being and pending more conclusive finds from Judah, it may serve as our next-placed example to illustrate—by way of analogy and with all due caution—how an extra-settlement Judahite *bamah* might have looked in the late Iron Age.[81] To stress unduly Qiṭmīt's "non-Judahite" character not only misrepresents the factual situation. It also obliterates a bulk of *potential* evidence for the history of Judahite religions, a religious history which cannot be understood in isolation from its broader regional context. In this sense, Qiṭmīt has also opened new perspectives for biblical scholars to think over the

81. But see B. Alpert Nakhai, "What's a Bamah? How Sacred Space Functioned in Ancient Israel," *BAR* 20, no. 3 (1993): 18-29, 77-78.

exilic and post-exilic history of the biblical image ban. We should not separate what belongs together as different aspects of ultimately one South Levantine historical reality: the statuary and the standing stones, the stands and the bowls, the figurines and the cooking-pots—nor, for that matter and period, "Yahweh of the South" and Qaus. But artifacts and images will reveal ancient religion only on the condition that we are willing to accept them plainly as serious witnesses.

II

Royal Cult

6

Sumerian Kingship and the Gods

JACOB KLEIN

According to the Sumerian King List, kingship was sent down from heaven twice in history: once before the flood, when it settled in Eridu,[1] and again after the flood, when it came to rest in Kiš.[2] This indicates that the Neo-Sumerian and early Old Babylonian kings wanted their subjects to believe that kingship had been a divinely ordained institution from time immemorial.[3] Modern scholarship, however, dismisses

1. Sumerian King List i 1-2, ed. Th. Jacobsen, *The Sumerian Kinglist*, AS 11 (Chicago: University of Chicago Press, 1939), 70f.: "When the kingship was lowered from heaven, the kingship was in Eridug."

2. Sumerian King List i 40-43, ed. Jacobsen, *Sumerian Kinglist*, 76f.: "After the flood swept thereover, when the kingship was lowered from heaven, the kingship was in Kiš."

3. The recently found version of the Sumerian Kinglist from the reign of Šulgi (cf. P. Steinkeller, "An Ur III Manuscript of the Sumerian King List," in W. Sallaberger et al., eds., *Literatur, Politik und Recht in Mesopotamien: Festschrift für Claus Wilcke* [Wiesbaden: Harrassowitz, 2003], 267ff.), indicates that the first recension of this composition is to be dated either to the early Ur III period (see already Cl. Wilcke, "Geneological and Geographical Thought in the Sumerian King List," in H. Behrens, D. Loding, M. Roth, eds., *dumu-e$_2$-dub-ba-a: Studies in Honor of Åke W. Sjöberg* [Philadelphia, 1989], 557-71; J.-J. Glassner, *Chroniques Mésopotamiennes* [Paris, 1993], 138; E. Flückiger-Hawker, *Urnamma of Ur in Sumerian Literary Tradition*, OBO 166 [Fribourg: University Press Fribourg, 1999], 41f.), or to the Sargonic period (cf. Steinkeller, "An Ur III Manuscript," 281-84). This recension must have opened with the post-diluvian section. The section containing the ante-diluvian dynasties was preserved only in a late manuscript (WB), dated by Jacobsen to the reign of Sin-magir of Isin (Jacobsen, *Sumerian Kinglist*, 5). Hence, the ante-diluvian section may be an addition from the Early Old Babylonian period.

The hoary antiquity of kingship is implied by many Sumerian myths and epics which tacitly assume that urban civilization in general, and kingship in particular, were created by the gods, or transferred to humanity, at the time of creation of mankind. Thus, for example, on the day of the creation of man the goddess Ninmaḫ fashions seven types of human being with bodily defects, of which at least four are assigned by Enki jobs associated with the king: the crippled servant, the blind singer, the sexless eunuch, and the barren harem concubine—cf. Th. Jacobsen, *The Harps That Once: Sumerian Poetry in Translation* (New Haven: Yale University Press, 1987), 160f.; Sh. Shifra and J. Klein, *In Those Distant Days: Anthology of*

this royal propaganda, demonstrating that in prehistoric times the Sumerian city-states were governed by some form of primitive democracy. According to current scholarly opinion, autocratic monarchy in Sumer developed gradually during the Early Dynastic period as a result of political and military pressures from the north on the small Sumerian city-states.[4]

Our information about the nature of Sumerian kingship in the Early Dynastic period (ca. 2700-2370 B.C.E.) is derived primarily from late literary sources, whose testimony is indirect, anachronistic, and tendentious. The earliest period for which we can learn about Sumerian kingship from contemporary documents is that of the First Dynasty of Lagaš, whose outstanding rulers commemorated in their royal inscriptions the history of their border disputes and wars with the neighboring city-state Umma.[5] From these inscriptions we learn that in the Early Dynastic III period (ca. 2500-2370 B.C.E.) Sumer consisted of a number of small states, each centered around a capital city. The city-state together with its population was conceived as the estate of the patron deity, who was worshipped in the central temple. The city was governed by a secular or a religious leader who was considered the earthly representative of the city god. One of the ruler's duties was to support the cult of the temple and to take part in it. The extent of the ruler's participation in the cult varied from city to city,

---

Ancient Near Eastern Poetry in Hebrew (Tel-Aviv: Am Oved, 1996), 84, ll. 58-78. In fact, a Neo-Babylonian Akkadian mythological fragment (*VS* 24, 92) tells of the creation of the human king (*māliku-amīlu*) immediately following the creation of the first common man (*lullû-amīlu*); cf. W.R. Mayer, "Ein Mythos von der Erschaffung des Menschen und des Königs," *Or* 56 (1987): 55-68. This late myth may have an Old Babylonian origin.

4. See Th. Jacobsen, "Primitive Democracy in Ancient Mesopotamia," *JNES* 2 (1943): 159-72; "Early Political Development in Mesopotamia," *ZA* 52 (1957): 91-140. His hypothesis that during the ED I period (ca. 2900-2700 BCE) the Sumerian city-states were organized in an amphyctiony (the "Kengir League"), whose members selected their leader in times of emergency with the sanction of Enlil in a democratic assembly (ukkin) at Nippur, cannot be confirmed from contemporary sources—cf. Cl. Wilcke, "Zum Königtum in der Ur III-Zeit," in *Le Palais et la Royauté*, ed. P. Garelli (Paris: P. Geuthner, 1974), 228f.; "Politische Opposition nach sumerischen Quellen," in *La voix de l'opposition en Mesopotamie*, ed. A. Finet (Brussels: Institut des Hautes Études de Belgique, 1973), 37-65. The emergence of Nippur as a national religious center seems rather to be the result of Enlil's supremacy in the Sumerian pantheon from the ED II period at the latest. See W. Sallaberger, "Nippur als religiöses Zentrum Mesopotamiens im historischen Wandel," in *Die orientalische Stadt: Kontinuität, Wandel, Bruch*, ed. Gernot Wilhelm, Saarbrücker Druckerei und Verlag (Saarbrücken, 1997), 147ff. From this period on, all monarchs who exercised hegemony in southern Mesopotamia showed Nippur utmost esteem by undertaking building projects in the city and by regularly dedicating war booty and cultic object to Enlil and its temples.

5. For the Early Dynastic royal inscriptions from Lagaš and elsewhere, see H. Steible, *Die altsumerische Bau- und Weihinschriften*, FAOS 5 1-2 (Wiesbaden: Franz Steiner Verlag, 1982). These texts are cited below from J. S. Cooper, *Sumerian and Akkadian Royal Inscriptions I: Presargonic Inscriptions* (New Haven: American Oriental Society, 1986).

and depended in some measure on his title and status. In Uruk the ruler carried the title en, "high priest / lord,"[6] and lived in the temple. This situation points to sacral kingship, wherein the political ruler was at the same time the supreme religious authority of the state. Indeed, the kings of Uruk were remembered as the human husbands of the love- and fertility-goddess Inanna, who had as such annually celebrated with the goddess the "sacred marriage" rite, a ceremony aimed at securing prosperity for the land. In other cities, the ruler, living in a palace of his own, was called lugal, "king,"[7] which points to a more secular type of kingship. Another wide-spread title known from this period is ensi(k), "city ruler," "governor" or the like,[8] a title particularly popular with the rulers of Lagaš. Since the latter also at times referred to themselves by the title lugal, it is generally assumed that these two royal titles are complementary and interchangeable: The term ensi(k) defines the status of the ruler vis-à-vis his city god, the ultimate owner of the city-state, and may be translated "steward." The term lugal, on the other hand, describes the position of the ruler in relation to his subjects as their political and military leader, its basic meaning being "master."[9]

Following Th. Jacobsen's groundbreaking studies of the development of early Mesopotamian monarchy,[10] it is now generally believed that the institution of en-ship preceded that of kingship, designated by the royal titles ensi(k) / lugal, which is a later development. However, the relationship between these two types of political systems is still a matter of debate.

One recent opinion holds that while the en was basically a religious ruler appointed by the god or goddess of his city (i.e., by the clergy) and did not enjoy the privilege of passing his position on to his posterity, the lugal and the ensi(k) were hereditary monarchs. According to this hypothesis, en-ship originated in prehistoric Uruk, whence it spread to northern Mesopotamia and Syria (i.e., Ebla). Beginning in the Early Dynastic II period hereditary kingship gradually superseded en-ship in

---

6. Akkadian *ēnum*, "high-priest," later equated with *bēlum*, "lord."

7. Literally "the great man," equivalent to Akkadian *šarrum*, "king."

8. Sumerian $ensi_2$(k) = Akkadian *iššakkum*, "governor," later "chief farmer."

9. Beside the usual translation of lugal as *šarrum*, "king," the Akkadians also translated it by *bēlum*, "master." Indeed, lugal may be used to define the relationship of a master to his slave, as well as that of the city god to the ruler, who was seen as his servant. See I. Winter, "'Idols of the King': Royal Images as Recipients of Ritual Action in Ancient Mesopotamia," *Journal of Ritual Studies* 6 (1992): 13-42; P. Steinkeller, "On Rulers, Priests and Sacred Marriage: Tracing the Evolution of Early Sumerian Kingship," in *Priests and Officials in the Ancient Near East: Papers of the Second Colloquium on the Ancient Near East—The City and Its Life*, ed. K. Watanabe (Heidelberg: Carl Winter, 1999), 112.

10. See above, note 4.

southern Mesopotamia and replaced it entirely with the rise of the Old Akkadian empire.[11]

According to another recent study of early Mesopotamian monarchy, the development of Sumerian kingship was conditioned by changes in Sumerian religion and cult. In the archaic period the Sumerian city-states were presumably dominated by female mother-goddess figures, patrons of male priestly rulers (en). These en-priests served as the human spouses of the city goddesses. Later the female deities were replaced by male deities as city-gods, and this shift caused a change in the form of government. The en-priests were replaced by secular political-military leaders, entitled ensi(k) / lugal, who acted as the stewards of the city gods and resided in royal palaces (é-gal) outside the old temple-quarter of the city.[12]

Whatever the precise reasons and factors behind the shift of political power from the en-priest to the ensi(k) / lugal may have been, once this shift had taken place the office of the en assumed a purely religious function and was gradually established in every major cultic center. Henceforth not only male en-priests served as votaries and spouses of female deities, but female en-priestesses were also installed as human spouses of male deities. The latter development probably began with the appointment of Enḫeduanna by her father, Sargon of Akkad, as en-priestess of the moon-god Nanna at Ur, an act which must have been a revolutionary religious innovation.[13]

Sumerian literature probably composed in the Ur III period (ca. 2100-2000 B.C.E.) assumes that the Early Dynastic priestly kings of Uruk had been divine or semi-divine beings, descended from gods. However, these descriptions may be in great part anachronisms generated by ideological interests. Judging from Early Dynastic and later sources from Lagaš, the Old Sumerian rulers were not in fact deified. In principle, they were considered ordinary human beings with a special relationship to the city god. As earthly administrators of the estates of the city gods, they formed the link between human society and the supernatural powers.[14]

---

11. See W. Heimpel, "Herrentum und Königtum im vor- und frühgeschichtlichen Alten Orient," *ZA* 82 (1992): 4-21. Once lugal prevailed in Sumer as a royal title, en came to designate a purely religious function ("high priest / priestess"), and ensi(k) became the title of the local city governor, subject to the authority of the king.

12. Cf. P. Steinkeller, "On Rulers."

13. P. Steinkeller, "On Rulers," 116-29. For a different opinion see Annette Zgoll, *Der Rechtsfall der En-ḫedu-Ana im Lied nin-me-šara*, AOAT 246 (Münster: Ugarit-Verlag, 1997), 99-102. According to Zgoll, the office of the en-priestess of Nanna in Ur was an ancient cultic practice, going back to the Early Dynastic period.

14. See, however, footnotes 43-45 below. For previous general studies of divine kingship in Mesopotamia, see Henri Frankfort, *Kingship and the Gods* (Chicago/London: University of

Rich and multifaceted information about Sumerian royal ideology is furnished for the first time in the Neo-Sumerian period.[15] The harbinger of this period is Gudea of Lagaš,[16] but the major sources of information come from the era of the Third Dynasty of Ur (ca. 2100-2000 B.C.E.). This period has left us a great number of contemporary administrative documents and monumental inscriptions which provide some evidence as to the actual nature of Sumerian kingship. On the other hand, we learn about the ideology of kingship in this period from a variety of literary texts preserved in quite accurate and reliable copies made in the Old Babylonian period.[17] Accordingly, I will offer here an outline of the political, religious, and cultural aspects of Sumerian kingship in the Ur III period. In my discussion I will pay special attention to the divinity of the Sumerian king and his role in the cult.[18]

As noted above, we have no clear evidence for the divinity of Sumerian kings in the Early Dynastic period. Proper divine kingship was introduced to Sumer by the second king of the Ur III Dynasty, Šulgi, who ruled from 2094-2047 B.C.E. We can infer from Šulgi's royal inscriptions, royal hymns, and year dates that he assumed divinity toward the middle of his reign. In this self-divinization Šulgi followed the precedent of

---

Chicago Press, 1948); and recently Ph. Jones, "Divine and Non-Divine Kingship," in *A Companion to the Ancient Near East*, ed. D. C. Snell (London: Blackwell Publishing, 2005), 330-42.

15. As J. N. Postgate observes in "Royal Ideology and State Administration in Sumer and Akkad," in *Civilizations of the Ancient Near East*, ed. J. Sasson et al. (New York: Scribners, 1995), 1:395-411, any account of Mesopotamian royal ideology must be one-sided and partial, for almost all our information derives from royal inscriptions and literature which the kings themselves commissioned in order to enhance their own legitimacy and image. Therefore, the sources at our disposal are to a great extent royal propaganda. Objective accounts or descriptions of kings and kingship are extremely rare, and we must therefore be careful to distinguish between royal ideology and royal reality. For a balanced approach to these historiographical problems, see recently W. W. Hallo, "New Directions in Historiography (Mesopotamia and Israel)," in *dubsar anta-men: Studien zur Altorientalistik. Festschrift für Willem H.Ph. Römer*, ed. M. Dietrich and O. Loretz (Münster: Ugarit-Verlag, 1998), 109-28.

16. For the royal inscriptions of Gudea, see A. Falkenstein, *Die Inschriften Gudeas von Lagaš I: Einleitung*, AnOr 30 (Rome, 1966); Edzard, *RIME* 3/1; Cl. Suter, *Gudea's Temple Building*, Cuneiform Monographs 17 (Groningen; Styx Publications, 2000).

17. Cf. W. W. Hallo, "Toward a History of Sumerian Literature," in *Sumerological Studies in Honor of Thorkild Jacobsen*, AS 20 (Chicago: University of Chicago Press, 1975), 187ff.; J. Klein, *Three Šulgi Hymns: Sumerian Royal Hymns Glorifying King Šulgi of Ur* (Ramat Gan: Bar-Ilan University Press, 1981), 68ff., 133f.; *The Royal Hymns of Shulgi King of Ur: Man's Quest for Immortal Fame*, Transactions of the American Philosophical Society, vol. 71, pt. 7 (Philadelphia, 1981), 27-32; "From Gudea to Šulgi: Continuity and Change in Sumerian Literary Tradition," in *DUMU.E2.DUB.BA.A: Studies in Honor of Åke W. Sjöberg*, ed. H. Behrens et al. (Philadelphia: University Museum, 1989), 291ff.

18. For a comprehensive survey of kingship in the Ur III period, see Cl. Wilcke, "Zum Königtum in der Ur III-Zeit." For an updated evaluation of the reign of Urnammu, founder of the dynasty, see Flückiger-Hawker, *Urnamma of Ur*, 28-67.

Naram-Sin, king of Akkad, who had reigned about a century and a half previously.[19]

The main evidence for the deification of the Neo-Sumerian kings is the use of the determinative diĝir, "god," which normally appears before names of deities. The names of these kings are written with the divine determinative in their inscriptions, date formulae, royal hymns, and so on. As noted above, the first king to apply the divine determinative to his name was Naram-Sin of the Old Akkadian dynasty, followed by his son Šarkališarri. This practice was later adopted by the kings of the Ur III dynasty, beginning with Šulgi, and taken over by all the kings of Isin, as well as some of the rulers of Larsa.[20] In addition, each of the Ur III kings, beginning from Šulgi, refers to himself as "the god of his land."[21]

Further important evidence for the deification of the Ur III kings comes from archeological excavations, as well as from contemporary administrative texts and votive inscriptions. These texts indicate that some of these kings, especially Šulgi and his grandson Šu-Sin, were worshipped in temples of their own during their lifetimes. Šulgi received offerings in temples erected especially for him in Lagaš, Umma, and Puzriš-Dagan, while Šu-Sin was similarly worshipped in Adab, Ešnunna, Girsu, and Ur. These temples were built in honor of the king by the local governor, just as the king constructed temples in honor of major gods.[22] Šulgi apparently also had a temple or shrine in his capital Ur. This fol-

19. While we do not have any explicit written reference to the circumstances of Šulgi's apotheosis, Naram-Sin's self-deification is explicitly reported in one of his inscriptions. According to Naram-Sin 10 (ed. D. Frayne, *Sargonic and Gutian Periods,* Royal Inscriptions of Mesopotamia, Early Periods, vol. 2 [Toronto: University of Toronto Press, 1993], 113-14), after having suppressed the Great Revolt of a coalition of Sumerian cities, this king assumed divinity at the request of his subjects, becoming thereby the tutelary deity of his capital city. The actual deification is presented as follows: "In view of the fact that he protected the foundations of his city from danger, (the citizens of) his city requested from Aštar in Eanna, Enlil in Nippur, Dagan in Tuttul, Ninḫursaĝ in Keš, Ea in Eridu, Sîn in Ur, Šamaš in Sippar (and) Nergal in Kutha, that (Naram-Sin) be (made) the god of their city, and they built for him a temple (dedicated) to him within Agade" (ll. 20-57). Note that Enlil appears only second in this list, after Aštar.

20. Ḫammurabi and his successors never used this determinative in their inscriptions, but the name of Ḫammurabi is occasionally written with the divine determinative in his royal hymns. This does not mean, however, that Ḫammurabi was considered deified.

21. See Cl. Wilcke, "Königtum in der Ur III-Zeit," 179.

22. For the worship of Šulgi and other kings in temples dedicated to them and in temples of other major gods, see J. Klein, *Three Šulgi Hymns*, 31, n. 43; P. Michalowski, "Charisma and Control: On Continuity and Change in Early Mesopotamian Bureaucratic Systems," in *The Organization of Power: Aspects of Bureaucracy in the Ancient Near East*, ed. M. Gibson and R. D. Biggs (Chicago: Oriental Institute, 1987), 65, nn. 41-42. For the temples dedicated to Šu-Sin, see D. Frayne, *Sargonic and Gutian Periods*, 321ff., nos. 11-15. For the worship of the Ur III kings in the cult, both in their lifetime and posthumously, see in general W. Sallaberger, *Der kultische Kalender der Ur III Zeit* I (Berlin, 1993), 63ff.; 85ff.; 96; 159f.

lows from the ninth hymn of the "Collection of Sumerian Temple Hymns," which is dedicated to a temple called "Eḫursaĝ of Šulgi of Ur."[23] The Eḫursaĝ is also mentioned in the "Disputation Between Tree and Reed" as the temple where the divine Šulgi sat in judgment between the two disputants.[24]

The worship of the Ur III kings is also indicated by the festivals and months called after them in the Ur Calendar, as well as by the gala and $gudu_4$ priests assigned to them in the cult.[25] Note, however, that these kings never had a shrine erected for them in Nippur, seat of the supreme god Enlil, nor did the cultic calendar of this city contain a month named after any of them. Such measures would have been considered hubris and would have met with the ardent opposition of the Nippur priesthood. Deified Sumerian kings were represented by statues erected in their own shrines as well as in the temples of major gods, especially the Ekur and other sanctuaries of Nippur.[26] These royal statues, just like those of gods, were animated and sanctified through a series of ritual acts, including the "mouth washing / mouth opening" ceremony, and received regular libations and food offerings together with the traditional gods. It may be assumed that the royal image, enshrined and worshipped in a temple of its own, depicted the king in a seated posture, whereas the royal statue placed in the temple of a god represented him standing, symbolizing the king's inferiority and submission to the deity whose favors he was seeking.[27]

---

23. Cf. Åke W. Sjöberg, *The Collection of the Sumerian Temple Hymns* (Locust Valley, NY: J. J. Augustin, 1969), 24, l. 134; 78, comment on l. 132.

24. *STVC* 58, reverse and duplicates. Note, however, that in the great self-laudatory royal hymn Šulgi B, the Eḫursaĝ seems to be referred to as a royal palace, the actual abode of the king. Cf. Šulgi B, 377-79 (cited from G. Haayer's manuscript—cf. G. R. Castellino, *Two Šulgi Hymns* [Rome: Istituto di studi del Vicino Oriente, 1972], 69):

> I Šulgi—my house, the Eḫursaĝ, the palace of palaces,
> The residence of my kingship, with great psalms of praise
> I make it towering like a lapis-lazuli mountain.

Perhaps the Eḫursaĝ, originally Šulgi's palace, was later converted into a temple following the king's deification or after his death. For the possibility that this temple is referred to in a cylinder seal as the "Eḫursaĝ of Enlil," see now N. Bellotto and D.M. Bonacossi, "Trois sceaux-cylindres appartenant à une collection privée et l'Ehursag d'Enlil," *RA* 91 (1997): 26-29.

25. See M. E. Cohen, *The Cultic Calendars of the Ancient Near East* (Bethesda: CDL Press, 1993), 68ff., 154f., 177f., 192ff.; W. Sallaberger, *Der kultische Kalender*, 197, 252.

26. Both Šulgi and Šu-Sin had their statues erected in the Ekur and other Nippur sanctuaries, and they as well as Amar-Sin and Ibbi-Sin appear frequently in animal offering lists pertaining to the Nippur cult. Cf. Cl. Wilcke, *RlA* 7, 120; W. Sallaberger, *Der kultische Kalender*, 75, 99f., 105ff., 199f., 212f., 272f.; I. Winter, "'Idols of the King,'" 33ff.

27. For a recent and most penetrating study of the Sumerian royal images, see I. Winter, "'Idols of the King.'" As she aptly points out, the presence of the royal image in the

A third very important source which attests to the divinity of the Neo-Sumerian kings is the royal hymns. The bulk of the approximately 150 known Sumerian royal hymns pertain to the kings of the Third Dynasty of Ur and the kings of Isin. Generally speaking, Sumerian "royal hymns" are of two types: hymns dedicated to gods with praise or prayer for a king, and genuine royal hymns addressed to the king or praising him.[28] Royal prayers are normally provided with liturgical notations ("stage directions") inserted in the text, as well as with generic subscripts. Genuine royal hymns, on the other hand, lack such notations and subscripts. It is generally assumed that whereas the royal prayers were regularly used in the temple liturgy, genuine royal hymns were rather part of the courtly ceremonial and were used in a more secular context.[29] It should be noted, however, that according to explicit statements in the royal hymns of Šulgi, his entire corpus, including the genuine "royal hymns," were commissioned to be recited in the temples, in his lifetime as well as after his death, thus perpetuating his memory in the temple liturgy. Šulgi also expressed the wish that his hymns be cultivated and transmitted to posterity by the scribal academies of Sumer.[30]

It is the genuine royal hymns in particular which attest to the divinity of the Neo-Sumerian kings: The very emergence of this genre is an indication of the divinity of these kings. The addressing to the king of hymns in which he is praised as a god and given divine attributes is a conscious application to the kings of a literary genre otherwise exclusively limited to the gods and their temples. The divinity of these kings also explains the fact that royal hymns were discontinued after the Old Babylonian period. This genre was apparently suppressed from the literary tradition on account of its close association with the abandoned concept of divine kingship.

The royal hymns, most of which became part of the tradition of the Nippur scribal school, reflect the ideology of Mesopotamian national unity also implied by the Sumerian King List. According to this ideology, in the divine assembly at Nippur the god Enlil conferred supreme executive power upon one of the local city gods, and this god in turn conferred it upon the king of his city. The kings who figure in the royal hymns regard themselves as the legitimate rulers of Sumer and Akkad, derive

---

god's sanctuary indicates the dependence of the ruler on the latter's favors, and at the same time testifies to a special, intimate, relationship between him and the divine. It makes the ruler's privileged mediating role between the gods and the people manifest.

28. The above classification of the Sumerian royal hymns is suggested here with due reservations. For the simplicity and inadequacy of this classification in many instances, see the recent discussion in Flückiger-Hawker, *Urnamma of Ur,* 12ff., with previous bibliography.

29. Cf. J. Klein, *Three Šulgi Hymns*, 25, n. 20; *Royal Hymns of Shulgi*, 18, n. 71.

30. See J. Klein, *Royal Hymns of Shulgi*, 18-21; "From Gudea to Šulgi."

their authority from Enlil, and brook no rivals to their rule. This ideology is also confirmed by literary tradition. The distribution of royal hymns shows that as a rule the Nippur tradition tends to honor only one dynasty at a time with this literary genre, even if other contemporary dynasties shared hegemony over Mesopotamia.[31] The same ideology is also reflected in the epic-mythological section of the "Lament over Sumer and Ur." This theological composition explains the fall of the Ur III empire as a direct result of the decision of the divine assembly in Nippur, presided over by An and Enlil, to take away hegemony from Ur and transfer it to another city, presumably Isin. Following this fateful and arbitrary decision, the patron deities of Ur, Nanna and Ningal, abandon their city and it falls prey to the enemy hordes.[32]

Another literary motif frequently invoked as proof of the divinity of the Ur III and Isin kings is their claim of divine lineage.[33] These kings repeatedly boast in their royal inscriptions and their royal hymns of being the offspring of gods and goddesses. Thus, for example, Šulgi constantly figures in his hymns as the son of the important Urukean goddess Ninsun and her human husband Lugalbanda. Consequently, he refers to himself as "the brother and friend of Gilgameš,"[34] the famous ancient king of Uruk who also figured in Sumerian mythology as the son of the above pair. Šulgi further widened his family ties with the divine world. He introduced to Ur the sacred marriage rite, which he borrowed from Uruk. In it he took the role of Dumuzi, the beloved spouse of the love- and fertility-goddess Inanna. This, in turn, made him the brother-in-law of the sun-god Utu, Inanna's divine brother.[35] As an incarnation of Dumuzi, he also speaks of the goddess Geštinana, Dumuzi's divine sibling, as "my sister Geštinana."[36]

To reinforce his ties with the pantheon of Uruk, Šulgi's poets composed a group of hymns which center on the major gods of this city and

---

31. For a comprehensive discussion and bibliography of the Neo-Sumerian royal hymns, see J. Klein, *Three Šulgi Hymns*, 21ff., 226ff. See also *Royal Hymns of Shulgi*, pp. 9ff.; M.-C. Ludwig, *Untersuchungen zu den Hymnen des Išme-Dagan von Isin* (Wiesbaden: Harrasowitz, 1990).

32. Cf. P. Michalowski, *The Lamentation over the Destruction of Sumer and Ur* (Winona Lake, IN: Eisenbrauns, 1989), 8ff., 59f.

33. For a comprehensive study of the divine lineage of the Sumerian kings which has not yet been superseded, see Å. Sjöberg, "Die göttliche Abstammung der sumerisch-babylonischen Herrscher," *Orientalia Suecana* 21 (1972): 87-112.

34. Cf. J. Klein, *Three Šulgi Hymns*, 49, passim; *Royal Hymns of Shulgi*, 10, passim.

35. Cf. Šulgi A 79 (J. Klein, *Three Šulgi Hymns*, 198f.): "With my brother (and) companion (= šeš ku-li-mu), the hero Utu, I drank beer in the palace, founded by An."

36. Cf. J. Klein, *Royal Hymns of Shulgi* , 10, 23, n. 113; Šulgi P 43-48; Šulgi C 92′. For the possibility that Ur-Nammu, the founder of the dynasty, already celebrated the sacred marriage rite with Inanna of Uruk, see Flückiger-Hawker, *Urnamma of Ur*, 38.

their support of Šulgi's kingship. In a small hymnal epic,[37] Šulgi's divine mother Ninsun intercedes in the divine assembly with the heaven-god An, her father, on behalf of Šulgi. She pleads with him to approve and legitimize the latter's kingship. As expected, An grants his approval to the king of her choice.[38] Another hymn, which probably commemorates Šulgi's installation of a statue of Gilgameš in the temple of the moon-god at Ur, describes the meeting of the two divine brothers, Šulgi and Gilgameš. In a dialogue they alternate in singing one another's praises and glory.[39] The sacred marriage between Šulgi and Inanna is the subject of a third hymn in which the divine lovers hold an amatory dialogue, inviting each other to Šulgi's fields and gardens, presumably in order to fructify them by means of various rites.[40]

Šulgi's descendants who ruled the Ur III empire after him seem to have abandoned the Uruk pantheon and adopted other gods as their divine parents.[41] The Isin kings, descended from Amorite families, based the legitimation of their kingship solely upon the Nippur religious establishment and, with a few exceptions, claim to be the sons of Enlil or the well-known Amorite deity Dagan.[42]

---

37. "Šulgi, Ninsun and An" (Šulgi P)—cf. J. Klein, *Royal Hymns of Shulgi*, 34ff. This hymn may have been composed on the occasion of Šulgi's coronation in Uruk.

38. The god An grants his approval in the following words: "Šulgi, the king of propitious reign, / For you, the goddess, may he perfect the cultic-norms, established for the kingship! / May he execute properly for you the statutes of the gods! / May he present you the offerings of the New Moon and the offerings of the New Year! / May you, yourself, bring to me daily his prayers!" (Šulgi P, Sect. b, ll. 5-9).

39. J. Klein, "Šulgi and Gilgameš: The Two Brother-Peers," in *Kramer Anniversary Volume*, ed. B. L. Eichler et al., AOAT 25 (Neukirchen-Vluyn: Neukirchener-Verlag, 1976), 271-92.

40. Cf. S. N. Kramer, "Inanna and Šulgi: A Sumerian Fertility Song," *Iraq* 31 (1969): 18-23, 40.

41. Šulgi's son Amar-Sin is referred to as "the beloved son of Nanna" (cf. Amar-Sin 17:18— D. Frayne, *Sargonic and Gutian Periods*, 265). His grandson Šu-Sin, on the other hand, calls Inanna's son Šara, patron of Umma, "his father" (ad-da-ni; cf. Šu-Sin 16:5—*Sargonic and Gutian Periods*, 327).

42. Išbi-Erra, Šū-ilišu, Išme-Dagan, and Lipit-Eštar, who belong to the same family, refer to themselves as sons of Enlil. Ur-Ninurta, who was descended from another family, is called "son of An" and also "son of Iškur." Iddin-Dagan (Išme-Dagan) and Urdukuga (thirteenth king of Isin) are called "son of Dagan." Enlil-bani, on the other hand, is called "the august son of Enki" (cf. Å. Sjöberg, "göttliche Abstammung," 95f.).

The theological concept of divine parentage seems to have become less important if not totally abandoned in Larsa and Babylon. According to Å. Sjöberg, Sin-iddinam of Larsa is still called "the mighty son/the first born of Iškur," and Abi-sare of Larsa is called "the exuberant one of his natural father (= Enlil) . . . born of Ninlil." However, references to divine parentage pertaining to Rīm-Sîn of Larsa and the kings of the First Dynasty of Babylon are equivocal. These rulers usually refer to themselves as śu-du$_{11}$-ga DN, "created by god so-and-so," or else refer to their personal god as diĝir-sa-dù (Akkadian *ilu bānû*), which may mean "the god who engendered (him)" or "the god who created (him)." For the ambiguity

The precise implication of these claims to divine parentage is obscured by a number of contradictory factors. First it should be observed that these claims are not an innovation of Šulgi, but are attested in the royal inscriptions of many Old Sumerian kings,[43] as well as in the inscriptions of Gudea, the most prominent ruler of Neo-Sumerian Lagaš,[44] and of Ur-Nammu, Šulgi's human father, founder of the Ur III

---

of these expressions, see J. Klein, "'Personal God' and Individual Prayer in Sumerian Religion," *AfO Beiheft* 19 (1982): 296.

43. According to the Sumerian King List (iii 1-11), Meskiağašer, the first king of the First Dynasty of Uruk (ED II Period), was the son of the sun-god Utu. His son Enmerkar also figures as the son of Utu in the epic "Enmerkar and the Lord of Aratta" (ll. 35, 215 et passim). However, this derives from a relatively late literary source, for the earliest copy of the Sumerian King List stems from the Ur III period (cf. n. 3 above).

The first Mesopotamian ruler to claim divine parentage in a royal inscription of his own was Mesilim, suzerain of Kiš, who lived about a century or so before Eannatum of Lagaš. In an inscription from Adab, Mesilim calls himself "the beloved son of Ninḫursağ" (J. S. Cooper, *Sumerian and Akkadian Royal Inscriptions*, 19, Ki 3.3). Eannatum of the First Dynasty of Lagaš claims to be the son of Ninğirsu, patron deity of his city (cf. Stele of Vultures—*Sumerian and Akkadian Royal Inscriptions*, 34, obv. v 1-5). Further, both he and other Old Sumerian rulers boast that they were nourished as infants on the faithful milk of Ninḫursağ. Enmetena, fifth ruler of Old Sumerian Lagaš, claims to have been the son of the goddess Ğatumdug (cf. Ent. 25:9-10). In another inscription he is called "son begotten by Lugalurub" (Inanna's husband) (cf. Ent. 35, 2:6-10; *Sumerian and Akkadian Royal Inscriptions*, 59, La 5.5a, cols. ii-iii). Similarly, his predecessor Enanatum I is called "son born of Lugalurub" (cf. Enanatum I 26, 1:14-18—*Sumerian and Akkadian Royal Inscriptions*, 47-54).

Lugalzagesi, governor of Umma who conquered all Mesopotamia in a swift attack and made Uruk his capital, is called "son born of Nisaba" (Stone Vessel Fragment 1:26-27—*Sumerian and Akkadian Royal Inscriptions*, 94, Um 7.1). On the other hand, Urukagina, the last ruler of Lagaš, refers to Nisaba as the "(personal) goddess of Lugalzagesi" (see Ukg. 16, 8:11-9:3—*Sumerian and Akkadian Royal Inscriptions*, 79, La 9.5, col. ix). Another Old Sumerian ruler of Umma, Lu-Utu, is called "son of Nininnam" (see *AnOr* 30/1, 16).

44. While Gudea never mentions his human father, he repeatedly refers to the goddess Ğatumdug as his divine mother, who gave birth to him in the sanctuary (Cylinder A 3:6-8— D. O. Edzard, *Gudea and His Dynasty*, Royal Inscriptions of Mesopotamia, Early Periods 3/1 [Toronto: University of Toronto Press, 1997], 70; cf. Statue F 1:12-2:1—op. cit., 47). These statements concerning Ğatumdug are contradicted by others. In the beginning of his temple hymn, Gudea refers to the goddess Nanše, Ninğirsu's sister, as "my mother" (see Cylinder A 1:29-2:3—*Gudea and His Dynasty*, 70; also 3:25; 5:25). And the epilogue of his hymn states that Gudea was born to Ninsun, an important goddess from the pantheon of Uruk, who is designated as "his divine-mother" (diğir-ama), and engendered by Ninğišzida, a chthonic deity, who is designated here and elsewhere as his "(personal) god" (see Cylinder B 23:18-21). Th. Jacobsen, *Harps*, 391, n. 16; 444, n. 62; and Cl. Wilcke, "Genealogical and Geographical Thought," 566, assume that the statements concerning Ğatumdug and Nanše are mere metaphors and that the official divine pair whom Gudea adopted as his parents were Ninsun and Ninğišzida. By relating himself to Ninsun, Gudea apparently aspired to legitimize his kingship, just the founders of the Ur III empire would do later. In addition to these claims of divine parentage, Gudea is referred to in his great temple hymn as "the god of his city" (Cyl. B i 5), which reminds us of Naram-Sin's title "god

dynasty.[45] Hence, this mythological motif seems to be a genuine Sumerian concept which had developed already in the Old Sumerian period, when kings were not yet deified.

Second, it has been observed that Sumerian kings occasionally refer to their divine "mother" and "father" simply as their "god" or "goddess" (diĝir) instead of calling them by the corresponding terms ama and a-a.[46] Furthermore, Sumerian kings seem never to have denied their human parents, and occasionally refer to them in their inscriptions and royal hymns in addition to their divine parents. Hence one gets the impression that the terms "father" and "mother" in this context are mere metaphors referring to the personal patron deities of the respective kings.[47]

In a series of literary *topoi* the royal inscriptions and royal hymns of the Neo-Sumerian kings stress the legitimation and support of their kingship not only by their patron deities but also by other major gods of the pantheon. Thus, for example, the kings claim that after having been born to their divine parents they were nurtured and raised by mother-goddesses. They had been selected for kingship from among the multitudes of the "black-headed people," endowed with superhuman qualities, such as perfect wisdom, immense physical power, heavenly beauty, etc., and invested at their coronation with all the insignia of kingship by the leading gods of the pantheon.[48]

The Neo-Sumerian kings are described as ideal rulers, righteous

---

of Akkad" (*il Akkade*). See further Cl. Suter, *Gudea's Temple Building,* 104f. Contrary to the former scholars, Edzard (*RIME* 3/1, 26-28) assumes that Gudea was not deified during his lifetime, because his name is never written with the divine determinative in contemporary documents, and there is no evidence for his receiving offerings as a living ruler.

45. Ur-Nammu claimed to be the son of the Urukean goddess Ninsun and the brother of Gilgameš; cf. Codex Ur-Nammu, Prol. 36ff. (M. T. Roth, *Law Collections from Mesopotamia and Asia Minor* [Atlanta: Scholars Press, 1997], 15); Ur-Nammu C 112-113 (Flückiger-Hawker, *Urnamma of Ur,* 218). But his name is never written with the divine determinative during his lifetime.

46. Thus some sources refer to Lugalbanda as Šulgi's "(personal) god," and others as his divine father (see Šulgi D 42—Klein, *Three Šulgi Hymns,* 74, 94). Similarly, in the Akkadian Gilgameš Epic VI 174 (cf. A. R. George, *The Epic of Gilgamesh* [London: Penguin Press, 1999], 53, l. 165), Lugalbanda is designated as the "(personal) god" of Gilgameš, whereas elsewhere he figures as his father. It was further observed that in one of his inscriptions Ur-Nammu refers to Ninsun as "his goddess" (Ur-Nammu 23:1-2—*Sargonic and Gutian Periods,* 58). We have seen a similar inconsistency in the religious terminology in the Gudea hymn (see note 44 above), and we also find it in a royal inscription of Sin-kāšid of Uruk, who likewise calls Lugalbanda "his god," and Ninsun "his mother."

47. So already W. W. Hallo, "The Coronation of Ur-Nammu," *JCS* 20 (1966): 137, n. 53.

48. For an extensive documentation of these *topoi* of legitimation, some of which are already attested in Old Sumerian royal inscriptions, see now Flückiger-Hawker, *Urnamma of Ur,* 22-58.

shepherds of their people, who uphold social and religious order in their land, protect the borders of Mesopotamia from barbarian invaders, and cause the multitudes of their people to dwell in peace, harmony, and prosperity. One of the most important tasks of the Neo-Sumerian king was to administer judgment to his people, like the sun-god Utu or Ištaran, the divine judges. As such, he had to prevent the strong from oppressing the weak and ensure that children honored their parents and their elder brothers.[49] For this purpose, Sumerian kings occasionally enacted socio-economic reforms and promulgated the earliest law codes in history.[50]

To ensure prosperity and stability in the land, the Neo-Sumerian king was responsible for the proper maintenance of the cult. For this purpose Šulgi established a central animal depot in Puzriš-Dagan (Drehem) near Nippur, whose main function was to provide sacrificial animals for the national temples in Nippur and Ur.[51] The same purpose was probably behind the establishment of the Ur III bala distribution system, which obliged the various city governors to deliver provisions to the Nippur and royal sanctuaries one month in each year.[52]

One of the major means of securing fertility and abundance for the land was the annual celebration of the *hieros gamos*, or sacred marriage rite. In this ritual, the Neo-Sumerian king, who represented the fertility god Dumuzi (Biblical Tammuz), married the love- and fertility-goddess Inanna (Semitic Ištar).[53]

---

49. See Klein, *Three Šulgi Hymns*, 32, 45, ll. 141-47, 164-65; 191, ll. 22-24. See, in general, M. Weinfeld, *Justice and Righteousness in Israel and the Nations* (Jerusalem: Magnes Press, 1985).

50. The earliest socio-economic reform in history was enacted by Urukagina of Old Sumerian Lagaš —see J. S. Cooper, *Sumerian and Akkadian Royal Inscriptions*, 70-77, with bibliography. The composition of the earliest law code was commissioned by Ur-Nammu of the Ur III dynasty. Another Sumerian law code, which survived only in fragmentary form, is Codex Lipit-Eštar of Isin (ca. 1934-1924 B.C.E.)—cf. M. T. Roth, *Law Collections from Mesopotamia and Asia Minor*, 13-35. For the theological background of these socio-economic reforms and law codes, especially in the Old Babylonian period, see now Jones, "Divine and Non-Divine Kingship," 335f.; 338f.

51. The temples of other Sumerian cities, however, were supported mainly by the local city governors.

52. In this context bala means "turn (of duty)." According to W. W. Hallo, "A Sumerian Amphyctiony," *JCS* 14 (1960): 88-114, this bala system originated in an ancient (ED Period) Sumerian amphyctiony, and it was a one-way procedure, by which the commodities were received from the governors and forwarded to the Nippur temples. However, in the view of P. Steinkeller, "The Administrative and Economic Organization of the Ur III State: The Core and the Periphery," in *The Organization of Power*, 27-29, this was a system of exchange whereby the governors received other commodities for their bala animal deliveries.

53. The *communis opinio*, that the female protagonist in the sacred marriage rite was a high priestess, has recently been questioned. Most probably the rite took a purely symbolic

Direct evidence for the sacred marriage rite is found only in Ur III and Early Old Babylonian literary texts. Sumerian epic literature, however, attributes statements concerning the performance of this rite already to Enmerkar, second king of the First Dynasty of Uruk. Furthermore, the god Dumuzi, the male protagonist in the sacred marriage rite, seems to have originated in the merger of two ancient royal figures: the deified shepherd-king Dumuzi, who, according to the Sumerian King List, ruled over the city of Bad-tibira before the flood, and his namesake, the deified fisherman who ruled over Uruk three generations after Enmerkar. Hence the sacred marriage rite probably originated in Early Dynastic Uruk, where it was customary for the priest-king (en) to marry the city-goddess Inanna. Later the human origin of Dumuzi was forgotten or ignored. However, several facts still attest to his origin: Throughout history Dumuzi appears as a passive, minor deity, a shepherd-king always inferior to his mate Inanna, who elevates him to be her husband. Furthermore, all the kings of the Third Dynasty of Ur and the Isin Dynasty impersonate him in the sacred marriage rite.[54] Finally, contrary to his central role in the literary sources related to the sacred marriage, his worship in Sumerian official cult was very limited.[55]

As P. Steinkeller has pointed out, by virtue of their assumption of the title en-Unu^{ki}-ga, "Lord of Uruk," Neo-Sumerian rulers were privileged to celebrate the sacred marriage with Inanna.[56] The Ur III kings performed the sacred marriage in Uruk, the home city of Inanna. This follows from a Šulgi hymn which describes the pilgrimage of the king to visit Inanna of Uruk, perhaps on the occasion of his coronation, and includes an elaborate love song chanted by the goddess upon seeing her royal bridegroom.[57] The Isin kings, on the other hand, who were not

---

form, whereby the king spent the night of the sacred wedding in the bed-chamber of the goddess, alone with the goddess's statue. Cf. J. Klein, "Sacred Marriage," *Anchor Bible Dictionary* (New York: Doubleday, 1992), 5:867; J. S. Cooper, "Sacred Marriage and Popular Cult in Early Mesopotamia," in *Official Cult and Popular Religion in the Ancient Near East*, ed. E. Matsushima (Heidelberg: Carl Winter, 1993), 87f.; P. Steinkeller, "On Rulers, Priests and Sacred Marriage: Tracing the Evolution of Early Sumerian Kingship," in *Priests and Officials*, 132ff.

54. Consequently, after their death all these kings impersonated the dead Dumuzi, who was believed to have descended to the netherworld, and was lamented during the month of Tammuz, in cultic funerary ceremonies. Cf. *TCL* 15, 8: 198-209; P.M. Witzel, *Tammuz Liturgien und Verwandtes* (Rome: Pontificio Istituto Biblico, 1935), 16-18; M. E. Cohen, *The Canonical Lamentations of the Ancient Near East* (Potomac, MD: CDL Press, 1988), 676ff.; Th. Jacobsen, *Harps*, 78; Sh. Shifra and J. Klein, *Anthology*, 417f.

55. For the history of Dumuzi's worship, see R. Kutscher, "The Cult of Dumuzi/Tammuz," *Bar-Ilan Studies in Assyriology Dedicated to Pinhas Artzi*, ed. J. Klein and A. Skaist (Ramat-Gan: Bar-Ilan University Press, 1990), 29-44.

56. P. Steinkeller, "On Rulers, Priests and Sacred Marriage," 130f.

57. J. Klein, *Three Šulgi Hymns*, 136ff.

always in control of Uruk, celebrated the sacred marriage in their own capital Isin with the city goddess Ninisinna, whom they identified with Inanna. From a long hymn which gives a detailed description of the sacred union between the king Iddindagan (ca. 1974-1954 B.C.E.) and Ninisina-Inanna, we learn that this ceremony took place on New Year's Day and involved a variety of ceremonies culminating in the union of the divine couple. In the course of the rite Inanna blesses the king with fertility and abundance for his land and with a long and prosperous reign.[58]

Another Isin king referred to in a fertility prayer is Išme-Dagan (ca. 1953-1935). In this text Inanna is asked to bless the stalls and sheepfolds with fertility for the sake of the king, as well as to grant him a long life. A duplicate of this prayer substitutes the name Dumuzi-Ušumgalanna for Išme-Dagan, which shows that the same hymn could be used in connection with a number of kings, each representing Dumuzi in the sacred marriage rite.[59]

According to majority opinion the sacred marriage was celebrated annually on New Year's Day, and its main purpose was to guarantee for the coming year abundance and fertility in nature as well as in human society. However, this was not thought to have been accomplished by sympathetic magic. Rather, the marriage with the goddess enabled the king—and through him the people—to establish personal and social ties to the gods, which in turn sustained and fostered fertility in the land.[60]

From this outline of the history and nature of Neo-Sumerian kingship it follows that the Ur III and Isin-Larsa kings were definitely deified in accordance with Šulgi's religious reforms. We have also seen that Šulgi did not invent the ideology of divine kingship but followed the precedent of the Old Akkadian king Naram-Sin. The motives of Naram-Sin and Šulgi for their self-deification are not clear, and different reasons have been suggested for this phenomenon. Most probably the apotheosis of these kings is connected with the formation of the empire: The constant unrest of the Sumerian cities, which had formerly been independent city-states, prompted these kings to assume divine status so that they could appoint the city rulers (ensiks) themselves, an act formerly held to be the prerogative of each city god.[61] In fact, the deification of the king not only made him overlord of the local governors, but also allowed him to usurp much of the economic power of the Sumerian temples.[62]

---

58. D. Reisman, "Iddin-Dagan's Sacred Marriage Hymn," *JCS* 25 (1973): 185-202.

59. See J. Klein, "The Sweet Chant of the Churn," in *dubsar anta-men*, 205-22.

60. J. Klein, "Sacred Marriage," 868; J. S. Cooper, "Sacred Marriage and Popular Cult," 91f.; Y. Sefati, *Love Songs in Sumerian Literature* (Ramat-Gan: Bar-Ilan University Press, 1998); P. Steinkeller, "On Rulers, Priests and Sacred Marriage," 135f.

61. C. J. Gadd, "Babylonia c. 2120-1800 B.C.," *CAH* I^3, 618f.

62. Cf. P. Michalowski, "Charisma and Control," 64ff.; P. Steinkeller, "The Administrative and Economic Organization of the Ur III State," 21ff.

From the Curse of Agade, a historiographical composition written in the Ur III period,[63] and other sources we learn that Naram-Sin, the Old Akkadian emperor, entered Mesopotamian historical tradition as a king of misfortune. Accordingly, it has been assumed that Naram-Sin's self-deification was considered by the Sumerian Nippur priesthood as an act of hubris.[64]

Consequently, the question had been raised: Why was Naram-Sin's self-deification considered to be an act of hubris, whereas Šulgi's self-deification a century and a half later was not met by any visible opposition? On the contrary, Šulgi was remembered as the third greatest royal figure of antiquity, next to Gilgameš and Sargon, so that his successors regarded him an ideal predecessor, worthy of imitation.[65] In fact, Šulgi gained a reputation as a divine king par excellence even outside of Sumerian religion, and far beyond his own age: In a first millennium "prophetic" text, he figures as a divine prophet alongside Marduk.[66]

William Hallo, in a stimulating study about Sumerian religion,[67] addresses himself to this problem. He argues that the emergence of the cult statue in Mesopotamia is to be dated to the Sargonic period. From this he concludes that the raising of the king to divine status threatened the fine balance between the secular and sacred power worked out by the Sumerians in the Early Dynastic age. Accordingly, he suggests that to restore that balance, the Sumerian religious establishment invested the great gods with royal status. To achieve this end, they changed the architecture of the temple so that it assumed the appearance of a royal palace; and for the first time they fashioned a life-size seated statue of the deity, looking to the worshipper like an enthroned king. Thus, according to

---

63. Cf. Jerrold S. Cooper, *The Curse of Agade* (Baltimore: Johns Hopkins University Press, 1983).

64. Cf. D. O. Edzard, "'Das Wort im Ekur' oder die Peripetie in 'Fluch über Akkade,'" in H. Behrens et al., eds., *Studies Sjöberg* (Philadelphia, 1989), 99-105. As a matter of fact, the only occasions in history in which Nippur did not keep its neutrality was when it participated in two revolts of Sumerian cities against Naram-Sin (Naram-Sin 2 vi 6-8; 6 vi 10′-12; cf. R. Kutscher, *The Brockmon Tablets . . . Royal Inscriptions* [Haifa: Haifa University Press, 1989], 13-14; A. Westenholz, *OSP* 2, p. 28). This may support Edzard's hypothesis that Nippur's religious establishment was sharply opposed to Naram-Sin's self-deification.

65. See J. Klein, "Šulgi and Išmedagan: Originality and Dependence in Sumerian Royal Hymnology," in *Bar-Ilan Studies in Assyriology Dedicated to Pinhas Artzi*, 65-136.

66. See R. Borger, "Gott Marduk und Gott König Šulgi als Propheten," *BiOr* 28 (1971): 1-24.

67. Cf. "Cult Statue and Divine Image: A Preliminary Study," in *Scripture in Context* II, ed. W. W. Hallo et al. (Winona Lake, IN: Eisenbrauns), 1-17; W. W. Hallo, "Texts, Statues and the Cult of the Divine King," *SVT* 40 (1988) 54-66; and idem, "Sumerian Religion," in *kinattūtu ša dārâti: Raphael Kutscher Memorial Volume* (Tel Aviv, Occasional Publications, no. 1) 1993, 15-35.

Hallo, the representation of the deity as a king is a distinctly Sumerian reaction to the Akkadian experiment with royal deification. Once divine cult statues were introduced, the religious establishment no longer felt threatened by the deification of kings.

On the basis of the above survey of Sumerian divine kingship, I would like to suggest a different solution to the above problem. We have seen that by assuming divinity, the Neo-Sumerian king rose above his people and the other city-rulers who were formerly his equals, acquiring over them absolute authority. However, vis-à-vis the gods of the pantheon, he always kept his inferior status. This inferiority is indicated by a number of mythological features which conform to a long established genuine Sumerian tradition. First, by adopting a pair of major deities as his "divine parents," the king demonstrates his inferiority and subordination to the realm of the gods, showing his dependence on their patronage. A similar attitude seems to be expressed by impersonating Dumuzi in the sacred marriage rite. As a Dumuzi figure, the king is the junior husband of Inanna, dependent on the love and blessing of the great goddess and ardently praying for her favors. The same attitude was demonstrated by installing the king's images in the gods' shrines, in a standing posture before their seated figures.[68]

Thus, while the Neo-Sumerian kings were considered as divinities, objects of worship, in the eyes of their human subjects, they saw themselves as semi-divine, inferior, beings vis-à-vis the genuine gods of the pantheon. In this way, it seems to me, they were able to keep the delicate balance between the political and religious power in their kingdom.

68. Cf. n. 27 above.

7

The Royal Cult in Ḫatti

HARRY A. HOFFNER

There are two possible interpretations of the phrase "royal cult": first, worship performed by or under the aegis of the king for the gods of his realm; and secondly, the organized worship of the king himself as a divine being. In regard to the first sense of the term "royal cult" we know next to nothing about the specific forms of any Hittite worship of the gods other than the official royally sanctioned and supported state cult.

The king was certainly the most important human figure in ancient Ḫatti, both as seen from textual evidence and from the monumental art. He occupied a central position in every sphere of public life, not the least in the official state cult, where he presided at the major festivals. It has been often noted that the king's presence at major religious festivals took precedence even over his duties as a battlefield commander, as witnessed by reports in the annals of king Muršili II that the king left the battlefield at crucial moments in order to return to Ḫattuša to preside over a festival.[1]

The King on Relief Scenes of Worship

Yazılıkaya

The importance of the king in the state cult is graphically illustrated by the reliefs in Chamber A of the chief Hittite outdoor sanctuary

1. See for example passages translated into German in A. Götze, *Die Annalen des Muršiliš* (Leipzig: J. C. Hinrichs, 1933), 139, 163, 189-91. Spanish translations in Alberto Bernabé and Juan Antonio Álvarez-Pedrosa, *Historia y Leyes de Los Hititas: Textos del Reino Medio y del Imperio Nuevo* (Madrid: Akal, 2000), 138-39, 145, 152-53. On the impossibility of delegating this duty to a subordinate see O. R. Gurney, *The Hittites* (New York: Penguin Books, 1990), 53. T. R. Bryce, *Life and Society in the Hittite World* (Oxford: Oxford University Press, 2002), 30-31, is wrong to assume a routine delegation of this duty, although as Gurney says, it was done in extreme emergencies and was admitted as a sin.

Yazılıkaya.[2] The reliefs show two long lines of gods and goddesses that converge on a central point, where the chief god, Teššub, and the chief goddess, Ḫebat, face each other. On a rock face exactly opposite to this central point the sculptor has carved the likeness of the only human depicted in this divine scene. The figure is that of King Tudḫaliya IV (c. 1237-1209 B.C.[3]), clothed in the garb of the sun-god, and standing on two mountain peaks.

The symmetry of the scene is remarkable: the human king, Tudḫaliya, confronts the divine king, Teššub, and his queen. The two male figures share significant features. Although the king is a human, like Teššub he bears iconography of deity. He is dressed exactly like the sun-god, who appears in the left-hand procession in the same chamber. As Teššub stands upon two deified mountains, so Tudḫaliya stands upon two mountain peaks, although unlike Teššub's mountains these are not portrayed anthropomorphically. As Teššub is king of the assemblage of deities represented on the walls of the chamber, so Tudḫaliya is king of the human worshippers who assembled in the central area of the chamber.

Alaca Höyük

At Alaca an unidentified king stands before an offering table, with the queen standing behind him.[4] Across the offering table is a pedestal on top of which is a standing bull figure, representing a storm-god. The king is dressed like the priests who appear on the same reliefs. He wears an ankle-length robe with sleeves, a skull-cap, and earrings.[5] Unlike them he also carries an inverted crook (Hittite *kalmuš*)[6] in his right hand. He holds

2. K. Bittel, *Die Hethiter: Die Kunst Anatoliens vom Ende des 3. bis zum Anfang des 1. Jahrtausends vor Christus* (Munich: C. H. Beck, 1976), figs. 232-34, 249.

3. It is presently impossible to establish an absolute chronology for the history of the Hittites. For the sake of convenience I have keyed the few references to dates in this essay to the chronological chart in the newly published history of the Hittites by Trevor R. Bryce, *The Kingdom of the Hittites* (Oxford: Clarendon Press, 1998), xiii-xiv. See his discussion of the subject on pp. 408-15.

4. K. Bittel, *Die Hethiter*, fig. 214.

5. On Hittite dress, see A. Goetze, "Hittite Dress," in *Corolla linguistica: Festschrift F. Sommer*, ed. H. Krahe (Heidelberg: Carl Winter, 1955), 48-62; and J. V. Canby, "Jewelry and Personal Arts in Anatolia," in *Civilizations of the Ancient Near East*, ed. J. Sasson et al. (New York: Scribners, 1995), 1673-84. On the priestly dress of the Hittite king, see S. Alp, "La désignation de lituus en hittite," *JCS* 1 (1947): 164-75; A. Goetze, "The Priestly Dress of the Hittite King," *JCS* 1 (1947): 176-85; and Th. P. J. van den Hout, review of P. J. Neve, *Ḫattuša—Stadt der Götter und Tempel* (Mainz: Philipp von Zabern, 1992), *BiOr* 52 (1995): 545-73.

6. On the Hittite *kalmuš* see S. Alp, "La désignation," and "GIŠ*kalmuš* 'Lituus' und ḪUB.BI 'Earring' in the Hittite Texts," *Belleten* 46 (1948): 320-24. For more recent textual documentation see J. Puhvel, *Hittite Etymological Dictionary*, vol. 4: K (Berlin: Mouton de

up his left hand in a gesture of greeting and veneration. The queen and priests hold up their right hands in the same gesture.[7]

Fraktin, Eflatun Pinar, Sirkeli

At Fraktin Ḫattušili III worships a god, while his queen Puduḫepa worships a goddess.[8] Both pour libations into a container sitting on the ground. At Sirkeli, on the River Ceyhan, King Muwatalli II is depicted in relief.[9] He is attired in the same priestly garb worn by the unnamed king at Alaca and Tudḫaliya IV at Yazılıkaya. No worshipped deity is shown on the relief unless that deity is the king himself.[10]

The King as Worshipper and Leader of Worship

We have just seen a few examples of graphic representations of the Hittite king at worship. But how were the deities worshipped by the king visually represented?

The Tangible Representation of the Deity

We have five sources of information about Hittite visual images of deities: rock reliefs, sculptured blocks (i.e., orthostats), relief vases, seal impres-

---

Gruyter, 1997), s. v. *kalmuš*; Harry A. Hoffner, Jr., "Thoughts on a New Volume of a Hittite Dictionary" *Journal of the American Oriental Society* 120 (2000): 70; and Gary M. Beckman, "'My Sun-God': Reflections of Mesopotamian Conceptions of Kingship among the Hittites," in *Ideologies as Intercultural Phenomena: Proceedings of the Third Annual Symposium of the Assyrian and Babylonian Intellectual Heritage Project held in Chicago, USA, October 27-31, 2000,* ed. A. Panaino and G. Pettinato, Melammu Symposia III (Milan: Università de Bologna & IsIAO, 2002), 42.

7. K. Bittel, *Die Hethiter*, figs. 212 and 214. Because others besides the king perform this gesture, it should not be equated with the important delegating-authorizing hand gesture that the king used in the cult (*QĀTAM dāi*), on which see David P. Wright, "The Gesture of Hand Placement in the Hebrew Bible and in Hittite Literature" *Journal of the American Oriental Society* 106 (1986): 433-46; Stefano de Martino and Fiorella Imparati, "La 'mano' nelle più significative espressioni idiomatiche ittite," in *do-ra-qe pe-re: Studi in memoria di Adriana Quattordio Moreschini*, ed. L. Agostiniani, M. G. Arcamone, O. Carruba, F. Imparati, and R. Rizza, (Pisa: Istituti editoriali e poligrafici internazionali, 1998), 175-85; Harry A. Hoffner, Jr., "Ancient Israel's Literary Heritage Compared with Hittite Textual Data," in *The Future of Biblical Archaeology: Reassessing Methodologies and Assumptions*, ed. James K. Hoffmeier and Alan R. Millard (Grand Rapids, MI: Eerdmans, 2004), 188-89.

8. K. Bittel, *Die Hethiter*, figs. 196 and 198.

9. K. Bittel, *Die Hethiter*, fig. 197.

10. K. Bittel, *Die Hethiter*, fig. 195.

sions showing worship, and verbal descriptions of cult images in cuneiform texts. These sources reveal various forms of divine representation.

Simple Stela

Judging from cult inventory texts from the reign of Tudḫaliya IV which record the replacing of earlier cult images by forms more acceptable to the current period, the earliest cult images were frequently simple stelae, perhaps with images carved in low relief and accompanied by a hieroglyphic inscription. These stelae were called *ḫuwaši*-stones, the Sumerogram for which was ZI.KIN. It is obvious that just such a representation of the state deities is found in the sanctuary of Yazılıkaya. And indeed some scholars have considered the entire relief-covered galleries of Yazılıkaya to be such a *ḫuwaši*.[11] Yet most examples of *ḫuwaši*-stones were probably free-standing stelae with bas reliefs, not huge galleries of reliefs on living rock walls. Thus, according to the texts, a *ḫuwaši* can be knocked over and even stolen.[12]

Theriomorphic Images

Cult inventories from Tudḫaliya's time record how these stelae were replaced or supplemented by images in the round made in precious metals.[13] Scenes on the orthostats at Alaca show the worshipped deity as a bull.[14] And although this bull figure is part of a rock relief or *ḫuwaši*, it imitated actual bull statuettes in the round used as cult images.

In a worship scene on the Old Hittite relief vase from Inandiktepe a deity portrayed as a bull standing on a pedestal (no. 18) receives worship from a male figure (no. 22) facing him and holding an elevated cup behind two other smaller persons who are in the act of killing a trussed-up kneeling bull.[15] The larger man holds the elevated cup in his right

11. See, for example, C. W. Carter, "Hittite Cult Inventories," Ph.D. diss., University of Chicago, 1962.

12. For knocked-over *ḫuwaši*'s see *CHD* L-N, 18. For possible stealing of a *ḫuwaši* see H. A. Hoffner, Jr., *The Laws of the Hittites: A Critical Edition* (Leiden: E. J. Brill, 1997), 116-17, 204-5. For a comprehensive examination of the evidence in cult inventories see Joost Hazenbos, *The Organization of the Anatolian Local Cults during the 13th Century BC* (Leiden: E. J. Brill, 2002), 174-75.

13. See Hazenbos, *Organization*, 173-90.

14. K. Bittel, *Die Hethiter*, fig. 214.

15. T. Özgüç, *Inandiktepe: An Important Cult Center in the Old Hittite Period* (Ankara: Türk Tarih Kurumu Basımevi, 1988), fold-out fig. 64 on p. 175; plt. H, panel 1.

hand and holds his left hand up in the same gesture of greeting and veneration used by the king on rock reliefs.

Cult inventories often mention drinking vessels as cult objects.[16] Recovered examples (*bibrū* from the Schimmel Collection) match the textual descriptions in the cult inventories.[17] A verbal description of a very similar cult image is found in a cult inventory text: "(Image of) the Storm-God of the (Royal) House: a silver bull's neck, (the animal shown) with forequarters, kneeling. His two festivals are in autumn and spring."[18]

Anthropomorphic Statues

Of the fully anthropomorphic statuettes made of gold described in cult inventories only a few small examples have been recovered.[19]

The King's Dress at Worship

The king's dress at worship is not uniform. On the reliefs at Alaca and Yazılıkaya it is an ankle-length priestly robe and skull-cap. At Fraktin it is a short kilt, dagger, and conical horned hat. In the cuneiform texts describing festivals the king's dress is not described. A term that apparently covers both his dress and his carried implements is the Hittite word *aniyatta*, sometimes translated "regalia." After the king leaves his palace, he proceeds immediately to the wash house (É DU_{10}.ÚS.SA), where he dons his *aniyatta* and his gold earrings, and proceeds from there to the place of worship.[20] But at times during the description of the festival itself there is mention of some item of his dress or equipment, such as his crook (*kalmuš*), which he carries in an inverted position, in contrast to deities, who, when they are shown with the crook, carry it with the curved end upward.[21] If this is a consistent contrast, it might mark the king as holder of *delegated* authority possessed *inherently* by the gods.

The King as High Priest

Building and Furnishing Temples

All temples were constructed under the direction of the king. A foundation ritual dating from the Old Kingdom shows how intertwined were

16. See Hazenbos, *Organization*, 173-74.
17. The *bibrū* are pictured in K. Bittel, *Die Hethiter*, figs. 169 and 178.
18. See *KUB* 38.2 ii 14-16.
19. K. Bittel, *Die Hethiter*, figs. 167-68 and 170-73.
20. For example, in *KUB* 2.13 i 1-4.
21. Bittel, figures 194 and 198.

the ideology of kingship and the ability to construct temples possessing the necessary numinous qualities.[22]

Maintaining Worship Places

Not all worship sites were temples in the strict sense of that word. Sacred springs were often furnished with reliefs and free-standing stelae, which had to be maintained. Identified sites of such sacred spring complexes are at Eflâtun Pınar,[23] and in Ḫattuša itself both at Temple 1 in the Lower City[24] and on the so-called Southern Citadel.[25]

In his instructions to the provincial governors the king explicitly laid this responsibility upon them, adding that written records should be kept of the current condition and staff of all worship sites in the governor's district.[26] Although the instructions for the governors date from as early as the Middle Hittite period (c. 1400-1350 B.C.), the first examples we possess of such records—the so-called "cult inventories"[27]—date from the end of the New Kingdom (c. 1260-1190 B.C.). They tell the names of deities worshipped, whether or not there was a temple building, the number and rank of the priestly staff, and what festivals were celebrated there in the course of a year.

Should any misfortune befall the royal family or the realm as a whole, oracular inquiries were instituted to determine the cause of divine anger.[28] Often the causes uncovered concerned failures in the cult: the neglect of a festival or damage done to a cult image. The king would immediately authorize steps to correct the abuse. But sometimes there was no immediate favorable response from the gods. During a plague that ravaged Ḫatti for twenty years, king Muršili II (c. 1321-1295 B.C.) instituted repeated oracular inquiries and responded to the results of

---

22. *KUB* 29.1 and duplicates (*CTH* 414), translated into English by A. Goetze in *ANET*, 357-58. See also F. Starke, "Halmašuit im Anitta-Texte und die hethitische Ideologie vom Königtum," *ZA* 69 (1979): 47-120; and M. Marazzi, "'Costruiamo la reggia, fondiamo la regalità': Note intorno ad un rituale antico-ittita (CTH 414)," *VO* 5 (1982): 117-69.

23. J. Börker-Klähn and Ch. Börker, "Eflatun Pinar. Zu Rekonstruktion, Deutung und Datierung," in *Jahrbuch des Deutschen Archäologischen Instituts* 90 (1975): 1-41; and K. Bittel, *Die Hethiter*, 222, fig. 257.

24. P. Neve, *Ḫattuša—Stadt der Götter und Tempel: Neue Ausgrabungen in der Hauptstadt der Hethiter* (Mainz: Philipp von Zabern, 1992), 79-80, Abb. 224-25.

25. P. Neve, *Ḫattuša*, 68-69, Abb. 194, 197-98.

26. See English translation of instructions to the governors about caring for such stelae and sacred springs in *ANET*, 210-11, and in *The Context of Scripture: Canonical Compositions, Monumental Inscriptions and Archival Documents from the Biblical World*, vol. 1, ed. W. W. Hallo and K. L. Younger (Leiden: E. J. Brill, 1997), 224, §§32-34.

27. C. W. Carter, "Cult Inventories."

28. See English translations in W. W. Hallo and K. L. Younger, eds., *Context*, 204-7.

each, without any relief. His anguish and confusion are evident in the so-called "plague prayers" he composed.[29]

Daily Worship

That the king worshipped the gods daily by means of formal prayers is shown by the colophon of the royal prayer texts, one of which reads as follows: "A scribe will speak this tablet daily to the deity and praise the deity."[30] That the daily prayer was actually spoken aloud by a scribe does not eliminate the fact that *what* was read were the king's own words. This daily worship of the deities took place in the privacy of the temple cella, where the statue of the deity stood.

The Festivals

General Introduction

In virtually all festival texts the king (and sometimes the queen) played a central role in the rituals. It was therefore extremely important that he be available. For this reason even in the midst of vital military campaigns the king would leave the scene of battle to return to the homeland for the celebration of major festivals.[31]Yet this didn't always mean returning to the capital city. For in the annals of Muršili II the king explains how he celebrated the "yearly festival" after he had finished the year's campaigning and entered winter quarters near the River Aštarpa.[32] However, there are some festival texts in which the chief celebrant is neither king nor queen, but a prince (DUMU LUGAL) or the high priestess referred to with the Sumerogram NIN.DINGIR.

Both king and people were very proud of the festivals by which they entertained and appeased their deities. In their daily prayer to the god Telipinu, the king and queen say: "You, Telipinu, are a noble god. Your worship is firmly established in the Ḫatti land. In no other land is it so (firmly established). Festivals and sacrifices, pure and holy, are presented

29. Historical treatment most recently in T. R. Bryce, *Kingdom*, 223-25. See translation by G. Beckman in W. W. Hallo and K. L. Younger, eds., *Context*, 156-60.

30. *KUB* 24.1 i 1-2, ed. O. R. Gurney, "Hittite Prayers of Mursili II," *AAA* 27 (1940): 3-163. Translation in Itamar Singer, *Hittite Prayers* (Atlanta: Society of Biblical Literature, 2002), 54.

31. See above in note 1.

32. *KBo* 3.4 ii 47-49 (decennial annals), edited in Götze, *Annalen*, 60.

to you in the Ḫatti land. . . . Lofty temples adorned with silver and gold are yours in the Ḫatti land. . . . Cups, rhyta, silver, gold, and precious stones are yours in the Ḫatti land. . . . Festivals too—the monthly festival, the festivals of the cycle of the year, ceremonies of winter, spring, and autumn . . . they celebrate for you in the Ḫatti land."[33] The passage just quoted mentions a monthly festival, most likely either at full or new moon, and seasonal ones scattered throughout the year. Some scholars maintain that the Hittites only distinguished three seasons: spring, autumn, and winter, with what we call summer consisting of the end of Hittite "spring" and the beginning of their "autumn." In this case, the above text indicates no season in which there was no festival. We have no text that contains a full and official cult calendar for the capital city.

Festivals were of varying length. For some that length is not stated in the preserved parts of the text. The longest known festival was the spring AN.TAḪ.ŠUM festival, which lasted for 38 days.[34]

The Names of the Festivals

The cuneiform texts speak of a "monthly festival" (Sumerian EZEN_4.ITU), a "yearly festival" (EZEN_4 MU-*TI*) and festivals of autumn and spring. The names of specific festivals often contain words for seasons of the year, meteorological phenomena such as rain, thunder, familiar agricultural activities such as plowing, reaping, cutting grapes, tools like the sickle, or harvested plants.[35]

The Seasonal Festivals

The most important spring festival celebrated the appearance of the AN.TAḪ.ŠUM plant. The most important autumn festival was that named the "Festival of Haste" (EZEN_4 *nuntarriyašḫaš*). Colophons tell us

33. *KUB* 24.1 i 18-27, ii 1-6. Translation adapted from A. Goetze, "Hittite Prayers," in *ANET*, 396-97. See also translation in Singer, *Hittite Prayers*, 54-55.

34. H. G. Güterbock, *Perspectives on Hittite Civilization: Selected Writings*, ed. H. A. Hoffner, Jr. (Chicago: Oriental Institute, 1997), 89.

35. Although eighty different names of festivals are listed in H. A. Hoffner, Jr., *An English-Hittite Glossary* (Paris: Klincksieck, 1967), 39-41, many may be alternate names for the same festival, and not all were royal or national festivals requiring the king's presence. See also H. G. Güterbock, "Some Aspects of Hittite Festivals," in *Comptes rendus de la 17e Rencontre Assyriologique Internationale* (Brussels: Comité Belge de Recherches en Mésopotamie, 1969), 175-80, reprinted in *Perspectives*, 87-90, esp. 88. A list of festival names occurring in cult inventories can be found in Hazenbos, *Organization*, 54-55.

this was celebrated "when the king returns from a (summer-long) campaign." During this festival the king was required to travel from one cult center to another over a prescribed route.[36] At each stop he presided over the worship of the local deities. It is called "the festival of haste" because the king's travel needed to be rapid in order to cover the entire route within the prescribed period.

Activities at the Festivals

What went on during a typical Hittite festival? And in particular what did the king do? First, we must understand that his roles as *builder* of the temple, *donor* of its most valuable furnishings,[37] and *observer* and *supervisor* of the rites were of equal importance to his function as an *active participant*. In fact, through the gesture of extending his hand toward another celebrant, the king figuratively performed many more of the concrete actions of worship than would appear at first glance.[38] From this point of view we must also include among his worshipping actions those performed by his subordinates. Prominent among these actions were those intended to *entertain* the deities.[39]

The Priests' and Performers' Actions: Entertaining the God

Such entertainment had many forms. First, the god's image was placed on a litter and brought out of his temple to a pleasant location in the countryside just outside the city. In that bucolic location the god was entertained. Musicians played for him.[40] We do not know the identity of

36. See discussion of the outline of activities of this festival in H. G. Güterbock, "Religion und Kultus der Hethiter," in *Neuere Hethiterforschung*, ed. G. Walser (Wiesbaden: Franz Steiner Verlag, 1964), 68-69. More recently see Ph. H. J. Houwink ten Cate, "Brief Comments on the Hittite Cult Calendar: The Main Recension of the Outline of the *nuntarrišḫaš* Festival, especially Days 8-12 and 15-22," in *Documentum Asiae Minoris Antiquae*, ed. E. Neu and Ch. Rüster (Wiesbaden: Otto Harrassowitz, 1988), 167-94; Silvin Košak, "The Hittite *nuntarrijashas*-Festival (CTH 626)," *Linguistica* 16 (1976): 55-64; M. Popko, "Ein neues Fragment des hethitischen 'nuntarijashas'-Festrituals," *AoF* 13 (1986): 219-23; and the discussion in V. Haas, *Geschichte der hethitischen Religion* (Leiden: E. J. Brill, 1994), 827-47.

37. Often from plunder taken in battle. See *KBo* 10.2 i 11-14, 37-40, ed. F. Imparati and Cl. Saporetti, "L'autobiografia di Hattusili I," *SCO* 14 (1965): 40-85; H. C. Melchert, "The Acts of Hattušili I," *JNES* 37 (1978): 1-22.

38. On the extended-hand gesture in both Hittite (*kešširan dāi-*) and Israelite (*sāmakh yadô*) ritual, see literature cited above in footnote 7.

39. The Hittite word for this was *tuškaratt-*, "entertainment, diversion."

40. See St. de Martino, "Music, Dance, and Processions in Hittite Anatolia," in *Civiliza-*

all terms for musical instruments used in the festivals. But the reliefs and relief vases show stringed instruments such as lyres, drums, tambourines, and flutes.[41] In most cases we can match these with words from the texts. Music soothed and pleased the gods.

But there were also contests of various types: athletic and otherwise.[42] The cult inventories mention wrestling, boxing, stone-throwing, foot-racing, and chariot racing. The Alaca reliefs show acrobatics and sword-swallowing,[43] which now can also be attested from newly published text fragments.[44]

There was also cult drama: mock battles in which one group called the "men of Maša," wielding "weapons of reed," fought against another group called the "Men of Ḫatti," who wielded weapons of bronze.[45] Of course, the "Men of Ḫatti" won! Another drama in the KI.LAM festival involved men from the city Tišaruliya.[46] The opening words of the Hittite myth of the great serpent identify the story as "the cult legend of the *Purulli*-Festival."[47] This would seem to indicate that the serpent story was actually acted out during the *Purulli*-Festival. One scholar has recently sought to identify characters in the myth with personages mentioned in the cult texts describing a festival for the Ḫattian goddess Tetešḫawi.[48] And other scholars believe that the mortal Ḫupašiya, who is the goddess

---

tions of the Ancient Near East, 2661-70; "Musik. A. III. Bei den Hethitern," *RlA* 8 (1997): 483-88; H. M. Kümmel, "Gesang und Gesanglosigkeit in der hethitischen Kultmusik," in *Festschrift Heinrich Otten*, ed. E. Neu and Ch. Rüster (Wiesbaden: Otto Harrassowitz, 1973), 169-78. See the depiction in K. Bittel, *Die Hethiter*, fig. 219.

41. For such musical instruments in art see Bittel, *Die Hethiter*, figures 141, 143, and 219.

42. On these contests, see C. W. Carter, "Athletic Contests in Hittite Religious Festivals," *JNES* 47 (1988): 185-87; H. Ehelolf, "Wettlauf und szenisches Spiel im hethitischen Ritual," *SPAW* (1925): 267-72; V. Haas, "Kompositbogen und Bogenschiessen als Wettkampf im Alten Orient," *Nikephoros* 2 (1989): 27-41; J. Puhvel, "Hittite Athletics as Prefigurations of Ancient Greek Games," in *The Archaeology of the Olympics*, ed. W. Raschke (Madison, WI: University of Wisconsin Press, 1988); and St. de Martino, "Music," 2661-70.

43. K. Bittel, *Die Hethiter*, 193, fig. 218.

44. See O. R. Gurney, "The Ladder-Men at Alaca Höyük," *AnSt* 44 (1994): 219-20; A. Ünal, "Boğazköy Kılıcıcın Üzerindeki Akadca Adak Yazısı Hakkında Yeni Gözlemler," in *Nimet Özgüç'e armağan: Aspects of Art and Iconography: Anatolia and its Neighbors*, ed. M. Mellink et al. (Ankara: Türk Tarih Kurumu Basımevi, 1993), 727-30.

45. See H. Ehelolf, "Wettlauf," 267-72.

46. See Th. P. J. van den Hout, "A Tale of Tissaruli(ya): A Dramatic Interlude in the Hittite KI.LAM Festival?" *JNES* 50 (1991): 193-202.

47. For recent translations, see W. W. Hallo and K. L. Younger, eds., *Context*, 150-51, and H. A. Hoffner, Jr., *Hittite Myths* (Atlanta: Scholars Press, second ed. 1998), 10-14. The text was edited by G. Beckman, "The Anatolian Myth of Illuyanka," *JANES* 14 (1982): 11-25.

48. See F. Pecchioli Daddi, "Aspects du culte de la divinité hattie Teteshapi," *Hethitica* 8 (1987): 361-80; F. Pecchioli Daddi and A. M. Polvani, *La mitologia ittita* (Brescia: Paideia Editrice, 1990), 39-55.

Inara's helper and lover in the story, represents the Hittite king.[49] There was even a role for ecstatic prophets piercing themselves in the course of festivals.[50]

Nor were the ceremonies of Hittite festivals devoid of comic elements. In the monthly festival a cook pours hot coals over the head of the chief of the performers.[51] And in another festival fragment, perhaps belonging to the same festival, the chief of the performers hits the cook on the head three times with a stick.[52] As the saying goes: "What goes around, comes around!" The king observed all these activities, and as the authorizing and supervising observer, he "offered" this entertainment to the god or gods being worshipped.

The King's Actions

But in addition to his passive participation in the role of donor, supervisor, and observer, the king often took an active part. The festival texts mention several specific actions.

When sacrificial bread is to be offered to the deity, a temple official (often the cup-bearer or the "table man") hands a representative loaf to the king, who breaks it and returns it. The official then places it on the king's behalf on the offering table. Although many times the libating is done by priests, there are occasions in the ritual when the king himself was expected to pour a libation. Often it is into a *ḫuppar*-vessel sitting on the ground. Once we are informed that the king poured libations thirteen times out of a window for a group of deities.[53] When the texts occasionally say that the king "offers" (*šipanti*) an animal sacrifice, it does not mean that he physically cuts the animal's throat. The immediate context makes it clear that he merely makes a gesture to authorize its killing. For it is then recorded that others drive the sheep out and cut its throat.[54]

At various points in the course of the festival rituals the king is given a wash bowl, washes his hands, and dries them on a linen towel.[55] This

---

49. See the summary of this view in F. Pecchioli Daddi and A. M. Polvani, *La mitologia*, 39-48.

50. Which reminds one of the description in the Hebrew Bible of such self-piercing by Canaanite cult practitioners: "Then they cried aloud and, as was their custom, they cut themselves with swords and lances until the blood gushed out over them" (1 Kings 18:28).

51. *KUB* 60.21:6-7 (*CTH* 591).

52. *KUB* 20.11 ii 12-13.

53. LUGAL-*uš⸗kan* ^{GIŠ}AB-*az arḫa kūš⸗pat* DINGIR.MEŠ-*aš* 13-ŠU *šipanti*, *KUB* 2.13 i 47-48.

54. *n⸗ašta* LUGAL-*uš* 1 UDU ^{d}*Šiwatti* ^{d}*Kuwanšaya šipanti n⸗ašta* 1 UDU *parā pennianzi n⸗an ḫattanzi*, *KUB* 2.13 ii 53-56.

55. ^{LÚ}ḪÚB *akugallit* KÙ.BABBAR *wātar pedāi* LUGAL-*uš⸗za QĀTI–ŠU ārri* GAL DUMU É.GAL LUGAL-*i* GAD-*an pāi* LUGAL-*uš⸗za QĀTI–ŠU ānši*, *KUB* 2.13 i 8-11.

action occurs at "seams" or boundaries in the ritual action, the washing being a necessary accompaniment of the passing from one phase to the next. It is ceremonial punctuation.

At other points in the ritual the king performs a gesture with his hand. Its literal translation is "the king places his hand." David Wright has compared this gesture to the expression *samakh yadô* in the Hebrew Bible.[56] It betokens the king's authorizing a subordinate to perform an act on his behalf. Usually he extends his hand and actually lays it on some object that has been held out to him. But sometimes the text indicates he does it "from a distance" (*tuwaz*).

Although this action is performed in the festivals by others beside the king,[57] nevertheless occasionally it is said that the king makes a signal with his eyes, to indicate that another person should perform a required action.[58] It is undoubtedly a gesture performed by a superior to his or her servants who act on his/her authority.

At strategic points in the proceedings the king (and sometimes also the queen) "drank" the deity. A vigorous dispute still exists between those who believe this means that he drank *to* (or *in honor of*) the deity and those who believe he actually imbibed the deity symbolically in the beverage consumed from the cup of the deity.[59] Since to take sides here and base my observations on only one opinion would make my summary less representative, I shall draw only those inferences that are possible from either interpretation. It has been generally ignored that, even if the drinking does not symbolize a royal imbibing of the deity's essence, no evidence suggests that anyone other than the king and queen did this. It was therefore more than a simple act of honoring the deity. It was an act appropriate only for the royal couple.

The act of *proskynesis* is perhaps the most typical gesture of worship in all religions. The Hittite king performs it regularly in festival descrip-

---

56. See above in footnote 7.

57. The GAL *MEŠEDI* signals with his eyes to an army commander in the festival *VS* 28.29 i 5.

58. LUGAL-*uš* IGI.ḪI.A-*it iyazi* $^{\text{LÚ.MEŠ}}$ŠU.I=*kan daganzipuš šanḫanzi*, "The king makes (a signal) with (his) eyes, and the sweepers sweep the floors," *KBo* 4.9 vi 14-15. This reminds one of Psalm 32:8, where "my eye is upon you" is in strophic parallelism with "and show you which way to go" (so the Jewish Publication Society's translation of the Tanakh). Such a signal would only work if the eyes of the other officials were always on the king's face during the ceremony. Cf. also *IBoT* 3.29:8-9, where the king signals with his eyes to the cupbearer.

59. See H. G. Güterbock, "To Drink a God," in *XXXIVème Rencontre Assyriologique Internationale* (Istanbul: Türk Tarih Kurumu, 1998), 121-29; A. Kammenhuber, "Heth. *hassus* 2-*e ekuzi* 'der König trinkt zwei,'" *SMEA* 14 (1971): 143-59; H. C. Melchert, "'God-Drinking': A Syntactic Transformation in Hittite," *JIES* 9 (1981): 245-54; J. Puhvel, "On an Alleged Eucharistic Expression in Hittite Rituals," *MIO* 5 (1957): 31-33.

tions. The exact posture of Hittite *proskynesis* is still unclear. The verb most commonly used in cult contexts is *aruwai-*, whose Akkadogram is the verb *šukênu(m)*. In non-cultic contexts we find the verbs *ḫaliya-* and *genuššariya-* describing the posture of submission before the Hittite king. The last of these is obviously related to the noun *genu*, "knee" and therefore means "to kneel." A gold figurine from Alaca shows a man in kneeling position with both knees on the ground.[60]

Unlike the "drinking" of the god, *proskynesis* was not an act peculiar to the king. Texts record others performing it to deities[61] and even persons performing it to a superior.[62] But it so thoroughly epitomizes formal worship that it can be used in a passing remark in an Old Hittite historical text *pars pro toto* to express the entire complex of actions making up formal worship.[63] No scene in the graphic art of the Hittites actually shows a king in *proskynesis*. This in spite of the fact that the texts often describe the action as taking place at the altar (*ištanani*), and most scenes of the king or queen worshipping show them standing (not bowing or kneeling) before an altar table. Evidently, although the king actually did bow in the presence of the gods, it was not appropriate to show him on public reliefs in that posture.

It is also remarkable that in the detailed description of the cultic activities of the king at no time is any act of speech or singing attributed to him.

The Cult of the Deceased King

In what sense were Hittite kings conceived as divine? For many scholars the whole subject of divine kingship in Ḫatti hangs on the idiom for a royal death. The most common way of saying in Hittite that the king or queen had died was "the king became a god." And logically, if the king *became* a god at death, he was not such during his lifetime. But although

---

60. K. Bittel, *Die Hethiter*, 71, plt. 46.

61. For example, two $GUDU_{14}$-priests of the city of Arinna (*KBo* 30.101 ii 1), the Head of the Royal Guard (GAL *MEŠEDI*, *IBoT* 1.36 i 23; see H. G. Güterbock and Th. P. J. van den Hout, *The Hittite Instruction for the Royal Bodyguard* [Chicago: Oriental Institute, 1991], 6-7), and even the unnamed worshipper ("lord of the house") in *KBo* 15.33 + 35 ii 39-42.

62. Subjects before the king in Laws §55, and one ordinary artisan to his patron: *n=ašta* ^{LÚ}NAGAR *išḫamanaz katta uizzi n=aš ANA* EN É[-*TIM U*]*ŠKEN*, "Then the carpenter descends by the rope and bows to the owner of the house," *KUB* 55.28 + Bo 7740 iii 17-19.

63. LUGAL-*uš* ^{URU}*Ḫattuša* DINGIR.DIDLI-*aš aruwanzi uet*, "The king returned to Ḫattusa to worship the gods," *KBo* 22.2 rev. 13′ (Zalpa text, ed. H. Otten, *Eine althethitische Erzählung um die Stadt Zalpa* [Wiesbaden: Otto Harrassowitz, 1973], 12-13).

the implications of the phrase "he became a god" are relevant, they do not end the discussion. If already during his lifetime the Hittite king had titles, iconography, roles, and prerogatives strongly suggesting deity, in what sense did the Hittites say that at his death he "became" a god?

The usual answer is that he received a cult, not unlike the ordinary cult of the ancestors carried on by private individuals, but on a grander scale. G. Beckman sees the situation as follows: "[The king's becoming a god] is simply an extension of the Hittite view of the power of the dead within a family. Just as the ghost of an ordinary person could cause trouble for survivors if the physical remains had not been properly disposed of . . . , so too could the unhappy spirit of a departed king adversely affect the fortunes of all of Khatti."[64] The analogy is only partial, and by "extension" Beckman probably means that—unlike the deceased king—the spirits of non-royal dead are not referred to as "gods" when they are mentioned in oracle texts as the cause of trouble to their surviving descendants.

It seems to me that textual evidence suggests several ways in which the king, even during his lifetime, but carrying over to his afterlife, was more like a god than a man.

The King as "My Sun-god"

The most common title of the Hittite king, even more common statistically than the title "king," is the term that lies behind the ubiquitous Sumerogram ^{d}UTU-*ŠI*, which has long been known to represent the Akkadian word *šamšī* "my sun-god."[65] There can be no doubt that the presence of the word "my" in this title indicates its origin and significance as an expression used in *addressing* a deity. The Hittite king was, at the very least, the main channel of the people's communication with the gods, their means of access to deity *par excellence*. In the sequence of royal titles "my sun-god" takes precedence over all other titles, even over the imperial title "great king" so highly prized and jealously guarded by Hittite kings. But when this earthly demi-god was described in festival texts in the act of worshipping, he is never styled "my sun-god," only as "the king" (LUGAL).[66]

---

64. "Royal Ideology and State Administration in Hittite Anatolia," *Civilizations of the Ancient Near East*, 531.

65. On the titles of the Hittite kings, see H. Gonnet, "La titulature royale hittite au IIe millénaire avant J.-C.," *Hethitica* 3 (1979): 3-108; J. Puhvel, "Hittite Regal Titles: Hattic or Indo-European?" *JIES* 17 (1989): 351-62.

66. V. Haas, *Geschichte*, 196, claims that the royal title identifying the king as *pontifex maximus* is Tabarna. But although this title occurs in annalistic texts and judicial decrees, it is notably absent from the festival descriptions.

And although it is a little risky to assume foreign influences without direct evidence, the very fact that ancient Egypt influenced Hittite monumental sculpture in the form of the huge sphinxes flanking the city gates at Ḫattuša and Alaca Hüyük, and in the royal aedicula in the form of the winged sun-disk, we may not be far off target to look to Egypt as the ultimate source of the Hittite royal title "my sun-god."

The King as Divinely Appointed Regent

To be sure, the Hittite king was not considered an equal to the gods and goddesses of Ḫatti, but their representative. A famous Old Hittite text, often quoted in assessments of Hittite kingship, expresses this concept well: "The land belongs only to the storm-god. But he has made the Labarna (the Hittite king) his administrator. . . . Let the Labarna keep administering the whole land with his hand!"[67] And although this text derives from the Old Kingdom, the faithful re-copying of it in the archives indicates its continuing validity. In New Hittite times, when the chief storm-god was reinterpreted as Teššub, we can see this textual assertion depicted in the scene from Chamber A of Yazılıkaya. King Tudḫaliya IV strikingly resembles King Teššub, but in the final analysis he is not his equal, but his earthly representative and administrator.

The King as Highest Priest

The king represented the gods in several ways. Principally, he functioned as the people's highest priest. One of the emperor's titles was "priest of the sun-goddess of Arinna and all the gods." And in one of Muršili's plague prayers he says to the gods: "I, Muršili, great king, your priest, your servant, am making this prayer to you."[68] The importance of the priestly title in the royal family is also illustrated by the conferring of the sobriquet "the priest" upon Šuppiluliuma I's son Telipinu, who became *appanage* king of Aleppo.[69]

The King's Purity

In ancient Israel not only Yahweh but also his priests had to maintain ritual purity, and the high priest in particular. But purity was not imposed

---

67. See G. Beckman, "Royal Ideology," 530.

68. First Plague Prayer obv. 5-6, edited by A. Götze, "Die Pestgebete des Muršiliš," *KIF* 1 (1930): 161-251; English translation in W. W. Hallo and K. L. Younger, eds., *Context*, 156-57; and in Singer, *Hittite Prayers*, 61.

69. See T. R. Bryce, "The Role of Telipinu, the Priest, in the Hittite Kingdom," *Hethitica* 11 (1991): 5-18, and *Kingdom*, 203-4.

on the king. In Ḫatti too priests maintained purity *while on duty* lest they defile the god they served. But the king was required to remain pure *at all times*. As the purity of the gods was jealously guarded, and those who violated it were severely punished, so also was the purity of the king's person. An entire text, quite similar in tone to one dealing with the purity of the gods,[70] deals with the protection of the king's purity.[71] Kitchen personnel who prepared the king's food had to swear each month that they had not given him impure food. The king's shoemakers were sworn to use only ox hides from the royal kitchen, taken from healthy animals slaughtered according to the rules of purity. The manufacturers of the king's chariot were sworn to use hides derived from the royal kitchen. The dispensers of drinking water to the king were sworn to prevent its contamination by even a single human hair. That violations of purity were not simply sanitation measures[72] such as might apply to any person may be seen from the king's statement that if a chariot is discovered to have been made from impure hides, "I, the king, will send that abroad or give it to one of my servants."[73] In other words, such an "impure" chariot would do no harm to anyone whose purity standards were not as high as the Hittite emperor's. Violators of these sworn precautions were executed.

The King as Judge

In the laws and the instructions to magistrates and other high officials involved in judicial duties it is required that certain serious legal cases be referred to the king's court. But it is significant that offenses that incurred impurity (such as the offense of *ḫurkel*[74]) were not referred to the king.[75]

---

70. *CTH* 264, edited by A. Süel, *Hitit kaynaklarında tapınak görevlileri ile ilgili bir direktif metni* (Ankara: Ankara Üniversitesi Dil ve Tarih-Coğrafya Fakültesi, 1985); English translations in *ANET*, 207-10, and in W. W. Hallo and K. L. Younger, eds., *Context*, 217-21.

71. *CTH* 265, edited by J. Friedrich, "Reinheitsvorschriften für den hethitischen König," in *Altorientalische Studien Bruno Meissner zum 60. Geburtstag gewidmet von Freunden, Kollegen und Schülern* (Leipzig: Otto Harrassowitz, 1928), 46-58; English translation in *ANET*, 207.

72. A. Ünal, "Ritual Purity versus Physical Impurity in Hittite Anatolia: Public Health and Structures for Sanitation According to Cuneiform Texts and Archaeological Remains," in *Essays on Anatolian Archaeology*, ed. T. Mikasa (Wiesbaden: Otto Harrassowitz, 1993), 119-39, tries to make a distinction between precautions against ritual impurity and public sanitation measures. But he does not apply that distinction to the measures taken to guard the king's sanctity.

73. See translation of the Instructions for Palace Personnel (*KUB* 13.3) in *ANET*, 207.

74. On the nature of this offence, see H. A. Hoffner, Jr., "Incest, Sodomy and Bestiality in the Ancient Near East," in *Orient and Occident. Essays Presented to Cyrus H. Gordon on the Occasion of his Sixty-fifth Birthday*, ed. H. A. Hoffner, Jr. (Neukirchen-Vluyn: Neukirchener Verlag, 1973), 81-90; "Legal and Social Institutions of Hittite Anatolia," in *Civilizations of the Ancient Near East*, 555-70.

75. Law §187. The Hittite Laws have been edited by H. A. Hoffner, *Laws of the Hittites*.

The King as Superhuman

It was believed that the gods had endowed the king with physical qualities far superior to those of ordinary mortals. Thus, in an incantation we read of him: "His body is new; his breast is new; his [head] is new. His [teeth] are those of a lion. [His] eyes are those of an eagle, so that he sees like an eagle."[76] The king's powers included extraordinary ability to judge difficult legal cases, power to intimidate and defeat his enemies on the battlefield, and protection by the gods against all attacks, whether by arms or by sorcery. A relief in Chamber B of Yazılıkaya shows the king in the protective embrace of his protective deity.[77] The same scene appears on some royal seals.[78]

Also reflecting the enormous gulf that separated an ordinary person from the king are the words of King Ḫattušili III in his famous "Apology."[79] There the king uses a special term that had come into general usage in the royal family only since his father Muršili II's reign, *parā ḫandandatar*. This term, which means something like "divine power" or "divine protection," bespeaks the numinous character of quasi-divinity that the Hittite kings in the Empire period shared only with the gods. The gods showed their *parā ḫandandatar* in spectacular displays of raw power, such as when the storm-god hurled his thunder-bolt at Muršili II's enemy, Uḫḫa-muwa, King of Arzawa, or when Šauška of Šamuḫa defeated emperor Muršili III (Urḫi-Teššub) at the hands of her favorite, Prince Ḫattušili. But Ḫattušili also boasts of himself: "Šauška, my lady, seized me by the hand and showed her *parā ḫandandatar* to me," and "because I was a man endowed with *parā ḫandandatar*, and because I walked before the gods in *parā ḫandandatar*, at no time did I ever commit any evil deed (characteristic) of mortals."[80] And although the sacred per-

---

English translations include *ANET*, 188-97, and H. A. Hoffner, Jr., "The Hittite Laws," in M. T. Roth, *Law Collections from Mesopotamia and Asia Minor* (Atlanta: Scholars Press, second ed. 1997), 211-47.

76. See *KBo* 21.22:27-28 and its discussion in A. Archi, "Auguri per il Labarna," in *Studia Mediterranea Piero Meriggi dicata*, ed. O. Carruba (Pavia: Aurora Edizioni, 1979), 27-52.

77. K. Bittel, *Die Hethiter*, fig. 253.

78. H. Gonnet, *Catalogue des documents royaux hittites du IIe millénaire avant J.-C.* (Paris: Éditions du Centre de la Recherche Scientifique, 1975).

79. Edited by H. Otten, *Die Apologie Hattusili III.: Das Bild der Überlieferung* (Wiesbaden: Otto Harrassowitz, 1981); new English translation by Th. P. J. van den Hout in W. W. Hallo and K. L. Younger, eds., *Context*, 199-204. See also the section dealing with this text in H. A. Hoffner, Jr., "Histories and Historians of the Ancient Near East: The Hittites," *Or* 49 (1980): 283-332.

80. Apology i 46-48, ed. H. Otten, *Apologie*—see preceding note; another English translation is by E. H. Sturtevant and G. Bechtel, *A Hittite Chrestomathy* (Philadelphia: Linguistic Society of America, 1935), 64-83.

son of the king made it necessary for him to be somewhat isolated from the general public, he could and did appear in public on solemn occasions. In this respect he was treated just like the cult images of the gods: they were kept in the privacy of the temple cellas, but brought out for public view at the great festivals.

The King's Afterlife

What Hittite textual evidence we have for the afterlife of mortals suggests a somewhat gloomy existence.[81] And it appears that this kind of afterlife was likely for non-royal persons, the rich as well as the poor. In the royal funerary rites, on the other hand, the king anticipates a very pleasant existence attended by all the accoutrements of a prosperous earthly life: land, cattle, luxury garments, fine food.[82]

The Cult of Deceased Kings

So far as we know, no cult offerings were made for living kings. But it is clear that deceased royalty—both kings and queens—received regular offerings and were represented in some way by images. When Muwatalli II moved his capital from Ḫattuša to Tarḫuntašša, he transferred there the cult images of the deceased kings.[83] Now it is true that throughout the ancient Near East there is evidence for a cult of deceased ancestors, royal or not. But, at least in Hittite texts, no ghost of an ordinary person is ever called a "god" (*šiu-* or *šiuni-*), but only a "dead one" (*akkanza*). There is surely no way in which one can explain what could be meant by the phrase "became a god" other than in these two prerogatives of deities: an assured afterlife in paradise and a continuing cult.

---

81. H. A. Hoffner, Jr., "A Scene in the Realm of the Dead," in *A Scientific Humanist: Studies in Memory of Abraham Sachs*, ed. E. Leichty et al. (Philadelphia: University Museum, 1988), 191-99.

82. See the excellent overview by H. Otten, *Hethitische Totenrituale* (Berlin: Akademie Verlag, 1958), 12-17, and the more detailed analysis by V. Haas, *Geschichte*, 216-30, 234-36. Brief summaries in English may be found in O. R. Gurney, *The Hittites* (Baltimore: Penguin Books, 1990), 137-40; M. Popko, *Religions of Asia Minor* (Warsaw: Academic Publications Dialog, 1995), 154-57; and Bryce, *Life and Society*, 176-77. The texts describing the royal funerary ritual have been edited by A. S. Kassian, A. Korolëv, and A. V. Sidel'tsev, *Hittite Funerary Ritual: šalliš waštaiš* (Münster: Ugarit Verlag, 2002).

83. For a historical analysis of this move see most recently T. R. Bryce, *Kingdom*, 251-55. On the cultic implications, see I. Singer, *Muwatalli's Prayer to the Assembly of Gods Through the Storm-god of Lightning (CTH 381)* (Atlanta: Scholars Press, 1996).

A Divine Being Offering Worship

But how, you ask, is the king's role as celebrant to be reconciled with his superhuman status while alive? How can a superhuman or semi-divine being offer worship? The answer to this can be found in the royal prayer texts and in the mythological literature. The royal prayers show us the king in his role of mediator and the people's means of access to the gods. To be sure, often the king seems to be praying only for his personal needs. See, for example, the prayers of Muršili II about his problems with his mother-in-law Tawananna. But more often the king prays as the embodiment of his people. In a prayer of Ḫattušili III the king presents requests to deities who are the children and grandchildren of more important gods, and asks them to relay these requests to their parents.[84] Here we have a clear case of gods praying to other gods. And, if it be granted that the royal petitioner is himself a god, we have a god praying to another god, who is asked to relay that prayer to still other gods. Again, the analogy of Egypt can be invoked. For Egyptian pharaohs, who were considered the divine sons of the sun-god, also offered prayers to their gods.

Furthermore, in the relief at Gâvur Kalesi two male figures wearing short kilts, daggers, and conical horned caps have the same dress as Ḫattušili III in the Fraktin relief.[85] The Gâvur Kalesi figures are thought by most to be gods. They stride toward a seated deity, who is probably their superior. They hold their hands up either in greeting or worship or both.

Summary

What can we say then about the royal cult in Ḫatti? We can say that a cult in the restricted sense of offerings made to the living king as a god appears not to have existed in Ḫatti during the lifetime of the monarch. As for the cult of deceased kings, we have no textual evidence for the form of the ceremonies, only for the names of the recipients and the identification of the animal sacrifices. And the names of royal recipients of these sacrifices included not only the emperors and empresses, but also the sons of the cadet branch of the family who ruled *appanage* kingdoms rather than succeeding to the imperial throne itself.[86]

---

84. English translation in *ANET*, 394.

85. K. Bittel, *Die Hethiter*, figs. 199-200.

86. For example, Pimpira, Ḫuzziya the "man of Ḫakmiš," Kantuzili, Karaḫnuili, Taki-Šarruma, and Šarri-Kušuḫ King of Carchemish—see H. Otten, "Die hethitischen 'Königslisten' und die altorientalische Chronologie," *MDOG* 83 (1951): 47-51; *Die hethitischen historischen Quellen und die altorientalische Chronologie* (Wiesbaden: Verlag der Akademie der

An indispensable part of any cult is an image to serve as the focus. Peter Neve excavated a relief showing King Tudḫaliya with a horned headdress and reconstructed its probable setting in a temple to that king in the Upper City.[87] In the Südburg area at Ḫattuša he cleared a *dromos* with a relief of Šuppiluliuma II at the back with a trench for offerings at his feet.[88]

Kings from Ḫattušili I on[89] speak of making images of themselves. Since it is sometimes specified that the image was donated to a deity's temple and set up there, it obviously had some cult function. But this function could have been to serve as the king's surrogate, always at worship before the deity, constantly performing prayers. Statues performed this function in Mesopotamia and in Egypt.

As noted above, no image of a Hittite king has yet been recovered or described in texts that shows him in a posture of kneeling or *proskynesis*. But representations on reliefs and seals show him either standing before the cult statue of a god or before an altar. And a familiar scene of seals and in Chamber B of Yazılıkaya shows the king in the protective embrace of a god, and although this is not worship, strictly speaking, it is the king in intimate concourse with a god.

In summary, the Hittite king not only led worship, but often performed it alone as the principal representative of his people. His physical presence at the major festivals shows that he was the indispensable link in the relationship between the people and their gods. In the course of time his special role, which included wearing garb associated with the sun-god and being shielded from all forms of impurity as a god or high priest would be, may have been extended to the point that he was regarded as a living demi-god. He was never worshipped by the people during his lifetime in the same manner as the well-known gods. But he enjoyed a cult after death. There is no evidence yet that this cult was performed by persons outside the royal family. But if it was more widespread, it was probably because the king was a father figure for the entire nation, and his death was experienced by all as what the texts describe it—"the great catastrophe"![90]

Wissenschaften und der Literatur zu Mainz, 1968) for a discussion of these sacrificial lists. The texts are listed under *CTH* 660-61 and *CTH* Suppl., p. 118.

87. P. Neve, *Hattuša*, 40-41, Abb. 100-4.

88. P. Neve, "Die Ausgrabungen in Boğazköy-Hattuša 1988," *AA* (1989): 271-332, and *Hattuša*, 70-77.

89. *KBo* 10.2 iii 21-22: "So I made this gold image of myself and set it up for the sun-goddess of Arinna, my lady"; and *KBo* 12.38 ii 4-10: "Tudḫaliya did not make this image of my father; I, Šuppiluliyama, great king, king of the Ḫatti land, made it." See also ibid. ii 18-19, and the study of this text by H. G. Güterbock, "The Hittite Conquest of Cyprus Reconsidered," *JNES* 26 (1967): 73-81.

90. Hittite *šalliš waštaiš*—see H. Otten, *Totenrituale*, 7-8.

8

Kingship and Divinity in Imperial Assyria

PETER MACHINIST

I. Introduction

The Assyrian state has been justly recognized, if not celebrated, for its military prowess and size—the state that achieved, arguably, the first really super-regional empire in the Middle East. Its center, as its written and iconographic sources give evidence—and as confirmed wherever we have testimony from the peoples which fell under its sway—was its ruler, the Assyrian king. How this king functioned administratively, that is, how the monarchic administration governed its core and its increasingly far-flung territories, has been one object of the intensive research that has focused on Assyriological matters, *sensu stricto*, over the last century. The other major object of this research has been the native conceptions of the king and the state he ruled, and how these conceptions were formulated and promulgated in what has come to be called Assyrian royal ideology.

It is this latter area that I want to examine in the present paper—more specifically, an aspect of the royal ideology that may fairly claim to be fundamental to the whole, the relationship of the Assyrian king to the divine. Kings, wherever they have appeared in history, have been understood to mediate between, and so to partake in some way of, the human world they govern and the divine world that furnishes the ultimate authority over the created order. Where, then, in this spectrum stood the Assyrian king? Especially, in what senses did he move in divine circles?

In treating this question, I will set the temporal focus on the Neo-Assyrian period, that is, the three centuries from the end of the tenth through the end of the seventh B.C., when the state reached its largest and most complex form and then collapsed. But I cannot leave out, in the process, the preceding Middle Assyrian centuries, particularly the late fourteenth through the thirteenth, when many of the conceptions and practices that later marked Neo-Assyrian kingship, as well as other Neo-Assyrian institutions, emerged.

II. Features of Assyrian Kingship

A variety of features from Assyrian royal tradition bear on the relationship of the king to the divine. Without trying to be exhaustive, let us examine those that appear to be most visible in the surviving, especially written, evidence—most directly illuminating of what the relationship could entail.

a. Representative of the Gods

The first feature is a set of three titles attested for Assyrian kings from the second millennium B.C. through the first: *iššiak* > *iššâk* ^{d}*Aššur*, *šakin* / *šakni*/ *šakan*/*šaknu* ^{d}*Enlil*, and SANGA. The titles provide a kind of ground-plane for measuring royal-divine connections in Assyria, and so have been repeatedly commented on, perhaps most prominently by M.-J. Seux, who has surveyed their patterns of occurrence.[1] They enter the Assyrian titulary at somewhat different points in the second millennium: *iššiak* ^{d}*Aššur* in the early Old Assyrian period prior to Šamši-Adad I, *šakin* ^{d}*Enlil* in that same period, but later, with Šamši-Adad I, and SANGA in the Middle Assyrian period, first attested with Aššur-uballiṭ I. Once these phrases become part of the Assyrian royal titulary, they often co-occur. Thus, *šakin* ^{d}*Enlil*, from Šamši-Adad I on, normally precedes *iššiak* ^{d}*Aššur*, while from Aššur-uballiṭ I on, SANGA increasingly appears with Aššur as SANGA ^{d}*Aššur*, so varying with the syllabically spelled *iššiak* / *iššakki* in the same construct. SANGA, accordingly, has been interpreted in this construct as a logogram for *iššakku*, alongside another and older logogram for *iššakku*, ENSÍ.[2] This interpretation may be correct at least in some cases where the variation with *iššakku* occurs in duplicate texts of the same inscription. However, other occurrences of SANGA as a royal title or part of a royal epithet, where the existence of syllabically spelled variants indicates that the reading is *šangû*, make one wonder whether a special exception

1. Seux, *Épithètes*, and his earlier "Remarques sur le titre royal assyrien *iššakki Aššur*," *RA* 59 (1965): 101-9. Also, of course, the relevant entries in the two major Akkadian dictionaries, *AHw* and *CAD*. In the following discussion of *iššiak* ^{d}*Aššur*, *šakin* ^{d}*Enlil*, and SANGA, the data are drawn, if not noted further, from these collections.

2. Note the special use of NU.ÈŠ in the epithet NU.ÈŠ ^{d}*Aššur*, which occurs only for Sargon II, and in which NU.ÈŠ represents, as Seux notes ("Remarques," 104-6), *nišakku*, clearly a form related to *iššakku* and probably a play, by Sargon's scribes, on it.

should be created for the locution SANGA ᵈ*Aššur*. Thus, even Seux and *CAD* Š/I agree that the occurrence of SANGA + adjective—attested are *ṣīru* and *ellu*—should be read *šangû ṣīru/ellu*. And SANGA is found in the spelling of the abstract noun, SANGA-*ūtu*, where again syllabic variants make it clear that the reading should be *šangûtu*.[3] Finally, the noun *šangû* alone is attested for the Assyrian king Aššurbanipal in a syllabic spelling, ˡᵘ́*šá-an-gu-ú-ku-nu*, where the suffix *–kunu* refers to the Assyrian pantheon, presumably including Aššur.[4]

All three terms appear to express in one way or another the notion of "administrator, acting as representative of a higher authority," in this instance, the king as administrative representative of the god to which the term is attached, or occasionally the pantheon as a whole. More specifically, all three terms have a considerable tradition of usage, going back to the third millennium B.C. in Sumerian in the Babylonian south, especially of the Ur III period. There *iššakku* < ensí is a ruler of a territory, under the Ur III empire the title for district governor; later from the Old Babylonian period on, it is "demoted" in status, though not essentially in meaning, to that of a tenant of the king, who works a plot of land given him or renewed for him by the king, and who must then pay the crown a certain "rental" fee.[5] *Šaknu*, which is "Sumerized" as šagan, likewise

3. To be sure, *CAD* Š/I, 384b, while aware of these data, raises the possibility that the spelling SANGA-*ti/su* when connected with Assyrian royalty may represent *iššakkūtu*, rather than *šangûtu*. And it notes at least one occurrence of *iššakkūtu* written syllabically, from the inscriptions of Esarhaddon: for the text, see R. Borger, *Esarh.*, 81:50, cited in CAD I/J, 267a, and Seux, *Épithètes*, 350. Strictly speaking, therefore, *CAD* is correct that one cannot decide definitively whether *iššakkūtu* or *šangûtu* is the reading for SANGA-*ti/su* as an Assyrian royal epithet. Yet the fact that there are a number of syllabic occurrences of *šangûtu* describing Assyrian kings, as against just one of *iššakkūtu*, gives, it would seem, the greater favor to *šangûtu* in this equation.

4. The reference of this suffix, however, is not absolutely clear, because the word to which it belongs occurs in a broken context, in a hymn of Aššurbanipal. The hymn is in the first instance directed to the goddess Nanaya, but note that in the line following the one mentioning our word the god Aššur is called on to bless Aššurbanipal. See edition in A. Livingstone, *Court Poetry and Literary Miscellanea*, SAA 3 (Helsinki: Helsinki University Press, 1989), 16-17: no. 5, 4-5.

5. The pre-Ur III, and indeed, original usage of ensí < *iššakku* is still debated, though the notion of some kind of administrator or manager is widely maintained. See recently T. Jacobsen, "The Term Ensí," *AulaOr* 9 (1991): 113-21, and P. Steinkeller, "On Rulers, Priests and Sacred Marriage: Tracing the Evolution of Early Sumerian Kingship," in *Priests and Officials in the Ancient Near East*, ed. K. Watanabe (Heidelberg: Universitätsverlag C. Winter, 1999), 112-16. For the Ur III situation, see, among others, W. Sallaberger, in *Mesopotamien: Akkade-Zeit und Ur III-Zeit*, by W. Sallaberger and A. Westenholz, OBO 160/3 (Freiburg: Universitätsverlag, 1999), 191-94. On *iššakku* in OB, a brief summary is given by D. O. Edzard, "Private Land Ownership and Its Relation to 'God' and the 'State' in Sumer and Akkad," in *Privatization in the Ancient Near East and Classical World*, ed. M. Hudson and B. A. Levine, Peabody Museum Bulletin 5 (Cambridge: Peabody Museum of Archaeology and Ethnology, Harvard University, 1996), 116 and 127-28, n. 36.

describes a royal official, although one with a range of possible duties and spheres of authority, depending on the particular context.[6] As for SANGA, this Sumerian term largely applies to an administrator, if not the chief administrator, of a temple complex, although there are some occurrences from the Ur III period where the secular ruler—ensí or even lugal—seems also to carry the title.[7]

In Assyrian usage, from the Old through the Neo-Assyrian periods, *iššakku* is strictly a royal title; *šaknu* and *šangû*, on the other hand, can also be used for officials as well as kings. Further, all three terms, when used of the king, are largely or exclusively attested in Assyrian tradition: exclusively, for *šangû*; nearly exclusively, for *šaknu*, except for one occurrence with Zimri-Lim of Mari (but in the construct *šakin* ^{d}*Dagan*);[8] and largely Assyrian, for *iššakku*.[9] In addition, when used of Assyrian kings, *iššakku* is always connected with the national god, Aššur; *šaknu*, correspondingly, always with Enlil, who came from the Babylonian south, but was adopted in Assyria in the second millennium B.C., evidently through the agency of Šamši-Adad I and gradually associated and in various contexts identified with Aššur. As for *šangû* with the Assyrian king, it is always associated with Aššur in the construct form, SANGA + DN (assuming, as above, that at least some of these instances are to be read as *šangû*, and not as *iššakku*), though in other phrases it can be connected with Enlil (*šangû ṣīru ša* ^{d}*Enlil*), with Ištar (in the abstract noun, *šangûtu*), and, more vaguely, with the Assyrian pantheon in general. Still, the bulk of the occurrences of *šangû* and *šangûtu* are with Aššur.

It is difficult to gain an exact sense of *iššakku* and *šaknu* as they are used with the Assyrian king, because they appear almost only as royal titles in the epithet sections of Assyrian royal inscriptions, thus, with essentially no explicative context. There is a slight exception in the single attestation of *iššakku* as an abstract noun, *iššakkūtu*. The text is part of a clause in the epithet section of one of Esarhaddon's inscriptions, describing his forefathers as: *iš-šak-ku-su-un eli* ^{d}*Aššur i-ṭi-bu-ma* "their *iššakku*-ship was pleasing/acceptable to Aššur."[10] But this clause really does not

---

6. This understanding of *šakin* in *šakin* ^{d}*Enlil* as the construct of the noun *šaknu*, meaning "administrative official," is widely maintained, e.g., by Seux, *Épithètes*, 280, and *AHw*, 1141a. But *CAD* Š/I, 179b-180a understands here the construct of the verbal adjective *šaknu*, "appointed." It is difficult to decide which analysis is correct, but finally, it is probably not important to do so, since both base forms come from the same root, *šakānu*, and in either case, *šaknu* carries the same notion of "appointed representative."

7. *CAD* Š/II, 382b.

8. I include within the Assyrian attestations Šamši-Addu I and his son, Yasmaḫ-Addu; the latter, however, was strictly king of Mari when the relevant attestation occurred: see *CAD* Š/I, 179b, 3b.

9. The Babylonian occurrences are significantly fewer, and mostly in the NB dynasty: see Seux, *Épithètes*, 110-16.

10. See in n. 3.

advance us beyond what we could conclude from the construct, *iššakki* ^{d}*Aššur*, namely, that the kings functioned as *iššakku* at the pleasure of Aššur, and that that role was connected in some way with that god.[11]

The only one of the three titles about which we can learn something is *šangû/šangûtu*, because its attestations involving the king cover more than simply stereotyped lists of royal epithets. On the one hand, as established by G. van Driel and especially B. Menzel, we see the king functioning as a major actor in rituals, sometimes—and this is clearest in one of the Neo-Assyrian texts for the ritual of the *apal-bīt-ili*—alternating with the priest who otherwise directs the ritual and who is designated *šangû;* it should be noted, however, that in these ritual texts, the king is identified as "king" (*šarru*), not as *šangû*.[12] Magen, moreover, has gathered and systematized the iconographic evidence, which shows the Neo-Assyrian king in a variety of cultic behaviors, particularly of purification,[13] and these representations, as she argues, may be correlated with various titles and phrases given to the king, for example, *išippu* "purification priest" and *mušaklil parṣi* "the one who performs perfectly the rites."[14] As for the *šangûtu* of the Assyrian king, there are texts that associate it with sanctuaries and their provision and maintenance, a role ordained for the king by the gods. Thus, an inscription of Sin-šar-iškun, near the end of Neo-Assyrian history, describes him: *šá . . . za-nin-*[*ut*] [*na*]*p-ḫar ma-ḫa-zi šá-an-gu-tu gi-mir eš-ret rē'û-u-ut* [. . . *epēšu*] [*i*]*q-bu-u-šú* "whom they (= the gods) commanded to exercise provision for all the shrines, *šangûtu* for all the sanctuaries, (and) shepherdship (for . . . .)."[15] While the sources at issue show the king as *šangû* particularly in the cult of the national god, Aššur, at the ancient capital at Assur, yet, as the Sin-šar-iškun inscription along with other texts reveals, the king can function as *šangû* in other cult centers also. Or, as van Driel felicitously phrases it, "We could perhaps say that he was a kind of honorary *šangû* of all the sanctuaries of his country."[16]

Given the above evidence, it makes sense, therefore, to translate *šangû* as "priest" and *šangûtu* as "priesthood," and to say that one of the roles of the Assyrian king is as chief priest of the realm. But the texts tes-

---

11. The same clause is found with *šangûtu*: *ša šangûssu eli ilū ti-ki rabīti i-ṭi-bu* "whose (=Aššurnaṣirpal II's) *šangûtu* was pleasing/acceptable to your (=Ištar's) great divinity" (A. K. Grayson, *RIMA* 1 [1987]: 194: no. 1, 11-12; cited in *CAD* Š/I, 383b, with related attestations).

12. G. van Driel, *Cult of Aššur*, 170-74; B. Menzel, *Tempel* I, 157-74, esp. 157-59.

13. U. Magen, *Assyrische Königsdarstellungen—Aspekte der Herrschaft*, Baghdader Forschungen 9 (Mainz am Rhein: Philipp von Zabern, 1986), 65-91.

14. See Seux, *Épithètes*, 109-10, 330-31; Magen, *Assyrische*, 65, 69-73. For other terms and phrases, see Magen, *Assyrische*, 65-91, and Menzel, *Tempel* I, 157-74.

15. Cited in Seux, *Épithètes*, 228-29, and thereupon in van Driel, *Cult of Aššur*, 173.

16. van Driel, *Cult of Aššur*, 174.

tify to another sense in which priesthood is understood with the king, and this is as rulership itself. The point here has been well seen by van Driel,[17] and is expressed in various ways: by the chronological phrase, *ina šurru šangûtiya* (written normally, SANGA-*ti-ia*) "in the beginning of my *šangûtu*,"[18] which occurs in the inscriptions of Šalmaneser I to indicate his accession, and corresponds to *ina rēš šarrūtiya* "in the beginning of my kingship" in other Assyrian royal inscriptions;[19] by such phrases as *išid* ^{giš}*kussî ša-an-gu-ti-ia* "the foundation of the throne of my *šangûtu*," which can alternate in similar fashion with *ina* giš*kussî šarru-(u)-ti*.[20] The connection is also apparent in the report of the Neo-Assyrian king, Sargon II, on his eighth campaign of conquest. The florid introduction here, which enumerates the audience of this report, begins with the god Aššur, "the father of the gods, the great lord," and concludes, in symmetrical fashion, with Sargon himself and the king's army—the king being identified not as king, but only as "the pure priest" (*šangî elli* [SANGA KÙ]), the servant who fears your great divinity."[21]

Behind this connection between priesthood and rulership is a notion that does not appear to be found, or at least articulated in the same way, in the contemporary Babylonian world to the south. The notion is that of the king as the steward of the gods, especially of the principal national god and eponym of the state, Aššur. Put another way, the state, and with its enlargement, the empire, may be imagined as the sacred realm of Aššur and his divine entourage, with the king as his earthly administrator. The formulation can yet be expressed at another level: Aššur remains the real and ultimate king; the human king is, then, his servant, mediator, administrative representative, responsible for the god's earthly possessions—a role that can be designated, depending, we may suppose, on the angle of vision chosen, as *šangû*, *iššakku*, or *šaknu*. The complex, multiple senses at work here are arguably best captured in the Assyrian coronation ritual, the surviving text for which appears to date, as many would suppose, to the Middle Assyrian period, perhaps the thirteenth century B.C. Here are two relevant segments of it:

> [l]ú*šangû*
> *ša Aššur ina pa-ni-šu-n*[*u* ...] *i-maḫ-aṣ a-ki-a i-*[*q*]*a-bi*
> *Aššur šar Aššur šar* [*a-di*] *bāb* d*A-zu-e i-q*[*a*]*-bi*

17. Ibid., 173.

18. On the discussion of whether this should be read, instead, *iššakkūtiya*, see n. 3.

19. *AHw*, 975 a-b, s.v. *rēšu(m)* D2; *CAD* Š/I, 383b, s.v. *šangûtu* b1′.

20. See Borger, *Esarh.*, 26 viii 26; 16 Ep. 12a 10. See also *CAD* Š/I, 383b, b1′.

21. See the recent edition of W. Mayer, "Sargons Feldzug gegen Urartu—714 v. Chr. Text und Übersetzung," *MDOG* 115 (1983): 68-69. I thank Louis D. Levine for calling these lines to my attention.

[a-di ku-lu-li]
a-na qaqqad šarri i-ṣa-li-ú-ni [[lú]*šangû*]
a-ki-a i-qa-b[*i*]
ma-a ku-li-li ša qaqqadi-ka ma-a Aššur [d][*N*]*in-lîl bēlē ša*
ku-lu-li-ka 1 ME *šanāte li-i*[*p-p*]*i-ru-ka*
šēp-ka ina É-kur ù qātē-ka [*i-n*]*a irat Aššur ili-ka lu ṭāb*
i-na ma-ḫar Aššur ili-ka ša-an-g[*u-ut*]*-ka ù ša-an-gu-ta*
ša mārē-ka lu ṭa-ba-a[*t*] *i-na e-šar-te*
[giš]*ḫaṭṭi-ka māt-ka ra-pi*[*š q*]*a-ba-a še-ma-a ma-ga-ra*
ki-it-ta ù sa-[*li*]*-ma Aššur lid-di-na-ku*

The priest of Aššur strikes [. . .] before them (= the Assyrian king and others in his entourage) (and) says the following:
"Aššur is king; Aššur is king." As far as the gate of Azu he says (this).

[While] he is setting [the headdress] on the head of the king, [the priest] says the following:
"May Aššur and Ninlil, the lords of your headdress,
cover you with the headdress for your head for a hundred
years. May your foot be acceptable in the Ekur and your
hands in the bosom of Aššur, your god. Before Aššur, your
god, may your *šangûtu* and the *šangûtu* of your sons be acceptable.
With your just scepter, enlarge your land. May Aššur grant you
(the capacity to) command, to hear, to answer (requests), truth,
and peace." [22]

The above lines, it should be emphasized, distinguish two kinds of *šangû*. The first is the non-royal priest who assists the king in this and various other parts of the ceremony. But this priest, then, calls upon the national divine couple, Aššur and Ninlil (the latter read in Neo-Assyrian as Mullissu), to establish the *šangûtu* of the new king and of his sons to follow. Note further that this *šangûtu* is linked to the fundamental duty of the king/*šangû*: to enlarge the territory of the realm—the quintessential imperial act. Finally, it should be emphasized, the sentiments expressed here are not exclusive to this text. As Lambert recently and succinctly has observed,[23] they are attested, most strikingly, from the beginning and end

22. K. F. Müller, *Das assyrische Ritual: Teil I. Texte zum assyrischen Königsritual*, MVAG 41/3 (Leipzig: J. C. Hinrichs, 1937), 8-9: col. I, 27-29; 12-13: col. II, 27-36. In col. II, 31, the verb *li-I*[*ip-p*]*i-ru-ka*, that is, a D Precative so restored by Müller, is restored as *li-t*[*ep-p*]*i-ru-ka* by *CAD* A/II, 167a, c. The latter is a Gtn Precative, and would be translated, "may they continually cover you." Either verb would work contextually, but it is not possible to make a final decision, since the disputed sign on the tablet is heavily damaged, and the copy of it, by E. Ebeling, *KAR* 135 obv II 8, is unclear.

23. W. G. Lambert, "Kingship in Ancient Mesopotamia," in *King and Messiah in Israel*

of Assyrian history. Thus, the first part of a seal of the Old Assyrian king Ṣilulu reads:

> *A-šùr*^{ki} *šar* (LUGAL) *Ṣi-lu-lu iššiak* (ENSÍ) *A-šùr*^{ki}
>
> Aššur is king. Ṣilulu is the *iššakku* of Aššur.[24]

And, from the last century of the Neo-Assyrian empire, the coronation hymn of Assurbanipal (668-627 B.C.) proclaims:

> ^{d}*Aš-šur šar* (LUGAL) ^{d}*Aš-šur-ma šar* (LUGAL) ^{m}*Aš-šur-bān-*[*apli . . . .*].
> ^{d}*Aš-šur bi-nu-ut qātē-šu*
> *ilāni rabûti lu-kín-nu palê-šú li-ṣu-ru* [*ša* ^{m}*Aš-šur-bā*]*n-apli šar māt Aš-šur* [*napšāti-šu*]
> ^{giš}*ḫaṭṭu i-šir-tu a-na ru-up-pu-uš māti u niš*[*ē-šu*] *lid-di-nu-niš-šú*
> *palû-šú li-te-diš* ^{giš}*kussî šarru-ti-šú a-na da-ra-a-ti lu-kín-nu*
>
> Aššur is king. Yea, Aššur is king. Assurban[ipal, the . . .] of Aššur, is the creation of his hands.
> May the great gods establish his reign. May they preserve [the life of] [Assurba]nipal, the king of Assyria.
> May they give him a just scepter to enlarge the land and [his] peoples.
> May his reign be renewed. May they establish his royal throne forever.[25]

To be sure, in the Ṣilulu and Aššurbanipal texts, *šangû* for the king is not mentioned, or at least not preserved.[26] But the associated title, *iššakku*, is; and otherwise, the texts display enough of the sentiments and language of the Middle Assyrian coronation ritual to be considered with it. Put together, thus, they parallel the long-lived usage of *iššakku*, *šaknu*, and *šangû* noted above, all testifying to an Assyrian ruling ideology of which, in Lambert's words, "the continuity of tradition is remarkable."[27] Indeed, it is an ideology that helps to give the whole of Assyrian history coherence.[28]

---

and the Ancient Near East, ed. J. Day, JSOTSup 270 (Sheffield: Sheffield Academic Press, 1998), 68.

24. Grayson, *RIMA* 1 (1987): 13: no. 1.

25. Livingstone, *Court Poetry*, 26-27: no. 11, 15-18.

26. In the Assurbanipal text, line 15 might contain it, but the critical word is broken. See Livingstone, *Court Poetry*, 26: no. 11, 15.

27. Lambert, "Kingship," 68.

28. Other echoes of this coronation ritual, or at least of the sentiments and language connected with it, may be found in the Neo-Assyrian period. One example is from the annals of Adad-narari II, wherein the king is described as being created by the gods, who make perfect his features, fill him with wisdom, decree his destiny, and then entrust him with scepter and *melammu*, making his name greater than all (other) lords: A. K. Grayson, *RIMA* 2 (1991): 147: 5-9.

b. Tukulti-Ninurta I and Change

This basic continuity, however, should not be confused with staticity. The growth of the Assyrian state in the Middle Assyrian period—the fourteenth through the eleventh centuries B.C.—to a state ruling states, that is, to an empire, brought with it an enlargement and consolidation of royal power. Reflecting this development, as A.K. Grayson showed, was an elaboration and rhetorical heightening of the descriptions of the king in his official inscriptions.[29] A first climax of this process, both politically and rhetorically, came in the reign of Tukulti-Ninurta I (1243-1207 B.C).[30] In his inscriptions we do find the familiar titles *šakin* ^{d}*Enlil, iššâk* ^{d}*Aššur*, and *šangû*.[31] There are also epithets, likewise appearing earlier in Assyria, that indicate more directly the closeness of king to deity, namely, the king as *migru* "favorite" and *narāmu* "beloved" of a particular god or gods.[32] And there is, finally, a continued focus on the king's military prowess and deeds.[33] Yet now, as well, there is something new for Assyrian tradition: a range of phrases celebrating the global reach of Tukulti-Ninurta's political and especially military ambitions, if not achievements, and, more immediately relevant to our present discussion, a range of phrases dramatically elevating the king's relationship to the gods. The most extravagant manifestation of this new status comes in the Tukulti-Ninurta Epic, the long narrative poem commissioned by the king to celebrate his victory and conquest of Babylonia and its ruler, Kaštiliaš IV. And within this Epic, perhaps the most acute illustration is provided by the hymn in the first tablet that introduces and praises the king (I 10′-27′). Here is the larger part of that text:

šar-ra-ḫat ma-am-lu-su tu-šá-a[*r*$^{?}$*-rap*$^{?}$ *la-a*] *a-di-ri pa-na ù ar-ka*
qa-e-da-at er-ḫu-su tu-ḫa-am-maṭ la-a še-mi-i šu-me-la ù im-na
gal-tu me-lam-mu-šu ú-sa-aḫ-ḫa-pu na-gab za-ia-a-ri
*šá kip-pat šārē erbette/arba*ʾ*i šá* IM.TU *i-ta-na-da-ru-uš pu-ḫur kal šarrāne*
ki-ma ^{d}*Ad-di a-na ša-gi-im-me-šu it-tar-ra-ru šadû*
ù ki-ma ^{d}*Nin-urta a-na ni-iš kakkē-šú ul-ta-nap-šá-qa ka-liš kibrātu*

---

29. A. K. Grayson, "The Early Development of Assyrian Monarchy," *UF* 3 (1971): 311-19.

30. Mesopotamian dates throughout this paper follow J. A. Brinkman, *apud* A. L. Oppenheim, *Ancient Mesopotamia: Portrait of a Dead Civilization*, rev. ed. by Erica Reiner (Chicago: University of Chicago Press, 1977), 335-48.

31. See especially Seux, *Épithètes, ad loc.*

32. Ibid., 162-68, 189-97. Both of these epithets, as the data in Seux make clear, ultimately derive from Babylonia, in Akkadian and Sumerian, being first attested there at the end of the third/beginning of the second millennia B.C.

33. Cf. the inscriptions in Grayson, *RIMA* 1 (1987), *ad loc.*

ina ši-mat ^{d}*Nu-dím-mud-ma ma-ni it-ti šēr ilāne mi-na-a-šu*
ina purussu bēl mātāte ina ra-a-aṭ šassuru ilāne ši-pi-ik-šu i-te-eš-ra
šu-ú-ma ṣalam ^{d}*Enlil da-ru-u še-e-mu pi-i nišē mi-lik māti*
ki-ma šá-a-šú ana pān re-de-e bēl mātāte ú-man-du-ú-uš i-ud ina šap-ti

---

ú-šar-bi-šu-ma ^{d}*Enlil ki-ma a-bi a-li-di ar-ki mār bu-uk-ri-šu*
a-qar ina ši-me-šu a-šar šit-nu-ni ra-sa-áš-šu an-dil-la
ul iš-nun ma-ti-ma ina šarrāne kul-la-ti qa-bal-šu ma-am-ma
ul iz-z[i-za-am]-ma ia-um-ma mal-ku ga-ba-ra-šu a-šar ta-ḫa-zi

Glorious is his vehemence; it scorches(?) the unfearing in front and rear.
Glowing is his aggressiveness; it burns the disobedient to the left and the right.
Frightful are his effulgences; they overwhelm all the enemies.
He who controls the entire four directions, the awe-inspiring one(?) — the assembly of all the kings fear him continually.
Like Adad when he thunders, the mountains tremble;
And like Ninurta when he raises his weapons, the regions (of the world) everywhere are thrown into continual panic.
By the fate (determined by) Nudimmud (= Ea), his mass is reckoned with the flesh of the gods.
By the decision of the lord of all the lands (= Enlil), he was successfully engendered through/cast into the channel of the womb of the gods.
He alone is the eternal image of Enlil, attentive to the voice of the people, to the counsel of the land.
Just as the lord of all the lands (= Enlil) designated him as head of the soldiers, so he praised (him) with his lips.

Enlil raised him like a natural father, after his first-born son.
He is (deemed) valuable in the price (reckoned) for him; the place where conflict (occurs) provides protection for him.
No one among all the kings ever competed with him in war.
There did not stand any prince (who was) his equal in battle.[34]

As just noted, these lines from the Epic stand out in two areas: praise of the king's global reach and prowess, and praise of his unequalled status before the gods. The global reach and prowess are articulated in lines

34. W. G. Lambert, "Three Unpublished Fragments of the Tukulti-Ninurta Epic," *AfO* 18 (1957-58): 48-51 + Taf. IV; edition in P. Machinist, "The Epic of Tukulti-Ninurta I: A Study in Middle Assyrian Literature" (Ph.D. diss., Yale University, 1978), 66-71. The present translation, in line 23′, also makes use of an unpublished fragment, which is taken up as well in the translation of B. R. Foster, *Before the Muses: An Anthology of Akkadian Literature*, 2d ed. (Bethesda, MD: CDL Press, 1996), 1:214-15.

12′-15′: note particularly the baroque syntax of 15′ describing the king's rule of the four quarters. Prowess also appears in lines 21′-23′, which emphasize the king's special affinity for the battlefield, unequalled by any other ruler. More numerous and striking in this selection from the Epic are the lines about king and the divine, 11′, 14′-20′, but it should be noted that these lines are not separated from those about global reach and prowess, rather juxtaposed and interwoven with them. Thus, Tukulti-Ninurta is depicted as exercising his warrior abilities like the two principal warrior gods, Adad and Ninurta (14′-15′), and by the use of the *melammu* (12′), the "effulgence" or "radiance," which is properly a divine attribute that makes its first appearance with Assyrian human kings in the reign of Tukulti-Ninurta. (Note also the related *namurratu* and *puluḫtu*, appearing elsewhere in the Epic, IIA 25′ and VA 20′, respectively.)[35] The king steps forth, indeed, as nearly a divine creature: given birth by the gods (17′); created of divine material—"reckoned with the flesh of the gods" (16′); proclaimed as the image of the principal director of the pantheon, Enlil (18′); and raised up by Enlil himself, just below the status of his first-born son (20′), who must here be Ninurta, thus echoing both the earlier reference to Ninurta as warrior (15′) and the king's own name, Tukulti-Ninurta, "my protection is Ninurta."[36]

But there is even more to the issue of divinity in these Epic lines, and that is signaled especially by the depiction of the king as *ṣalmu* "image" of Enlil (18′). For *ṣalmu* is not simply a reflection, metaphorically, of another, and that other's character or capabilities, but something concrete: a manufactured object like a statue, in this instance one of Tukulti-Ninurta that is supposed, in some way, to suggest, and participate in, the presence of his divine guardian, Enlil. Put another way, these lines make clear that one mark of the king as divine child is that he, his body, serves as the statue of the god. The point is underscored by the other language in these lines. Thus, the deliberate ambiguity in 17′ of *ina ra-a-aṭ šassuru ši-pi-ik-šu i-te-eš-ra*, referring both to the "engendering" of the king in the divine "womb" and to his being "cast/poured out" as the metal of a statue in a "channel/mould." And the description in line 16′ of the king's body, "his

35. On these terms, see E. Cassin, *La splendeur divine* (Paris/Le Haye: Mouton & Co., 1968); more recently, I. Winter, "Radiance as an Aesthetic Value in the Art of Mesopotamia (with some Indian Parallels)," in *Art: The Integral Vision. A Volume of Essay in Felicitation of Kapila Vatsyayan* (New Delhi: D. K. Printworld [P] Ltd., 1994), 123-32, and "Images of Gods and Kings: What Cannot Be Represented Visually . . . ." (forthcoming).

36. Note the Tukulti-Ninurta I inscription published by K. Deller, A. Fadhil, and K. M. Ahmad, "Two New Royal Inscriptions Dealing with Construction Work in Kar-Tukulti-Ninurta," *Bagh. Mitt.* 25 (1994): 460-61, 469: IM 57821, obv 7, which speaks of the king as: *šu-tùq du-un-ni geš-ru šá tu-kúl-ta-šu* ^{d}*Nin-urta* "the one of overweening strength, the fierce, whose protection is Ninurta."

mass," as *šēr ilāne* "the flesh of the gods," which points not only to the divine birth, but to the statue, exactly as in the Erra Myth, where the prized and exotic *mesu*-wood used for making divine statues is called *šēr ilāne*.[37]

Tukulti-Ninurta's new language and imagery for global prowess and divinity were not the original creation of his court. They represent a borrowing from the Akkadian and Sumerian traditions of the Babylonian south, traditions beginning already in the later third millennium B.C.[38] Here one will find the phrases about rule over the four quarters and unmatched battle valor, and particularly the notion of the divine status of the king. Admittedly, the exact form and meaning of this latter notion vary with the range and setting of the southern texts at issue, yet certain expressions of it run through all of these that coincide with those of lines 16′-20′ of the Tukulti-Ninurta Epic. They describe birth and nurture, telling of the king as a creature begotten, suckled, endowed with special talents by some deity or deities, including the possession of the properly divine *melammu*—and the related *puluḫtu* and *namurratu*—and labeled as their son. And the very form of the royal hymn, describing as here the king directly and emphasizing his divine status and, not occasionally, his military strength, is also a southern creation, at home especially in the Old Akkadian through the Isin-Larsa periods of the later third–early second millennia B.C. These southern features in Tukulti-Ninurta thus continue an interest, attested earlier in the Middle and Old Assyrian periods, to take from the south such features as the royal titles, *iššakku*, *šaknu*, and *šangû* and epithets like *migru* and *narāmu*. The difference now is that this southern borrowing is much larger and more intensively exploited, in keeping with Tukulti-Ninurta's political and military effort to control Babylonia.

And yet if these features in Tukulti-Ninurta's Epic are ultimately southern, they were not simply taken over mechanically and unchanged. So in line 20′, the king is said to have been raised by Enlil "like (*ki-ma*) a natural father"; Enlil is not labelled, straight-out, the natural father. Similarly, Tukulti-Ninurta's "mass" (*mi-na-a-šu*) is in line 16′, in a play on this noun, "reckoned with (*ma-ni it-ti*) the flesh of the gods"; a more direct equation of the king's mass with divine flesh is not given. And, finally, there is no explicit deification of the king's name here—no prefix of din-

37. See L. Cagni, *Erra*, 74-75: I 150; recent translation in Foster, *Before the Muses* II, 765. This line was originally brought to my attention in the present context by my teacher, Prof. William W. Hallo.

38. See Machinist, *Epic of Tukulti-Ninurta I*, 180-208. Additional discussion of expressions of divinity or at least of closeness to the gods may be found in n. 116 below and in Esther Flückiger-Hawker, *Urnamma of Ur in Sumerian Literary Tradition*, OBO 166 (Fribourg: University Press Fribourg, 1999), 46-55.

gir—as we know occurred for certain earlier southern kings, especially of the Old Akkadian and Ur III periods. All of these suggest, in sum, a certain hesitation on the part of Tukulti-Ninurta and his scribes as to the full deification of kings that at least the late third and early second millennia of Babylonian history offered. Evidently, the pull of a more conservative Assyrian tradition, reflected in the description of the king as the god's administrator—*iššakku, šaknu, šangû*—was still strong.

One should add that the picture the Tukulti-Ninurta Epic gives us is confirmed, though in a more laconic and less heightened way, in the king's inscriptions. Here too we find phrases drawn from Babylonian tradition, describing the king's global reach and prowess: *šar kibrāt erbette/ arbaʾi* "king of the four quarters," which, it would appear, line 13′ from the Epic above playfully echoes; and the king "unequalled" (using a form of *šanānu*) in war, as in the Epic's lines 22′-23′ (this language of "inequality," it should be added, appears first in the inscriptions of Tukulti-Ninurta's predecessor and father, Šalmaneser I[39]). As for the king's divine-like "radiance," it also occurs in his inscriptions, though there only as *puluḫtu*,[40] not also as *melammu* and *namurratu* as in the Epic. And while Tukulti-Ninurta as the *ṣalam* ᵈ*Enlil* does not occur in his inscriptions, he is there described, in phrases again well ensconced in earlier Babylonia, as *lipit qāt* ᵈ*Adad* "the creation/work of Adad," and ᵈ*Šamšu kiššat nišē* "sun(-god) of all the people"; note also the phrase, combining two of the foregoing, *ša kibrāt erbette arki* ᵈ*Šamaš irteʾû* "the one who shepherds the four quarters after Šamaš."[41] Finally, the kinds of hesitation about divine status of which the Epic gives evidence have at least one echo elsewhere in the period of the king. This is the personal name, Šarru-ki-iliya "the king is like my god," attested in a ration list from the Assyrian garrison site of Kulišḫinaš in the Upper Ḫabur area; the text cannot be precisely dated, but other texts found with it come from the thirteenth century B.C., including the reign of Tukulti-Ninurta.[42]

39. Seux, *Épithètes*, 117.

40. Grayson, *RIMA* 1 (1987): 236: no. 1, iv 7.

41. Machinist, *Epic of Tukulti-Ninurta I*, 181, 394 n. 67; *CAD* L, 201, s.v. *liptu* A, c; also R. Labat, *Le caractère religieux de la royauté assyro-babylonienne* (Paris: Librairie d'Amérique et d'Orient, 1939), 228-33 for the king and Šamaš in the Sumero-Babylonian south.

42. See P. Machinist, "Provincial Governance in Middle Assyria and Some New Texts from Yale," *Assur* 3/2 (Nov. 1982), 8-9: YBC 12862, rev 15: LUGAL-*ki-i*-DINGIR-*ia*. One may also mention an inscription of Tukulti-Ninurta I, Grayson, *RIMA* 1 (1987): 271-74: no. 23. Grayson argues ("Early Development," 316 n. 38) that in the introductory section of this inscription, which lays out the honorific epithets of the king, it is unclear whether those epithets that elsewhere describe deities are here associated with the deities or with the king himself. Grayson raises the possibility that this ambiguity is "intentional in order to lend more divine aura to the Assyrian king's image." If Grayson is right about the ambiguity of

c. The Legacy of Tukulti-Ninurta I in the Neo-Assyrian Period

The language and themes about Assyrian royalty that are first attested, and in all likelihood were inaugurated, in the reign of Tukulti-Ninurta I did not die with him. Indeed, they are to be found, directly or indirectly, in subsequent reigns, both Middle and Neo-Assyrian.

Consider first global reach and military prowess. A quick glance at the two major Akkadian dictionaries, *AHw* and *CAD*, and the collection of M. J. Seux, *Épithètes*, makes clear that the title *šar kibrāt erbette*, and its variations, become almost a commonplace after Tukulti-Ninurta: it is significant, however, that they are barely attested in Babylonia of this same period, even in the Neo-Babylonian empire after Assyria's fall.[43] Even more, the grandiloquent elaboration of this title in the Tukulti-Ninurta Epic above, line 13′, finds its echoes in such phrases from later Assyrian royal texts as *kullat kibrāt erbette/arbaʾi* "the totality of the four quarters" or *ša napḫar malkē kibrāte tāḫāssu ezzu idurūma* "of whom all the princes of the regions trembled at his fierce battle."[44] This proclamation of global sovereignty, as in the Tukulti-Ninurta Epic, is regularly connected with the gods who are understood to grant it to the king.[45] Similarly commonplace in the later Assyrian texts, though again not the later Babylonian, is the language in the Epic, lines 22′-23′, describing the "unequalled" valor of the king in battle; and this, again, can be connected with the gods.[46] Indeed, one of these later passages about valor, from a letter-prayer of Esarhaddon, has almost verbatim identity with the Epic lines:

> ⸢*šá*⸣ *ma-ti-ma ina šarrāne kul-lat na-ki-ri la is-ḫu-ru la iš-nu-u qa-bal-šú mam-ma-an*
> [*la iz*]-*zi-zu maḫ-ru-uš-šú a-a-um-ma* ⸢*mal*⸣-*ku ga-ab-ra-šú a-šar ta-ḫa-zi*

---

these lines and the intentional design of this—both not so certain—then one might ask further: is the intentional ambiguity for the purpose not simply of lending the king divine aura, but also of holding back on the full assertion of that aura?

43. Seux, *Épithètes*, 305-8. In Neo-Babylonia, this title is atttested only with the king Nabonidus, who otherwise shows much interest in Assyrian royal tradition, especially of Aššurbanipal.

44. Seux, *Épithètes*, 349, 313-14; 35.

45. The examples are legion. One of them is the recurrent phrase about Tiglath-pileser I in his inscriptions: *ša* ᵈ*A-šur kakkū-šu ú-šá-ḫi-lu-ma a-na mu-ʾu-ru-ut kib-rat erbetti šum-šu a-na da-riš iš-qu-ru* "whose weapons Assur sharpened and whose name he pronounced eternally for directing the four quarters" (Grayson, *RIMA* 2 [1991]: 13: no. 1, i 36-38, and passim).

46. Seux, *Épithètes*, 116-20, 253, 287, 288, 312, 313, 314, 334-35, 368. On the connection with the gods, see, e.g., a passage from an inscription of Tiglath-pileser I: *i-na si-qir* ᵈ*En-líl ma-ḫi-ra la-a i-šu-ú* "by the command of Enlil, he has no rival" (Grayson, *RIMA* 2 [1991]: 13: no. 1, i 44).

Against whom no one of the kings of all the enemies has ever turned to take up war again,
Before whom no prince ever stood (who was) his equal in battle.[47]

As for king and divinity, here too the post-Tukulti-Ninurta period stands in a continuous line with what that monarch offered in his inscriptions and Epic. For one thing, older royal epithets originating before Tukulti-Ninurta, like *migru* "favorite" and *narāmu* "beloved" of the gods, remain in play, as they do in contemporary, first-millennium Babylonia.[48] But the apparent innovations of Tukulti-Ninurta's era are found as well. The first of these is the theme of the king's birth and/or nurture by the gods. It appears in a number of later royal texts, scattered over different types that include annals, prophecies, and hymns to deities.[49] For example, early in the Neo-Assyrian period, the introduction to the inscriptions of Tukulti-Ninurta II (890-884 B.C.) affirms:

ša ina šassur um-mi ki-ni-[iš . . .]
n[ab]-ni-ti a-na nab-ni-ti EN.MEŠ *uš-[tennû]*

(the gods) who faithfully [noticed me(?)] in my mother's womb
(and) altered my features to lordly features.[50]

The most numerous, and most elaborate, attestations of this theme appear in the last century of Neo-Assyrian rule, during the reigns of the Sargonid kings, especially Aššurbanipal. Here are representative instances:

a-na-ku ^{d}*Ištar ša* $^{ur[u}$*Arba-ìl]*
sa-ab-su-ub-ta-k[a]
ra-bi-tu a-na-ku
mu-še-ni[q]-ta-ka
de-iq-tú a-na-ku

I am Ištar of [Arbela].
I am your great midwife.
I am your effective wet nurse.[51]

---

47. Borger, *Esarh.*, 103 68 II 27-28; cf. Seux, *Épithètes*, 288 and n. 132; *CAD* G, 3b s.v. *gabarû*, 2. In the Esarhaddon text, *iš-nu-u* "take up (war) again" may be an error for *iš-nu-nu* "compete (in war)," given *iš-nun* in the parallel line of the Tukulti-Ninurta Epic. This correction, moreover, appears to make better sense in the context.

48. Seux, *Épithètes*, 162-68, 189-97.

49. It also can be found in first-millennium B.C. Babylonian royal texts, specifically of the Neo-Babylonian dynasty: see Labat, *Le caractère*, 55-56.

50. Grayson, *RIMA* 2 (1991): 165: no. 1, 18-19.

51. Prophecy for Esarhaddon, in S. Parpola, *Assyrian Prophecies*, SAA 9 (Helsinki: Helsinki University Press, 1997), 7: no. 1.6, III 7′, 15′-18′.

a-na-ku abu-ka ummu-ka
bir-ti a-gap-pi-ia ur-ta-bi-ka

I (= Ištar of Arbela) am your father (and) your mother.
I have raised you between my wings.[52]

[šarru be-lí ṣa-la]m ^{d}Marduk šu-ú
[šarru] be-lí a-bat-su ki-i šá ilāni
[ga-am-rat x x]x *šēr ilāni ^{d}Šamaš*
[xxxx]x *šarru be-li*

The king, my lord, is the image of Marduk.
The king, my lord—his word is final like that of the gods.
. . . the flesh of the gods, Šamaš
. . . the king, my lord.[53]

ul i-di aba u um-me ina$^{!}$ ⌈bur$^{!}$⌉-ki$^{!}$ $^{d!}$ištarāti$^{!}$-ia ár-ba-a ana-ku
it-tar-ru-un-ni-i-ma ilāni rabûti kīma la-ʾe-e

^{d}be-lit ^{uru}Ni-ná-a um-mu a-lit-ti-ia
taš-ru-ka šarru-u-tu šá la šá-na-a-ni
^{d}be-lit ^{uru}Arba-ìl ⌈ba$^{!}$⌉-[ni]-⌈ti⌉-ia taq-ba-a balāṭi da-ra-a-te

I knew no (human) father or mother; I grew up on the knees of my goddesses (= Ištar of Nineveh and Ištar of Arbela).
The great gods brought me up like a baby.

The Lady of Nineveh, the mother who bore me,
granted me kingship without equal.
The Lady of Arbela, who created me, ordered (for me) everlasting life.[54]

ṣe-eḫ-ru at-ta ^{m}Aššur-bān-apli ša ú-maš-šir-u-ka ina muḫḫi ^{d}šar-rat Ninua^{ki}
la-ku-u at-ta ^{m}Aššur-bān-apli ša áš-ba-ka ina bur-ki ^{d}šar-rat Ninua^{ki}
er-bi zi-ze-e-šá ina pi-ka šak-na 2 te-en-ni-iq 2 ta-ḫal-líp ana pa-ni-ka

You were a child, Aššurbanipal, when I left you to the care of the Queen of Nineveh (= Ištar of Nineveh).
You were a baby, Aššurbanipal, when you sat on the knees of the Queen of Nineveh.
Her four teats are placed in your mouth: two you suck; two you milk to your face.[55]

52. Prophecy for Esarhaddon, in Parpola, *Assyrian Prophecies*, 18: no. 2.5, III 26′-27′.

53. Letter to Esarhaddon or Aššurbanipal, in S. W. Cole and P. Machinist, *Letters from Priests to the Kings Esarhaddon and Assurbanipal*, SAA 13 (Helsinki: Helsinki University Press, 1998), 43: no. 46, rev 11-14.

54. Hymn from Aššurbanipal to the Ištars of Nineveh and Arbela, in Livingstone, *Court Poetry*, 12-13: no. 3, obv 13-14, rev 14-16.

55. Dialogue between Aššurbanipal and Nabu, in Livingstone, *Court Poetry*, 34: No. 13, 6-8.

In the above examples, divine attachment to the king takes several forms, which can, but need not, co-occur, and which recall, but are not necessarily identical with, the language of the Tukulti-Ninurta Epic: a deity, usually goddess, or deities can create or give birth to the king, can nurture him by giving him suck on her knees, can be called, thus, mother and/or father, sometimes with the explicit denial of human parentage; and the king, in turn, can apparently be associated with the flesh of the gods. Other examples, not given above, can label the king *mār ilišu* "son of his god," though this label can be found also with non-royal persons.[56]

This language of divine parentage is, in Assyria, almost exclusively a royal idiom. But an exception occurs with those high Assyrian officials who in the first half of the eighth century B.C., before the accession of Tiglath-pileser III, achieved unusual freedom of expression and, we presume, power in the absence of strong monarchic control. The most well documented, and perhaps most powerful, of these was the commander-in-chief (*turtānu*), Šamši-ilu, who like the other officials has left us a series of royal-like inscriptions.[57] One of the latter, from Šamši-ilu's provincial capital at Til Barsip, includes a reference to a successful military campaign, carried out by him, as he says, *i[na qi]-bit abi A[š-š]ur bēlu rabû u šaqīt[u] ummu É-šar-ra ašaritti ilāni* ^d^*Mullissu* "at the command of the father, Aššur, the great lord, and the exalted mother of Ešarra, foremost among the gods, Mullissu."[58] This looks very much like the references to divine parents in the texts above, but what is missing is explicit personalization, as in: *my* father and mother. Do we have here, therefore, something different: a more generalized reference to Aššur and his consort, Mullissu, as the father and mother, i.e., supreme heads, of the pantheon, and so of the state? Or is the sense still to be Šamši-ilu's father and mother, wherein the absence of the personal pronoun or the like may be

56. Seux, *Épithètes*,160 and 159 n. 28. In the latter, Seux properly observes that *mār ilīšu* can be used with commoners as well as with royalty, since it describes first and foremost the relationship between the human individual in question and the personal god who watches over him; the phrase, thus, does not by itself indicate that the human involved is divine. I would, however, disagree with Seux's larger conclusion from this discussion, when he says that a statement of divine parentage per se "ne peut constituer un element essentiel dans la question de la divinisation des souverains" (159 n. 28). For the fact is that *elaborated* statements of divine parentage and nurture like those cited in our text are not normal, if found at at all, with commoners; they appear to be centered on royalty.

57. On these high officials, see A. K. Grayson, *RIMA* 3 (1996): 200-201; idem, "Assyrian Officials and Power in the Ninth and Eighth Centuries," *State Archives of Assyria Bulletin* VII/1 (1993): 19-52; idem, in *CAH* ² III/1 (1982), 273-79. For Šamši-ilu in particular, see most recently R. Mattila, *The King's Magnates*, SAAS 11 (Helsinki: Neo-Assyrian Text Corpus Project, 2000), 110-11 with reference to earlier literature on 110 n. 7; elsewhere in the book the sources for others of these high officials are presented and discussed.

58. Grayson, *RIMA* 3 (1996): 233: no. 2010, 13.

understood as a mark of reticence, to avoid any explicit equalization with what a king could say? It is not possible, finally, to decide. In any case, the issue of reticence, one will recall, was evident even in Tukulti-Ninurta I's own expression of his divine status, and we find that echoed as well in subsequent Assyrian royal tradition. Thus, in a colophon attested in several inscriptions of Aššurbanipal, we read: ᵈ*Nabû* ᵈ*Taš-me-tu*$_4$ . . . *ki-ma a-bi u um-mi ú-šar-bu-u-šú* "Nabu and Tasmetu . . . raised him like a father and mother."[59]

A second feature of the Tukulti-Ninurta language of king and divine also recurs among later Assyrian kings. This is the description of the king's "radiance" or "effulgence." The several terms that appear in Tukulti-Ninurta's texts for this phenomenon—*melammu*, *namurratu*, and *puluḫtu*—and which go back, as we have seen, to the underlying Sumero-Babylonian tradition, continue in later Assyrian royal inscriptions, where they become increasingly frequent. They are joined there by two other terms, *namrirru* and *šalummatu*, which are also rooted in earlier Sumer-Babylonia, though there only for gods, not so far for kings, and in any case are not attested for Tukulti-Ninurta I.[60] Together, these Assyrian texts make clear that the radiance is something that strikes awe and even terror into all who encounter it and so its possessor. It is fiery—a quality brought out in the Tukulti-Ninurta Epic, where the line in which it appears, 12′, parallels two others, 10′-11′, that tell of the king burning his enemies. This same juxtaposition of images occurs also in the later Assyrian inscriptions, as well as in other kinds of texts, both Babylonian and Assyrian.[61] And of these, the annals of Tiglath-pileser I show some very close echoes of the Tukulti-Ninurta phraseology:

ša me-lam-mu-šu kibrāte ú-saḫ-ḫa-pu
nab-lu šur-ru-ḫu šá ki-ma ti-ik
ri-iḫ-ṣi a-na māti nu-kur-te šuz-nu-nu-ma

Whose radiance overwhelms the regions,
Glorious flame which like a rainstorm
is sent down against the hostile land.[62]

One other point: the radiance, as noted earlier, is properly and originally a divine property, handed over by the gods to the human king. This trans-

---

59. H. Hunger, *Kolophone*, 100: no. 323: 3; also 105: no. 336:3; 107: no. 341:2.

60. See *CAD* N/I, 237-38; Š/I, 283-85a. There are other terms for "radiance" as well, but they are either not yet attested for Assyrian kings—so *birbirru* (*AHw*, 1127b-28a, 1548b; *CAD* B, 245-46a)—or they are not yet attested for kings altogether, but only for gods and holy objects like temples and cities—so *šarūru* (*AHw*, 1193b-94a; *CAD* Š/II, 141-43).

61. Cassin, *La splendeur divine*, 75-76.

62. Grayson, *RIMA* 2 (1991): 13: no. 1, I 41-43; cf. 17, III 2.

fer, in fact, is directly stated in the annals of the early Neo-Assyrian king Adad-narari II, which seem to describe it as part of the coronation ceremony:

> *arki ilāni rabûti i-ši-mu-ma* ^giš^*ḫaṭṭa mu*[*r-te-ʿa-at*] [*nišē*] *a-*[*na*] *qa-ti-ia ú-me-el-lu-ú eli šarrāni* [*šu*]*-ut a-ge-e iš-šu-u-ni me-lam-me šarru-ti i-pi-ru-ni* . . .

> After the great gods had decreed (my) destiny, had put into my hands the scepter for shepherding the people, had raised me in front of crowned kings, (and) had put on my head the radiance of kingship . . .[63]

A third royal-divine feature that continues after Tukulti-Ninurta I is the king as representation—often, specifically, as image (*ṣalmu*)—of the god. The primary sense here is the king as reflection of the capacity and character of the god; and this, as we have seen, has a long background in the earlier Sumero-Babylonian south, remaining alive there into later periods, even as it develops in Assyria. In post-Tukulti-Ninurta Assyria, it should be noted, there are a few examples of humans other than the king as representation, but these turn out to be, in one way or another, part of the royal entourage: so Naqia/Zakutu, the wife of Sennacherib and queen-mother of Esarhaddon,[64] and, once, a royal exorcist (*āšipu*).[65] By far, however, the bulk of the occurrences of humans as divine representations in Assyria after Tukulti-Ninurta have to do with the king, and all come from official royal inscriptions or letters and reports to the king from his advisors. These occurrences connect the king with the gods Marduk/Bel or Šamaš, or speak more generically about the king and any god. We have already considered several examples here; let us now look at a few more. Thus, for Marduk/Bel, two examples, as Parpola has observed, appear to make the connection in terms of Marduk's capacity for mercy and care.[66] In one, the royal advisor Adad-šumu-uṣur, writes to his lord, Esarhaddon, to express his gratitude for the king's acknowledgement of the loyalty Adad-šumu-uṣur and his family have shown the

63. Ibid., 147: no. 2, 7-9. Note also the coronation hymn of Aššurbanipal, in which the various gods give the king certain of his governing capacities and instruments; Nergal, in this listing, provides him with *šalummatu* (Livingstone, *Court Poetry*, 27: no. 11, rev 7.

64. See S. Parpola, *Letters from Assyrian and Babylonian Scholars*, SAA 10 (Helsinki: Helsinki University Press, 1993), 14: no. 17, rev 1, in which the authority of Naqia's word is compared to that of the gods; the same comparison is made with the word of the Assyrian king, in Cole and Machinist, *Letters*, 43: no. 46, rev 12-13.

65. G. Meier, "Der zweite Tafel der Serie *bīt mēseri*," *AfO* 14 (1941-1944): 150-51: 225-26.

66. S. Parpola, *Letters from Assyrian Scholars to the Kings Esarhaddon and Assurbanipal. Part II: Commentary and Appendices*, AOAT 5/2 (Neukirchen-Vluyn: Neukirchener Verlag, 1983), 112 *ad* 125: 18f.

monarchy and so for the king's willingness to retain him and his family in the royal entourage. As a way of crystallizing his expression of the royal kindness and mercy, Adad-šumu-uṣur says:

> *abu-šú šá šarri be-li-ia ṣa-lam ^{d}beli-ma šu-ú*
> *ù šarru be-li ṣa-lam ^{d}beli-ma šu-ú*
> *ina pi-i ša 2 bēlē-⸢ni$^{!}$-ia$^{!}$ i$^{!}$⸣-[t]uq-ta*
> *man-nu ú-ḫar ú-šá-an-na man-nu i-šá-na-an*
>
> The father of the king, my lord, was the image of Bel,
> and the king, my lord, is the image of Bel.
> From the command (mouth) of my two lords, this (honor) has fallen to me.
> Who could repeat (this) later; who could equal it?[67]

More explicit about Marduk, the king, and mercy is the second example, from an astrological report addressed to one of the Neo-Assyrian Sargonid kings, perhaps Esarhaddon:

> *^{d}bēlu re-mi-nu-ú qar-rad ^{d}Marduk*
> *ina mūši i-zu-uz-ma*
> *ina še-e-ri it-tap-šar*
> *šar kiššati ṣa-lam ^{d}Marduk at-ta*
> *a-na libbi urdu-ni-i-ka*
> *ki-i tar-ᶜu-ú-bu ru-ᶜu-ub-ti*
> *šá šarri bēli-ni ni-il-ta-da-ad*
> *u su-lum-mu-ú šá šarri ni-ta-mar*
>
> The merciful Lord, the warrior Marduk, was angry at night
> but relented in the morning. O King of the World! You are
> the very image of Marduk; you were angry with your servants;
> we suffered the anger of the king our lord, (but) we (also) saw the king relent.[68]

As for Šamaš, the connection with the Neo-Assyrian king is expressed in a variety of ways. These include the royal epithet that first appeared in Tukulti-Ninurta I's inscriptions, *Šamšu kiššat nišē* "Šamaš of all the people,"[69] the simpler equation of the king with Šamaš, as in the

---

67. Parpola, *Letters from Assyrian and Babylonian Scholars*, 181: no. 228, obv 18-21. In line 20, *i-tuq-ta* is the defectively written Neo-Assyrian G perfect of *maqātu*, 3. m.sg. with dative 1. sg. (= *ittuqta*).

68. H. Hunger, *Astrological Reports to Assyrian Kings*, SAA 8 (Helsinki: Helsinki University Press, 1992), 189: no. 333, obv 5′-rev 6.

69. Seux, *Épithètes*, 284; S. M. Maul, "Der assyrische König—Hüter der Weltordnung," in *Gerechtigkeit*, ed. J. Assmann, B. Janowski, and M. Welker (Munich: Wilhelm Fink Verlag, 1998), 70 and n. 31.

assertion, *šarru bēlī* ᵈ*Šamaš* "the king, my lord, is Šamaš,"[70] or the labelling of the king as the "image" (*ṣalmu*) of the god.[71] From the texts where these expressions occur, it becomes evident that the king is considered Šamaš especially as he displays, in clear and public manner, his sovereign control and order over the known world, just as the god manifests the light of his rule over the world.[72] This point about sovereignty is best illustrated in two passages, both connected with Esarhaddon. In the first, from a royal inscription, the king asserts:

> *ul-tu qé-reb tam-tim* ˡᵘ́*nakrūti-ia ki-a-am iq-bu-(u)-ni*
> *um-ma šēlebu la-pa-an* ᵈ*Šamaš e-ki-a-am il-lak*
>
> From the midst of the sea my enemies said:
> "Where can the fox go from before Šamaš (= the king)?"[73]

In the second passage, the royal advisor Adad-šumu-uṣur, tries to persuade the sickly Esarhaddon to leave the confines of the palace, whether literally darkened or not, and show himself, and so, implicitly, his authority, to his court:

> *a-ta-a šá-ni-ú ina ūmi*
> *an-ni-e* ᵍⁱˢ*paššuri ina pa-an*
> *šarri be-li-ia la e-rab*
> *a-na* ᵈ*Šamaš*
> *šar ilāni*
> *man-nu* [*id-du-ru*]
> *ūmu-k*[*al*] ⸢*mu-šú*⸣

---

70. In the letter ABL 633 + K 11448 rev 33, cited in Parpola, *Letters . . . Part II*, 130 *ad* 143 r4 f.

71. Parpola, *Letters from Assyrian and Babylonian Scholars*, 159: no. 196, rev 4-5. An additional observation by Parpola should be noted here (*Letters . . . Part II*, 130 *ad* 143 r4 f.), namely, that the frequent logogram for "king" in Assyrian texts, MAN, i.e., the sign for the number 20, comes from the usage of this sign as the mark of the sacred number of Šamaš and so as an alternative designation of the god himself. However, we must be careful not to invest too much significance into each occurrence of MAN for "king": that in origin the usage may come from the connection with Šamaš does not have to mean that it (always) connotes a "sun-king."

72. The focus, in other words, may lie perhaps more on the public manifestation of sovereignty than on the manifestation of justice, as in earlier, southern Mesopotamian comparisons of Šamaš and the king (for the latter, see Labat, *Le caractère*, 228-33). The difference, however, cannot be pressed, because there are Assyrian texts that, while not describing the king as Šamaš or his image, nonetheless associate Šamaš with the king as a god who gives the king the capacity for justice: see Maul, "Der assyrische König," 66, citing an inscription of Esarhaddon (Borger, *Esarh.*, 2: I 31-36) in which Sin and Šamaš are said to provide just and right decisions as the basis of the king's own activity.

73. Borger, *Esarh.*, 58: A V 24-25, as cited in Parpola, *Letters . . . Part II*, 130 *ad* 143 r4 f.

e-da-ar tu-ú-ra
ši-it-ta ú-ma-ti
šarru bēl mātāti ṣa-al-mu
ša ᵈŠamaš šu-ú mi-ši-il
ūme ú-ta-da-ar

Why, then, today, for the second time, has the table not been brought before the king, my lord? Who is in the dark longer than Šamaš, the king of the gods—staying in the dark for a full day and a night, even for two days? The king, the lord of all the lands, is the very image of Šamaš. He should be in the dark for (only) half a day.[74]

Sovereignty also appears in other passages associating the king with Šamaš, although not calling him Šamaš or the image of Šamaš. Note, for example, the introductory line of Aššurbanipal's coronation hymn:

ᵈŠamaš šar šamê u erṣetim a-na re'-u[t kib-r]at erbe-tim liš-ši-ka

May Šamaš, the king of heaven and earth, elevate you to the shepherdship of the four quarters.[75]

The issue of the king as representative of the gods is perhaps most subtly expounded in another letter by the royal advisor Adad-šumu-uṣur, to his lord, Esarhaddon. This letter has been discussed repeatedly because its content is so intriguing—and difficult. The most difficult part is the concluding proverb about the king and his representativeness, lines rev 9-13, which, in turn, picks up language from earlier in the letter, obv 18-rev 3. Here are the two parts and their connecting lines:

šarru be-li am-ru
ša ilāni rabûti šu-u
ṣillu šá šarri bēli-iá
ina muḫḫi gab-bi de-iq
šu-nu le-e-lu-u-ni
ina ṣilli ṭābi da-an-qi
ša šarri bēli-iá li-du-lu

---

74. Parpola, *Letters from Assyrian and Babylonian Scholars*, 159: no.196, obv 14-rev 6.

75. Livingstone, *Court Poetry*, 26: no. 11, obv 1. M. Arneth, "'Möge Šamaš dich in das Hirtenamt über die vier Weltgegenden einsetzen.' Die 'Krönungshymnus Assurbanipals' (SAA II, 11) und die Solarisierung des neuassyrischen Königtums," *Zeitschrift für Altorientalische und Biblische Rechtsgeschichte* 5 (1999): 45, notes in his discussion of this coronation hymn that it is the first line of the text that mentions Šamaš, only then to be followed by lines that specify what Aššur and his consort, Šerua, give to the king as ruler. This order of presentation, Arneth suggests, indicates, along with various other evidence, that "in die assyrische Königsideologie werden bei Assurbanipal massiv Šamaš-Vorstellungen eingetragen."

né-me-el-šú-nu šarru be-li
le-e-mur mār mārē-šú-nu
ki-i an-ni-im-ma ina pa-an
šarri be-li-ia li-du-lu
[*š*]*a qa-bu-ni am-me-ú*
[*m*]*a-a ṣilli ili a-me-lu*
[*u*] *ṣilli* [lú]*a-me-le-e*
[*a*]*-me-lu: šarru: šu-u*
[*k*]*al*[!] *mu-uš-šu-li šá ili*

The king, my lord, is the one chosen by the great gods; the shadow of the king, my lord, is effective in regard to everything. As for them (= two officials mentioned earlier in the letter), may they come up here and wander around in the good and effective shadow of the king, my lord. May the king, my lord, see them prosper, and may their grandchildren wander around, similarly, before the king, my lord.

Now as to that saying, "The shadow of the god is man, and the shadow of man is man": (this 'man' [i.e., the *amēlu* that is the predicate] is) the king, (for) he is the likeness in every way of the god.[76]

To understand the proverb is to recognize that it is actually a set of two interlocked statements, which have the same syntactic structure: the first, "The shadow (*ṣillu*) of (the) god is man (*amēlu*)," and the second, "the shadow (*ṣillu*) of man (*amēlu*) is man (*amēlu*)." The point, thus, is to explain the first statement in relation to the second. This is done through two wordplays. The first involves *amēlu*, meaning here, I would suggest, both "human being"—any human, or the class of creatures called human—and "ruler/king," the latter a restricted and, in this Neo-Assyrian context, an older, even archaic sense of *amēlu*.[77] The second wordplay involves *ṣillu*: "shadow" in the sense both of "likeness/image" and of "protection/protector." Given these wordplays, the *amēlu* that is the predicate of each statement, i.e., the *amēlu* that is "the shadow of (the) god" and "the shadow of the (other) *amēlu*," must be the king. He is, in other words, the "shadow," i.e., the image, of the god—*ilu* here means any god, and so the notion of divinity in general—as he is the "shadow," i.e., the protection, of the other *amēlu*, which is any human and so humanity in general (cf. the previous part of the letter, edge 20-rev 3). This equation is, in fact, made explicit by Adad-šumu-uṣur, the writer of the letter, in rev 12, where he specifies that the predicate *amēlu* is *šarru* "the king": note the punctuation of the colon mark before *šarru*, to indicate *šarru*'s explanatory function—a usage and format taken from the scholastic list tradition.

76. Parpola, *Letters from Assyrian and Babylonian Scholars*, 166: no. 207, edge 18-rev 13.
77. See *CAD* A/II, 57b, s.v. *amīlu*, d, which collects examples from OB and MB (Amarna).

Adad-šumu-uṣur, then, sums up the matter in his last clause, *šu-u . . . ili* of rev 12-13, which also is preceded by a colon, to mark it as an explanation of *šarru*. Here, in asserting that the king is "the likeness in every way of (the) god," our writer is saying, I would propose, that the king can function as the "shadow/protection" of humanity, because he gets this ability from (the) god, whose "shadow/image" he is and who is the ultimate source of "shadow/protection" over the human world.

There is another sense in which image is associated with the Assyrian king, and this furnishes the last category we will discuss of the connection between king and divine. Here it is the king himself who has a *ṣalmu*, a physical image of himself, just as the gods have. This idea and practice are again old, with a long history in Mesopotamia reaching back at least to the third millennium B.C. in the Sumero-Akkadian south and continuing into later Assyria as well as Babylonia.[78] In Assyria, the practice seems to be first attested in the Middle Assyrian period, though the evidence is modest: the lines about the birth/manufacture of Tukulti-Ninurta I in his epic, discussed above, are one indication; another is the altar base from Aššur with Tukulti-Ninurta I twice in relief.[79] Only in the Neo-Assyrian period does the practice become common, indeed, elaborate.[80] In any case, both in Assyria and in Babylonia, *ṣalmu* can include not only sculpture in the round, i.e., a statue, but other fashioned objects like reliefs and drawings, as on walls of public buildings and especially on stelae.[81] As statue, *ṣalmu* is attested for gods and, among humans, significantly if not largely for royalty.[82] In both regions as well, the royal *ṣalmu* seems to

---

78. The bulk of the textual data are gathered up in the standard dictionaries: *PSD* 1: A/III, 161-66, s.v. alam, 1.3-1.6.4; *AHw*, 1078b, s.v. *ṣalmu(m)*, 2; *CAD* Ṣ, 80a- 84a, s.v. *ṣalmu*, a2′-b4′. The iconographic evidence, but sculpture in the round only, is surveyed in A. Spycket, *La statuaire du Proche-Orient ancien*, Handbuch der Orientalistik 7/1/B 2 (Leiden: E. J. Brill, 1981), 83-91, 146-59, 187-203, 204-13, 235-56, 294-305, 363-72. Among a number of studies may be mentioned: W. W. Hallo, "Texts, Statues, and the Cult of the Divine King," in *Congress Volume. Jerusalem 1986*, ed. J. A. Emerton, VTSup 40 (Leiden: E. J. Brill, 1988), 54-65; also I. J. Winter, in such articles as "'Idols of the King': Royal Images as Recipients of Ritual Action in Ancient Mesopotamia," *Journal of Ritual Studies* 6/1 (Winter, 1992): 13-42; "The Body of the Able Ruler: Toward an Understanding of the Statues of Gudea," in *DUMU E$_2$-DUB-BA-A: Studies in Honor of Åke Sjöberg*, ed. H. Behrens et al. (Philadelphia: University Museum, 1989), 573-83; and "Art *in* Empire: The Royal Image and the Visual Dimensions of Assyrian Ideology," in *Assyria 1995*, ed. S. Parpola and R. M. Whiting (Helsinki: Neo-Assyrian Text Corpus Project, 1997), 359-81. An attempt at a kind of grammar of Assyrian royal representation is offered by Magen, *Assyrische*.

79. For this base, see, e.g., A. Moortgat, *The Art of Ancient Mesopotamia* (London/New York: Phaidon, 1969), pls. 246-47.

80. See n. 78.

81. *AHw*, 1078b-1079a, s.v. *ṣalmu(m)*; *CAD* Ṣ, 78b-85b, s.v. *ṣalmu*.

82. *AHw*, 1078b, s.v. *ṣalmu(m)*; *CAD* Ṣ, 79a-82a, s.v. *ṣalmu*. This leaves out occurrences designating figurines used in magical and related rituals, which do involve more than roy-

work in three possible ways. In the first, the *ṣalmu*, normally as statue or as stela dominated by a relief of the king,[83] serves as a votive in a sanctuary, thus allowing the king to worship a god or the pantheon.[84] The *ṣalmu*, again as statue or relief stela, can also itself serve as the object of recognition, respect, and obeisance from the king's human subjects—a function immediately suggested by the public display of these monuments, often larger than human size, in the Assyrian core urban settlements as well as in the conquered centers.[85] Here we are clearly reminded of the respect accorded the images of the gods, but how close the analogy is we shall have to see. The third possible function is the *ṣalmu* as a relief or drawing within a larger carved narrative, showing the king in some characteristic activity, including worship, and so eliciting respect for his authority from the onlooker.

Now the division among these three functions of the royal *ṣalmu* is not sharp. One measure of their overlapping character is the fact that in any one of them the king can appear—though he need not—in a posture of venerating the gods (see below). Moreover, all three functions rest on a common notion, which is thus fundamental to what the *ṣalmu* is, namely, a part of the essence—the being, the order of existence—of the person or deity which it represents, and for which it can so stand. The connection here may be illustrated in a text from the Neo-Assyrian king Aššur-naṣirpal II, which uses the word *tamšīlu*, "likeness," to describe the way in which the king's *ṣalmu* represents him:

> *ṣalam šarru-ti-ia tam-šil bu-na-ni-a ina ḫurāṣē ḫu-še-e u abnē eb-bi ab-ni*
> *ina ma-ḫar* d*Ninurta bēli-ia ú-še-zi-iz . . . .*

> My royal image, with the likeness of my features, in red gold and pure stones
> I created and stationed it before Ninurta, my lord.[86]

---

alty. On the meaning of *ṣalmu*, see further, Winter, "Art *in* Empire," especially 364-67, who revises and extends the formulation in *CAD* Ṣ. Her main point, quite correctly, is that *ṣalmu* carries everywhere the sense of "image," which can then be realized in a number of different forms, both three- and two-dimensional; *ṣalmu* is not, therefore, only a statue.

83. It is often difficult from the textual evidence alone, i.e., without the actual *ṣalmu*, to decide which is being referred to. See M. Cogan, *Imperialism and Religion: Assyria, Judah and Israel in the Eighth and Seventh Centuries B.C.E.*, SBLMS 19 (Missoula, MT: Scholars Press, 1974), 58 n. 100. Also Winter, "Art *in* Empire," 365-66; 378 n. 13.

84. For the Neo-Assyrian period, see Parpola, *Letters . . . Part II*, 10-11.

85. Cogan, *Imperialism*, 59; Winter, "Art *in* Empire," 375.

86. Grayson, *RIMA* 2 (1991): 291: no. 30, 76-78; called to my attention and discussed by J. Westenholz, "The King, the Emperor, and the Empire: Continuity and Discontinuity of Royal Representation in Text and Image," in *The Heirs of Assyria*, ed. S. Aro and R. M. Whiting, Melammu Symposia 1 (Helsinki: Neo-Assyrian Text Corpus Project, 2000), 111, 113. On the vocabulary here, in particular *tamšīlu* and *bunnannû*, see also Winter, "Art *in* Empire," 367-73, as well as *AHw* and *CAD*, *ad loc.*

The connection is also reflected in the fact the language for manufacturing an image, both of a god and of a king, and for giving birth to the actual king or god, is often transferred from one to the other. That is, the *ṣalmu* is often said to be "born" (Akkadian *alādu*; Sumerian tu_4), while the king or god can be talked about as being "constructed/poured out" (Akkadian *šuklulu/šapāku*). As we have seen, this transfer is manifest in the description of Tukulti-Ninurta I in his epic. It returns in the Neo-Assyrian period, as in a passage from the annals of Adad-narari II:

> . . . ᵐ*Adad-nārāri rubû na-a-du ki-niš ib-nu-ni* [. . .]
> ⸢*nab-ni-te*⸣ *a-na nab-ni-ti bēlū-ti uš-te-en*$_6$*-nu-ú ši*⸢*kín bu-na-ni*⸣*-ia i-še-riš*
> *ú-šék-li-lu-ma*
> *zu-mur bēlū-ti-ia iš-pu-uk* ⸢*ta*⸣*-ši-im-*⸢*ta*⸣ . . .

> . . . Adad-narari, attentive prince, they (= the gods) duly created me . . .
> They changed (my) shape to a lordly shape; they constructed with perfect correctness the form of my features,
> and poured wisdom into my lordly body . . .[87]

Let us look more closely at the properties of the Assyrian royal image that give it a divine-like character. One is exemplified by the lines of the Adad-narari II text just cited, and the lines of the Tukulti-Ninurta I Epic that they echo. It is that the gods themselves are the ones to have formed the king, and so his image, giving them features of lordliness and perfection that, by implication, no ordinary human possesses. But the connection with divinity cannot only be read textually; it can also be seen on the physical *ṣalmu*, as, for example, in a frequent form of the Neo-Assyrian royal stela where the king is depicted with one arm raised and his index finger pointed straight (*ubāna tarāṣu*), in a gesture of veneration toward the divine symbols above him. These symbols often number five, and can be represented simultaneously as pendants on the necklace of the venerating king: star (Ištar), lightning (Adad), moon crescent (Sin), winged sun-disk (Šamaš), and horned crown (Aššur).[88]

Other textual evidence speaks to the possible divine-like functioning, indeed power, of the Assyrian royal image. The first comprises a couple

87. Grayson, *RIMA* 2 (1991): 147: no. 2, 5-7. In this text note especially *nabnītu*, *šiknu*, and *šuklulu*, all of which can be used to describe physical images as well as persons: see *AHw* and *CAD*, *ad loc*. For other manifestations of the close connections, indeed almost interchangeability, between image and royal person, see Z. Bahrani, "Assault and Abduction: The Fate of the Royal Image in the Ancient Near East," *Art History* 18 (1995): 374-80.

88. The parade example here is the "Nimrud" or "Great Monolith" of Aššurnaṣirpal II. See Winter, "Art *in* Empire," 372, who points out the occurrence of the divine symbols both in the field above the relief of the king and on his necklace; also Magen, *Assyrische*, 45-55. See the further discussion of this monolith below.

of god-lists, Neo-Assyrian in their present form, but with sections, at least, that may well go back to Middle Assyrian times. These enumerate the deities, including their *ṣalmu*, at particular Assyrian sanctuaries—the better known of the lists is the so-called "Götteradressbuch" for the sanctuaries in the old capital at Aššur—and among the entries is the object, mentioned several times, $^{(d)}$*ṣalam šarri* "the (divine) image of the king," which can appear both with and without the divine prefix.[89] Once the *ṣalmu* of a specific king is listed, namely, *ṣalam* ^{m}*Tukulti-apil-ešarra* "the image of Tiglath-pileser."[90] The fact, then, that the god-lists record royal images, sometimes explicitly marked as divine, alongside deities and their images suggests that these royal images were treated as part of the divine world. What function they had in these lists is not finally clear, but it is possible that they were some kind of votive, giving homage to the regular deities, while at the same time they could also have been themselves the objects of respect or obeisance from humans.[91]

A clearer sense of the royal image as object of respect and obedience, even veneration, may be found in several other texts. Two are loan contracts from Tell Halaf in the later seventh century B.C., i.e., toward the end of the Neo-Assyrian period.[92] They mention at the beginning of the list of witnesses to their transactions two gods, Nabu and Šamaš, and in third place, the *ṣalam šarri* "image of the king"—the latter marked as divine in one of the contracts (No. 112), but not in the other (No. 113), suggesting the same kind of free alternation exhibited by this phrase in the god-lists. Whatever the alternation, one should observe that the three witnesses are

---

89. In the "Götteradressbuch" the $^{(d)}$*ṣalam šarri* appears with the temples of Anu, Adad, Ištar-aššuritu, and Gula (Menzel, *Tempel* II, T150: 57, 60; T151: 80; T153: 105). Note also the Sammeltafel IIIR 66 (= K. 252), which gathers lists of gods connected, apparently, with various Assyrian festivals and other cultic festivals (so Menzel, *Tempel* I, 145-46, as against the view of R. Frankena, *Tākultu*, especially 1-5, who considers all the different elements of this tablet to describe the *tākultu* festival). In this Sammeltafel, the ^{d}*ṣalam šarri* appears at least twice, in different lists of gods: one is connected with the town of Arbela (Menzel, *Tempel* II, T120-121: VII 35′); in the other, the affiliation is evidently broken away (Menzel, *Tempel* II, T119-120: VI 29).

90. In the "Götteradressbuch": Menzel, *Tempel* II, T147: 12. Which Tiglath-pileser is being referred to is not certain; Frankena, *Tākultu*, 29, 112, thinks it is the first, but does not explain why.

91. See further below on the relief stelae with altars from Aššurnaṣirpal II and Aššurbanipal. The sense of votive may perhaps be inferred from certain summarizing phrases that appear in another Neo-Assyrian listing of gods, which is part of a ritual for the *tākultu* festival. This mentions a variety of images of humans, including both rulers and commoners, none of which has the divine prefix, and all of which are brought into the sanctuary, along with the images of a large group of gods, to participate in the *tākultu*: [*ṣa*]*lmāni šá mal-ki u ru-bi-i ṣalmāni šá ḫu-up-še* "the images of princes and rulers, the images of commoners" (Menzel, *Tempel* II, T138: 19-20).

92. A. Ungnad, in J. Friedrich et al., *Tell Halaf*, 62-64 + Taf. 23, 26: nos. 112-13.

regarded as a group, separate from the (ordinary) human witnesses who then follow; indeed, in one of the contracts (No. 112), though again not in the other (No. 113), the two groups of witnesses are separated by the date formula. A similar function for the royal *ṣalmu* appears in the vassal treaties of Esarhaddon. In them the guardians of the treaties and so of the oaths sworn as part of it by the vassals are said to be Aššur and the other great gods, and then the *ṣalmu*'s of the king, of the crown prince, Aššurbanipal, and, apparently, of the other royal son(s)(?) (none of these has the divine prefix).[93] Finally, we may point to a third Tell Halaf contract, which offers still another indication of the royal statue's divine-like power. Here one of the human witnesses to the contract bears the name Ṣalam-šarri-iqbi "the image of the king has spoken" (No. 108).[94] The same name, though not necessarily the same person, occurs in a number of other Neo-Assyrian documents as well, once again with the dingir sometimes preceding and sometimes not.[95] Furthermore, as Arthur Ungnad, the editor of the Tell Halaf texts, pointed out, this name falls into a pattern that otherwise uses explicitly the names of deities: thus, ^{d}Adad-iqbi, or ^{d}Aššur-iqbi.[96] We may thus assume that in this name pattern, the royal image, like these gods, was understood to have the capacity not simply to "speak," but to "reveal authority," in the sense, perhaps, of having commanded the birth of the human bearing the name.

The view we have been discussing, that the royal image in Neo-Assyrian times could have special, divine-like power, has been recognized by a number of scholars.[97] But how far to take this view has been disputed. In particular, did the respect paid to the royal image, especially in statue or stela form, involve worship? Mordechai Cogan denies this, even while accepting the general proposition, as he puts it, of "the heightened significance" of these images.[98] For one thing, he argues, the textual evidence about the stelae does not "tell of demands for their worship or describe ritual instituted upon their erection."[99] This matches, Cogan adds, the actual archaeological evidence of Assyrian royal statues and

---

93. Brought to my attention by Magen, *Assyrische*, 44; for the text, see S. Parpola and K. Watanabe, *Neo-Assyrian Treaties and Loyalty Oaths*, SAA 2 (Helsinki: Helsinki University Press, 1988), 44-45: no. 6, 397-404.

94. Ungnad, in Friedrich, *Tell Halaf*, 57-59 + Taf. 22: no. 108.

95. K. Tallqvist, *APN*, 205; *CAD* S, 82a s.v. *ṣalmu*. A new example was added recently from another site in the Ḫabur Valley, Til Barsip: S. M. Dalley, "Neo-Assyrian Tablets from Til Barsib," *Abr-Nahrain* 34 (1996-1997): 84: T 14, 14, here without the dingir prefix.

96. Ungnad, in Friedrich, *Tell Halaf*, 58-59.

97. E.g., ibid.; also the cautious formulation of A. K. Grayson, in *CAH* ^{2} III/2 (1991), 195-96.

98. Cogan, *Imperialism*, 59.

99. Ibid., 60.

stelae, which show no indication of having been worshipped. The one possible indication that there may be more is, for Cogan, no such indication at all. This is the "Nimrud or Great Monolith" of Aššurnaṣirpal II at the entrance to the Ninurta temple in Kalah/Nimrud, the only excavated royal stela, in Cogan's view, with an altar in front of it. Echoing Kurt Galling, Cogan asserts that the altar in question—a round structure with three legs shaped like lions' feet, positioned opposite the base of the stela—was not for offerings to the stela, but, as the dedicatory inscription to Bel on the altar indicates, for offerings to that god.[100]

Cogan's caution on the significance of the Assyrian royal images does give pause. There is, indeed, no surviving textual evidence, for example, of *mīs/pīt pî* rituals which were normally used to animate divine images, also to animate these royal images; the latter, however, is attested much earlier, from the latter third millennium B.C. in the Sumerian south, for the statues of Gudea, king of Lagash.[101] On the other hand, Steven Cole has pointed to at least one text, an *akītu* (= New Year) ritual tablet (VAT 10464) from the city of Assur in the Neo-Assyrian period, in which the king is depicted as making sacrifices, including something "before the image of the king" (*pa-an ṣalam šarri*); the phrase here corresponds, it appears, to other lines in this tablet that likely describe sacrifices "before" (*pa-an*) a variety of deities (col. V: 6′-9′, though all that is preserved of these lines is *pa-an* + a divine name. Now this practice of sacrifice before royal images, as Cole observes, is an old southern Mesopotamian institution, attested in the latter half of the third and the first half of the second millennia B.C.[102] In the case of Neo-Assyria, the practice may also be attested iconographically, but to affirm this requires that we return to the "Nimrud/Great Monolith" of Aššurnaṣirpal II, and reconsider the analysis of it given by Cogan and Galling. That analysis needs serious revision.

Already in 1936, C.J. Gadd of the British Museum, where the Aššurnaṣirpal stela and altar are conserved, noted that the altar has no inscription on it—the attribution resulting from a mistaken confusion with another Neo-Assyrian altar.[103] This has more recently been confirmed by

---

100. Ibid., 58, referring to K. Galling, *Der Altar in den Kulturen des alten Orient: Eine archäologische Studie* (Berlin: Karl Curtius Verlag, 1925), 43-44.

101. For the Gudea statues, see M. Civil, *apud* E. Reiner, "Another Volume of Sultantepe Tablets," *JNES* 26 (1967): 211. For the *mīs/pīt pî* rituals for divine images, see C. Walker and M. Dick, *The Induction of the Cult Image in Ancient Mesopotamia: The Mesopotamian* Mīs Pî *Ritual*, SAA Literary Texts I (Helsinki: Neo-Assyrian Text Corpus Project, 2001).

102. Cole, in Cole and Machinist, *Letters to Priests*, xiii-xiv, who provides a concise, yet comprehensive survey of royal images. For the text of VAT 10464, see *loc. cit.*, xxiii: n. 27, referring to Menzel, *Tempel* II, T80: 10′-11′.

103. C. J. Gadd, *The Stones of Assyria* (London: Chatto & Windus, 1936), 129 *ad* 118805, arguing against E. Nassouhi, "Les autels trepieds assyriens," *RA* 22 (1925): 88-89. The other

Julia Börker-Klähn, in her authoritative study of ancient Near Eastern stelae and rock reliefs.[104] Without the dedicatory inscription, therefore, one is free to take the natural step—a step fortified by the text of the *akītu* tablet discussed by Cole—of supposing that the altar is, indeed, for offerings to the stela of Aššurnaṣirpal. This, in fact, was the view advanced by the discoverer of the "Nimrud/Great Monolith," A. H. Layard,[105] and reaffirmed by Börker-Klähn.[106] Yet if so, it must be observed that the Aššurnaṣirpal depicted on the stela is in the familiar gesture of adoration of the gods described above: his left hand grasping a mace and his right raised with his index finger pointed straight above toward the group of five divine symbols, which are also on his necklace. Apparently this same gesture can be found in another attested Neo-Assyrian example of a king in relief on a stela with an altar in front—an example that Cogan does not mention, but that is pointed out, among others, by Börker-Klähn. In this case, we do not have the actual monuments, rather a representation of them on a wall relief of Aššurbanipal from his North Palace in Nineveh, Room H; but the representation is unmistakable.[107]

What, then, should we say about the worship of royal images on public display in the Neo-Assyrian period? The *akītu* text and the two archaeological examples of relief stela and altar do suggest such worship, *if* by worship can be meant the recognition and homage that are expressed by offerings. There is, indeed, nothing physical that would distinguish these altars from others of the same types used for deities in the Neo-Assyrian period.[108] There is a further point here as well. It is that in our two archaeological examples the Assyrian king is depicted on his stela not as a god looking down on his worshippers, but as someone worshipping the gods.

---

altar is 118870, whose text is given by Grayson, *RIMA* 2 (1991): 351-52: no. 98; the god mentioned there is ^{d}BAD = Enlil.

104. J. Börker-Klähn, *Altvorderasiatische Bildstelen und vergleichbare Felsreliefs*, Textband, Baghdader Forschungen 4 (Mainz am Rhein: Philipp von Zabern, 1982), 182: no. 136.

105. A. H. Layard, *Discoveries among the Ruins of Nineveh and Babylon* (New York: Harper & Brothers, 1853), 302, with drawing on 303 of the altar *in situ* in front of the temple.

106. Börker-Klähn, *Altvorderasiatische*, no. 136 in Textband, 182, and in Tafelband.

107. Ibid., no. 228 in Textband, 217, and in Tafelband. The main publication now is R. D. Barnett, *Sculptures from the North Palace of Ashurbanipal at Nineveh (668-627 B.C.)* (London: British Museum, 1976), 41 + pl. XXIII: slabs 8-9(?). From the plates in these two publications, the wall relief does not picture in full detail the relief of the king on the stela; for example, no divine symbols can be made out. As for the altar, it looks different from the one on the Aššurnaṣirpal II Monolith, having an overhanging flat slab on top of a rectangular trunk, and a kind of battlement on top of the slab. This altar is positioned below, i.e., in front of, the stela, apparently on some kind of processional way.

108. Thus, for the round altar before the Nimrud/Great Monolith of Aššurnaṣirpal II, compare the altar 118870, also of Aššurnaṣirpal II, with the inscription dedicated to Enlil (see n. 103).

If, thus, the king through his stela image is to receive worship from his human subjects, it is by virtue of his capacity to mediate between them and the *full* gods, those whose basic residence is beyond earth. In other words, the king's image, as suggested above for the god-lists, is both votive and venerated at the same time.[109]

III. Conclusions

We have wandered through a number of different features belonging to the ideology of Assyrian kingship in the Middle and especially Neo-Assyrian periods—features that proclaim the relation of the king to the divine world. So the king as "representative or administrator" of the gods, expressed through the titles *iššakku*, *šaknu*, and *šangû*; the king as divinely birthed and/or nurtured; the king adorned by divinely based "radiance" or "effulgence"; and the king as "image" (*ṣalmu*) of the god, having himself an "image." We have also looked at more general epithets describing the royal-divine relationship, like "favorite" (*migru*) and "beloved" (*narāmu*), as well as at two other features that, while not explicit about this relationship, are often associated with it because understood as the gift of the gods: the king as master of military prowess and sovereign over a global expanse. Now these features, we saw, have their roots in the Sumero-Babylonian south, of the later third and early second millennia B.C., and the process of transmitting them to the Assyrian north must have begun in that period, with significant milestones being the reigns of the Old Assyrian king Šamši-Addu I (1813-1781 B.C.) and the Middle Assyrian Tukulti-Ninurta I (1243-1207 B.C.). This is not to say that Assyria simply copied the south. In the peculiar association of *šangû* with the king, it went its own way; and the emphasis that it developed, in the official literature and art of the Middle and particularly Neo-Assyrian periods, on ever more elaborate strings of royal epithets, mentioning, *inter alia*, royal "radiance/effulgence," the royal "image," and royal military prowess and global reach—all this appears, at least in the surviving evidence, to be much more than the kings in contemporary Babylonia put forward.[110] As we have observed, a key figure in this

109. Cogan, *Imperialism*, 59-60: n. 104, comes close to this view in his alternative suggestion about royal images, which is grounded, as he says, in the discussion by H. Frankfort, *Kingship and the Gods* (Chicago: University of Chicago Press, 1948), 295-312. But Cogan applies his suggestion only to the *ṣalmu* as statue, not as relief stela, and maintains that "in no way do these circumstances prove that the kings were worshipped as gods." More on the latter point in the conclusions below.

110. Compare the Middle and Neo-Assyrian royal inscriptions with those from Kassite and first millennium B.C. Babylonia, as conveniently gathered in the admittedly anti-

heightened presentation of the royal ideology was Tukulti-Ninurta I, and the achievements of his reign seem to have provided the fountainhead for the Neo-Assyrian period, within the practices of the Sargonid Assyrian kings of the seventh century B.C. served, perhaps, as another high point.

The above list of features, it should be recalled, is not exhaustive; it represents those that seem to be most visible to us in the evidence, especially the written evidence, for the relation between king and divine and, arguably, most evocative of it.[111] The critical issue, finally, is what do these features all mean for the conception of Assyrian kingship. One could argue, perhaps, that they mean little, on the basis that their long history of use, back through Assyrian history to the third millennium B.C. in the south, made them empty rhetoric, dead cliches, by the time they passed at least into late Neo-Assyrian hands. But this argument could easily be reversed, namely, that their long history was, rather, a mark of their importance to Assyrian kingship, which needed these features in the constant quest to reaffirm its legitimacy as much in the eyes of its practitioners, the monarch and his court, as in the eyes of its subjects and outsiders. This reverse argument, indeed, can be confirmed when we remind ourselves, yet again, of the variations and elaborations these features underwent, for example, in Tukulti-Ninurta I's adaptations of them from southern models, or in the expostulations of the advisor Adad-šumu-uṣur to his lord Esarhaddon, on the king as divine shadow. For such variations and elaborations bespeak not transmission of dead cliches, but active concern with what the features signify and how best they can be articulated.

I would conclude, then, that our features do tell us about Assyrian kingship and divinity, and this appears to be what most modern scholars accept as well. But in asking about the king and the divine, modern opinion has ranged between two poles. One pole, represented by A.T. Olmstead, speaks of "the central fact of the empire, the worship of the deified ruler."[112] At the other end is the rejection of divinity as an appropriate

---

quated collection of D. D. Luckenbill, *Ancient Records of Assyria and Babylonia*, 2 vols. (Chicago: University of Chicago Press, 1926-1927). More up-to-date editions, although they do not yet cover all the periods represented in Luckenbill, are those of Grayson, *RIMA* 1 (1986): 2 (1991), and 3 (1996), and G. Frame, *RIMB* 2 (1995). To be sure, the claims of the Neo-Babylonian royal dynasty begin to approach the grandiloquence of the Assyrian kings, but still do not match it.

111. Among other features that could be noted is the epithet *dandannu* "almighty" (*CAD* D, 87a; noted by Grayson, in *CAH*² III/2 [1991], 195), which is attested only with deities and the Neo-Assyrian kings

112. A. T. Olmstead, *History of Assyria* (Chicago: University of Chicago Press, 1923), 104; quoted in Cogan, *Imperialism*, 57. Deification has also been championed recently by Simo Parpola, as part of a distinctive thesis about the development of a kind of mystery religion in Assyria—its efflorescence coming in the Neo-Assyrian period—in which the king

and meaningful description of the Assyrian king, however much it is acknowledged that there are expressions of his exalted status, above that of other humans, in the ancient sources. Mordechai Cogan is an example of this point of view, as we have seen,[113] but it is reflected directly or indirectly in the majority of treatments of Assyrian culture and society.

Now some of the features we have examined do indicate that the Assyrian king, from the Middle Assyrian Tukulti-Ninurta I on through the monarchs of the Neo-Assyrian period, was not simply an exalted man, but someone with a place in the divine world—or more precisely, his place in the divine was part of his exaltation. Thus, the king as a divinely nurtured, even birthed, child; his mass reckoned with the flesh of the gods; himself the image of a particular god, exhibiting a divine "radiance/effulgence" and having his own physical image like the gods, which can be listed with the gods in god-lists and business contracts, can form like them elements in certain patterns of human personal names, can occasionally be prefixed by the divine logogram, and can apparently be sacrificed to on facing altars—it is difficult to deny that these look to some kind of divine status for the king, all the more because outside of the gods they are found only, or almost exclusively, with the king.

Yet holding us back from this divine status are several other features we have observed as well. The first is the long-standing and regular description of the king as the gods' "representative" or "administrator." To be sure, the concept of "representative/administrator" need not be incompatible with divinity—the more senior gods can certainly have lesser gods as their deputies—yet in this case it does seem to point in a terrestrial direction, if only because the three terms used, *iššakku*, *šaknu*, and *šangû*, are otherwise applied to human officials and not attested for

---

functioned as a divine savior figure, the god Aššur was the ultimate divine reality, offering an inclusive monotheism summing up all the other gods, and the sacred tree was a, if not the, principal symbol of the whole. This religion, then, is supposed to lie behind the fundamental features of Jewish, Christian, and Muslim theology. Parpola discusses the thesis just outlined in a number of publications, of which the most elaborate is *Assyrian Prophecies*, xiv-xliv, and the most recent, with reference to the others, are "Monotheism in Ancient Assyria," in *One God or Many? Concepts of Divinity in the Ancient World*, ed. B. N. Porter, Transactions of the Casco Bay Assyriological Institute 1 (2000), 165-209, and "The Mesopotamian Soul of Western Culture," *Bulletin of the Canadian Society for Mesopotamian Studies* 35 (Sept., 2000): 29-34. The thesis is argued with great learning and ingenuity, but I have grave doubts about it, beginning with the lack of explicitness in the ancient sources for many aspects of it. For a more elaborate critique, see J. S. Cooper, "Assyrian Prophecies, the Assyrian Tree, and the Mesopotamian Origins of Jewish Monotheism, Greek Philosophy, Christian Theology, Gnosticism, and Much More," *JAOS* 120 (2000): 430-44, which the author kindly made available to me in advance of publication. See also the review of *Assyrian Prophecies* by B. N. Porter in *BiOr* 56 (1999): 685-87, 689-90.

113. Cogan, *Imperialism*, 56-60.

any of the divine pantheon per se.[114] Second, the divine logogram (Sumerian dingir), as we have seen, is found before the phrase *ṣalam šarri* "image of the king," but it is not found always. And it never occurs before the names of the Assyrian kings themselves. Indeed, in the god-lists and the business contracts, it is the *ṣalmu* of the king that is mentioned, not the king directly, whereas the gods there listed are given both by name of the god alone and, less frequently, by name of the god and his *ṣalmu* or emblem.[115] We may also recall the wording in the Tukulti-Ninurta I Epic and several inscriptions of Aššurbanipal, where the gods are not the parents of the king, but raise him *like* father and mother, and similarly, the Middle Assyrian personal name, which reads "The king is *like* my god" (Šarru-ki-iliya). All this qualified language, in turn, becomes only more meaningful when it is contrasted with certain earlier periods of history in the Sumero-Babylonian south. Here, and most particularly in the Old Akkadian and Ur III dynasties, explicit deification does appear: the kings, while still living, have the dingir before their names, their deification process can be described, and, over against the modest archaeological evidence that Assyrian royal images could be sacrificed to, we have much fuller, indeed, explicit, data that the earlier monarchs had temples built for their worship.[116] In the Assyrian realm, in sum, the royal-divine relationship clearly had limits.[117]

---

114. See the attestations in *AHw* and *CAD, ad loc.*

115. See, e.g., Menzel, *Tempel* II, T 120-121: VII 1'-40'.

116. The clearest and fullest instances of this deification are the Old Akkadian king, Naram-Sin, where it is first attested, and Šulgi, the second king of the Ur III dynasty. But there are other monarchs of both dynasties and of Babylonian dynasties that follow where some indication of deification can be found. See, e.g., J. J. Glassner, *La chute d'Akkadé*, Berliner Beiträge zum Vorderen Orient 5 (Berlin: Dietrich Reimer Verlag, 1986), 8, 14-19; Sallaberger and Westenholz, *Mesopotamien*, 54, 56, 152-56; C. Wilcke, "Zum Königtum in der Ur III-Zeit," in *Le palais et la royauté (archéologie et civilisation)*, ed. Paul Garelli, CRRA 19 (Paris: Librairie Orientaliste Paul Geuthner, 1974), esp. 179-80; J. Klein, *Three Šulgi Hymns*, Bar-Ilan Studies in Near Eastern Languages and Culture (Ramat-Gan: Bar-Ilan University Press, 1981), 29-36.

117. This matter of limits, and the dire consequences of not observing them, is addressed quite directly in the eighth campaign report of the Neo-Assyrian king, Sargon II. At one point in it, the king contrasts his own behavior, as one "who preserves truth, not transgressing the limits (set) by Aššur and Šamaš" (*na-ṣir kit-ti la e-ti-iq i-te-e* d*A-šur* d*Šamaš*), with that of his enemy, Rusa, king of Urartu, "who had transgressed the limits (set) by Šamaš and Marduk" (*ša i-te-e* d*Šamaš* d*Marduk e-ti-qu-ma*) and whom Sargon consequently defeats as the agent of the offended gods (Mayer, "Sargons Feldzug," 82-85: 148, 156). It is interesting to compare this with the Sumerian poem now labelled the Curse of Agade (see the edition by J. S. Cooper, *The Curse of Agade*, JHNES (Baltimore: Johns Hopkins University Press, 1983). Written well after the reign of the Old Akkadian Naram-Sin, the first king, as we have seen, for whom explicit deification is attested while he was alive, this poem has a forceful condemnation of the king for blasphemous behavior against the gods. The particular god offended is Enlil, the head of the pantheon, whose sanctuary in Nippur, according to

The issue, then, of king and divine in Assyria is complicated. If there are features that suggest that the king does have entry into the divine world, there are others that evince hesitation about his status there: that suggest, at the very least, that he was not so fully a god as the other members of the pantheon were. To this we must add that the picture may not have been a uniform and stable one. In other words, we should keep open the possibility—which at present I am not able to resolve—that because a feature like divine birth and nurture is not attested, or not attested as elaborately, for every Assyrian monarch from Tukulti-Ninurta I on, this may not be an accident of discovery, but point to individual historical differences in the calibration of the official royal ideology.

At the least, it appears, we should not conceive of the Assyrian king as either/or: as either divine or human. Put another way, we should not assume that the explicit deification and worship of the king especially in Old Akkadian and Ur III times is the only definition of how divinity may work with human kingship. We need, rather, to find a more flexible definition, a framework of discussion, that allows for variation on the issue historically. Let me propose, then, a framework. It would take as the fundamental point the designation of the Assyrian king that does seem to be constant and ubiquitous through most of Assyrian history, namely, the king as the "representative/administrator" of the gods, or, in a complementary way, his simultaneous function as both votary of the gods and venerated among his human subjects. What these usages reflect is a view of the king as the primary nexus between heaven and earth: the lynchpin that allows the two realms to communicate with and sustain each other. Viewed from heaven, the king is the principal divine emissary to his earthly community; viewed from earth—and the earth here, of course, is the earth as realized in the territory controlled by the king—he is the principal emissary of his community before the pantheon. Such a dual view was not unique to Assyria; it is probably to be found, in one formulation or another, in virtually every tradition of human kingship.[118] The degree and explicitness of divinity, then, would vary with which of the two views is given the greater emphasis and with how exclusively the king is conceived as the nexus to heaven. In the Assyrian case, one may argue, this duality came to be important, and so was elaborated and heightened, precisely as it came to form the core of an ideology that would correlate

---

the poem, Naram-Sin destroyed when he could not get permission from Enlil to build his own temple in Agade for the goddess Inanna. This charge, to be sure, is historically quite doubtful, but underlying it—although here too there is no certainty—may be a criticism of Naram-Sin for crossing the line into explicit self-deification.

118. There is, e.g., a parallel, but not entirely congruent formulation in late antiquity and medieval and early modern Europe discussed by E. H. Kantorowicz, *The King's Two Bodies: A Study in Medieval Political Theology* (Princeton: Princeton University Press, 1957).

with and reinforce the expansion of the state into an empire, beginning in Middle Assyrian times and reaching its climax in the later Neo-Assyrian, or Sargonid, period (end of the eighth-seventh centuries B.C.), when the Assyrian emperor was, in fact, *the* ruler in the world known to him. Construed ideologically, and promulgated through all manner of inscription and iconography, this expansion was presented as a task that no other human could undertake, for it involved nothing less than the establishment and defense of the orderly world, the cosmos, against the chaos of the outside: even more, the ceaseless effort to eliminate that chaos by expanding into it and remaking it as order. But the expansion was never a task that the king alone conceived and executed; he was regularly depicted as fulfilling the directive of the imperial god, Aššur, and pantheon, over against his enemies, who were often described as acting, blasphemously, on their own.[119] This expansion, in short, was a task that only a god-man could execute, and the fact that he was god *and* man reflected both the possibility and yet the fragility and limits of his power as regulated by the far greater power of the pantheon.

What is going on here is perhaps best elucidated by analogy to the ways in which the physical images and other representations of the Assyrian king were constructed. As Irene Winter has acutely observed, the *ṣalmu* of the king exhibited an array of conventional traits that had come to mark kingship, such as elaborate beards and musculature, within which particular features can be discerned that were intended to catch the individuality of the actual human king being represented.[120] Similarly, Stefan Maul has remarked that the Neo-Assyrian royal seal, dating at least from Shalmaneser III, remained unchanged in its iconography, regardless of the particular documents—reflecting, in turn, the particular human king who was their authority—on which the seal was impressed.[121] In both *ṣalmu* and seal, thus, we encounter the conjunction of the *office* of kingship, signified by the conventional features, with the *individual* Assyrian monarch, signified by the features that were individualizing. It was this kingly office

119. See, e.g., M. Liverani, "The Ideology of the Assyrian Empire," in *Power and Propaganda: A Symposium on Ancient Empires*, Mesopotamia 7 (Copenhagen: Akademisk Forlag, 1979), 297-317; building on Liverani, P. Machinist, "Assyrians on Assyria in the First Millennium B.C.," in *Anfänge politischen Denkens in der Antike*, ed. K. Raaflaub, Schriften des Historischen Kollegs, Kolloquien 24 (Munich: R. Oldenbourg, 1993), 77-104, esp. 83-91; and H. Tadmor, "World Dominion: The Expanding Horizon of the Assyrian Empire," in *Landscapes: Territories, Frontiers and Horizons in the Ancient Near East. Part I*, ed. L. Milano et. al., CRRA 44 (Padua: Sargon, 1999), 55-62.

120. Winter, "Art *in* Empire," esp. 369-76.

121. S. M. Maul, "Das 'dreifache Königtum'—Überlegungen zu einer Sonderform des neuassyrischen Königssiegels," in *Beiträge zur Kulturgeschichte Vorderasiens: Festschrift für Rainer Michael Boehmer* (Mainz am Rhein: Philipp von Zabern, 1995), 395-402 + Taf. 33 a-c.

that in a sense the individual monarch put on, when, in the coronation ceremony, the gods gave him the capacity to rule and the particular instruments and symbols of that rule. By reason of its durative, transpersonal character, then, the office may be considered divine; and this is why the *ṣalam šarri* as one of the physical representations of the office could, even if not always, be prefixed with the divine determinative, while the name of the individual king could never have such a prefix. The office, in short, was not a natural endowment of the individual king; it was a gift of the true gods, to whom he, as their earthly representative, had to remain attentive and obedient.

9

Israel's Royal Cult in the Ancient Near Eastern *Kulturkreis*

ZIONY ZEVIT

The congeries of ideas associated with the notion of "Royal Cult" in Israel at the beginning of the twenty-first century is more muddled than it was in the mid-twentieth century. By mid-century, historians had come to appreciate that the kingdoms of ancient Iraq were intertwined politically and economically with those of Syria-Palestine during both the second and first millennia B.C.E. while research into the languages, writing systems, legal conventions, representational art, and literatures of different peoples throughout both regions revealed many shared languages, legal practices, social norms, and mythic traditions.[1] These discoveries sanctioned hypothesizing a common, general Syro-Palestine-Mesopotamian *Kulturkreis*, "cultural zone."[2]

The *Kulturkreis* hypothesis, nourished by generalizing insights drawn from anthropology on the one hand and the history of religions on the other, posited that the philological and archaeological data demonstrated the existence of a common pattern of ancient Near Eastern culture in early antiquity. Although ethno-linguistic fault lines in the *Kulturkreis* divided it into different areas—Semitic versus non-Semitic, West Semitic

1. Although not ignored, Egypt tends to be marginal to this discussion because of the nature of the written materials involved, and, I suspect, because of a dearth of scholars trained in both Egyptology and cuneiform studies. In this essay, I do not factor Egyptological data into the discussion because no claims have been advanced and no data presented supporting any connection between Egyptian conceptions of the Royal Cult and those of ancient Israel.

2. Cf. the essays of H. Polotsky and E. A. Speiser published in parts II and III of *At the Dawn of Civilization: A Background of Biblical History* (= *The World History of the Jewish People, First Series: Ancient Times*), ed. E. A. Speiser (Tel Aviv: Massadah Publishing Co., 1964), 98-266.

versus East Semitic, alphabet versus cuneiform, Aramaic versus Canaanite—the hypothesis proved and remains useful. It justified assuming that what was explicit and apparent in one part of the zone must have existed in all parts so that what was attested partially in one specific area within the zone could be imagined more completely by filling in lacunae with information from a different part, even if deriving from a different chronological horizon. This was akin to how concepts such as *Western civilization, Muslim civilization, Chinese civilization, modernity, post-modernity* and the like are employed today.

Applied to the institution of monarchy in Israel, it supported homogenizing conceptions of kingship throughout the ancient Near East identifying the result as the common conception and claiming, on that basis, that not only were Israelite kings involved in cultic matters, but that they were considered divine. This opinion, characterized as a conclusion of the "myth and ritual school," was associated with the work of S. H. Hooke and A. R. Johnson in England, and with S. Mowinckel, I. Engnell, and G. Widengren in Scandanavia.[3]

This particular application of the *Kulturkreis* hypothesis is no longer popular in the study of Israelite religion even though it persists in discussions of *Psalms*. It does, however, remain useful for explicating the "divine" or "quasi-divine" status of some figures in Late Antiquity: Alexander the Great, Antiochus Epiphanes, Julius Caesar, Augustus, and Jesus. Despite my disclaimer about its popularity, in his recent history of Israelite religion, R. Albertz finds the concept useful. He characterizes it as follows:

> In the Near East the king was regarded in one way or another as more or less directly God's representative on earth: as God's creation, the son of God, the image of God or even God himself, who imposed divine rule outside the state and established divine order within, thus guaranteeing the existence of the state.[4]

A few pages later he writes: "In accordance with the conception of sacral kingship, the Davidides as a matter of course also had cultic functions, like the Jebusite kings before them." He continues to argue, using David as a paradigmatic example, that the king was priest, performing sacri-

---

3. Cf. H. F. Hahn, *The Old Testament in Modern Research with a Survey of Recent Literature by H. D. Hummel* (Philadelphia: Fortress Press, 1966), 78-82, and the comments of Hummel on pp. 277-78.

4. R. Albertz, *A History of Israelite Religion in the Old Testament Period*, vol. 1 (Lousiville, KY: Westminster John Knox Press, 1994), 116. It is noteworthy how Albertz employs the word/designation "God" ahistorically in the section cited, rendering the concept useful for ready borrowing into Yahwism.

fices, acting as a cultic vehicle of the divine spirit, and a mediator of revelation.[5] The selection of David as paradigm is particularly unfortunate since he was a "pre-Temple" figure. Furthermore, even in Temple ritual, every Israelite slaughtered his own animal and cannot be a signifier of priestly status. (This is discussed below in greater detail.)

Contrary to Albertz's characterization, no longer is there a broad consensus about what constituted the general, ancient Near Eastern pattern of kingship. A number of factors contribute to this: good philology and critical self-appraisal have led to the reevaluation of the meaning of texts that encouraged the original hypotheses, calling earlier interpretations into question; the climate of contemporary scholarship prefers emphasizing the particular and the unique; and finally, awareness that new texts can undermine any general statement discourages scholars from formulating such statements. The conception born of homogenization has been pasteurized. It is therefore necessary to consider the rubric "royal cult" as covering three distinct topics: 1) the king's involvement in cultic matters, 2) the king as a cultic functionary, and 3) the king as a focus of cultic activity, either as a person or as a deified being.

Jacob Klein informs us about the Neo-Sumerian period. In elite literature, the king supported state cults at Nippur and at Ur, they portrayed themselves as high priests, and the DINGIR determinative before their names suggests deification. The question with which he leaves us is whether or not the DINGIR and expressions translatable as "sons of gods" in some texts reflect living, dynamic myth or metaphor, conceptions of metaphysical reality or charismatic personae.[6]

Harry Hoffner, drawing also on official type texts representing elite perspectives at ancient Hattusha (modern Boghazkoy), presents a similar picture. The king was the priest of the realm, officiating at major festivals throughout his domain. He was nominally responsible for supplying the stuff of offerings, sponsoring festivals and cultic entertainment, ensuring that rites were performed, and was deemed culpable when the gods expressed their displeasure through natural or military disasters. Although kings or queens were said to have "become a god" on their demise, Hoffner notes that they were not considered to have become anything like the great gods. Rather, their cult may have cared for their needs in death just as did the family, ancestor cults of all dead Hittites.[7]

Peter Machinist's kings are more closely allied to those of Klein than to those of Hoffner. Neo-Assyrian kings too busied themselves with cultic matters and temples, but Assyrian royal tradition designated them as

5. Albertz, *A History of Israelite Religion*, 121.
6. Cf. Klein, this volume, pp. 115-31.
7. Cf. Hoffner, this volume, pp. 132-51.

"chief priest/functionary (shangu)" of the god Ashur, labelled them with the DINGIR determinative, and assigned them some special birth or nurture by the gods. The mix of temporal and cultic authority, that of king and priest, made the king a divinely appointed potentate with cultic obligations. Machinist notes that living kings were not worshipped as gods, but leaves unanswered the question of what exactly their deification implied. His study does not resolve whether their deification was a matter of archaic metaphor or of living myth.[8]

In each of the three cultures examined, kings were involved in cultic affairs and in each they were considered high priests and functioned in that capacity. In both Sumer and Assyria, the kings were identified as being of divine parentage and as being deified in their lifetime. Among the Hittites, the kings were deified only after death.

Literary sources from ancient Israel bearing on the subtopics of "royal cult," as explained above, are restricted to those in the Bible, but are scattered in different genres from various documents with different literary histories. Although the sources may be deemed elitist in that they were most likely not circulated widely during the Iron Age, their concilience reveals that Israelite conceptions of kingship—at least Judahite ones—differed from others examined in this volume.

Were Israelite Kings Involved with Cultic Matters?

The *locus classicus* for a description of their activities is 1 Kings 12: 28-33 where the Deuteronomistic historian, an individual who lived in the seventh-sixth centuries B.C.E. summarizes the cultic involvement of Jeroboam I, a king of the tenth century B.C.E.:[9]

1. He placed a small bull image in shrines at Bethel and Dan.
2. He declared these two shrines to be official pilgrimage objectives, alternatives to Jerusalem.
3. He established *bāttê bāmôt* (reading *bty* for MT's *byt*), shrines of some sort with altars which could be served by priests.
4. He enfranchised and confirmed as priests males from non-Levitical lineages, and these served at the new *bāmôt* as well as at Bethel, an older, established shrine.

---

8. Cf. Machinist, this volume, pp. 152-88.

9. For the purpose of this paper, this historian may be characterized as the individual living at the end of the seventh century who is usually characterized in research as Dtr I. An extensive treatment of this appears in the author's *The Religions of Ancient Israel: A Synthesis of Parallactic Approcahes* (London: Continuum, 2001), 439-79. For the nonce, cf. Z. Zevit, "Deuteronomistic Historiography in I Ki 12–II Ki 17 and the Reinvestiture of the Israelite Cult," *JSOT* 32 (1985): 57-73.

5. He affected a change in the cultic calendar.
6. He officiated at the Bethel altar, though not a Levite and not a priest.

Elsewhere, but in a different fashion, the historian notes that Ahab, a king of the ninth century "... established the evil/wrong in the eyes of YHWH ... *walking in the sins of Jeroboam* ... and ... he erected an altar for Baal in the house of Baal which he built in Samaria. And Ahab made/dedicated an Asherah ..." (1 Kings 16: 30-33).

By pruning these passages of the Deuteronomistic evaluative comments, we are left with the events to which they refer. Thus, in addition to maintaining Jeroboam's precedent of cultic involvement and maintaining institutions that he established, Ahab extended his involvement, constructing a temple or shrine for Baal, erecting an altar for it, and he also put up an Asherah.[10] All acts of piety. Ahab was an Israelian monarch of the northern kingdom not of Jeroboam's lineage, but scion of a usurping family, the Omrides. His activities, however, followed the institutional pattern established by the founder of the northern monarchy.

It is harder for us to discern the engagement of Judahite monarchs in cultic affairs. Solomon built the temple in his own back yard, and also put up *bāmôt* for Astarte of Sidon, Chemosh of Moab, and Milkom of the Ammonites on the Mount of Olives (1 Kings 11:5-7). The evidence is sparse, but it is likely that after Solomon's death (and the secession of the northern tribes) in 922 B.C.E., Judahite kings were not proactive in cultic matters. That changed in the days of Jehoram and his son Ahaziah in the middle of the ninth century, four kings (Rehoboam, Abijah, Asa, Jehoshaphat) and almost 80 years later. I conclude this cautiously on the basis of an *absence* of any statement to the contrary by the Deuteronomistic historian who was the critical reader of ancient records, noting innovative activity regularly when it occurred.

His comment about Jehoram is telling: "He went in the way of the kings of Israel just as the house of Ahab did because a daughter of Ahab became his wife, and he did the evil in the eyes of YHWH" (2 Kings 8:18a). A similar remark prefaces his summary of Ahaziah's career (2 Kings 8:27). I take the historian to mean that Jehoram (and later Ahaziah) acted in some cultic matters, claiming privileges that he, the Deuteronomistic historian, recognized as prerogatives wrongfully arrogated by Israelian kings as epitomized by the behavior of Jeroboam, the first northern monarch. Furthermore, the historian attributed this added authority directly or indirectly to the influence of a woman. He has nothing negative to say about the fact that the king assumed this power, only about what was achieved by its application. If this evaluation of the state-

10. It is unnecessary to clarify what is meant by "Asherah" in this context. For a summary of recent discussion, cf. *ABD* 1:485-86.

ment is correct, Judahite kings first assumed new authority in the middle of the ninth century B.C.E.

The Deuteronomistic historian mentions Ahaz's innovations in the cult of the Jerusalem temple, towards the last third of the eighth century B.C.E. He changed the shape of some appurtenances, specifically removing basins from lavers and the great basin, the *yam,* from the back of its stand. More significantly, he had a new altar constructed and instituted that it replace the old one in regular ritual. He then usurped for his private use the old altar which he ordered placed to the side of the new one. The historian describes him also as one who "went in the way of the kings of Israel" (2 Kings 16:2).[11] This comment reflects a particular, but not necessarily widely shared, Judahite conception of what royal practice ought to have included and excluded.

Data presented in the studies of Klein, Hoffner, and Machinist indicate that in Sumer, Hatti, and in Assyria during the Neo-Assyrian period kings initiated observances at some centers, stopped them at others, forced priests to obey their commands with regard to cultic matters. Phoenician inscriptions inform us that kings built and rebuilt sanctuaries, established celebrations, influenced the cultic calendar, and dedicated new images in established shrines (cf. KAI 4,5,6,7,26).

Like other potentates, Israelian and Judahite kings had access to wealth, influence over many servitors, and they controlled armies, i.e., men in their employ whose labor could be utilized for public works projects favored by the king. Biblical texts suffice to indicate that the kings of Israel from the tenth century and of Judah from the middle of the ninth century acted like their more powerful royal counterparts and contemporaries in Mesopotamia in that they were involved in cultic affairs, politics, and construction.

Did Israelite Kings Officiate in the Cult?

In Israelite sacrificial lore, as comprehended through Priestly legislation extant in Leviticus, blood manipulation was what counted in all animal offerings presented in the temple, and this occurred at the altar. Individu-

---

11. The activities of Ahaz had far-reaching results, influencing blood rituals prescribed in the P document. Ostensibly, these were accepted as valid by the Deuteronomistic historian. See Z. Zevit, "Philology, Archaeology, and a Terminus a Quo for P's *ḥaṭṭā*ʾ*t* Legislation," in *Pomegranates and Golden Bells: Studies in Biblical, Jewish, and Near Eastern, Ritual, Law, and Literature in Honor of Jacob Milgrom,* ed. D. P. Wright et al. (Winona Lake, IN: Eisenbrauns, 1995), 34-38.

als presenting animals, slaughtered and butchered their own offerings. They collected the requisite blood and gave it to a priest who took it to the altar for tossing, sprinkling or pouring. The priests also placed the meat on the altar, overseeing the burning process by which the animal products placed on the altar became sweet savor. The altar was their exclusive province.

The Deuteronomistic historian included only one narrative in his essay about a Judahite king manipulating blood on the altar. That king was Ahaz, mentioned already in the preceding section. Ahaz clearly busied himself with cultic matters that were of interest to the historian who commented: " . . . He did not do the proper thing in the eyes of YHWH his god like David his ancestor and he went in the way of the kings of Israel . . ." (2 Kings 16: 2-3).

The Deuteronomistic historian notes that after returning from Damascus and viewing the new altar that he had ordered built, Ahaz officiated in an act of dedication. He burnt his own *ʿōlāh*-offering and *minḥāh*-grain offering on it, poured out his libation and threw the blood of his peace offerings, *wayyizrōq ʾet dam-haššĕlāmîm ʾăšer lô* on it (2 Kings 16: 13). The historian's report merits scrutiny. It observes that Ahaz burnt the most important of his sacrifices, his own *ʿōlāh*-offering, but does not mention that he manipulated the blood at the altar. From its silence about the blood, I assume that a priest did it in accord with standardized ritual procedures in Jerusalem (cf. Lev. 1: 5, 9) and that it did not merit mention. Only with regard to the lesser *šĕlāmîm* did Ahaz exercise priestly prerogative with regard to the blood. The report does not mention who officiated when the proper sacrificial parts were burnt on the altar in accord with standardized procedures (cf. Lev. 3: 1-5). Here too I assume that a priest did it.

According to my interpretation, Ahaz performed only certain parts of different rituals while leaving the remaining parts to regular officiants. This interpretation is simply a by-product of the report. The historian's point in describing Ahaz' selective officiating at the altar among his other cultic activities was to illustrate its peculiarity. This emphasizes its special place in the annals of the Judahite cult at Jerusalem. It was the exception; not the rule.

The singularity of Ahaz's act is reinforced by legislation in Leviticus 4 datable to the late or post-Ahaz period, the late eighth century B.C.E.[12] In a section regarding the *ʾāšām* offering, those who have to bring particular types of an *ʾāšām* are listed in the following order: priest, whole congrega-

---

12. Zevit, "Philology, Archaeology, and a Terminus a Quo," 30-32, 38.

tion, and *nāśîʾ* (v. 22), an archaic term for tribal leader. In the time of the monarchy, the Judahite king was the *nāśîʾ par excellence* of the southern tribal kingdom. He is instructed to kill his goat and present the blood to the officiating priest, just like everybody else (vv. 24-25).

Less significant but sometimes cited in discussion of the sacred status of the Israelite monarch is the enigmatic Psalm 110:4, part of a dynastic oracle:

nišbaʿ YHWH wĕlōʾ yinnāḥēm	"YHWH has sworn, he will not revoke,
ʾattāh kōhēn lĕʿôlām	you are a priest for ever,
ʿal dibrātî malkî-ṣedeq	in the manner/according to the command of Malchi-Zedeq."

This verse has a long, glorious history of eisegesis. On the surface, it suggests that YHWH ordained the king to be his priest, like the *šangu* in Assyria. The Hebrew, however, can also be translated as being addressed to Malchi-Zedeq and rendered: "You are a priest forever according to my command, Malchi-Zedeq." The text of the poem is uncertain and I simply cite the verse but choose not to factor it in to the following discussion.[13]

In comparison with what prevailed in Sumer, Hatti, and Assyria, evidence bearing on the role of king as a cultic functionary in ancient Israel is mixed. Although biblical data disallow inferring that Judahite kings functioned as priests during the Iron II period, this is not the case for the northern kingdom of Israel.[14] There, the pattern was quite different, kings officiated regularly. Jeroboam reportedly "ascended the altar" (1 Kings 12: 32,33) and I assume that those described by the Deuteronomistic historian as "following in his ways"—the eighteen kings who reigned in the northern kingdom—did so also. With regard to this sparse evidence, northern kings conformed to templates of involvement described in the articles of Klein, Hoffner, and Machinist.

13. Even if the text with all its mythic overtones is comprehended as directed to the king, it indicates nothing about what the poet thought a priest-king in Judah should do or be. In any event, this notion—if that is what the psalmist intended—is an isolate within the body of Israelite literature and inscriptions available to researchers at this time.

14. It may be inferred from stories in Judges and Samuel and from remarks by the Deuteronomistic historian about the kings of Judah, that individuals offered their own sacrifices at ad hoc or established local shrines throughout the Iron Age. A prescriptive rule in Exod. 20:24 provides for this when the sacrifices are *ʿōlôt* and *šĕlāmîm*. Thus, it is not extraordinary to find a few pre-temple kings involved in such activities: Saul (1 Sam. 13:9-12), David (2 Sam. 6:12-19; 24:25), and Solomon (1 Kings 3:15). 1 Sam. 13:9, 2 Sam. 24:25, and 1 Kings 3:15 specify that the offerings were *ʿōlôt* and *šĕlāmîm*. None of these texts describes the manipulation of blood, which was a distinct priestly task and one that was supposed to have been performed only on the temple altar. 1 Samuel 14: 31-35 does not address sacrifice but proper slaughter. Even in the temple, individuals slaughtered their own sacrifices.

Were Israelite Kings the Focus of Cultic Activity? Were They Considered Divine?

The first of these questions is easier to answer than the second, but the second is more interesting. It raises a host of other questions in its wake: What does it mean to the contemporary scholar to say that a king was divine or deified? Was he accorded public honors similar to those accorded deities on conventionally scripted occasions? Was he perceived as god-like with regard to particular attributes such as knowledge or power or was he capable of functioning as a divine agent performing feats considered beyond human capacity such as healing or granting agrarian or human fertility? And if divine, what did it mean within the culture and how was it expressed there?

Biblical evidence bearing on the comprehension of the king as an object of veneration—all of it from Psalms—is sparse, but enticing. In its extant formulation, the psalter is a Jerusalem composition and so I broach the topic in the context of what the two preceding sections identified as Jerusalemite norms. We lack data for the northern kingdom. With few exceptions, the contents of the psalter are dated *linguistically* to the pre-exilic period.[15]

Among its compositions are poems celebrating the deity YHWH as king, and a collection labeled by scholars Royal Psalms. These celebrate kings of the Davidic dynasty in various ways in their relationship with YHWH. Such psalms, are of course, not surprising inasmuch as the Jerusalem temple was a five minute up-hill walk from the palace.

The case for deification actually rests on a few lines. In Psalm 2:7, the speaking voice of the king is quoted addressing his enemies:

ʾăsappĕrāh ʾel ḥōq	I will tell *in truth*
YHWH ʾāmar ʾēlay	YHWH said to me:
bĕnî ʾattāh	"You are my son;
ʾănî hayyôm yĕlidtîkā	I, this day, birthed you."

The implicit inverse of this declaration is a statement that the king might make: "I said to YHWH, 'You are my father; you, this day, birthed me.'" Something like this actually is cited in Psalm 89:27. After YHWH is quoted reciting all the good things that he did and will do for the king such as strengthening him, guiding him, striking down his enemies, and

15. D. A. Robertson, *Linguistic Evidence in Dating Early Hebrew Poetry* (Missoula, MT: Society of Biblical Literature, 1972); A. Hurvitz, *The Transition Period in Biblical Hebrew: A Study in Post-Exilic Hebrew and Its Implications for the Dating of Psalms* (Jerusalem: Bialik Institute, 1972) [Hebrew].

allowing the king to achieve glory by means of his name (vv. 20-26), he prescribes a statement for the king: "He will call me: 'You are my father, my god, rock of my salvation.'"

Whatever is meant by Psalm 2:7, it is clear that the adult king was not born a deity or a son of the deity. This is all the more obvious from a line in the J epic describing the conception and birth of Cain (Gen. 4:1):

wattahar wattēled ᵓet-qayin	and she conceived and birthed Qayin
wattōᵓmer	and said:
qānîtî ᵓîš ᵓet-YHWH	"I created a man with YHWH."

Eve's language in this statement is very specific; yet nobody interprets this to mean that Cain was semi-divine. Since there is no evidence that Israelite mythopoesis ever imagined YHWH as sexed, Eve's expression in Genesis can only have been a metaphor, and not an erotic one, at that.[16]

In Psalm 2:7 and 89:27, the father-son language may have expressed adoption, but even that does not solve the problem. What did it mean to be adopted by a deity in ancient Israel? In Rome, Augustus claimed divinity because he was the nephew and adopted son of Julius Caesar who had been designated a god.

In Psalm 89:26, YHWH declares that among the beneficent deeds that he will perform for the king is the following:

weśamtî bayyām yādô	"I will place his hand against Yam/sea
ûbannĕhārôt yĕmînô	and against Neharot/rivers, his right (hand).

16. Tikvah Frymer-Kemsky points out that YHWH, although usually presented as a social male, is not portrayed as sexed. She determines on the basis of cross-cultural comparisons within the ancient Near Eastern *Kulturkries* and inner-cultural comparisons within the literature of the Tanakh, that sexuality was not part of the divine order as conceived by Israel (cf. *In the Wake of the Goddess* [New York: Free Press, 1992], 187-89). The "not sexed" of her determination means that YHWH did not combine or contain within himself maleness and femaleness; he was neither bisexual nor androgynous. These categories simply were irrelevant.

Archaeological discoveries of inscriptions from Khirbet el Qom and Kuntillet ʿAjrud referring to both YHWH and the goddess Asherah pose a problem. Once the category of feminine-female is associated with YHWH, it elicits the presence of the polar correlative, masculine-male and opens up, at least theoretically, the likelihood of a mythic tradition involving sexuality. If, however, Frymer-Kemsky's conclusion be maintained, it is possible to analyze the role of Asherah asexually. This type of analysis may go against what is conceived as contemporary common sensibilities and common sense arguments, but is defensible on both linguistic and phenomenological grounds. Cf. V. Eller's application of L. Wittgenstein notions of "language games," and of the relationship between language and experience in culture, to the problem of YHWH's gender (*The Language of Canaan and the Grammar of Feminism* [Grand Rapids: Eerdmans, 1982], 6-47).

This verse alludes to Baal's victory over Prince Yam/Judge Nahar in the well known Ugaritic myth. A historicized metaphor in Psalm 89, it clearly evoked a particular type of relationship in that Baal was the son of El. This verse leads in to v. 27 cited above, suggesting, at least on some level, that the sonship of the king to YHWH was like that of Baal to El. This (over)reading of the psalm should not be pressed; the same image of control over Yam-Nahar is used in Psalm 24: 2 to define YHWH's cosmic authority. Thus, even if no Israelite would associate Psalm 89:26 with an (Israelite form of a Canaanite version of the) Ugaritic myth, someone familiar with psalmody could connect it with the metaphor in Psalm 24, a liturgy portraying YHWH's entrance into his temple as cosmic king, and arrive at a similar conclusion.

This association was made in Late Antiquity by the author of Mark. In Mark 4:39, Jesus orders the raging sea to become still while in Mark 6: 49-51 he walks on the sea (cf. Job 9:8).[17] That the author of Mark could make this association may be explained two ways: 1) It reflected a persistent, ancient tradition within the folk religion that read these texts literally from early through late antiquity. 2) The evangelist remythologized the metaphor in Psalms owing to conceptions of deity and of human-divine kings current in the Roman empire and provided it with a new application.

In Psalm 2:7 and 89:27 mentioned above, I suspect that the father-son language had more to do with expressing the relationship of tutorial deity to king than anything else. Similar language was also used in prophetic groups to express the relationship between followers and the prophet leader. This is clearly its intent in a dynastic oracle preserved in 2 Samuel 7:14 where YHWH speaks:

ʾănî ʾehyeh lô lĕʾāb	"I will become a father for him
wĕhûʾ yihyeh lî lĕbēn	and he will become a son for me."

The imagery of YHWH as "father" in some tutelary role is obvious in other biblical passages also. Compare Exodus 4:22 and Jeremiah 3:19, and especially 2 Kings 2:12 where Elisha calls out after the departing Elijah, "*ʾābî ʾābî* . . . "[18] Accordingly, the image in Psalm 89:26, even if picked up as an allusion to El-Baal, would have been understood as expressing the

17. F. R. McCurley, *Ancient Myths and Biblical Faith: Scriptural Transformations* (Philadelphia: Fortress Press, 1983), 34-62.

18. It is in this sense that the word was picked up by Christian speakers of Aramaic dialects as titles that emerged in European languages after some "Latinization" as French *abbé*, "priest," English *abbot*, "head of monastery," and Hungarian *apáca*, "nun" (see Y. Kutscher, *Words and Their History* [Jerusalem: Kiryath Sepher, 1965], 1-2 [Hebrew]).

granting of power rather than as an allusion to a relationship in which power was transmitted along with some divine "stuff" in a sexual manner.

I admit, however, to a modicum of methodological prejudice in this interpretation. I cannot imagine how a king who could not officiate at the altar could have been considered divine in any way. (This conclusion, however, is valid only with regard to the kingdom of Judah. We lack data bearing on this issue from northern Israel.)

Assuming that the psalms comprised part of the set liturgy in the Jerusalem temple, then the presence of the genre "Royal Psalms" with prayers on behalf of or in favor of the Judahite kings indicates not that they were objects of veneration but rather that they were objects of cultic concern.[19] Some archaeological evidence suggests that Judahite kings may have been provided with particularly impressive funeral rites and ritual fires, but this may be understood as befitting a rich, powerful, person who was not only king but also the head of the tribe of Judah.[20] In sum, nothing in the culture of ancient Israel as known from extant texts and artifactual remains indicates that the king had any attributes distinguishing him from his subjects as a human being.

Compared with the treatment of kings in the religions of Sumer, Hatti, and Assyria, Judahite religion is quite distinct. Judah's kings were not "DINGIRIZED" in any unambiguous way in their lifetime nor were they deified after death. Accordingly, based on arguments from numerous texts that do shed some light on an implicit theory of Judahite kingship, the questions posed at the beginning of this section can be answered in the negative.[21] With regard to the overall question of "Royal Cult" in Israel analyzed as three distinct topics, an analysis of extant data warrants concluding that there was only partial congruity between Judah and the vague general pattern of the ancient Near Eastern *Kulturkreis* during the Neo-Assyrian period.

---

19. The following are usually classified as Royal Psalms: Psalms 2, 18, 20, 21, 33, 45, 60-61, 63, 68, 72, 78, 79, 110, 132, 144.

20. Y. Aharoni, *The Archaeology of the Land of Israel* (Philadelphia: Westminster Press, 1982), 239; and cf. Jer. 34:5; 2 Chron. 16:14; 21:19.

21. We are unable to answer the questions posed at the beginning of this section about Israelian kings. No data bearing on this subject directly is known. Even though an argument could be made that northern Israel was within the ancient Near Eastern *Kulturkreis* during the height of Neo-Assyrian domination, no evidence for Neo-Assyrian cultic colonialism there is known.

10

Moses as Equal to Pharaoh[1]

GARY A. RENDSBURG

Two of the least understood passages in the otherwise rather straightforward account of the Israelites in Egypt are Exodus 4:16, 7:1:

Exodus 4:16 והיה הוא יהיה לך לפה ואתה תהיה לו לאלהים
"And it will be, he will be to you as a mouth, and you will be to him as a god"

Exodus 7:1 ראה נתתיך אלהים לפרעה ואהרן אחיך יהיה נביאך
"Look, I have set you as a god to Pharaoh, and Aaron your brother will be your prophet"

Some translations of the Bible and most commentaries to the book of Exodus misunderstand the true sense of these verses.[2] The plain meaning of אלהים, of course, is "god" (with upper case "G" or lower case "g") and thus it should be understood in these two verses as well.

The background for comprehending the import of these passages is the very essence of Egyptian religion. Unlike other cultures in the ancient Near East, where kings were considered human (serving as human agents of the gods, but human nevertheless),[3] in Egypt the Pharaoh was

1. This article represents a portion of my research on Exodus 1-15 in the light of Egyptian literary and magical texts conducted at the Center for Advanced Judaic Studies of the University of Pennsylvania during the 1997-98 academic year. My thanks to all associated with the center for the warm reception and for an environment that is extremely conducive to scholarly pursuits. In addition, an oral version of this paper was presented to the Hebrew University Bible Department Symposium in December 1998; my thanks to my colleagues in Jerusalem for their feedback.

2. See, e.g., the compromising terms in JPSV "in God's stead," and in NJV "the role of God."

3. The few exceptions from Akkad, Sumer, and Hatti do not disprove this general statement. For a recent treatment about Hatti, see T. P. J. van der Hout, "Tutḫalija IV. und die Ikonographie hethitischer Grosskönige des 13. Jhs.," *BO* 52 (1995): 545-73 (reference

considered divine.[4] This unique position of the Pharaoh clearly was known to the Israelites, and thus the author of Exodus describes Moses in the unique position of having achieved divine status as well. Hierarchy in ancient Israelite religion can be schematized as per Figure 1:[5]

FIGURE 1

God	——	Yahweh/Elohim
Prophet	——	Moses
Priest	——	Aaron

The highest level that any human being can achieve in Israelite religion is prophet, one who receives direct communications from God. Beneath this rank is the rank of priest, one who receives communications through the more indirect method of Urim and Thummim. In other ancient Near Eastern cultures, ordinary human beings can achieve the level of the divine in very special cases. The best known example from Egypt is the great sage Imhotep, who was deified by later generations;[6] and the best known example from Mesopotamia is the legendary hero Gilgamesh.[7] Parallel cases from Greece include Herakles and Prometheus.[8]

In Israel the elevation of a human being from human status to divine

---

courtesy of Gary Beckman). For Sumer, with brief reference also to Naram-Sin of Akkad, see J. Klein, "Shulgi of Ur: King of a Neo-Sumerian Empire," *CANE* 2:846-48; as well as his contribution to the present volume.

4. For general treatment, see the excellent essays in D. O'Connor and D. P. Silverman, eds., *Ancient Egyptian Kingship* (Leiden: E. J. Brill, 1995). For a recent study devoted to one aspect of the Pharaoh's divine status, see F. Abitz, *Pharao als Gott in den Unterweltsbüchern des Neuen Reiches*, OBO 146 (Göttingen: Vandenhoeck & Ruprecht, 1995). Some Egyptologists are more reserved in their remarks; see, e.g., E. Hornung, *Conceptions of God in Ancient Egypt: The One and the Many* (Ithaca: Cornell University Press, 1982), 140-42; and R. J. Leprohon, "Royal Ideology and State Administration in Pharaonic Egypt," *CANE* 1:274-75. The basic point remains, however, that statements such as "Long live the Horus, Strong Bull who causes the Two Lands to live . . . Horus of Gold . . . King of Upper and Lower Egypt" present the Pharaoh in unambiguous terms as divine. The cited passage is relatively standard; see, for example, H. W. Fairman and B. Grdseloff, "Texts of Ḥatshepsut and Sethos I inside Speos Artemidos," *JEA* 33 (1947): 21-22.

5. I first heard the general point being made here, and was shown the accompanying graphic depiction of the point, from my mentor Cyrus H. Gordon when I was a graduate student at New York University in the late 1970s. As far as I know, Gordon never published the idea. I am happy to present the point as the springboard to this article and to expand upon it with much additional material.

6. On the sage Imhotep, see conveniently D. Wildung, "Imhotep," *LÄ* 3 (1980): 145-48.

7. For a survey of the data, see J. M. Tigay, *The Evolution of the Gilgamesh Epic* (Philadelphia: University of Pennsylvania Press, 1982), 13-14.

8. See conveniently A. Schachter, "Heracles," and K. Dowden, "Prometheus," both in S. Hornblower and A. Spawforth, *The Oxford Classical Dictionary*, 3rd edition (Oxford: Oxford University Press, 1996), 684-86 and 1253-54 respectively.

status certainly was heretical. For while the covenant concept in ancient Israel meant that the relationship between man and God was extremely close, the gap between the two could never be bridged. Paradoxically, the other cultures in the ancient Near East viewed their gods as distant, operating in their own world replete with theogony and theomachy,[9] and yet the larger gap could be bridged. The standard theology of the Bible, however, is set aside in the case of Moses's appearance before Pharaoh. The summit conference between the two leaders of the two peoples demands that the two appear as equals.[10] Accordingly, since Pharaoh was understood to be a god by his people, for the purposes of this story, Moses is elevated to divine status. This is the plain meaning of the two passages cited at the outset.[11]

Thus, Moses the prophet par excellence is elevated to god, and consequently Aaron the priest par excellence is elevated to prophet (the latter notwithstanding the fact that the priesthood of Aaron is an element not stated until much later in the book of Exodus [28:1-3, etc.]; however, this may serve to explain the presence of the word הלוי "the Levite" in Exodus 4:14).[12] In the words of the two verses, Aaron will serve Moses as his "mouth" (the metaphorical usage in 4:16) and his "prophet" (the more direct usage in 7:1). Figure 1 above may be altered to portray these promotions in the manner of Figure 2:

9. See, e.g., the succinct remarks of M. Weinfeld, "Israelite Religion," in M. Eliade, ed., *The Encyclopaedia of Religion* (New York: Macmillan, 1987), 7:481.

10. As with nations today: when one country sends a head of state, the other does likewise; when one country sends a foreign minister, the other follows suit; and so on.

11. If this were simply a case of Aaron serving as a spokesperson for his brother Moses encumbered by a speech impediment or with difficulties speaking, as some scholars have suggested, then one would be ready to accept the words פה "mouth" and נביא "prophet" figuratively, with no further discussion necessary. But the application of the term אלהים to Moses in these passages informs us that something much grander is present, namely, promotion to divine status, and thus one needs to understand the epithets attributed to Aaron literally: they notify the reader that he too has been elevated in rank, to the level of prophet. The only other place in the Bible where the word "God" is applied to a human being confirms the point. I refer to Isaiah 9:5 with the expression אל גבור "God Hero" as one of the elements of the name of the king (Psalm 45:7 is subject to varying interpretations). This entire section of Isaiah is heavily indebted to the Egyptian coronation ritual, as seen first by G. von Rad, "Das judäische Königsritual," *TLZ* 72 (1947): 211-16, and recently confirmed by J. J. M. Roberts, "Whose Child Is This? Reflections of the Speaking Voice in Isaiah 9:5," *HTR* 90 (1997): 115-29. My thanks to Israel Knohl of the Hebrew University for reminding me of the importance of this passage as a support for the main point being argued herein and for sending me to the Roberts article.

12. Interestingly, Abraham ibn Ezra understood that Aaron's promotion to prophet must entail a concomitant promotion for Moses. However, the great medieval commentator could not countenance Moses' elevation to divine status, and therefore he inferred that Moses was elevated to an angel. See ibn Ezra's comments at Exodus 4:16.

FIGURE 2

God	——	
Prophet	——	Moses
Priest	——	Aaron

These promotions, of course, are only temporary. They are for the specific instance of appearing before Pharaoh. And while the Bible never states explicitly that Moses is reduced to prophet and Aaron to priest, this is implicit from the major traditions of the Torah (for Moses, see Deuteronomy 34:10; for Aaron, see Exodus 29). Here we may note that temporary promotion of this sort has an analogy in the modern military, as the famous cases of George Custer and Orde Wingate illustrate.[13]

These passages truly are remarkable. They indicate the extent to which the biblical author was willing to reflect the Egyptian background of the story. Literary flavor overrides biblical theology. If the exigency of the moment calls for Moses's elevation to the divine plane, even if this position violates a basic tenet of the ancient Israelites, the biblical author was ready and willing to present the episode in just such a manner.

The depiction of Moses as the equal to Pharaoh is not limited to these two verses. Rather, as we shall see, there are a number of instances where the biblical author portrays Moses in this manner. We begin our survey with the birth story of Moses in Exodus 2:1-10. Virtually every treatment of the story in the secondary literature discusses this story as an example of the "exposed-infant motif,"[14] and further notes the particularly close parallel between this episode and the birth legend of Sargon of Akkad.[15] But the nature of biblical literature suggests that we should look not to Mesopotamia to explain a feature in a story set in Egypt, but rather to

13. George Custer was elevated from the rank of captain to brigadier general at the battle of Gettysburg in 1863, then to major general later in the Civil War, but after the war received his regular commission of lieutenant colonel. Details may be found in the standard biographies, e.g., J. Monagahn, *Custer: The Life of General George Armstrong Custer* (Boston: Little Brown, 1959); and J. D. Wert, *Custer: The Controversial Life of George Armstrong Custer* (New York: Simon & Schuster, 1996). Orde Wingate received several temporary promotions during his remarkable career in the British army, first as lieutenant colonel in Sudan in 1941, then as major general in Burma in 1943. A recent biography is T. Royle, *Orde Wingate: Irregular Soldier* (London: Weidenfeld & Nicolson, 1995).

14. The most detailed treatment of Exodus 2:1-10 is that of B. Childs, "The Birth of Moses," *JBL* 84 (1965): 109-22. For a general treatment of the exposed-infant motif, see D. B. Redford, "The Literary Motif of the Exposed Child," *Numen* 14 (1967): 209-28.

15. For translation with notes, see B. R. Foster, *Before the Muses: An Anthology of Akkadian Literature*, 2nd ed. (Bethesda, MD: CDL Press, 1996), 2:803-4; and B. R. Foster, "The Birth Legend of Sargon of Akkad," in W. W. Hallo, ed., *The Context of Scripture* (Leiden: E. J. Brill, 1997), 1:461. The most extensive treatment is B. Lewis, *The Sargon Legend*, ASORDS 4 (Cambridge, MA: American Schools of Oriental Research, 1980).

Egypt.[16] Accordingly, it is more apposite to consider the birth account of Horus from Egyptian tradition, especially, as we shall see below, since this story alone includes a crucial factor present in the Moses story. But first we need to discuss the role of Horus in the religion of ancient Egypt.

As with most ancient pantheons, the essence of any particular god is very fluid. But the one element that remains with Horus throughout the course of ancient Egyptian history (from the Old Kingdom through the Ptolemaic and Roman periods) is his role as the god of kingship represented by a falcon. The Pharaoh, in turn, is seen as the living embodiment of this god, that is, as Horus incarnate.[17] Accordingly, any myth about Horus is in essence a story about the Pharaoh as well.

The account of Horus's birth is recorded in true story form only in Plutarch's *Isis and Osiris*, and in very abridged form in P. Jumilhac dated to the Ptolemaic period. Because the latter is a native Egyptian text (while the former is not), and because the latter is curt in its exposition, it is preferable to utilize P. Jumilhac to present the germane material. A large section of the papyrus is concerned with the origin of various divine names. When the text reaches the name Anubis, we read as follows:[18]

> Another version: Seth was ranging about looking for Horus when he was a child in his birthplace at Khemmis. His mother hid him in a papyrus-thicket, and the coverlet of Nephthys was over him. She hid him as "the royal-child (*inpw*) who is in the papyrus-thicket," and so his name Anubis (*inpw*) came into being, and Mehet-imy-wet became his cult image.
>
> Another version: He was sailing about in a boat (*inp*) of papyrus, and Isis said to Thoth, "Let me see my son who is hidden in the marshes." Thoth said, "See him." And Isis said, "Is that him (*in p3y pw*)?" And that is how his name Anubis (*inpw*) came into being, a name which on that account is given to every royal-child (*inpw*).

The aforementioned fluidity of the pantheon is reflected in this text: note that there is an attempt to identify Horus and Anubis, two gods who are otherwise distinct in Egyptian religion. But the main point is clear:

---

16. Mesopotamian literary texts should serve to illuminate sections of the Bible with a Mesopotamian context; see, e.g., P. Machinist, "Assyria and Its Image in the First Isaiah," *JAOS* 103 (1983): 719-37. Similarly, Persian material is relevant to the book of Esther; see, e.g., C. H. Gordon, "The Substratum of Taqiyya in Iran," *JAOS* 97 (1977): 192.

17. For a survey, which also extends the discussion to include later developments such as the divinity of Jesus, see J. K. Hoffmeier, "Son of God: From Pharaoh to Israel's Kings to Jesus," *Bible Review* (June 1997): 44-49, 54.

18. J. Vandier, *Le Papyrus Jumilhac* (Paris: Centre National de la Recherche Scientifique, 1962), 117.

Horus the son of Isis was hidden by his mother in a papyrus basket among the marshes to protect him from his wicked uncle Seth.[19]

The basic story of Horus is as follows, for which see also Figure 3 with the family tree representing the *dramatis personae* of the myth. In a battle between the two brothers Seth and Osiris, the former, representing the forces of evil and chaos,[20] kills the latter, representing goodness. Osiris thus becomes the god of the dead. Osiris's wife, Isis, was pregnant with Osiris's seed before this battle occurred. The widowed Isis now flees to the Delta where she is able both to hide from Seth and to give birth to Horus. Here Isis suckles the child and protects him. On occasion Isis must leave the newborn Horus unprotected, and at times he is attacked by snakes and scorpions, but always he survives, especially when other deities, most prominently Isis's sister Nephthys, serve as guardians and protectors of the young Horus. At myth's end, Horus reaches adulthood and is ready to fight against Seth in order to avenge the death of his father Osiris.

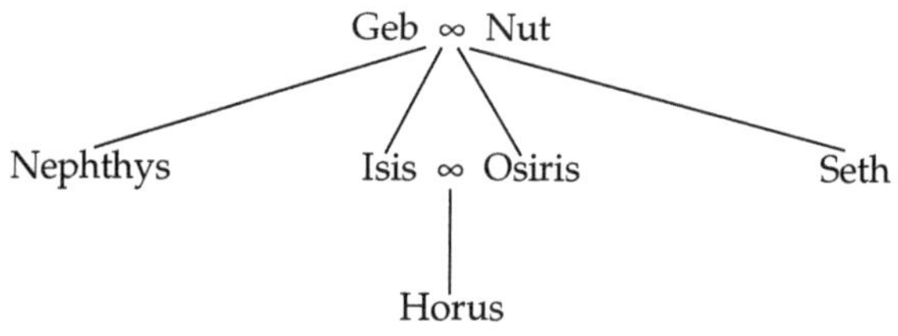

FIGURE 3: Family tree of the principle Egyptian deities involved in the myths of Horus.

---

19. Because this text is known only from the very late period, Redford ("The Literary Motif of the Exposed Child," 221-24) proposed that the Egyptians borrowed this specific version of the exposed-infant motif during the Greco-Roman period "when literary cross-fertilization had been going on for a long time" (p. 223) with the result that "Egypt had been sufficiently exposed to both Hebrew and Classical literature for influences from those sources to have crept into the age-old myths" (pp. 223-24). See also his brief statements in an earlier article: D. B. Redford, "Exodus i 11," *VT* 13 (1963): 415. But elements of the Horus-Seth conflict and the Isis-Horus relationship appear already in the Pyramid Texts from the Old Kingdom and in the Coffin Texts from the Middle Kingdom; for documentation, see J. G. Griffiths, *The Conflict of Horus and Seth* (Liverpool: Liverpool University Press, 1960), 1-27; for brief treatment, see D. Meeks and C. Favard-Meeks, *Daily Life of the Egyptian Gods* (Ithaca, NY: Cornell University Press, 1996), 85-86. For a direct response to Redford's 1963 article, see W. Helck, "Tkw und die Ramses-Stadt," *VT* 15 (1965): 48. The only element of the Horus birth story that appears for the first time in late texts is the specific mention of the papyrus basket. In short, there is little or no basis for Redford's contention.

20. For general introduction, see H. te Velde, *Seth, God of Confusion* (Leiden: E. J. Brill, 1967).

Above I noted that the Horus story alone shares a crucial factor with the Moses story, as opposed to the main theme of the other exposed-infant accounts from antiquity. In the typical version of this motif, the goal is for the parents to be rid of the child that is exposed to nature.[21] This clearly is not the case in the Moses and Horus birth stories. Only in these two versions do the parents (or to be more specific, the mother) seek the salvation of the child, rather than its destruction. Moses's mother, Jochebed (see Exodus 6:20; her name is not given in Exodus 2:1-10), seeks to protect her newborn son from the wicked machinations of the Pharaoh; just as Horus's mother, Isis, seeks to protect her newborn son from the machinations of the child's wicked uncle Seth. This point has not been taken into account in the scholarly literature about the folkloristic parallels to the Moses birth story. In light of this important connection, we may conclude that the biblical story has its closest parallel by far, if not its only true parallel, in the Horus birth story.

Still other parallels may be cited. The role of the mother is emphasized in both stories:[22] with Horus, Osiris is dead of course, and Isis is forced to act on her own; with Moses, the mother is the active participant, and the father appears only in Exodus 2:1 and never again in the story. The mother's hiding of the child is present in both versions: with Isis this is an important element in the story;[23] in Exodus 2:2-3 this is noted with the twofold use of the root צפן "hide." A second female appears in both stories as a protectress of the newborn: with Horus, it is his aunt Nephthys; with Moses, it is his sister Miriam (again, not named in Exodus 2:1-10, but prominently present). In both stories an emphasis is placed on the suckling of the child: for Isis and Horus the best representation is in the artwork (for one of many examples, see Figure 4[24]); in the biblical account, see Exodus 2:7-9 where Miriam arranges for Jochebed to nurse Moses.

The sum of the evidence is clear: not surprisingly, a biblical story set in Egypt echoes a well-known and popular myth from Egypt. Further-

21. This point has been noted by N. M. Sarna, *Exploring Exodus* (New York: Schocken, 1986), 29-31; and N. M. Sarna, *The JPS Torah Commentary: Exodus* (Philadelphia: Jewish Publication Society, 1991), 267-68. Sarna did not take into consideration the similarity between the Moses and Horus stories to be noted presently.

22. Admittedly, this is true of the Sargon birth story as well.

23. Again, see the brief treatment in Meeks and Favard-Meeks, *Daily Life of the Egyptian Gods*, 85-86.

24. Walters Art Gallery (Baltimore) 54.416. For an additional illustration, see S. Quirke and J. Spencer, *The British Museum Book of Ancient Egypt* (London: British Museum Press, 1994), 68.

FIGURE 4: Bronze statuette of Isis nursing Horus (WAG 54.416). Courtesy The Walters Art Gallery, Baltimore.

more, the biblical writer utilized the venerable Horus myth in order to present Moses as the equal to Pharaoh. The young Moses is akin to the young Horus, the latter a mythic equal of the living Pharaoh. At the same time, the Pharaoh of the biblical story has been transformed from his Egyptian mythological position of the persecuted, that is, Horus, to that of the persecutor, that is, Seth.

The next episode in the Moses story that demands our attention is Exodus 4:1-5. Atop Mt. Horeb (see Exodus 3:1), Moses is informed by God that he will be the leader of the Israelites in their efforts to gain freedom from Egyptian bondage. Moses issues a series of objections as to why he is unqualified for this position.[25] One of the objections is that the people will not believe him, but rather they will say לא נראה אליך יהוה

25. The last of these objections, in fact, is Moses' inability to speak, a point which serves as the springboard for the verse with which I began this article, namely, Exodus 4:16.

"Yahweh did not appear to you" (Exodus 4:1). In response to Moses's objection, God empowers Moses with the ability to turn his shepherd's staff into a snake and back again into a staff (vv. 2-4). When Moses and Aaron appear before Pharaoh several chapters later, they accomplish this act, though now the text reads תנין "crocodile" instead of נחש "snake" (Exodus 7:9-10). There has been some debate on the meaning of the word תנין, but "crocodile" must be the intended animal, as the descriptions in Ezek 29:3-4, 32:2 indicate quite clearly.[26] Support for this conclusion comes from the Middle Egyptian story of the Wax Crocodile, a portion of the Tales of Wonder cycle preserved on P. Westcar dated to the Hyksos period. In this story, the magician-priest Webaoner fashions a wax crocodile seven fingers long, turns it into a real crocodile seven cubits long, and then converts it back into the wax crocodile. At the same time, however, we have evidence for snake-staffs (see immediately below), and thus we conclude that the two interrelated biblical pericopes (Exodus 4:1-5 and Exodus 7:8-12) echo an important aspect of Egyptian culture, namely, the belief that select individuals could transform inanimate objects into animate reptiles (and back again).

I append here several notes to this discussion. First, note that the Egyptian magician-priests are able to duplicate this "trick" in Exodus 7:11-12 without difficulty. Of course, an important distinction is present in the biblical text. Moses and Aaron are able to accomplish this task, and the following plagues as well, simply because they have been so empowered by God, whereas the Egyptian magician-priests must resort to their magical spells (בלהטיהם), consistent with our knowledge of ancient Egyptian magic.[27] Second, note that Aaron's staff swallows the staffs of the Egyptian magician-priests, in accord with the common Egyptian reference to swallowing as an indication of control and power.[28] Third, on the question of the snake of Exodus 4:1-5 versus the crocodile of Exodus 7:8-12, from a unified literary point-of-view (in contrast to a source-

---

26. For full discussion, notwithstanding a contrary opinion, see C. Cohen, "Ha-Muvan ha-ʾAḥer shel ha-Tannin ha-Miqraʾi—'Naḥaš' ʾo 'Timsaḥ'?" in B. Z. Luria, ed., *Sefer Prof. H. M. Y. Gevaryahu: Meḥqarim ba-Miqraʾ u-ve-Maḥshevet Yiśraʾel*, vol. 2 (Jerusalem: Ha-Ḥevra le-Ḥeqer ha-Miqraʾ be-Yiśraʾel, 1991): 75-81.

27. On Egyptian magic in general, see R. Ritner, *The Mechanics of Ancient Egyptian Magical Practice* (Chicago: Oriental Institute of the University of Chicago, 1993), and G. Pinch, *Magic in Ancient Egypt* (Austin: University of Texas Press, 1994).

28. A particularly interesting example is found on the exterior right panel of Tutankhamun Shrine III, where the snake portrayed is called "he who swallows the forms"; see A. Piankoff and N. Rambova, *The Shrines of Tut-Ankh-Amon*, Bollingen Series XL/2 (New York: Pantheon Books, 1955), 89 and figure 32 = plate 36. For other examples and brief discussion, see S. B. Noegel, "Moses and Magic: Notes on the Book of Exodus," *JANES* 24 (1996): 45-59.

FIGURE 5: Line drawing of The Spearers of Apopis, from the tomb of Rameses VI in the Valley of the Kings. Reproduced from A. Piankoff and N. Rambova, *The Tomb of Ramesses VI* (New York: Pantheon Books, 1954), p. 200, figure 60, with kind permission of Princeton University Press.

critical approach), it is possible to see in the latter pericope an "upgrade." Note that in Exodus 4 Moses appears as God to Aaron and a snake is involved; whereas in Exodus 7 Moses appears as God to Pharaoh and a crocodile is involved. In addition, note the collocation of the two creatures in the following passage from the hand of Sarenput I, the mayor of Elephantine during the 12th Dynasty: *iw.i r.f m msḥ ḥr mw m ḥf3w m t3 m ḫfty m ẖrt-ntr* "I shall be against him as a crocodile on the water, as a snake on the land, and as an enemy in the necropolis."[29] Furthermore, on occasion Egyptian artwork presents a combination creature, as seen, for example, in Figure 5 taken from the tomb of Rameses VI in the Valley of the Kings at the west bank of Thebes.[30] In short, most likely an ancient reader of these sections was not distracted by the difference between נחש and תנין, certainly not to the extent that modern commentators appear to be bothered by the different words.

Most of the documentation discussed thus far comes from Egyptian literary remains, though the last example serves as an excellent segue into the field of Egyptian art. For with the next item to be discussed, namely, snake-staffs, the evidence comes wholly from Egyptian artwork. I use the term "snake-staff" to refer to a staff held in the hand like any other staff, but one which has the features of a snake. A comprehensive presentation of the material is both unnecessary, because snake-staffs appear so ubiquitously, and impractical, since space concerns allow for only a sampling of the evidence. An entire series of snake-staffs may be seen on the upper

29. L. Habachi, *The Sanctuary of Heqaib*, Elephantine 4 (Mainz am Rhein: P. von Zabern, 1985), 36-37.

30. A. Piankoff and N. Rambova, *The Tomb of Ramesses VI* (New York: Pantheon Books, 1954), fig. 60 on p. 200.

31. For general description of the stela, see L. Kákosy, "Metternichstele," *LÄ* 4 (1982): 122-24; and J. F. Borghouts, "Witchcraft, Magic, and Divination in Ancient Egypt," *CANE* 3:1781.

FIGURE 6: Back of the Metternich Stele (MMA 50.85), with registers two through six presenting a series of individuals (most likely, gods) each holding a snake-staff. Courtesy The Metropolitan Museum of Art, New York, Fletcher Fund, 1950.

portion of the back of the Metternich stela from the 30th Dynasty (see Figure 6), with registers two through six presenting a series of individuals (most likely gods) each holding a snake-staff.[31] Another example appears on the funerary papyrus of Muthetepi, chantress of Amun, from Thebes during the 21st Dynasty (P. BM 10010), specifically at the vignette accompanying Spell 182 of the Book of the Dead, where four different gods are portrayed holding snake-staffs.[32]

The above material places the story of Exodus 4:1-5, 7:8-12 within the context of Egyptian culture, but it also suggests that Moses (and Aaron too) is presented in the image of an Egyptian magician-priest. This is true in other places as well, and I plan to write a follow-up article on this image in the book of Exodus.[33] But now I wish to return to Moses as equal to Pharaoh, and thus I put forward here a specific use of the snake-staff, namely, its presence in the ceremony of the Pharaoh driving the calves. This ritual has been studied in detail by A. Egberts, with the following summation: "The scenes depicting the rite of driving the calves are attested from the early Vth Dynasty to the beginning of the Roman

32. See R. O. Faulkner, *The Ancient Egyptian Book of the Dead*, ed. C. Andrews (Austin: University of Texas Press, 1990), 178-79.

33. Here I have in mind not only the Wax Crocodile parallel, but, among others, parallels from the Setne Khamwas cycles (especially the reference to three days of darkness in P. BM 604 verso) and from the Boating Party incident from the Tales of Wonder text of P. Westcar (in particular, the separating of the waters). For other items of interest, see Noegel, "Moses and Magic: Notes on the Book of Exodus."

period. Throughout this long history the vignettes of the scenes remained essentially the same. The king holds a straight rod in his right hand. The rod is kept in a more or less horizontal position. The end of the rod is often shaped like a snake's head, especially from the Ramessid period onwards."[34] See Figure 7 for an example.[35] A typical accompanying text, such as the following from Edfu, reads: "Ptolemy VII, the beneficent god, Horus with careful mind, guarding his small cattle, watching over his calves when treading the threshing-floor. Long live the good god, who holds fast the rope and brandishes the stick behind the calves."[36] The

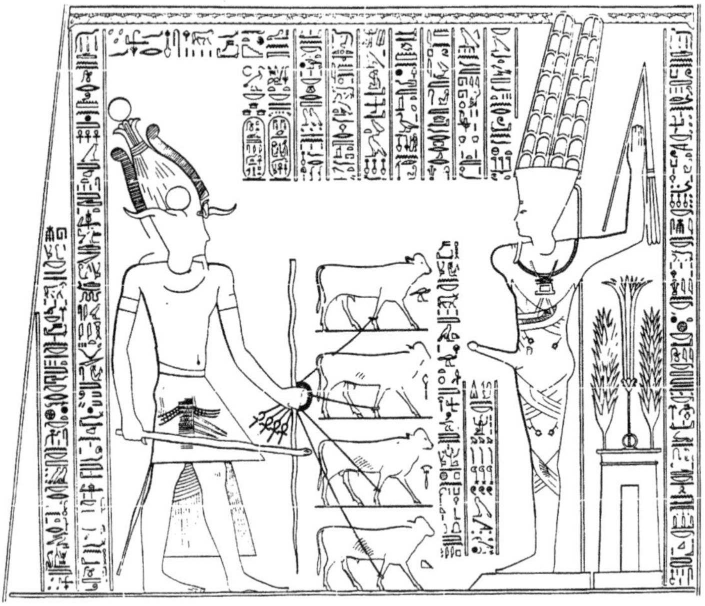

FIGURE 7: Line drawing of a scene depicting the Driving of the Calves, from Karnak Temple. Originally appeared in P. Clère, *La porte d'Éuergète à Karnak II, Planches* (Mémoires publiés par les Membres de l'Institut français d'archéologie orientale du Caire LXXXIV) (Cairo: Institut français d'archéologie orientale, 1961), Plate 44. See also A. Egberts, *In Quest of Meaning: A Study of the Ancient Egyptian Rites of Consecrating the* Meret-*Chests and Driving the Calves* (Leiden: Nederlands Instituut voor het Nabije Oosten, 1995), vol. 2, plate 109. Reproduced here with kind permission of the Institut français d'archéologie orientale, Cairo.

34. A. Egberts, *In Quest of Meaning: A Study of the Ancient Egyptian Rites of Consecrating the* Meret-*Chests and Driving the Calves* (Leiden: Nederlands Instituut voor het Nabije Oosten, 1995), in particular vol. 1, p. 437.

35. This scene is from Karnak; reproduced from Egberts, *In Quest of Meaning*, vol. 2, plate 109.

36. A. M. Blackman and H. W. Fairman, "The Significance of the Ceremony *ḥwt bḥsw* in the Temple of Horus at Edfu," *JEA* 35 (1949): 98-112, in particular 105.

ancient Egyptians appear to have understood this ceremony in a variety of ways, one of which was pastoral. The passages which accompany the vignettes (dating mainly from the Greco-Roman period, as in the text just cited, but in some cases from earlier exemplars) "stress the capacities of the king as herdsman."[37] The portrayal of the king as herdsman is not limited to Egypt, of course; it is a common motif found throughout the Near East.[38] But what makes the connection between the Pharaoh as depicted in the ceremony of driving the calves and Moses as portrayed in the book of Exodus especially close is the emphasis on the staff, especially a staff which is at once both staff and snake. In short, the Egyptians commonly portrayed the Pharaoh wielding a staff in an act of animal husbandry, and thus the Bible incorporates this motif into its presentation of Moses. The staff is mentioned first in Exodus 4:2, where it clearly is nothing more than the staff with which Moses had been shepherding the flocks of his father-in-law Reuel/Jethro.[39] (Note, incidentally, that the difference between the Pharaoh's cattle and Moses's sheep is an accurate reflection of the difference between the bovines in the Nile Valley and the caprids among the denizens of the eastern desert, Sinai, etc.).

The account in Exodus 4:1-5 includes another detail that is well illustrated in Egyptian artwork. Once the staff has been turned into a snake, God instructs Moses שלח ידך ואחז בזנבו "send forth your hand and grab (it) by its tail" (v. 4). Obviously, the usual manner of grabbing a snake is by the neck behind the head, but in this case Moses is instructed to grab the snake by the tail. This feature of the biblical story parallels the portrayal of Horus on the many amuletic stelae that have been found from ancient Egypt. Of the many examples that could be utilized, I present here the famous British Museum example (EA 36250) dated to the 6th-3rd centuries B.C.E. (Figure 8), and the front of the aforementioned Metternich stela (Figure 9).[40] These objects d'art consistently portray Horus (in fact,

37. Egberts, *In Quest of Meaning*, 438.

38. See, e.g., the statement in "Shulgi, King of the Road": "I am a shepherd, the pastor of the 'black-headed [people],'" translation of J. Klein, *Three Shulgi Hymns* (Ramat-Gan: Bar-Ilan University Press, 1981), 85.

39. See S. E. Loewenstamm, "Maṭṭeʰ," *ʾEnṣiqlopedya Miqraʾit* 4 (1962): 828.

40. Both examples appear in many standard works. For the former, see, e.g., P. Montet, *Everyday Life in Ancient Egypt* (Philadelphia: University of Pennsylvania Press, 1981), plate XIII (facing p. 282); and Pinch, *Magic in Ancient Egypt*, 20. For the latter, see, e.g., Borghouts, "Witchcraft, Magic, and Divination in Ancient Egypt," *CANE* 3:1781. For an illustration of an additional example, see Quirke and Spencer, *The British Museum Book of Ancient Egypt*, 84. For general treatments, see P. Lacau, "Les statues 'guérisseuses' dans l'ancienne Égypte," *Monuments et mémoires: Fondation Eugène Piot* 25 (1921-22), 189-209; K. C. Seele, "Horus on the Crocodiles," *JNES* 6 (1947): 43-52; and L. Kákosy, "Horusstele," *LÄ* 3 (1980): 60-62.

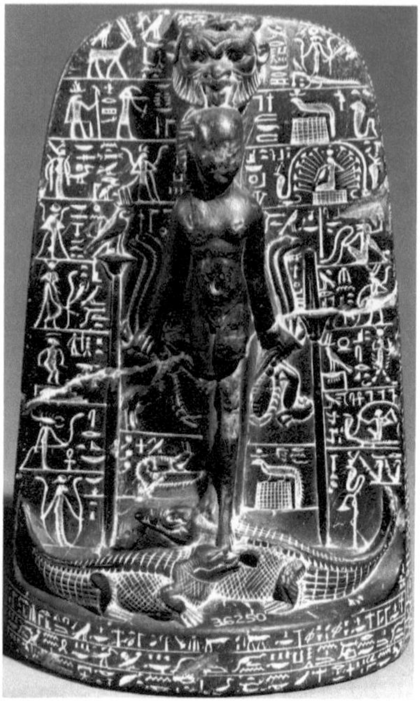

FIGURE 8: British Museum EA 36250, a magical stela depicting the young Horus handling snakes by the tail. © Copyright The British Museum, and reproduced here with their kind permission.

FIGURE 9: Front of the Metternich Stele (MMA 50.85), with the young Horus handling snakes by the tail. Courtesy The Metropolitan Museum of Art, New York, Fletcher Fund, 1950.

the young Horus) handling most prominently snakes but also other creatures (scorpions, etc.) by the tail. When we recall once more that the Pharaoh is Horus incarnate, we understand the biblical story's goal of presenting Moses as the equal to Pharaoh. Furthermore, note that in the ceremony of the driving of the calves discussed above, the Pharaoh is consistently portrayed holding the staff-with-snake's-head at the very end (again, see Figure 7).

One must be careful not to push evidence too far, and so with all due caution I take the opportunity to point out another feature in the biblical story that may be germane. At the moment when Moses and Aaron are ready to appear before Pharaoh, the text stops to inform us of the ages of the two heroes. Moses, we learn, is 80 years old at this point (Exodus 7:7). No doubt there is an attempt here at an internally consistent chronology, since the wandering period lasts 40 years and Moses dies at the age of 120. But the very fact that Moses's age of 80 years is noted immediately before his appearance before Pharaoh is significant,[41] I believe, in light of the following. One of the classic texts that relates the struggle between Horus and Seth is the Late Egyptian story called "The Contendings of Horus and Seth" preserved on P. Chester Beatty I (recto) dated to the 20th Dynasty. In the course of the story, Thoth writes a letter to Re-Atum in which he states "What shall we do about these two people, who for eighty years now have been before the tribunal, and no one knows how to judge between the two?"[42] As I remarked above, the Moses birth story places Moses in the traditional role of Horus, and it transforms Pharaoh into the traditional role of Seth. As the Exodus narrative progresses from the birth account to the initial appearance of Moses before Pharaoh, 80 years have passed. I admit that this item may be coincidental (and thus mark my words at the start of this paragraph), but given the other material surveyed above and the echoes of Egyptian texts throughout these chapters, I am inclined to see the reference to Moses's age of 80 years in Exodus 7:7 as yet another reverberation of Egyptian literature and mythology. Moses and Pharaoh have struggled for 80 years, à la Horus and Seth; and it is now time for the climactic event.

In the above pages I have noted a number of topoi shared by the story in Exodus 1-15 and Egyptian art and literature. An overarching theme may be noted as well. A well-known genre in Egyptian literature is the *Königsnovelle*, the basic elements of which are as follows: "The pattern

---

41. Moses already has appeared (with Aaron) before Pharaoh in Exodus 5:1-5, but this is a brief scene only. The long uninterrupted narrative of Moses before Pharaoh commences at Exodus 7:8.

42. Translation of M. Lichtheim, *Ancient Egyptian Literature* (Berkeley: University of California Press, 1976), 2:215.

became a stereotyped one: first, the motivation is given for some royal activity, often of a ritual or military nature, and is frequently received through the medium of a dream; next, the king's plans are outlined to a gathering of courtiers and officials, who are usually sceptical and hesitant; and, finally, the exploit is successfully accomplished."[43] Siegfried Herrmann sought to observe the *Königsnovelle* in biblical material that relates the history of David and Solomon.[44] But most biblical scholars have not been convinced by his analysis.[45]

As far as I am able to determine, no one has suggested the Moses story as an example of *Königsnovelle*. But if any segment of biblical literature is to be seen as related to this Egyptian literary genre, it certainly is the Moses narrative viewed as a whole. Moses has a task to undertake, namely, the freeing of the Israelites from Egyptian bondage. There are major obstacles in his path, but most noteworthy is the fact that the situation gets worse before it gets better. I refer to the setback caused by Moses's first appearance before Pharaoh (Exodus 5), an audience that resulted in the king's command that the Israelites produce the same daily quota of bricks but without the Egyptians supplying them with the straw necessary for the manufacturing process. This leads to the people (or at least the Israelite foremen) vilifying Moses (and Aaron) for making matters worse (Exodus 5:21). Only after this initial setback does the situation improve, à la the pattern of the *Königsnovelle*, eventuating in the achievement of the goal, the liberation of the Israelites from slavery.

There is one final item in the account of Moses's life that parallels the Egyptian portrayal of the Pharaoh. I refer to one of the most enigmatic passages in the Torah, Exodus 34:29-30 קרן עור פניו, an expression which has engendered much discussion throughout the centuries.[46] Most mod-

43. R. J. Williams, "Egypt and Israel," in J. R. Harris, ed., *The Legacy of Egypt*, 2nd ed. (Oxford: Clarendon, 1971), 273. The *Königsnovelle* genre was identified first by A. Hermann, *Die ägyptische Königsnovelle*, Leipziger ägyptologische Studien 10 (Glückstadt: J. J. Augustin, 1938).

44. S. Herrmann, "Die Königsnovelle in Ägypten und in Israel," *Wissenschaftliche Zeitschrift der Karl-Marx-Universität Leipzig* 3, *Gesellschafts- und Sprachwissenschaftliche Reihe* 1 (1953-54): 51-62.

45. For a convenient summary of the different opinions, see P. K. McCarter, *II Samuel*, AB 9 (Garden City, NY: Doubleday, 1984), 212-15.

46. For an extremely thorough review of the Forschungsgeschichte on this expression, see W. H. Propp, "The Skin of Moses' Face—Transfigured or Disfigured?," *CBQ* 49 (1987): 375-86. A more popular version of this article appeared as "Did Moses Have Horns?" *Bible Review* 4, no. 1 (1988): 30-37, 44. My thanks to Ted Lewis for bringing these two articles to my attention. In addition, Propp offered his own suggestion concerning the phrase, positing that קרן עור פניו refers to the skin of Moses's face becoming dry and hard. This is an original proposal, but I do not believe that the evidence mustered by Propp is sufficient support for his interpretation. My own proposal follows presently.

FIGURE 10: Head of Amenhotep III with erased horn of Amun, from the Luxor Temple. Photograph by Lanny Bell, appearing originally in *Journal of Near Eastern Studies* 44 (1985), p. 266, Figure 4. Reproduced here with kind permission of Lanny Bell.

ern translations read something like "the skin of his face was radiant" (thus the NJV), in accordance with ancient Jewish interpretation: Targum Onqelos and Targum Pseudo-Yonatan understood the verse this way (both use the noun זיו "radiance"), and Sifre Zuta 27:20 says plainly שקרנים היו יוצאין מפני משה כקרנים שיוצאין מגלגל חמה "the 'horns' that came out from the face of Moshe were like the 'rays' that come out of the disk of the sun." But I am not sure that this is the original intent of the verse.[47] Instead, I propose that we return to the idea expressed in Jerome's Vulgate, the source for Michaelangelo's famous sculpture of Moses, and translate this phrase as "the skin of his face was horned." In support of this rendering, I point to an Egyptian parallel of great potential. Various pharaohs of the 18th and 19th Dynasties are portrayed with "a ram's horn curled around the king's ear and onto his cheek," representing, it appears, either the deification of the king or the pharaoh's *ka*-aspect.[48] For examples, see Figure 10, a picture of Amenhotep III, and Figure 11, a picture of Rameses II, both from the walls of the Luxor Temple.[49] In light of this trend among New Kingdom pharaohs, we should accept the biblical

---

47. There is no case of the verb קרן "shine," either in biblical Hebrew or in post-biblical Hebrew. The Hiphʿil form in Psalm 69:32 can mean only "send forth horns"; and B. Hullin 60a refers to the same verse. As to the noun קרן "ray, beam," scholars often look to קרנים in Habakkuk 3:4 for help, claiming that it means "rays" there, collocated with נגה "brightness" and אור "light." But note that the form is in the dual, which makes the meaning "horns" almost certain. Moreover, the context of Habakkuk 3:4 is that of the horned demon Hebyon; see C. H. Gordon, "*Ḥby*, Possessor of Horns and Tail," *UF* 18 (1986): 129-32. The earliest source for the noun קרן "ray, beam" is the passage from Sifre Zuta cited above, followed by later midrashim, Shemot Rabba 47 and Tanḥuma Ki Tissa 37. The earliest sources for the verb קרן "shine" are still later piyyutim.

48. L. Bell, "Luxor Temple and the Cult of the Royal *Ka*," *JNES* 44 (1985): 251-94, esp. 268-69 (see nn. 84-85 for detailed bibliography). I am indebted to David O'Connor of the New York University Institute of Fine Arts for calling this parallel to my attention.

49. Bell, "Luxor Temple and the Cult of the Royal *Ka*," 266-67.

FIGURE 11: Head of Rameses II, with the horn of Amun, from the Luxor Temple. Photograph by Lanny Bell, appearing originally in *Journal of Near Eastern Studies* 44 (1985), p. 267, Figure 5. Reproduced here with kind permission of Lanny Bell.

statement at face value, understand "the skin of his face" as the cheek,[50] and interpret the passage as a final reference to Moses as the equal to Pharaoh.

I have attempted to show in this essay that the author of the Exodus narrative patterned his portrayal of Moses after the Egyptian understanding of the Pharaoh, thus presenting the former as the equal to the latter. This suggests that not only did the Israelite author possess a knowledge of ancient Egyptian motifs, both textual and artistic, but also that the author could assume a reasonable level of understanding by his readership. Accordingly, one may wish to ask: by what means and at what period did such knowledge enter the Israelite general population? We cannot delve into this important question with any detail here at article's end. But we can point out—and I take the opportunity to do so because not all scholars of the ancient world realize the obvious—that the relationship between Egypt and Israel/Canaan was continual. We have a large amount of documentation for the period of Israel's emergence, that is, the Late Bronze and Early Iron Ages. In the one direction there is ample evidence for Israelites and others from Canaan living in Egypt, specifically in the eastern Delta, for extended periods.[51] In the other direc-

50. I do not venture into a discussion here of the unique word מסוה occurring in Exodus 34:33-35. The standard interpretation is "veil," but "mask" also is possible. For the latter, see A. Jirku, "Die Gesichtsmaske des Mose," *ZDPV* 67 (1943): 43-45.

51. For general discussion, see G. A. Rendsburg, "The Early History of Israel," in, *Crossing Boundaries and Linking Horizons: Studies in Honor of Michael C. Astour on His 80th*

tion we may note the Egyptian presence in Canaan during the New Kingdom period and/or the process of "elite emulation" by local peoples in Canaan.[52] But even in the later period, that is, the early and mid-1st Millennium during which time the majority of the Bible was written, there is continued contact with Egypt. References such as 1 Kings 3:1; 10:28-29; 11:40; 12:2-3; 2 Kings 17:4; Hosea 7:11; etc., are all well known and need no elaboration here.[53] The bottom line is that at no time in ancient Israelite history would its population, especially the literati and the intelligentsia, have lacked the knowledge to create and appreciate the biblical account with its remarkably accurate reflection of Egyptian religion.

Birthday, ed. G. D. Young, M. W. Chavalas, and R. E. Averbeck (Bethesda, MD: CDL Press, 1997), 433-53. In addition to the material adduced there, note also the linguistic evidence, collected by J. E. Hoch, *Semitic Words in Egyptian Texts of the New Kingdom and Third Intermediate Period* (Princeton, NJ: Princeton University Press, 1994).

52. See, e.g., C. Higginbotham, "Elite Emulation and Egyptian Governance in Ramesside Canaan," *TA* 23 (1996): 154-69.

53. Even Donald Redford, a scholar who sees little of historical value in the biblical record ("Some day evidence may be produced on Solomon's trade in horses or on his marriage to Pharaoh's daughter. Until then these must remain themes for midrash or fictional treatment"), admitted that "Nevertheless, there is good evidence that both Judah and Israel communicated regularly with Egypt." See D. B. Redford, *Egypt, Canaan, and Israel in Ancient Times* (Princeton, NJ: Princeton University Press, 1992), 311, 335 for the two quotations respectively. The linguistic evidence which supports the second of Redford's statements is collected in Y. Muchiki, *Egyptian Proper Names and Loanwords in North-West Semitic*, SBLDS 173 (Atlanta: Society of Biblical Literature, 1999). For a review of Redford's book, with critique of his treatment of the biblical material, see G. A. Rendsburg, "Review Essay of Donald B. Redford, *Egypt, Canaan, and Israel in Ancient Times*," in *Approaches to Ancient Judaism*, new series, vol. 7, ed. J. Neusner, South Florida Studies in the History of Judaism 110 (Atlanta: Scholars Press, 1995), 203-14. In addition, there is mounting archaeological evidence to support the claim that Israel had continued contact with Egypt throughout the Iron Age. For a comprehensive treatment of a single corpus of data, see C. Herrmann, *Ägyptische Amulette aus Palästina/Israel*, OBO 138 (Göttingen: Vandenhoeck & Ruprecht, 1994). The Egyptian material found in Canaan continues to grow with each season of excavation; see, e.g., R. Arav and M. Bernett, "An Egyptian Figurine of Pataikos at Bethsaida," *IEJ* 47 (1997): 198-213; and D. Sweeney, "The Man on the Folding Chair: An Egyptian Relief from Beth Shean," *IEJ* 48 (1998): 38-53.

III

Temples

11

Parallelism in Popular and Official Religion in Ancient Egypt

CAROLYN ROUTLEDGE

Common to the study of ancient Near Eastern religions is the assumption that these religions were each divided into two distinct entities that can be described as "official religion" and "popular religion." In scholarship on these cultures the division in religious practice is connected intimately to social class, with official religion being the domain of the elite and popular religion that of the masses. This assumption has caused some researchers to attempt to "recover" popular religion.[1] While such a separation can be useful in some types of analysis, the tendency to make a bipartite division in religion based on social class leaves many aspects of religious practice unexamined or unexplained. This study addresses one of these areas of difficulty for the study of ancient Egyptian religion, namely the ritual use of the ancient Egyptian state temple.

The most prominent settings for ritual in ancient Egypt were the great state temples, best known today from the ruins at Karnak and Luxor. It generally is understood by Egyptologists that the rites that took place within these state temples reflected official religious practice. It also is common for scholars to consider this official religion to be limited to the elite in ancient Egyptian society. This implies that the state temples of ancient Egypt served only the elite—leaving a prominent, costly, and potent architectural structure with but a single use in society. The aim of this study is to focus on how society defines and integrates its social

1. E. g., A. Sadek, *Popular Religion in Egypt During the New Kingdom*, Ägyptologische Beiträge 27 (Hildesheim: Gerstenberg, 1988); K. Van der Toorn, *Family Religion in Babylonia, Ugarit, and Israel: Continuity and Change in the Forms of Religious Life* (Leiden: E. J. Brill, 1995); J. Berlinerblau, *The Vow and the "Popular Religious Groups" in Ancient Israel* (Sheffield: Sheffield Academic Press, 1996).

groups through religious activity. Such a focus will be relevant to the task of rethinking the proposed dichotomy between popular and official religion for ancient Egypt as well as for the religions of the ancient Near East in general.

Definitions

Across scholarly studies, what constitutes popular and official religion is not developed consistently. Sometimes popular religion is equated with the practices of the masses,[2] local practices,[3] or religion for personal benefit.[4] Most scholars studying ancient Egypt understand official religion to represent the religion of the state temples as practiced by the king and the elite and not by the general populace.[5] Popular religion represents the religion practiced in the home and at "popular" shrines by the general populace.[6] Sometimes connected to these categories is the notion that official religion favors state gods like Amun and Ptah in formal rites that benefit the state, the king, and possibly the bureaucracy while popular religion favors domestic gods like Bes and Taweret in magical rites that benefit the individual and/or the family.[7] It also is common to suggest that official and popular religion were relatively separate systems within Egyptian religion.[8]

---

2. P. Vrijhof, "Conclusion," in *Official and Popular Religion: Analysis of a Theme for Religious Studies*, ed. P. Vrijhof and J. Waardenburg (The Hague: Mouton, 1979), 691-92.

3. J. Goody, *The Logic of Writing and the Organization of Society* (Cambridge: Cambridge University Press, 1986), 24-26. These last two descriptions seem to parallel theories of the "great" and "little" traditions. See R. Redfield, "Peasant Society and Culture," in *The Little Community and Peasant Society and Culture* (Chicago: University of Chicago Press, 1960), 41-42.

4. P. Vrijhof, "Conclusions," 692-93.

5. A. Sadek, *Popular Religion*, 1; T. G. H. James, *An Introduction to Ancient Egypt* (London: British Museum Press, 1979), 132-33, 139.

6. A. Sadek, *Popular Religion*, 2; G. Pinch, *Votive Offerings to Hathor* (Oxford: Griffith Institute, 1993), 325; S. Morenz, *Egyptian Religion*, trans. A. Keep (Ithaca, NY: Cornell University Press, 1973), 102.

7. A. R. David, *The Ancient Egyptians* (London: Routledge & Kegan Paul, 1982), 143; G. Englund, "Gods as a Frame of Reference," in *The Religion of the Ancient Egyptians: Cognitive Structures and Popular Expressions*, ed. G. Englund (Uppsala: Acta Universitatis Upsaliensis, 1989), 24; J. Borghouts, "Magical Practices among the Villagers," in *Pharaoh's Workers: The Villagers of Deir el Medina*, ed. L. Lesko (Ithaca, NY: Cornell University Press, 1994), 120.

8. L. Holden, "The People's Religion," in *Egypt's Golden Age*, ed. R. Freed (Boston: Museum of Fine Arts, 1982), 296-98; G. Englund, "Gods as a Frame of Reference," in *The Religion of the Ancient Egyptians*, 8-9; idem, "The Treatment of Opposites in Temple Thinking and Wisdom Literature," in *The Religion of the Ancient Egyptians*, 88.

Egyptian Temple Religion

The best known form of the Egyptian temple is that of the New Kingdom processional temple. These temples had a standardized plan and daily ritual practice. The inner temple consisted of a series of courtyards placed before an enclosed shrine surrounded by a series of small rooms. Outside this inner temple, but within a temenos wall, were work areas, priests' houses, a sacred lake, and sometimes other cult installations like small shrines and barque stations. The standard ritual of these temples mirrored a human daily schedule featuring three meals and morning bathing and dressing.[9] These temples were built at state expense and granted land and other sources of income by the pharaoh. For a variety of reasons,[10] Egyptologists have long suggested that state temples were closed to the general public. Supposedly only the king and the priests had access to the temple and only the king or high priest witnessed and/or performed the daily rites. The logical outcomes of this exclusion have been clearly articulated over time by a number of Egyptologists from varying theoretical perspectives. For example, more than one hundred years ago A. Erman wrote, "The state and the priesthood are alone responsible for (the temple's) prosperity, and in this matter the people are but the 5th wheel to the coach."[11] Over fifty years later H. Fairman wrote, "The (daily rituals) were always celebrated within the temple by a limited number of priests, and the laity and general public had no access to them."[12] Similarly, É. Droiton theorized, "Just as the mighty Egyptian would not open his dwelling to be invaded by the mob, so the god reserved entry into his

---

9. A. Moret, *Le rituel du culte divin journalier en Égypte* (Geneva: Slatkine Reprints, 1988); H. Fairman, "Worship and Festivals in an Egyptian Temple," *Bulletin of the John Rylands Library* 37 (1954): 165-203.

10. Early work on temple access was based on three primary criteria: the statements of the ancient Graeco-Roman author, Chaeramon, that temples were inaccessible to all but priests—see P. Van der Horst, *Chaeremon, Egyptian Priest and Stoic Philosopher: The Fragments Collected and Translated with Explanatory Notes* (Leiden: E. J. Brill, 1984), 17; the modern interpretation of the ancient concepts behind the temple structure (as in Droiton's description of the temple as the god's private house); and the idea that restricted participation in temple cult was part of an evolutionary pattern of the evolution either of religion—see, e.g., P. Renouf, *The Origin and Growth of Religion as Illustrated by the Religion of Ancient Egypt* (New York: Scribners, 1880), 86—or of human cognition—see H. Frankfort, *Kingship and the Gods.* (Chicago: University of Chicago Press, 1948), 81-82, 123-25, 151; H. Fairman, "Worship and Festivals in an Egyptian Temple," 174. In current considerations of temple access the first two criteria are still examined, but evolutionary schema of religion or human cognition are less popular.

11. A. Erman, *Life in Ancient Egypt*, trans. H. M. Tirard (London: Macmillan, 1894), 273.

12. H. Fairman, "Worship and Festivals in an Egyptian Temple," 174.

temple to his own intimates . . . The people took no part in the ceremonies performed in the temple."[13]

Current reasoning, while drawing on modern theories, maintains the basic conclusions of these earlier scholars. For example, S. Quirke states:

> The closest analogy to the Egyptian temple thus becomes not the church or mosque in which the faithful congregate to offer prayers and hymns but the power station in which society produces the energy it needs to function and survive. An Egyptian temple is a machine for the preservation of the universe, a technical operation that requires technical staff and knowledge and thereby excludes the great majority of the population in order to ensure that the crucial task of survival is never impaired.[14]

In this view, the ancient Egyptians understood the temple as a machine for the preservation of the universe and felt that special training was necessary for those humans involved in its operation.

In a number of influential studies J. Baines[15] sets a widely accepted theoretical basis for the current understanding of temple cult by closely linking official religion with literacy. He suggests that literacy, confined to the elite bureaucracy of ancient Egypt, was a prerequisite for participation in official cult practices. J. Baines and C. Eyre estimate this literate group to have made up no more than one percent of the population in ancient Egypt.[16] Baines draws a number of conclusions from this basic situation: 1) "Most of what is known about ancient Egypt relates to the small elite; there is little direct evidence for the lives and attitudes of the rest of the people."[17] 2) "Temples and other major structures on which this (elite) system was displayed related chiefly to the official cults . . . whose relevance for most people was rather limited. The privileged

---

13. É. Droiton, *Religions of the Ancient Near East,* trans. M. Loraine (New York: Hawthorn, 1959), 39, 41.

14. S. Quirke, *Ancient Egyptian Religion* (London: British Museum Press, 1992), 70.

15. J. Baines and C. Eyre, "Four Notes on Literacy," *Göttinger Miszellen* 61 (1983): 65-96; J. Baines, "Literacy and Ancient Egyptian Society," *Man n.s.* 18 (1983): 572-99; idem, "Interpretations of Religion: Logic, Discourse, Rationality," *Göttinger Miszellen* 76 (1984): 25-54; idem, "Practical Religion and Piety," *Journal of Egyptian Archaeology* 73 (1987): 79-89; idem, "Restricted Knowledge, Hierarchy, and Decorum: Modern Perceptions and Ancient Institutions," *Journal of the American Research Center in Egypt* 27 (1990): 1-23; idem, "Society, Morality, and Religious Practice," in *Religion in Ancient Egypt: Gods, Myths, and Personal Practice,* ed. B. Shafer (Ithaca, NY: Cornell University Press, 1991), 123-200; idem, "Kingship, Definition of Culture, and Legitimation," in *Ancient Egyptian Kingship,* ed. D. O'Connor and D. Silverman (Leiden: E. J. Brill, 1995), 3-47.

16. J. Baines and C. Eyre, "Four Notes on Literacy," 67.

17. J. Baines, "Society, Morality, and Religious Practice," 124.

received the rewards of divine beneficence and returned gratitude, while the rest suffered misfortune in greater measure and had no official channel for interacting with deities."[18] 3) "Literacy was also necessary for the proper performance of temple ritual, which involved a lector priest."[19]

We can conclude then that there are two factors that keep official religion separate from the general populace and their practices: literacy and physical access to state temples.

Comparative Evidence

The issue of popular and official religion is of concern to the fields both of religious studies and of anthropology, with reference to many cultures both ancient and modern. In general, the division of religion into popular and official systems has proven itself theoretically interesting, but rather difficult to apply to actual religious practice. The most interesting examples of such studies, and the most comparable to ancient Egyptian religion and society, come from polytheistic kingdoms in the Far East like Taiwan and China. For example, in K. Schipper's 1985 study of vernacular and classical ritual in Taiwanese Taoism, he found that Taiwanese society divided religious practitioners into two levels—popular (vernacular) and official (classical). When Schipper examined the actual practice of these religious officials, however, he found that it did not justify positing two distinct types of religion. Rather, he found that rituals from the two categories could be performed side by side or one directly after the other, and—more significantly—that hybrid rituals mixing elements from popular and official practice were also performed.[20] Additionally, he noted that the primary difference between popular and official rituals was in form and not content.[21] Taken together these observations undermine any attempts to suggest sharp divisions between these categories in relation to knowledge and access.

As for the hypothesis that literacy was necessary for participants in official religion, the work of several scholars on ritual specialists suggests the utility of separating what can be termed "practical literacy" from "symbolic literacy."[22] Practical literacy refers to the ability to read and

18. J. Baines, "Society, Morality, and Religious Practice," 126-27.

19. J. Baines, "Literacy and Ancient Egyptian Society," 585.

20. K. Schipper, "Vernacular and Classical Ritual in Taoism," *Journal of Asian Studies* 45 (1985): 35-36.

21. K. Schipper, "Vernacular and Classical Ritual," 33-34.

22. Cf. D. Johnson, "Communication, Class, and Consciousness in Late Imperial China," in *Popular Culture in Late Imperial China*, ed. D. Johnson, A. Nathan, and E. Rawski (Berkeley: University of California Press, 1985), 56, esp. fig. 1; J. Hayes, "Specialists and

interpret texts while symbolic literacy denotes a situation where the appearance of literacy is more important than true ability. Someone who was symbolically literate could be partially literate or totally illiterate but able to employ alternate methods such as memorization to do his or her job. While literacy might be an ideal requirement for specific aspects of ritual, much as Egyptologists propose, field work in countries such as China suggests that such ideal requirements can be overcome through various strategies. In Chinese funerary ritual, J. Watson finds that priests who were supposed to be literate were in fact only semi-literate and pretended to read the ritual texts laid out during the ceremony.[23] In reality, instead of reciting written texts they recited memorized chants.

While this study does not suggest that a parallel situation existed in ancient Egypt, it does take into consideration that literacy was not *necessarily* a barrier to participation in the performance of temple ritual. That symbolic literacy may have played a role in ancient Egyptian society is indicated by the use of memorization, textual cues in writing for partial literacy, and artistic representations for the illiterate.

That strategies such as memorization were used in ancient Egypt is indicated in the tomb biography of Nekhebu.[24] In his appeal to the living for offerings, Nekhebu tells the reader, "then recite to your children on the day of my traveling there (the necropolis) the words of the invocation offering for me."[25] This text hints at the education of children in proper ritual practices before they could read. They would be taught the proper words to say for the dead and possibly when and where to recite them.

Memorization may even have been aided by the ways in which key ritual texts were written. Indeed, parts of certain prayers and offerings are often written in a highly symbolic form of hieroglyphs. For example, the invocation offering was introduced by the words *ḥtp di nzw* ("an offering which the king gives"), written in a graphic and recognizable form and placed in predictable locations within decorative schemes. The items that appear in these offering lists are often depicted in symbols like an ox head (GSL F1) in place of the standard writing *kꜣw* ("ox") and a duck head (GSL H1) in place of the standard writing *ꜣpdw* ("fowl").[26] This form

Written Materials in the Village World," in *Popular Culture in Late Imperial China,* 92-94; S. Naquin, "Funerals in North China: Uniformity and Variation," in *Death Ritual in Late Imperial and Modern China,* ed. J. Watson and E. Rawski (Berkeley: University of California Press, 1988), 63-66.

23. J. Watson, "Funeral Specialists in Cantonese Society: Pollution, Performance, and Social Hierarchy," in *Death Ritual in Late Imperial and Modern China,* 119.

24. Urk I, 215-21.

25. Urk I, 218.3-4.

26. See for an example of a typical offering list, A. Gardiner, *Egyptian Grammar,* 3rd ed. (Oxford: Griffith Institute, 1957), 172.

of writing would make it simple for someone to learn to identify the location of such an offering, recognize the abbreviated and more pictographic writings, and recite memorized prayers cued by the symbols.

Another indication that partial literacy may have played a role in temple ritual is found in the occurrence of the *rḫyt*-bird symbol (GSL G24) in the forecourts of many state temples. This hieroglyph is used as a determinative for *rḫyt*, the word for subjects or commoners.[27] The *rḫyt* - bird may have served to indicate those areas which the general populace was allowed to enter to worship.[28] As such, the symbol could have been "read" by those not able to understand the complex hieroglyphic inscriptions found on temple walls and doorways.[29]

Given these indications, it is possible that many Egyptians were able to participate in what would appear to be activities that required full literacy, by being "symbolically literate." The symbolically literate could have been partially literate or illiterate, but both could be considered "ritually literate." In this way, literacy could have held a symbolic importance in ritual activity without being a practical barrier to participation. This ritual literacy would not need to be indicative of advanced study, but could represent standard cultural usage common to most native Egyptians cutting across social classes. Thus, in the study of ancient Egyptian society, we should take seriously Rawski's warning: "We close a potentially important area of inquiry if we draw a sharp line between educated and uneducated that correlates with belief systems."[30]

M. Bloch's study of the ritual of the royal bath in Madagascar helps in understanding how societies function in relation to ritual and social status.[31] Bloch makes an important point in relation to our concerns here. Royal—and by extension official—rituals and symbols are developed and lent significance through connection with their popular counterparts.[32] For example, during the bath ritual the king bathed and then sprinkled the courtiers with some of the bath water in blessing. When the king had finished, a signal was given and the head of each household

---

27. Wb II, 447.

28. L. Bell, "Luxor Temple and the Cult of the Royal Ka," *JNES* 44 (1985): 275.

29. For further examples of hieroglyphic and artistic representations addressed to an illiterate or partially literate audience, see B. Bryan, "The Disjunction of Text and Image in Egyptian Art," in *Studies in Honor of William Kelly Simpson*, ed. P. Der Manuelian (Boston: Museum of Fine Arts, 1996), 1:161-68.

30. E. Rawski, "Problems and Prospects," in *Popular Culture in Late Imperial China*, 402.

31. M. Bloch, "The Ritual of the Royal Bath in Madagascar: The Dissolution of Death, Birth and Fertility into Authority," in *Rituals of Royalty: Power and Ceremonial in Traditional Societies*, ed. D. Cannadine and S. Price (Cambridge: Cambridge University Press, 1987), 271-97.

32. M. Bloch, "Royal Bath," 271, 274.

bathed only the upper part of his head in his own house and then sprinkled his family members in blessing.[33] In this way all partook in the ritual without physical access to the main rite. It also is significant that the ritual featured the sharing and modification of symbols in such a way as to cut across class structures while affirming those very structures through the manner and location of individual participation.

While this is a simplified look at several scholars' sophisticated analyses, it provides a starting point for a reevaluation of the relationship between ancient Egyptian religion and society. First, the necessity for literacy in official religious practice remains to be demonstrated. Second, given the possible discontinuity between the ideal requirement of literacy and the practical reality of religious practice, it is necessary to reexamine the idea that there were barriers to access to state temples. Third, the existence of parallel religious beliefs and practices in Egyptian religion would undermine an exclusive separation of official and popular practice.

Ancient Egyptian Religious Practice

People in the Outer Courts

As stated above, most scholars suggest that the people were excluded from the state temples and from participation in the rites conducted in them. An exception to this consensus is A. Gardiner. In his study of the Ritual of Amenhotep I, a script for the daily ritual in state temples, he suggested that the public gathered in the outer courts of the temple to chant hymns at appropriate times during the morning and evening rites.[34] This suggestion was ignored in scholarship until quite recently when some scholars, following a variety of evidence, began to affirm that the populace was admitted relatively freely to the outer courts of the temple.[35] While a thorough review of the evidence supporting this position is

33. M. Bloch, "Royal Bath," 280-82.

34. A. Gardiner, *Hieratic Papyri in the British Museum*, Third Series, Vol. 1 (London: British Museum, 1935), 91-92.

35. L. Bell, "Luxor Temple and the Cult of the Royal Ka," 251-94; J.-M. Kruchten, *Les annales de prêtes de Karnak (XXI-XXIIImes dynasties)* (Leuven: Universitaire Stichting van Belgie, 1989), 245-47; F. Dunand and C. Zivie-Coche, *Dieux et hommes en Égypte, 3000 av. J.C.–395 apr. J.C.: anthropologie religieuse* (Paris: A. Colin, 1991), 117-19; C. Routledge and L. Hitchcock, "Constructing Religious Practice: Ritual and Space in Egyptian Architecture," paper read and distributed at AAR/SBL Annual Meeting, San Francisco, 1992; G. Pinch, *Votive Offerings to Hathor*, 356-59; L. Bell, "The New Kingdom 'Divine' Temple: The Example of Luxor," in *Temples of Ancient Egypt*, ed. B. Shafer (Ithaca, NY: Cornell University Press, 1997), 127-84.

beyond the scope of this paper, I want to highlight some of the more persuasive evidence.

The first piece of evidence is a series of New Kingdom inscriptions located on walls and statues in the open courts of state temples like those of Karnak, Luxor, and Ptah at Memphis,[36] which indicate that petitions of the people were heard at these locations. An early example is found on a pair of statues of Amenhotep son of Hapu (reign of Amenhotep III) from an open court of the Karnak temple:

> Oh southerners and northerners, every eye that looks upon the sun disc, who come northwards and southwards to Thebes in order to pray to the lord of the gods, come to me, I will report your speech to Amun in Ipet-sut.[37]
>
> Oh people of Karnak, those who desire to see Amun, come to me, I will report your petitions. I am the herald of this god. King Nebmaare gave me to report the speech of the Two Lands.[38]

These and similar inscriptions on doorways, walls, and statues do not suggest restrictions on who could enter the outer courts of temples. In a building inscription concerning the Ptah temple in Memphis, Ramesses II says, "I opened your open court to the north with two noble walls in front of you; their double doors are like the horizon of the sky causing the people of low station to adore you."[39] The entry to his open court at the Luxor temple bears an inscription that addresses "the people" in an inclusive manner:

> The great door of the King of Upper and Lower Egypt Woser-maat-re-stepenre, whom the common people (*rḫyt*) worship in the mansion of Ramesses Meriamun in the house of Amun; all lands, the Southland and Upper Egypt all together, so that they may adore this good god.[40]

Access into the back area of the temple seems to have been restricted to priests celebrating the rites, as indicated by more restrictive door

---

36. L. Habachi, *Features of the Deification of Ramesses II* (Gluckstadt: J. J. Augustin, 1969), 18-20, 41-42; L. Bell, "Luxor Temple and the Cult of the Royal Ka," 270-71; A. Sadek, *Popular Religion in Egypt*, 16-18, 45-47.

37. Urk IV, 1833.12-16.

38. Urk IV, 1835.3-5.

39. KRI II, 278-79.

40. KRI II, 610.

inscriptions.[41] While people were not excluded from entry into the courts, they were not free to participate directly in the presentation of the ritual offerings in the daily rites exemplified by the Ritual of Amenhotep I. Entry into the open courts would allow them to see the temple decoration and texts including scenes of propaganda like that of the king ritually executing foreign prisoners and scenes of the daily ritual being performed by the king.[42] Seeing these scenes would give people knowledge about what went on in the inner parts of the temple. It can therefore be concluded that people had limited access to state temples, were excluded from direct participation in the daily rites for the cult statue, but allowed to perform personal rites within the state temple to state gods. Restricted entry into the temple also would allow the experience of a hierarchy of access and participation.

Parallel Worship

Four major areas of ancient Egyptian ritual practice reveal aspects of parallel worship; state temples, non-state temples, domestic cult, and festivals. These ritual loci will be compared with "official" religious practice and analyzed for overall similarities.

State Temples

Letters from the scribe Dhutmose to his son recovered from the Deir el-Medina workmen's village strongly suggest that people of all social classes could participate in a rite in the open courts of state temples that could be perceived as directly parallel to the daily ritual performed on the god's statue in the sanctuary. Scribes such as Dhutmose were probably important mid-level members of Egyptian society. The first letter mentions a large range of people (women, children, low social rank) and a reason to go to the open courts of temples:

> Another message, for the female citizen Tanedjem, Nana, Henutaa, Irymut, Isis, Baketmut, Kerinefer, Tanedjem, Taseper, the boatman, and the people all together . . . when this letter reaches you, go to the open court

---

41. See, e.g., H. Fairman, "The Kingship Rituals of Egypt," in *Myth, Ritual, and Kingship: Essays on the Theory and Practice of Kingship in the Ancient Near East and Israel*, ed. S. Hooke (Oxford: Clarendon Press, 1958), 74-104.

42. See C. Routledge, "Constructing Religious Practice," forthcoming; and summary in B. Shafer, "Temples, Priests, and Rituals: An Overview," *Temples of Ancient Egypt*, 243 n. 36.

> of Amun of the Thrones of the Two Lands. Take the children with you and flatter him and ask him to rescue me.[43]

A second letter indicates what was to be done in the outer court, "Moreover, do not be weary taking water to his open court and presenting it to him to rescue me."[44] In a third letter we are given an indication of how often one might go to the outer court:

> I am standing in his open court daily, I am not growing weak, I am presenting in their names, saying "give to you very many favors before the general, your lord."[45]

> "Do not weary of taking water to Amun of the Thrones of the Two Lands." I do it two or three times in 10 days. I am not weary in taking water to him.[46]

Here we see that water could be offered frequently in the open courts for health, a safe return, or to appease the god.

The offering of libations of water was one of the foundational rites of ancient Egyptian temple ritual and the main method of purification of kings and priests. People offering such a libation in the forecourt would be partaking in a parallel rite that would allow them to feel that they were dealing directly with a deity in the same manner as the official practitioners. In her study of Hathor votive offerings, G. Pinch observes a similar cross-over in what are sometimes designated official and popular rites.[47] This form of non-elite worship—libations, the offering of incense, burning of fowl, and musical offerings—is shown in New Kingdom stelae and textile paintings dedicated to Hathor.[48] Pinch notes that these activities seem very official, with formulaic requests of the goddess, and that some were modeled on funerary inscriptions.[49] The official nature of these activities indicates the connection of non-elite practice to what is normally considered official practice.

Non-State Temples

In non-state temples too the laity could feel that they were participating in parallel religious activities. A number of small local chapels are known,

---

43. LRL, 2.5-7, 2.9-12.
44. LRL, 5.14-15.
45. LRL, 31.11-13.
46. LRL, 32.2-4.
47. G. Pinch, *Votive Offerings to Hathor*, 356-60.
48. G. Pinch, *Votive Offerings to Hathor*, figs. 7-15.
49. G. Pinch, *Votive Offerings to Hathor*, 98-101, 126, 356.

primarily from the sites of Amarna—including the workmen's village—and Deir el-Medina. Due to recent excavations at Amarna, this type of chapel has recently received detailed study.[50] The use of these sanctuaries is not entirely clear and the distribution of such chapels across ancient Egypt outside of these towns is debated. However, interesting parallels between rituals in state temples and in these chapels may be identified.

There are strong indications in textual sources from Deir el-Medina that the rites in these chapels were maintained by the workmen themselves, with priests selected from the village. A. Bomann claims that the worship in these chapels indicates that "the ordinary man was carrying on his own religion quite independent of the state."[51] However, if architectural form, iconographic content of the decoration, dedication to state gods like Amun, and evidence for rites practiced in these chapels are considered, it becomes evident that the religion of these chapels is parallel to, not independent of, official religion.

Close examination of the basic architectural form of these chapels reveals similarities to that of the state temple. It is important to compare the entire area within the walls of the state temple. Then it can be seen that these two structures share the same linear plan of sanctuary, porch, and forecourt, with preparation and storage areas on the side.[52] The major difference between the state temples and the chapels is one of scale, not plan, with the state temples being of course much larger.

The decorative elements in the chapels were not well preserved, but the remains that have been recovered indicate wall paintings appropriate to normal temple iconography. These elements include fragments of the figures of a man accompanied by a woman holding a sistrum, Nekhbet vultures holding *šn*-signs, winged solar discs,[53] *serekh* (palace facade) patterns,[54] and a file of fatted bulls.[55] These elements are all standard in scenes appropriate for state gods. In addition, water basins, incense burners, and offering tables of the type standard for state temples, but in cheaper materials—e.g., clay rather than gold—were found in these chapels.

All of the evidence for rites, both textual and architectural, suggests

---

50. See, e.g., B. Kemp, *Amarna Reports I-III* (London: Egypt Exploration Society, 1984-86); A. Bomann, *The Private Chapel in Ancient Egypt* (London: Kegan Paul International, 1991).

51. A. Bomann, *Private Chapel*, 74.

52. Cf. B. Kemp, *Amarna Reports III*, figs. 0.1, 7.1; D. Wildung, *Egypt, from Prehistory to the Romans*, trans. I. Taylor, Taschen's World Architecture Series (Cologne: Taschen, 1997), 98, 135, 139, 140, 145.

53. A. Bomann, *Private Chapel*, 57-58.

54. A. Bomann, *Private Chapel*, 10.

55. A. Bomann, *Private Chapel*. 69.

that the rituals performed in these temples conformed to state practice, but on a smaller scale. The materials offered by the people included water, bread, beer, fowl, incense, fish, melon, nuts, cattle, goat, and possibly pork.[56] Textual evidence suggests that workmen were given days off to celebrate private feasts to gods at these chapels.[57] It thus appears that in the New Kingdom people could have access to daily ritual and state gods in parallel rites at local chapels.

Domestic Cult

Evidence for domestic cult in ancient Egypt is not extensive and again is mostly drawn from Deir el-Medina and Tell el-Amarna. Houses at Deir el-Medina present evidence for the worship of deities and deceased family members (*ꜣḫ-iḳr-n-rꜥ* busts and stelae).[58] These houses at Deir el-Medina contained shrines where villagers could worship for personal reasons. These shrines housed state gods like Amun, Ptah, Hathor, and Sobek; local gods like Amenhotep I and Meretseger; domestic gods like Taweret and Bes; and ancestors represented by stelae, ancestor busts, and inscriptions on libation tanks and offering tables.[59] While there is little direct indication of the character of the rites performed in the houses, archaeological remains and texts on the stelae and offering tables suggest a standard ritual like the daily temple offerings of food, flowers, and libations. R. Demarée points to the instructions in the calendar of Lucky and Unlucky days: "Make a *prt-ḫrw*-offering to the *ꜣḫw* and give food in accordance with their list . . . Make *prt-ḫrw*-offerings to the *ꜣḫw* in your house; make *ꜣḫt*-offerings to the gods."[60] He also adduces the inscriptions on libation basins and offering tables referring to *ꜣḫ-iḳr-n-rꜥ* found in the houses to support the idea that offering rituals were conducted in the home.[61] A good example occurs on an offering table and libation basin dedicated to Irtynefer found in house C.VI:

56. A. Bomann, *Private Chapel*, 58.

57. A. Sadek, *Popular Religion in Egypt*, 193-96.

58. R. Demarée, *The ꜣḫ-iḳr-n-Rꜥ-Stelae—on Ancestor Worship in Ancient Egypt* (Leiden: Nederlands Instituut voor het Nabije Oosten, 1983); F. Friedman, "On the Meaning of Some Anthropoid Busts from Deir el-Medina," *Journal of Egyptian Archaeology* 71 (1985): 82-97; A. Sadek, *Popular Religion in Egypt*, 77-78; F. Friedman, "Aspects of Domestic Life and Religion," in *Pharaoh's Workers: The Villagers of Deir el Medina*, ed. Leonard H. Lesko (Ithaca, NY: Cornell University Press, 1994), 95-117.

59. See R. Demarée, *The ꜣḫ-iḳr-n-Rꜥ-Stelae*, 285-90; F. Friedman, "Anthropoid Busts," 80-85; "Aspects of Domestic Life and Religion," 111-17.

60. R. Demarée, *The ꜣḫ-iḳr-n-Rꜥ-Stelae*, 272.

61. R. Demarée, *The ꜣḫ-iḳr-n-Rꜥ-Stelae*, 287.

> Offering table: An offering which the king gives to Osiris, Foremost of the Westerners, the good god, that they may give everything good and pure to the *ka* of Irtynefer.
>
> Libation-basin: An offering which the king gives to Atum, lord of the Two Lands, the Heliopolitan, that he may give "receiving of offering bread before Re" for the *ka* of Irtynefer.[62]

The ancestor cult in homes not only reflects the temple statue cult, but also funerary cults. Both R. Demarée and F. Friedman trace household feeding cults to early food offerings to the spirits of the dead at the tomb.[63] Therefore, the ancestor cult in the homes of Deir el-Medina, and possibly elsewhere, suggests another series of parallels: first with the royal ancestor cult as practiced for the king at Abydos,[64] and second with funerary rites that bridge official and popular practice (i.e., opening of the mouth, *ḥtp-di-nzw*, and food offerings).

Festivals

Various Egyptian festivals parallel rituals from Madagascar presented by M. Bloch. Ancient Egypt had an extensive festival calendar for state temples requiring participation by the king and the bureaucracy (elite). Unfortunately, while the names of many of these festivals are known, details allowing a reconstruction comparable to Bloch's ritual description are unavailable. In general, it can be said that people seem to have participated in a number of state festivals, although often only on a single day of a multi-day festival (e.g., Sokar, Opet).[65] These festivals usually involved feasting, the appearance of divine statues, and sometimes ritual plays and oracles.

The festival providing the best comparison with Bloch's material is the "Beautiful Festival of the Valley." The practices in this festival hint at parallel rites that cut across social status and would have promoted a sense of unified religious practice. Statues from the east-bank temple of Karnak were brought over to the mortuary temples on the west bank, where the dead were remembered in a series of rites. These rites seem, like the ritual of the royal bath on Madagascar, to demonstrate parallel practice from the king right down to the peasants of the Theban region.[66]

---

62. R. Demarée, *The ³ḫ-iḳr-n-Rᶜ-Stelae*, 148-49.
63. R. Demarée, *The ³ḫ-iḳr-n-Rᶜ-Stelae*, 205; F. Friedman, "Anthropoid Busts," 86-91.
64. A. R. David, *Religious Ritual at Abydos (c. 1300 BC)* (Warminster: Aris & Phillips, 1973), 145-200.
65. See A. Sadek, *Popular Religion in Egypt*, 167-91.
66. S. Schott, *Das schöne Fest vom Wüstentale: Festbräuche einer Totenstadt*, Abhandlun-

The core of the festival was, in L. Bell's words, "a sort of annual family reunion during which ancestors were reintegrated into the family and bonds between the living and the dead were strengthened."[67] The central feature of the ritual was an all-night meal at the family tomb featuring offerings to the dead.[68] What integrated state, king, and people was the participation of all these levels of society in the same basic rituals. Amun-Re traveled from Karnak to the Hathor shrine at Deir el-Bahri and visited the royal funerary cult centers in the vicinity.[69] The king celebrated the funerary banquet with his royal ancestors,[70] while the people celebrated the banquet with their own forebears. A further connection was made through objects and offerings brought into contact with the state god that were redistributed to the people.[71]

Conclusions

It is clear that within ancient Egyptian religious practice there are numerous points where "popular" and "state" religion parallel each other. State temple rituals, both restricted and open, non-state temple rituals, and domestic rituals all share significant elements of practice and belief structures. This parallelism is expressed in the offering of similar objects, in a similar manner, with similar prayers. Parallel and mixed practices also can be identified in the celebrations of the Beautiful Festival of the Valley. In fact, there seems to have been an intentional mixing of genres, as well as a mixing of what we might see as personal and state aims. It may therefore be said that an analysis of Egyptian religious practice as a bipartite religion with official and popular levels misses much of its complexity and meaning. In the rituals of state and non-state temples and in the

---

gen der Geistes- und Sozialwissenschaftlichen Klasse, Jahrgang 1952, Nr. 11 (Wiesbaden: Franz Steiner, 1952), 90; A. Sadek, *Popular Religion in Egypt*, 180-81; G. Pinch, *Votive Offerings to Hathor*, 10, 351.

67. L. Bell, "The New Kingdom 'Divine' Temple," 136.

68. S. Schott, *Das schöne Fest*, 80-82. This practice can be compared with the Canaanite death rites called *marzēaḥ*. Note royal and common participation, the meal at night involving the living and divine ancestors, and the consumption of alcoholic beverages. Cf. T. Lewis, *Cults of the Dead in Ancient Israel and Ugarit*, Harvard Semitic Monographs 39 (Atlanta: Scholars Press, 1989), 80-98, 171-72; B. Schmidt, *Israel's Beneficent Dead: Ancestor Cult and Necromancy in Ancient Israelite Religion and Tradition*, Forschungen zum Alten Testament 11 (Tübingen: Mohr, 1994), 62-66.

69. S. Schott, "The Feasts of Thebes," in *Work in Western Thebes 1931-33* , ed. H. Nelson and U. Hölscher, Oriental Institute Communications 18 (Chicago: University of Chicago Press, 1934), 73.

70. S. Schott, *Das schöne Fest*, 29.

71. L. Bell, "The New Kingdom 'Divine' Temple," 137; S. Schott, *Das schöne Fest*, 57-58.

Beautiful Festival of the Valley, the multiple positions of a person in society were expressed and affirmed through the participation in religion, rather than through exclusion.

I am not suggesting that there were no class distinctions in the organization of state temples or that religion played no role in social structure in ancient Egypt. Rather, I argue that in the social fabric of Egyptian society the complex relationship between groups was integrated and defined through state temples and religious practice. This was not a bipartite religious system practiced by two non-communicating groups. Treating religious practice as an integrated whole allows a wider role for the temple in ancient Egyptian society and explains the willingness of the people to participate in the economic, political, and religious life of those temples. Indeed, the construction of consent, or "hegemony," [72] is a much stronger force in legitimizing a given social order than is direct coercion. As C. Bell has stated, religious practices and rituals are central elements in the ideological systems that create and negotiate tacit consent between social groups with potentially different interests.[73] Such central social dynamics are neglected when a bifurcation of religious practice is assumed.

This study has examined how religious practice was integrated across social groups within ancient Egypt. Such an approach contrasts with the tendency of scholars of both Egypt and of the wider ancient Near East to assume a fundamental division between "popular" and "official" religious practice. At almost every level, careful attention to the ways in which religious practices were integrated has taken us further in understanding both the evidence at hand and the role of religious practice in ancient Egyptian society. Clearly, attention to parallel practices in religion as an integrative and defining force in society holds great potential for future research on the ancient world.

---

72. J. Femia, *Gramsci's Political Thought: Hegemony, Consciousness, and the Revolutionary Process* (Oxford: Clarendon Press, 1981), 24, 37-39.

73. C. Bell, *Ritual Theory Ritual Practice* (Oxford: Oxford University Press, 1992), 204-18.

12

Reflections of Ptah and Memphite Theology from the Soil of Palestine

Iconographic and Epigraphic Evidence[1]

OTHMAR KEEL

It is a commonplace that Palestine was a kind of bridge between the two main cultural areas of the ancient Near East. We should not underestimate the steady flow of traffic crossing this bridge. It peaked during the Thirteenth through Nineteenth Dynasties, as well as under the Twenty-fifth and Twenty-sixth and rarely dried up completely. Since there was probably not much private commercial exchange, the influence exercised by this traffic must have originated mainly in palaces and temples.

The sensibilities of our secular world lead us to concentrate on the influence of palaces and political powers and to neglect the influence of temples and their symbol systems. But every living religion experiences a steady flow of impulses from outside, which it takes in, assimilates, digests, transforms, or rejects. Since the rediscovery of the ancient cultures of Egypt and Mesopotamia scholars have realized time and again that the Bible contains many symbols, notions, ideas, and even shorter or longer texts which have close counterparts in ancient Syria, Mesopotamia, or Egypt. Numerous comparative studies deal with this phenomenon.

---

1. In the lecture I gave in Philadelphia in May 1998 I dealt in addition with two other cult centers. One was the temple of Amun in Tanis, which I related to post-Ramesside mass production. Stefan Münger will elaborate on this subject in his Ph.D. thesis. The other was the temple of Sin at Harran. The relevant material has now been published in O. Keel, *Goddesses and Trees, New Moon and Yahweh*, JSOTSup 261 (Sheffield: Sheffield Academic Press, 1998), 59-120 and figs. 1-115. Cf. also M. Bernett and O. Keel, *Mond, Stier und Kult am Stadttor*, OBO 161 (Fribourg: Universitätsverlag, 1998).

Drawings here not taken from acknowledged sources have been made by Inés Haselbach, Hildi Keel-Leu, and Ulrike Zurkinden.

Less extensively discussed are the channels that directed this flow to Palestine. My assumption is that one of these was constituted by the messengers, diplomats, merchants, mercenaries, and others who traveled from Palestine to neighboring countries. These men were probably not ignorant of the splendor and wonders of the famous sanctuaries of the cities where they stayed for one reason or another.[2] And as always in ancient times, visitors to sanctuaries often brought home some of the blessings of these particular places—in the form of relics (flowers, leaves, fruits, water, stones, earth; for the latter see 2 Kings 5: 17), or in that of amulets (pendants, figurines, seal-amulets, etc.). In turn, all sorts of people from Egypt and Syria brought amulets with them to Palestine as protective or life-enhancing devices.

While as far as I can see we have in the Bible no reports of such visits to sanctuaries outside Palestine/Israel, the archaeology of Palestine/Israel has produced a wealth of Egyptian amulets (scarabs and other stamp-seals, figures of faience and bronze, etc.). The presence of these artifacts must be explained. Some may have been imported by Egyptians or Syrians. Others may have been brought back from Egypt by Canaanites, Philistines, Judaeans, or Israelites. Or—as we will see—they may have been copied in Palestine from Egyptian originals. Connected with the flow of these symbols was most probably a bundle of notions, concepts, and ideas. How much the bearers really knew about the symbolic system whose elements they brought to Palestine most probably differed from case to case. It is improbable, however, that the people who carried these objects were totally uninformed about the items they valued so highly.

Middle Bronze Age IIB: Canaanite Interest in the God of Memphis

One of the cults of which many traces can be found in Palestine is that of Ptah, whose main temple was in Memphis.[3] It seems that the first

2. D. Wildung, "Besucherinschriften," *Lexikon der Ägyptologie* 1:766-67. Most of the inscriptions of New Kingdom visitors were made by local scribes. They are done in ink, since people did not yet dare to engrave their names. Not every foreign visitor carried the instruments necessary for creating such an inscription, and their main purpose was probably to bring home something from the sanctuary rather than to leave traces of the visit behind. The formulae of these inscriptions hint at esthetic, historical, and religious interests. W. Helck is hardly justified when he declares that only the two first motives were real, while the religious one was purely traditional—see "Die Bedeutung der ägyptischen Besucherinschriften," *ZDMG* 102 (1952): 39-46. This judgment is based on the writer's own secular sensibilities.

3. C. M. Zivie, "Memphis," *Lexikon der Ägyptologie* 4:24-41; H. te Velde, "Ptah," *Lexikon der Ägyptologie* 4:1177-80.

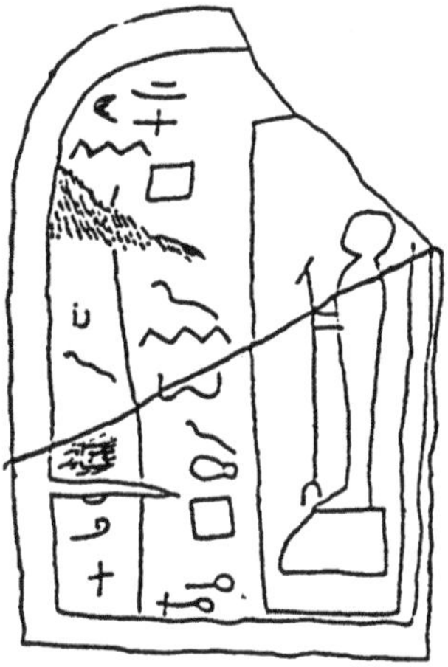

FIGURE 1

FIGURE 2

FIGURE 3

recorded contacts between Asiatics and the cult of Ptah took place in Serabit el-Khadem in central Sinai. There is evidence to show that expeditions to this site set out from Memphis in the time of Amenemhet III (1818-1772).[4] Ptah is not mentioned in Serabit el-Khadem before this period, but he is prominent there during the reigns of this king and his successor Amenemhet IV (1772-1762).[5] Two Middle Kingdom stelae mentioning Ptah without a royal name[6] probably also belong to one of these reigns. At this time Ptah was worshipped not only by Egyptians but also by Asiatics. A small stele found in Serabit el-Khadem shows a proto-Sinaitic inscription beside a depiction of Ptah in his shrine (fig. 1).[7]

4. Ch. Bonnet, F. Le Saout, and D. Valbelle, "Le temple de la déesse Hathor, maîtresse de la turquoise, à Sérabit el-Khadim. Reprise de l'étude archéologique et épigraphique," *Cahiers de la Recherche de l'Institut de Papyrologie et d'Egyptologie de Lille* 16 (1994): 15-29; Ch. Bonnet and D. Valbelle, *Le sanctuaire d'Hathor maîtresse de la turquoise. Sérabit el-Khadim au Moyen Empire* (Aoste: Musemeci editeur, 1996), 10-12 and 39-41.

5. A. H. Gardiner, T. E. Peet, and J. Černy, *The Inscriptions of Sinai* I. Introduction and plates (London: Egypt Exploration Society, 1952), II. Translations and Commentary (London: Egypt Exploration Society, 1955), nos. 114, 120, 124-26.

6. Gardiner, Peet, and Černy, *Sinai*, nos. 136 and 140.

7. Gardiner, Peet, and Černy, *Sinai*, no. 351; Y. Leibovitz, "The Cult of Ptah with Non-Egyptians," *EI* 4 (1956): 64-67 (Hebrew), vi (English summary); B. Sass, *The Genesis of the Alphabet and Its Development in the Second Millennium B.C.*, Ägypten und Altes Testament 13 (Wiesbaden: Otto Harrassowitz, 1988), 20-22, nos. 351, 137, figs. 32, 37-39; O. Keel, "Der ägyptische Gott Ptah auf Siegel-Amuletten aus Palästina/Israel. Einige Gesetzmässigkeiten bei der Übernahme von Motiven der Grosskunst auf Miniaturbildträger," in O. Keel, H. Keel-Leu, and S. Schroer, *Studien zu den Stempelsiegeln aus Palästina/Israel*, OBO 88 (Fribourg: Universitätsverlag, 1989), 287-88, fig. 21.

Scarabs with the name of Ptah, the Memphite god of craftsmanship, found in Palestine were probably produced by Asiatic craftsmen with commercial or other links to Egypt, particularly Memphis. A number of examples are characterized by a border of three paired oblong scrolls, with a loop at the upper end enclosing the name of Ptah. To this group belong examples from Jericho (**fig. 2**),[8] Lachish (**fig. 3**),[9] Shiqmona (**fig. 4**),[10] and from Tell el-Yahudije (**fig. 5**).[11] A surface find from Apheq has only two paired scrolls instead of three, and the name of the god is written twice (**fig. 6**).[12] Many more instances of this type are found in museums and collections, most of them unpublished.[13]

It is typical for this group to put the name of the god at the top of the decoration. The rendering of the hieroglyphs shows some un-Egyptian elements. The *t* in Ptah is sometimes almost square (cf. fig. 4), sometimes upside down (cf. fig. 3). The signs in the cartouche of fig. 3 do not make sense. Although the cartouche in fig. 5 has the correct rendering of the throne name of Sesostris I, the way the *k*³ is written is un-Egyptian. D. Ben-Tor has shown that this is a typical Canaanite feature.[14] While the upside-down *t* might be a mistake, it could also be an attempt at a more elegant presentation.[15] The *t* is sometimes inverted even on scarabs of Egyptian manufacture.[16] It is hardly a sufficient reason to claim that the Canaanite engravers did not understand what they copied.[17]

---

8. D. Kirkbride, "Scarabs," in K. M. Kenyon, *Excavations at Jericho* II: *The Tombs Excavated in 1955-58* (London: British School of Archaeology at Jerusalem), 609, fig. 287, 10.

9. O. Tufnell et al., *Lachish IV (Tell ed-Duweir): The Bronze Age* (London: Oxford University Press, 1958), pl. 30, 36.

10. O. Keel, *Corpus der Stempelsiegel-Amulette aus Palästina/Israel. Von den Anfängen bis zur Perserzeit. Einleitung*, OBO.SA 10 (Fribourg: Universitätsverlag, 1995), 241, fig. 563.

11. F. L. Griffith, *The Antiquities of Tell el Yahûdîyeh and Miscellaneous Work in Lower Egypt during the Years 1887-1888*. EEF 7 (London: Egypt Exploration Fund, 1890), pl. 10,1; O. Tufnell, with contributions by G. T. Martin and W. A. Ward, *Studies on Scarab Seals and their Contribution to History in the Early Second Millennium B.C.* (Warminster: Aris & Phillips, 1984), pl. 51, 3028.

12. O. Keel, *Corpus der Stempelsiegel-Amulette aus Palästina/Israel. Von den Anfängen bis zur Perserzeit. Katalog*, Bd. 1. OBO.SA 13 (Fribourg: Universitätsverlag, 1997), Afek no. 37.

13. O. Keel, *Corpus 1995*, §§569-70. Eight examples are published in O. Keel "Egyptian Deities in Middle Bronze Age Palestine," in Shmuel Aḥituv and Eliezer Oren, eds., *Aharon Kempinski Volume. Studies in Archaeology and Related Disciplines* (Beer-Sheva 15) (Beer-Sheva: Ben-Gurion University of the Negev Press, 2002), 210-12 and figs. 7-12 and 14-15.

14. D. Ben-Tor, "The Relation between Egypt and Palestine in the Middle Kingdom as Reflected by Contemporary Canaanite Scarabs," *IEJ* 47 (1997): 171 and 173, fig. 4.

15. Cf. the very common *nb* at the bottom of scarab decorations.

16. For example, a scarab from Lachish with the throne name of Amenophis III shows the epithet *tyt R'*, "sign, image of Re"; the *t* in *tyt* is inverted. See R. Giveon, "The Scarabs (Lachish V)," in Y. Aharoni, *Investigations at Lachish: The Sanctuary and the Residency (Lachish V)* (Tel Aviv: Gateway Publishers, 1975), 71 and pl. 16, 12 and 35, 9.

17. One might compare the very often very imperfect English orthography of people whose mother tongue is not English.

FIGURE 4

FIGURE 5

FIGURE 6

FIGURE 7

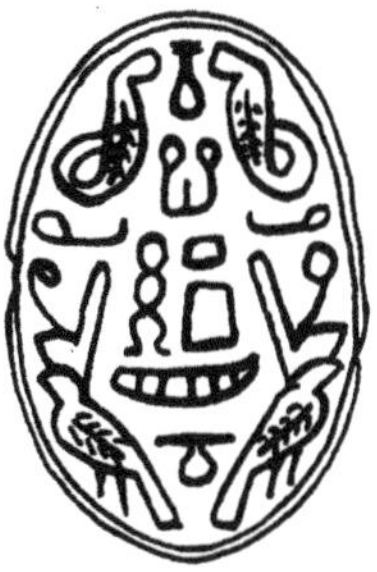

FIGURE 8

FIGURE 9

Fig. 7, a scarab from Gezer, has no scroll border.[18] On a scarab from Beth-Zur, "Ptah" occupies the central position instead of the top (**fig. 8**).[19] The name of Ptah may also be intended on a rather fragmentarily preserved scarab picked up as a surface find on Tell Keisan by children of Kibbutz Yasᶜur (**fig. 9**).[20] The only Middle Bronze Age scarab I know with the name of Ptah included in a horizontal arrangement comes from a tomb in Afula (**fig. 10**).[21] All the scarabs found in this tomb are definitely of early Fifteenth-Dynasty date.

It also seems to me that most of the other scarabs bearing the name of Ptah listed above originated in the early Fifteenth Dynasty. The fine linear engraving, the side types (d13 and d14 as distinguished from e6a), the border of paired spirals, and many other features fit very well into this period.[22] There should be a thorough investigation into the

18. R. A. S. Macalister, *The Excavations of Gezer: 1902-1905 and 1907-1909* (London: Palestine Excavation Fund, 1912), 3, pl. 204b, 8.

19. O. R. Sellers et al., *The 1957 Excavations at Beth-Zur* (New Haven: American Schools of Oriental Research, 1968), 81f., fig. 30a, pl. 41a; two more scarabs with the name of Ptah were found in Atlit (cf. O. Keel, *Corpus 1997*, Atlit nos. 38 and 42).

20. Photographs of this scarab were found among the notes and impressions left by the late Prof. Raphael Giveon. No measurements are available.

21. O. Keel, *Corpus 1997*, Afula no. 4.

22. O. Keel, *Corpus 1995*, §§111, 327, 329, 508.

FIGURE 10

FIGURE 11

FIGURE 12

FIGURE 13

FIGURE 14

FIGURE 15

archaeological (pottery) context of these scarabs, which cannot be done here. If my assumption is correct, these scarabs bear witness to the interest taken by Canaanite artisans in the Egyptian god of craftsmanship. The phenomenon fits well into the general picture of Canaanites settling and working in the eastern delta and establishing close relations between this region and Palestine, particularly its southern part. It was this development which led to the establishment of the Fifteenth Dynasty.

There are two Palestinian scarabs exhibiting iconographic elements in addition to the name "Ptah." On one from the Jerusalem antiquity market the name of the god is flanked by two z^3-signs above a *nb* (**fig. 11**).[23] These hieroglyphs may be read as an expression of personal devotion: "Ptah (is my) lord and (my) protection." The aspect of personal piety is enhanced by the two devotees kneeling beneath the name and holding a papyrus flower.[24] The other was found in tomb 1021 on Southern Tell el-

23. O. Keel and Ch. Uehlinger, *Altorientalische Miniaturkunst: Die ältesten visuellen Massenkommunikationsmittel. Ein Blick in die Sammlungen des Biblischen Instituts der Universität Freiburg Schweiz* (Fribourg: Universitätsverlag, 1996), 79, fig. 104a.

24. Keel, *Corpus 1995*, §§561-62, 615-17.

Far^cah (**fig. 12**).[25] The female figure here may be identified by her Red Crown as Neith (*Nt*), who had a sanctuary in Memphis "north of the wall."[26] Her association with the Memphite Ptah should come as no surprise. The lotus in her hand, however, is an element more appropriate for a devotee, and despite the Red Crown,[27] just such a worshipper may be represented here.

Besides the name of Ptah, we also find his image on Middle Bronze Age Palestinian scarabs. The earliest is that depicted on a scarab said to originate from ᶜAin Samija (**fig. 13**).[28] It shows the god with a devotee in front of him. In contrast to the usual direction for the main figure, the god faces to the left. This feature and the absence of the tassel at the neck are also found on the stele from Serabit el-Khadem (cf. fig. 1). An additional un-Egyptian feature is a branch between the god and the devotee. A similar representation appears on an unpublished scarab (**fig. 14**).[29] Though in this instance the tassel in the neck is not missing, some small mistakes suggest that this scarab too is a Canaanite product: The lower end of the scepter of dominion is not forked properly. The tassel and the feet are too long. The un-Egyptian branch already seen in fig. 13 is now found underneath the god. The linear style of the engraving and the features of the scarabs suggest that the items of figs. 13 and 14 belong to the early Fifteenth Dynasty.

In contrast to the items just mentioned, the design of another unpublished scarab (**fig. 15**)[30] does not show linear engraving but is hollowed out. Though this feature can be found earlier, it becomes common only in the Fifteenth Dynasty.[31] The d6 side is equally characteristic for the Fifteenth Dynasty. All the scarabs of the early Hyksos king *Jᶜqbhr* whose side-type is known to Ward have d6 sides.[32] Again Ptah exhibits some un-Egyptian features: There is the remnant of a uraeus-serpent. The tassel at

25. J. L. Starkey and L. Harding, *Beth-Pelet II: Prehistoric Fara. Beth-Pelet Cemetery* (London: British School of Archaeology in Egypt, 1932), pl. 43, 9.

26. H. Bonnet, *Reallexikon der ägyptischen Religionsgeschichte* (Berlin: de Gruyter, 1952), 513; R. El-Sayed, *La déesse Neith de Saïs I: Importance et rayonnement de son culte, II. Documentation*, Bibliothèque d'étude 86, 1-2 (Cairo: Institut français d'archéologie orientale, 1982), 39-41.

27. O. Keel, *Corpus 1995*, §562.

28. O. Keel, "La glyptique," in *Tell Keisan (1971-1976): Une cité phénicienne en Galilée*, ed. J. Briend and J. B. Humbert, OBO.SA 1 (Fribourg: Universitätsverlag, 1980), 262, fig. 68; O. Keel, M. Shuval, and Ch. Uehlinger, *Studien zu den Stempelsiegeln aus Palästina/Israel III: Die Frühe Eisenzeit. Ein Workshop*, OBO 100 (Fribourg: Universitätsverlag, 1990), 179, fig. 14.

29. British Museum EA 40015.

30. British Museum EA 39745.

31. O. Keel, *Corpus 1995*, §329.

32. W. A. Ward in O. Tufnell, *Studies on Scarab Seals*, pl. 57, 3221-31.

FIGURE 16

FIGURE 17

FIGURE 18

the neck starts at the lower part of the head. The shapelessness of his body is equally un-Egyptian. On a final example of this group originating in the former Matouk Collection and now at the Department of Biblical Studies of the University of Fribourg (**fig. 16**),[33] the shape of the god is more in accordance with classical Egyptian standards than on fig. 15. Still the tassel and the beard are missing. The hollowed-out engraving and the two cobras in front of the god are typical of the Fifteenth Dynasty.[34] In all four instances shown in figs. 13-16 the scepter of dominion is held in the correct way.

This is not the case with another Fifteenth-Dynasty group of scarabs. Except for the scarab in fig. 18, which was bought in Jerusalem in 1978, the origin of these items is totally unknown. All of them exhibit hollowed-out engraving. With the exception of fig. 17 they have simple side-types and trapezoidal heads. They show Ptah flanked by two falcons with spread wings (**fig. 17**),[35] by a falcon and a standing anthropomorphic falcon-headed deity (**fig. 18**),[36] a kneeling anthropomorphic falcon-headed deity (**fig. 19**),[37] two kneeling anthropomorphic falcon-headed deities (**fig. 20**),[38] or a kneeling anthropomorphic falcon-headed deity and a cobra (**fig. 21**).[39] All five instances depict Ptah holding the scepter of dominion in the wrong direction. Except for fig. 17, he is shown without the characteristic tassel and on all without beard. The group was produced by non-

33. F. S. Matouk, *Corpus du Scarabée Egyptien. Vol. II: Analyse thématique* (Beirut: Impremerie Catholique, 1977), 379, no. 272; O. Keel, "Der ägyptische Gott Ptah," 289-92, fig. 27.

34. O. Keel, "Der ägyptische Gott Ptah," 289f., fig. 26.

35. F. S. Matouk, *Corpus*, 378, no. 245 = O. Keel, "Der ägyptische Gott Ptah," 293, fig. 34.

36. O. Keel, "La glyptique," 263, fig. 71 = "Der ägyptische Gott Ptah," 293, fig. 36 = O. Keel, M. Shuval, and Ch. Uehlinger, *Studien*, 179, fig. 17.

37. British Museum EA 43096.

38. E. Hornung and E. Staehelin, *Skarabäen und andere Siegelamulette aus Basler Sammlungen* (Mainz: Phillip von Zabern, 1976), 399, no. MV 21 = "Der ägyptische Gott Ptah," 293, fig. 35.

39. British Museum EA 46523.

FIGURE 19

FIGURE 20

FIGURE 21

Egyptians, most probably Canaanites. It shows a continuing interest in Ptah, though combined with the falcon or the falcon-headed deity, the god most popular on Fifteenth-Dynasty scarabs. The falcon is closely connected with kingship,[40] as is the falcon-headed figure.[41] To represent Ptah flanked by falcons and/or falcon-headed deities qualifies him as king.[42] A similar eagerness to indicate the superiority of Ptah can be found on a certain type of Ramessid scarabs (cf. figs. 60-63).[43]

It seems that it was the Canaanites,[44] who were used to representing the picture of deities on cylinder-seals, who began to put the name and image of the great god of Memphis on scarabs. We do not find either name or image of Ptah[45] or of any other major deity on scarabs of certain

---

40. O. Keel, *Studien zu den Stempelsiegeln aus Palästina/Israel* IV, OBO 135 (Fribourg: Universitätsverlag, 1994), 94f.

41. O. Keel, M. Shuval, and Ch. Uehlinger, *Studien*, 243-80.

42. O. Keel, "Der ägyptische Gott Ptah," 292-99.

43. The lion-headed Sakhmet is not represented on Middle Bronze Age seal-amulets from Palestine. Attention can be drawn to a typical Middle Bronze Age cowroid in Basel (O. Keel, *Corpus 1995*, §186) without known provenance (*Corpus 1995*, §593, fig. 465). The object shows Sakhmet or another lion-headed goddess in linear engraving. Sakhmet was closely associated with Ptah for the first time during the New Kingdom; see H. Sternberg, "Sekhmet," *Lexikon der Ägyptologie* 5:323-33.

44. Besides the representations already mentioned, there are a few more which may possibly be identified as Ptah, but they have not been included here because this identification is far from certain: for example, O. Keel, *Corpus 1997*, Tell el-ʿAğul no. 954 = "Der ägyptische Gott Ptah," 290, fig. 25; A. Ben-Tor, *The Scarab: A Reflection of Ancient Egypt* (Jerusalem: Israel Museum, 1989), 69, fig. 40; J. L. Haynes and Y. Markowitz, *Scarabs and Design Amulets: A Glimpse of Ancient Egypt in Miniature*, nfa Classical Auctions, Inc., New York, December 11, 1991, no. 64 = DBF SK 1991.10. For a cylinder seal with a Ptah-like figure, see E. Porada, *Corpus of Ancient Near Eastern Seals in North American Collections, vol. I. The Collection of the Pierpont Morgan Library* (New York: Pantheon Books, 1948), no. 999 = O. Keel, "Der ägyptische Gott Ptah," 288, fig. 22.

45. There is one exception: On a private name scarab that belonged to a man named "Sa-Ptah" ("son of Ptah"), we find the picture of the god. See A. Ben-Tor, "Scarabs Bearing Titles and Private Names of Officials from the Middle Kingdom and the Second Intermediate Period (c. 2050-1550 B.C.E.)," *Israel Museum Journal* 7 (1988): 39, no. 11, pl. 2, 11 = O. Keel, "Der ägyptische Gott Ptah," 290, fig. 29a. This usage can be explained by the name of the owner and is thus not a real exception to the rule.

Egyptian manufacture of this period. This did not change before the New Kingdom. The scarabs previously discussed here thus testify to the Middle Bronze Age Canaanites' fervor and enthusiasm for Egyptian culture in general and for the god of Memphis in particular. The predilection for this god may be explained by trade connections with Memphis and by the fact that many of the Canaanites coming to Egypt during the Thirteenth and Fifteenth Dynasties were craftsmen. Canaanite scarabs with the name and image of the craftsman's god Ptah were expressions of the local artisans' admiration for this Egyptian deity and Egyptian craftsmanship, and of their personal piety in respect to Ptah.

Ptah scarabs are found all over the country, from Tell el-Farʿah in the southern coastal plain to Shiqmonah near Haifa in the north, from the coastal plain to inland sites such as Beth-Zur, Jericho, and Afulah.

Late Bronze Age I-IIA: Court Propaganda: The Pharaoh Beloved of Ptah

A different distribution pattern characterizes the Eighteenth-Dynasty Ptah seal-amulets. They originate from a few places that must be considered strongholds of Egyptian administration: five from Lachish, two from Tell el-ʿAğul, two from Shechem, and two from Beth-Shan. One each comes from Gezer and from the northern Timnah. The message that the Ptah seal-amulets of the Eighteenth Dynasty convey is also completely different from that of the Ptah scarabs of the Fifteenth Dynasty. The message is now political. About 15% (ca. 100 items) of the stamp seal-amulets of the Eighteenth Dynasty found in Palestine/Israel are engraved with the name of Amun, the main god of the Eighteenth Dynasty and the patron god of the reigning family. Amun's name is not found on a single scarab of the previous period. Next to Amun comes Hathor (20 items—3%), followed by Ptah (13 items—2%), and Month (7 items—1%). Ptah the patron of Memphis is thus the male god second after Amun, though eclipsed by a very wide margin. In sharp contrast to Amun, he is almost exclusively represented by his image. In company with Amun and a falcon-headed deity, he can be seen on a rectangular piece of Amenophis II (**fig. 22**).[46] On the recto of an oval piece of the same Pharaoh, the king offers a pointed loaf, while on the verso, the name of Ptah is written before him (**fig. 23**).[47] In this case the god must be understood as the addressee of the offering.

---

46. O. Tufnell et al., *Lachish IV*, pls. 37/38, 317 = O. Keel, "Der ägyptische Gott Ptah," 313, fig. 111.

47. O. Keel, *Corpus 1997*, Tell el-ʿAğul, no. 272 = "Der ägyptische Gott Ptah," 301, fig. 64.

FIGURE 22

FIGURE 23

A third item bearing the name of Amenophis II and an image of Ptah is a square prism from Lachish (**fig. 24**).[48] One side shows the standing Ptah with his name written in front of him and *nfr* beneath it.[49] On a number of Eighteenth-Dynasty stamp seal-amulets we have the image of Ptah standing and a few hieroglyphs in front of him, which may be abbreviated forms of well-known epithets of the god. Thus the *nfr* on the Lachish prism may mean "of beautiful appearance" (*nfr <ḥr>*). This epithet is found on a rectangular plaque with domed top from Shechem from the time of Amenophis III (**fig. 25**).[50] On a scarab from Lachish, he is called *nfr <ḥr> nb t^{3}wy* (**fig. 26**).[51] On a rectangular plaque from Tell el-ʿAğul with the name of Amenophis III written on the verso, the recto may be

48. O. Tufnell et al., *Lachish IV*, pl. 37/38, 295; R. Hestrin, B. Sass, and O. Ophel, "The Lachish Prism Inscription—Proto-Canaanite or Egyptian?" *IEJ* 32 (1982): 104-6.

49. The very worn figure holding the sign of life on another side of the same prism may represent the king and he may be related to the god. Thus we would have a similar constellation as on the preceding piece. The problem is that the king in this case would approach the god from behind.

50. Ch. Clamer, 1981, "A Late Bronze Age Burial Cave near Shechem," *Qad.* 14 (1981): 34.

51. O. Tufnell et al., *Lachish IV*, pl. 35/36, 244 = O. Keel, "Der ägyptische Gott Ptah," 290, fig. 31.

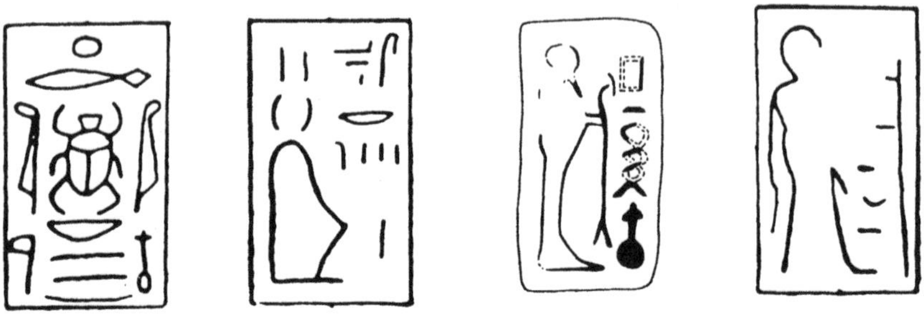

FIGURE 24

FIGURE 25

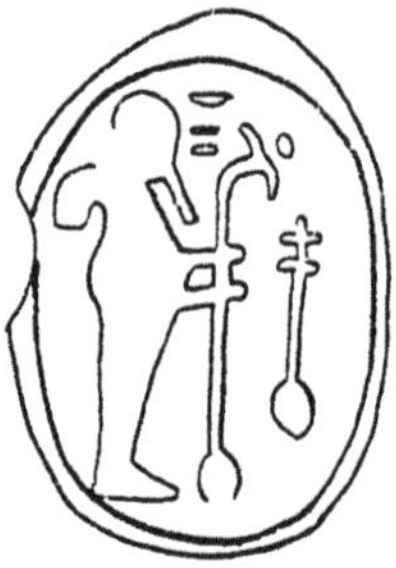

FIGURE 26

FIGURE 27

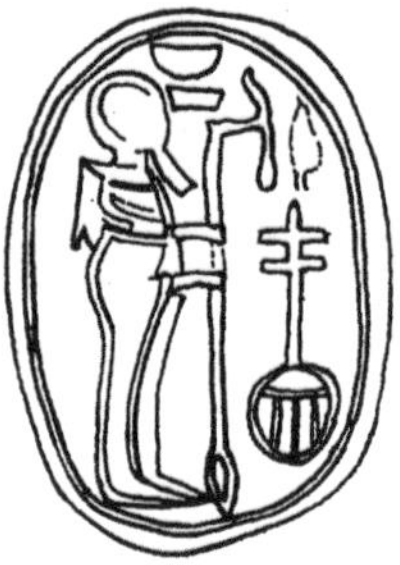

FIGURE 28

FIGURE 29

FIGURE 30

read as "Lord of truth" (*nb m3ʿt*) and "of beautiful appearance" (*nfr ḥr*) (**fig. 27**).[52] The same epithets are clearly written in front of the god on a scarab from Timnah North (**fig. 28**).[53] Twice we see the sign of life and the *djed*-pillar in front of his image (**figs. 29-30**).[54] They may be understood as abbreviations of the two well-known epithets "Lord of life" (*nb ʿnḫ*) and "The noble *Djed*-pillar" (*ḏd špsj*).[55]

While eleven items represent Ptah by his image together with his name, or replace the latter with one or two epithets, only four show the name of the god without an accompanying image. Once we find it in connection with the throne name of Amenophis III, who is said to be "beloved of Ptah, the Lord of Truth" (**fig. 31**).[56] The same formula, *mry Ptḥ nb m3ʿt*, is found on an oval plaque, this time without a royal name.[57] Once we have on one side of an oval piece: "Ptah (is my) Lord," while on the other there is the name "Amun-Reʿ" (**fig. 32**).[58] Finally we must mention an occurrence of the formula, "Ptah perfect with favors" (*Ptḥ nfr ḥzwt*) (**fig. 33**).[59]

Seal-amulets of the Eighteenth Dynasty depict the god with one or two of his epithets. Characteristic for this dynasty, particularly for the time of Amenophis III (1390-1353), is the combination of the name of the king and the image (and name) of the god on the same seal-amulet, suggesting that the king is *mry Ptḥ*, "Beloved of Ptah," as the inscription on some scarabs explicitly says. These scarabs were most probably produced at the court and sold or donated to Egyptian officials or to Canaanites in the service of Egypt. To carry such an item signified loyalty toward the pharaoh whose name or image was on the object. At the same time it implied that the bearer was loved and protected by the pharaoh and the god—in this case by that Ptah whose love for the pharaoh the object proclaims.[60]

---

52. O. Keel, *Corpus 1997*: Tell el-ʿAğul, no. 847 = "Der ägyptische Gott Ptah," 314, fig. 122.

53. A. Mazar and G. L. Kelm, *Timnah: A Biblical City in the Sorek Valley* (Winona Lake, IN: Eisenbrauns, 1995), 63, fig. 4.30 and 80, fig. C13. For "Lord of Truth" alone, see O. Tufnell et al., *Lachish II (Tell ed-Duweir): The Fosse Temple* (London: Oxford University Press, 1940), pl. 32A-B, 20 = O. Keel, "Der ägyptische Gott Ptah," 309, fig. 101.

54. Philadelphia, University Museum, Inv. no. 29-104-69 = O. Keel, "Der ägyptische Gott Ptah," 295, fig. 48; S. Horn, "Scarabs and Scarab Impressions from Shechem-III," *JNES* 32 (1973): 281-89 = O. Keel, "Der ägyptische Gott Ptah," 295, fig. 49.

55. O. Keel, H. Keel-Leu, and S. Schroer, *Studien*, 294f.

56. O. Keel, *Corpus 1995*, 90, fig. 153.

57. A. Rowe, *The Four Canaanite Temples of Beth-Shan I: The Temples and Cult Objects* (Philadelphia: University Museum, 1940), 84 and pl. 37, 20.

58. S. Ben-Arie, D. Ben-Tor, S. Godovitz, "A Late Bronze Age Burial Cave at Qubeibeh, near Tel Lachish," *ʿAtiqot* 22 (1993): 82-83, fig. 6.

59. O. Tufnell et al., *Lachish IV*, pl. 39/40, 376.

60. Sakhmet is never shown together with Ptah on Eighteenth-Dynasty seal-amulets from Palestine.

FIGURE 31

FIGURE 32

FIGURE 33

Late Bronze Age IIB: Ptah Venerated by the Pharaoh and as the God of the Memphite Theology

The Nineteenth Dynasty, like the Fifteenth, has left us mainly scarabs. Other shapes are much less numerous than in the Eighteenth Dynasty. These scarabs continue to exhibit the image of Ptah combined with a few hieroglyphs that can be interpreted as abbreviations of epithets of this deity. In contrast to the production of the Eighteenth Dynasty, the image is no longer combined with the name of a king. Now it is not the relationship of the god to the king that is important, but the god himself. Several times we find the image of Ptah with a *djed*-pillar before him; on top of the pillar is the figure or the feather of Maʿat (**figs. 34-36**).[61] Four examples show only the feather of Maʿat before the god (**fig. 37-39**),[62]

61. E. Grant, *Rumeileh: Being Ain Shems Excavations (Palestine) III* (Haverford, PA: Haverford College, 1934), fig. 3, 2; J. L. Starkey and L. Harding, *Beth-Pelet II*, pl. 55, 286 = A. Rowe, *A Catalogue of Egyptian Scarabs, Scaraboids, Seals and Amulets in the Palestine Archaeological Museum* (Cairo: Institut français d'archéologie orientale, 1936), no. 810; W. M. F. Petrie, *Beth Pelet I: Tel Fara* (London: British School of Archaeology in Egypt, 1930), pl. 12, 172; cf. also J. L. Starkey and L. Harding, *Beth-Pelet II*, pl. 52, 167; W. A. Ward, "Cylinders and Scarabs from a Late Bronze Temple at ʿAmman," *ADAJ* 8-9 (1964): 51 and pls. 21-22.

62. J. L. Starkey and L. Harding, *Beth-Pelet II*, pl. 48, 14 = A. Rowe, *Catalogue*, no. 721; O. Keel, "Der ägyptische Gott Ptah," 309, fig. 99; Starkey and Harding, *Beth-Pelet II*, pl. 49, bottom row, second from left = Rowe, *Catalogue*, no. 720. Cf. also Petrie, *Beth Pelet I*, pl. 31, 11; 308f., figs. 97-101.

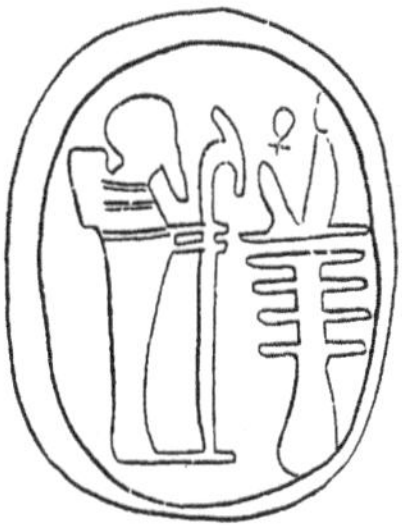

FIGURE 34

FIGURE 35

FIGURE 36

FIGURE 37

FIGURE 38

FIGURE 39

and one the squatting figure of Maʿat (**fig. 40**).[63] There is only one example of an isolated *djed*-pillar in this position.[64] The holiness of the god is emphasized by a huge uraeus-serpent in front of him (**fig. 41**),[65] and once by an additional *nfr*-sign (**fig. 42**).[66] On one seal the protecting uraeus is behind Ptah (**fig. 43**).[67] A new shape is represented by finger rings, which show nothing but the image of the god (**fig. 44**).[68]

While on all the previous scarabs and finger rings the god was represented standing, one scarab shows him enthroned. The combination of

---

63. O. Tufnell et al., *Lachish II*, pl. 32A/B, 20.

64. Deir el-Balaḥ, Tel Aviv, Institute of Archaeology, ex-Dayan Coll., no. 241 = O. Keel, "Der ägyptische Gott Ptah," 295, fig. 51.

65. O. Tufnell et al., *Lachish IV*, pl. 39/40, 360.

66. Deir el-Balaḥ, Tel Aviv, Institute of Archaeology, ex-Dayan Coll., no. 229 = O. Keel, "Der ägyptische Gott Ptah," 314, fig. 119.

67. W. M. F. Petrie, *Anthedon Sinai* (London: British School of Archaeology in Egypt, 1937), pl. 31, 11 = O. Keel, "Der ägyptische Gott Ptah," 309, fig. 98.

68. T. Dothan, "Aspects of Egyptian and Philistine Presence in Canaan during the Late Bronze-Early Iron Age," in *The Land of Israel: Cross-Roads of Civilizations. Proceedings of the Conference Held in Brussels from the 3rd to the 5th December 1984 to Mark the Twenty-Fifth Anniversary of the Institute of Archaeology Queen Elisabeth of Belgium and the Hebrew University of Jerusalem*, ed. E. Lipiński (Leuven: Uitgeverij Peeters, 1985), 63-65 and figs. 5-6 = O. Keel, "Der ägyptische Gott Ptah," 290, fig. 32. Cf. Keel, *Corpus 1997*, Abu Hawam, no. 8; Tell el-ʿAğul, no. 194.

FIGURE 40

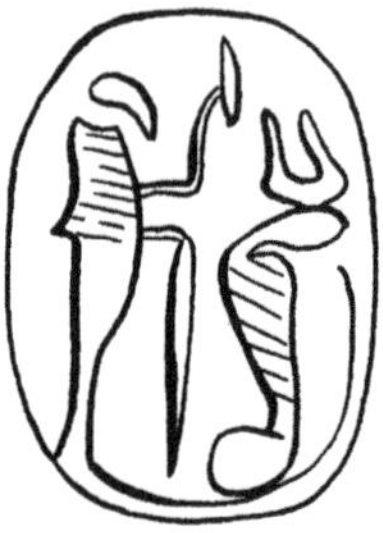

FIGURE 41

FIGURE 42

FIGURE 43

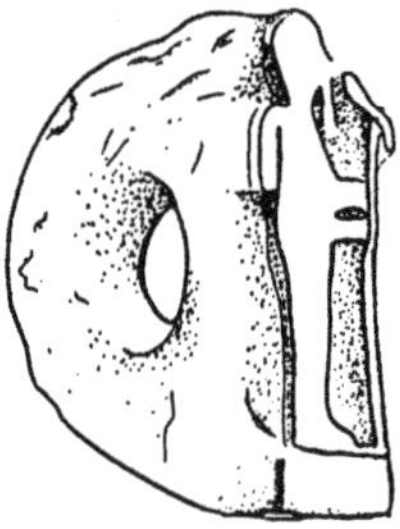

FIGURE 44

FIGURE 45

FIGURE 46

FIGURE 47

FIGURE 48

FIGURE 49

FIGURE 50

FIGURE 51

his name with the epithet *nb t*^{3}*wy*, "Lord of the Two Lands," emphasizes that he is represented as king (**fig. 45**).[69] On two other Ramessid scarabs the god is depicted in an archaic squatting position, once with a uraeus in front (**fig. 46**)[70] and once with undecipherable hieroglyphs (**fig. 47**).[71]

As already mentioned, Nineteenth-Dynasty stamp seal-amulets do not connect the name of the king to Ptah as was done on Eighteenth-Dynasty objects. God and king, however, are related in a new way. The reason the old practice was abandoned and replaced by a new one is probably that the main production centers of scarabs were no longer the workshops of the royal court but those of the temples. W. M. F. Petrie found large numbers of unfinished scarabs in the court of the Nineteenth-Dynasty Ptah temple in Memphis.[72] The iconography of many of the scarabs from this period does not display the god in splendid isolation, but presents miniature copies of scenes known from temple reliefs. The king was the only son, servant, and priest of the gods. He was represented time and again in these functions on the wall reliefs in the temples. Now he can also be seen in this role on scarabs. The motif of the smiting of an enemy in front of the god is typically carved on the outer walls of a temple (**fig. 48**).[73] Other scenes translated from monumental to miniature scale on scarabs are particular cult scenes typical of the inner walls of the temples. They include the presentation of a *rḫyt*-bird (**fig. 49**),[74] of two wine jars (**fig. 50**),[75] of cloth (*rdyyt mnḥt*) (**fig. 51**),[76] or more commonly that of a figure of the goddess Maʿat, which constitutes a summary of the correct execution of all cultic and other commitments of the pharaoh

69. A. Biran and O. Negbi, "The Stratigraphical Sequence at Tel Ṣippor," *IEJ* 16 (1966): pl. 22D-E = O. Keel, "Der ägyptische Gott Ptah," 290, fig. 30.

70. R. A. S. Macalister, *The Excavations of Gezer. 1902-1905 and 1907-1909* (London: Palestine Exploration Fund, 1912), vol. 3, pl. 204b, 11 = A. Rowe, *Catalogue*, no. 691.

71. J. L. Starkey and L. Harding, *Beth-Pelet II*, pl. 50, 58 = R. Giveon, *Egyptian Scarabs from Western Asia from the Collection of the British Museum*, OBO.SA 3 (Fribourg: Universitätsverlag, 1985), 48-49, no. 79. Giveon sees an empty cartouche(?) and *wsr*; B. Jaeger (oral communication) proposes "elements of the god's name: *p* (rounded) and *t* and beneath it an *wsr*. The element above could also be a *z*^{3}, 'protection,' in combination with *wsr*: 'Ptah is a mighty protection.'"

72. W. M. F. Petrie, *Memphis I* (London: British School of Archaeology in Egypt, 1909), pl. 28, 14. For the king in front of Ptah as a typical subject of Ramessid scarabs, see B. Jaeger, *Essai de classification et datation des Scarabées Menkhéperrê*, OBO.SA 2 (Fribourg: Universitätsverlag, 1982), 199, §§1336-40.

73. O. Keel, "Der ägyptische Gott Ptah," 304-5, fig. 79; cf. also figs. 78 and 80-81.

74. R. Giveon, *The Impact of Egypt on Canaan: Iconographical and Related Studies*, OBO 20 (Fribourg: Universitätsverlag, 1978), 100 and fig. 52a-c = O. Keel, "Der ägyptische Gott Ptah," 302, fig. 75.

75. O. Keel, "Der ägyptische Gott Ptah," 301, fig. 65.

76. O. Keel, "Der ägyptische Gott Ptah," 301, fig. 66.

(fig. 52-53).[77] A generalization almost completely absent from temple walls but very common on scarabs shows the pharaoh occupied not with some specific ritual but with empty hands lifted in adoration (**figs. 54-57**).[78] In a few cases the figure of the king is replaced by the cartouche with his name (**figs. 58-59**).[79]

The message of these scarabs is to advertise the excellence of the sanctuary and the piety of the king, who is the foremost worshipper of Ptah and an example to all pious people who come to Memphis to worship the god. To carry such an item signified a participation in this summit of king and god and a part in the blessing emanating from this harmony on the highest level.

Beside these miniature copies of scenes from temple walls, we find two additional subjects that seem not to be found among temple decorations. One shows Ptah turned to the right as the main figure.[80] In front of him stands the sun god Re grasping the scepter of dominion held by Ptah (**figs. 60-63**).[81] The position of Re on these scarabs is taken on others by the pharaoh. A scarab from Gezer shows the sun god to the left and the pharaoh to the right grasping the scepter of the god (**fig. 64**).[82] A scarab from Tell el-Farᶜah-South exhibits basically the same arrangement, save that the position of Re is here held by Amun (**fig. 65**).[83] Another scarab from the same site shows Amun on the right looking left. With one hand

---

77. O. Keel, "Der ägyptische Gott Ptah," 302, figs. 69-70; cf. also figs. 71-72.

78. O. Keel, "Der ägyptische Gott Ptah," 306, figs. 85, 93, 90 = Deir el-Balaḥ, Tel Aviv, Institute of Archaeology, ex-Dayan Coll., nos. 214 and 91; cf. also 84 = J. L. Starkey and L. Harding, *Beth-Pelet II*, pl. 52, 135; 86 = P. L. O. Guy, *Megiddo Tombs* (Chicago: University of Chicago Press, 1938), pl. 131, 3; 87 = F. J. Bliss, *A Mound of Many Cities: Tel el Hesy Excavated* (London: Palestine Exploration Fund, 1898), 79, fig. 125; 88 = Deir el-Balaḥ, Tel Aviv, Institute of Archaeology, ex-Dayan Coll., no. 329; 89 = Deir el-Balaḥ, Tel Aviv, Institute of Archaeology, ex-Dayan Coll., no. 303; 92 = O. Keel, *Corpus 1997*, Akko, no. 73; 93-94; 95 = R. A. S. Macalister, *Gezer*, vol. 3, pl. 121, 20.

79. J. L. Starkey and L. Harding, *Beth-Pelet II*, pl. 57, 345 = O. Keel, "Der ägyptische Gott Ptah," 301, fig. 67; Keel, *Corpus 1997*, Aschkelon, no. 40. Although the throne name of Thutmosis III is in the cartouche on this scarab, it is nevertheless Ramessid.

80. H. Schäfer, *Von ägyptischer Kunst*. 4. verbesserte Auflage und mit einem Nachwort versehen von E. Brunner-Traut (Wiesbaden: Otto Harrassowitz, 1964), 308f.

81. O. Keel, "Der ägyptische Gott Ptah," 293, figs. 37 = W. M. F. Petrie, *Beth Pelet I: Tel Fara* (London: British School of Archaeology in Egypt, 1930), pl. 12,1 62; 38 = Keel, *Corpus 1997*, Tell el-ᶜAğul, no. 295; 40 = O. Tufnell et al., *Lachish IV*, pl. 39, 353; 41 = Keel, *Corpus 1997*, Akko, no. 73; cf. also 39 = J. L. Starkey and L. Harding, *Beth-Pelet II*, pl. 50, 48; 42; 43 = Deir el-Balaḥ, Tel Aviv, Institute of Archaeology, ex-Dayan Coll., no. 302; 46 = Starkey and Harding, *Beth-Pelet II*, pl. 55, 289; 47. Figs. 44 = Petrie 1930: pl. 12,163, and 45 = Starkey and Harding, *Beth-Pelet II*, pl. 52, 165, show the falcon-headed deity holding his own scepter.

82. R. A. S. Macalister, *Gezer*, vol. 3, pl. 208, 6.

83. J. L. Starkey and L. Harding, *Beth-Pelet II*, pl. 52, 140 = O. Keel, M. Shuval, and Ch. Uehlinger, *Studien*, 18, fig. 5

FIGURE 52

FIGURE 53

FIGURE 54

FIGURE 55

FIGURE 56

FIGURE 57

FIGURE 58

FIGURE 59

FIGURE 60

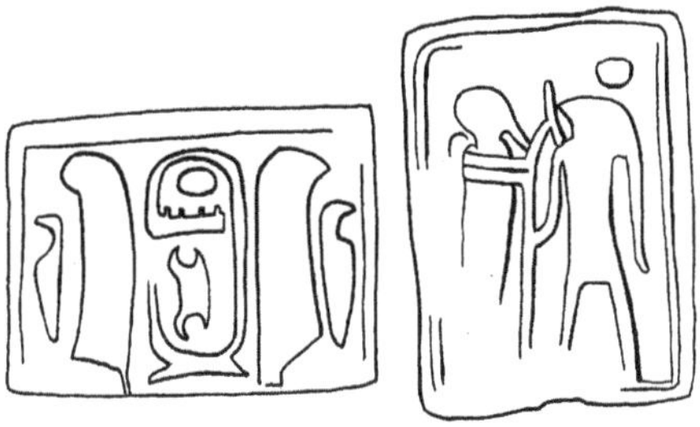

FIGURE 61

FIGURE 62

FIGURE 63

FIGURE 64

FIGURE 65

FIGURE 66

FIGURE 67

Rameses II grasps the scepter of the god, while lifting the other in a gesture of adoration (**fig. 66**).[84] This arrangement indicates the pharaoh's participation in the god's power and in his government of the world. As in these scenes the king is subordinated to the god whose scepter he grasps, in the same way Re-Harakhti is subordinated to Ptah.[85]

Another arrangement that places Ptah in a dominating position represents him with two *djed*-pillars. On each *djed*-pillar is a *ba*-bird (**figs. 67-70**).[86] According to the Book of the Dead (Spell 17, section 21) and other

---

84. J. L. Starkey and L. Harding, *Beth-Pelet II*, pl. 52, 121 = R. Giveon, *Egyptian Scarabs from Western Asia from the Collection of the British Museum*, OBO.SA 3 (Fribourg: Universitätsverlag, 1985), 28-29, no. 20.

85. Ch. Eder, *Die ägyptischen Motive in der Glyptik des östlichen Mittelmeerraumes zu Anfang des 2. Jts. v. Chr.* (Leuven: Uirgeverij Peeters, 1995), 127, n. 17, interprets my position that the priests of Memphis endeavored to win as many adherents as possible for their cult and rejects this idea with the remark that there is no proof of missionary activities by the priests of Ptah. Both this summary of my position and its interpretation as missionary activity are equally incorrect. Eder offers no interpretation of his own for Re-Harakhti's grasping of the scepter of Ptah.

86. O. Keel, "Der ägyptische Gott Ptah," 295, fig. 52 = F. James, *The Iron Age at Beth Shan: A Study of Levels VI-IV* (Philadelphia: University Museum, 1966), 317, fig. 100, 6; 54 = Jabne, IAA 60-953; 55 = A. Rowe, *Catalogue*, no. 718; 57; cf. also 53 = O. Tufnell et al., *Lachish III (Tell ed-Duweir). The Iron Age* (London: Oxford University Press, 1953), pl. 43, 28 ; 56 = E. D. Oren, *The Northern Cemetery of Beth Shan* (Leiden: E. J. Brill, 1973), 246, fig. 51, 14; N.

FIGURE 68

FIGURE 69

FIGURE 70

sources, the two *ba*-birds may in certain cases represent Re and Osiris as the main gods of the world above and the world below.[87] The composition with Re grasping the scepter of Ptah hints at the subordinate position of the falcon-headed deity, most probably Re. Ptah with two *djed*-pillars before him conveys the message that he is the primordial god, a position held in Heliopolis by Re-Atum.

The superiority of Ptah over Re and Atum, respectively, as "Ur- und Allgott" is the subject of the famous "Memphite Theology."[88] The text is said to have been copied on the order of Shabaka (716-702) from a worm-eaten document[89] and inscribed on a slab of black granite to be placed in the temple of Ptah at Memphis. The text was later used for some time as a millstone and was badly damaged.[90] J. H. Breasted, who was the first to

---

Zori, *An Archaeological Survey in the Beth Shan Valley. The 17th Archaeological Convention* (Jerusalem: Israel Exploration Society, 1962), 171 and pl. 19, 4-5; an unpublished piece from Musmus near Megiddo (IAA 48-1406); B. Jaeger, *Essai*, 194, §§1314-15. A scarab found in 1962 at Deir Alla shows just one *djed*-pillar with a *ba*-bird in front of Ptah and Sakhmet.

87. The birds normally represent Shu and Tefnut, the two primordial deities along with Atum. See O. Keel, "Der ägyptische Gott Ptah," 294-98. Tefnut is not "moisture," as traditionally claimed (for example, by G. Hart, *A Dictionary of Egyptian Gods and Goddesses* [London: Routledge and Kegan Paul, 1986], 213); no text validates this assumption; see S. Bickel, *La cosmogonie égyptienne*, OBO 134 (Fribourg: Universitätsverlag, 1994), 169. J. Assmann, "Rezeption und Auslegung in Ägypten. Das 'Denkmal memphitischer Theologie' als Auslegung der heliopolitanischen Kosmogonie," in *Rezeption und Auslegung im Alten Testament und in seinem Umfeld*, ed. R.G. Kratz and Th. Krüger, OBO 153 (Fribourg: Universitätsverlag, 1997), 130, suggests that her essence is rather "fire."

88. For the text see H. Junker, "Die Götterlehre von Memphis (Schabaka-Inschrift)," *APAW.PH* 23, Jg. 1939 (1940); for translations, see J. A. Wilson in *Ancient Near Eastern Texts relating to the Old Testament*, ed. J. B. Pritchard (Princeton, NJ: Princeton University Press, 1955), 4-6, and M. Lichtheim, *Ancient Egyptian Literature. Vol. I: The Old and Middle Kingdoms* (Berkeley and Los Angeles: University of California Press, 1973), 51-57.

89. H. Altenmüller, *Lexikon der Ägyptologie* 1:1065-66, repeatedly calls it a "papyrus," although Breasted already insisted that the text speaks only of a written document—inscribed on wood, papyrus, or something else. See J. H. Breasted, "The Philosophy of a Memphite Priest," *ZÄS* 39 (1901): 41.

90. British Museum, inventory no. 498.

edit and translate the text, thought that the original has "to be dated in or *before* the beginning of the New Kingdom."[91] K. Sethe proposed a date at the beginning of the dynastic history of Egypt.[92] A. Erman wanted to date it to the time when Memphis became the capital of Egypt at the beginning of the Old Kingdom.[93] H. Junker saw reason to put it in the Fifth Dynasty.[94] H. Altenmüller still argued for a date at the very end of the Old Kingdom.[95] F. Junge altered course radically and tried to understand the document as a compilation from the time of Shabaka based on various older documents.[96]

H. A. Schlögl has demonstrated that the combination of Ptah with Tatenen found in the "Memphite Theology" is typical of the time of Rameses II (1279-1213).[97] In his short monograph on Rameses II Schlögl assumes that the author of the text was Khaemwese, a son of Rameses II and a very active high priest of the temple of Ptah at Memphis.[98] "There he held an almost royal position. He built the Ramessid temple of Ptah; he proclaimed and organized the first five *Sed*-festivals of Rameses II. He left numerous monuments at Memphis and at other places . . . His erudition and 'archaeological' activities earned him the reputation of a magician . . . "[99] It is, of course, impossible to know if Khaemwese indeed composed the original hymn. What we are able to say is that the activities of Khaemwese must have created a climate favorable for the writing of a text like the "Memphite Theology."

The text had always been understood as a proclamation of the superiority of the patron god of Memphis. J. Assmann rejects this interpretation as polemic and understands the text as an interpretation or exegesis of the Heliopolitan cosmogony.[100] His statements suggest that polemic and

---

91. J. H. Breasted, "The Philosophy of a Memphite Priest," 43.

92. K. Sethe, *Dramatische Texte zu altägyptischen Mysterienspielen* (Leipzig: J. C. Hinrichs, 1928), 2-5 and 70.

93. A. Erman, "Ein Denkmal memphitischer Theologie," *Sitzungsbericht aus der königlich-preussischen Akademie der Wissenschaften* 43 (1911): 924.

94. H. Junker, "Die Götterlehre von Memphis," 6-8.

95. *Lexikon der Ägyptologie* 1:1068-69.

96. F. Junge, "Zur Fehldatierung des sogenannten Denkmals memphitischer Theologie oder der Beitrag der ägyptischen Theologie zur Geistesgeschichte der Spätzeit," *MDAIK* 29 (1973): 198, 201-3.

97. H. A. Schlögl, *Der Gott Tatenen: Nach Texten und Bildern des Neuen Reiches*, OBO 29 (Fribourg: Universitätsverlag, 1980), 110-17. J. P. Allen, *Genesis in Egypt: The Philosophy of Ancient Egyptian Creation Accounts* (New Haven: Yale Egyptological Seminar, 1988), 43, accepted his argumentation, as did K. Koch, *Geschichte der ägyptischen Religion: Von den Pyramiden bis zu den Mysterien der Isis* (Stuttgart: W. Kohlhammer, 1993), 377-82.

98. H. A. Schlögl, *Ramses II. (rm 425)* (Reinbeck bei Hamburg: Rohwolt, 1993), 115. For Khaemwese see Ch. Maystre, *Les grands prêtres de Ptah de Memphis*, OBO 113 (Fribourg: Universitätsverlag, 1992), 147-56 and 308-34, nos. 107-46.

99. F. Gomaa, *Lexikon der Ägyptologie* 1:898.

100. "Bisher hat man immer angenommen, daß es sich bei diesem Text um eine

interpretation signify opposition, but these modes of discourse are not at all mutually exclusive. To the contrary, a tremendous amount of polemic—between Jews and Christians, between Catholics and Protestants—has taken the form of interpretation of Scripture. Assmann argues that the Heliopolitan cosmogony had long been a basic pan-Egyptian myth, not limited to Heliopolis. Whoever wanted to think and speak about cosmogonic topics had to use it. But if the myth was indeed pan-Egyptian, why was the myth not repeated in its original form in Memphis? Why was Ptah given precedence over Atum? In the "Memphite Theology" Atum is not just replaced by Ptah as a kind of local adaptation, but he is set at a superior level. Conceiving through his heart, he brings into being by his tongue the entire world, of which Atum is a part.

Another scholar has objected that the sons and relatives of Rameses II were high priests at various temples, and that polemic was therefore out of the question. But excluding rivalry between brothers does not make any more sense than postulating a sharp opposition between interpretation and polemic.

The "Memphite Theology" sheds light on the Ramessid scarabs displaying the subordination of Re to Ptah, as well as those depicting Ptah as a primordial god in the company of Shu and Tefnut (figs. 60-63 and 67-70). This fact corroborates the dating of the "Memphite Theology" to the Ramessid period. A further point of contact between Ramessid Ptah scarabs and the "Memphite Theology" will be furnished by a scarab type illustrated here in figs. 88-90.[101]

The similarity of the concept of creation by thought and speech to the Greek notions of νοῦς and λόγος was already noticed by J. H. Breasted.[102] K. Koch compared at length the notions of the creative word of God in the "Memphite Theology," in the cult traditions of Jerusalem, which are most probably much earlier than the Psalms where they appear, and in Genesis chapter 1.[103] J.P. Allen says, "The opening words of John's Gospel, devoid of their Christian implications, could easily have been appreciated by the

---

polemische Überbietung der heliopolitanischen Weltentstehungslehre handelt. Ich möchte dagegen zeigen, daß dieser Text vielmehr eine Auslegung der heliopolitanischen Kosmogonie darstellt"(J. Assmann, "Rezeption und Auslegung," 126, cf. also p. 127).

101. D. B. Redford, *Egypt, Canaan and Israel in Ancient Times* (Princeton, NJ: Princeton University Press, 1992), 399-400, asserts that "it is not until the period of cultural renewal of the 24th to the 26th Dynasties . . . that such sophisticated treatises as the Memphite Theology have any impact on the outside world," but he was not aware of the material adduced here. That does not, however, mean that the text had no later impact during the Twenty-sixth Dynasty, for example on the creation text of Genesis chapter 1.

102. J. H. Breasted, "The Philosophy of a Memphite Priest," 54.

103. K. Koch, "Wort und Einheit des Schöpfergottes in Memphis und in Jerusalem," *Zeitschrift für Theologie und Kirche* 62 (1965): 251-93, reprinted in *Studien zur alttestamentlichen und altorientalischen Religionsgeschichte* (Göttingen: Vandenhoeck & Ruprecht, 1988), 61-105.

FIGURE 71

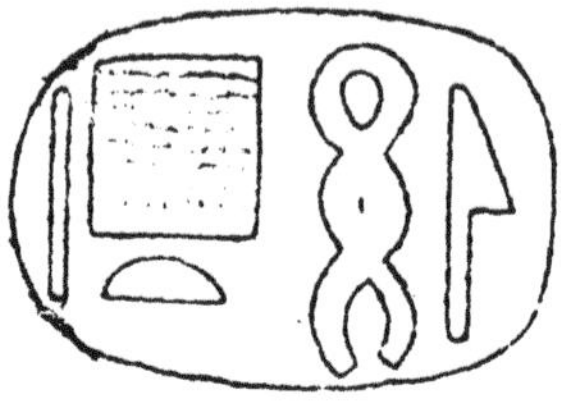

FIGURE 72

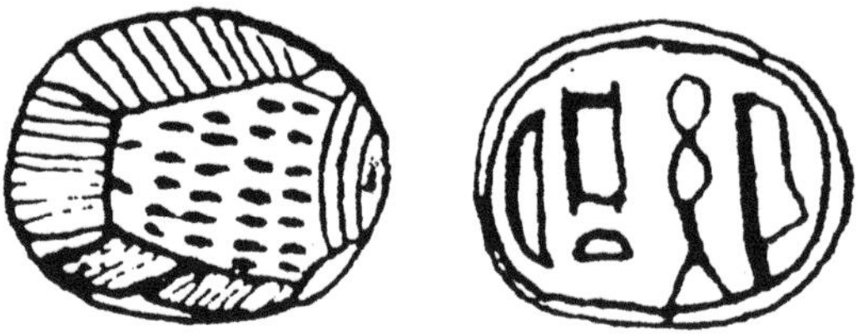

FIGURE 73

Egyptian author(s) of the 'Memphite Theology' as a summary of their own view of creation:

> In the beginning was the Word,
> and the Word was with God,
> and the Word was God.
> He was in the beginning with God.
> Through him all things came into being,
> and of all that has come into being not one thing came into being except
> through him.[104]

In contrast to the Eighteenth Dynasty, the Nineteenth Dynasty produced not only scarabs with the image of Ptah, but also scarabs with the name of the god as the only decoration of the base. During the Eighteenth Dynasty this practice was reserved for Amun, but in the Nineteenth Dynasty Amun had to share this privilege with Ptah. More than 20 scarabs and fish scaraboids from controlled excavations in Palestine display the divine name in a horizontal arrangement. The name is usually accompanied by the hieroglyph of the flowering reed, phonetic *j*, and a *nb* sign (**figs. 71-73**).[105] Some pieces show a Maʿat feather instead of the flow-

---

104. John 1:1-3; see Allen, *Genesis in Egypt*, 46.

105. O. Keel, *Corpus 1997*, Tell el-ʿAğul, no. 250; Aseka, no. 29; J. L. Starkey and L. Harding, *Beth-Pelet II*, pl. 55, 281 = A. Rowe, *Catalogue*, no. S. 69. Cf. also Oren, *Northern Cemetery*, 126, no. 11 and fig. 51, 21; Beth-Shan, University Museum, Inv. no. 29-104-27; Deir el-Balaḥ, Tel Aviv, Institute of Archaeology, ex-Dayan Coll., no. 256; W. M. F. Petrie, *Beth*

FIGURE 74

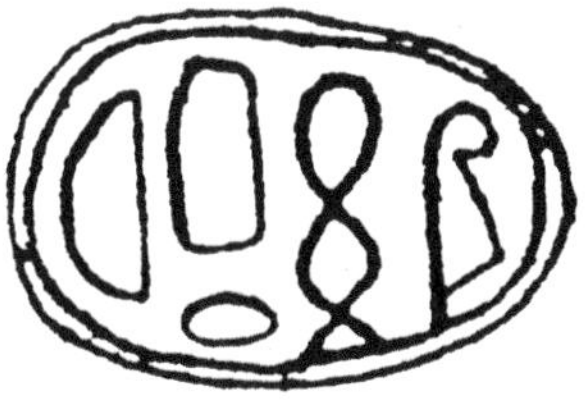

FIGURE 75

FIGURE 76

FIGURE 77

FIGURE 78

ering reed (**figs. 74-75**).[106] In these cases the composition can be read as "Ptah (is the/a) Lord of truth." Perhaps the flowering reed is to be understood as a "Bedeutungsäquivalent"[107] of the Maᶜat feather. Beside these two variants there are others—with two flowering reeds, with a flowering reed and a Maᶜat feather, and so on (**figs. 76-78**).[108]

Apart from the group of seal-amulets with the name of Ptah and the epithet "Lord of truth" in horizontal arrangement, there is a second type with the same in a vertical arrangement (**figs. 79-81**).[109] A particular type of Ramessid scarab with vertical arrangement divides the base into three

---

Pelet I, pl. 22, 212; Starkey and Harding, *Beth-Pelet II*, pl. 48, 7 = A. Rowe, *Catalogue*, no. 776; pl. 50, 60 = R. Giveon, *Egyptian Scarabs from Western Asia*, 50-51, no. 81; pl. 55,303 = A. Rowe, *Catalogue*, no. 778; 57, 352.

106. Deir el-Balaḥ, Tel Aviv, Institute of Archaeology, ex-Dayan Coll., no. 257; J. L. Starkey and L. Harding, *Beth-Pelet II*, pl. 57, 386.

107. O. Keel, *Corpus 1995*, §473.

108. Deir el-Balaḥ, Tel Aviv, Institute of Archaeology, ex-Dayan Coll., no. 245; W. M. F. Petrie, *Beth Pelet I*, pl. 12, 175; J. L. Starkey and L. Harding, *Beth-Pelet II*, pl. 53, 197 = R. Giveon, *Egyptian Scarabs from Western Asia* 1985: 38-39, no. 49. Cf. also Deir el-Balaḥ, Tel Aviv, Institute of Archaeology, ex-Dayan Coll., no. 366; W. M. F. Petrie, *Beth Pelet I*, pl. 12, 174; 22, 185 = A. Rowe, *Catalogue*, no. S.31; Starkey and Harding, *Beth-Pelet II*, pl. 50, 88; 53, 195; 55, 283 = A. Rowe, *Catalogue*, no. 775; 57, 355; Tel Ridan, IAA 74-2012.

109. Deir el-Balaḥ, Tel Aviv, Institute of Archaeology, ex-Dayan Coll., no. 332; J. L. Starkey and L. Harding, *Beth-Pelet II*, pl. 53, 198 = R. Giveon, *Egyptian Scarabs from Western Asia*, 38-39, no. 48; pl. 57, 350. Cf. also O. Keel, *Corpus 1997*, Tell el-ᶜAğul, no. 195, 289; Starkey and Harding, *Beth-Pelet II*, pl. 53, 194 and 196; R. A. S. Macalister, *Gezer*, vol. 3, pl. 208, 18; Y. Leibovitz, "Cult of Ptah," 66.

FIGURE 79

FIGURE 80

FIGURE 81

or occasionally four registers (**figs. 82-84**).[110] The central register or—if there are four, one of the central registers—contains the throne name of Thutmosis III, *Mn-ḫpr-rᶜ*, with an additional element. The upper register shows the name of Ptah flanked by two Red Crowns. This element is sometimes so debased that it may be recognized only by analogy.

The plinth of an archaizing Ramessid scarab is engraved with *anra*-signs and exhibits the name of Ptah (**fig. 85**)[111] in a way very similar to its placement on Middle Bronze Age scarabs (cf. figs. 2-10). A scarab of the Nineteenth Dynasty, or perhaps of the late Eighteenth Dynasty, shows in the central register the formula *mry* <*J*>*mn-rᶜ*, "beloved of Amun-Re." The two flanking registers contain the name Ptah. To the right the name is combined with *mry Ptḥ*, "beloved of Ptah" (**fig. 86**).[112] Another scarab—also organized in three vertical registers—reads in the center <*J*>*mn-rᶜ ḏt*, "Amun-Re of eternity" or "Amun-Re forever," and to the left: <*J*>*mn-rᶜ nfr ḥzwt*, "Amun-Re is perfect/rich with/of favors." To the right is the name of Ptah (**fig. 87**).[113]

While already during the Eighteenth Dynasty there is a rich variety of seal-amulets with religious formulae accompanying Amun,[114] those with Ptah are characteristic of the Nineteenth Dynasty. Six or seven examples from Palestine exhibit the maxim: *mdw*<*t*> *nb*<*t*> *nfr*<*t*> *dd Ptḥ ḥrs m*

110. O. Keel, *Corpus 1997*, Tell el-ᶜAğul, no. 297; E. D. Oren, *The New Encyclopedia of Archaeological Excavations in the Holy Land*, 2nd ed. (Jerusalem: Karta, 1993), 1330; J. L. Starkey and L. Harding, *Beth-Pelet II*, pl. 50, 62 = Giveon, *Egyptian Scarabs from Western Asia*, 42-43, no. 58. Cf. also O. Keel, *Corpus 1997*, Tell el-ᶜAğul, no. 294; Aschdod, no. 48; Starkey and Harding, *Beth-Pelet II*, pl. 55, 254 = A. Rowe, *Catalogue*, no. 506. For this type of scarab, see B. Jaeger, *Essai*, 193-94, §§1308-13.

111. J. L. Starkey and L. Harding, *Beth-Pelet II*, pl. 52, 149 = Giveon, *Egyptian Scarabs from Western Asia*, 22-23, no. 5.

112. O. Keel, *Corpus 1997*, Tell el-ᶜAğul, no. 290.

113. Deir el-Balaḥ, Tel Aviv, Institute of Archaeology, ex-Dayan Coll., no. 341.

114. Cf. for example O. Keel, *Corpus 1997*, Afek, no. 8; Tell el-ᶜAğul, nos. 224, 313, 553.

FIGURE 82

FIGURE 83

FIGURE 84

FIGURE 85

FIGURE 86

FIGURE 87

wsr, "Ptah rewards every good deed generously" (**figs. 88-90**).[115] This formula emphasizes the positive aspect of retribution. Retribution in a more general sense is one of the functions which the "Memphite Theology" attributes to Ptah: "(*Thus justice was given to*) him who does what is liked, (*and injustice to*) him who does what is disliked. Thus life was given to him who has peace, and death was given to him who has sin."[116]

The uniqueness ("Einheit") of the creator god and creation by thinking and speaking are not the only characteristics that Ptah has in common with the god of the Bible. In addition, Ptah, like YHWH, is a god who assures justice, rewards the righteous with life, and punishes wrongdoers with death. Here we have one more element connecting the Ramessid production of Ptah seal-amulets with the "Memphite Theology."

Apart from these seal-amulets, a few small amuletic figures of Ptah,

115. O. Keel, *Corpus 1997*, Tell Abu Farağ, no. 1; Tell el-ʿAğul, no. 291; Aschdod, no. 45. Cf. also Afek, no. 35 (which may be identical with Aschdod, no. 45); J. L. Starkey and L. Harding, *Beth-Pelet II*, pl. 50, 40; 53, 216 = Giveon, *Egyptian Scarabs from Western Asia*, 38-39, no. 50; G. L. Harding, "An Early Iron Age Tomb at Madeba," *PEFA* 6 (1953): 33 and pl. 5. For further parallels see E. Drioton, "Maximes morales sur des scarabées égyptiens," *Collection Latomus* 28 (1957): 9-11; E. Hornung and E. Staehelin, *Skarabäen*, no. 716B.

116. J. A. Wilson in *Ancient Near Eastern Texts*, 5, upper right column.

FIGURE 88

FIGURE 89

FIGURE 90

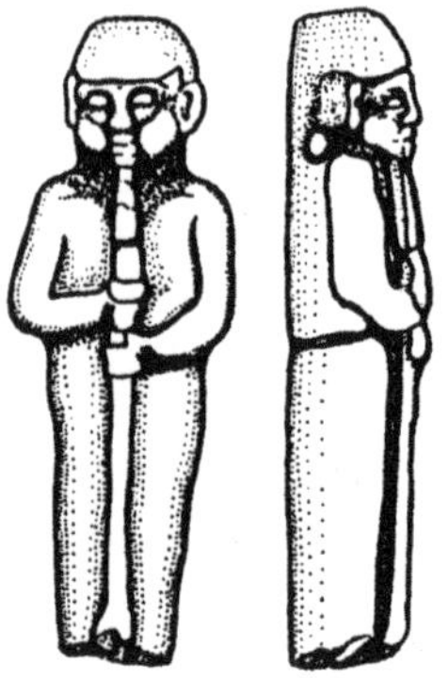

FIGURE 91

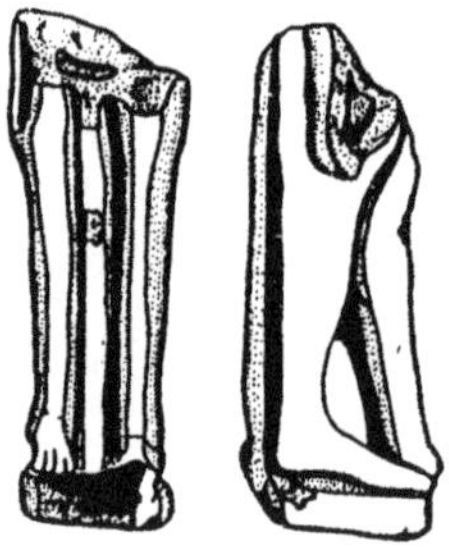

FIGURE 92

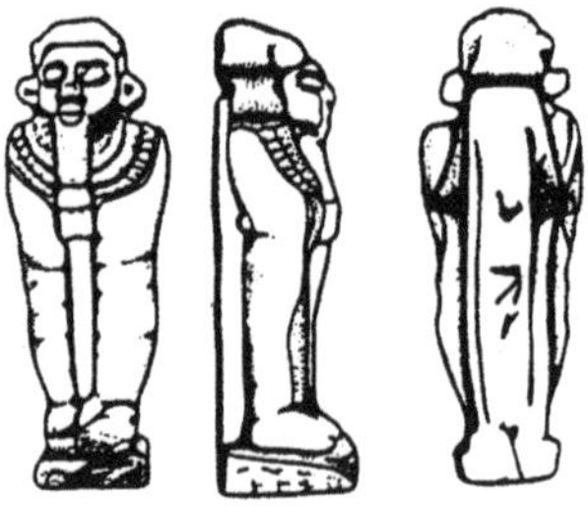

FIGURE 93

FIGURE 94

FIGURE 95

or rather fragments of such figures made of composite material, have been excavated in Palestine. Three of them come from levels contemporary with the Nineteenth and Twentieth Dynasties (**figs. 91-92**).[117] Two more items were produced in this same period but found in a much later (sixth-fifth-century) context (**fig. 93**).[118]

On some Nineteenth-Dynasty seal-amulets Ptah is shown together with his consort Sakhmet in scenes copied from temple walls.[119] A typical Ramessid carnelian[120] scarab damaged along the border shows Ptah turned to the left. Behind him is Sakhmet and a second figure that cannot be identified (**fig. 94**).[121] One would, of course, expect Nefertem here, but the figure exhibits no feature characteristic of this god. On another carnelian scarab (**fig. 95**)[122] we find Ptah—as expected—turned to the right. "Facing him is a goddess (perhaps Sekhmet) adorned in a tunic; she holds a crude papyrus scepter in her right hand and the *ʿnḫ* (*ānkh*) symbol of 'life' in her other hand. On her head is a debased crown of Lower Egypt with solar disk above."[123] P.L.O. Guy gives a somewhat different description: "Sekhmet but with horns of Hathor added to her sun disk and carrying basket of Bastet." The sun disk above the head is unambiguous. The horns of Hathor are more probable than a debased Red Crown, the sign of life more probable than the basket of Bastet, but according to my impression the spot is just damaged. Most intriguingly the head of the goddess looks more like the head of a snake than that of a lioness. Anthropomorphic goddesses with the head of a snake and cow horns with the sun disk between are not uncommon during the Nineteenth and Twentieth Dynasties.[124]

---

117. R. A. S. Macalister, *Gezer*, vol. 3, pl. 210, 19 = A. Rowe, *Catalogue*, no. S.268 = Ch. Herrmann, *Ägyptische Amulette aus Palästina/Israel: Mit einem Ausblick auf ihre Rezeption durch das Alte Testament*, OBO 138 (Fribourg: Universitätsverlag, 1994), 236, KatNr. 199; W. M. F. Petrie, *Beth Pelet I*, pl. 33, 379 = Herrmann, *Ägyptische Amulette*, 236-39, KatNr. 200; cf. KatNr. 201.

118. Ch. Herrmann, *Ägyptische Amulette*, 238, KatNr. 202; 239, KatNr. 203.

119. Cf. figs. 52 and 57 above, and O. Keel, "Der ägyptische Gott Ptah," 302, fig. 69 and 306, fig. 91.

120. O. Keel, *Corpus 1995*, 144-45, §§373 and 375.

121. E. Grant, *Bet Shemesh*, 89, second row from top, third from left, and 150, no. 105 = O. Keel, "Der ägyptische Gott Ptah," 313, fig. 116.

122. A. Rowe, *Catalogue*, no. 719 = P. L. O. Guy, *Megiddo Tombs*, pl. 131, 1.

123. A. Rowe, *Catalogue*, 172.

124. B. Bruyère, *Mert Seger à Deir el Médineh* (Cairo: Institut Français d'Archéologie Orientale, 1930), 164, fig. 88; 170, fig. 91; M. Tosi and A. Roccati, *Stele e altre epigrafi di Deir el Medina* (Turin: Edizioni d'arte Fratelli Pozzo, 1972), 274, no. 50035; H. M. Stewart, *Egyptian Stelae, Reliefs and Paintings. Part One: The New Kingdom* (Warminster: Aris & Phillips, 1976), pl. 28, 2—Rennutet (without headgear) in front of Ptah.

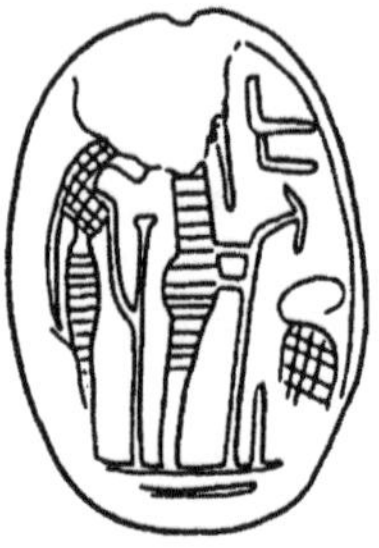

FIGURE 96

FIGURE 97

FIGURE 98

FIGURE 99

On a third Ramessid scarab Ptah again looks to the right. Behind him is Sakhmet (**fig. 96**),[125] who though damaged can be clearly identified.[126] On a Nineteenth-Dynasty rectangular plaque crowded with deities and symbols of protection and regeneration, a standing Ptah occupies one of the small sides (**fig. 97**).[127]

On a beautiful human-face scaraboid as crowded as fig. 94, Ptah appears not among other Egyptian gods but among Canaanite deities. These may be identified as Reshef and Astarte or Anat (**fig. 98**).[128] A frag-

125. W. M. F. Petrie, *Gerar* (London: British School of Archaeology in Egypt, 1928), pl. 19, 49 = O. Keel, "Der ägyptische Gott Ptah," 313, fig. 114.

126. A standing Sakhmet alone is twice represented on finger rings—see R. Giveon, "The Egyptian Objects," in *Akko Tombs near the Persian Gardens*, ed. S. Ben-Arie and G. Edelstein (Jerusalem: Department of Antiquities and Museums, 1977), 70-71—and once on an *udjat*-eye scaraboid—J. L. Starkey and L. Harding, *Beth-Pelet II*, pl. 64, 64. A squatting Sakhmet alone is found on a scarab—see Starkey and Harding, *Beth-Pelet II*, pl. 50, 66 = A. Rowe, *Catalogue*, no. 839.

127. J. L. Starkey and L. Harding, *Beth-Pelet II*, pl. 53, 212 = O. Keel, "Der ägyptische Gott Ptah," 313, fig. 112

128. O. Keel, *Corpus 1997*, Akko, no. 3; E. Lipiński, "Egypto-Canaanite Iconography of Reshef, Ba'al, Ḥoron, and Anat," *Chronique d'Egypte* 71/142 (1996): 257.

FIGURE 100

mentary stele from the time of Merenptah, successor of Rameses II, found at Memphis shows Astarte behind Ptah (**fig. 99**).[129] On a Late Bronze Age IIB cylinder seal found at Deir Alla we have once more Ptah in the company of one or perhaps two Canaanite gods (**fig. 100**).[130] The smiting god is most probably the weather and war god Baʿal. The small figure in front of this god may be a minor deity or a human prince. These last two examples show the popularity of Ptah not just among Egyptians in Late Bronze Age Canaan but also among the local inhabitants of the region.

Ptah is also reflected in the ivories found in Late Bronze IIB Megiddo, which had once belonged to a female singer of Ptah (**fig. 101**).[131] The woman was also a singer of the prince of Ashkelon (*ʾ3 wr n-Isqrn*). As St. Wimmer has demonstrated, it is impossible to understand *ʾ3 wr n-Isqrn* as an epithet of Ptah and to reason that there must have been a Ptah temple at Ashkelon.[132]

There are almost ten times more Ptah seal-amulets from the Nineteenth Dynasty[133] as from the Eighteenth. During the later dynasty Ptah gained tremendously in popularity, and there are about 100 Ptah seal-amulets known from this period (in contrast to 13 from the previous dynasty)—almost as many as Amun seal-amulets. The distribution pattern follows that of the Eighteenth Dynasty, although other places now

129. W. M. F. Petrie, *Memphis I*, pl. 15, 37 = Y. Leibovitz, "Cult of Ptah," 65, fig. 1. In the Ramessid story "Astarte and the Tribute of the Sea" (trans. J. A. Wilson in *Ancient Near Eastern Texts*, 17-18) Astarte is the daughter of Ptah.

130. P. Amiet et al., *Der Königsweg* (Mainz: Philipp von Zabern, 1997), 116, no. 119 = O. Keel, "Der ägyptische Gott Ptah," 313, fig. 113.

131. G. Loud, *The Megiddo Ivories* (Chicago: University of Chicago Press, 1939), no. 380; cf. also nos. 379 and 381-82. The texts are translated and discussed by J. A. Wilson on pp. 12-13.

132. St. Wimmer, "Egyptian Temples in Canaan and Sinai," in *Studies in Egyptology Presented to Miriam Lichtheim*, ed. S. Israelit-Groll (Jerusalem: Magnes Press, 1990), 2:1092-93, against J. C. de Moor, *The Rise of Yahwism*, 2nd ed. (Leuven: Peeters, 1997), 68.

133. Only a few seem to date from the Twentieth Dynasty.

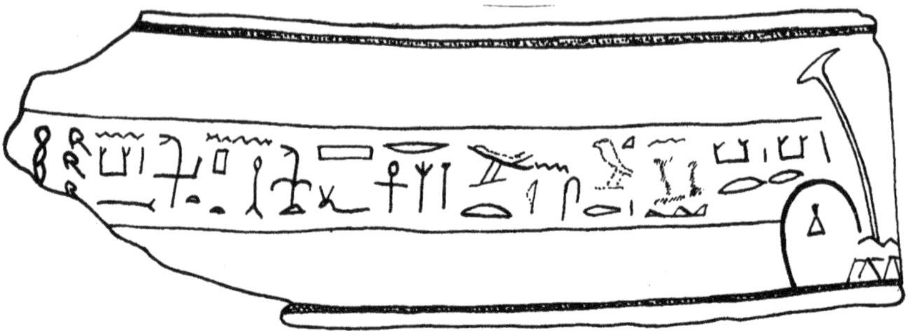

FIGURE 101

become prominent. About 35% were found at Tell el-Farʿah South, 12% at Deir el-Balaḥ, 8% at Tell el-ʿAğul, and 16% from other sites in the southern coastal plain. This means that on the whole 71% of the material originates from this area. An additional 13% come from the Shephelah. The remaining 16% were found at Acco, Megiddo, and Beth-Shan. The concentration in the southern coastal plain is conspicuous: Almost half of the material originates in the two centers of Tell el-Farʿah South and Deir el-Balaḥ. The mountain areas have yet to produce a single item.

The Iron Age: Ptah and Sakhmet during the Twenty-sixth Dynasty

Ptah is absent from the seal-amulets of the Twenty-first through Twenty-fifth Dynasties found in Palestine, and—it seems—in Egypt as well. The same is true of amulet figures.[134] He reappears on scarabs of the Twenty-sixth Dynasty (664-525). A scarab shows him squatting accompanied by the epithet *ꜣwy ḥzwt*, "rich of/with favors" (**fig. 102**).[135] On another scarab Ptah sits on the throne holding the usual scepter of dominion (**fig. 103**).[136] In front of him is a cartouche with *mn-kꜣ*<*w*>*-rʿ*, the birth name of Mycerinus, sixth pharaoh of the Fourth Dynasty, who built the smallest of the three pyramids at Giza. One cannot say that he was a very impressive ruler, so why is his name quite common on scarabs of the Twenty-sixth Dynasty?[137] The reason is most probably that parts of his funerary temple

134. Ch. Herrmann, *Ägyptische Amulette*, 236.

135. W. M. F. Petrie, *Beth Pelet I*, pl. 43, 521; cf. J. Vercoutter, *Les objets égyptiens et égyptisants du mobilier funéraire carthaginois* (Paris: P. Geuthner, 1945), nos. 64-65 and 209.

136. W. M. F. Petrie, *Beth Pelet I*, pl. 43, 518, who completely misinterprets this item.

137. Cf. O. Keel, *Corpus 1997*, Achsib, nos. 52-53, 130; Aschkelon, no. 93; W. M. F. Petrie, *Beth Pelet I*, pl. 43, 519; R. Giveon, *Scarabs from Recent Excavations in Israel*, OBO 83 (Fribourg: Universitätsverlag, 1988), no. 64.

FIGURE 102

FIGURE 103

FIGURE 104

FIGURE 104

FIGURE 105

and equipment were restored at this time.[138] This place must also have become a pilgrimage site.

Fig. 104[139] shows again an enthroned Ptah. The rectangular throne looks rather un-Egyptian. Instead of the traditional scepter of dominion, the god holds a bent flower. In front of him squats the goddess Maʿat. Together with the *nb* in the exergue, the goddess is part of Ptah's age-old epithet "Lord of truth." Another typical Twenty-sixth-Dynasty scarab[140] shows again what seems to be an enthroned Ptah (**fig. 105**).[141] This time he holds the flail, an old royal symbol. Facing him is his consort, the lion headed Sakhmet, with the papyrus scepter. On **fig. 106**[142] Ptah and Sakhmet stand facing each other. Between them is a third person. One is, of course, tempted to identify it as Nefertem, but here too, as on fig. 92, no feature characteristic of this god can be discovered. The plinth of **fig. 107**[143] is divided into two registers like that of fig. 104. In the upper regis-

---

138. J. Leclant, "Fouilles et travaux en Egypte et au Soudan, 1967-1973," *Or* 38 (1969): 252.

139. O. Keel, *Corpus 1997*, Achsib, no. 21.

140. The double pronotum line is typical. The line between the elytra is simple.

141. O. Keel, *Corpus 1997*, Akko, no. 194.

142. O. Keel, *Corpus 1997*, Akko, no. 106.

143. B. Brandl in O. Keel, *Corpus 1997*, Achsib, no. 133.

FIGURE 106

FIGURE 107

ter Horus is shown as a squatting child flanked by two falcons. In the lower register stands Ptah, while behind him is a goddess, probably Sakhmet, and in front of him a third deity who cannot be identified.

There are significant differences between the representations of Ptah on scarabs of the New Kingdom and on those of the Twenty-sixth Dynasty. First, the scarabs originating from the later period are much less numerous than the New Kingdom examples. Second, Sakhmet comes to play a much more prominent role: While only three scarabs show Ptah without Sakhmet, Sakhmet is found alone on at least eight scarabs from this period.[144] A third characteristic is the total absence of the figure of the pharaoh. While the Eighteenth-Dynasty seal-amulets attested Ptah's love for the king, the Nineteenth-Twentieth-Dynasty scarabs produced by the temple workshop exhibited the love of the king for Ptah. On Twenty-sixth-Dynasty Ptah scarabs the king simply does not exist. At the same time the iconography is less strict, less canonical, than it was during the New Kingdom. The seal-amulets testify to the private cult of visitors to the sanctuary and holy places in its neighborhood.[145] These seal-amulets were probably not produced by the temple itself but by private souvenir workshops.[146] The distribution of these few items is limited to the coast, although this time as far north as Akhziv.

144. O. Keel, *Corpus 1997*, Achsib, nos. 30, 52-53; Akko, no. 71; Aschkelon, no. 88; G. Schumacher, *Tell el-Mutesellim I* (Leipzig: Rudolf Haupt, 1908), 138-39, fig. 208e; R. Giveon, *Scarabs from Recent Excavations*, no. 64; O. Tufnell, in K. M. Kenyon and T. A. Holland, *Excavations at Jericho V: The Pottery Phases of the Tell and Other Finds* (London: British School of Archaeology in Jerusalem, 1983), 766-68, fig. 353, 5.

145. Among these visitors were Asiatics, as shown by a stele from the Michailidis collection mentioned by Y. Leibovitz, "Cult of Ptah," vi.

146. For the question of the use of Ptah in Hebrew theophoric names mentioned in the Bible, see M. H. van Voss, "Ptah," *Dictionary of Deities and Demons in the Bible*, ed. K. van der Toorn, B. Becking, and P. W. van der Horst, 2nd ed. (Leiden: E. J. Brill, 1999), 668-69.

13

The ʿAin Dara Temple and the Jerusalem Temple

JOHN MONSON

The Jerusalem temple stood at the center of Israel's religious consciousness for over 1000 years. From the time of Solomon it was inseparable from the theology of Zion reflected in the Psalms, Isaiah, and the apocalyptic literature. Even after the destructions of 586 B.C.E. and 70 C.E., this central shrine continued to animate the sacred literature and spiritual longings of the Jews. While the biblical description of the temple remains unchanged, from time to time archaeology provides a significant advance in our understanding of this famous edifice. The ʿAin Dara temple of northern Syria represents one such advance which hitherto has been overlooked.

Although both temples are worthy of independent investigation, a comparative study of their architecture and iconography is useful for several reasons. First, certain features of the ʿAin Dara temple shed new light upon the Jerusalem temple as it is described in the Hebrew Bible. Due to the almost complete lack of archaeological evidence for the Jerusalem temple, any reconstruction must rely heavily upon the corpus of excavated temples from the ancient Near East, to which ʿAin Dara has recently been added. It is now possible to propose many connections between the finds at ʿAin Dara and obscure temple terms from the Bible which have for decades challenged linguists and archaeologists alike. A second benefit of a comparative analysis between the Jerusalem and ʿAin Dara temples is that it offers an unusually rich case study in the correlation of religious text and artifact, which is the subject of this volume. ʿAin Dara also has broader implications for the history of Jerusalem which will be explored at the conclusion of the essay.

A popular version of this article (though with many photographs) appeared in J. Monson, "The New Ain Dara Temple: Closest Solomonic Parallel," *BAR* 26.3 (2000): 20-35, 67.

In the following pages the architecture of the preexilic Jerusalem temple is examined in four sections. A brief consideration of the relevant biblical texts is followed by an analysis of comparative temple architecture with an emphasis on ʿAin Dara. In the next section several correlations are made between biblical terms and temple features from ʿAin Dara and elsewhere. Finally, the findings of this study are brought to bear upon issues of methodology, the cultural origin of the Jerusalem temple, and the current debate concerning the United Monarchy of Israel.

Text: Temple Accounts in the Hebrew Bible

The Hebrew Bible contains over one hundred words related to architecture and building. A large percentage of this vocabulary is associated with the Jerusalem temple. The main features of the temple can be determined by examining 1 Kings 6-7, 2 Chron. 3-4, and Ezek. 40-43, despite discrepancies among these accounts.[1] As pointed out by A. Hurowitz, these passages represent the most detailed building account in the ancient Near East.[2] The authors of the Kings account provide the reader with a meticulous and technical word picture of the temple.

The temple was built at the center of a large courtyard which was accessible by gates on all sides. Already in the Judean monarchy there appear to have been inner and outer courts which were later surrounded by chambers (Jer. 36; Ezek. 42). The description makes it clear that the central part of the temple was built according to the long-room (or *Langraum*) plan.[3]

The building had three divisions, each originally 20 cubits wide. The porch (*ʾûlām*) was 10 cubits long and was reached by a stairway. It was differentiated from the interior of the temple by its large pillars, not by a

1. The main attributes have been noted by numerous commentators, including A. Hurowitz, "Inside Solomon's Temple," *BR* 10, no. 2 (1994): 25-37, 50; J. Gray, *I Kings I & II: A Commentary*, OTL (London: SCM, 1963), 149-213.

2. *I Have Built for You an Exalted House: Temple-Building in the Bible in Light of Mesopotamian and Northwest Semitic Writings*, JSOT Supplements 115 (Sheffield: Sheffield Academic Press, 1992), 246.

3. The differences between long-room and broad-room temples are explained in note 20 below. Architecture and buildings figure prominently in biblical poetry and narrative, and in texts early and late. In the case of the temple account in 1 Kings, the authors appear to have shared with their readers a rather sophisticated knowledge of construction techniques and building components, as evidenced in the variety of terms and the frequency of parallel forms. They chose to emphasize the extraordinary aspects of the temple and used the vocabulary which was in their source documents selectively. Editors and interpreters have been trying to understand the specialized terminology ever since.

doorway.[4] The main hall (*hêkāl*) was 40 cubits long. It was entered through ornate wooden doors of ten-cubit width. The position of the windows and the precise construction of the roof are ambiguous in the biblical account. The Holy of Holies (*dəbîr*) most likely constituted a cube with sides of 20 cubits each, but many details were left out of the biblical text.[5]

When these proportions are taken at face value, the building measured 70 x 20 cubits and was 30 cubits high. If the royal cubit of 52.5 cm is taken, the width of the main temple was approximately 12 m and its length roughly 40 m.[6] The height of the main structure was approximately 15 m and the side structure was at least half that height. According to the descriptions in Kings and Ezekiel the central shrine was enclosed on three sides by multistoried side chambers which enveloped the hall and the holy of holies.

The construction materials and ornamentation of the temple are relatively easy to ascertain from the biblical accounts. Fine ashlar masonry was used throughout, and the roof was constructed from large beams. The walls and floors were lined with cedar. Cherubs, palmettes, floral patterns, and window frames lined the walls of the two interior rooms (1 Kings 6:29; 2 Chron. 3:7). The doors to both rooms were also finished with ornate patterns.[7]

Despite the length of the biblical record, there are several obstacles which hinder any attempt to reach a precise understanding of the temple using the written sources alone. The first obstacle is the nature of the biblical accounts themselves. They are selective and it seems that they were not intended to provide a complete description of the temple. For reasons

---

4. The height of the porch is not provided in any of the accounts. The porch was also distinguished from other parts of the temple by the lack of wood paneling and its style of masonry. In contrast to the remainder of the temple, it was built with the ashlar and timber technique used in the courtyards of the temple and palace (1 Kings 7:12).

5. According to several scholars, the Holy of Holies of the Tabernacle itself was erected inside the *dĕbîr*. See R. E. Friedman, "The Tabernacle in the Temple," *BA* 43(1980): 241-48. For an archaeologically informed discussion of the symbolism found in the temple of Solomon, see E. Bloch-Smith, "'Who Is the King of Glory?' Solomon's Temple and Its Symbolism," in *Scripture and Other Artifacts: Essays in Bible and Archaeology in Honor of Philip J. King*, ed. M. Coogan et al. (Louisville, KY: John Knox, 1995), 18-31.

6. For the most compelling interpretation of the cubit, see G. R. H. Wright, *Ancient Building in South Syria and Palestine*, vol. 1, Handbuch der Orientalisti (Leiden: Brill, 1985), 118. A careful discussion of the cubit can be found in G. Barkay, "Two Biblical Building Terms in the Light of Archaeology" (unpublished paper, 1998). For reasons that are unclear, the author of Ezekiel measured twenty cubits for the depth of the *ʾûlām*. Perhaps he or she included the flanking piers, the frontal staircase, or part of the floor which protruded into the courtyard.

7. See Hurowitz, "Inside the Temple" (n. 1), and J. Strange, "The Idea of Afterlife in Ancient Israel: Some Remarks on the Iconography in Solomon's Temple, " *PEQ* 117 (1985): 35-40.

unknown, the authors chose to leave out many details.[8] Furthermore, the passages are disjointed and may have been edited numerous times.[9] The versions offer little help. The LXX version of 1 Kings 6-7 differs from the MT version on many points; Gooding has shown the MT to be more reliable, but there are places in each version where the logic of the description is difficult to follow.[10] A second obstacle is that the three biblical accounts are most likely separated by several hundred years during which the temple may have undergone several additions. Third, the temple accounts contain many technical terms which are poorly attested elsewhere. These include *ḥallônîm/ôt ʾaṭumîm/ôt, migrāʿâ, məzûzôt ḥămišît, mābôʾ, kātēp, ʾattîq, ʾayil, ṣəlāʿ*, and others.[11]

In sum, the large size of the biblical description is inversely proportional to the meager quantity of relevant archaeological evidence discovered in Jerusalem to date. Not one piece of the architecture from the rich biblical accounts has been discovered to inform a reconstruction of the preexilic temple. A precise understanding of the temple must therefore be sought not in the biblical accounts alone but also in the comparative architecture from Israel and surrounding regions.[12]

Artifact: ʿAin Dara Among the Temples of the Levant

The temples of the Levant do not exhibit a singular building plan. This fact may be attributed to the geographical position of Canaan and Syria

8. Thus Ezekiel emphasizes the courtyards and gates, whereas these same features go unmentioned in 1 Kings. Instead, 1 Kings emphasizes unusual aspects of the pillars, relief, and gilding, etc.

9. In 1 Kings 6, e.g., there is no progression from outside to inside or front to back, and the reader is required to make his or her own connections between the data that are provided.

10. See W. Gooding, "Temple Specifications: A Dispute in Logical Arrangement between the MT and LXX," *VT* 17 (1967): 143-72. The Rabbis themselves struggled with the temple terminology, which is understandable as they had no archaeological parallels to consult. Commenting upon 1 Kings 6:10 Rashi writes, "I have no idea what these terms are. . . ."

11. In the English Revised Standard Version these terms are identified in the following manner: *ḥallônîm/ôt ʾăṭumîm/ôt* = blocked windows; *migrāʿâ* = support; *mĕzûzôt ḥămišît* = five sided doors; *mābôʾ* = entrance; *kātēp* = side; *ʾattîq* = pillars; *ʾayil* = pier; *ṣēlāʿ* = side wing.

12. Many attempts have been made. Kitchen, for example, found Egyptian recessed chambers of different widths which provide a good parallel for the recessed side chambers described in Solomon's Temple (1 Kings 6:5-6, 8,10; "Two Notes on the Subsidiary Rooms of Solomon's Temple," *EI* 20 [1989]: 107-12). In a similar study A. Millard, following Noth, explained the technical terms for doorways by contrasting them with descriptions of lintels and doorways from elsewhere in the Levant. See "The Doorways of Solomon's Temple," *EI 20* (1989): 135*-39*.

between the great centers of ancient civilization and to the trade and ethnic diversity which this region fostered. Increasingly refined reconstructions of the Jerusalem temple have been possible with each addition to the corpus of comparative architecture, most of the temples being found in territories north of the Israelite heartland. The flow of cultural influence from northern Syria to Israel is known from the earliest phases of the archaeological record. According to 1 Kings 6-7 the temple design was mediated through Phoenician artisans.[13] As early as 1939, A. Alt observed that the architecture of the Jerusalem temple belonged to the traditions of the northern Levant.[14] In subsequent years it has been shown that Iron Age public architecture from northern Syria has much in common with the buildings attributed to Solomon in the Hebrew Bible.

The discovery of Tell Tayanat in 1936 provided the first clear parallel to the Jerusalem temple, a fact which was reflected in the writings of G. E. Wright and L. Vincent.[15] Royal compounds were discovered not only at Tayanat but also at Megiddo, Zinjirli, Alalakh, and Hamath. They dated to the second and first millennia B.C.E. and conformed very well to the biblical description of Solomon's regal-ritual center in Jerusalem.[16]

---

13. Note especially Solomon's connection to Hiram of Phoenicia (2 Kings 5:1). Two seminal articles on this subject were written by D. Ussishkin: "Solomon and the Tayanat Temples," *IEJ* 16 (1966): 104-10; "Solomon's Palace and Building 1723," *IEJ* 16 (1966): 174-86. For earlier studies, see G. E. Wright, "The Significance of the Temple in the Ancient Near East: III The Temple in Syria-Palestine," *BA* 7 (1944): 65-77; L. Waterman: "The Damaged Blueprints of the Temple of Solomon," *JNES* 2 (1943): 284-94.

14. "Verbrietung und Herkunft des syrischen Tempeltypus," *PJ* 35 (1939): 83-99. The impact of parallels from excavations can be seen by comparing the temple reconstructions of the late nineteenth century with those of the early twentieth century. See Th. Busink, *Der Tempel von Jerusalem von Salomo bis Herodes: Eine archäologische-historische Studie unter Berücksichtigung des westsemitischen Tempelbaus. I Der Tempel Salomos* (Leiden: Brill, 1970), 44-58. The general accuracy of interpretations by K. Möhlenbrink (*Der Tempel Salomos, BWANT* 4 [Stuttgart: W. Kohlhammer, 1932]), C. Watzinger (*Denkmäler Palästinas, I* [Leipzig: J.C. Hinrichs, 1933]), and others was later confirmed with each new parallel unearthed in the northern Levant. In 1932 the closest parallels Möhlenbrink could find were in the Assyrian temples, which proved to have little in common with the Jerusalem temple (*Der Tempel*, 40-47). No preexilic tripartite temples were known at that time, so he was forced to conclude that the layout of the Jerusalem temple—as well as its biblical description—were later innovations (ibid., 10; 152-53).

15. G. E. Wright, "Solomon's Temple Resurrected," *BA* 4 (1941): 17-31; H. Vincent, *Jérusalem de l'Ancient Testament* (Paris: J. Gabalda, 1956).

16. The association of temple and palace in one building compound had been well-attested in Mesopotamia and Egypt. It proved to be a popular layout in the Levant as well, as noted by D. Ussishkin, "Solomon's Palace and Building 1723," *IEJ* 16 (1966): 174-86. In 1971 Th. Busink collected into one monograph all known parallels (*Der Tempel* [n. 14]). Despite the numerous similarities between the biblical description and Canaanite and Syrian temples, he considered many of the features in the Jerusalem temple to be Israelite innovations, a point on which we disagree (ibid., 617).

To date no Israelite temples have been found, with the possible exception of Arad. Many have argued that this complex has much in common with Solomon's. (See the contribution by W. G. Dever in the present volume.) In my view, its contribution to our understanding of the Jerusalem temple has been greatly over-estimated. While it does provide important evidence of Israelite worship outside of Jerusalem during the Judahite monarchy, the Arad "temple" bears very little resemblance to the *Langhaus* symmetrical temples at Tell Tayanat, ʿAin Dara, and Jerusalem. It is of irregular shape, has no central axis, and has a main room to which a new wing and a new door were added in later phases. Even the position of the altar along the northern wall of the courtyard is unusual. Despite the similarities, including altar, niche, and pillar bases, architecturally the Arad shrine has little in common with the Jerusalem temple.

Nevertheless, the assemblage of temples has expanded significantly in the past several decades. We may now identify 26 buildings whose primary features are shared with the Jerusalem temple.[17] The following components were found in all but two of the temples.[18] They were built upon a leveled terrace or elevated platform on the acropolis of the city and were separated from the communities in which they were built, usually by a temenos wall. Each was constructed in front of a courtyard, and in most of the temple compounds an altar stood near the porch with a stone basin nearby. Standing stones or *maṣṣēbôt* of varying size were erected at or near the entrance to many of the temples.[19] Most of these

---

17. They range in date from the third to first millennia B.C.E. and include: Munbaqa, Emar, Ebla D, Mari, Chuera, Ḥayyat, Kittan, ʿAin Dara, Tayanat, Ebla B1, N, Hazor A, Ur, Hazor H, Dabʿa, Alalakh I, Hamath, Shechem, Megiddo, Haror, Alalakh VII, IV, Byblos II, Carchemish, Lachish P, Beth Shean VI, and the temenos at Dan.

18. The most comprehensive typologies proposed to date include A. Mazar, "Temples of the Middle and Late Bronze Ages and the Iron Age," in *The Architecture of Ancient Israel*, ed. A. Kempinski and R. Reich (Jerusalem: Israel Exploration Society , 1992), 161-87; V. Fritz, *Tempel und Zeit: Studien zum Tempelbau in Israel und zu dem Zeltheiligtum der Priesterschrift*, WMANT 47 (Neukirchen-Vluyn: Neukirchener Verlag, 1977); M. Ottoson, *Temples and Cult Places in Palestine*, Uppsala Studies in Ancient Mediterranean and Near Eastern Civilizations 12 (Uppsala: Almqvist & Wiksell, 1980).

19. See the contribution by E. Bloch-Smith in the present volume. See too A. Biran and J. Naveh, "The Tell Dan Inscription: A New Fragment," *IEJ* 45 (1995): 1-3.

A minority of temple courtyards contained scattered pits. Some of them were used as *favissae* (e.g., Lachish Fosse temple, A. Mazar, *Archaeology of the Land of the Bible* [New York: Doubleday, 1990], 254-55), but others are unexplained. Their function may have been to collect runoff from the altar. A more intriguing possibility is that these pits were formed by sacred trees that originally occupied the courtyards. The association between temples and sacred trees is well documented in the Hebrew Bible and ancient Near Eastern literature. See E. Bloch-Smith, "'Who Is the King of Glory?' Solomon's Temple and Its Symbolism," (n. 5) 24, and L. E. Stager, "Jerusalem and the Garden of Eden," *EI* 26 (1999) 183*-94* and "Jerusalem as Eden," *BAR* 26, no. 3 (2000): 36-47, 66. At Avaris M. Bietak discovered a residue of acorns upon the courtyard altar (*Avaris: Capital of the Hyksos. New Excavation*

sanctuaries belong to the "Syrian Temple Type," a symmetrical, *Langhaus* plan consisting of a porch and one or two rooms.[20] Every temple in this corpus has a porch and main hall or cella. The most sacred place is differentiated from the rest of the cella either by higher elevation (dais) or by a niche in the back wall. Standing stones or images of the deity are placed in the innermost shrine, as seen at ʿAin Dara and Hazor H. Many of the buildings are built *in antis*, with extending walls or tower-like protrusions on either side of the entrance. The doorways are all very similar, with elevated thresholds (often formed from a single stone block) and well-designed door sockets. Beyond these common traits, the temples possess various combinations of secondary features such as porch design, pillar position, number of rooms, layout of the inner shrine, ornamentation, and presence or absence of side chambers.

The temples can be seen as hybrid forms of architecture, each consisting of a basic symmetrical floor plan and a cluster of secondary features which reflect the various cultures of the ancient Near East.[21] In our view, therefore, the Jerusalem temple and its closest parallels do not comprise a single category. Rather, each can be viewed as a *Langhaus* temple reflecting Syrian and Canaanite styles which were appropriated for the particular religious heritage of the cult in each respective city or state.

The Jerusalem temple represents one configuration of this hybrid style. Its features reflect both the Canaanite and north Syrian building traditions. According to the biblical account, Solomon's temple incorporated all of the primary features identified above (platform, courtyard, porch, *Langhaus* layout, ornate doorways, etc.). The secondary elements built into the symmetrical, long-room design included side chambers on three sides, a porch with monumental staircase, two flanking piers, and two pillars. The interior likely comprised a large room with a separate, elevated holy of holies along the pattern of ʿAin Dara and Ebla B1 and N. The square wooden cube of innermost shrine was separated either by a screen or by a wall of wood or stone. Each of these features reflects the influence of surrounding cultures and is attested in the 26 temples noted above.

Results [London: British Museum, 1996], 36). The evidence of a sacred grove raises the possibility of the same phenomenon at Munbaqa, Emar, and Hazor H, which also share a common origin in MB II culture.

20. Based upon layout we may loosely divide Near Eastern temples into two categories which are culturally derived. In Canaan the preferred style was the broad room from the fourth millennium until the early second millennium B.C.E. The *Langhaus* tradition, on the other hand, is indigenous to northern Syria and spans the fourth millennium B.C.E. to the first century C.E. These points were noted by A. Mazar ("Temples" [n.18], 169).

21. The *Langhaus* floor plan with *antae*, e.g., probably originated in Mesopotamia or Anatolia, whereas the lion pilasters are most at home in the neo-Hittite kingdoms of northern Syria.

The ʿAin Dara Temple

The spectacular ʿAin Dara temple in northern Syria represents an important new resource for studying the Jerusalem temple. In my view it should supersede the Tayanat temple as the most significant parallel to Solomon's temple discovered to date. Its date, state of preservation, and stunning similarity to the biblical temple are unique among the shrines of the Levant. This neo-Hittite sanctuary, located 67 kilometers northwest of Aleppo in Syria, dates to the early first millennium B.C.E. It was published by A. Abu Assaf in 1990, but is still relatively unknown.[22] Many of its features were hitherto unattested in the archaeological record. These can now be correlated with several enigmatic words found in the biblical description of the Jerusalem temple, a fact which has been largely ignored to date.[23]

The temple stands on the acropolis of the tell, but there is no clear association with a palace or public building as at sites such as Tayanat and Zinjirli. Abu Assaf identified three building phases within Level VII, to which the temple belongs. He determined the following stages in construction: Phase I, 1300-1000 B.C.E.; Phase II, 1000-900 B.C.E.; Phase III, 900-740 B.C.E.[24] The main building was constructed in phases I and II, which are identical except for the addition in Phase II of basalt piers on the facade, cella, and entrance. Side chambers were added in Phase III.

A brief description of the temple is necessary before we associate its features with those of the Jerusalem temple. The courtyard floor in front of the temple was well-constructed with limestone slabs arranged in frames of basalt, giving a decorative effect.[25] The temple was founded upon a large elevated platform whose outer surfaces were lined with basalt blocks engraved with sphinxes and mythic creatures. The floors of the porch and vorcella are built on a stone foundation which raises them 70 cm above the orthostat walls of the terrace.[26] A monumental staircase of four steps connects the courtyard to the porch of the temple.[27] This

---

22. *Der Tempel von ʿAin Dara*, Damaszener Forschungen 3 (Mainz am Rhein: Philipp von Zabern, 1990).

23. As noted below, I have identified thirty-three features shared by the Jerusalem and ʿAin Dara temples. Fewer than half of them are discussed in this paper .

24. *Der Tempel von ʿAin Dara*, 39-41. These were delineated not by pottery but by parallel sculpture from Carchemish, Zincirli, and other Neo-Hittite sites. It is very difficult to evaluate this phasing because the publication does not record the stratigraphy and pottery of the temple. See more recently A. Abu Assaf, "Die Kleinfunde aus ʿAin Dara," *Damaszener Mitteilungen* 9 (1996): 47-111.

25. A large, trough-like water basin stands 11 meters southeast of the temple entrance. It no doubt supplied water for the temple activities.

26. *Der Tempel von ʿAin Dara*, Abb. 15

27. The front of each step is decorated with interwoven ribbons in relief. A short parapet on either side of the staircase has the same design (ibid. Taf. 9a, 10).

front room takes the form of a niche between two large projections which may have supported towers and staircases. Large ornate reliefs of lions, winged sphinxes, palmettes, and guilloche patterns flank the staircase, and there is a winged lion on either side.[28] The first threshold at the entrance has been carved with a pair of meter-long footprints. A second step with only one footprint completes the ascent into the next room. Perhaps the footprints represent a great deity entering its abode, but it is noteworthy that all the gods depicted on the temple reliefs are wearing shoes and sandals.[29]

The two inner rooms of the temple are also reached by way of large limestone stairs. The vorcella (or "antechamber") of the temple is twice as wide as it is deep (15.5 x 6 m). The entire room is lined with large basalt orthostats which have been engraved with flowery ribbon patterns.[30] Two panels on the east and west walls are engraved with triple-indented frames bordered by guilloche. These bring to mind representations of window frames in the Nimrud palace ivories and elsewhere.[31]

The main hall of the temple is square and very large, measuring approximately 16.6 x 16.7 meters. It is reached by three stairs, each decorated with a chain-like border. The doorway is 3.8 m wide and has a single footprint on the limestone threshold. There is a carved lion profile on each of the door posts. Although this room was largely destroyed by later construction, it is clear that the design of orthostat wall with mudbrick superstructure is similar to the wall construction at Alalakh, Shechem, and Megiddo temples.

A large elevated ledge opposite the entrance occupies the rear third

---

28. As in the Tell Tayanat temple, the two pillars on the porch are slightly inset, but whether they supported a roof it is impossible to say. These features are reminiscent of the entryway to the well-known *bīt ḫilāni* palace of Hazor. See A. Ben Tor et al., "Excavating Hazor. Part II: Did the Israelites destroy the Canaanite city?" *BAR* 25 (1999): 22-39.

29. See Bloch-Smith, "'Who Is the King of Glory?' Solomon's Temple and Its Symbolism" (n. 5), 21, 23 and T. J. Lewis, "Divine Images and Aniconism in Ancient Israel," *Journal of the American Oriental Society* 118 (1998): 40.

30. It is curious that there are no orthostats along the southeastern and southwestern corners of the vorcella. The excavator speculates that there was a doorway in each of these 2.5 meter gaps (Abu Assaf, *Der Tempel von ʿAin Dara*, Abb. 13). These doorways would have allowed access to stairways and upper levels of the towers at the front of the temple. The eastern wall of the vorcella and the cella confirms this hypothesis. It was partially hollowed and had two layers of masonry with stones jutting out for support (Abb. 13). Circular holes in two of these walls supported a wooden construction, possibly a staircase (fig. 35B).

31. There are two horizontal openings inside each frame with a rounded molding in between. Inside each is a carved figure-eight pattern. This accords well with R. D. Barnett's description of the famous panel at Nimrud with "triply-recessed embrasure, which is closed up to half its height by a horizontal sill supported on three small columns with polygonal shafts and leaf capitals. Above it there appears a woman's head wearing a heavenly Egyptian wig." See *Assyrian Sculpture in the British Museum* (Toronto: McClelland and Stewart, 1975), 172 and pl. IV.

of the main hall. It was originally reached by a ramp on the central axis of a platform which extended from a niche in the back wall of the cella. Facing the entrance there were wall panels with depictions of bull-men and genies.[32] Behind the platform the rear wall of the room has a shallow niche which is of the same width as the temple porch (11.5 m). The ledge and podium were at one time blockaded from the remainder of the cella. This can be determined from two sockets in the western wall and one on the northern wall which are in line with the elevated area in the back of the room.[33] The holes can be interpreted as brackets for supporting a wooden cross wall which separated the adyton or "Holy of Holies."[34]

In the final building stage (Phase III) a raised corridor was built against three sides of the temple (900-740 B.C.E.). This is one of the most splendid features of the ʿAin Dara temple.[35] The walkway is preserved to a height of 1.5 m and is lined with over 80 relief panels.[36] The size and position of the two-tiered basalt blocks are strong indications that the hallway had a second story. Large piers at regular intervals provided additional support for the wood and mudbrick construction of the upper floors. The side structure was entered by two doors on the facade, one on each side of the main entrance to the temple.[37] The exquisite workmanship on the interior and exterior walls of the side chambers shows us that they could not have functioned merely as storage space. Rather they were an integral part of the temple architecture and its ceremonial function.

---

32. Abu Assaf, *Der Tempel von ʿAin Dara*, Taf. 43-45.

33. Ibid., 16 and Taf. 15c.

34. A similar internal screen was constructed in the second millennium temples at Emar and Munbaqa. Descriptions and illustrations are found in V. Fritz, "Temple Architecture: What Can Archaeology Tell Us about Solomon's Temple?" *BAR* 13 (1987): 38-49. See also J. Margueron's description of the Emar temples: "Quatre campagnes de fouille à Emar (1972-1974): un bilan provisoire," *Syria* 52 (1975): 53-85.

35. The foundations of this addition are not connected to the main part of the temple, which indicates that it was a later building phase of the temple. The masonry was laid upon the preexisting temple platform which extended beyond the new construction.

36. The iconography of this building warrants an entire monograph. Wall reliefs of sphinxes, lions, and floral patterns are known from Hittite and neo-Hittite palace construction, but they are used much more extensively at ʿAin Dara. Abu Assaf cites specific parallels to neo-Hittite cities (*Der Tempel von ʿAin Dara*, 40-41). Note especially the sphinxes, bull-men, and procession scenes on the orthostats at Alaca Höyük, Tell Halaf, and Zinjirli which have conveniently been assembled by R. Naumann, *Architecture Kleinasiens* (Tübingen: E. Wasmuth, 1955), 77, figs. 57-59; 62. The individuals on the wall relief at ʿAin Dara bear a remarkable resemblance to those on the walls of the *ḫilāni* building at Zinjirli as reported by F. von Luschen, *Ausgrabungen in Sendschirli, IV. Mittheilungen aus den orientalischen Sammlungen* (Berlin: George Reimer, 1911), Abb. 150.

37. The thresholds of the entryways were positioned 1.3 meters above the courtyard, meaning that in antiquity there must have been a stairway which has since been removed. Today only the western door is preserved, but it is flanked by four impressive winged lions (Abu Assaf, *Der Tempel von ʿAin Dara*, Taf. 6; 34-38).

In summary, because of its date, design, and unusual state of preservation, the ʿAin Dara temple provides unique insight into the *Langraum* Syrian temple type to which the Jerusalem temple belongs. It bears many close similarities not only to second millennium temples such as Emar, Munbaqa, and Ebla (Temple D) but also to the temple of Solomon and the eighth century temple from Tell Tayanat.[38] Jerusalem's temple can be viewed, like ʿAin Dara, as a mixture of architecture and art from Syria and Canaan which was appropriated for a particular religious heritage, in this case, the Jerusalem cult.

If the ʿAin Dara temple represents a significant new resource for the study of Solomon's temple, it has yet to be mined for parallel material. The two temples are roughly contemporary and they share many elements, including approximate size, broad foundation platform, inset pillars on the porch, an elevated inner shrine, multistoried side chambers, detailed reliefs, and carved windows which offer no opening to the outside world. These similarities may inform a new interpretation of several features in the biblical temple.

Correlation of Text and Artifact: Reconstructing the Jerusalem Temple

The biblical terminology and the corpus of excavated temples offer an ideal case study for examining the nexus between *realia* and text. The rich vocabulary of temple architecture in the Hebrew Bible should, we believe, reflect at least in part the cultural realities of the first millennium context which it claims to describe. In order to evaluate this hypothesis, the vocabulary must be related to the features identified in the archaeological record. In our view, the most productive text-artifact analyses do not favor one discipline to the exclusion of the another. Rather, two bodies of evidence, the textual and archaeological, are examined independently before they are combined in an ongoing dialectic.[39]

---

38. Within the typology ʿAin Dara is a link between the fourteenth- to twelfth-century temple at Hazor H and the eighth-century temple at Tel Tayanat. It combines the basalt orthostats and broad-room vorcella of Hazor with the side *antae*, porch, and separate adyton found at Emar, Ebla, and ultimately Tayanat. Not only this, but the gate-like walls flanking the porch are large enough to be towers, meaning that the temple may also have been built with the tower-gateway element found at Megiddo and Shechem.

39. There is a relatively small number of text-artifact studies which are firmly planted in both archaeology and linguistics. See, e.g., P. Weadock, "The Giparu at Ur," *Iraq* 37 (1975): 101-22 and E. Porada, "Battlements in the Military Architecture and in the Symbolism of the Ancient Near East," in *Essays in the History of Architecture Presented to Rudolph Wittkower*, ed. D. Fraser et al. (Bristol: Phaidon Press, 1967), 1-12. Similar integrative

The correlations proposed in the following pages were reached by means of this two-layered methodology. The primary referent from archaeology is the ʿAin Dara temple (**fig. 1**), although many features of other temples could also be considered.[40] The primary text is 1 Kings 6-7, though Ezekiel and Chronicles are also incorporated. The overlap in architecture between these two databases is extraordinary indeed. ʿAin Dara possesses 33 out of the 65 architectural elements mentioned in the biblical temple passages. No other building excavated to date has so many features in common with the biblical description of the Jerusalem temple. The most noteworthy parallels are summarized here, though many more could be noted.

Approach/ *məsillâ, mābôʾ*. It is difficult to determine a precise referent for these terms, but the biblical context indicates that both are graded approaches to the temple, which typically stood at a high elevation within the city.[41] This is an element of almost every temple in the Levant, and ʿAin Dara is no exception.[42]

Courtyard/ *ḥāṣēr*. The original temple of Solomon is recorded as having an inner court (*heḥāṣēr happənîmît*, 1 Kings 6:36) and an outer court in front of the temple (*heḥāṣēr haggədôlâ*, 1 Kings 7:9; 8:64). The distinction is preserved in Ezekiel's description, although many more courts are envisioned there (Ezek. 46:23; Ezek. 42:8). The courts of the temple have many features in common with proper buildings. The inner and outer courts of the visionary temple were built with the same timber and stone construction used in the *ʾûlām* (1 Kings 7:11). They possessed gates and entrances (Ezek. 40:14; 8:7), rooms (Ezek. 42:8), four corners (*miqṣōaʿ*, Ezek. 46:21), even pillars (*ʿammûdîm*, Ezek. 42:6) and entryways (*ʾûlām*, Ezek. 40:31).[43]

ʿAin Dara has a flagstone courtyard with no indication of the courtyard perimeter. The flagstones fit tightly together with no need for

---

investigations of Israelite architecture are fewer still, e.g., B. Halpern, *The First Historians* (San Francisco: Harper & Row, 1988), 37-75. Typically the subject is handled primarily from the standpoint of *either* language *or* archaeology.

40. See my dissertation, "The Jerusalem Temple: A Case Study in the Integration of Text and Artifact," Ph.D. diss., Harvard University, 1999.

41. *mābôʾ*: 2 Kings 16:18; 2 Chron. 23:13; Jer. 38:14, Ezek. 46:19. In our view *mĕsillâ* refers to the final ascent toward the gates of the temple courtyard (1 Chron. 26:16; 2 Chron. 9:11). See the excellent study of N. Tidwell, "No Highway! The Outline of a Semantic Description of *mesillâ*," *VT* 45.2 (1995): 251-69.

42. At most temple sites an esplanade, or open area, surrounded the sanctuary (e.g., Hazor, Area H temple), but in some temples the temenos wall is formed by the outer walls of adjacent buildings (e.g., Megiddo 2048).

43. Some of these elements, such as gates and pillars, were also present in the Tabernacle as it is described in Exodus 27 and 38. The only temple courtyard with temenos walls and gate from the southern Levant is Hazor H, Stratum 1b, discovered by Y. Yadin, *Hazor: The Schweich Lectures, 1970* (London: Oxford University Press, 1972), 75-83.

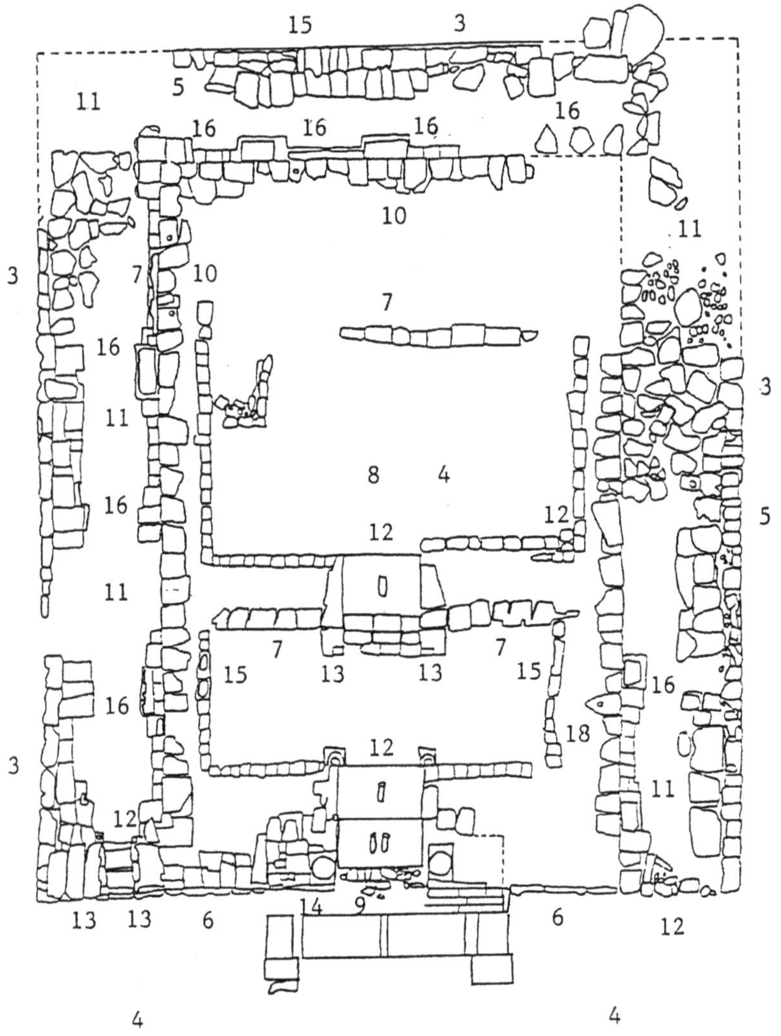

FIGURE 1: The ʿAin Dara temple and biblical temple terms. Plan follows A. Abu-Assaf (1990: Taf. 18).

1. Courtyard/חָצֵר
2. Foundation/מוּסָד
3. Terrace Platform/גֹּבַהּ
4. Paved Floor/רִצְפָּה, אֶרֶץ, קַרְקַע
5. Exterior Wall/קִיר
6. Facade Wall/כָּתֵף
7. Wall Panels/שְׂדֵרֹת
8. Hall/Cella/הֵיכָל, אוּלָם
9. Porch/אוּלָם
10. Holy of Holies/דְבִיר
11. Side Chambers/צְלָעוֹת
12. Door/פֶּתַח, חֲמִשִׁית, מְזוּזוֹת, סַף, מִפְתָּן
13. Piers/אֵלִים
14. Pillar/עַמּוּד
15. Window/חַלּוֹנֵי שְׁקֻפִים אֲטֻמִים
16. Pilasters and Piers/מִגְרָעוֹת
17. Upper Floor/יָצוּעַ, עֲלִיָּה
18. Staircase/לוּל, מַעֲלֶה, מַעֲלָה

cement. A large basin is an additional point of similarity with the Jerusalem Temple.[44] Other good parallels have been found at Beth-shean, Hazor Temple H, and Tel Dan. At Hazor the inner court of Stratum 2 was reached through a gateway with flagstone stairs and a porch.[45] The walls of the court were of substantial size, a fact which also corresponds to the biblical description of the walls which lined the *ḥāṣēr* (1 Kings 7:11). A second, more impressive correlation is found at Tel Dan, where A. Biran discovered a sequence of long rooms which defined the courtyard of the sacred precinct on its western side.[46]

Foundation and Terrace Platform/ *mûsād, gōbah.* Archaeological evidence for temple foundations (*môsədôt)* and platform (*gōbah*) can be found at numerous sites. The ʿAin Dara temple was constructed atop a limestone platform of 70 cm height. Its outer surfaces were lined with basalt reliefs. Since the temple of Solomon was also built on a rounded hilltop, it no doubt required a similar platform. Such a feature is alluded to in Ezek. 41:8, 13-14.[47] The foundation platform at Tayanat raised the temple 45 cm above the height of the adjacent courtyards. At Temple 2048 at Megiddo the landing was over 2 m high and was constructed from rubble and stone fill with ashlars on the borders.[48] The most impressive temple foundation is the high place at Dan. Although the original structure has been removed, in our opinion the platform must have supported a stone, brick, and wood construction, because the first three courses were left intact. Additional evidence of large foundation material was excavated at the palaces of Megiddo, where the proportions of construction are comparable to those described in 1 Kings 7:10.[49]

---

44. As noted above, courtyard pits at several temples may have been formed by uprooted tress. Biblical evidence for sacred gardens in the temple precinct is found in Pss. 92:12-14; 52:8, as noted by L. E. Stager ("Jerusalem and Eden," 183-86). The *ʾăšērîm* as sacred emblems are well documented in the biblical text (e.g., 2 Kings 23). These sacred trees in the garden temples represented not only the fertile tree of life but also, according to the biblical polemicists, pagan idols, as evidenced in their complete destruction during various religious reforms in Judah (e.g., 2 Kings 18:24; 23:14). Stager rightly associates "the oak of the *maṣṣēbâ*" with the standing stone and pits in the courtyard of the temple at Shechem (Judges 9)

45. Y. Yadin, *Hazor: The Schweich Lectures* (n. 43), fig 19.

46. *Biblical Dan* (Jerusalem: Israel Exploration Society, 1994), 204-17.

47. Traces of the Second Temple platform have been discovered east of the Dome of the Rock in Jerusalem, but the possibility of a tenth-century platform is controversial. L. Ritmeyer, "The Ark of the Covenant: Where It Stood in Solomon's Temple," *BAR* 22 (1996): 46-55, 70-73.

48. The Dagan temple at Mari, together with the temples of Alalakh VII and Hazor Temple H, were also constructed upon flattened ledges which elevated the temples slightly above the surrounding surfaces (as noted above).

49. "Costly and large. . . of eight and ten cubits." See buildings 1723 and 1482 (R.

Paved Floor/ *riṣpâ, ʾereṣ, qarqaʿ*. The latter two Hebrew expressions are general signifiers of floors. They are homonyms with earth and ground, which is appropriate in that the vast majority of temples in the Levant were discovered with earthen floors. It is possible that many temple floors were originally lined with wood. According to the Kings account, the floors of the Jerusalem temple were inlaid with planks of cedar. Evidence of this practice was found in several Hittite palaces.[50] A similar technique was used in Building 1723 at Megiddo.[51] *Riṣpâ* refers specifically to stone pavement (e.g., Ezek. 42:3). It may be compared to the limestone flooring throughout the courtyard and interior of the ʿAin Dara Temple.

Facade Wall/ *kātēp*. From the context of this word in 1 Kings 6:8 it may be surmised that this word specifically represents the side walls of the temple facade. If the analogy of ʿAin Dara is followed, doorways to the ambulatory were located on either side of the facade, a possibility which is not ruled out in the biblical text (1 Kings 6:8). In the porch of the ʿAin Dara temple the wall is engraved with reliefs of large mythic creatures, guilloche, and sphinxes. The two side walls do not meet but are adjoined to recessed door frames on either side.

Wall Panels/ *śədērôt*. As noted above, the remarkable reliefs on the exterior and interior of the ʿAin Dara temple bear motifs which accord well with the iconography described in the Bible. Such reliefs lined the Jerusalem temple as well, but they were carved in wood because local limestone was less conducive to fine relief, and there was no basalt available in the vicinity of Jerusalem. The *śədērôt* may well have been wall

---

Lamon and G. Shipton, *Megiddo I* [Chicago: University of Chicago Press, 1939], 17-27, 50). The stones of the foundations were roughly cut in contrast to the ashlar masonry above floor level. Broad timbers were set against the stone foundations for the purpose of holding the irregular boulders in place. The wall foundations identified in the temples of the Levant range in width from 1.5 to 5.1 meters. Some have been traced to a depth of 1-2 meters. In many instances the foundations are slightly wider than the wall, and the lowest course of ashlars is set back 15-20 centimeters. Extensive foundation material is exposed at ʿAin Dara. The side chambers were built upon large limestone blocks. The remains accord well with Ezek. 41:8, where *mûsād* is a support for the *ṣĕlāʿôt*, or side chambers.

50. They are described by Naumann, *Architecture* (n. 36), 145-48.

51. Lamon and Shipton, *Megiddo I*, 17-21. Indirect evidence of a comparable cedar floor has been discovered by A. Ben Tor in the severely burned palace at Hazor dating to the second millennium B.C.E. (personal communication). There is adequate room between the orthostats and the floor for an additional surface which was removed or burned at the time of the palace's destruction. The complete absence of stone leads to the conclusion that the floor was originally constructed of wood. Hence, evidence of wood floors at Kültepe, Hattusas, Zinjirli, and Megiddo not only illuminate the biblical text, but also raise the likelihood that many of the temples in the Levant once had wood flooring which has since been stripped away.

panels lining the side chambers of the temple (1 Kings 6:9).[52] The socles attached to the inner walls of the ambulatory at ʿAin Dara explain this feature by analogy. There the side structure was accessible through doors on either side of the facade. Such an access in the Jerusalem temple would explain Athaliah's hasty exit from the building through the *śədērôt*, or "wood paneled walls" of the ambulatory (2 Kings 11:13-14).

Porch/ *ʾûlām*. The small porch of the ʿAin Dara temple, like the entrances to many second millennium temples, was integrated with an open courtyard and was reached via a monumental staircase (*maʿăleh*). The *ʾûlām* was narrower and shallower than the rooms of the temple, which is one reason we consider it to be part of the facade and not an internal division of the temple. With large piers on either side, it more closely resembled a gate or doorway than a room. Reliefs of human figures and cherub creatures lined the rabbeted frame of the entrance and facade wall (*kātēp*). The *ʾûlām* of Jerusalem's temple, likewise, served as a transitional passageway linking the courtyard to the temple proper. The porch door in the ʿAin Dara temple was two-leafed, as indicated by the sockets inside the vorcella. In typical Syrian tradition, the porch also had massive pillar bases flanking the rabbeted doorway. Like the columns in the Tell Tayanat temple and the *bīt ḫilāni* palaces, the position of these pillar bases is indicative of load-bearing columns. From this it is reasonable to conclude that the Jerusalem temple had the same configuration.[53]

Hall, Cella/ *hêkāl, bayit*. According to the biblical description in 1 Kings 7: 31ff., the *hêkāl*, or main hall, of Solomon's temple measured approximately 11 x 21 m and was the center of cultic activity. It housed the lamp stands, a small incense altar, and a table for the "bread of presence." The biblical *hêkāl* was paneled with wood and had windows on either side. There were also pilasters on either side. Each was 6 cubits wide, and they were positioned at regular intervals (*ʾêlîm*, Ezek. 41:1). Once again ʿAin Dara provides a dramatic parallel. The corresponding room at ʿAin Dara is roughly square-shaped.[54] It is not as well-preserved

---

52. A similar but less convincing proposal is made by B. Eshel: "*ʿAtîqîm, śĕdrôt, and mĕśdĕrôn* in Biblical Hebrew," *Leshonenu* 37 (1973): 8-9. He understands the *śĕdērôt* to be covered walkways between the temple and the priestly chambers. Unfortunately this translation does not reflect the archaeological evidence. While several of the temples stood adjacent to courtyards and casemate structures (e.g., Alalakh VII and Tell ed-Dab'a), long covered walkways and promenades were likely introduced only in Persian period.

53. In the view of J. Ouellette, the *ʾûlām* of the temple is nothing other than a copy of the porch taken from contemporary *bīt ḫilāni* palaces ("The Temple of Solomon," Ph.D. diss., Hebrew Union College, Cincinnati, 1966, 11-13; 102-13). While the pillars and staircases may be similar, we note that the *bīt ḫilāni* porches are much longer and narrower.

54. Approximately 16.6 x 16.7 meters. Although both temples are supposedly tripartite, the ʿAin Dara temple has four rooms if a screened holy place is separated from the main

as other parts of the building, but the lower panels of basalt relief can still be seen lining the walls. The images include carved windows and mountain gods. In addition, the remains of an elevated podium, a niche, and sockets for a secondary wall are clearly visible. The podium and its original screen may be compared to the innermost enclosure, or *dəbîr*, of the Jerusalem temple. Additional examples of the *hêkāl* include the palace halls at Megiddo (Buildings 1723 and 6000) and the large central rooms of the temples at Ebla and Emar.[55] In each case the *hêkāl* functioned as an inner court and the main center of activity in the building, royal or sacred.

Innermost Shrine/ *dəbîr*. The relationship between the *hêkāl* and *dəbîr* in the Jerusalem temple continues to elude clarification. The *dəbîr* is described as a wooden cube measuring 20 cubits on each side (1 Kings 6:20; Ezek. 41:3-4). It is unclear from the biblical accounts whether it was a shrine within the 40 cubit length of the *hêkāl* (perhaps separated by a thin screen) or an independent room separated from the hall by a solid wall as in the Tayanat temple.[56] The width of this wall is unaccounted for in the biblical description, and in the archaeological record walls in this position are of varying widths. The majority of temples in the Levant have a niche or elevated podium along the back wall. At Ebla Temple D, Munbaqa, Hazor H, and ᶜAin Dara there is evidence that the podium was screened off from the remainder of the cella.[57] In most cases only a shallow area along the back wall is detached from the rest of the building. Representations of the gods may have been placed behind the screens, similar to the *maṣṣēbôt* flanking the niche at Arad. The adyton at ᶜAin Dara was significantly larger, occupying over one third of the floor space in the cella.

We may conclude that the *dəbîr* of Solomon's temple as described in the Bible has much more in common with the screened podiums at ᶜAin Dara and Hazor Temple H than with the thick-walled adyton at Tell Tayanat. Unfortunately, the ruins of Syrian temples, even when they are

---

hall. The vorcella, or middle room, is clearly too small to be equated with the main hall of the Israelite temple. I thank Amihai Mazar for bringing this matter and Yadin's comments to my attention (Yadin, *Hazor*, 75-83).

55. See D. Ussishkin, "Solomon's Palace," and J. Margueron, "Emar."

56. Opinion is split on the matter, but the first view is far more popular. It is espoused by various scholars, including J. Ouellette, "The Temple of Solomon" [n. 53]; R. Friedman, "The Tabernacle in the Temple" [n. 5]; V. Fritz, "Temple Architecture" [n. 34]; M. Ottosson, *Temples and Cult Places* [n. 18], 112; and Th. Busink, *Der Tempel* [n. 14], Abb. 48.

57. The best example is the well-preserved screen at Hazor Temple H, Strata 2 and 1a, which was discovered by Y. Yadin (*Hazor*, 75-83). See also the analysis of M. Ottosson (*Temples and Cult Places* [n. 18], 28) and the recent discussion of the Tabernacle by F. M. Cross in *From Epic to Canon: History and Literature in Ancient Israel* (Baltimore: Johns Hopkins University, 1998), 85-90.

considered alongside the biblical text, do not provide conclusive evidence as to the nature of the *dəbîr*. Nevertheless, ʿAin Dara's elevated podium with attachments for a separate screen is a commanding parallel for the biblical Holy of Holies. It is elevated, is reached by steps, and it originally housed the image of a deity.

Side Chamber/ *ṣəlāʿôt*. Generations of commentators have tried to determine the precise nature of the *ṣəlāʿôt* adjoining Solomon's temple. The term is usually interpreted collectively as "side structure" or "side chambers." A third lexeme, *yāṣûaʿ*, seems to refer to the superimposed layers of the side structure.[58]

The outer hallway represents one of the most dramatic contributions which the ʿAin Dara temple brings to our understanding of the Israelite temple. Until the discovery of ʿAin Dara no side corridors were available for comparison with the *ṣəlāʿôt* of the biblical text. The multistoried hallways which flank the temple make it possible to propose an impressive correlation between text and artifact. The side rooms are the first examples of the ambulatory described in the biblical accounts to be preserved above foundation level. First, the structure in both buildings surrounded the temple on three sides. At ʿAin Dara the wings envelope the porch, vorcella, and cella whereas at Jerusalem they only encompassed the *hêkāl* and *dəbîr* (1 Kings 6:5). Parallel rows of socles on either side of the side structure at ʿAin Dara were certainly wide enough to support two or three floors above. These relief-lined piers, or *migrāʿôt*, could easily have supported mud brick piers which narrowed with increasing elevation.[59]

Door/ *petaḥ, məzûzâ, ḥămišît, sap, miptān*. Each of these terms in the biblical temple has a convincing counterpart at ʿAin Dara. There the *petaḥ* of each room measured approximately 3.8 m in width. Both door frames had *məzûzôt*, or side posts, in the form of lion profiles. These are characteristic of neo-Hittite architecture but are also attested at the temple in area H at Hazor. The limestone *sap* and *miptān* at ʿAin Dara provide a worthy means of reconstructing the shaking doorposts in the vision of Amos (9:1) and the position of the "keepers of the threshold" in the Jerusalem cult (2 Kings 22:4). By considering the superhuman footprints on the thresholds, one can speculate as to the manner in which the august deity of ʿAin Dara was understood to enter his abode. In similar fashion,

---

58. According to our interpretation of 1 Kings 6:6, the word *yāṣûaʿ* is used to describe the "stories" which make up the side chambers, or *ṣĕlāʿôt*.

59. The foundation of the side structure is 5.50 meters wide. The basalt bases of the side walls range from 1-1.5 meters in thickness, which leaves a walkway of 2.5 to 3 meters width. These dimensions are close to the 5 cubit width of the side wing as it is described in 1 Kings 6:6. The corridors in the Syrian temple also provide fine counterparts to the biblical *ganzak*, a type of casemate room in the side chambers (1 Chron. 28:11).

Yhwh's omnipotence was communicated through the size of the *dəbîr* and cherub throne of the Jerusalem temple.[60]

In the light of ʿAin Dara I would like to propose a revised interpretation of the expressions *ḥămišît* and *rəbiʿît*. In my view they signify the ornate, recessed door frames of the temple (1 Kings 6:1-33). Even the most basic door frames in the buildings of the ancient Near East had single recesses, as the necropolis of Silwan in Jerusalem reveals.[61] Luxurious buildings throughout the Mediterranean world incorporated this style, as seen, for example, in the Nimrud ivories and Tamassos tombs.[62] Rabbeted facades were known in the Levant already from the Middle Bronze Age IIA, as demonstrated in the facades of the Ḥayyat temple and Ashkelon gate, as well as later temples at Alalakh and Tayanat.[63] At ʿAin Dara the door between the *ʾûlām* and the vorcella was of the *rəbiʿît* type, a door with four recesses. The *faux* windows also incorporated recesses in their frames.

Pillar/ *ʿammûd*. The pillars at the entrance to the ʿAin Dara temple, like those in the Tell Tayanat temple, seem to have had an architectural function in addition to their cultic significance. In our view this same arrangement was found in the Jerusalem temple, despite the discrepancy between the height of the pillars and the height of the roof. There is very little direct evidence of column shafts and capitals in the temples of the Levant except for the Egyptian columns at Lachish Temple P and the *tīmōrâ* capitals (so-called "proto-aeolic").[64] In order to visualize the capitals we must rely almost entirely upon models and reliefs, but we can infer that a majority of column shafts and capitals in temple architecture were fashioned from wood.[65]

---

60. Cf. Psalm 24. See also Bloch-Smith, "'Who Is the King of Glory?' Solomon's Temple and Its Symbolism" (n. 5), 24-26.

61. D. Ussishkin, *The Village of Silwan: The Necropolis from the Period of the Judean Kingdom* (Jerusalem: Israel Exploration Society, 1993), ills. 47, 94, and 108.

62. *ANEP* 586 and 590-91; See also J. Margueron, "'Maquettes' architectuales de Meskene-Emar," *Syria* (1976) 193-232 and figs. 4, 7, 9.

63. S. Falconer and B. Magness-Gardiner, "Community, Polity, and Temple in a Middle Bronze Age Levantine Village," *JMA* 7, no. 2 (1994): 127-64. C. L. Woolley, *Alalakh: An Account of the Excavations at Tell Atchana in the Hatay, 1937-1949* (Oxford: Oxford University Press, 1955), pl. XIII.

64. The components of the column are the base, the shaft, and the capital. The latter is represented by no fewer than four words in Hebrew. *Rōʾš*, *ṣepet*, and *kōteret* are nondescript words which refer to capitals. *Kaptôr* is used in the detailed descriptions of the ornamentation on the capitals Jachin and Boaz in the Jerusalem temple.

65. E.g., R. Naumann (*Architecture* [n. 36], 139: Abb. 150b-c.) Pillars in other structures are very well represented. Stone columns still stand in the dwellings and storehouses at Hazor, Beer-sheba, Megiddo, Tell Batashi, and many other sites (L. Herr, "Tripartite Pillared Buildings and the Market Place in Iron Age Palestine," *BASOR* 272 [1988]: 47-67). Evi-

Jachin and Boaz of the Jerusalem temple belong to the Levantine tradition of symbolic porch pillars as attested in the ubiquitous column bases flanking the entrances to most temples of the Levant. Measuring 18 cubits, the columns were built to proportions for which there are no comparisons in the ancient Near Eastern world.[66] They have been interpreted variously as columns with dedicatory inscriptions, representations of the doorways into the divine abode, and flowering trees representing the virile attributes of the divinity. Based upon the layout of parallel temples, the pillars were both symbolic and functional.[67] The symbolic function is at least in part derived from the role of gateways in cultic ritual, as seen in Psalm 24.[68]

Window/ *ḥallôn, ḥallônê šəqupîm ʾăṭumîm*. Besides the all-encompassing term *ḥallôn*, very few window types are mentioned in the Bible. It is a feature in both public (2 Kings 9:30) and private architecture (Josh. 2:15; Joel 2:9; Eccles. 12:3). The Israelite tombs at Silwan in Jerusalem again provide rare examples of architecture which is seldom preserved elsewhere in the archaeological record.[69] The limited terminology of windows in Solomon's temple is very technical and obscure. Among the most difficult is the phrase *ḥallônê šəqupîm ʾăṭumîm*. Most commentators translate this term as "framed, blocked windows," or "framed, latticed windows," on the basis of etymologies. A bewildering number of theories have been proposed, and some scholars consider any attempt at translation to be exercise in futility.

---

dence for wood pillars was summarized by Y. Shiloh (*The Proto-Aeolic Capital and Israelite Ashlar Masonry*, Qedem 11 [Jerusalem: Hebrew University, 1979], 43-44), and R. Reich ("Building Materials and Architectural Elements," in *The Architecture of Ancient Israel*, ed. E. Netzer, A. Kempinski, and R. Reich [Jerusalem: Israel Exploration Society, 1992], 10).

66. They occupy a disproportionate percentage of the temple vocabulary in 1 Kings 6:1-38; 7:13-51 and 2 Chron. 3–4, and are described in some detail in Jer. 52:17-23 as well. These massive pillars were gilded in bronze and had highly decorative capitals. The literature on this topic is vast and a large number of reconstructions have been offered. See especially Busink, *Der Tempel* (n. 14), 299-321, and S. Yeivin, "Jachin and Boaz," *PEQ* 91 (1959): 6-22.

67. For discussion on the purpose of the pillars, see Hurowitz, *Exalted House*, 257-58; Bloch-Smith, "'Who Is the King of Glory?' Solomon's Temple and Its Symbolism" (n. 5) , 19-23; and C. Meyers, "Jachin and Boaz in Religious and Political Perspective," *CBQ* 45 (1983): 174.

68. See F. M. Cross, *Canaanite Myth and Hebrew Epic* (Cambridge, MA: Harvard University Press, 1973), 91-99.

69. The openings of certain burial troughs are reached through windows hewn in the rock. The window frames consist of right and left jambs (60 centimeters deep) and a narrow 14 centimeter sill along the bottom. See Ussishkin, *The Village of Silwan* (n. 61), 3, 100 and figs. 75, 64.

Figure 2: "Recessed, blocked window" (חַלּוֹנֵי שְׁקֻפִים אֲטֻמִים) at ʿAin Dara. Drawn from Taf. 42b in A. Abu-Assaf (1990).

The framed windows carved in stone represent one of the most noteworthy finds at ʿAin Dara **(fig. 2)** because they match perfectly the biblical phrase noted above (1 Kings 6:4). These "decorative windows" are not lacking in any detail. They are located on the inner walls of the vorcella and cella. Each has a recessed, indented frame on each side, including the top, where it is slightly arched. Horizontal figure eight-shaped ribbons fill the upper half of each window. These may indeed represent the kind of window lattice described in 1 Kings 6:4-5 and elsewhere in the Hebrew Bible. Some of the windows have been carved with side posts which are attested in the Phoenician ivories at Samaria, Arslan Tash, Nimrud, and Khorsabad.[70] A beautiful stone replica of this window style from

70. At ʿAin Dara, one relief depicts a god standing adjacent to a post of a window or doorway (Abu-Assaf, *Der Tempel von ʿAin Dara*, Taf 4b; 39b). Compare the ivories described by E. Stern, "Phoenician Architecture," 306-7, and R. Barnett ("Lions and Bulls in Assyrian Palaces," in *Le Palais et la Royauté Archéologie et Civilization*, ed P. Garelli, XIXe Rencontre Assyriologique Internationale [Paris: Geuthner, 1974] 441-46).

Episkopi on Cyprus also bears some similarity to both the biblical expression and the windows at ʿAin Dara.[71]

In light of the language in the biblical phrase, we may infer that the "framed, blocked windows" of Solomon's temple were decorative stone reliefs such as the ones at ʿAin Dara. There the beautifully crafted *faux* windows are the Syrian version of Solomon's *ḥallônê šəqupîm ʾăṭumîm.* Ezekiel speaks of similar windows, *ḥallônîm ʾăṭumôt*, which were no doubt carryovers from the Solomonic windows (Ezek. 40:16; 41:16, 26). There were most likely additional windows and openings in the Jerusalem temple which allowed light to enter.[72] These may have been the inspiration for the beautiful windows which were replicated in stone and singled out in the biblical accounts on account of their unusual appearance. In sum, I would like to suggest that the windows at ʿAin Dara provide the solution to a riddle which has eluded commentators for generations.

Pilaster and Pier/ *ʾayil, migrāʿôt.* Pier construction in Syria and Israel reached the height of its popularity in the late Iron Age. Here again the ʿAin Dara temple contains excellent examples. Many piers and socles of basalt stone protruded at regular intervals from the side walls of the ambulatory.[73] We may associate these piers with the *migrāʿôt* of 1 Kings 6:6.[74] The piers at ʿAin Dara are 8 m apart, protrude 0.5 to 1 m into the walkway, and have an average width of 2.5 m. These measurements are surprisingly close to the width of the pilasters of the *hêkāl* described in Ezek. 41:1 (six cubits or approximately 3 m). At ʿAin Dara the size of the pilasters in the ambulatory leaves little doubt that they supported one or two upper stories of the building. Voids and ledges by which the second floor was attached to the *migrāʿôt* have unfortunately weathered away in all but one place, but a better-preserved example was found at Ugarit.[75] The pilasters at ʿAin Dara are almost identical in size to those mentioned in Ezek. 41:6.

A second type of pilaster is represented by the biblical word *ʾayil.*

---

71. Y. Shiloh, *The Proto-Aeolic Capital and Israelite Ashlar Masonry*, pl. 19. Note also the small window socket from Zinjirli (R. Naumann, *Architecture* [n. 36], 166, fig. 194). One function of the window frames was to secure window coverings. Such coverings or shutters may have been fastened to the window frame or built onto a pivot for easy opening and closing.

72. The presence of blocked windows does not preclude real windows in other parts of the temple which have not been preserved

73. Abu Assaf, *Der Tempel von ʿAin Dara*, Taf. 7c and 6a.

74. L. E. Stager arrives at a similar conclusion ("Jerusalem and Eden," 6 and fig. 4).

75. G. Hult, *Bronze and Ashlar Masonry in the Eastern Mediterranean*, Studies in Mediterranean Archaeology 66 (Göteborg: Paul Aströms, 1983), 29-31.

This term is attested most frequently in the vision of Ezekiel where it can designate the sides of a building or a gateway.[76] In our view, the *ʾayil* was a squared, engaged pillar whose main function was to support the wall or to frame a doorway or gate. This feature is well-documented not only at ʿAin Dara but also in the gate complexes of Iron Age Israel and the palace architecture of Syria and Mesopotamia from the second and first millennia B.C.E.[77]

In sum, ʿAin Dara provides evidence for two types of support documented in the biblical temple. The *migrāʿôt* at ʿAin Dara are pilaster supports with basalt reliefs built into the ambulatory. The *ʾêlîm* are comparable piers built into the doorways and gate-like facade of the temple. In its classic form this style consisted of engaged stone piers capped with palmette capitals. And indeed, one of the *migrāʿot* at ʿAin Dara bears the *tīmōrâ* design. The so-called *tīmōrâ* or palmette pattern has been found on such capitals throughout the southern Levant, including Transjordan.[78]

Upper Levels/*ʿăliyyâ, yāṣûaʿ*. The most common Hebrew designation for the upper level of a building is *ʿăliyyâ*. Its semantic range is very broad.[79] Like domestic houses, palaces, and gates, the temple had an *ʿăliyyâ*, (1 Chron. 28:11). The upper levels of the side hallways (*ṣəlāʿôt*) have a designation which is different from the typical expression for the upper floors of buildings. *Yāṣûaʿ* is an enigmatic term, which in our view denotes the levels of the side corridors in the Jerusalem temple. Each *yāṣûaʿ* was attached to the walls of the main temple building by means of *migrāʿôt* which we have identified as piers or socles (1 Kings 6:10). The ʿAin Dara temple doubtless had upper stories built upon the side chambers and piers of the facade. There the evidence for this feature is found in

---

76. Here it appears exclusively in the plural, a fact that verifies the archaeological picture of matching piers at the entrance of a gate or monumental doorway.

77. In monumental architecture ashlar piers provided stability and a frame for fieldstone fill. See E. Stern, "The Phoenician Architectural Elements during the Iron Age and the Persian Period," in *The Architecture of Ancient Israel*, ed. E. Netzer, A. Kempinski, and R. Reich (Jerusalem: Israel Exploration Society, 1992), 303. For parallels at Mari see E. Heinrich, *Die Tempel und Heiligtümer im Alten Mesopotamien: Typologie, Morphologie und Geschichte*, Denkmäler antiker Architectur 14 (Berlin: de Gruyter, 1982), 162.

78. I. Negueruela, "Proto-Aeolic Capitals from Mudeibi'a in Moab," *ADAJ* 26 (1982): 395-400.

79. When in construct with *pinnâ* (Neh. 3:31) and *gāg* (Prov. 21:9; 25:24) the word refers to a corner tower or the meeting of the wall and the roof (cf. *gēbîm* above). In the Ehud narrative three distinct rooms are attributed to Eglon's palace. Among them are the *misdĕrôn*, apparently a hallway connecting several rooms (Judg. 3:24), and the *mĕqērâ*, an upper room in which the king had a special chair (Judg. 3:20); see T. Jull, "*Mqrh* in Judges 3: A scatological reading," *JSOT* 81 (1998): 63-75.

the flooring of the outer corridors and possibly in the voids in one of the piers which most logically was designed for wooden inserts.

Staircase/ *lûl, maʿăleh, maʿălâ.* A monumental staircase, or *maʿăleh,* is found in most of the temples mentioned above, but the one at ʿAin Dara is exceptional for its high quality and the gigantic footprint in the first threshold. The biblical term for the ascent between the levels of the side chambers is very difficult to translate. It need not be assumed that the *lûl-lîm* were "spiral staircases" or "trap doors," much less that they were ladders.[80] In our view, this hapax legomenon is a staircase with a return and not a ladder or winding staircase as some interpreters have argued. Our translation is based upon tower and palace staircases at north Syria and Abu Assaf's description of the grooves and braces in the eastern wall of the vorcella at ʿAin Dara. The large piers of the facade could easily have housed staircases, and an ascent in either location would perfectly match the arrangement noted in 1 Kings 6:8: ". . . one went up by the *lûllîm* to the middle story, and from the middle story to the third." The staircase at ʿAin Dara is therefore a compelling parallel for part of Solomon's temple which until recently could only be reconstructed in theory

Summary. A walk through the ʿAin Dara temple affords the visitor a chance to visualize many aspects of the Jerusalem temple, in some cases to a high level of detail. A spectacular edifice in its own right, ʿAin Dara provides clarification for over 33 terms in the biblical temple description. Like the Jerusalem temple it is a hybrid form, but in a unique state of preservation. Even the massive footprints on the threshold cause one to reconsider the deity that was worshipped in that place (perhaps Ishtar or Baal Hadad, or some other deity?) and to understand better the Israelite's concept of the God who entered the temple in Jerusalem (cf. Ps. 24:7).

Conclusions

In the preceding pages we have noted a high degree of overlap between the biblical terminology of the Jerusalem temple and the excavated architecture of temples in the Levant. A number of temple terms from the Bible were clarified by comparison with the ʿAin Dara temple in particular. Most significant are the side chambers, the recessed doors, the blocked windows, and the piers in the side chambers. Of special importance is the conclusion that the ambulatory described in the biblical accounts is not

80. G. Dalman, *Arbeit und Sitte, vol. IV: Das Haus.* (Hildesheim: Schriften des Deutschen Palästina-Instituts, 1939), 87. The only other parallels for this hapax are Mishnaic Hebrew *lûl,* "room with stairs" (M. Jastrow, *Dictionary of the Targum,* [1903; repr. New York: Judaica Press, 1971], 698) and Arabic *lūl, laulab,* "spiral staircase, screw" (W. Baumgartner and L. Koehler, *Hebräisches und aramäisches Lexikon zum Alten Testament,* 3rd ed. [Leiden: Brill, 1953], 498). In later Hebrew the word also denotes "trap door" (Ouellette, "The Temple of Solomon," [n. 53], 34).

exceptional at all. It belongs to a long-standing tradition of temples with multi-storied side chambers which spans the fourth through first millennia B.C.E. Together with ʿAin Dara these may warrant a new temple category altogether. Although the superstructures of the temples are not preserved, I have identified seven temples with foundations wide enough to serve as supports for a second story.

Several methodological issues also emerge from the current study. It has been my goal to correlate select features of Syrian temples with the Hebrew vocabulary of the Jerusalem temple. The task is hampered by the fact that Israelite architecture has been treated primarily in excavation reports, individual articles, or within broader surveys of material culture.[81] The subject is typically analyzed from the standpoint of *either* language *or* archaeology rather than strenuous consideration of both. In contrast, the most productive text-artifact analyses do not favor one discipline to the exclusion of the another. Rather, they combine text and artifact in an ongoing dialectic.

In preparing this paper, for example, two bodies of evidence (archaeological remains and biblical terminology) were examined independently before they were brought together. This two-stage methodology created a nexus between text and artifact which helped to clarify several of the more enigmatic features in the Jerusalem temple. Such an approach might yield even more favorable results if applied to categories of *realia* whose biblical descriptions are less technical and which contain words of more frequent occurrence.

Although this study is not primarily concerned with the origin of the temple, several observations are worthy of note. First, the Jerusalem temple represents one configuration of a hybrid, long-room temple style. Its features belong to both the Canaanite and north Syrian building traditions. The origin of the temple should therefore not be sought in Phoenicia or northern Syria alone. Rather, its various components reflect a combination of local traditions and cultural borrowing from farther afield. The influence of the Syrian long-room plan and the iconography of Phoenicia, Syria, and Egypt are undeniable. But in the end, neither the Jerusalem temple nor any of its closest parallels are traceable to a single, monolithic temple tradition.

A second observation on origins is that the Jerusalem temple and its parallels bear a striking resemblance to the design and layout of gates throughout the Levant. The similarity of design is noticeable in temples

81. See C. Watzinger, *Denkmäler* [n. 14]; G. E. Wright, *Biblical Archaeology* (Philadelphia: Westminster, 1957); A. Mazar, *Archaeology of the Land of the Bible* (New York: Doubleday, 1990). There are only two monographs which treat architecture in a comprehensive manner: G. R. H. Wright, *Ancient Building*; A. Kempinski et al., *The Architecture of Ancient Israel* (Jerusalem: Israel Exploration Society, 1992).

and gates from the Middle Bronze through Iron Ages. The correspondence between Middle Bronze temples and gates at Shechem and Megiddo cannot be accidental and requires explanation. Likewise, the ʿAin Dara and Tayanat temples share similarities of floor plan, size, and facade with contemporary Iron Age gates in Israel and Syria. The origin of the Jerusalem temple's internal divisions may therefore be traced at least in part to gate architecture in the Levant dating to the second and first millennia B.C.E. The implications of this interpretation are many, and I plan to address them elsewhere.[82]

Finally, our discussion also has a bearing on the date of the Jerusalem temple. The date and design of the ʿAin Dara temple provide new evidence which chronologically anchors the Temple of Solomon in the cultural traditions of the 10th century B.C.E. The traditional date of Solomon early in the Iron Age II is not an issue for those who accept the United Monarchy as an historical fact. This view is still widely held, despite the difficulty of discerning the archaeological phases of the 10th and 9th centuries B.C.E. In recent years, however, these longstanding assumptions have been challenged. There is no longer any consensus concerning the nature of United Monarchy in ancient Israel and its archaeological reflex.[83] Many scholars question whether there was a Solomonic kingdom at all, much less a temple in Jerusalem.[84]

---

82. For now, the following tentative observations can be made. First, the designation "Tower Temple," which includes the temples of Megiddo and Shechem, should in our view be replaced with the name "Gate Temple." Second, gateway architecture has much to tell us about the design of the temple facade and doorways, as well as its theological significance. The door frames between the piers of ancient Near Eastern gates and temples were often rabbeted, which explains the biblical description of temple doorways with four or five recessed frames. Because most of the gateways are assumed to have had large mud brick arches, it is plausible (but not provable) that the entrance to the Jerusalem temple included an arch. Perhaps the best way to visualize the facade of the Jerusalem temple is by viewing the impressive Middle Bronze Age gateways at Ashkelon, Alalakh, and Tel Dan. Third, the iconographic and theological connection between temple and gate should not be underestimated. The temple was literally a gate into the cosmic realm.

83. E.g., M. Gelinas, "United Monarchy–Divided Monarchy: Fact or Fiction?," in *The Pitcher is Broken: Memorial Essays for Gösta W. Ahlström*, ed. S. Holloway and L. Handy (Sheffield: JSOT Press, 1995), 227-37. Solomon's building projects are a central part of this discussion. Monumental architecture from Megiddo, Hazor, Gezer, and smaller sites has been associated with the building projects of 1 Kings 6–9 ever since Y. Yadin proposed the connection in 1958. See W. Dever, "Monumental Architecture in Ancient Israel in the Period of the United Monarchy," in *Studies in the Period of David and Solomon and Other Studies*, ed. T. Ishida (Tokyo: Yamakawa-Shuppansha, 1982), 269-306. The six-chambered gates and occupation levels at Hazor, Megiddo, and Gezer would seem to coincide with the account in 1 Kings 9:15 which mentions these cities by name. At Megiddo, in particular, two palaces with elaborate masonry testify to a grand scale of architecture with cultural origins in the northern Levant. There is considerable debate as to the age of these palaces, but until recently the views of Yadin have prevailed (A. Mazar, "Temples," [n. 18] 382).

84. The debate reflects an ever-widening divide between so-called "minimalists" and

In my view, a comparative study of the architecture of the Solomonic temple is therefore not only valid, but also timely. The current study presents some additional difficulties for those who would revise the chronology of the United Monarchy and downplay the biblical tradition. Here the usefulness of a temple typology— and the place of ʿAin Dara within it— is analogous to the contribution of palaeography in the recent debate over the date of the Siloam inscription.[85] A broad-based typology is not easy to overturn. The three phases at ʿAin Dara span the early Iron Age through the eighth century B.C.E. The middle one is a bridge in the temple sequence between the Late Bronze temple of Hazor H and the eighth-century temple at Tell Tayanat. Its many similarities to the biblical temple corroborate the traditional tenth century date of Solomon's central shrine. The Jerusalem temple therefore takes its place comfortably within the typology of Iron Age temples despite the dearth of architectural remains in Jerusalem.[86]

"maximalists" regarding the degree to which the Hebrew Bible accurately portrays the history of Israel. For the former see G. Wightman, "The Myth of Solomon," *BASOR* 277 (1990): 5-22 and T. Thompson, *Early History of the Israelite People from the Written and Archaeological Sources* (Leiden: Brill, 1992). For the latter see W. Dever, "Archaeology, Ideology, and the Quest for an 'Ancient' or 'Biblical' Israel," *BA* 61 (1998): 39-52. Finkelstein and others have proposed a complete reworking of the stratigraphy ("The Archaeology of the United Monarchy: An Alternative View," *Levant* 28 [1996]: 177-88). According to this revised chronology, the architecture of Megiddo, Hazor, etc., which was previously attributed to the period of Solomon is shifted to the ninth century. In our view this proposal creates as many difficulties as it solves.

85. See R. Hendel, "The date of the Siloam inscription: A rejoinder to Rogerson and Davies," *BA* 59, no. 4 (1996): 233-37. For the most recent discussions see *Jerusalem in Bible and Archaeology: The First Temple Period*, ed. A. Vaughn and A. Killebrew, Society of Biblical Literature Symposium Series 18 (Atlanta: Society of Biblical Literature, 2003) and I. Finkelstein and N. Silberman, *David and Solomon: In Search of the Bible's Sacred Kings and the Roots of the Western Tradition* (New York: Free Press, 2006).

86. New data continue to shed light upon Solomon's temple and the broader tenth-century debate. Most recently, an impressive temple has come to light atop the citadel at Aleppo in Syria, less than 70 kilometers from ʿAin Dara (J. Gonnella, W. Khayyata, K. Kohlmeyer, *Die Zitadelle von Aleppo und der Tempel des Wettergottes* [Münster: Rhema, 2005]). The general design of the temple and the details of its iconography are so reminiscent of the ʿAin Dara Temple that, in my view, the two are likely to have been built by the same king, employing the same craftsmen. Shalmaneser III mentions his sacrifice to the storm god Hadad after his conquest of Aleppo in 853 B.C.E. The phasing of the relief correlates nicely with that of ʿAin Dara and, indirectly, with the biblical account of Solomon's temple.

14

Were There Temples in Ancient Israel?

The Archaeological Evidence

WILLIAM G. DEVER

Introduction

Any answer to the question posed in the title of the paper obviously depends upon the answers given to two prior questions: (1) What do we mean by "temple"?; and (2) How do we assess the evidence in the sources at our disposal, in this case archaeology in particular?

Toward a Functional Definition of a "Temple"

Although Syro-Palestinian archaeologists have been concerned (one might say preoccupied) with locating and excavating temples for more than a century now, one must ask whether most archaeologists would *recognize* one if they saw it. Therein may lie the problem. Almost nowhere in the literature can one find even a working definition of the term "temple," much less a comprehensive model.[1] Only on the basis of such a

1. One of the best studies suggests only that the temple in the ancient world "signifies a residence"; cf. C. Meyers, "Temple, Jerusalem," *Anchor Bible Dictionary*, ed. D. N. Freedman (New York: Doubleday, 1992), 6:351. For other treatments, although similarly with minimal definition, see V. Fritz, "Temple Architecture: What Archaeology Can Tell Us About Solomon's Temple," *Biblical Archaeology Review* 13, no. 4 (1987): 38-49; E. Bloch-Smith, "'Who Is the King of Glory?' Solomon's Temple and Its Symbolism," in *Scripture and Other Artifacts: Essays on the Bible and Archaeology in Honor of Philip J. King*, ed. M. D. Coogan, J. C. Exum, and L. E. Stager (Louisville, KY: Westminster John Knox Press, 1994), 18-31. Horowitz has dealt with the biblical and other ancient Near Eastern textual data on temple-building, but he virtually ignores the archaeological data, and does not even raise the issue

"model" could we test hypotheses that might determine whether or not a given installation may be a temple, or reveal how it once might have functioned within the larger ideological and socio-economic system.

The key word here is not "ideology," but "*function*." That is not because ideology is less significant (we archaeologists are not really "vulgar materialists"), but because (1) actual function is an expression of a temple's structure and furnishings, and these are the attributes best reflected in the archaeological record; and (2) even *intended* function can *best* be recognized in form, perhaps even more so than in texts, since the latter are often excessively idealistic. Thus we shall ask presently whether a building corresponding to the Solomonic Temple described in somewhat fantastic terms in Kings ever actually existed.

You will see at the outset that I am taking a *phenomenological* approach to this topic, an approach for which few archaeologists would make any apology.[2] A temple *is* what it *does*. And even if it is largely a symbol, a temple communicates a social reality, one that reflects its essence.

Since I do not wish to ignore texts, but rather to involve them in a dialogue with artifacts, let me begin with a philological observation. In all the West Semitic languages and dialects of Canaan and later Israel, the common and usually exclusive term for "temple" is "house" (*bêt*). This is true, for instance, in the Ugaritic texts of the Late Bronze Age; in the Iron Age Aramaic royal inscriptions of Bar-Rakkab and others; and, of course, throughout the Hebrew Bible, as well as in Hebrew ostraca and other non-Biblical materials.[3] Indeed classical Hebrew has no word for "temple" other than *bêt*, "house." Solomon's temple is no exception. To be sure, its main hall is designated a *hêkāl* in I Kings, often translated as "nave." The Hebrew, however, is transparently derived from Sumerian É.GAL, which the later Assyrians rendered as *ekallu*, "temple" or *bītu rabû*, the "Great House."[4]

---

of whether Solomon's Temple actually existed. See V. Horowitz, *I Have Built You an Exalted House: Temple Building in the Bible in Light of Mesopotamian and Northwest Semitic Writings* (Sheffield: Sheffield Academic Press, 1992).

2. Cf. W. G. Dever, "The Contribution of Archaeology to the Study of Canaanite and Israelite Religion," in *Ancient Israelite Religion: Essays in Honor of Frank Moore Cross*, ed. P. D. Miller, P. D. Hanson, and S. D. McBride (Philadelphia; Fortress Press, 1987), 209-42. Full references to other relevant literature will be found here.

3. See generally G. A. Barroi, "Temples," in *Interpreter's Dictionary of the Bible*, ed. G. A. Buttrick (New York: Abingdon Press, 1962), 561-68; cf. also Horowitz, *Exalted House*, chapters 1-6.

4. Barrois, "Temples," 561. The only other biblical term that might be construed as referring to a temple in our definition here is *miškan*, from the root *škn*, "to dwell," but it almost always refers to the Tabernacle, or "temporary abode" of God—which the Solomonic temple was designed precisely to replace.

Thus everywhere in the Iron Age—in the Aramaean states, in Phoenicia, in Israel, and elsewhere—a "temple" was any structure that was deliberately conceived and moreover served as the "house of a deity." Since this was usually the national deity, many temples in the Southern Levant were "state temples" of monumental style and proportions. But there were certainly others, local structures that merit the designation "temple." It is neither size, form, nor location that determines whether a structure may be considered a temple, but rather its capacity to *function* as the "house" of the deity, with all the ramifications of that concept.

As any adequate description should, ours both includes and excludes, that is, it specifies. A god's temple or proper "house" is not a household cult-corner, a small outdoor shrine, an open-air sanctuary (all of which are now attested in several examples), or even a large "high place," such as the well known 9th cent. B.C.E. installation at Tel Dan, which I would consider a clear full-scale example of what the Hebrew Bible means by a *bāmâ*.[5] I Kings 12:31 does refer to *bêt (bāttê?) bāmôt*, something like "houses/temples of/on high places," at Dan or elsewhere, but the texts are ambiguous, and I would suggest that the latter Biblical editors were uncertain exactly what the now-condemned "high places" were.[6]

To put it somewhat simplistically, a *real* house suitable for a deity—the place where he resides and where his presence on earth is effectively felt—should have sizeable proportions, walls, a roof, several rooms, a monumental entrance, iconography expressive of the deity's persona and activities, and furnishing or cult paraphernalia appropriate to the carrying out of both public and private rituals. Above all, a structure defined as a "temple" should yield evidence that the deity was conceived as *residing* there symbolically, not merely as having been venerated at that particular place.[7]

---

5. See, with full references, W. G. Dever, "The Silence of the Text: An Archaeological Commentary on 2 Kings 23," in *Scripture and Other Artifacts: Essays on the Bible and Archaeology in Honor of Philip J. King*, ed. M. D. Coogan, J. C. Exum, and L. E. Stager (Louisville, KY: Westminster John Knox, 1994), 143-68; idem, "Ancient Israelite Religion: How to Reconcile the Differing Textual and Artifactual Portraits?" in *Ein Gott allein? JHWH-Verehrung und biblischer Monotheismus in Kontext der israelitischen und altorientalischen Religiongeschichte*, ed. W. Dietrich and M. A. Klopfenstein (Freiburg: University of Freiburg, 1994), 105-25; idem, "Folk Religion in Early Israel. Did Yahweh Have a Consort?" in *Aspects of Monotheism: How God Is One*, ed. H. Shanks (Washington, DC: Biblical Archaeology Society, 1997), 27-56. For the Dan "high place," see A. Biran, ed. *Dan I: A Chronicle of the Excavations, the Pottery Neolithic, the Early Bronze and the Middle Bronze Age Tombs* (Jerusalem: Nelson Glueck School of Biblical Archaeology, 1996), 32-49.

6. For the burgeoning literature on "high places," see now B. Alpert-Nakhai, "What's a Bamah? How Sacred Space Functioned in Ancient Israel," *Biblical Archaeology Review* 20, no. 3 (1994): 19-29.

7. Cf. B. Levine, "On the Presence of God in Biblical Religion," in *Religions in Antiquity: Essays in Memory of Erwin Ramsdell Goodenough*, ed. J. Neusner (Leiden: E. J. Brill, 1968), 71-87.

By these "functional" criteria, I find only two temples attested archaeologically in ancient Israel, that is, in Iron Age Palestine west of the Jordan, namely the 10th-6th cent. B.C.E. Temple in Jerusalem, and the 9th-8th (?) cent. B.C.E. structure at Tel Arad. There may once have been a functioning temple at Beersheba, but none of the relevant data were found in primary context, and Aharoni's argument was based almost entirely on circumstantial and largely negative evidence. And the 8th cent. B.C.E. Ajrûd sanctuary, while clearly cultic in nature, does not exhibit the full range of features that our definition of "temple" would require.[8]

King Solomon's Temple in Jerusalem: Fact or Fancy?

You may find it peculiar that I begin an archaeological discussion with the so-called "Solomonic Temple" in Jerusalem. It is well known that no physical evidence of such a structure survives. Nor is any evidence ever likely to be found, since the Temple Mount where it presumably once stood is off-limits for many reasons and almost certainly will never be investigated in detail by archaeologists. On the basis of the lack of direct archaeological witness, plus a growing skepticism about the historicity of the Biblical texts among "revisionist" Biblicists and others, many scholars have come to regard the Biblical stories of Solomon's Temple in Jerusalem as little more than myths. They believe that the descriptions of this building are simply royalist and priestly propaganda, much of it dating not to the Iron Age but to the Persian or even the Hellenistic era, when the Hebrew Bible is alleged by such "revisionists" to have been composed.[9]

Yet I would argue that no historian who knows even the rudiments of Syro-Palestinian archaeology can any longer dismiss the accounts in I Kings 6-9 as entirely fanciful (although they are, of course, somewhat exaggerated). We now possess a mass of archaeological data that provide a *Sitz im Leben* (not merely a *Sitz im Literatur*), that is, a *real*-life context in which virtually every detail of the Biblical description, despite linguistic

---

8. For references to Beersheva and Kuntillet ʿAjrûd, see Dever, "Silence of the Text."

9. The literature on "revisionism" is too vast to cite, but for orientation see W. G. Dever, "Will the Real Israel Please Stand Up? Archaeology and Israelite Historiography: Part I," *Bulletin of the American Schools of Oriental Research* 297 (1995): 61-80; idem, "Philology, Theology, and Archaeology: What Kind of History Do We Want, and What Is Possible?" in *The Archaeology of Israel: Constructing the Past, Interpreting the Present*, ed. N. A. Silberman and D. Small (Sheffield: Sheffield Academic Press, 1996), 290-310; L. L. Grabbe, ed., *Can a "History of Israel" Be Written?* (Sheffield: Sheffield Academic Press, 1996). For Solomon in particular, see Dever, "Archaeology and the 'Age of Solomon.' A Case- Study in Archaeology and Historiography," in *The Age of Solomon: Scholarship at the Turn of the Millennium*, ed. L. T. Handy (Leiden: E. J. Brill, 1998), 217-51.

difficulties, can be illuminated, indeed explained. And it is instructing that the 30 or more comparative examples of archaeologically attested Bronze and Iron Age temples in Syria-Palestine date almost exclusively to the 15th-8th cents. B.C.E., *not* later, when the Biblical writers are supposed to have "invented" the stories. (What are the statistical odds that they did so—and got the details right?)

The salient features of the Solomonic temple, based at this point solely on the Biblical accounts, can be represented in chart form as follows.

No.	Features or characteristics	References in 1 Kings, 2 Chronicles
1.	Tripartite plan, with three successive rooms along a single axis	1 Kings 6:3; 2 Chron. 3:3-9
2.	Construction in Phoenician style	1 Kings 7:13, 18; 2 Chron. 2:1-16
3.	Overall dimensions of *ca.* 30 by 90 feet, 45 feet high; vestibule and inner sanctum 20 by 20 feet, nave 50 by 20 feet	1 Kings 6:2; 16, 17; 7:9, 10; 2 Chron. 3:3,4
4.	Foundation walls *ca.* 8 feet thick	1 Kings 6:2
5.	Construction of fitted, quarry-dressed foundation stones; reinforcing wood beams inserted every three courses in superstructure; inner walls lined with decorated cedar panels; cedar roof beams	1 Kings 6:6-18; 36
6.	Two bronze columns with capitals flanking entrance of vestibule, elaborately decorated (pomegranates, lilies)	1 Kings 7:15-22; 2 Chron. 3:15-17
7.	Interior decoration of wooden panels carved with gourds, palm trees, cherubs, open flowers, and chains, some overlaid with gold leaf	1 Kings 6:15-32; 2 Chron. 3:5-17
8.	Two carved olivewood, gold-overlaid cherubs in the inner sanctum, 15 feet high and 15 feet from wingtip to wingtip	1 Kings 6:23-28; 2 Chron. 3:10-13
9.	Furnishings of building and forecourt include cast bronze paneled and spoke-wheeled braziers, some with open top, *ca.* 4 feet high; decorated with wreaths, lions, oxen, cherubs, and palm trees	1 Kings 7:27-37; 2 Chron. 9:1-10
10.	Pots, shovels, basins, firepans, and snuffers for offerings	1 Kings 8:48-50; 2 Chron. 4:11-22

Here I can only mention in passing the wealth of archaeological corroboration that we now possess for the Solomonic temple (listed here in reference to the features as numbered in the above table).

(1) The supposedly enigmatic tripartite or "long room" temple plan turns out to be the standard Late Bronze and early Iron Age temple plan throughout Syria and Palestine, with nearly 30 examples now archaeologically attested. Even the dimensions, proportions, and details fit the

FIGURE 1: Reconstruction of the Solomonic Temple (adapted from G. E. Wright, *Biblical Archaeology* [Philadelphia: Westminster Press, 1948], fig. 92).

norm.[10] The "Phoenician" derivation in Kings and Chronicles thus turns out to be quite plausible; there was no native tradition of monumental architecture in Israel's earliest phases of urbanization in Iron IIA, so models had to be borrowed from neighboring peoples in the centuries-old Canaanite tradition.

(2) The dressed masonry with interlaced wooden beam construction seems odd at first glance; but we now know that it was typical of Middle-Late Bronze Age construction in monumental buildings throughout Canaan, with particularly close parallels coming from palatial buildings at Alalakh and Ugarit, as well as at Late Bronze Age Hazor in northern Palestine.[11] Such construction was apparently a practical device for protecting heavy masonry walls with a flexible "break-joint," as in modern construction. As for the Biblical description of "sawn" or chisel-dressed masonry blocks, produced in finished form at the quarries and fitted together at the site "without the sound of a hammer," that also seems odd. So it is, unless one happens to know that *precisely* such dressed, pre-fitted masonry—known as "ashlar" to archaeologists—has been found to characterize monumental or "royal" constructions in Israel *precisely* in, and only in, the 10-9th centuries B.C.E. The finest examples of such ashlar masonry come from Dan, Hazor, Megiddo, Samaria, and Gezer, all of which were probably administrative centers in some sense in the 10th-9th

10. See further Dever, "Contribution," 222-27; cf. also Fritz, "Temple Architecture."

11. Y. Shiloh, *The Proto-Aeolic Capital and Israelite Ashlar Masonry*, Qedem 11 (Jerusalem: Institute of Archaeology, The Hebrew University of Jerusalem, 1979).

centuries B.C.E., and thus under royal administration (cf. I Kings 4). The introduction of such ashlar masonry into Israel is now thought by some to have been due to the "Sea Peoples," Philistines and others, who brought with them, or at least were acquainted with, Mycenaean-style ashlar masonry in Cyprus in the late 13th century B.C.E. Thence it came to the Phoenician coast where it was probably adopted locally. Once again, the Hebrew Bible's references to "Phoenician" artisans and craftsmen in stone makes perfect sense, and the 10th century B.C.E. date is just what we would expect for early Phoenician-Israelite contacts. As for the implication of an unusual style of pre-fitting the stones at the quarry, one must cite ashlar blocks discovered at Megiddo and Gezer precisely in 10th century B.C.E. contexts in monumental buildings and city gates, which exhibit *identical* geometric masons' marks and even traces of red chalk-lines, that is, evidence of advance quarry-fitting (as Yigal Shiloh long ago pointed out).[12]

(5) The Biblical description of lower courses of masonry combined with upper courses overlaid with wooden panels remained mysterious, unparalleled until modern archaeological discoveries provided the answer. At Middle Bronze Age Ebla and at Late Bronze Age Alalakh in Syria, as well as at Late Bronze Age Hazor in northern Palestine, we now have examples of monumental architecture featuring lower dadoes of black basalt (volcanic) stone orthostats, with regularly-spaced drilled holes on the upper sides that are obviously mortises for tenons on the end of wooden panels that were once attached to the orthostats.[13] Once again, the Biblical descriptions, though thought later, are uncannily accurate for the late LB-early Iron Age.

(6) The two columns with elaborate capitals at the entrance of the Solomonic temple, so prominent that they receive the names "Boaz" and "Jachin," in the Hebrew Bible, are also not unique. The standard Middle Bronze, Late Bronze, and Iron Age bipartite and tripartite temples now known throughout Canaan exhibit just such columns, as revealed by two typical surviving column bases flanking the entrance at the vestibule or entrance-porch (the "temple-in-antis" plan that is well known even down to Classical times).[14] The description of the elaborate decoration of the capitals is not entirely clear, but the motifs fit with the rest of the decor (see no. 7 below). Elsewhere, in simpler 10th-9th century B.C.E. royal con-

---

12. Ibid., 63-66.

13. L. Woolley, *Alalakh: An Account of the Excavations at Tell Atchana in the Hatay, 1937-1949* (Oxford: Oxford University Press, 1975), 59-73; Y. Yadin, *Hazor: The Head of All Those Kingdoms* (London: Oxford University Press, 1972), 67-105.

14. Cf. many examples in Shiloh, *Proto-Aeolic Capital*, 40-43; cf. also Bloch-Smith, "King of Glory," 22.

structions, the carved "palmette" capital (previously called "proto-Aeolic"), usually not free-standing but engaged, is typical; it almost certainly represents the stylized "tree-of-life" that goes back to common Late Bronze Age Canaanite motifs (below).

(7) All the motifs of the interior decoration of the temple and its furnishings, formerly subject only to speculation, are now well attested in Canaanite art and iconography of the Late Bronze and Iron Ages. The reference to "chains" is not entirely clear, but it recalls the familiar Late Bronze Age Minoan *guillôche* design, featuring a running row of spirals turning back upon themselves, as for instance on a basalt offering basin from the Area H temple at Hazor. "Open flowers" almost certainly refer to lilies or papyrus blossoms, both of which are exceedingly common motifs in the Late Bronze Age. They are also well represented on numerous Iron Age ivories, such as those from 9th-8th century B.C.E. Samaria, on many seals, and on the painted storejars from the 8th century B.C.E. sanctuary at Kuntillit ᶜAjrûd in the Sinai. "Pomegranates," commonly associated with fertility in the ancient Near East, have Late Bronze-Iron Age parallels in pendants on bronze braziers (below), on a cultic bowl from Lahav, and on many seals. They also appear on ivory priests' wands from several sites, including the now famous 8th century one from chance finds in Jerusalem, bearing the Hebrew inscription "Set apart for the priests of the Temple of . . . h" (restore "Yahweh"), which in all probability comes from the Temple of Solomon.[15]

(8) The term "cherub" now presents no problem whatsoever, although long misunderstood as some sort of chubby, lovable winged creature shooting darts into lovers. The Biblical "cherub" is simply a "mixed creature" of the sort widely known from the 3rd millennium B.C.E. onward in the ancient Near East, usually with the body of a lion, a human head, and wings. From early times the cherub is one of the principal iconographic representations of deities and kings, often occurring in pairs bearing on their backs the king seated on his throne. Such "lion-thrones" occur in Palestine on a well-known 12th century B.C.E. ivory panel from Megiddo, showing a Canaanite king receiving a procession. Later Iron Age examples of cherubs include those on one register of the

---

15. N. Karageoghis, *Cyprus* (Geneva: Nagel Publishers, 1968), figs. 182-85; idem, *Cyprus from the Stone Age to the Romans* (London: Thames and Hudson, 1982), fig. 102; idem, *Les anciens Chypriotes: Entre Orient et Occident* (Paris: Éditions Errance, 1990), 157; Shiloh, *Proto-Aeolic Capitals*, 30-43; O. Keel, *The Symbolism of the Biblical World* (Winona Lake, IN: Eisenbrauns, 1997), fig. 224; A. Lemaire, "Probable Head of Priestly Scepter from Solomon's Temple Surfaces in Jerusalem," *Biblical Archaeology Review* 10, no. 1 (1987): 24-29. See further Bloch-Smith, "King of Glory," 22. It should be noted that the authenticity of this scepter has recently been called into question.

10th century B.C.E. terra cotta cult stand from Taʿanach, on one of the painted storejars from ʿAjrûd (a seated female figure, in my judgment Asherah), on the Samaria and other ivories, and on numerous seals.[16] The symbolism of a *pair* of cherubs, a supposedly "pagan" motif, in the inner sanctum of the Jerusalem temple is now clear. Israel's national god Yahweh sat enthroned on a lion-throne just like all the other deities of the ancient Near East, except that he was invisible—an exceptionally powerful statement of his spiritual presence in his "house."

(9) The references to "lions," of course, overlap with references to cherubs, but the lion often appears in its own right in the Late Bronze and Iron Ages, often carrying a nude female deity riding on its back, almost certainly Asherah. This goddess is widely known in ancient texts as the "Lion Lady" and is much favored in iconography from Egypt all the way to Mesopotamia. Palestinian Iron Age examples of the lion motif would include an ivory box from Megiddo, both 10th century B.C.E. cult stands from Taʿanach, the storejars at Kuntillet ʿAjrûd, several Samaria ivories, and many seals, especially the well known Megiddo seal of "the servant of Jeroboam."[17] "Oxen" may refer to bulls or bull calves. The bull was commonly associated in the Levant with the preeminent Canaanite male deity El, whose titles and imagery were borrowed in early Israel and associated with the new national god Yahweh, as Cross and others have shown. One recalls the famous "golden calf" set up at Mt. Sinai, and again at Bethel when the northern kingdom seceded. Actual Iron Age examples of bulls in cultic context in Palestine include a beautiful bronze bull from a 12th century B.C.E. Israelite open cult-place (the Biblical "high place") in the territory of Mannaseh, an animal on one of the Taʿanach stands, carrying a winged sun-disk on his back (some think it a horse), and many examples on 8th-6th century B.C.E. seals.[18]

Finally, the reference to "palm trees" is clear, as we have seen in discussing the temple's columns and capitals above. Following the late Yigal Shiloh's work on "palmette" capitals, as well as that of Ruth Hestrin and others, the meaning of the familiar "tree" imagery is now beyond doubt. We finally understand the frequent prohibition in the prophetic and

---

16. Keel, *Symbolism*, 81-86, 126, 127, 169-71, 191-93; Shiloh, *Proto-Aeolic Capitals*, 35, 36. For the ʿAjrûd lion/cherub motif, see W. G. Dever, "Asherah, Consort of Yahweh? New Evidence from Kuntillet ʿAjrûd," *Bulletin of the American Schools of Oriental Research* (1984): 29-37. See also Bloch-Smith, "King of Glory," 23-25.

17. See generally n. 16 above. On the Taʿanach stand, see P. W. Lapp, "Taʿanach," *Encyclopedia of Archaeological Excavations in the Holy Land*, ed. M. Avi-Yonah (Jerusalem: Massada Press, 1975) 4:1139-47.

18. A. Mazar, "The 'Bull Site': An Iron Age Open Cult Place," *Bulletin of the American Schools of Oriental Research* 247 (1982): 27-42. On the Taʿanach stand, see n. 17 above. For other representations of bull column-bases or thrones, see Keel, *Symbolism*, figs. 183, 237, 292.

Deuteronomistic literature of trees (*ʾăšērîm*) and the denunciation of Asherah and her hilltop "groves," vividly expressed in the descriptions of Israel's fornication with strange gods "under every green tree and on every high hill" (Isaiah 57: 3-13). Given the capitals that depict the drooping fronds of the palm tree's crown, the columns themselves are clearly stylized palm trees. Indeed we have several Iron Age *naoi*, or terra cotta temple models, that have just such a pair of tree-columns flanking the entrance, complete with Palmette capitals. One comes from 10th century B.C.E. levels at Tell el-Farʿah North, Biblical Tirzah, which for a time in the 9th century B.C.E. served as the capital of the northern kingdom. Others are known from Transjordan.[19] All have other related temple motifs as well, especially the dove, associated with Asherah/Tanit in the Phoenician world; or the "stars of the Pleades," again an Asherah-symbol. A clear example of a Phoenician *naos* is the one from Idalion in Cyprus, probably late 6th century B.C.E., which has two full-represented palm-capitals flanking the doorway, and a nude female standing in the doorway, no doubt Asherah (known as "Astarte" in Cyprus and associated with "Adonis," Semitic *ʾAdon*, "Lord," or the equivalent of Canaanite-Israelite Baʿal).[20]

I have presented here a relatively small sampling of archaeological examples of the individual motifs of the Solomonic temple enumerated in Kings and Chronicles, but we have a number of more or less complete Iron Age temples that may provide even more instructive comparisons. The one usually cited (but of course ignored by the "revisionists") is the small 9th-8th century B.C.E. temple at Tell Tayinat in northern Syria, excavated by the University of Chicago in the 1930s and long since fully published. It is a tripartite building, similar to the Biblical description in both plan and size, exhibiting two columns with lion-bases at the portico. The inner sanctum (the Biblical *dĕbîr*, or "Holy of Holies") has a podium on the rear wall for a representation of the deity. The excavators presented ample evidence for ashlar construction, as shown in some reconstructions.[21] Other examples of Syrian temples from the 9th-8th centuries B.C.E. include the recently-discovered marvelous 9th-8th century B.C.E. acropolis temple at the Aramaic capital of ʿAin Dara, in northern Syria near the Turkish border. [See the article by J. Monson in this volume.] Few archae-

19. See Shiloh, *Proto-Aeolic Capitals*, 27-50; cf. now R. Hestrin, "The Lachish Ewer and the 'Asherah,'" *Israel Exploration Journal* 17 (1987): 212-23; idem, "Understanding Asherah—Exploring Semitic Iconography," *Biblical Archaeology Review* 17, no. 5 (1991): 50-59. For the *naoi*, see, with references, Dever, "Folk Religion," 30-34.

20. P. Gaber, with W. G. Dever, "Was Adonay in Cyprus?" *Odyssey* 2 (1998): 48- 55.

21. See references in n. 10 above. Fritz, "Temple Architecture" is an easily accessible discussion.

ologists or Biblical scholars are aware of this temple, but I have visited it many times. It is of tripartite style, decorated in and out with carved basalt orthostats featuring lions and cherubs. The most stunning feature is a series of four *giant* footsteps carved into the threshold and then the entrance into the main hall—first a pair of feet side by side, then higher up a single left foot followed by a single right foot—the god entering "his house."[22] The effect is overpowering.

The Arad Temple

Between 1962 and 1967 the late Yohanan Aharoni excavated an Iron Age structure at Tel Arad, eighteen miles east of Beersheba. This structure and its interpretation have since become a notorious crux in Syro-Palestinian archaeology—indeed symptomatic of the fundamental epistemological dilemma of "Biblical archaeology" in the minds of its many critics.[23]

The Essential Data

Let us try to separate hard facts (and there *are* some) from fancies. (1) First, the structure is a tripartite building, its rooms arranged along a longitudinal axis. It has a large outer courtyard with a prominent stone altar, probably unroofed to judge from its size. The next room is a much smaller chamber, its only features low benches around the walls. The third room is quite small, slightly elevated and approached by two steps. On either side are two flanking, stylized "horned" altars, on top of which traces of an oily "organic substance," later analyzed as animal fat, were

---

22. See n. 10 above.

23. No final reports have appeared, but the best syntheses are Z. Herzog et al., "The Israelite Fortress at Arad," *Bulletin of the American Schools of Oriental Research* 254 (1984): 1-34; idem, "Arad—An Ancient Israelite Fortress with a Temple to Yahweh," *Biblical Archeology Review* 13, no. 2 (1987): 10-35; D. W. Manor and G. A. Herion, "Arad," *Anchor Bible Dictionary*, ed. D. N. Freedman (New York: Doubleday, 1992), 1:331-36; and, secondarily, Y. Aharoni, "Arad," *Encyclopedia of Archaeological Excavations in the Holy Land*, ed. M. Avi-Yonah (Jerusalem: Masada Press, 1975), 1:74-89. For the principal critiques, see Y. Yadin, "A Note in the Stratigraphy of Arad," *Israel Exploration Journal* 15 (1965): 180; O. Zimhoni, "The Iron Age Pottery of Tel ʿEton and Its Relation to the Lachish, Tell Beit Mirsim and Arad Assemblages," *Tel Aviv* 12 (1985): 63-90; A. Mazar and E. Metzer, "On the Israelite Fortress at Arad," *Bulletin of the American Schools of Oriental Research* 263 (1986): 87-91; D. Ussishkin, "The Date of the Judaean Shrine at Arad," *Israel Exploration Journal* 38 (1988): 142-57. For attempts of leading biblical scholars to use the Arad material, see, e.g., R. Albertz, *A History of Israelite Religion in the Old Testament Period. Volume 1: From the Beginnings to the End of the Monarchy* (Louisville, KY: Westminster John Knox, 1994), 180-81.

reported to have been found. Against the back wall of this "inner sanctum" there was apparently one, then later two, large roughly dressed stone stelae, one smaller than the other. The original one had been tinted with a red substance, possibly red ochre. Later all these stelae had been overturned and covered by fills.

(2) Several items of the temple's original paraphernalia were recovered, although uncertainties stemming from Aharoni's faulty stratigraphy make it impossible to determine their precise date and phasing.[24] A terra cotta offering stand representing a stylized tree may belong to Str. X, undoubtedly 8th cent. B.C.E. Two shallow platters inscribed with the Hebrew letters *qof kap* (probably a abbreviation for *qōdeš kōhănîm*, "consecrated for the priests"), found near the base of the altar, were attributed by Aharoni variously to Str. V or VIII, but both stratigraphy and paleography suggest the latter date, i.e. late 8th cent. B.C.E. A miniature bronze lion was discovered beside the altar, but I can find no information about its precise stratigraphic context (it may also be 8th cent. B.C.E.).[25]

B. Interpretation

The tripartite plan itself had originally suggested to Aharoni that the Arad structure was indeed the temple that he had admittedly been looking for at Arad, following his "discovery" of temples at Lachish and Beer-sheba (much debated). We saw above that this basic tripartite structural form was characteristic of Late Bronze and Iron Age temples throughout the Southern Levant, not least of the Solomonic temple in Jerusalem.

Secondly, what remains of the Arad building's furnishings strongly suggests cultic activities appropriate to a temple, but to no other structure of which we know.

The two inscribed plates at the base of the altar, despite some controversy over the exact meaning of the Hebrew inscription,[26] can only be interpreted as offering-platters. They would have been especially consecrated for temple service, that is, for the "care and feeding of the god in his house," as everywhere in Semitic religion from early times.

The finely-modeled bronze lion may have originally belonged to a well known class of zoomorphic weights. In use in this context, however,

---

24. See references in n. 23 above.

25. For critical discussion, see Herzog et al., "Israelite Fortress," 15-19; Mazar, "Israelite Fortress"; Ussishkin, "Judaean Shrine;" Manor and Herion, "Arad," 333-34.

26. Cf. references in n. 25 above; and add F. M. Cross, "Two Offering Dishes with Phoenician Inscriptions from the Sanctuary in Arad," *Bulletin of the American Schools of Oriental Research* 235 (1979): 75-78.

the lion inevitably recalls the familiar iconography of Asherah, the "Lion Lady." In many Late Bronze Age representations she is depicted riding on the back of a lion. In the Iron Age and later, iconography as well as texts often personify Asherah as the "Lion Lady."[27] Thus we may have once had a *pair* of deities at Arad, as elsewhere.

The stelae in the inner sanctum are perhaps the most significant, especially with regard to the perception of the presence of the god or gods in their "house." Although the preliminary reports are far from clear, it appears that there once stood somewhere a single, red-painted monolith in the inner sanctum (Str. XI?), while later (Str. X-IX?) there was a pair of monoliths against the rear wall, one smaller than the other (in the present reconstruction of the site, replicas of these two are where they supposedly once stood). I think that there can no longer be any doubt that such stelae are precisely the *massebot*, or "standing stones" of the Hebrew Bible, which we always associated in the tradition with epiphanies, sacrifice, covenant-making, and the making of vows. Iron Age examples of such *massebot* include those found at Dan, Tell el-Far^cah N., and other sites, as my student Beth Alpert-Nakhai has recently shown—all of them going back to a long Bronze Age tradition.[28] [See the article by E. Bloch-Smith in this volume.] And in the Arad temple we have by the 8th cent. B.C.E. or so a *pair* of *massebot*; if one is Yahweh, as must be the case, then the other represents his consort Asherah.[29]

The problem here is that all three (?) of these stelae, together with the two stylized "horned" incense altars at the entrance to the inner sanctum, were found not *in situ*, but overturned and covered by a deep fill after the temple had gone out of use, that is, by the end of Str. VII (below). Aharoni had claimed that the two altars, at least, were carefully turned over on their sides and deliberately covered over by a plaster surface, and the published photographs bear him out that far. The original position of the one or two stelae is less clear, but they, too, were somehow put out of use by the end of Str. VII.

Aharoni, of course, saw in these changes in phasing the well-known attempt at the abolishment of local shrines first under Hezekiah in the late 8th cent. B.C.E. (Str. VIII), and then again in the late 7th cent. B.C.E. under Josiah (the final abandonment at the end of Str. VII).[30]

---

27. See references in n. 17 above. For another opinion that the two Arad *massebot* symbolize a pair of deities, see A. Mazar, *Archaeology of the Land of the Bible, ca 10,000-586 B.C.E.* (New York: Doubleday, 1990), 497.

28. See Alpert-Nakhai, "Bamah," and references there.

29. On the cult of Asherah, with full references, see Dever, "Consort of Yahweh?"

30. Cf. Herzog et al., "Israelite Fortress," 22-26; Ussishkin, "Judaean Shrine," 151-53; Manor and Herion, "Arad," 332-34.

Aharoni has sometimes been held up to ridicule as a parade example of the uncritical linking of archaeological data and a naive reading of the Biblical text—the worst of "Biblical archaeology's" many abuses. Some Biblical scholars, however, have seized upon Aharoni's interpretation as one of the rare examples when archaeological discoveries can be directly and legitimately correlated with historical events in, or at least lying behind, the Biblical text. Unfortunately, the difficulty in dating Str. VIII-VII, along with the absence of final published reports, make the kinds of precise correlations that would be required impossible.

As an archaeologist with no particular Biblical interpretation to defend, I would argue that despite differing interpretations the following, minimal statements may be made with confidence on a strictly *archaeological* basis. (1) At one time there was one or more than one stela in the inner sanctum, which must be understood in the Biblical world view as symbolic of the presence of a deity or deities in the temple or "house." (2) At some later time, whether in Str. VIII or by the end of Str. VII, these *massebot* were abolished, and the temple was put out of use. (3) The little pottery that has been published suggests to me independently that Str. VIII should be dated, as Aharoni thought, to the late 8th cent. B.C.E., since it is comparable to that of Lachish III, destroyed by Sennacherib in 701 B.C.E.[31] The pottery of Str. VII then looks to me to be 7th cent. B.C.E. generally.[32] (4) In the light of the ceramic dates suggested here, Aharoni's correlation of the final phases of the Arad temple with the period of the Biblical Hezekiah and Josiah is not at all unreasonable in principle.

Venturing beyond what I think is an archaeological consensus, I would go so far as to suggest that in the light of what we now know of the extent of "popular" religious syncretism in Judah, the Biblical accounts of efforts at reform, however motivated by later Deuteronomistic propaganda, are not in themselves far-fetched. For instance, in an analysis of II Kings 23, a detailed account of Josiah's supposed reforms, I have shown that virtually every detail of this notoriously difficult condemnation of "popular religion" can be illuminated by archaeological data from the

31. The only Arad pottery that is published is Herzog et al., "Israelite Fortress," figs. 5-29, which I insisted upon having as then-editor of the *Bulletin of the American Schools of Oriental Research.* Zimhoni, Mazar, and Ussishkin (above, n. 23) then commented. For the Str. VII pottery, see fig. 22; note especially such typically *late* eighth/early seventh cent. B.C.E. forms as the rilled-rim cooking pot (fig. 22:6), "hippo" storejars (fig. 22: 18, 19), and simple jugs (fig. 22: 10). So also Mazar and Netzer, "Israelite Fortress," 84, 90; Ussishkin, "Judaean Shrine," 150, 151; Zimhoni, "Iron Age Pottery," 84, 85.

32. See Herzog et al., "Israelite Fortress," fig. 25; note the very late shallow plate (fig. 25: 1) and the stump-based lamp (fig. 25: 14). Mazar and Netzer, Ussishkin, and Zimhoni all date Str. VII to the seventh cent. B.C.E. as well; see "Israelite Fortress," 88-90; Ussishkin, "Judaean Shrine," 152, 153; Zimhoni, "Iron Age Pottery," 84, 85.

8th-6th cents. B.C.E.[33] Does this "corroborate" the Biblical story? Of course not, certainly not in its theological dimensions, but it does caution us against dismissing Biblical historiography out of hand, simply because we moderns are skeptical. Sometimes the Biblical writers could and did produce a plausible history of actual events. That will be unwelcome news to the "revisionists," but then most presentations of *data* are to these "troublers of Zion," who are increasingly becoming ideologues, indeed demagogues.[34] It is the *archaeological* data, of which they are so conspicuously ignorant, that decisively refute them.

One matter of interpretation of the Arad temple remains, although that may be of interest only to specialists, namely the overall chronological framework. Since precise correlations with Biblical and other texts, and therefore historical "dead reckoning," are premature pending final publication (if ever), I would argue that we can only go on the scant pottery published thus far, principally in *BASOR* 254 (1984). The Arad pottery published there has been analyzed by Zeev Herzog and Miriam Aharoni, by David Ussishkin, by Amihai Mazar, by the late Orna Zimhoni, and by myself.[35] Without going into the complex details of late Judean ceramic typology, the essential differences of opinion can be presented succinctly in chart form.

Str.	**Y. Aharoni 1967, 1968, 1975**	**M. Aharoni 1981; 1985**	**Herzog *et al.* 1984**	**Zimhoni 1985**	**Mazar 1986**	**Ussishkin 1988**	**Dever**
XII: Bamah?	12th-11th c.	12th-11th c.	12th-11th c.	10th c.	10th c.?		10th c.
XI: Temple?	late 10th c.	late 10th c.	late 10th c. (925 B.C.E.)	9th c.	9th c.		mixed, 10th-8th c.
X: Temple *refounded?*	9th c.	1981 = late 9th/8th c. 1985= early 8th c.	mid-9th c.	early 8th c.	8th c.	8th c.	early 8th c.
IX	early 8th c.	mid 8th c.	8th c.	mid 8th c.	8th c.	8th c.	mid 8th c.
XIII	late 8th c.	late 8th c.	late 8th c.	late 8th c.	late 8th c	late 8th c.	late 8th c.
VII	7th c.	7th c.				Temple founded	
				7th/6th c.	7th/6th c	7th/6th c	7th/6th c.
VI	7th/6th c.	(586 B.C.E.) 7th/6th c.			(586 B.C.E.)		

33. See Dever, "Ancient Religion" and "Silence of the Text."

34. See the references in n. 9 above.

35. See nn. 32, 33 above, and add M. Aharoni, "The Pottery of Strata 12-11 of the Iron Age Citadel at Arad," *Eretz-Israel* 15 (1981): 181-204 (Hebrew); idem, "On the Israelite Fortress at Arad," *Bulletin of the American Schools of Oriental Research* 258 (1985): 73.

A glance at this convenient chart, which is not duplicated elsewhere, reveals several significant convergences. (1) The "high" chronology of Aharoni and his associates for the early strata at Arad (Str. XII-X) is strongly contested by several leading scholars who are experienced stratigraphers and have specialized in Iron age pottery. (2) There is general skepticism regarding an "early *bāmâ*." (3) Only when we come to Str. VIII—relatively late in the temple's history—is there an overall consensus: the late 8th cent. B.C.E. And one scholar, Ussishkin, would place the founding of the temple even later, in Str. VII-VI.[36] (4) Aharoni's description of a "radical alteration" of the temple, which he attributed to Hezekiah's reputed reforms in the late 8th cent. B.C.E., is possible, but unproven. Not only is his "higher chronology" suspect, but the evidence for such things as the "surfacing over" of the two incense altars and the stelae, as first reported by Aharoni and then later by Herzog *et al.*, is conflicting.[37] (5) The only *overall* agreement among critics is that in Str. VII-VI, in Josiah's time in the late 7th cent. B.C.E., there stood a tripartite temple at Arad, after which (i.e., in Str. VI), the structure went out of use. It *could* have been abolished by Josiah, or, alternatively, it could have been destroyed by the Neo-Babylonians in 587/586 B.C.E. (6) Zimhoni's lowering of dates for Str. XI and the *presumed* founding of the temple seems the most radical (i.e., 9th cent. B.C.E.), but it does not necessarily conflict with either Mazar's or my dates (mine even allowing for an 8th cent. B.C.E. possibility).

Finally, I should note that while Aharoni's Israeli colleagues have been especially harsh in criticism of his faulty stratigraphic methods (including the lack of any sections) and have not hesitated to lower his ceramic dates accordingly, sometimes radically, they have *not* addressed what I consider the essential problem, namely the fact that the pottery as published is far from stratigraphically secure, and therefore it may not be homogeneous—indeed, it often appears to be *mixed*. Zimhoni, for instance, has confronted the problem, but only obliquely, arguing that the pottery of the critical Str. X- VIII is so close in date that the major forms overlap. Elsewhere, and more recently, she has argued for a similar "long continuity" of ceramic forms in the north, in the 10th-9th cent. B.C.E.[38]

I am somewhat doubtful of this, on principle. I suspect, rather, that many of the published assemblages, even from some contemporary exca-

---

36. Ussishkin, "Judaean Shrine," 155.

37. Cf. Herzog et al., "Israelite Fortress," 22, 23; Mazar and Netzer, "Israelite Fortress," 89; Ussishkin, "Judaean Shrine," 154, 155; Manor and Herion, "Arad," 334. For a photograph showing the two square altars and the *massebot* lying on their sides, with the overlying debris/fill partially sectioned through, see Herzog et al., "Israelite Fortress," fig. 24.

38. Cf. Zimhoni, "Iron Age Pottery"; idem, "Two Ceramic Assemblages from Lachish Levels III and II, *Tel Aviv* 17 (1990): 3-52.

vations, are *stratigraphically mixed*. If true, that would mean that "intrusive" sherds from below, and even perhaps from above, have given a misleading impression of a *long* time-span for some ceramic sequences, whereas the actual use-period may have been much shorter. Thus I would regard the published pottery of Arad Str. XI as neither "10th cent. B.C.E." (Aharoni, Herzog *et al.*) *or* "9th cent. B.C.E." (Zimhoni, Mazar), but *both*, i.e., mixed—with some forms clearly dating even to the 8th cent. B.C.E. as far as I am concerned.[39]

Only full publication of the pottery, plus *much* more sophistication than revealed in the latest ceramic analyses, will confront the above issues adequately. Meanwhile, the date of the destruction or abandonment of the Arad temple is much clearer than the date of its foundation. Nevertheless, "Solomonic" or not (which I doubt), the Arad temple, as our *only* surviving, archaeologically-attested ancient Israelite temple, provides us with unique and invaluable insight into the nature of actual Israelite religious belief and practice—not simply the "official" cult portrayed so idealistically by the writers and final redactors of the Hebrew Bible.

Were there "temples" in ancient Israel? Of course! Indeed, the very attempt in the Hebrew Bible to *deny* by and large the existence of local sanctuaries and temples outside of Jerusalem is our best evidence that they did exist. Archaeology only confirms what we should have known all along—and would have known, had we been "reading between the lines" in the Biblical texts.

---

39. See note 31.

IV

Monotheism, Monolatry, and Polytheism

15

Monotheism in Ancient Egypt

JAMES P. ALLEN

Ancient Egypt has long been regarded as the paragon of polytheism, and deservedly so. The list of gods in a recently published dictionary of the ancient Egyptian language contains more than 1400 names, ranked from "major" to "obscure." While most of the names fall into the latter category, some five dozen can be considered gods of the first or second rank, worshipped in temples or mentioned in texts throughout most of ancient Egyptian history. Egypt's world view was basically polytheistic for the entire lifetime of its ancient religion, from the fourth millennium B.C.E., when its gods first appear in recognizable images, to the fifth century C.E., when Christians finally closed the last of the ancient temples. In fact, polytheism was so much a part of Egyptian thought that the early Christian Egyptians easily tolerated the plural word "gods" in their own personal names.

Yet despite its fundamental and persistent polytheism, ancient Egypt also gave birth to the world's earliest recorded monotheistic religion—that espoused by the pharaoh Akhenaten at the end of the fourteenth century B.C.E.—the era known as the Amarna Period, from the modern name of Akhenaten's capital city. The focus of this religion was the natural phenomenon of light, which Akhenaten saw as the prime force in the universe. At the beginning of his reign Akhenaten depicted this force as, and identified it with, the traditional Egyptian sun-god Re-Harakhti—that is, the sun (Re) appearing as ruler of the world at dawn (Harakhti). But the god was given a new didactic name, which was to serve as the credo of Akhenaten's religion: "The living one, Re-Harakhti, who becomes active in/from the Akhet (the space just below the visible horizon) in his identity of the light that is in the sun-disk." By Akhenaten's third year, the traditional depiction of Re-Harakhti, as a falcon or falcon-headed human, had been abandoned and replaced by the image of the sun disk (or Aten, the Egyptian word for "sun-disk") with multiple rays. This change served to disassociate Akhenaten's theology even further from traditional notions of divinity. It also emphasized the abstract nature of his god: the new image was not an icon to be worshipped but merely a large-scale version of the hieroglyph for "light."

Akhenaten's religion seems to have begun as another example of Egyptian henotheism, the practice of stressing the primacy of one god over all others. The didactic name of the new god was written in two cartouches, like those of the pharaoh, indicating his domination in the pantheon. The god's rule was proclaimed by means of a jubilee festival, like that celebrated by pharaohs in their thirtieth regnal year. Eventually, however, the new god was proclaimed not just as the greatest but as the only god, "with no other except him" (as Amarna texts say). The names, images, and avatars associated with the traditional gods—even the word *nṯr* "god" itself—were avoided. At this point the new religion moved from henotheism to true monotheism.

Akhenaten's monotheism differs from that of other religions in the nature of its god. Unlike the transcendent deity of Judaism, Christianity, or Islam, Akhenaten's god is dependent on nature: it comes into the world only through the medium of a natural phenomenon, the disk of the sun ("in his identity of the light that is in the sun-disk," as the didactic name puts it). It is also more a natural force than a personal god: though it can be prayed to and worshipped, it never speaks to its worshippers in return.

In other respects, however, Akhenaten's creed has some of the classic features of monotheistic religions. Like ancient Israelite religion, Christianity, and Islam, it is a secondary religion, one that arose in contrast to existing beliefs. It is also a revealed religion—the first to be documented in history. The Amarna texts constantly speak of Akhenaten's "teaching of life," and Akhenaten's own hymn to the god proclaims "you are in my heart, and there is no other who knows you except your son, Akhenaten." Like many monotheistic religions, Akhenaten's religion eventually lost its tolerance for other conceptions of divinity. Sometime after his ninth year, the pharaoh began an active campaign of persecution against other forms of Egyptian religion, erasing the names of individual gods and changing the plural "gods" to the singular "god" on monuments throughout Egypt. At the same time he purged the didactic name of his own god from any possible association with the traditional religion. The name now became "The living one, the sun, ruler of the Akhet, who becomes active in/from the Akhet, in his identity of the light that comes in the sun-disk." This alteration replaced the name Re-Harakhti by the neutral expression "the sun, ruler of the Akhet;" substituted a neutral word for "light" in place of the original word *šw*, which was also the name of one of the Egyptian gods; and divorced the notion of the god from its physical medium by changing "the light that is in the sun-disk" to "the light that comes in the sun-disk."

The contrast between Akhenaten's monotheistic theology and traditional Egyptian polytheism is so striking that it is difficult to judge the relationship between them. Some Egyptologists have seen little in common between the two. To James Henry Breasted, writing in the early years of the last century, Akhenaten's religion was an enlightened precursor of Judeo-Christian monotheism, preached in vain to a world still enthralled by the darkness of polytheism.[1] Other scholars, however, have made a more reasoned attempt to understand how the idea of monotheism might have arisen within a polytheistic world view. One prominent early theory argued that Egyptian religion had originally been monotheistic and had only "degenerated" into polytheism after the founding of the Egyptian state; in this view, Akhenaten's theology could be seen as an attempt to return Egyptian religion to its monotheistic roots.[2]

The arguments for a primitive monotheism of this sort have long been discredited,[3] but the notion has persisted that monotheism itself might have existed in some form within Egyptian religion before Akhenaten.[4] Proponents of this view have pointed to a number of textual features suggesting that Egyptian theologians had begun to perceive an underlying unity beneath the multiplicity of their gods as early as the Middle Kingdom, some seven centuries before Amarna.

Egyptian wisdom literature, which appears at the beginning of the second millennium B.C.E., rarely refers to individual gods of the Egyptian pantheon. Instead, it normally uses just the term *nṯr* "god" or "the god":

> Great is the blessing of god . . .
> He makes the ignorant become the wise,
> the hater become the lover.
> He makes the small surpass the great,
> the one at the end be first, . . .
> He teaches the dumb to speak
> and opens the ears of the deaf.
>
> ("Teaching of a Man for his Son")

---

1. J. H. Breasted, *The Dawn of Conscience* (New York: Scribner's, 1933), 305-6.

2. See H. Junker, *Die Götterlehre von Memphis*, Sitzungsberichte der Preussischen Akademie der Wissenschaften, Philosophisch-historische Klasse 1939 (Berlin: de Gruyter, 1940); É. Drioton, *La religion égyptienne dans ses grandes lignes* (Cairo: Éditions de la Revue du Caire, 1945), and idem, "Le monothéisme de l'ancienne Égypte," *Cahiers d'histoire égyptienne* 1 (1945): 149-68.

3. H. Brunner, "Monotheismus," *Lexikon der Ägyptologie* 4 (Wiesbaden: Harrassowitz, 1980), 200.

4. E. Otto, "Monotheistische Tendenzen in der altägyptischen Religion," *WO* 2 (1955): 99-110; S. Morenz, *Die Heraufkunft des transzendenten Gottes in Ägypten*, Sitzungsberichte der Preussischen Akademie der Wissenschaften 109, 2 (Berlin: Akademie-Verlag, 1964).

Passages such as this sound almost biblical, and can easily suggest that the Egyptian writer had in mind a single divine authority similar to the god of the Bible.

Ancient Egyptian cosmogonies consistently refer to a single god as the origin of all creation, though in this case by name rather than anonymously. In early texts this is most often the god Atum, the primal singularity who evolved into the multiplicity of creation; or the sun god Re, the ultimate evolution of Atum, whose rising at the first dawn began the process of life. In the centuries immediately preceding Akhenaten, however, Egyptian theologians focused their attention on the god Amun as the prime cause. Unlike creators such as Atum and Re, who are a part of the world they have created, Amun was seen as transcendent, existing apart from creation. The very name Amun means "hidden," a reference to the notion that the god's true being cannot be perceived in the immanent phenomena of nature. Whether the creator was viewed as immanent or transcendent, however, his existence reflects a primal monotheism. It can also be seen as evidence for the underlying unity of the divine. This is particularly evident in the case of Atum: though he evolved into the forces and elements of the created world—which the Egyptians recognized as gods—he continues to exist as a single god in his own right.

Egyptian theologians regularly solved such conceptual paradoxes by means of syncretism, the practice of combining one or more gods into a composite deity, who bore the names of the component gods but was conceived and addressed as a single being. Re-Harakhti, for example, combines the natural force of the sun (the god Re) with the power of kingship (the god Harakhti, or Horus of the Akhet) in a theoretical construct that expresses the role of the sun as the dominant force in nature. Similarly, the god Re-Atum expresses the unity of the original material source of the world (Atum) with its ultimate evolution, the sun. Such constructs allow for the simultaneous experience of the divine as both singular and diverse, in much the same way that the notion of the Trinity allows Christians to understand three distinct aspects of god within a single deity.

Underlying the practice of syncretism is the realization that one god can also be seen as an aspect or manifestation of another. The Egyptian term is *ba*—the form in which or the means by which something can be perceived. Most Egyptian syncretisms involve only two or three gods, but in theory, at least, all the gods could be understood as *ba*s of a single deity. Evidence for such a conception of divinity can be seen in the text known as the "Litany of Re," first attested about two hundred years before Akhenaten, in which the god Re is addressed "in all his evolutions" as 75 different gods. It also appears in a somewhat different form as early as the Pyramid Texts, about 2400 B.C.E., where the deceased king, united with Re, is said in turn to "become completed in/as every god" (Spell 215).

Cosmogony and syncretism reflect two theoretical solutions to the problem of the one and the many, as Jan Assmann has pointed out.[5] The relationship can be seen either as one of generation, in which the one produces the many, or as one of emanation, in which the one is present in the many. In ancient Egypt both relationships existed simultaneously, although theories of emanation were most thoroughly developed by Ramessid theologians, after the Amarna revolution. In Amarna monotheism itself, however, the concept of the *ba*, or emanation of the god, is absent. Only generation is present: the god continually recreates the multiplicity of the world, but always exists apart from his creation. In this sense, too, Akhenaten's religion is comparable to more familiar forms of monotheism.

It is tempting to see the theory of emanation as the Ramessid Period's answer to Amarna monotheism, as Assmann does. Before Amarna the dominant theory was in fact one of generation, but the notion of emanation was not a Ramessid invention. The practice of syncretism, which is predicated on the idea that two or more deities can share a single identity, goes back to the earliest periods of Egyptian history, and the cosmogony of Atum, which is the ultimate expression of emanation, is already fully developed in the Pyramid Texts of the mid-third millennium. Like the multiple gods of traditional Egyptian religion, differing perceptions of the unity of god also seem to have existed in harmony within the traditional religion for much of its history.

Amarna religion can be viewed as a logical culmination of one such perception—that which understood the one god as the generative source of all gods, in the same way that a parent generates his or her children. Ramessid theology is a logical culmination of the other view—that the one god is present, as emanation, in the multiplicity of all the gods.

In a sense, what I am suggesting here is a Hegelian synthesis between two opposing theses of modern Egyptology. One thesis sees Akhenaten's ideas as totally derivative of concepts already present in Egyptian theology well before Amarna.[6] The other thesis, proposed by Erik Hornung, views Akhenaten's theology—and his monotheism—as a radical innovation.[7]

---

5. J. Assmann, *Moses the Egyptian: the Memory of Egypt in Western Monotheism* (Cambridge, MA: Harvard University Press, 1997), 192-207.

6. The most extreme expression of this view is F. J. Giles, *Ikhnaton* (Rutherford, NJ: Fairleigh Dickinson University Press, 1970).

7. E. Hornung, *Der Eine und die Vielen* (Darmstadt: Wissenschaftliche Buchgesellschaft, 1971), trans. J. Baines as *Conceptions of God in Ancient Egypt* (Ithaca, NY: Cornell University Press, 1982); idem, "Monotheismus im pharaonischen Ägypten," in *Monotheismus im Alten Israel und seiner Umwelt*, ed. O. Keel, Biblische Beiträge 14 (Freiburg: Universitätsverlag, 1980), 84-97.

By far the most influential interpretation in modern Egyptology is the latter. Hornung dismisses features such as those I have just described as evidence for Egyptian monotheism outside of Amarna. The use of the neutral term *nṯr* "god" in wisdom literature, for example, is plausibly explained as an attempt at generalization, making the texts universally applicable no matter which god the reader understands by the term. The uniqueness of the creator is seen as explicitly contrastive with the diversity of his creation: oneness is a negative concept, a feature of the pre-creation universe, in contrast to the multiplicity of daily human experience. Rather than reflecting an underlying sense of the oneness of god, syncretism is understood, in Hornung's words, as a "counter-current to monotheism," which keeps henotheism from turning into monotheism by showing that a single god is not isolated from all others.[8]

This analysis of the evidence is a more informed version of earlier theories such as that espoused by Breasted. Like Breasted, however, Hornung is then forced to see the monotheism of Amarna as essentially alien to traditional Egyptian religion: in his words, "Monotheism does not arise from the gradual accumulation of 'tendencies' in that direction, but requires a radical about-turn of thought, such as occurred under Akhenaten."[9]

Hornung is certainly right in pointing out the distinction between Akhenaten's monotheism and the earlier understanding of god, but the difference was not necessarily as severe as he supposes. What was radical about Akhenaten's theology was not its proclamation of the oneness of god but its insistence on exclusivity. Traditional Egyptian religion, like Egyptian thought, reflects a polyvalent logic: different explanations of a phenomenon are seen as complementary rather than mutually exclusive. To take but one example, creation accounts centered on Atum, Re, Amun, or a number of other gods are not competing cosmogonies, as earlier Egyptologists thought, but rather complementary explanations of the creation—different facets of an essentially uniform understanding of how the world came into being. In the same way, the polyvalent logic of Egyptian thought could easily have allowed an appreciation of the underlying oneness of god to coexist with traditional Egyptian polytheism—and in fact, the evidence suggests that it did so, long before Akhenaten.

The well-established henotheism of traditional Egyptian religion does not in itself rule out the simultaneous appreciation of god as one, any more than it excludes a polytheistic world view. The best evidence for this is the phenomenon of syncretism, which unites the simultaneous

8. E. Hornung, *Der Eine und die Vielen*, 89.

9. E. Hornung, "Monotheismus im pharaonischen Ägypten," 91.

view of god as both many and one. In the same way, the creator of Egyptian cosmogonies continued to exist as a single god despite the multiplicity of his "evolutions."

This is not to say that Egyptian religion was essentially a disguised monotheism, monotheism with a polytheistic face. In fact, insofar as it was appreciated at all, the perception of god as essentially one was probably limited to a few Egyptian theologians at any one time. For ordinary Egyptians, however, it may well be that the *experience* of god was essentially monotheistic. While they continued to understand the world around them in polytheistic terms, they also related to the divine one god at a time—not by simply selecting one of the many Egyptian gods to relate to, but rather by identifying their uniform notion of "god" with a particular god, depending on the particular situation. This, I think, rather than—or in addition to—simple pragmatism, is the reason for the use of the neutral term *nṯr* in wisdom texts. The authors of these texts are not espousing a particular theology but are reflecting instead their appreciation of humanity's relationship to the divine in general—not "a god" of polytheism or "the god" of henotheism but simply "god."

In this understanding of the world, what Akhenaten invented was not the notion that god is one but the belief that god is *only* one. Insofar as monotheism is defined as exclusive in this way, his religion is in fact the first recorded instance of true monotheism. But this is not the same as saying that Akhenaten was the first to appreciate the underlying oneness of god. What Akhenaten introduced to the world is rather the first recorded instance of univalent logic—the notion that one and only one explanation of reality can be true. It is this characteristic, rather than his understanding of the divine, that was new and radical in Egyptian thought; and it is this feature of Akhenaten's teaching, more than any other, that ultimately doomed his religion to failure.

16

Concepts of God in Israel and the Question of Monotheism

NILI FOX

The nature of Israelite religion in the monarchic period has been described by assorted terms: monotheism, monolatry, henotheism, and polytheism. Essentially, the process of labeling is based on divergent interpretations of the biblical and archaeological evidence. Some of the controversy actually centers on common variants found in definitions of the terms, thereby focusing on philosophical issues.[1] To complicate mat-

1. The following definitions are based on a combination of scholarly interpretations (Theodore Ludwig, "Monotheism" in *EncRel* 10:68-76; Manfried Vogel, "Monotheism" in *EJ* 12:260-63; W. Holsten, "Henotheismus" and "Monolatrie" in *Die Religion in Geschichte und Gegenwart*, 3rd ed., ed. K. Galling (Tübingen: J. C. B. Mohr, 1959-65), 3:225, 4:1105-6; Michiko Yusa, "Henotheism" in *EncRel* 6:266-67; Zwi Werblowsky, "Polytheism" in *EncRel* 11:436-39). They are clearly based on Western thought and only serve as basic categories for discussion purposes.

MONOTHEISM presupposes the unity of the divine-oneness in all aspects of the godhead. God is the creator of the world yet is distinct from it. In the strict sense, God is perceived as perfect, everlasting, and all-powerful. God is a personal deity worthy of being worshipped by all creatures. A distinction is drawn between stages of monotheism. Explicit monotheism maintains a definite denial of the existence of other gods while implicit monotheism, the earlier phase, does not.

MONOLATRY understands the oneness of the godhead only in reference to worship because ontologically there is a plurality of gods. The exclusive worship of a god within a certain social group is enforced by prohibitions of allegiance to other deities.

HENOTHEISM is conceptually similar to monolatry in that a single god is worshipped even though a plurality of gods is acknowledged. The terms henotheism and monolatry are often used interchangeably since distinctions in meaning are blurred. Henotheism is sometimes distinguished from monolatry in that allegiance to a specific deity is temporary rather than long-lasting. Thereby, only at a certain time and place is devotion offered exclusively to a single deity.

POLYTHEISM indicates the recognition and worship of a plurality of gods, each independent and co-eternal. The system is often perceived in terms of a pantheon with a clearly

ters, inherent in religions are aberrations that cross boundaries and blur the categories. For example, can or should a system be labeled monotheistic if it incorporates other divine beings, regardless of their stature *vis-à-vis* the Supreme God? How is such a system to be understood? These questions are repeatedly raised in studies on "Israelite monotheism."[2]

The goal of the present investigation is not simply to reevaluate the biblical and archaeological material yet again, but rather to approach the problem with additional data in hand. One discipline that can be utilized to study religions in antiquity is anthropology. Information derived from cultural studies of religious concepts and practices, specifically those pertaining to monotheistic ideas in non Jewish, Christian, or Islamic societies, can be analyzed in terms of belief systems and ritual processes. It should be noted *a priori* that these do not serve as models per se for the religion of ancient Israel. Clearly, no historical connections have been established between the cultures in question nor are similarities in environment and social structure factors for comparison. In general, cultural attributes of different societies, both ancient and modern, are particular and must be viewed primarily in their own setting, even if they tend to display certain universal human characteristics. Yet despite the limitations, studies of living peoples offer alternatives for understanding the complexities of religion.

Anthropological Theories on the Development of Monotheism

In the late nineteenth and early twentieth century, the two prevailing schools of thought on the development of monotheism were influenced by evolutionist views. The anthropologist Edward Tylor and his followers held that monotheism, the apex of complexity, evolved from earlier stages of polytheism. The most primitive phase, animism, the worship of

---

defined stratification of the divinities. The position of chief god, however, is not consistently occupied by the same deity. Polytheism is characterized by a highly developed mythology.

2. Especially applicable to this study are Baruch Halpern's interpretations in "'Brisker Pipes than Poetry': The Development of Israelite Monotheism," in *Judaic Perspectives on Ancient Israel*, ed. J. Neusner, B. A. Levine, E. S. Frerichs (Philadelphia: Fortress, 1987), 77-115; "Jerusalem and the Lineages in the Seventh Century BCE: Kinship and the Rise of Individual Moral Liability," in *Law and Ideology in Monarchic Israel*, ed. B. Halpern and D. W. Hobson, JSOT Supplement 124 (Sheffield: Sheffield Press, 1991), 11-107 (especially 77-91). Other recent pertinent studies include, among others, Adrian Schenker, "Le monothéisme israélite: un dieu qui transcende le monde et les dieux," *Biblica* 78 (1997): 436-48; Mark Smith, *The Origins of Biblical Monotheism: Israel's Polytheistic Background and the Ugaritic Texts* (New York: Oxford University Press, 2001); idem, *The Early History of God: Yahweh and the Other Deities in Ancient Israel* (Grand Rapids: Eerdmans, 2002).

countless spirits, was followed by the worship of mainly anthropomorphic deities, a more complex form of polytheism.[3] In answer and opposition to this theory, the "Ur-monotheism" group, led by Andrew Lang and Wilhelm Schmidt, asserted that belief in a supreme being was original to humankind and that polytheism was a later development, the result of contamination and degeneration.[4]

Evolutionist theories about monotheism have not been borne out by rigorous ethnographic studies and consequently were abandoned. It was found instead that monotheistic and polytheistic ideas could actually coexist within a single society. Paul Radin's work is important in this area.[5] Radin discovered that the notion of a Supreme, Creator God is prevalent in the Native American and Polynesian societies he investigated. Yet he noticed that when it came to actual worship, most members of the society had no difficulty worshipping other divinities, sometimes to the exclusion of the Supreme Deity. What is most revealing is his observation that religious thought varies markedly between different groups in society. For example, among the Native American Dakota tribe, what is perceived as a pantheon by most members of the society is explained as aspects of the Supreme God by certain members of the tribe. The latter point of view is the creed of the priests. In contrast, among the populace the sixteen aspects of the godhead are perceived as sixteen distinct deities.[6] Based on his research, Radin concluded that monotheistic ideas were manifest among the intellectuals or philosophers of society, in simple cultures the shaman, medicine man, and priest. Radin explained this phenomenon as the expression of a certain temperament of individuals who picture the world as a unified whole postulating some First Cause.[7] Radin assumed that a limited number of explicit monotheists exists in every society, no matter how simple or complex, but that their ideas frequently are restricted to a special group. It seems that the moment the idea leaves the protected atmosphere of its creators, it is transformed into notions hardly envisioned by the originators.[8] Therefore, for modern historians of religion the issue is not the inception of a monotheistic philosophical view,

---

3. Edward Tylor, *Primitive Culture: Researches into the Development of Mythology, Philosophy, Religion, Language, Art, and Custom*, vols. 1 and 2 (London: J. Murray, 1913 [originally 1871]), esp. 2:331-55.

4. Andrew Lang, *The Making of Religion* (New York: AMS, 1968 [originally London, 1898]), esp. 173-293; Wilhelm Schmidt, *The Origin and Growth of Religion: Facts and Theories* (New York: Lincoln MacVeagh, 1931), esp. 167-290.

5. Paul Radin, *Monotheism among Primitive Peoples*, 2nd ed. (Basel: Ethnographical Museum, 1954); idem, *Primitive Religion: Its Nature and Origin* (New York: Viking, 1937), 254-67.

6. Radin, *Monotheism*, 19-21.

7. This idea is supported by Robin Horton's findings on conversion in Africa ("African Conversion," *Africa* 16 [1971]: 103).

8. Radin, *Primitive Religion*, 266-67.

but rather the question of how it prevails as a religion and is actualized in practice. Although Radin's theory that monotheistic ideas are attested cross-culturally remains unproven, his observations about diverse understandings of the divine within a single culture is instructive for comprehending how systems of religion can operate in society.

Concepts of God in Africa

A variety of studies of traditional African religions are also instructive for the purpose of this inquiry because they present a picture of beliefs and practices that seem to cross categories of religious systems and often appear paradoxical. John Mbiti, who has researched African religions extensively, examined cult practices and ideas about God in close to 300 African peoples who follow traditional native religions.[9] His findings are based on data derived from a combination of published fieldwork researched by anthropologists (dated mostly to the mid-twentieth century, although some are early twentieth or late nineteenth century), unpublished papers, and oral testimony. Although some of the data are fragmentary and the reliability of certain sources is questionable, the bulk of the information is believed to be accurate and seems to reflect native African thought rather than the syncretism of Christian or Moslem concepts.[10] For most African people God is omniscient, omnipresent, and omnipotent. Expressed ontologically, God is the origin and the sustainer of all things. While African religion is certainly not homogeneous, every ethnic group seems to hold the notion of God as the Supreme Being.[11] Among some groups, God bears one name but in other societies he, or occasionally she, is known by many names, mostly epithets such as creator, almighty, master of all things, giver of light, etc.[12] The Ashanti, who inhabit Ghana and the Ivory Coast, claim that God is pre-eminent—calling him "Alone the Great One"—the source of power for all things. The earth, however, the first creation of God, is personified as a great-breasted goddess who is second to God in power.[13] Ashanti religion features a pantheon of major and minor divinities through whom God manifests himself. Allegedly these divinities all originate from God.[14] The religion

9. John Mbiti, *Concepts of God in Africa* (New York: Praeger, 1970); idem, *African Religions and Philosophy*, 2nd ed. (Oxford: Heinemann, 1990).

10. The possibility that in antiquity ideas were diffused from Egypt and/or Semitic cultures into greater Africa and that these influenced traditional African religions at some point in time cannot totally be discounted.

11. Mbiti, *African Religions*, 29-38.

12. Mbiti, *Concepts*, 327-36.

13. Surprisingly few African people attribute a wife or goddess consort to God.

14. Mbiti, *Concepts*, 144.

of the Yoruba of Nigeria shows similar concepts. Bolaji Idowu, who studied Yoruban religion and is himself of Yoruban descent, notes that in contrast to polytheism, God in Yoruban belief is not just one of the deities who happens to be the chief god in a particular place or time. Rather, God, called "Sky God" or "Supreme God," is apart and wholly other. It is believed that he has existed from the very beginning as the ruler of the world.[15] Other divinities are God's ministers, carrying out, each in his or her office, the functions connected with the creation and theocratic government of the earth.[16] Prayer is often directed to the various divinities. The veneration of divinities and spirits other than God pervades the religious systems of African peoples. A common belief is that the divinities and spirits are intermediaries between humans and God.[17] Their dependence on God, however, is not always apparent and perceptions about them probably vary among individuals in society.

Notably, while lesser divinities and spirits are commonly identified with natural phenomena, God is not. An expression of God's supremacy above natural forces is reflected in a proverb of the Banyarwanda of Rawanda asserting that "the plant protected by God is never hurt by the wind."[18] Banyarwanda pronounce blessings and oaths in the name of God and pray to him in distress, invoking him as the "God of Rawanda." Interestingly, they believe that God's goodness precludes the need for sacrifices. Instead, they make offerings to the two main spirits believed to collaborate with God and who are sent by him to eat the sacrifices.[19] Although members of a number of African ethnic groups bring offerings and sacrifices to divinities and spirits other than the Supreme God, these practices cannot be attributed to a notion that God is unreachable. Quite the opposite. Many African peoples emphasize God's moral attributes: pity, mercy, kindness, justice, and righteousness.[20] Notably, as far as is known, there are no images or physical representations of the Supreme God in these or any other traditional African religions.[21] This is not the case for lesser divinities.[22]

---

15. E. Bolaji Idowu, *Olódùmarè: God in Yoruba Belief* (London: Longmans, 1962), 21, 58; E. McClelland, *The Cult of Ifá Among the Yoruba* (London: Ethnographica, 1982), 11.

16. Idowu, *Olódùmarè*, 203.

17. E. Bolaji Idowu, *African Traditional Religion* (New York: Orbis, 1973), 170-71; Mbiti, *Concepts*, 121-23; *African Religions*, 74-77.

18. Mbiti, *Concepts*, 9.

19. Mbiti, *Concepts*, 121.

20. Mbiti, *Concepts*, 31-42.

21. Mbiti, *African Religions*, 34.

22. Among the Yoruba, for example, images of deities other than Olodùmaré (= Olorun), the Supreme God, are regularly depicted in various media. These are integral components of the cult. See McClelland, *Cult of Ifá*, 14, 15, 21, 34, 81.

The examples just cited, a mere sampling of the data, seem to indicate that in African religions the conception of divinity does not comfortably fall into the usual paradigm for polytheism.[23] At the same time, in most cases, since the Supreme God is complemented and supplemented by other divinities, the term monotheism, certainly in a strict sense, is inappropriate. Idowu has coined the term "diffused monotheism" to describe the belief system of the Yoruba and most other African ethnic groups. He defines diffused monotheism as a form of monotheism in which God delegates certain portions of his authority to particular divine functionaries who work as they are commissioned by him.[24] These divinities derive their power from God even if in actual worship they are treated as autonomous, each with his or her own priesthood and set of rituals. More important, the leader of the community is the head of all the cults, none of which has meaning apart from the Supreme God.[25]

Idowu maintains that since God is conceived as the absolute sovereign of the universe, African religion is essentially monotheistic. In some cases, however, monolatrous rather than monotheistic ideas are detectable, especially when God is identified as the deity of a particular ethnic group. An example from Robert Lystad's study of the Ashanti illustrates the point. An Ashanti couple was unsuccessful in their attempts to bear children. Appeals to their gods, including Nyame, the Ashanti Supreme God, had failed. The couple turned to Christianity, trying as they put it, the "Christian Nyame" whose desire and ability to answer prayers for children had gained some fame.[26] Although the personal name Nyame was transferred to the Christian God, an apparent distinction was made between the two and it is unclear whether these individuals perceived Nyame as the universal God. The issue is undoubtedly complex.

YHWH and the Nature of the Heavenly Host in Israel

The label "diffused monotheism," while not the perfect solution to problems inherent in the categorization of religions manifesting both polytheistic and monotheistic characteristics, is useful for describing certain patterns of belief and worship. As such, it seems worthwhile to test its

---

23. See the definition of polytheism in note 1.
24. Idowu, *Olódùmarè*, 135-36.
25. On one level the divine structure reflects the socio-political structure or vice versa.
26. Robert Lystad, *The Ashanti* (New Brunswick, NJ: Rutgers University, 1958), 181.

applicability, with modification, to the definition of Israelite religion in the monarchic period, especially during periods of influential leaders and their advocates.

A few biblical scholars have maintained that Israelite religion was essentially monotheistic from the time of Moses, even if only implicitly so. Yehezkel Kaufmann and William Foxwell Albright, two champions of this school of thought, support their view by referring to specific ideas in the biblical text, or, in some cases, a lack of certain notions. Without detailing a well-known argument, their main points may be summarized as follows: 1. For Israel, a single God, known by the name YHWH, existed all along. 2. YHWH did not derive from a primordial realm, rather, he is the source of all there is. 3. Since he transcends the universe, in contrast to the gods of other nations, he is not subject to the cosmic order. 4. In addition, he cannot be controlled by rituals of magic.[27] Proponents of the "original monotheism" theory explain the idolatrous practices reported in the Bible as gross exaggerations of perfectionist prophets, as periodic aberrations provoked by foreigners or foreign influence, and as folk preoccupation with fetishes. In that light, archaeological remains, especially the female pillar figurines found in abundance at 8th-7th century B.C.E. Judean sites are classified as amulets or fetishes.[28]

The notion of fetishism requires comment. Unlike an idol which is regarded as an image, symbol, or residence of a deity, a fetish is defined as an inanimate object that is worshipped because of its inherent magical powers. Usually the term is applied to charms and amulets that form a subordinate part of a religious complex.[29] Tylor and his followers applied the term incorrectly to African worship of divinities and spirits that were somehow attached to inanimate objects.[30] Essentially, their misinterpretation resulted from a lack of understanding of what they called pagan African religions. They mistakenly assumed that the status of divinity was actually appropriated to the objects themselves.

Regarding the religion of ancient Israel, no concrete evidence exists that the various images mentioned in the Bible in connection with Israelite, Canaanite, and foreign cults, or the figurines discovered in archaeological excavations, fit the category fetish.[31] Nor can the seem-

---

27. See especially, Y. Kaufmann, *The Religion of Israel from Its Beginnings to the Babylonian Exile*, trans. M. Greenberg (New York: Schocken, 1960), 60-149, 229-31; William F. Albright, *Archaeology and the Religion of Israel*, 5th ed. (Garden City: Doubleday, 1969), 93-168.

28. Kaufmann, *Religion of Israel*, 144; Albright, *Archaeology and the Religion of Israel*, 111-12.

29. *A New English Dictionary on Historical Principles* (Oxford: Clarendon, 1901), 4: 176; Geoffrey Parrinder, *West African Religion* (London: Epworth, 1949), 9.

30. Tylor, *Primitive Culture*, 2:143-83.

31. For a contrasting opinion, see Jeffrey Tigay, *Deuteronomy* (New York: Jewish Publication Society, 1996), 53, 433-34.

ingly generic and often derogatory designations תרפים, פסלים, עצבים, גלולים, אלילים be taken as proof that "the idolatrous cults were obscure, featureless, and not really known to Israel," as Yehezkel Kaufmann assumes.[32] Although the biblical writers often use these terms in derision to emphasize the impotence of these divinities, that evaluation reflects personal beliefs that the objects represent non-gods. But it is not proof that most Israelite worshippers shared those views. Modern notions asserting that idolatry entails nothing more than veneration of the object itself are generally not supported by studies of religious beliefs among living peoples.[33] As for the labels attached to biblical "idols," it is possible that at least some of them identify types or classes of divinities and spirits.[34] For example, the תרפים that Rachel stole from her father's home (Gen. 31:30-35), those that Michal laid in David's bed to impersonate him (1 Sam. 19:13), and the ones housed in Micah's private shrine (Judg. 17:5; 18:14), have long been recognized as belonging to a class of minor divinities or spirits revered and consulted as family gods. Like the תרפים, the אלילים, עצבים, גלולים, and פסלים probably represent varieties of anthropomorphic statuary.[35] Apparently, while certain classes of minor divinities were known by these generic expressions, individual divinities were named, as implied by the prophet Zechariah's observation that the עצבים bore names (Zech. 13:2).

Other terms, such as אשרים/אשרות, בעלים, and עשתרות, which appear as singular and plural nouns, seem to designate more specific types of divinities. Differentiation in meaning between the singular and plural forms, however, is not always apparent. In the case of the title בעל, in certain contexts the singular form clearly refers to the chief West Semitic storm and fertility deity Baᶜal. Temples for בעל were built in Samaria and Jerusalem and priests and prophets served in the cult (e.g., 1 Kings 16:32; 18:22; 2 Kings 11:18).[36] In contrast to the single form בעל, the plural form

---

32. Kaufmann, *Religion of Israel*, 144.

33. Distinctions in religious concepts within any given society must always be considered (see Radin, above). Therefore, it can be assumed that some members of society do attribute divine status to objects that are actually meant to symbolize or house the divinity.

34. It is possible that different types or classes of divinities were distinguished by their shape or mode of manufacture (e.g. גלולים = circular shape [גלל], perhaps like the female pillar figurines from eighth-seventh century B.C.E. Judean sites; פסלים = hewn or carved [פסל] images of wood or stone; עצבים = shaped or formed [עצב II BDB 781] of precious metal—silver and gold (plate ?), e.g., Hos. 8:4; 13:2; Pss. 115:4; 135:15). Since these terms were imbued with contemptuous connotations they may have lost their original meaning.

35. See, for example, פגרי גלוליכם, "the corpses of your *gilulim*" (Lev. 26:30).

36. See John Day, "Baal" *ABD* 1:545-49. In the monarchic period these references are concentrated in accounts of the reign of Ahab in Israel, Jehu's subsequent purge of the Baᶜal cult in Israel, and the interlude in Judah when Ataliah sat on the Davidic throne. Probably, this particular Baᶜal was of Phoenician origin, imported by Jezebel. Smith identifies him as

בעלים, which is more widely attested biblically, seems to denote a generic designation for a class of lesser divinities, no doubt male.[37] Like the עצבים, the בעלים apparently also bore personal names, as is indicated by the prophet Hosea, "I will remove the names of the בעלים from Israel's mouth and they will no longer be remembered by their names" (Hos. 2:19). The names of these gods were probably recited in worship. As Baruch Halpern suggests, quite possibly they represent the cults of a variety of deities who were members in YHWH's heavenly assembly, but subordinate to him.[38]

In the case of עשתרות/עשתרת, the distinction between the plural and singular forms of the noun may parallel that of בעל/בעלים. The singular form, עשתרת, is identified with the proper noun Astarte, the name of the Canaanite goddess who was a consort of Baᶜal.[39] According to the Deuteronomistic Historian (DH), construction of a shrine for עשתרת was initiated by Solomon for his foreign wives (1 Kings 11:5, 33). The shrine seems to have survived until the mid-seventh century when it was destroyed by Josiah as part of his cult cleansing reform (2 Kings 23:13). Notably, the plural עשתרות is mentioned together with references to בעלים (Judg. 2:11-13; 10:6; 1 Sam. 7:4; 12:10). As such, עשתרות may refer to a class of female divinities worshipped in conjunction with male בעלים.

Defining אשרים/אשרות has elicited extensive discussions in light of inscriptional evidence. Based on verbs associated with these terms in the Bible, it is generally agreed that אשרים/אשרות were trees or wooden poles utilized as cult objects, often situated alongside altars and מצבות, "standing stones" (Deut. 16:21-22; 1 Kings 14:23; 2 Kings 17:10). In addition,

---

Baᶜal Shamem (*Early History*, 65-79). Apparently, altars and shrines for Baᶜal operated in the later monarchy as well (e.g. 2 Kings 21:3; Jer. 19:5).

37. In the Deuteronomistic historical books the plural form בעלים is attested primarily in accounts of the premonarchic period (Judg. 2:11; 3:7; 8:33; 10:6, 10; 1 Sam. 7:4; 12:10). As such, they seem to refer to local gods worshipped by Israelites. However, there is no reason to assume that the worship of local Baᶜal type deities ceased later in the monarchic period. In addition to the mention of בעלים in conjunction with Ahab's reign (1 Kings 18:18), the term also appears in the prophecies of Hosea and Jeremiah (Hos. 2:15, 19, 11:2; Jer. 2:23; 9:13). Jeremiah actually states that the worship of בעלים has a long tradition, having been transmitted from generation to generation (Jer. 9:13). That the term בעלים in fact indicates multiple Baᶜal types is evident from Hosea's remark that they were known by different names (Hos. 2:19). It should be noted that the Chronicler regularly employs the term בעלים rather than בעל, even in his parallel accounts of Kings where the singular form appears (2 Chron. 17:3; 24:7; 28:2; 33:3; 34:4). The one exception is in his account of the coup against Ataliah during which the temple of בעל was destroyed and Matan the priest of בעל was murdered (2 Chron. 23:17). The same holds true for אשרה/אשרים/ות.

38. See Halpern, "Brisker Pipes," 93-95; idem, "Jerusalem and the Lineages," 83-84.

39. John Day, "Ashtoreth" *ABD* 1:491-94. The goddess עשתרת is discussed further below as a possible candidate for the Queen of Heaven.

אשרים/אשרות are paired with various iconic statuary such as עצבים (2 Chron. 24:18) and בעלים (Judg. 3:7) that probably represent male divinities.[40] The feminine gender of אשרים/אשרות can be deduced from the meaning of the singular noun אשרה which is connected to the goddess by that name, Asherah (Athiratu), the consort of El in Ugaritic literature.[41] While the precise nature of the plural forms אשרים/אשרות is uncertain, biblical attestations of the singular form, אשרה, seem to refer to the Canaanite-Israelite goddess or to her symbol.[42] An אשרה stood in the capitals of Samaria (1 Kings 16:33; 2 Kings 13:6) and Jerusalem (1 Kings 15:13; 2 Kings 21:7), minimally in certain periods. A פסל, "sculpted image," of אשרה was erected in the Jerusalem Temple by Manasseh (2 Kings 21:7) and women in the Temple compound wove clothes for the statue (23:7).[43] During Ahab's reign in Israel, prophets of אשרה served in her cult (1 Kings 18:19).

Additional information on the nature of אשרה has been gleaned from Hebrew epigraphic sources. Several inscriptions from Kuntillet Ajrud and Khirbet el-Qôm mention blessings invoking YHWH and his אשרה. The interpretation of these inscriptions remains hotly debated, especially on issues surrounding the identity and functions of the אשרה. A number of scholars, including Ze'ev Meshel, Andre Lemaire, and Jeffrey Tigay explain this אשרה as a cult object or shrine associated with the worship of YHWH.[44] Thereby, אשרה is understood as a common noun, not a deity name, and the pronominal suffix "his" is simply affixed to an object. Without specifically referring to these inscriptions, Bernard Lang

---

40. In Isaiah אשרים is paired with חמנים (Isa. 17:8; 27:9). Usually חמנים are defined as "incense altars," based on the verbal root חמם, "to heat" (KB 1:329). Ceramic cult stands that could have been used as incense altars are attested from various sites in Israel. Of the most famous are those from Taanach which are decorated with various images including male and female figures (*NEAEHL* 4:1431-32). An alternate definition, "sun pillars" (BDB 329), is less convincing.

41. John Day, "Asherah" in *ABD* 1:483-87.

42. Theologically, any distinction between the goddess (depicted anthropomorphically) and symbols identified by her name is only significant if the symbol had already lost its original meaning.

43. The MT states that the women wove בתים, literally "houses," but usually translated as "coverings." Asa's mother is said to have made a מפלצת for the אשרה (1 Kings 15:13). The exact meaning of the term מפלצת, usually translated as "abhorrent thing," is unknown.

44. Ze'ev Meshel, *Kuntillet ʿAjrud—A Religious Center from the Time of the Judaean Monarchy on the Border of Sinai* (Jerusalem: Israel Museum, 1978), 13; André Lemaire, "Les inscriptions de Khirbet el-Qôm et l'ashérah de YHWH," *RB* 84 (1977): 603-8; Jeffrey Tigay, *You Shall Have No Other Gods: Israelite Religion in the Light of Hebrew Inscriptions* (Atlanta: Scholars Press, 1986), 26-30; idem, "Israelite Religion: The Onomastic and Epigraphic Evidence" in *Ancient Israelite Religion*, ed. P. D. Miller, P. D. Hanson, S. D. McBride (Philadelphia: Fortress, 1987), 173-75.

expands on this idea by defining the term אשרה, whenever it appears, as YHWH's power of blessing made visible in a form of vegetation.[45] In contrast, others scholars, including Mordechai Gilula, William Dever, Saul Olyan, Judith Hadley, and Ziony Zevit, to mention just a few, staunchly maintain that אשרה should be identified with the Semitic goddess, even if the reference in the inscriptions is to her cult symbol.[46] Christoph Uehlinger argues another angle based on an analogy from an Eblaite text that records a donation brought before the statues of Rashap and his consort Adamma. He suggests that in the Hebrew inscriptions not only does "his אשרה" refer to the cult statue of the goddess אשרה, but that יהוה refers to a statue as well, one of YHWH.[47] An alternate solution to the problem is attempted by Kyle McCarter who explains YHWH's אשרה as the idea of hypostasis, the concretization of abstract aspects of a god into semi-independent or independent deities.[48] Although not explicitly stated by McCarter, his interpretation implies that the cult object represents a divinity, albeit one who belongs to the heavenly host of YHWH. This solution corresponds to ideas observed in African religious systems where aspects of the Supreme God are manifested in various forms, each aspect viewed as a separate lesser divinity.[49] If we accept this theory as

45. Bernard Lang, *Monotheism and the Prophetic Minority* (Sheffield: Almond, 1983), 39.

46. Mordechai Gilula, "To YHWH Shomron and His Asherah," *Shnaton* 3 (1978-1979): 134-37; William Dever, "Asherah, Consort of Yahweh? New Evidence from Kuntillet ʿAjrud," *BASOR* 255 (1984): 21-37; Saul Olyan, *Asherah and the Cult of Yahweh in Israel* (Atlanta: Scholars Press, 1988), esp. 23-37; Judith Hadley, *The Cult of Asherah in Ancient Israel and Judah: Evidence for a Hebrew Goddess* (Cambridge: Cambridge University Press, 2001), 38-53; Ziony Zevit, *The Religions of Ancient Israel: A Synthesis of Parallactic Approaches* (London: Continuum, 2001), 650-51. For a more complete summary of recent scholarly discussion of issues pertaining to Asherah, see Smith, *Early History*, 125-47.

47. Christoph Uehlinger, "Anthropomorphic Cult Statuary in Iron Age Palestine and the Search for Yahweh's Cult Images" in *The Image and the Book: Iconic Cults, Aniconism, and the Rise of Book Religion in Israel and the Ancient Near East*, ed. K. van der Toorn (Leuven: Peeters, 1997), 140-42. This argument, however, seems highly speculative since no images identifiable as YHWH have yet come to light nor are such images mentioned in the biblical text. Interestingly, in African religions, for which a plethora of images exist, there are no images of the Supreme God. A similar convention may have been prevalent in ancient Israel in the latter monarchic period.

48. P. Kyle McCarter, "Aspects of the Religion of the Israelite Monarchy: Biblical and Epigraphic Data," in *Ancient Israelite Religion*, ed. P. D. Miller, P. D. Hanson, S. D. McBride (Philadelphia: Fortress, 1987), 146-49; idem, "The Religious Reforms of Hezekiah and Josiah," *in Aspects of Monotheism: How God is One*, ed. H. Shanks and J. Meinhardt (Washington, DC: Biblical Archaeology Society, 1997), 76-80. The idea that divinities can be hypostases or refractions of a Supreme God was already suggested by E. E. Evans-Pritchard in connection with Kwoth, the Supreme God of the Nuer (*Nuer Religion* [Oxford: Clarendon, 1956], 48-52, 118-22).

49. This system seems to differ from the syncretism which in Mesopotamia generated the notion of a supreme god, aspects of whom were identified with other well-known deities. A good example of this phenomenon is illustrated in a god list from the Neo-

viable, we can conclude that even though אשרה symbolized a distinct divine being, homage paid to her was ultimately given to YHWH.[50] It cannot be assumed, however, that such a perception of אשרה was prevalent in Israel and Judah in all periods or that it was held by all sectors of society. Certainly in the reigns of Ahab, Manasseh and certain other kings, the role of אשרה at the royal court seems to have been that of an independent deity.

Based on the above discussion, we may infer that the terms אשרים/אשרות, בעלים, and עשתרות refer to classes of local Canaanite-Israelite deities rather than to the major gods of Israel's neighbors. A list in the book of Judges that distinguishes these divinities from the national gods of the surrounding peoples—the Arameans, Phoenicians, Philistines, Moabites, and Ammonites (Judg. 10:6) strengthens the argument.[51] Although Israel is repeatedly condemned for abandoning YHWH (ויעזבו את יהוה) to worship these divinities, it should not be assumed that YHWH was excluded from Israelite worship. Rather, the phrase "to abandon YHWH" seems to indicate the adoption of improper or incorrect Yahwistic rituals, as defined by these thinkers. Samuel's entreaty to the people to remove the "foreign" deities and to worship YHWH לבדו, "alone" (1 Sam. 7:3-4) implies that אשרים/אשרות, בעלים, and עשתרות were indeed incorporated into the cult of YHWH.

A type of Israelite religion that tolerated the diffusion of aspects of the realm of YHWH's authority to divinities at his court should not be relegated to popular religion alone. According to the Bible, all sectors of society during the monarchic period were condemned for improper worship, including kings, officials, priests and prophets. The prophet Jere-

---

Babylonian period that names important deities who were previously independent gods as aspects of Marduk, each serving a different function (CT 24 50, BM 47406, obverse). For a discussion of this and similar texts, see W. G. Lambert, "The Historical Development of the Mesopotamian Pantheon: A Study of Sophisticated Polytheism," in *Unity and Diversity: Essays in the History, Literature and Religion of the Ancient Near East*, ed. H. Goedicke and J. Roberts (Baltimore: Johns Hopkins University, 1975), 197-98.

The post-Amarna theology (mid fourteenth century) in Egypt is somewhat comparable to this later Mesopotamian idea. In Egypt it is expressed by hymns describing Amun-Re as the One who makes himself into a million. For the latest discussion on the topic, see Jan Assmann, "Mono-, Pan-, and Cosmotheism: Thinking the 'One' in Egyptian Theology," *Orient* 33 (1998): 130-49.

50. Perhaps this is what Klaus Koch means when he calls *asherah* a "mediating entity," entity being somewhat ambiguous ("Aschera als Himmelskönigin in Jerusalem," *UF* 20 [1988]: 99-100). Othmar Keel and Christoph Uehlinger adopt this definition in their 1992 volume *Gods, Goddesses, and Images of God in Ancient Israel*, trans. T. H. Trapp (Minneapolis: Fortress Press, 1998), 236-37, 278).

51. Judges 10:6 seems to belong to the polemics of a later hand (Robert Boling, *Judges* [New York: Doubleday, 1965], 193; Smith, *The Early History of God*, 127).

miah, for example, accuses these groups of the veneration of trees and stones, no doubt references to אשרות and מצבות (2:26-27), and the defilement of the Temple with forbidden cult objects (32:32ff.). Furthermore, condemnation is not limited to the kings of northern Israel, who are systematically rejected by the DH.[52] More than half of the kings of Judah receive a negative evaluation as well, although that appraisal is based on later stricter standards.[53] Concerning the general populace, it is impossible to ascertain what percentage followed the fluctuating model of the royal leadership, how many consistently adhered to practices in keeping with exclusive Yahwism, perhaps due to the influence of a particular king, priest, or prophet, and how many understood members of YHWH's host to be independently functioning gods and goddesses. Certainly social context played a role in the religious expressions of the people. Practices observed at officially sanctioned cult sites, for example, need not have mirrored personal beliefs.[54]

Israelite Polytheism

Based on the evidence, it can be argued that certain groups of divinities worshipped by Israelites were components of Yahwism and may have represented local gods who belonged to the circle of YHWH's host.[55] Indeed, the existence of a host surrounding YHWH, albeit one comprised of anonymous beings some of whom represented the forces of nature, is a concept generally accepted in biblical theology (e.g., 1 Kings 22:19; Isaiah

---

52. Jeroboam I (1 Kings 13:33), Nadab (15:26), Baasha (15:34), Elah (16:13), Zimri (16:19), Omri (16:25), Ahab (16:30), Ahaziah (22:53), Jehoram (2 Kings 3:2), Jehu (10:29), Jehoahaz (13:2), Jehoash (13:11), Jeroboam II (14:24), Zechariah (15:9), Menahem (15:18), Pekahiah (15:24), Pekah (15:28) and Hoshea (17:2).

53. Rehoboam ("Judah" 1 Kings 14:22), Abijam (15:3), Joram (2 Kings 8:18), Ahaziah (8:27), Ahaz (16:2), Manasseh (21:2-9), Amon (21:20), Jehoahaz (23:32), Jehoiakim (23:37), Jehoiachin (24:9) and Zedekiah (24:19).

54. Beth Alpert Nakhai observes from archaeological evidence that cult paraphernalia in private domestic sites differ from those at officially sanctioned sites and even secondary sites with public access. She stresses the eclectic forms of worship in monarchic Israel and Judah, some of which seem to preserve ancient traditions dating to the pre-state period (*Archaeology and the Religions of Canaan and Israel* [Boston: ASOR, 2001], 176-93). Ziony Zevit, who also argues for a multiplicity of religious practices in ancient Israel, identifies two classes of cult sites: the larger ones planned and controlled by a central authority, and local ones displaying the initiative of few persons (*Religions of Ancient Israel*, 654-58).

55. Mark Smith points to the general absence of a divine family in Israel (in contrast to that at Ugarit), especially one lacking active second-tier deities. He cautions, however, that the biblical vision of a collapsed pantheon is exaggerated for the preexilic period (*Origins of Biblical Monotheism*, 48-50, 78).

6). In contrast, when the Bible specifies principal "foreign" gods, they do not fit the category "YHWH's host." For example, worship of the Phoenician Baʿal at the time of Ahab and his descendants, both in Israel and Judah (1 Kings 16:31-32; 2 Kings 11:18), as well as periodic worship of the national gods of Israel's neighbors, such as Milkom of the Ammonites and Kemosh of the Moabites (1 Kings 11:5-7; 2 Kings 23:13), bespeaks a polytheistic system. As suggested by the account of Elijah on Mt. Carmel (1 Kings 18:16-46), the cult of Baʿal with its functionaries and shrines was actually considered a threat to the survival of Yahwism.[56]

Other divinities such as Tammuz, the Queen of Heaven, and astral deities penetrated Israelite religion in the latter monarchic period. The roles of these divinities and their relationship to YHWH, however, are difficult to define. Not all qualify as major deities in their native cults but they do hold independent status. The question is whether in Israel they functioned independently or were members of YHWH's host. For example, Tammuz (Dumuzi), who is known from Mesopotamian literature as a minor vegetation divinity whose death was lamented in the summer,[57] is the object of Israelite devotion condemned by the prophet Ezekiel. A bird's eye view of Tammuz worship in Ezekiel's vision of a scene on the Temple mount describes women sitting at the Temple gate wailing for Tammuz (Ezek. 8:14). This singular biblical attestation of Tammuz worship suggests that the deity was of relatively minor importance even in Israel. The fact that he was worshipped within the Jerusalem Temple precinct intimates that his devotees viewed the cult as a component of Yahwism.

Defining astral worship in Israel is more complex. Worship of astral deities, which reflects Syro-Palestinian as well as Mesopotamian cult practices,[58] is listed in the Bible among the transgressions of the Northern Kingdom at the time of its fall (2 Kings 17:16) and as a corruption of Judean cult practices from the late eighth century to the destruction of Jerusalem (Zeph. 1:5; 2 Kings 21:3, 5; Jer. 8:2; 19:13). In general, the astral deities, צבא השמים, "heavenly host," are grouped together, though occasionally the sun and moon are specified individually. Apparently, shrines to these divinities were housed on the flat rooftops of private homes and

---

56. Lang believes that the main threat was economic, resulting in a financial loss to the priesthood of YHWH (*Monotheism*, 26-27). While the economic impact of the Baʿal cult on Yahwism is not measurable, certainly a developed and functioning cult of a chief god such as Baʿal could have challenged YHWH's role as the national God of Israel, especially following the extermination of the prophets of YHWH at the hands of Jezebel (1 Kings 18:4).

57. Lowell Handy, "Tammuz" in *ABD* 6:318.

58. Mordechai Cogan and Hayim Tadmor, *II Kings* (AB; New York: Doubleday, 1988), 266.

those of the royal compound (Zeph. 1:5; Jer. 19:13). According to the DH, in the reign of Manasseh, altars to the צבא השמים were even erected in the courtyards of the Temple (2 Kings 21:3, 5). Since personal names are not attached to astral deities in the Bible they cannot be positively identified as Mesopotamian or Syro-Palestinian divinities and may actually represent both. While there is no explicit evidence that astral deities were considered members of YHWH's host, it is likely that they were worshipped side by side with YHWH and other gods (Zeph. 1:5).[59]

A deity of significance who may have been associated with astral worship is the Queen of Heaven. She is identified with different goddesses known by that epithet, the Semitic Astarte or Anat or the Mesopotamian Ishtar.[60] Whatever her true identity(s), the Queen of Heaven qualifies as a major deity. Her worship is described in the book of Jeremiah in the context of the last days of the monarchy and again in the exile in Egypt. A dialogue between the prophet Jeremiah and a group of Judeans in Egypt provides a rare opportunity to view rituals and their underlying ideology from what may be a popular perspective (Jer. 44:15-19). As reported, rituals associated with her worship included the baking of cakes and the pouring of libation offerings. Interestingly, when Jeremiah appeals to the people to abandon these practices they respond in the negative, claiming that the rites are part and parcel of their tradition, having been performed by their forefathers and also at the royal court by kings and ministers. Their response reveals that the cult was not limited to the so-called "common folk" in a family cult setting. More importantly, the people observe that when these rituals were performed they experienced prosperity, and only when they ceased those practices were they beset with disaster. A cause and effect relationship between cult practices and events in their lives leads these Judeans to conclude that adherence to a YHWH-alone religion is inadequate. Although it remains unclear from the narrative in Jeremiah the nature of the relationship between the cults of the Queen of Heaven and that of YHWH, it does appear that in the minds of her worshippers the goddess' power was independent from that of YHWH.[61]

---

59. See Adele Berlin's discussion in *Zephaniah* (AB; New York: Doubleday, 1994), 71-77.

60. Philip Schmitz, "Queen of Heaven," in *ABD* 5:586-88. Moshe Weinfeld presents a strong argument for identifying the Queen of Heaven with Ishtar ("The Worship of Molech and of the Queen of Heaven and Its Background," *UF* 4 [1972]: 149-54).

61. According to Moshe Weinfeld ("The Worship of Molech and of the Queen of Heaven," 133-54), Molech worship should also be connected with the cult of the Queen of Heaven and astral deities. Weinfeld maintains that the biblical name Molech is simply a distortion of the title מלך, "king," a common epithet attached to various deity names known from non-Hebrew sources. In the Assyrian-Aramean cult, Adad/Hadad, often designated

The prevalence in some periods but not in others of certain cults seems to reflect foreign influence. In the case of Tammuz, the Queen of Heaven, and possibly astral deities, Assyrian, Babylonian and/or Aramean inspiration is probable, especially during the late eighth, seventh, and early sixth centuries. Worship of Phoenician Baʿal and its proliferation both in Israel and Judah, specifically in the ninth century, can be traced to the marriage of Ahab and the Sidonian princess Jezebel which promoted political, economic and cultural relationships with the Phoenician city-states.

Monotheism vs. Monolatry

If we view Israelite religion through biblical lenses, relegating polytheistic practices to aberrations, and focus on what constitutes "proper" biblical Yahwism, we find a system definable as essentially monolatrous with some monotheistic features. While the national gods of Israel's neighbors were openly recognized,[62] they were deemed inferior to YHWH. These beliefs are reflected in two references in Deuteronomy noting that when YHWH chose Israel as his people, he assigned other divinities to the remaining nations (Deut. 4:19; 32:8 [LXX & Q]. The notion that YHWH was in a position to apportion national groups to the gods demonstrates his superiority over the other deities. A similar idea is expressed by the prophet Micah in his depiction of YHWH as the judge of a multitude of nations, despite the fact that each has its own gods (4:2-5). Although YHWH's divine status is not unique, he is frequently portrayed as incomparable: "Who is like you among the gods, YHWH?" (Exod. 15:11).[63]

---

as "king," is paired with Ishtar, called the "queen of heaven." Weinfeld posits that Assyrian and/or Aramean influence in the eighth-seventh centuries introduced these divinities into Israelite worship. At the same time, the more familiar Baʿal may have acquired the title מלך as well (Jer. 32:35). While Weinfeld's theory is tempting, it hardly resolves the enigmatic nature of the designation Molech and will therefore be excluded from our discussion. For a concise and up-dated summary of the issues and theories, see George Heider, "Molech" in *ABD* 4:895-98.

62. For example, the potency of Kemosh as national god of Moab seems to be reflected in the account of the war between Moab and an Israel/Judah alliance in the reigns of Jehoram and Jehoshaphat. In the final battle, the nearly victorious Israelites are suddenly overcome when the desperate Moabite king sacrifices his eldest son to Kemosh who responds favorably (2 Kings 3:26-27).

63. For a similar interpretation of these and other passages, see Schenker, "Le monothéisme israélite," 438-47. The possibility that Psalm 82 actually attests to the deposal of these gods, an idea reflecting a progression toward monotheism, is suggested by Matitiahu Tsevat,"God and the Gods in Assembly: An Interpretation of Psalm 82," in *The Meaning of the Book of Job and Other Biblical Studies* (New York: Ktav, 1980), 131-47.

A key issue centers on the dating of monotheistic rhetoric in texts that appear chronologically ambiguous. For example, several hymns in the books of Psalms and Samuel portray YHWH as the sole God and the creator of the world (e.g., Pss. 33; 36; 2 Sam. 7:22; 22:32).[64] This particular genre of literature lends itself to these kinds of expressions of praise and devotion. A hymn, for example, is often composed in honor of a particular deity even by worshippers of multiple deities. In contrast, declarations of the oneness of YHWH in Deuteronomy and other Deuteronomistic literature seem more indicative of theological precepts held by certain Israelite thinkers. Explicit monotheistic assertions are found in Deuteronomy 4:35,39 in reference to the revelation at Sinai and redemption from Egypt: "You (the Israelites) have been shown so that you know that YHWH is God, there is none besides him;" "YHWH is God in the Heavens above and on the earth below, there is no other." These texts cannot be dated with confidence to any earlier than the seventh century and may actually be later.[65] Similar proclamations, but in liturgical contexts, are attributed by the DH to two Judean kings: Solomon in the context of the dedication of the Temple (1 Kings 8) and Hezekiah in a petition to God for deliverance from the Assyrians (2 Kings 19:15-19). Again, dating the proclamations of the oneness of YHWH in these prayers is problematic, as is the dating of other portions of these passages.[66] But whether they date to the late monarchy or to the exilic period (a narrow time difference), it appears that the theology is explicitly monotheistic, especially as stated by Hezekiah in his petition. The latter not only recognizes YHWH as creator

64. 2 Sam 7:22 is generally attributed to Deuteronomistic expansion. See M. Weinfeld, *Deuteronomy and the Deuteronomic School* (Oxford: Clarendon Press, 1972), 37-38. Likewise, 2 Sam 22:32 also contains later features, though possibly as early as the seventh century. P. K. McCarter, Jr. sees its closest analogies in Deutero-Isaiah, especially Isa. 45:5 (*II Samuel* [New York: Doubleday, 1984], 469). For a list of texts revealing monotheistic creed, see Weinfeld, *Deuteronomy*, 331.

65. Scholarly opinion on these passages varies as well. Jeffrey Tigay, for example, believes that late preexilic and exilic explicit monotheistic rhetoric was the result of the socio-political situation of the time, though the monotheistic idea had been implicit since the time of Moses (*JPS Torah Commentary Deuteronomy* [Philadelphia: Jewish Publication Society, 1996], 433-35). In contrast, Alexander Rofé argues for an exilic date for Deut. 4:32-40, a time when God's historic act of redeeming Israel from Egypt became proof of his uniqueness (*Deuteronomy, Issues and Interpretation* [London: T&T Clark, 2002], 17-21).

66. For a summary of the issues pertinent to Solomon's prayer, see Mordechai Cogan, *1 Kings* (New York: Doubleday, 2000), 292-93. M. Weinfeld considers most of Solomon's prayer exilic, though he identifies verses 12-13 as "original," comparable to the temple dedication of Gudea (*Deuteronomy*, 35). Concerning Hezekiah's prayer, Weinfeld asserts that the creation motif dates it to exilic and post-exilic liturgy (p. 39). Gary Knoppers, on the other hand, considers the latter preexilic, seeing a version of Solomon's prayer in Hezekiah's petition (*Two Nations under God: The Deuteronomistic History of Solomon and the Dual Monarchies*, vol. 1 [Atlanta: Scholars Press, 1993], 104). The circular reasoning behind the dating of these and other passages is obvious.

and sole God, but he reasons that the Assyrians triumphed over the gods of the nations they conquered because those deities are non-gods—merely wood and stone creations of men. While the polemical character of this message is evident, the underlying philosophy is clearly monotheistic.

In sum, we find only isolated expressions of monotheistic ideas in a scant number of biblical texts of uncertain date. Generally, the existence of a plurality of divinities was not categorically denied in the pre-exilic period. Notably, however, such denial was not essential for the ultimate proliferation of a YHWH-alone religion. After all, the distinction between strict monotheism and monolatry is purely philosophical since the ritual process of the two is identical—worship of deities other than the One is prohibited. Thus, the prophets and other proponents of strict Yahwism, who consistently decry improper cult practices, could actually attain their goal by establishing a pure state of monolatry.[67] Philosophical musing is for intellectuals, and for those who themselves may have been monotheists, radical monotheism would be an outgrowth of radical monolatry. Not surprisingly, the strongest biblical evidence for monotheism is found in the writings of the exilic prophets, in particular Deutero-Isaiah. Amidst an altered social structure that characterized the exilic period, in the face of a fallen monarchy and Temple, prophets and priests had the opportunity to set the direction of the official religion, at least for a core of followers.[68] The belief that YHWH would redeem a repentant Israel, despite his disassociation from the national territory, gave new meaning to monotheistic concepts.

Conclusions

While the limited biblical and archaeological data inspire caution in drawing conclusions about the nature of Israelite religion in the monarchic period, the following can be inferred from the evidence at hand.

(1) In general, identifying mainstream Israelite religion is limited by the selective texts that comprise the biblical corpus, a small collection of

---

67. According to Halpern, prophets like Jeremiah went as far as to assault all symbolism, even if part and parcel of the Yahwistic cult ("Brisker Pipes," 99).

68. Mark Smith suggests that beginning in the late seventh century, as a result of political weakness and defeat, the disruption of Judean social structure impacted its traditional theology. To offset the ultimate loss of land and nationhood, "the cosmic status of its deity soared in its literature" (*Origins of Monotheism*, 164-65). While it is possible that intellectuals in society reacted in this manner, the record in Jeremiah expressing Judean popular sentiments (44:15-19) actually demonstrates the opposite.

epigraphic material, and the cult objects recovered in archaeological excavations. The picture that emerges suggests that in certain respects Israelite ideas about their religion differed from those prevalent in Egypt, Syria, Mesopotamia, and Ugarit. Both in Judah and in Israel, in most periods, YHWH was viewed as the Supreme God in a national if not universal sense. Still, other divinities were worshipped in concert with YHWH. Since in the eyes of most biblical writers these other divinities were non-gods, their specific roles remain elusive. Possibly, some of these divinities functioned as intermediaries in their capacity as members of YHWH's host. Perhaps, then, the term diffused monotheism or, more appropriately diffused monolatry, is applicable to what may be construed as mainstream Israelite religion. Clearly, Israelite religion in the pre-state and even monarchic periods does not fit snugly into most academically-constructed paradigms of polytheism, monotheism, or monolatry. Yet, as shown by analogies with living African peoples, it is a tenable system.

(2) What can be said about Israelite monotheism in its stricter sense? Searching for evidence of monotheism in pre-exilic Israel or Judah resembles the excavation of a community dump where isolated sherds of a specific type are only found in mixed assemblages. In other words, distinguishing monotheism from monolatry in the biblical text is a frustrating endeavor. Still, it is noteworthy that all extant sources, both biblical and archaeological, demonstrate that with rare exceptions YHWH maintained the role of Supreme God throughout the monarchic period.[69] Essentially, the ongoing conflict between both official and popular worship on one hand and YHWH purists on the other, centered around issues of "correct" Yahwistic worship rather than the more fundamental question, is YHWH the God of Israel? Noticeably, although YHWH is not the sole object of veneration in Israel, both among the populace and the leadership, conceptions of him are imbued with monotheistic ideas.

(3) Ancient Israel should be viewed as a diverse society exhibiting variant religious expressions.[70] As shown, what has been labeled diffused monotheism or monolatry coexisted with polytheistic cults, at least among certain groups in certain periods. Radical monolatry at best was an ideal promoted by prophets and other reformers who in their own

69. Jeffrey Tigay's work on the onomastic and epigraphic material, which reveals the proliferation of Yahwistic PNs, lends support to that conclusion (*You Shall Have No Other Gods*, 5-20, 47-89).

70. I cannot accept Baruch Halpern's thesis that late eighth- and seventh-century centralization of government and cult aimed at breaking down kinship and village obligations (reflected in Deuteronomic law) also eliminated intermediary gods and ancestors from the cult ("Jerusalem and the Lineages," 75-91). His conclusion is not only conjectural but his analysis ignores the religious heterogeneity in society borne out by textual, archaeological, and anthropological evidence.

minds may actually have perceived YHWH in monotheistic terms. What percentage of the general population fit into each group is unknown, though our sources suggest that a sizable portion of Israelites recognized YHWH as the Supreme National God and worshipped him, if not exclusively, then in concert with other divinities who seem to qualify as members of his host.

www.ingramcontent.com/pod-product-compliance
Ingram Content Group UK Ltd.
Pitfield, Milton Keynes, MK11 3LW, UK
UKHW041432180426
11947UKWH00007B/399

9 781930 675780